FOUNDATIONS

OF

PSYCHONEUROIMMUNOLOGY

FOUNDATIONS
OF
PSYCHONEUROIMMUNOLOGY

Edited by

Steven Locke
Robert Ader
Hugo Besedovsky
Nicholas Hall
George Solomon
Terry Strom

N. Herbert Spector, Consulting Editor

ALDINE
Publishing Company
New York

ABOUT THE EDITORS

Steven Locke, M.D., Harvard Medical School
Robert Ader, Ph.D., University of Rochester School of Medicine and Dentistry
Hugo Besedovsky, M.D., Medical Research Institute of Switzerland
Nicholas Hall, Ph.D., George Washington University College of Medicine
George Solomon, M.D., University of California, San Francisco
Terry Strom, M.D., Harvard Medical School
N. Herbert Spector, Ph.D., National Institutes of Health

Aldine Publishing Company
200 Saw Mill River Road
Hawthorne, New York 10532

Library of Congress Cataloging in Publication Data

Main entry under title:

Foundations of psychoneuroimmunology.

A collection of articles reprinted from various sources.
Includes index.
1. Neuropsychiatry—Addresses, essays, lectures.
2. Neuroimmunology—Addresses, essays, lectures.
I. Locke, Steven. [DNLM: 1. Allergy and Immunology—collected works. 2. Neurology—collected works.
3. Psychophysiology—collected works.   QW 505 C614]
RC344.C54   1985   616.07'9   84-24559
ISBN 0-202-25138-1 (lib. bdg.)

Printed in the United States of America
10 9 8 7 6 5 4 3 2 1

CONTENTS

I   NEUROIMMUNOMODULATION

II BEHAVIOR AND IMMUNE FUNCTION

PREFACE

Islands and cities situated at the intersection of trade routes often become centers of civilization and creativity. Interdisciplinary research is an analogous phenomenon in science. The cross-fertilization encouraged by the combined participation of many scientific specialties facilitates revolutionary conceptual leaps, conveying "hybrid vigor" to our knowledge. The burgeoning field of *psychoneuroimmunology* represents the emergence of an important new interdisciplinary area whose roots lie in neuroscience, immunology, ethology, psychology, neurology, anatomy, psychiatry, epidemiology, and endocrinology, As stated by Ader, "The assumption of an autonomous immune system is no longer tenable . . . the immune system, like all other physiological systems functioning in the interests of homeostasis, is integrated with other psychophysiological processes; as such, it is subject to regulation or modulation by the central nervous system" (Ader, 1981).

The idea for this collection of research reports was conceived over a dinner attended by researchers interested in the interaction of brain, behavior, and immunity during the 6th World Congress of the International College of Psychosomatic Medicine in Montreal in 1981. The perceived need for *Foundations of Psychoneuroimmunology* was based on the wide dispersion of this knowledge among the world's scientific journals; Locke and Hornig-Rohan noted in their annotated bibliography, *Mind and Immunity: Behavioral Immunology (1976–1982)*, that papers in psychoneuroimmunology were scattered among more than 200 journals world-wide (Locke and Hornig-Rohan, 1983). Even this bibliography, with its more than 1400 abstracts, does not provide a complete coverage of the extant literature.

Papers were selected by the Board of Editors to represent important contributions to the state of our knowledge published prior to 1979. Most of the selected papers represent novel or creative research efforts of their era. Many have earned their "classic" status because they have stood the test of time. Others were selected because they heralded growth in new directions, pursued later by others. Most of the papers chosen are original reports; review articles were intentionally excluded except where they summarized a stream of work emanating from a single laboratory spanning several years. In an effort to make this an international effort, we included papers judged "classic" that were not originally published in English. Thus, the paper by Korneva and Khai (1963) and by Metal'nikov (1926) were ably translated by Ria Olsen and Robert Radway, respectively, of Language Consultants, Wellesley Hills, Massachusetts.

The reader will notice variability in the layout, typography, and quality of reproduction of the represented articles. These problems are inherent in a publication of this sort. Since this is a collection of classics, we have endeavored to provide the manuscripts in their original form or, when the originals were impossible to obtain, they were reprinted from the best copies available. We chose not to reset the type (except for a small number of papers) to achieve a more aesthetic design because it would have substantially raised the cost of the book and thereby reduced its distribution and, ultimately, its usefulness. Similarly, we chose to reproduce the Author's names and scientific terminology exactly as they appeared in the original for the sake of authenticity.

Undoubtedly, there will not be universal agreement with our selection. There may be other excellent papers worthy of inclusion that were inadvertently overlooked and for this, we apologize. We encourage readers of this collection to share with us their impressions of our selection and to call to our attention additional papers we have omitted.

Steven Locke
Robert Ader
Hugo Besedovsky
Nicholas Hall
George Solomon
Terry Strom

INTRODUCTION

During the 1970's, the remarkable complexity of regulatory networks operating entirely within the immune system became apparent. Therefore, it is not surprising that a growing literature, which strongly suggests that homeostatic and regulatory influences "outside" of the immune system may also alter immunity, has been overlooked by some immunologists. Nevertheless, a broad variety of evidence—some phenomenological, some mechanistically oriented—indicates that neuroendocrine influences upon immunity do indeed exist and that some of the mechanisms by which this feedback takes place have been elucidated.

Feedback endows the immune system with a remarkable capacity for autoregulation. Immunoregulation has become a central issue in contemporary immunology. Mechanisms intrinsic to the system such as those mediated by different subsets of T cells, by antibodies, including their idiotypic determinants, monokines, lymphokines, etc., constitute a level of autoregulation. This autoregulation confers a degree of autonomy to the immune system. Our growing understanding of these processes has, however, reinforced the necessity to identify the limits of this autonomy. In fact, processes essential for the functioning of immunological cells such as metabolism, transport of substances, allosteric changes in membranes, lymphoid cell proliferation and transformation, lymphokine synthesis are affected by several hormones and neurotransmitters. These facts by themselves constitute evidence for the existence of a level of neuroendocrine immunoregulation, superimposed on and interwoven with autoregulation.

Neuroendocrine and certain neurochemical systems have, in some instances, well documented but poorly characterized effects upon the immune system. This is due in part to the fact that many aspects of each discipline are also poorly characterized so that any attempt to formulate integrative models has to be speculative at best. Nonetheless, some pioneering work has been conducted over the years and when the results of seemingly disparate studies are interpreted collectively with the objective of formulating a unifying hypothesis of neuroendocrine modulation of immunity, some important consistencies are to be found in what at first appears to be an inconsistent literature. The effects of corticosteroids upon immunity have been documented by some investigators through functional, anatomical, and histological assessment of the immune system. Correlations between the effects of electrolytic lesions and stimulation of brain regions that regulate the hypothalamic-hypophyseal-adrenal (HPA) axis and the immune system are, in general, consistent with perturbations of the HPA as well as other hormonal circuits. Other investigators have concentrated their efforts not simply upon neural influences upon immunity, but also upon the immunologic signals that trigger neuroendocrine pathways. When all of this information is considered collectively, it is apparent that there is considerable evidence in support of bidirectional neuroendocrine-immune circuits that have the potential to profoundly influence the course of immunogenesis and immunity.

In the present volume of *Foundations of Psychoneuroimmunology*, several papers have been collected which are judged to be representative examples of the effect of manipulation of the brain, endocrine, and autonomic mechanisms on immune processes. Other papers provide clear examples that the links of central nervous system (CNS) structures with the immune system are by no means unidirectional. For example, immunological cells can emit messages to the CNS causing a neuroendocrine immunoregulatory response. The papers selected for inclusion in this volume are representative of the approaches that have been taken in an attempt to elucidate the mechanisms by which emotional states and mental processes might influence the course of disease. The data considered as a whole constitute an important body of evidence for permanently operating feedback mechanisms involving both immune and neuroendocrine mechanisms. On this basis, psychosocial influences on immunity can be better understood. External stimuli and/or intrinsically generated signals processed by the brain can affect the immune response by changing the "set point" of brain immunoregulatory mechanisms resulting in immunosuppression or potentiation. The results are not always definitive, but they are provocative and in many instances have provided the rationale for more systematic penetrating investigations.

The studies that deal more specifically with behavior illustrate the impact of a variety of behavioral and psychosocial factors on immune responses. The available neuroendocrine data provide a foundation for supposing that behavioral processes of adaptation would, in fact, influence immunoregulatory processes. Behavioral studies will, in turn, stimulate further research on the neuroendocrine mechanisms mediating the effects of behavior on the immune system. From another perspective, these behavioral studies suggest that psychosocial factors influence health and disease via the immune system.

Thus far, the majority of behavioral studies have involved the effects of "stress" in laboratory animals. Some of those included in this volume are representative of several investigations that have used similar behavioral manipulations (such as the series of experiments of Rasmussen and his colleagues on avoidance conditioning or noise on infectious disease processes). Studies of "stress" effects, however, are becoming more sophisticated in light of data such as that reported by Monjan and Collector (1977) indicating a biphasic immune response and a dissociation of adrenal and immune responses during the course of extended exposure to "stressful" stimulation. "Stress" research remains of experimental and clinical interest and has been the subject of several papers in psychoneuroimmunology in the last few years. These data indicate that both humoral and cell-mediated immune responses may be suppressed and/or enhanced by a variety of environmental circumstances.

Whether or not they should be classified under the rubric of "stress," the impact of psychosocial factors on immune responses is also documented by the early studies of differential housing (Solomon, 1969; Vessey, 1964) which have led to similar experiments in recent years and the studies of prenatal and early life experiences (Solomon, Levine, & Kraft, 1968) which, given the rapid growth of psychoneuroimmunology, can be expected to reawaken interest in a developmental perspective to the field.

The most dramatic studies of behavioral modulation of immunity in terms of central nervous system function are those indicating that immunologic reactivity can be modified by learning. The paper by Dolin et al. (1960) is one of the last of the studies from Europe and Asia that began more than 50 years ago with Metal'nikov and Chorine (1926). Research in the United States on behaviorally conditioned alterations on immune function began with the study by Ader and Cohen (1975). Conditioning effects have since been replicated and extended by several investigators and the conditioning paradigm has been applied to the immunopharmacotherapy of an autoimmune disease in mice and to dramatic reductions in histamine levels by classical (Pavlovian) techniques. These studies and the other behavioral studies included in this volume have precipitated new research on the role of personality factors, psychosocial influences, and a variety of behavioral interventions in the modulation of immune responses and reinforce the notion that processes of adaptation are integrated biopsychosocial processes that include the immune system.

The studies that have dealt with the relationship of psychosocial factors and human immune function have been provocative though often methodologically flawed. In fairness to those researchers whose pioneering work has had widespread appeal and has generated considerable interest, the ethical problems raised by the use of humans in such research have often hobbled the investigators. This limitation is therefore reflected in the paucity of published research on the direct effects of behavioral manipulations on human immune function in experimental designs. This void is partially filled by some recent epidemiologic studies on human populations, mostly retrospective, but a few, prospective. Many of the human studies represented in this volume report findings obtained from weaker, correlational designs. Nevertheless, these studies have raised provocative questions about the relative influence of both state and trait factors in determining immune status.

"Immunopsychiatry" can be thought of as encompassing the variety of immunologic abnormalities reported in conjunction with mental illness and the production of mental symptoms as a result of immune processes, particularly autoimmune and allergic. If the central nervous system (CNS) and the immune system are intimately linked, as all the papers in the volume suggest in one way or another (and recent work more convincingly suggests), then it follows that severe emotional disturbance and mental dysfunction may be accompanied by immunologic abnormalities. In other words, major perturbation in one system might be expected to be reflected in some perturbation in the other.

A variety of immunologic abnormalities has been reported in conjunction with mental illness, particularly schizophrenia. These findings include: abnormalities in levels of immunoglobulins (first documented by Solomon and co-workers, 1966); the presence of autoantibodies to a variety of self components (first reported by Goodman and co-workers, 1963), including the presence of antibrain antibodies that might be expected to have functional significance (first reported by Fessel, 1963 and later significantly elaborated upon by Heath, 1976 and by the Janković group in Yugoslavia, 1973); abnormal heterophile antibodies; deficient immune responsivity; hypersensitivity to gluten (Dohan, 1966); and morphologic and functional abnormalities of immunologically competent cells (structural changes first being noted by the great hematologist Damashek in 1930 and convincingly demonstrated by Fessel and Hirata-Hibi, 1963). The significance of whatever the immunologic aberration to the etiology or pathogenesis of mental illness, especially schizophrenia, remains quite unclear; indeed, such abnormalities may be epiphenomena.

It is important that work in this field be interpreted with great care and caution. The true importance of brain, neuroendocrine, and immune system interactions *in vivo* remains unknown. We hope that this collection of papers may serve to bring attention to the close interrelationship of the nervous and immune systems and that it may also stimulate others to explore this relationship with scientific rigor.

ACKNOWLEDGMENTS

The editors wish to express their appreciation to a number of individuals and organizations whose assistance and support contributed substantially to the production of this collection. Suggestions for included papers were provided by Joan and Myrin Borysenko and N. Herbert Spector. Mady Hornig-Rohan and Jane Leserman provided valuable editorial assistance. Janice Rand helped locate and photocopy the papers deep in the stacks of the Francis H. Countway Medical Library, an invaluable Boston resource. The Division of Computer Medicine at Beth Israel and Brigham and Women's Hospitals graciously made available its wordprocessing and Paperchase utilities, facilitating production of the work. The principal editor (Steven E. Locke) received administrative support and encouragement from the Department of Psychiatry, Beth Israel Hospital, Harvard Medical School, and was supported in part by a Young Investigator Award from the National Cancer Institute (CA-21955).

The most important source of support and assistance came from assistant editor Claudia Dorrington, whose mastery of organization and communication was largely responsible for the completion of this work.

CONTRIBUTORS TO THIS VOLUME

Ader, R.
Bartop, R. W.
Besedovsky, H.
Black, S.
Burbaeva, G. Sh.
Bussard, A. E.
Byers, L. W.
Cantell, K.
Canter, A.
Carpenter, C. B.
Chang, S.-S.
Cheido, M.
Chen, C. H.
Chorine, V.
Cluff, L. E.
Cohen, N.
Cobb, E. K.
Collector, M. I.
Daniels, J. C.
Dameshek, W.
Da Prada, M.
del Rey, A.
Devoino, L.
Dohan, F. C.
Dolin, A. O.
Dougherty, T. F.
Eliseeva, L.
Eremina, O.
Evans, A. S.
Fabris, N.
Felix, D.
Felsenfeld, O.
Fessel, W. J.
Filipp, G.
Fischer, C. L.
Flerov, B. A.
Frank, J. A.
Fröberg, J.
Gisler, R. H.
Goodman, M.
Gottlieb, J. S.
Granström, M.

Greer, W. E.
Haas, H.
Haggerty, R. J.
Hamilton, D. R.
Heath, R. G.
Hess, R.
Hildemann, W. H.
Hill, C. W.
Hirata-Hibi, M.
Horvat, J.
Hultin, E.
Humphrey, J. H.
Idova, G.
Ignatov, S. A.
Imboden, J. B.
Isaković, K.
Ishigami, T
Janković, B. D.
Jensen, M. M.
Johnsson, T.
Karlsson, C.-G.
Kasl, S. V.
Keller, H. H.
Keller, M.
Khai, L. M.
Kiloh, L. G.
Kimzey, S. L.
Kolyaskina, G. I.
Kopp, H. G.
Korneva, E. A.
Kraft, J. K.
Krupp, I. M.
Krylov, V. N.
Lavender, J. F.
Lazarus, L.
Levi, L.
Levin, W. C.
Levine, S.
Liljekvist, J. I.
Lozovsky, D. V.
Luckhurst, E.
Luk'ianenko, V. I.
Luparello, T. J.

Maestroni, G. J. M.
Marsh, J. T.
Mazié, J. C.
Medawar, P. B.
Merrill, J. P.
Metal'nikov, S.
Mettrop, P. J. G.
Meyer, R. J.
Mihailović, Lj.
Miller, J.
Mitrović, K.
Monjan, A. A.
Moos, R. H.
Morgan, E. E.
Mostarica, M.
Müller, J.
Niederman, J. C.
Niven, J. S. F.
Palmblad, J.
Park, C. D.
Penny, R.
Pierpaoli, W.
Rakic, Lj.
Rasmussen, A. F.
Ritzmann, S. E.
Rosenblatt, M.
Schenkel-Hulliger, L.
Solomon, G. F.
Sorkin, E.
Sparrow, E. M.
Stein, M.
Strander, H.
Strom, T. B.
Sytkowski, A. J.
Szentivanyi, A.
Unger, P.
Vartanian, M. E.
Veskov, R.
Vessey, S. H.
Visser, P.
White, A.
Wister, R., Jr.

I

NEUROIMMUNOMODULATION

A. Neuroanatomy, Neurophysiology, and Immunity

Chapters 1 through 9

B. Neuroendocrinology, Neuropharmacology, and Immunity

Chapters 10 through 20

1

ANAPHYLAXIS AND THE NERVOUS SYSTEM
PART III.

Geza Filipp and Andor Szentivanyi

B ILATERAL focal lesion of the tuberal region of the hypothalamus protects the guinea pig against anaphylactic shock.[1,2]

We may define our next problem by asking whether it is the first (specific) or the second (nonspecific) phase of the anaphylactic shock that is affected by tuberal lesion. The absence of shock may be caused by inhibition of antibody production, by inhibition of tissue products that cause shock, or by a decreased reactivity of the shock organs in the tuberal-injured animal.

In this paper we report an examination of the production of antibodies and the union of antigen and antibody in the tuberal-injured animal.

I. The Effect of Tuberal Lesion of the Hypothalamus on the Production of Antibodies in Guinea Pigs.

Three methods were used: (1) the Schultz-Dale test; (2) the determination of precipitin levels; and (3) experiments on passive transfer.

Schultz-Dale experiments:*—In these experiments we used eighty-three guinea pigs weighing 300 to 400 g. We operated upon forty-nine of them using the Horsley-Clarke stereotaxic technique, modified by Szentagotai. The test guinea pigs together with thirty-four control guinea pigs were sensitized subcutaneously on the seventh day after tuberal lesion, with bovine serum globulin containing 33 mg protein/0.5 ml saline. The sensitizations were repeated twice at two-day intervals.

On the seventeenth day after the last sensitization, we bled the animals by cutting the carotids, and carried out Schultz-Dale experiments on the surviving intestines of the animals. Because of the well-known high margin of error of the Schultz-Dale test, we examined several small pieces of intestine and, in addition, checked histamine sensitivity. In every other respect we followed the classic procedure of the Schultz-Dale test.

The results are shown in Table I. The difference in reactivity between the tuberal-injured and the control groups is so large as to be significant without doubt.

From the Department of Internal Medicine, University Medical School of Debrecen, Debrecen, Hungary

*For the devoted co-operation of Drs. M. Keszthelyi and P. Demeny, Department of Internal Medicine, University Medical School of Debrecen, Debrecen, Hungary, we wish to express our sincere thanks.

Precipitin Production:—We produced tuberal lesion in twenty guinea pigs, reserving twenty for controls. Seven days after tuberal lesion, we sensitized both groups with 0.3 ml of undiluted horse serum. Fourteen days after sensitization the animals were bled and from the serum thus

TABLE I. SCHULTZ-DALE EXPERIMENTS

Groups	Number of Animals	Schultz-Dale Positive	Schultz-Dale Negative
Tuberal-injured group	49	5	44
Control group	34	26	8

TABLE II. PRECIPITINS IN GUINEA PIGS

Number of Animal	Tuberal-injured Group	Control Group
1	0	800
2	200	800
3	0	1600
4	0	1600
5	0	1600
6	400	3200
7	200	800
8	100	1600
9	0	3200
10	0	1600
11	100	800
12	0	1600
13	400	800
14	0	1600
15	0	3200
16	0	800
17	0	800
18	400	1600
19	100	800
20	0	3200

obtained we determined precipitin by ring test. The results are shown in Table II. To be sure, the ring method of precipitation is not an exact procedure. However, the differences between the tuberal-injured and the control groups shown in Table II can, without doubt, be considered significant.

Experiments with Passive Transfer:—From among forty guinea pigs with an average weight of 300 g to 400 g, twenty were assigned the role of donors and twenty served as recipients. Ten of the donor guinea pigs underwent destruction of the tuberal region. On the seventh day following operation, we sensitized them, together with ten control animals, by subcutaneous injection of 0.3 ml of undiluted horse serum. On the fourteenth day following this injection, we bled both the tuberal-injured and the control donor animals and then intraperitoneally sensitized twenty normal guinea pigs with two to three ml of this serum, depending on the size of the receiving animal. Twenty-four hours after the introduction of antibody we challenged by intravenous injection of 0.5 to 1.0 ml of homologous antigen.

While the transfer experiment with sera derived from injured animals was successful in only two cases, we obtained positive transfer with all sera from the control animals. Thus, in contrast with the control animals, only two tuberal-injured animals disposed of enough circulating antibody to sensitize passively.

All three experiments show that production of antibodies in the tuberal-injured guinea pig is greatly diminished.

II. The Effect of Tuberal Lesion of the Hypothalamus on Antigen-Antibody Union.

On the basis of these results, the antianaphylactic effect of tuberal lesion may seem to be explainable solely by inhibition of antibody production. However, in some of our experiments[2] the tuberal lesion was made on previously sensitized animals (that is, animals provided with antibodies) which also showed lack of anaphylactic reactivity. For this, two alternative explanations are available: (1) the production of antibodies in previously sensitized tuberal-injured animals is inhibited and the antibodies existing prior to turberal lesion had been metabolized; (2) the inhibition of the production of antibodies is not the only way by which tuberal lesion interferes with the anaphylactic mechanism. We proceeded to the examination of this possibility.

An approach seemed to be offered by the technique of the passive anaphylactic shock in tuberal-injured animals. In this case, the inhibition of antibody production does not enter into the experiment.

Homologous passive anaphylaxis.—We divided thirty-nine guinea pigs of an average weight of 300 to 400 g into three groups: (1) thirteen guinea pigs we subcutaneously sensitized with 0.3 ml of undiluted horse serum twice at three-day intervals; (2) we set tuberal lesions in thirteen normal (unprepared) guinea pigs; and (3) thirteen guinea pigs served as controls for Group (2). The thirteen guinea pigs of the first group were bled on the fourteenth day following the second sensitizing injection. By intraperitoneal injection of 3.0 ml we sensitized one guinea pig of Group (2) (tuberal-injured) and one of Group (3) (normal controls) with the serum of each of the donors.

Twenty-four hours after the introduction of the antibody, we challenged by intravenous injection of 1.0 ml of homologous antigen. Out of thirteen tuberal-injured animals, eleven showed no shock, one reacted with mild shock and one with lethal shock. This animal which reacted with lethal shock showed no injury in the hypothalamus on examination of the brain (probably because of some mishap during operation). Of the control animals, ten reacted with lethal shock and three with severe shock.

Heterologous passive anaphylaxis.—We immunized two rabbits as donors by four intravenous injections of 2 to 8 ml of undiluted horse serum in gradually increasing quantities at three-day intervals. Fifteen days after the last injection, we found the precipitin level of the rabbits to be 1/2560 by ring test. With the antiserum from these animals we passively sensitized eleven tuberal-injured and ten control guinea pigs. The animals operated on were sensitized five days after operation. Each animal received 5 ml of rabbit serum intraperitoneally and was challenged twenty-four hours later with 1.0 ml of antigen given intravenously.

Of the eleven tuberal-injured animals, two reacted with lethal and three with mild shock, while the rest showed no reaction. By contrast, out of ten control animals, nine died in acute shock and only one survived after a fairly severe shock.

It appears that bilateral focal lesion of the tuberal region inhibits not only the active but also the passive anaphylactic shock.

THE EFFECT OF TUBERAL LESION ON THE ANTIBODY LEVEL
IN RABBITS AFTER SHOCK

Information was collected on antibody levels after shock in normal and tuberal-injured animals. We chose rabbits rather than guinea pigs for this second series of experiments for the reason that rabbits are good producers of circulating antibody. Moreover, we wished to learn whether the effect of tuberal lesion could be produced in rabbits.

First group:—We injected twenty-one rabbits, male and female, weighing 2.5 to 3 kg, first with 4.0 ml of undiluted horse serum intraperitoneally; two days later, 6.0 ml intravenously; and after three days, 2.0 ml subcutaneously and 3.0 ml by intraperitoneal injection. Eleven of the sensitized animals were tuberally injured on the fifteenth day following the first injection; ten animals were kept as controls. On the fourth day after the tuberal lesion (that is, on the nineteenth day after the first injection) we reinjected intravenously 4.0 ml of homologous antigen into both the animals operated on and the control animals. Immediately before and after the reinjection, we took blood from the tuberal-injured and control rabbits in order to determine precipitin levels.

In Table III we present the reaction after challenge and the precipitin levels before and after reinjection. Eight of the tuberal-injured animals remained without reaction, two reacted with mild and one with lethal shock. As to the control animals, two reacted with lethal shock, five with long-lasting severe shock, two with very mild shock, and one remained without reaction. Both the tuberal-injured animals and the controls had high titers of precipitin before provocation of shock, which declined after the provocation of shock in nine cases to zero, in two cases to half or to a quarter of the original titer.

Second group:—Furthermore, we sensitized ten guinea pigs weighing, on the average, 400 g, by subcutaneous injections of undiluted horse serum. After eighteen days we tuberally injured five of the guinea pigs, keeping the other five as controls. Both groups were challenged by intravenous injection on the twenty-third day with 1.0 ml of homologous antigen. None of the tuberal-injured animals showed anaphylactic symptoms, while all the control animals died in shock. About an hour after

TABLE III. THE EFFECT OF TUBERAL LESION ON
ANTIGEN-ANTIBODY UNION IN RABBITS

Tuberal-injured Animals			
		Precipitin Titers	
Number of Animal	Effect of Reinjection	Before Reinjection	After Reinjection
1	Lethal shock	800	0
2	No reaction	1600	0
3	No reaction	1600	0
4	Mild shock	1600	400
5	No reaction	800	400
6	No reaction	1600	0
7	No reaction	800	0
8	Mild shock	?	0
9	No reaction	?	0
10	No reaction	1600	0
11	No reaction	1600	0

Control Animals			
		Precipitin Titers	
Number of Animal	Effect of Reinjection	Before Reinjection	After Reinjection
1	Severe shock	1600	0
2	Severe shock	1600	200
3	Lethal shock	1600	0
4	Severe shock	3200	0
5	No reaction	1600	400
6	Lethal shock	1600	0
7	Severe shock	800	0
8	Mild shock	800	0
9	Mild shock	1600	0
10	Severe shock	1600	0

challenge we killed the tuberal-injured animals with CO and made Schultz-Dale experiments with small intestinal pieces. From each animal several small intestinal pieces were tested and in each case we also determined sensitivity to histamine. After adding homologous antigen to the bath water of the apparatus, in no case did we observe any contraction of the intestinal preparation.

This experiment was repeated with twenty guinea pigs. Of these, we tuberally injured ten animals; ten served as controls. On the twenty-third day following the sensitization, they were challenged as described in the preceding paragraph. Of the ten tuberal-injured animals, one reacted with severe shock, one with fairly severe shock, two with mild shock and six remained without shock. Nine of the ten control animals died in shock and one recovered after a very severe shock.

As with the first group, Schultz-Dale experiments were carried out. In one out of ten tuberal-injured animals, addition of a homologous antigen to the bath water caused intestinal contractions. Intestinal preparations from ten control animals showed reactivity in two cases.

CONCLUSIONS

The following conclusions can be drawn from an investigation of the mechanism of the antianaphylactic effect of tuberal lesion:

1. Antibody production in tuberal-injured guinea pigs is significantly reduced. This is true both for circulating and tissue-fixed antibodies.

2. In view of the fact that the antianaphylactic effect of tuberal lesion manifests itself in sensitized animals provided with antibody, the inhibition of antibody production cannot be the only effect of tuberal lesion.

3. This conclusion is borne out by our observation that tuberal lesion inhibits not only active but also passive anaphylactic shock in the guinea pig (both with homologous and heterologous antibody).

4. In rabbits, as well as in guinea pigs, anaphylactic reactivity is impaired by tuberal lesion.

5. Anaphylactic challenge produces a marked decrease in circulating, precipitating antibody to a similar degree in rabbits with tuberal lesions and in controls.

6. Sessile antibody is reduced both in nonoperated guinea pigs and those with tuberal lesions to a similar degree. This was shown by testing preparations made from the intestines of challenged animals in the Schultz-Dale apparatus.

7. We conclude from these data that the anti-anaphylactic effect of tuberal lesion is not related to an impairment of the ability of available antibody to react with antigen.

REFERENCES

1. Filipp, G.; Szentivanyi, A.; and Mess, B.: Anaphylaxis and the nervous system —I. Acta Medica Academiae Scientiarum Hungaricae, Tom. III, Fasc. 2, 103, 1952.

2. Szentivanyi, A. and Filipp, G.: Anaphylaxis and the Nervous System—II. Annals of Allergy, 16:143-151, 1958.

This chapter was part of a series of articles which appeared in the following publications:

Filipp, G., Szentivanyi, A., and Mess. B. (1953). Anaphylaxis and nervous system. I. Acta Med. Hung. III/2, 163–170.

Szentivanyi, A., and Filipp, G. (1958). Anaphylaxis and nervous system. II. Ann. Allergy 16, 143–151.

Filipp, G. and Szentivanyi, A. (1958). Anaphylaxis and nervous system. III. Ann. Allergy 16, 306–311.

Filipp, G. and Mess. B. (1969). Role of the thyroid hormone system in suppression of anaphylaxis due to electrolytic lesion of the tuberal region of the hypothalamus. Ann. Allergy 27, 500–505.

Filipp, G. and Mess. B. (1969). Role of adrenocortical system in suppressing anaphylaxis after hypothalamic lesion. Ann. Allergy 27, 607–610.

Filipp, G. (1973). Mechanism of suppressing anaphylaxis through electrolytic lesion of the tuberal region of the hypothalamus. Ann. Allergy 31, 272–278.

2

EFFECTS OF INTRAVENTRICULARLY INJECTED ANTI-N. CAUDATUS ANTIBODY ON THE ELECTRICAL ACTIVITY OF THE CAT BRAIN

Lj. Mihailović and B. D. Janković

IT is well known that anti-tissue antibodies, when injected into an animal of the donor species, may exhibit the selective affinity for the homologous organ and produce certain modifications in its morphological and functional state[1]. The damaging effects of anti-tissue antibodies have been demonstrated in different organs[2]. However, no information could be found in the literature available concerning the physio-pathological events associated with an *in vivo* collision between anti-brain antibodies and the corresponding nervous tissue. Bearing in mind the high complexity of morphological and functional organization of the brain, a series of immuno-electro-physiological experiments has been undertaken to investigate the possible differential reactivity of various cerebral structures when exposed to the action of different brain region anti-sera. The present communication, as a part of these investigations, is a preliminary report concerning only some of the effects of intraventricularly administered anti-n. caudatus antibody on the electrical activity of various parts of the cat brain.

Cats operated under 'Nembutal' anæsthesia were used. Surface and depth, 'Teflon'-insulated silver and stainless steel electrodes ($0 \cdot 005$–$0 \cdot 01$ in. in diameter), respectively, were implanted into various regions of the brain (frontal cortex, frontal white matter, n. caudatus, hippocampus, hypothalamus, thalamus and brain stem reticular formation). Needle electrodes for the interior of the brain were introduced by means of a Horsley-Clarke stereotaxic instrument. All electrodes were implanted into the left cerebral hemisphere, while the cannula was inserted into the right lateral ventricle, according to the method of Feldberg and Sherwood[3]. Electrical activity was recorded throughout the experiment using a 12-channel Reega-Alvar electroencephalograph. Details regarding recording and stimulation technique have been published elsewhere[4].

The cat n. caudatus was carefully dissected, homogenized, mixed with Freund adjuvant and injected subcutaneously into rabbits ($1 \cdot 0$ gm. of fresh tissue per kgm. body-weight). The γ-globulin from the immune rabbit sera was separated by the method of Basset *et al.*[5]. Immune rabbit γ-globulin was investigated by diffusion-gel[6] and complement fixation reaction[7], in which the saline extract of n. caudatus tissue was used as antigen. The reaction between n. caudatus antigen and the corresponding immune rabbit γ-globulin revealed 2–3 precipitin lines in the agar and a titre of 1/128–1/256 in the complement fixation test. Normal rabbit γ-globulin, taken prior to the immunization, did not show any serological activity with antigen prepared from the n. caudatus tissue.

The cats were divided into three groups: the first (experimental group) was treated with immune rabbit γ-globulin; the second (control group) received normal rabbit γ-globulin, and animals from the third (control group) were injected with physiological solution in order to evaluate the possible influence of volume of injected fluid. Two to three injections of 0·3 ml. daily, with an interval of 60 min. between the injections, were administered on four successive days. Total protein content of immune rabbit γ-globulin injected into an animal of the first group was 46·08 mgm., while that of normal γ-globulin administered to an animal of the second group amounted to 60·24 mgm.

Some of the results are illustrated in Fig. 1. In both control groups no essential change in electrical activity of various cerebral structures investigated could be noticed. Records made in the course of normal γ-globulin application, as well as the records taken at intervals within the period of one month following the last injection, were found to be fairly comparable with the activity recorded prior to the γ-globulin administration (Fig. 1*A*). However, in the experimental group of animals, intraventricular application of anti-n. caudatus γ-globulin was followed by pronounced modification in electrical activity. The evolution of electrographic disturbances seemed to pass through three consecutive stages. The first stage was characterized by the appearance of spikes and high-voltage sharp waves localized in the n. caudatus. These transient irritative abnormalities become apparent on the third day of antibody administration, and disappeared two to three days afterwards. The second, also transient stage was characterized by slight general accentuation of background activity and by sporadic appearance of diffuse abnormalities consisting of bursts of 4–6/sec. high-voltage waves, in all leads. Such activity outlasted the disappearance of spikes and sharp waves in n. caudatus for several days. The third stage was characterized by gradual slowing down, progressive decrease in the amplitude and almost complete disappearance of spontaneous electrical activity of the caudate nucleus within a month

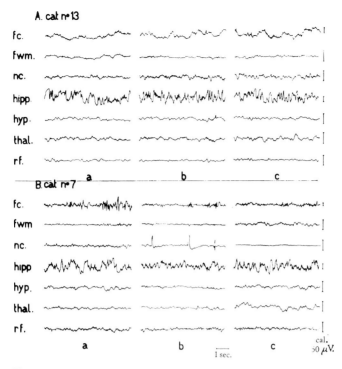

A. cat n° 13

fc.			
fwm.			
nc.			
hipp.			
hyp.			
thal.			
rf.			

a   b   c

B. cat n° 7

fc.			
fwm			
nc.			
hipp			
hyp.			
thal.			
rf.			

a   b   c

cal.
1 sec.   50 µV.

Fig. 1. *A*, Records made (*a*) before administration, (*b*) following the third day of injecting, and (*c*) eight days after the last injection of normal rabbit γ-globulin. *B*, Records taken (*a*) prior to antibody application, (*b*) after the third day of injecting, and (*c*) seven days following the last intraventricular injection of anti-n. caudatus γ-globulin. *fc*, frontal cortex; *fwm*, frontal white matter; *nc*, n. caudatus; *hip*, hippocampus; *hyp*, hypothalamus; *thal*, thalamus; *rf*, brain stem reticular formation; for explanation, see text

after antibody administration (Fig. 1*B*). Such an evolution of electrographic abnormalities was reflected in modification of potentials in n. caudatus evoked by acoustic stimuli, as well as in the change of activity propagated to n. caudatus during seizures induced by electrical stimulation of the hippocampus. It should be emphasized that no change in electrical activity of the caudate nucleus could be observed in animals treated with anti-hippocampus antibody (unpublished experiments).

In a previous paper[7] it was found that lipids from various regions of cat brain lack individual specificity but are all highly organ-specific. That is why, in the present experiments, the saline extract of n. caudatus containing mainly protein components has been used as antigen in preparing the corresponding anti-serum. N. caudatus was chosen because it forms the wall of the lateral ventricle and could be, therefore, easily attacked by the intraventricular route and thus brought into prolonged contact with antibody injected into the cerebrospinal fluid. This, of course, could not be assured adequately if the antibody were administered by a systemic route[8]. Diffuse electrographic abnormalities reported here were also observed following intraventricular administration of some other anti-brain region sera, such as anti-hippocampus, and should be, therefore, considered as nonspecific manifestations. However, the initial irritative phenomena, followed by a progressive decrease in electrical activity, strictly confined to n. caudatus, strongly suggest that anti-n. caudatus antibody has definite affinity towards the homologous nervous tissue.

This work has been supported in part by a grant from the Yugoslav Foundation for Scientific Research, contracts No. 490/1 and No. 202/1.

Institute of Pathological Physiology,
Medical School, and Microbiological Institute,
School of Pharmacy,
University of Belgrade.

[1] Pressman, D., and Sherman, B., *J. Immunol.*, **67**, 21 (1951). Bale, W. F., and Spar, L. I., *ibid.*, **73**, 125 (1954). Anigstein, L., McConnell, K. P., Whitney, D. M., Pappas, P., Portman, O. W. and Barnes, W., *Tex. Rep. Biol. Med.*, **12**, 945 (1954).

[2] Metshnikoff, E., *Ann. Inst. Pasteur*, **14**, 369 (1900). Joanović, Dj., in *Allergie*, 707 (Georg Thieme Verlag, Stuttgart, 1957). Masugi, M., *Beitr. Path. Anat.*, **91**, 82 (1933).

[3] Feldberg, W., and Sherwood, S. L., *J. Physiol.*, **120**, 3 P (1953).

[4] Mihailović, Lj., and Delgado, J. M. R., *J. Neurophysiol.*, **19**, 21 (1956).

[5] Basset, C. A. L., Campbell, D. H., Evans, V. J., and Earle, W. R., *J. Immunol.*, **78**, 79 (1957).

[6] Ouchterlony, P., *Acta Path. Microbiol. Scand.*, **32**, 231 (1953).

[7] Janković, B. D., Isaković, K., and Mihailović, Lj., *Int. Arch. Allergy*, **17**, 211 (1960).

[8] Stern, L., Kassil, G. N., Lockshina, E. S., Romel, E. L., and Zeitlin, S. M., *C.R. Soc. Biol.*, *Paris*, **99**, 360 (1928).

3

THE EFFECT OF THE DESTRUCTION OF AREAS WITHIN THE HYPOTHALAMIC REGION ON THE PROCESS OF IMMUNOGENESIS*

E. A. Korneva and L. M. Khai

Introduction

It has been previously demonstrated that the sympathoadrenal system plays a significant role in the regulation of the immunogenesis process, exerting a stimulating influence on the process of antibody formation and the elimination of an antigen (Khai and Korneva, 1960, 1961; Korneva and Khai, 1961). The mechanism of the influences of the sympathoadrenal system on immunogenesis may be acceptable only if we admit the possibility of their being mediated by the central nervous system.

Taking into consideration the facts discovered in recent years pointing toward the influence of the sympathoadrenal system on the functional state of the reticular formation of the brain stem, especially its adrenergic structures [Bonvalett *et al.*, 1954; Rothballer, 1956; Anokhin, 1957; Karamyan, 1959; Anokhina-Itskova, 1961; Megun (Magoun), 1961], we consider it probable that the influence of the sympathoadrenal system on the process of immunogenesis may be mediated through these structures.

In recent years a large number of studies have been accumulated regarding the physiology of the hypothalamus. As a result of numerous studies the hypothalamus is now considered as a center of vegetative innervation [Ranson and Magoun, 1939; Grinshtein, 1946; Gel'gorn (Gellhorn), 1948; Hess, 1954; Tonkikh, 1961]. Many authors have studied the influence of the interstitial brain tissue on the metabolism of substances, including proteins (Leschke, 1919; Zhislina and Perel'muter, 1939), and noted the role of the hypothalamus in the regulation of protein metabolism (Ternovskii and Mogil'nitskii, 1925; Shargorodskii, 1948). These and other data enable us to suppose that the hypothalamus also takes part in the regulation of immune reactions, although such an hypothesis has been expressed only analogously (Zil'ber, 1958; Zdrodovskii, 1961).

Only very recently have we seen in the literature extremely interesting but, unfortunately, isolated works devoted to an experimental clarification of the influence of the interstitial brain tissue on the blood antibody content (Kanda, 1959; Petrovskii, 1961). Using the method of stimulating the brain through chronically implanted electrodes, the authors established that, in animals with previously developed antibodies, and in which their titer had reached a steady state, the stimulation of several zones of the hypothalamus [the infundibulum (stalk of the

*Translated from the original Russian article *Sechenov Physiological Journal of the USSR* **XLIX** (No. 1), 1963, by Robert Russell Radway, for Language Consultants, Wellesley Hills, Massachusetts.

neurohypophysis), the zone of the grey eminence, and the sympathetic zone], leads to a brief increase in the titer of agglutinins. Electrical irritation of the parasympathetic zone of the hypothalamus leads to a decrease in the quantity of agglutinins in the blood of the animals. Since the observed changes occur quickly, and after 1 or 2 hours the level of antibodies returns to the initial value, it is difficult to assume that the effect is caused by shifts in the production of antibodies. Rather, we should speak of their redistribution in the body.

The focus of the current study is a clarification of the role of the hypothalamus and the thalamic structures in the regulation of immune reactions. We must emphasize that, although hundreds of studies have been devoted to the functional characteristics of the hypothalamus, the question of its participation in the regulation of the immunogenesis process is essentially only proposed.

Procedure

Experiments were carried out on 57 rabbits, each of which was subjected to the destruction of various areas of the hypothalamus and other structures of the forebrain and the mesencephalon.

The destruction of the areas of brain tissue was usually carried out to the right of the midline by a steady electric current of 1 mAmp for 30 seconds through a monopole electrode reliably insulated along its entire length, except for a sharp point which was left bare over a distance of 0.5 to 0.7 mm. The ground electrode was located on the rabbit's ear. The procedure used made it possible to destroy limited areas of brain tissue, usually in a size range 1–1.5 mm.

The electrode was embedded in the brain using a Horsley-Clark stereotaxic apparatus. An atlas by Sawyer and co-authors, with corrections by R.M. Meshcherskii and I. A. Chernevskii (1959) was used to determine the coordinates.

Prior to the operation, the animals were anesthesized using urethane (0.7 g/kg) or hexanal (used in combination with morphine). The animals survived the operation easily, their appetite was quickly restored, and the rabbits were lively, and sometimes exhibited heightened excitability.

A foreign protein—horse serum in the quantity of 0.25 ml/kg—was introduced into a vein in the rabbits 4 or 5 days after the destruction of various areas of brain tissue. During the month following injection of the antigen we investigated the dynamics of its elimination and the process of antibody formation, the presence of which was determined in the blood by the reaction of complement binding (prolonged binding at low temperature). The intensity of the reaction was evaluated using a four-cross system.

The experiments were carried out on eight series of rabbits, each series of which contained 6–9 animals.

In two series of rabbits daily body temperature measurements using a contact thermometer were made in the morning hours. The instrument probe was held on the skin surface for 3 minutes. Thermometer measurements were made on control (intact) animals for comparison.

Research Results

We could observe four types of immune reactions from among the animals of all the test series: in one group of rabbits the dynamics of elimination of the antigen and the production of antibodies could not be distinguished from normal; in the second group we noted some reduction in the production of antibodies; in the third group we noted a sharp depression in the production of antibodies and a significant retention of foreign protein in the blood; the fourth group was characterized by a complete absence of complement-binding antibodies and an extended retention of the antigen in the blood.

Using these serological characteristics as a basis, we divided all of the experimental rabbits into four corresponding groups. The characteristics of the processes of elimination of foreign protein and of the formation of antibodies in the animals of these groups are shown in Fig. 3.1.

On the average, the freeing of the organism from foreign antigens and the production of antibodies for a specified dose of antigens proceeded with strict regularity: the quantity of antigens in the blood for a dose of 0.25 ml/kg fell to zero by day 7–9, antibodies were first detected 5–7 days after the introduction of the protein, reaching a maximum quantity between day 15–20. After the twentieth day, the quantity decreased, and around 30 days from the time of introduction of the foreign antigen there were usually few antibodies in the blood, or they were entirely absent.

These regular rules in our experiments were characteristic for the control (unoperated on) animals and for rabbits of the fourth group.

As we see in Fig. 3.1, the degree of change in the dynamics of the immune processes in animals of the various groups was diverse—from complete agreement with the control graph to absolute inhibition of production of antibodies, which was expressed by an absence of antibodies in the blood during the entire length of the experiment and by an extended retention of foreign protein in the body of the animal (up to day 15).

An histological inspection of the localization of areas of destruction in the animal brain shows that for each of the groups in the study there was a characteristically defined localization of destruction.* Among the animals with a complete depression of the process of antibody formation the zone of destruction of brain tissue was limited and was situated (according to the atlas of Sawyer and co-authors) in the region of the dorsal hypothalamic field, usually at level P = 4 (Fig. 3.2).

Figure 3.2a demonstrates brain destruction typical for rabbits of this group. As we see in Fig. 3.2 the area of necrosis is restricted; at high magnification a proliferation of the glial tissue and complete destruction of the nerve cells is seen. The center of destruction is located in the cell structure comprising the grey paraventricular substance and occupies only a small area of the anterior hypothalamus.

After the destruction of the brain tissue on the boundary of this area, we noticed a sharply expressed depression of antibody production in the animals; the freeing of the body from foreign protein was decreased (rabbits of the second group).

In those cases where the areas of necrosis were localized in other regions of the hypothalamus, the thalamic structures, the caudate nucleus, the anterior commissure, and several other

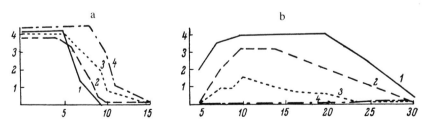

FIGURE 3.1. The dynamics of antigen elimination (a) and of formation of antibodies (b) in rabbits of the various groups. The ordinate axis shows days into the experiment; the abscissa shows the intensity of the reaction showing the presence of antibodies and antigen in the blood. (1) Shows rabbits of the fourth group and the controls; (2) shows the third group; (3) shows the second group; (4) shows the first group.

*The histological studies were carried out by M. V. Kovalenkova, to whom the authors extend their deep thanks.

Hypothalmic Region Destruction on Immunogenesis   **13**

a

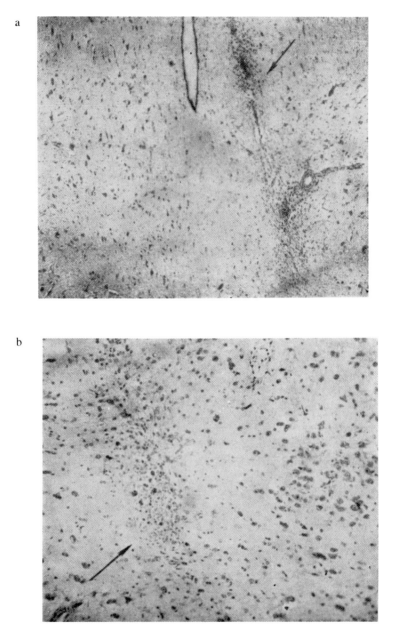

b

FIGURE 3.2. A microphotograph of sections of the brain of rabbits of the first (I) and second (II) groups at small a (ocular 10 × objective 10 and ocular 10 × objective 1) and large b (ocular 10 × objective 20 and 7 × objective 10) magnifications. Arrows show areas of necrosis.

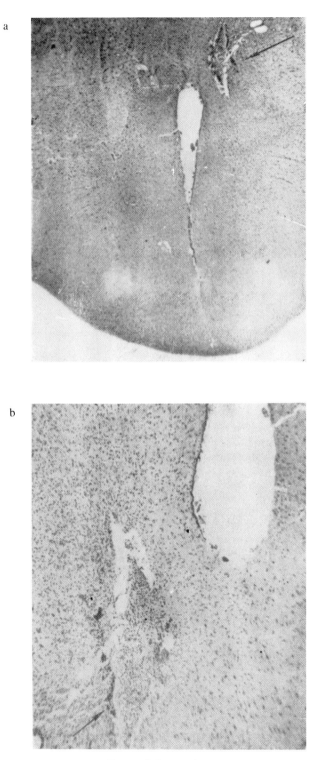

FIGURE 3.2. (continued)

formations of the forebrain and the mesencephalon, the dynamics of the immune process did not differ from normal (rabbits of the fourth group). In some cases (rabbits of the third group), we could establish a slight depression in antibody production and an insignificant retention of antigen in the blood (Fig. 3.3).

We should note that in a number of animals the destruction was located slightly forward of the level shown in Fig. 3.3. A complete suppression of antibody formation was not observed in these animals, and a corresponding localization of the centers of destruction was not plotted on the diagram.

The experiments carried out form a basis for the assumption that there is a limited area, situated in the region of the dorsal hypothalamic field, which is specifically related to regulation of the immunogenesis process. The destruction of this area leads to a depression of antibody production.

It is difficult for us to judge the extent to which the observed influences are specific, and the role of the structures being studied in regulating the processes of the metabolism of substances, in general, and of protein metabolism, in particular.

The animal's body temperature may serve as in indirect indicator reflecting the level of metabolism of substances in the organism since there is a corresponding increase or decrease in body temperature with significant changes of metabolism. Moreover, located in the grey para-ventricular substance of the hypothalamic region are structures participating in the thermoregulation process (Arnson and Sachs, 1885; Isenschmidt and Schnitzlar, 1914; Tomas, 1934; Vainberg, 1946) which may be disturbed as a result of the intervention carried out. Hence, we made a daily temperature measurement of the animals in two of the experimental groups (15 animals). It was established that the body temperatures of the rabbits which had been operated on differed little from the temperature of the control (intact) animals. Occasionally, we could establish a certain lability of body temperatures in the experimental animals compared with the control animals (Fig. 3.4).

The data derived bear witness to the absence of significant shifts in the intensity of overall substance metabolism and of the absence of destruction of thermoregulation in the rabbits which were operated upon.

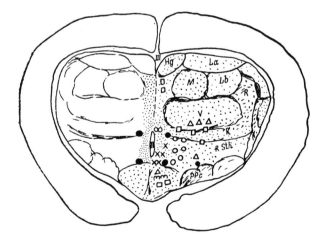

FIGURE 3.3. A diagram of the location of areas of destruction of brain tissue in rabbits of the various groups. ×, First group; ○, the second group; △, the third group; and □, the fourth group.

A Discussion of the Results

We established the fact that the hypothalamic structures, especially formations of the anterior hypothalamus, influenced the production of antibodies and the process of elimination of an antigen from the blood of rabbits.

In many respects, the interpretation of the facts presented is complicated since the question of immunogenesis regulation in this plane has not been experimentally studied, and the information in the literature regarding this question is extremely scanty.

Since at the present stage of research it does not appear possible to explain the essence and mechanism of the observed phenomena, we may only state certain considerations in this regard. First, the question arises as to how we may evaluate the area that we discovered in terms of function based on cellular structure and how this participates in the regulation of the immunogenesis process.

Immunogenesis is a complicated reaction which includes complex physiological processes involving many organs and systems. We may suppose that the area found in the region of the dorsal hypothalamic field plays a definite role in the integration of processes directed toward the organization of defensive reactions of this type, in the same way that separate structures of the grey eminence are considered responsible for the regulation of heat formation and output. This concept is supported by contemporary views on the activities of the subcortical structures, especially of the nuclear formations of the reticular formations of the brain stem, which provides a specific direction and a modality of action, i.e., is integrative.

In addition, there is a need to study in what manner, and through which systems, the transfer of influences takes place from the hypothalamus to the organs producing antibodies.

Recent work has established that the hypothalamus, its anterior divisions, in particular, is connected to the thalamic structures by underlying formations of the brain stem and the spinal

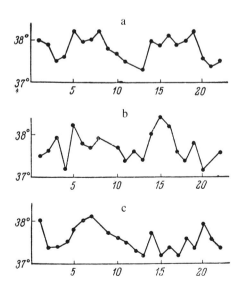

FIGURE 3.4. Temperature graphs of the rabbits of various experimental groups. Along the ordinate axis are the days of the experiment. Along the abscissa are body temperatures (°C) (a) first group; (b) second group; and (c) control group.

chord (Ranson and Magoun, 1939; Murphy and Gellhorn, 1945a; Hess, 1954). There are also ascending links, passing from the hypothalamus to the sections of the brain lying above, including the cortex of the large hemispheres* (Kennard, 1943; Murphy and Gellhorn, 1945b; Nakao, 1958). We cannot rule out that the influences of the hypothalamus on the organs taking part in the production of antibodies is transmitted through the structures designated and then through the peripheral branches of the vegetative nervous system. However, direct experiments in this regard have not been carried out, and the question requires further study.

The most appropriate current representation of regulation of the immunogenesis process is the supposition that there is an hormonal path for the transfer of influences from the hypothalamus to the cells of the reticuloendothelial system.

As studies by Porter (1952, 1953) and Buomon et al. (1957) have shown, the anterior hypothalamus stimulates the secretion of adrenocorticotropic hormones of the hypophysis and possibly a somatotropic hormone which, in turn, stimulates antigen formation (Schellin et al., 1954; Gurevich, 1960). Consequently, we may think that there are structures situated in the zone of the dorsal hypothalamic field that normally exert a stimulating influence on the production of the somatotropic hormone of the hypophysis. It is possible that the destruction of this zone of the hypothalamus leads to a decrease in secretion of the hormone, which causes a depression in antibody production.

Although this hypothesis agrees well with the data of other authors who have investigated the influence of hormones of the hypophysis and of the adrenal cortex on antibody production, it does not explain the complete absence of complement-binding antibodies in the blood of the animals. All of the researchers who have studied the influence of the hormone systems mentioned have noticed only a slight decrease in immune reactions.

As shown by Nagareda (1954), even removal of the entire hypophysis does not cause a significant reduction in the production of antibodies during various periods after the operation (from 12 hours to 60 days). Consequently, the hypophysis is not the sole pathway by which influences of the central apparatuses of the nervous system on the process of immunogenesis are transmitted; apparently, they may also be mediated through other structures. The data derived make it possible to assume that the influences of the hypothalamus on the process of antibody formation are transmitted both by nervous and hormonal pathways. The hypothesis formulated indicates paths for further research on the question rather than suggesting specific mechanisms for the observed phenomena.

The cause of the appearance of such a pronounced depression of immunological reactions, even with unilateral destruction of anterior hypothalamus structures, remains unclear. Evidently, research into the degree of compensation for the destroyed function following uni- and bilateral destruction would help clarify this question.

In conclusion, we should mention that the problem of the regulation of immunological reactions has recently been given more attention (Zdrodovskii, 1961). Characteristically, in considering the role of the hypothalamus-hypophysis system in the regulation of the process of immunogenesis, and underscoring the major role of the hypothalamus in this process, the author has not yet cited studies regarding this subject which completely reflect the contemporary state of the question.

The data which we have obtained provide a real basis for the inclusion of the hypothalamus in this diagram and underscore the role of the nervous system in regulating the immunogenesis process.

*Typographical error in the Russian original.

Conclusions

1. Destruction of the hypothalamus in the area of the dorsal hypothalamic field, for example, at level P = 4 (according to the atlas of Sawyer and co-workers), leads to a complete depression of production of complement-binding antibodies and prolonged retention of antigens in the blood.

2. Destruction of the hypothalamic and thalamic stuctures at the boundary with the dorsal hypothalamic field, or partially within its limits, but at other levels (P = 2, P = 3), leads to a sharp depression in the process of antibody formation and significant retention of antigen in the blood.

3. Destruction of brain tissue in other areas of the hypothalamus and also in the forebrain and mesencephalon does not bring about any changes in the dynamics of immunogenesis, or insignificantly lowers production of antibodies and inhibits the removal of foreign protein from the body.

References

Anokhin, P. K. (1957). *Fiziol. Zh. SSSR*, **43** (No. 11) 1072 (Physiological Journal of the USSR).

Anokhina-Itskova, I. P. (1961). *Fiziol. Zh. SSSR*, **47** (No. 2) 154 (Physiological Journal of the USSR).

Aronson, E. and Sachs, I. (1885). *Arch. Ges. Physiol.* **37**, 625.

Bonvallet, M., Dell, P., and Hiebel, I. (1954). *EEG Clin. Neurophysiol.* **6**, 119.

Boumon, P. R., Gaarenstroom, J. H., Smelik, P. G., and De Wied, D. (1957). *Acta Physiol. Pharmacol. Neurol.* **6**, 268.

Gel'horn (Gellhorn), E. (1948). "Regulator Functions of the Autonomic Nervous System." Moscow.

Grinshtein, A. M. (1948). "Paths and Centers of the Nervous System." Moscow.

Gurvich, G. A. Cited in P. F. Zdrodovski L.-M. (1961).

Hess, W. R. (1954) "Diencephalon." NY.

Isenschmidt, R. and Schnizler, W. (1914). *Arch. Exp. Pathol.* **76** (No. 1–2), 202.

Kanda, R. (1959). *J. Bacteriol.* **14** (No. 3), 223.

Karamyan, A. I. (1959). *Fiziol. Zh. SSSR*, **45** (No. 7), 778.

Kennard, M. A. (1943). *J. Neurophysiol.* **6** (No. 5), 405.

Khai, L. M. and Korneva, E. A. Ezhegodn. IEM for 1959 350 pub. IEM L, 1960 Ezhegodn, IEM for 1960 307 pub. IEM L 1961 (Yearbook of the Institute of Experimental Medicine).

Korneva, E. A. and Khai, L. M. (1961). *Fiziol. Zh. SSSR*, **47** (No. 10), 1298.

Leschke, J. (1919). *Zs. Klin. Med.* **87**, 99.

Megun (Magoun), G. (1961). "The Vigilant Brain." Moscow (Bodrstvuyushchii Mozg.).

Meshcherskii, R. M. and Chernevskaya, I. A. (1959). *Fiziol. Zh. SSSR*, **45** (No. 9), 1152.

Murphy, I. P. and Gellhorn, E. (1945a). *J. Neurophysiol.* **8** (No. 6), 431.

Nagureda, S. I. (1954). *Immunology* **73**, 88.

Nakao, H. (1958). *Amer. J. Physiol.* **194** (No. 2), 411.

Petrovskii, N. I. (1961). *Zh. Mikrobiol. Epidemiol.* (No. 10), 213 (Journal of Microbiology and Epidemiology).

Porter, R. W. (1952). *Amer. J. Physiol.* **169** (No. 3), 629.

Porter, R. W. (1953). *Amer. J. Physiol.* **172** (No. 3), 515.

Ranson, S. W. and Magoun, H. W. (1939). *Ergeb. Physiol.* **41**, 56.

Rothballer, A. B. (1956). *EEG Clin. Neurophysiol.* **8**, 63.

Sawyer, C. H., Everett, I. W., and Green, I. D. (1954). *J. Comp. Neurol.* **101** (No. 3), 801.

Schellin, U., Hessalsjö, R., Paulsen, F., and Mallgren, J. (1954). *Acta Pathol. Microbiol. Scand.* **35**, 6.

Shargorodskii, L. (1948). Ya. Sb. Mauchn. tr. Posvyashch. E. K. Seppy, 84, Medgiz. (A collection of scholarly works dedicated to E. K. Sepp.)

Ternovskii, V. N. and Mogil'nitskii, B. N. (1925). "The Anatomy of the Vegetative Nervous System and Its Pathology." Moscow and Leningrad.

Thomas, A. (1934). *Rev. Neurol.* **6**, 71.

Tonkikh, A. V. (1961). Thesis. I. All-Union Conference on the Physiology of the Vegetative Nervous System and the Cerebellum, 156, Erevan.

Vainberg, I. S. (1946). "The Role of the Nervous System in Thermoregulation." Leningrad.

Zdrodovskii, P. F. (1961). Problems of Infection and Immunity, Medgiz. (State medical publishing house.)

Zhislina, S. and Perel'muter, P. (1939). *Vopr. Neirokhirurg* **2** (No. 2), 53 (Questions of neurosurgery).

Zil'ber, L. A. (1958). "Bases of Immunology." Moscow.

4

EFFECT OF HYPOTHALAMIC LESIONS ON RAT ANAPHYLAXIS

Thomas J. Luparello, Marvin Stein, and C. Dick Park

LUPARELLO, THOMAS J., MARVIN STEIN, AND C. DICK PARK. *Effect of hypothalamic lesions on rat anaphylaxis.* Am. J. Physiol. 207(4): 911–914. 1964.—The present study investigated the effect of anterior and posterior hypothalamic lesions on lethal anaphylaxis in the rat. Three groups of animals—control, posterior hypothalamic lesioned, and anterior hypothalamic lesioned—were sensitized to ovalbumin and subsequently challenged with various doses of the antigen. Dose-mortality curves were plotted for the control and two experimental groups. The three curves were demonstrated to be parallel. Ovalbumin was significantly less potent in the animals with anterior hypothalamic lesions than in both the control rats and those with posterior lesions. The protective action of anterior hypothalamic lesions against lethal anaphylaxis in the rat is discussed in terms of neuroendocrine processes, parasympathetic-sympathetic effects and antibody formation.

electrolytic lesions   hypothalamus   anaphylaxis
CNS influence on anaphylaxis

T HERE IS A GROWING BODY of literature indicating that the central nervous system is related to hypersensitive mechanisms, and specifically anaphylaxis. Freedman and Fenichel (7) tested the effect of midbrain lesions on the course of anaphylaxis in the guinea pig and found that bilateral lesions in the midbrain reticulum, at the level of the superior colliculus, prevented anaphylactic death. Szentivanyi and Filipp (6, 20, 21) have reported that lethal anaphylactic shock in the guinea pig can be prevented both by bilateral focal lesions in the tuberal region of the hypothalamus and by electrical stimulation of the mammillary region. They noted that the protective effect of hypothalamic lesions was greatest in what they referred to as the tuberal region and that it diminished in proportion to the distance from this area. Further in-

vestigation is required of the specific areas of the hypothalamus that may be related to lethal anaphylaxis.

The mechanisms by which central nervous system lesions inhibit the development of anaphylaxis have not been defined. The effect of an alteration of hypothalamic processes on guinea pig anaphylaxis could be species specific and related to a modification in the responsivity of the shock tissue, i.e., the bronchioles. In order to investigate this question further, the present report is concerned with the effect of hypothalamic lesions on a species with a different major shock organ in anaphylaxis. The albino rat was chosen since in this species anaphylactic shock is accompanied by congestion and hemorrhage of the small intestine, without major pulmonary changes (18). In contrast, in guinea pig anaphylaxis there are changes in the lungs, without pathology in the intestines.

METHODS

Male albino Sprague-Dawley rats (175–240 g) were used in all phases of this study. Seventy rats were injected intraperitoneally with 25 mg ovalbumin in 1.0 ml of physiological saline solution, with 0.5 ml *Hemophilus pertussis* (Wyeth) vaccine as an adjuvant. Thirteen days after sensitization the animals were challenged with ovalbumin in 0.5 ml saline administered intravenously by means of the tail vein. The rats were divided into seven groups, each consisting of ten animals, and each of the groups receiving one of the following challenging doses of ovalbumin: 4.00, 2.00, 1.00, 0.50, 0.250, 0.125, and 0.062 mg. The rats treated in this manner comprised the control group.

A second group of 36 rats was sensitized as previously described, and on the 7th postsensitization day bilateral lesions were placed in the hypothalamus with the aid of a Stellar-Johnson stereotaxic apparatus. With the head leveled in the instrument the following coordinates were used for directing the electrode: 4.0 mm anterior to the ear bars, 0.75 mm lateral to the superior sagittal sinus, and vertically 8.0 mm from the dorsal brain surface. These coordinates were intended for localization of the electrode tip in the posterior hypothalamus. Lesions were made by an anodal d-c current of 2 ma passed for 10 sec through the electrode tip; the stainless steel electrode was 0.01 in. in diameter and insulated except at the tip. The

This investigation was supported in part by National Institute of Neurological Diseases and Blindness Grant NB-04857.

This work was done during the tenure of Special Fellowship ESP-15,620 from the National Institute of Allergy and Infectious Diseases and of Career Development Award K3-MH-15,620 from the National Institute of Mental Health.

Reprinted from *American Journal of Physiology,* **207** 911–914, 1964 by permission of the American Physiological Society.

TABLE 1. *Lethal effects of ovalbumin in control and hypothalamic-lesioned rats*

Treatment of Rats	Challenging Dose, mg Ovalbumin										Slope Function	LD₅₀, mg
	0.062	0.125	0.25	0.5	1.0	2.0	4.0	5.0	6.0	8.0		
Control	0/10*	2/10	3/10	2/10	5/10	7/10	10/10				3.16	0.80 (0.50–1.28)†
Posterior lesions				2/8		3/5	10/12	11/11			2.15	0.92 (0.51–1.62)
Anterior lesions				0/10	3/10		7/13		8/10	8/10	2.84	3.0 (2.0–4.5)

* Mortality ratio. † 95% Fiducial limit.

ground connection was made at the ear bar of the stereotaxic instrument. Rats treated in this manner will be referred to as the group with posterior lesions. Six days postoperatively (13 days postsensitization) the animals were challenged with an intravenous injection of ovalbumin as previously described. Eleven of the rats were injected with 5.0 mg ovalbumin, twelve animals with 2.0 mg, five animals with 1.0 mg, and eight animals with 0.5 mg. Following this phase of the experiment, all the operated animals were decapitated and the heads were placed in 10% formalin. The sites and magnitudes of the lesions were determined histologically.

A third group of 53 rats was sensitized in the same manner, and on the 7th postsensitization day lesions were made as before except that the lesions were intended for the anterior hypothalamus. The coordinates were anterior 7.0 mm, 0.75 mm lateral to the superior sagittal sinus and vertically 8.5 mm from the brain surface. Six days postoperatively the animals were challenged as were the previous groups. Ten of the animals were injected with 8.0 mg ovalbumin, ten animals with 6.0 mg, thirteen animals with 4.0 mg, ten animals with 1.0 mg, and ten of the animals with 0.5 mg. As in the previously described group the brains were examined histologically. The animals of this group will be referred to as those with anterior lesions.

Dose-effect curves were plotted for each of the three groups of animals. The goodness of fit of the line for each curve was determined by testing the heterogeneity of the data by the chi-square test. The slope function, LD_{50}, and potency ratios of ovalbumin in the control and operated rats were determined from these curves in order to compare the sensitivity of the three groups of animals to ovalbumin. These values were computed according to the method of Litchfield and Wilcoxon (12).

RESULTS

In the control and experimental animals who developed lethal anaphylactic shock, the course followed a fairly uniform pattern, as described by Sanyal and West (18). The animals showed progressive symptoms characterized by marked prostration, weakness, cyanosis, and convulsions. Death occurred most often within 1 hr, but in some cases after as long as 6 hr. Animals who developed anaphylactic shock but who did not die exhibited

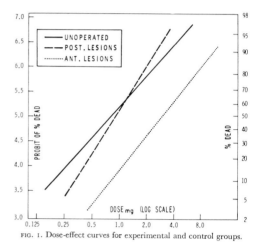

FIG. 1. Dose-effect curves for experimental and control groups.

ecchymotic changes in the wall of the small intestine. The majority of the rats dying from anaphylactic shock showed severe congestion of the entire intestine with blood and mucus in the lumen; however, some of the rats with fatal anaphylaxis had minimal changes in the intestine.

The response of the control group to the various doses of ovalbumin can be seen in the mortality ratios in Table 1. A dose-effect curve was plotted from these values (Fig. 1). The slope function of the line was 3.16 and the LD_{50} was 0.80 mg (Fig. 1, Table 1).

The mortality ratios of the animals with posterior hypothalamic lesions are presented in Table 1. Figure 1 shows the dose-effect curve for this group, with a slope function of 2.15 and an LD_{50} of 0.92 mg. Histological examination of the brains of those animals with lesions intended for the posterior hypothalamus revealed that the lesions were primarily in the mammillary and premammillary regions. None of the lesions extended anteriorly beyond the posterior aspect of the ventromedial nucleus, nor posteriorly beyond the interpeduncular fossa. Figure 2 presents a schematic diagram of the areas of the hypothalamus involved in the study.

The mortality ratios of the group with anterior hypo-

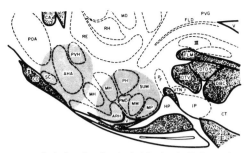

FIG. 2. Sagittal section of rat brain following the DeGroot atlas. The lightly shaded areas correspond to the anterior and posterior hypothalamic lesions as described in the text.

TABLE 2. *Comparison of potency between control and experimental groups*

Comparison Between Groups	Potency Ratio*	Significance of Diff. in Potency
Anterior lesions/control	3.75	$P < 0.001$
Anterior lesions/posterior lesions	3.33	$P < 0.001$
Posterior lesions/control	1.12	NS

* Potency ratio = LD_{50_1}/LD_{50_2} where LD_{50_1} is the larger value.

thalamic lesions are also seen in Table 1, including the slope function of 2.84 and LD_{50} of 3.0 mg. These values were calculated from the dose-effect curve shown in Fig. 1. Histological examination of the brains in this group revealed that these lesions were all centered in the anterior hypothalamic area. None of the lesions extended anteriorly beyond the preoptic area at the coronal level of the anterior commissure, nor posteriorly beyond the midportion of the ventromedial nucleus (Fig. 2).

The dose-effect curves of the three groups have been compared in Fig. 1. A test for parallelism revealed that the three curves did not differ significantly. The potency ratios between the groups are shown in Table 2, and it can be seen that ovalbumin was significantly ($P < 0.001$) less potent in the animals with anterior hypothalamic lesions than in both the control rats and those with posterior lesions.

DISCUSSION

The findings of the present study have demonstrated that lesions of the hypothalamus afford significant protection against lethal anaphylactic shock in the rat. These results indicate that the effect of hypothalamic lesions on the course of anaphylaxis is not species specific and limited to the guinea pig. The findings also suggest that the mode of action of hypothalamic lesions in preventing lethal anaphylaxis is not specifically related to a modification of the major pathophysiological change in guinea pig anaphylaxis, i.e., bronchiolar obstruction. In the rat, anaphylactic shock is accompanied by hemorrhage and congestion of the small intestine without major pulmonary changes.

A variety of factors may be involved in the protective action of hypothalamic lesions on rat anaphylaxis. The effect of hypothalamic lesions could be related to specific anatomical areas concerned with neuroendocrine processes. The adrenal cortex appears to be involved in the natural resistance of rats to the development of anaphylaxis. Adrenalectomized, sensitized rats are as susceptible to the induction of anaphylactic shock as are guinea pigs (5). The loss of resistance in sensitized, adrenalectomized rats can be partially restored by the administration of

adrenal cortical extracts or cortisone. It has been suggested that in the hypothalamus there are inhibitory and facilitative systems with respect to the control and release of ACTH (3). In the present study the anterior hypothalamic lesions may have provided protection against lethal anaphylaxis by an increase in ACTH and adrenal cortical activity. It has been reported that the anterior hypothalamus is involved in the inhibition of ACTH production, and a lesion in this area could result in an increased pituitary-adrenal response and subsequent modification of anaphylaxis. It must be pointed out, however, that Porter (16) has found a decrease in corticosterone release following anterior hypothalamic lesions in the rat.

Stimulation and lesion studies, as well as recordings of electrical activity under stress, have demonstrated that the posterior zone of the hypothalamus of the rat mediates the pituitary-adrenal cortical response to stress (9, 17, 19). In the present study the posterior lesions were extensive, and in most cases the entire posterior hypothalamus was ablated. It is therefore noteworthy that posterior lesions did not increase the susceptibility to fatal anaphylaxis. Further studies are necessary to clarify the relationship between hypothalamic lesions and anaphylaxis from the standpoint of ACTH and adrenal cortical activity.

Several studies (1, 2, 4) have indicated that the anterior region of the hypothalamus regulates the secretion of thyroid-stimulating hormone (TSH) by the hypophysis. Electrolytic lesions in this area induce in the rat low plasma levels of TSH and decrease thyroid function (4). Similar lesions were found in the present study to be associated with increased resistance to anaphylaxis in the rat. A number of investigators have demonstrated in the rat and guinea pig a relationship between thyroid physiology and the anaphylactic process. Leger and Masson (11) noted that the resistance to the anaphylactic reaction was increased in thyroidectomized rats when egg white was used as the antigen. Similar findings were observed by Nilzen (13, 14, 15) in the guinea pig following thyroidectomy or administration of I^{131}. He found that suppression of thyroid activity of guinea pigs sensitized to egg albumin inhibited local and systemic anaphylaxis and abolished circulating precipitins.

The protective action of hypothalamic lesions on the course of anaphylaxis may also be involved with an alteration in antibody production. A number of recent studies have indicated that the hypothalamus may play a role in determining antibody levels. Korneva and Khai (10) reported that hypothalamic lesions tended to decrease antibody production in rabbits, and in guinea pigs it has been found that there is a decrease in reagin following tuberal lesions. There is some question, however, as to whether hypothalamic modification of antibody titers is a major factor in altering the course of anaphylaxis. Szentivanyi (6) has found that lesions in the tuberal region protected guinea pigs from lethal anaphylaxis even when passive antibody transfer techniques were used.

It has been demonstrated that lesions in the anterior hypothalamus reduce parasympathetic discharge while posterior lesions diminish sympathetic effects (8). The findings of the present study may be related to modification of the tonic autonomic activity in the sympathetic-parasympathetic nervous system, and its effect on the gastrointestinal and cardiovascular systems.

The processes which may be involved in modifying lethal anaphylaxis by means of hypothalamic lesions are complex. Further study is required which will consider the effect of stimulation of specific areas of the hypothalamus on anaphylaxis as well as a consideration of the role of neuroendocrine processes, antibody formation, histamine release, and sympathetic-parasympathetic activity.

REFERENCES

1. BOGDANOVE, E. M., AND N. S. HALMI. Effects of hypothalamic lesions and subsequent propylthiouracil treatment on pituitary structure and function in the rat. *Endocrinology* 53: 274–291, 1953.
2. BOGDANOVE, E. M., B. N. SPIRTOS, AND N. S. HALMI. Further observations on pituitary structure and function in rats bearing hypothalamic lesions. *Endocrinology* 57: 302–313, 1955.
3. BOVARD, E. W. A concept of hypothalamic functioning. *Perspectives Biol. Med.* 5: 52–60, 1961.
4. D'ANGELO, S. A., AND R. E. TRAUM. Pituitary-thyroid function in rats with hypothalamic lesions. *Endocrinology* 59: 593–596, 1956.
5. DEWS, P. B., AND C. F. CODE. Effect of cortisone on anaphylactic shock in adrenalectomized rats. *J. Pharmacol. Exptl. Therap.* 101: 9, 1951.
6. FILIPP, G., AND A. SZENTIVANYI. Anaphylaxis and the nervous system, part III. *Ann. Allergy* 16: 306–311, 1958.
7. FREEDMAN, D. X., AND G. FENICHEL. Effect of midbrain lesions in experimental allergy. *Arch. Neurol. Psychiat.* 79: 164–169, 1958.
8. GELHORN, E. H. NAKAO, AND E. S. REDGATE. The influence of lesions in anterior and posterior hypothalamus on tonic and phasic autonomic reactions. *J. Physiol., London* 131: 402–423, 1956.
9. HARRIS, G. W. Central control of pituitary secretion. In: *Handbook of Physiology. Neurophysiology.* Washington, D. C.: Am. Physiol. Soc., 1960, sect. 1, vol. II, chapt. 39, pp. 1007–1038.
10. KORNEVA, E. A., AND L. M. KHAI. Influence of hypothalamic lesions on antibody production. *Fiziol. Zhur. SSR* 49 (1): 42–47, 1963.
11. LEGER, J., AND G. MASSON. Factors influencing an anaphylactoid reaction in the rat. *Federation Proc.* 6: 150–151, 1947.
12. LITCHFIELD, J. T., JR., AND F. WILCOXON. A simplified method of evaluating dose-effect experiments. *J. Pharmacol. Exptl. Therap.* 96: 99–113, 1949.
13. NILZEN, A. The influence of the thyroid gland on hypersensitivity reactions in animals. I. *Acta Allergol.* 7: 231–245, 1954.
14. NILZEN, A. The influence of the thyroid gland on hypersensitivity reactions in animals, II. *Acta Allergol.* 8: 57–61, 1955.
15. NILZEN, A. The influence of the thyroid gland on hypersensitivity reactions in animals, III. *Acta Allergol.* 8: 103–111, 1955.
16. PORTER, J. C. Secretion of corticosterone in rats with anterior hypothalamic lesions. *Am. J. Physiol.* 204: 715–718, 1963.
17. PORTER, R. W. Hypothalamic involvement in the pituitary-adrenocortical response to stress stimuli. *Am. J. Physiol.* 172: 515–519, 1953.
18. SANYAL, A. K., AND G. B. WEST. Anaphylactic shock in the albino rat. *J. Physiol., London* 142: 571–584, 1958.
19. SLUSHER, M. A. Dissociation of adrenal ascorbic acid and corticosterone responses to stress in rats with hypothalamic lesions. *Endocrinology* 63: 412–419, 1958.
20. SZENTIVANYI, A., AND G. FILIPP. Anaphylaxis and the nervous system, part II. *Ann. Allergy* 16: 143–151, 1958.
21. SZENTIVANYI, A., AND J. SZEKELY. Anaphylaxis and the nervous system, part IV. *Ann. Allergy* 16: 389–392, 1958.

5

EFFECT OF INTRAVENTRICULAR INJECTION OF ANTI-BRAIN ANTIBODY ON DEFENSIVE CONDITIONED REFLEXES

B. D. Janković, Lj. Rakic, R. Veskov, and J. Horvat

IT has been suggested that intraneuronal storage of information is based on the production of specific proteins following changes in RNA base composition, so that the neurones of an experienced animal differ biochemically from the neurones of a naïve one[1-3]. It can therefore be assumed that the molecular and biological properties of RNA and proteins make them probable substrates for intraneuronal storage of information. On the other hand, it has been shown that the *in vivo* interaction between anti-brain antibodies and brain antigens results in a series of electrical and behavioural changes[4-6]. Because of its specificity an antibody reacts differentially with cells and subcellular constituents, and with molecules which are otherwise indistinguishable by physical and chemical methods. These properties of antibodies make possible the functional dissection of the nervous system. Thus we have investigated the relationship between brain proteins and learning processes using immuno-neuro-physiological techniques. We report here the *in vivo* effect of anti-brain protein antibodies on defensive conditioned reflexes in the cat.

Brain proteins were prepared as follows. Cat brain was removed, quickly frozen, homogenized in 0·14 M saline (1 mg of tissue to 2 ml. of saline), kept at 0° C for 3 h and then centrifuged at 3,000 r.p.m. for 20 min. The supernatant was dialysed overnight against redistilled water. The proteins were precipitated by cold ethanol at −10° C, centrifuged, redissolved in saline and lyophilized. In the same way proteins were isolated from cat liver. Lyophilized brain and liver proteins were treated with a 3 : 1 mixture of ethanol and ether to separate out phospholipids[7]. The residues were dried over phosphorus pentoxide in a cold room and used as antigens. In 100 mg of brain protein fraction there was 97 mg of protein[8], 2 mg of RNA and 0·1 mg of DNA. The liver protein fraction was composed of 96 mg of protein, 3 mg of RNA and 0·2 mg of DNA.

Immune sera were prepared by injecting rabbits with brain protein or liver protein incorporated in complete Freund's adjuvant. The mixture of antigen and adjuvant was injected into the toe-pads of each leg (20 mg of protein was administered to each rabbit), and 20 days later each animal received a 20 mg intraperitoneal injection of corresponding antigen without adjuvant. A further group of animals was given a single injection of adjuvant alone and served as the control. The sera were separated, pooled and heated at 56° C for 20 min. Anti-brain protein and anti-liver protein antibodies were identified by a diffusion gel technique, passive haemagglutination using formalinized erythrocytes, complement fixation and quantitative precipitin. Anti-brain antibodies were present only in anti-brain sera. The gamma globulin fraction was isolated from pooled sera by the method of Coons[9], passed through sterile Seitz-filter and lyophilized. Dried gamma globulins from anti-brain, anti-liver and normal rabbit serum (obtained from animals injected with adjuvant alone) were dissolved in distilled water (75 mg of protein/ml.) before injection into the lateral ventricle of the cat brain.

Bipolar electrodes were implanted in cortical and subcortical sites of naïve cats, together with a cannula directed toward the right lateral ventricle. The electroencephalogram (EEG) was recorded from these leads, and the electromyogram (EMG) was recorded through silver disk electrodes attached to the dorsum of the right hind leg. After being allowed to recover from surgery for at least a week, the cats were trained in defensive conditioned reflexes according to the following schedule. Each animal was permitted 1 week of preconditioning to become accustomed to the training environment (sound-proof room, personnel, diffuse illumination, standard temperature, and so on), after which it was habituated to the "positive" conditioned stimulus (800 Hz, 3 s duration) through a speaker positioned approximately 1 m from the animal's head. Between twenty-eight and forty trials were carried out each day for between 8 and 17 days. The criterion used was the disappearance of EEG and EMG activation on positive tone. The animal was then subjected to the same 3 s tone and after 2·5 s an electrical shock (100 Hz lasting 0·5 s) of sufficient intensity to produce leg flexion was applied. A minimum of thirty trials a day were continued for each cat until it was trained to show an EMG response to positive tone alone in at least 90 per cent of trials for 3 consecutive days. The last trial each day was reinforced with shock following the principles of classical conditioning. After conditioning, a second "negative" stimulus (700 Hz lasting 3 s) was introduced randomly into the trials with the positive tone. These particular trials were reinforced with shock either occasionally or at the end of daily training, and training was continued for fifteen to twenty more sessions until there was differentiation of responses to the tones, judged by the ability of the cat to respond correctly in 92–100 per cent of trials for 3 consecutive days. During habituation—training for the establishment of defensive conditioned reflexes and differentiation—each animal was given an intraventricular injection of 0·2 ml. of saline every second day. Fully trained cats received through a cannula

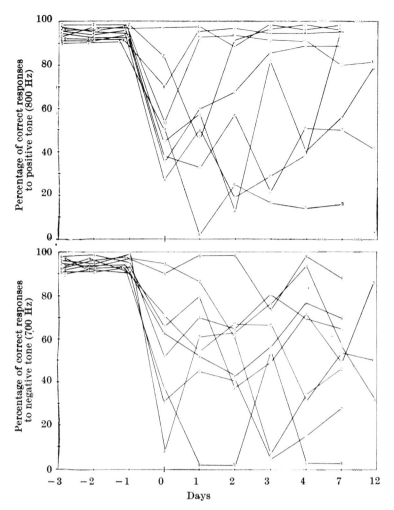

Fig. 1. Effect of intraventricular injection of anti-brain antibody on defensive conditioned reflexes of nine cats (Nos. 2–10). The injection was given on day 0. Top, response to positive tone; bottom, response to negative tone. Calculations of correct and incorrect responses to positive and negative tone are based on leg flexion and EMG activity.

a single injection of 0·2 ml. of anti-brain protein, anti-liver protein or normal gamma globulin. Electrical activity and behaviour were recorded before injection, immediately after the injection and on subsequent days. Defensive conditioned reflexes were tested immediately after injection and every day thereafter. At the end of the experiment, the cats were killed and nervous tissue was inspected histologically.

The results (Fig. 1) show that the intraventricular injection of anti-brain antibody produces significant changes in conditioned responses immediately after the administration and on subsequent days. The type and degree of incorrect response varied from day to day and from cat to cat. Most animals failed to respond correctly to both tones. Several cats exhibited an inadequate response to positive tone, while others demonstrated a loss of differentiation. These changes persisted in some animals for as long as 27 days, and retraining was unsuccessful. Intraventricular injection of anti-liver antibody, normal gamma globulin and saline produced no effect on defensive conditioned reflexes (Table 1). Histological examination of brain sections revealed no pathological changes. The EEG activity recorded during the training of cats and before and after intraventricular administration of anti-brain antibodies will be published later.

Although there have been no definite suggestions as to the way the biosynthesis of RNA, DNA and protein could be involved in learning, the neural correlate of learning must include structural changes at the cellular, subcellular and molecular levels[10]. There is a high degree of turnover of cerebral proteins[11], and brain proteins certainly play an important part in neuronal function[12]. According to Schmitt[13], very small change might induce the combination in quaternary conformation of neural soluble acidic proteins. Bogoch[14] described specific protein changes related to the learning phenomenon, and stated that the information is coded in the glycoproteins of the brain. On this basis, it can be assumed that given information causes not only the accumulation of RNA in the functioning neurones[1], but also the production of new protein perhaps by modifying sites of protein synthesis. In immunological terms, a protein molecule with a new or altered antigenic identity could be formed during learning. It should be said, however, that the antigens used in this study to produce anti-brain antibodies were derived from cats which were not previously familiar with the conditioned stimuli. The activity of antibodies thus obtained was therefore probably not directed toward the total molecule of a "learning-linked protein" but rather to a portion of it. Consequently, it seems reasonable to expect that an anti-brain antibody which was formed after immunization with a brain protein from cats trained to perform a given task would act more specifically and would differentiate between two different types of learning.

Several specific antigenic materials, particularly proteins, were isolated from nervous tissue[15-17]. The exoplasm of squid contains at least fourteen antigens, and anti-axoplasm antibodies can block the propagation of action-potential[18]. It has been suggested that there are more than 100 proteins of different size and charge in the human brain[19,20]. The antigenic material used in this experiment contained different brain proteins, and so the anti-brain immunoglobulin injected into the cerebral cavity of trained cats represented a mixture of anti-brain antibodies which were probably capable of differentiating between nerve cell constituents. But, except for the behavioural

Table 1. LOSS OF DIFFERENTIATION IN TRAINED CATS FOLLOWING INJECTION OF ANTI-BRAIN ANTIBODY

Group	No. of cats	Response to positive tone			Response to negative tone		
		Total stimuli	Correct (per cent)	Incorrect (per cent)	Total stimuli	Correct (per cent)	Incorrect (per cent)
Injected with saline (3 consecutive days)	9	448	424 (94·6)	24 (5·4)	450	422 (93·7)	28 (6·3)
Injected with normal gamma globulin	4	256	240 (93·7)	16 (6·3)	268	252 (94·2)	16 (5·8)
Injected with anti-liver antibody	7	398	383 (96·2)	15 (3·7)	375	353 (94·4)	21 (5·6)
Injected with anti-brain antibody	9	1,231	697 (56·6)	534 (43·4)	1,054	580 (55·0)	474 (45·0)

phenomenology, this work can offer no evidence that anti-brain immunoglobulin entered the nervous tissue or that its effect on brain function was truly a neuronal one. Experiments to elucidate the mechanism, site and specificity of anti-brain antibody interference in the learning process are in progress.

This work was supported by grants from the Federal Scientific Fund, Belgrade, and from the National Institutes of Health, US Public Health Service.

Institute of Microbiology and
Institute of Biochemistry,
University of Belgrade.
Immunology and Neurophysiology Units,
Institute for Biological Research,
Belgrade, Yugoslavia.

[1] Hydén, H., in *The Cell: Biochemistry, Physiology, Morphology* (edit. by Brachet, J., and Mirsky, A. E.), **4**, Ch. 5 (Academic Press, New York, 1962).

[2] Hydén, H., and Egyházi, E., *Proc. US Nat. Acad. Sci.*, **48**, 1366 (1962).

[3] Hydén, H., and Lange, P. W., *Proc. US Nat. Acad. Sci.*, **53**, 946 (1965).

[4] Mihailović, Lj., and Janković, B. D., *Nature*, **192**, 665 (1961).

[5] Mihailović, Lj., and Janković, B. D., *Neurosci. Res. Prog. Bull.*, **3**, 8 (1965).

[6] Janković, B. D., Rakić, Lj., Janjić, M., Mitrović, K., and Ivanuš, J., *Pathol. Europ.*, **2**, 87 (1966).

[7] Schneider, W. C., *J. Biol. Chem.*, **161**, 293 (1945).

[8] Lowry, O. H., Rosenbrough, N. J., Fau, A. L., and Randall, R. S., *J. Biol. Chem.*, **193**, 765 (1951).

[9] Coons, A. H., in *General Cytochemical Methods* (edit. by Danielli, J. F.), 399 (Academic Press, New York, 1958).

[10] Bullock, T. H., and Quarton, G. C., *Neurosci. Res. Prog. Bull.*, **4**, 191 (1966).

[11] Waelsch, H., and Lajtha, A., *Physiol. Rev.*, **41**, 709 (1961).

[12] Schmitt, F. O., and Davison, P. F., *Neurosci. Res. Prog. Bull.*, **3**, 55 (1965).

[13] Schmitt, F. O., in *The Neurosciences: A Study Program* (edit. by Quarton, G. C., Melnechuk, T., and Schmitt, F. O.) (Rockefeller Univ. Press, New York, in the press).

[14] Bogoch, S., *Neurosci. Res. Prog. Bull.*, **3**, 38 (1965).

[15] Milgrom, F., Tuggac, M., and Campbell, W. A., *J. Immunol.*, **92**, 82 (1964).

[16] McCallion, D. T., and Langman, J., *J. Embryol. Exp. Morphol.*, **12**, 511 (1964).

[17] Klee, C. B., and Sokoloff, L., *Proc. US Nat. Acad. Sci.*, **53**, 1014 (1965).

[18] Huneeus-Cox, F., *Science*, **143**, 1036 (1964).

[19] Bogoch, S., Rajam, P. C., and Belval, P. C., *Nature*, **204**, 73 (1964).

[20] Rajam, P. C., and Bogoch, S., *Immunology*, **11**, 211 (1964).

6

NEURO-ENDOCRINE CORRELATES OF IMMUNE RESPONSE
I. Effect of Brain Lesions on Antibody Production, Arthus Reactivity and Delayed Hypersensitivity in the Rat

B. D. Janković and Katarina Isaković

Abstract. Bilateral symmetrical electrolytic lesions were produced in the following areas of the rat brain: hypothalamus, reticular formation, thalamus, superior colliculus, caudate nucleus and amygdaloid complex. Brain-lesioned and control sham-lesioned animals were immunized 24 h after operation with bovine serum albumin, and examined for antibody production, Arthus reactivity and delayed skin hypersensitivity 10, 20 and 30 days after sensitization. The intensity of Arthus and delayed skin reactions, and the rate of circulating antibody formation were significantly reduced only in hypothalamus-lesioned and reticular formation-lesioned rats.

This study provides strong evidence for a relationship between the activity of some brain structures and the function of the immune system. It has been postulated that neural, endocrine, lymphatic and non-lymphatic components cooperate in the lymphatic microenvironment and constitute true functional units of the immune potential. Taking into account neuro-endocrine and lympho-endocrine communications and relations, three possible explanations were proposed for the changes in immunological responses which might be accomplished by electrolytic damage of hypothalamic and reticular formation areas of the rat brain.

Introduction

The fundamental assumption underlying the great majority of experimental and theoretical approaches to analysis of immune mechanisms is that an immunological experience produces specific alterations in lymphatic cells. It is a general belief that the function of the immune system

[1] This work was supported by the US Public Health Service grant 6X9803 from the National Institutes of Health, Bethesda, Md., and by grants from the Republic Fund for Research of SR Serbia, Belgrade.

Reprinted from *Intern. Arch. Allergy Appl. Immunol.* **45**, 360–372 (1973).

under normal conditions is determined by the type, maturity and arrangement of lymphatic cells and their ability to cooperate in processes by which immune informations are transmitted from one cell to another. However, it is now obvious that the immune response depends not only on anatomical, physiological and biochemical properties of lymphatic cells, but also on a variety of nonlymphatic components, cellular or molecular, of the lymphatic microenvironment [11]. Consequently, our understanding of the mode by which the immune system operates will remain very imperfect without the exploration of immune response in relation to the nervous and endocrine system.

In this connection, mention should be made of two sharply distinct aspects of immunoneurology: one concerns the structural and functional 'dissection' of the nervous system by means of anti-brain antibody and various immunological tools [10], and the other deals with the role of the nervous system in immunity. Some ingenious pioneering attempts in the latter domain of research by Russian and French scientists are described in MÉTALNIKOV's book [21]. BESREDKA [2] was first to study the nervous origin of anaphylactic symptoms, and much earlier work was concerned with anaphylaxis [7, 15, 18, 32]. The present paper represents a continuation of our initial efforts [12, 13] to link together the nervous, endocrine and immune system, and to establish the relationship between the function of some brain structures and the performance of immune response. This initial study encompasses the production of antibody, Arthus reactivity and delayed skin hypersensitivity in rats with electrolytic lesions in the hypothalamus, reticular formation, thalamus, superior colliculus, caudate nucleus and amygdaloid complex.

Materials and Methods

Electrolytic lesions. Female Wistar rats weighing 210 ± 10 g were used in the experiment. An anodal stainless steel electrode was inserted into the brain structure, under nembutal anaesthesia, using David Kopf's stereotaxic instrument for the rat. Coordinates described in KÖNIG and KLIPPEL's atlas of the rat brain [16] served as a guide in the placement of electrodes. Bilateral symmetrical brain lesions were produced by means of 1 mA direct current for 10 sec. Sham-lesioned rats served as controls. All the surgical procedures used with the brain-lesioned rats were performed, except that no current was applied through electrodes. This group of 51 animals was composed of six different groups of rats with sham-lesioned hypothalamus, reticular formation, thalamus, superior colliculus, caudate nucleus or amygdaloid complex, respectively. It should be pointed out at the start that we were prima-

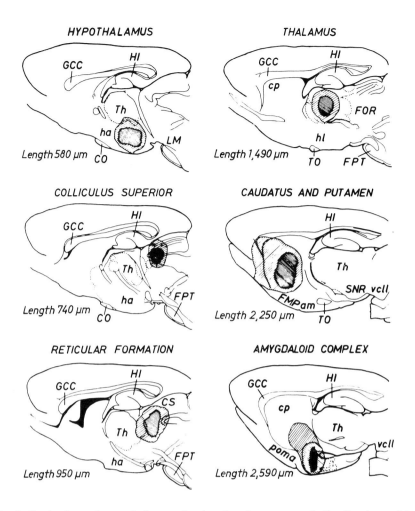

Fig. 1. Sagittal sections of the rat brain showing areas of distribution of lesions in the hypothalamus, thalamus, superior colliculus, caudate nucleus, reticular formation and amygdaloid complex. Abbreviations according to KÖNIG and KLIPPEL [16]: am = nucleus amygdaloideus medialis; CO = chiasma opticum; cp = nucleus caudatus putamen; CS = colliculus superior; FMP = fasciculus medialis prosencephali; FOR = formatio reticularis; FPT = fibrae pontis transversae; GCC = genu corporis callosi; ha = nucleus anterior hypothalami; HI = hippocampus; hl = nucleus lateralis hypothalami; LM = lemniscus medialis; poma = nucleus preopticus magnocellularis; SNR = substantia nigra, zone reticulata; Th = thalamus; TO = tractus opticus; vcll = nucleus ventralis caudalis lemnisci lateralis.

rily interested in obtaining general information about the relationship between the central nervous system and immune reactivity which would justify further studies in this direction. Therefore, lesions were purposely distributed within a brain region (fig. 1) rather than concentrated to a small circumscribed target consisting of a group of neurons. Because of this approach and the known limitations of lesion technique [28], a large number of animals was included in each group so as to enable results to be evaluated more correctly.

Electrolytic lesions were produced in areas of the hypothalamus, reticular formation, thalamus, superior colliculus, caudate nucleus and amygdaloid complex (fig. 1). Information on the extent of nervous tissue destruction were obtained by *post mortem* histological examination of the brain. For this purpose, the brain was fixed in formalin, embedded in paraffin and a cross-section was cut every 40 μm in the area of the lesion. Sections were stained with haematoxylin and eosin, and examined microscopically. Brains of control sham-lesioned rats were treated in an identical manner.

Immunization. Brain-lesioned and sham-lesioned rats were immunized with crystalline bovine serum albumin (BSA). The antigen-adjuvant mixture was made up of one volume of saline containing BSA and one volume of complete Freund's adjuvant (1.5 vol of Arlacel A, 8.5 vol of Draceol mineral oil and killed tubercle bacilli at a final concentration of 6 mg/ml). Each rat was injected subcutaneously into the left hind foot-pad with 0.1 ml (0.5 mg of BSA) of this stable water-in-oil emulsion 24 h after surgical treatment.

Antibody determination. Blood samples were obtained from the retro-orbital sinus 10, 20 and 30 days after immunization. The content of anti-BSA antibody in sera was determined by a modification of Takátsy's microhaemagglutination technique using formalinized sheep erythrocytes. The plastic plates were left for 18 h at room temperature prior to final reading. Antibody determination in each serum was performed twice to ensure accurate end-point of anti-BSA activity.

Skin testing. 10, 20 and 30 days after immunization, and always before the bleeding, rats of all groups were skin-tested with 30 μg of BSA in 0.1 ml of saline, injected intradermally in the depilated flank. Arthus reaction was read at 3, and delayed reaction at 24 h. Diameters of reactions and haemorrhages were recorded, and the degree of oedema and induration was graded from 0 to $+++$.

Results

Arthus reactivity to BSA. Statistical evaluation of results (Student's t-test) showed that Arthus reactions were significantly lower in rats which lesions in the hypothalamus and reticular formation 10, 20 and 30 days after immunization (fig. 2). This suppression of Arthus reactivity was particularly pronounced in rats of the reticular formation group. Animals with lesions in the area of the thalamus, superior colliculus, caudate nucleus or amygdaloid complex developed Arthus reactions closely comparable to those of sham-lesioned rats.

Delayed skin reactions to BSA. Figure 3 illustrates the development and intensity of delyed hypersensitivity response. Typical delayed reactions at 24 h were observed in all rats 10 and 20 days after immunization with BSA in adjuvant. However, in animals with lesioned hypothalamus

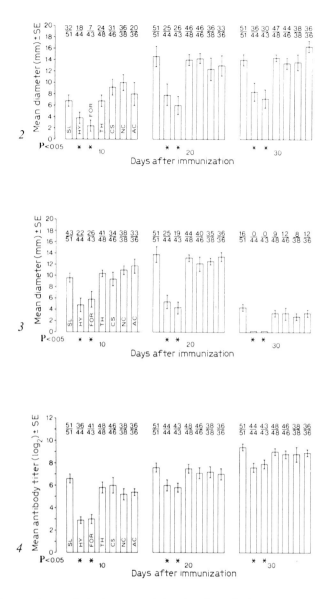

Fig. 2. Comparison of Arthus reactivity in sham-lesioned (SL) rats, and in rats with electrolytic lesions in areas of the hypothalamus (HY), reticular formation (FOR), thalamus (TH), colliculus superior (CS), caudate nucleus (NC) and amygdaloid complex (AC). Student's t-test was applied for statistical analysis and p values less than 0.05 are given (asterisks). The upper series of numbers shows: number of responders (nominator) and number of rats in group (denominator).

Fig. 3. Comparison of delayed skin-hypersensitive reactions in sham-lesioned (SL) and brain-lesioned (HY, FOR, TH, CS, NC and AC) rats.

Fig. 4. Comparison of anti-BSA antibody production in control sham-lesioned (SL) rats, and in rats with electrolytic lesions in different brain structures (HY, FOR, TH, CS, NC and AC).

Neuro-Endocrine System and Immune Response   35 and reticular formation, the degree of induration was markedly reduced, and histological examination of representative skin samples from the site of reaction revealed a mild subcutaneous oedema, and occasional small perivenous aggregates of mononuclear cells in the dermis.

Anti-BSA antibody production. The direct current lesioning of hypothalamic and reticular formation areas induced a considerable reduction in the production of circulating antibody at 10 days (fig. 4). After 20 and 30 days of immunization, rats exhibited a tendency towards increased antibody synthesis. However, statistical analysis of data showed that the antibody-producing capacity of those rats was still significantly lower than in sham-lesioned animals and in rats with lesioned thalamus, superior colliculus, caudate nucleus and amygdaloid complex.

Discussion

The data presented here show that electrolytic lesions of hypothalamic and reticular formation areas disrupted to a great extent performance of both humoral and cell-mediated immunity in the rat. On the other hand, rats with lesions in the thalamus, superior colliculus, caudate nucleus and amygdaloid complex displayed normal immune reactivity following stimulation with a protein antigen. So far as the hypothalamus is concerned, these results are in agreement with earlier reports showing that local lesions of the hypothalamus protected guinea pigs [7, 32], rats [18] and rabbits [15] from lethal anaphylactic shock. In contrast to these results, unusually high and identical titres of antibody were described in hypothalamus-lesioned, sham-lesioned and hypophysectomized rats [33].

From observations of the kind presented here, it may be deduced that the hypothalamus and reticular formation are involved in immune processes. In this regard, the relationship between the hypothalamus and endocrine glands [30] is of particular interest. Some endocrinological facts bearing directly upon immunity should, therefore, be mentioned, before attempting to outline the mechanisms underlying the suppression of immune responsiveness in hypothalamus-lesioned and reticular formation-lesioned animals. Thus, LUDIN [17] described a decline of antibody production in hypophysectomized rats, but KALDEN et al. [14] stated that pituitaryless animals develop normal immune reactivity. Various aspects of the effect of corticosteroids on antibody formation have been reviewed by MCMASTER and FRANZL [20], and since then corticosteroid-induced impairment of immune capacity has been reported from several laboratories [5, 6, 8, 25]. Hormonally deficient animals have made new experimental undertakings possible in the domain of immuno endocrinology [1, 26], and the importance of the thymus-hypophysis axis for immunological maturation was emphasized recently [27]. Manifestations of cell-mediated immunity are also influenced by hormones, e.g. skin homograft survival was longer in animals treated with cortisone [22, 35], and in the monkey injected with progesterone [24].

In the light of foregoing observations it is clear that some portions of the nervous and endocrine system are associated with the immune system. It is, therefore, reasonable to suppose that representatives of those three systems constitute structural and functional units of the immune machinery of the body. Indeed, the lymphatic microenvironment is composed of both lymphatic and non-lymphatic elements (reticular cells, neurons, etc.) which are associated according to their specific properties [11]. Biologically active substances which are obviously operating in the lymphatic microenvironment [4] maintain, increase or suppress the excitability of cells by exerting chemical influences on the mechanisms involved in the synthesis of antibody or in the creation of 'sensitized cells'. In the lymphatic microenvironment, all elements are in dynamic equilibrium, and functional relationships are somehow established between lymphatic and non-lymphatic cells in such a way that the activation of one kind of cells is subsequently reflected on the other cells. Accordingly, an immunological stimulus will cause alterations and the establishment of new interconnections between cellular and molecular constituents of the lymphatic microenvironment. Viewed in this way, either the neural, endocrine or lymphatic component may be critical in determining the immune response.

Pursuing this line of thought, one is tempted to try to answer the principal question raised by this study: How might the lesions of the hypothalamus and reticular formation influence the activity of the immune system so as to diminish its potential? Obviously, the interplay between the brain function and immune capacity cannot be explained without taking into consideration the endocrine influence on immune response, and the relationship between the hypothalamus and endocrine glands [30]. Although the risk of simplification cannot be avoided, it is appropriate to introduce here three possible explanations which are not mutually exclusive.

(a) The first explanation deals with the relationship between the lymphatic tissue and the anterior hypothalamus, hypophysis, glucocorti-

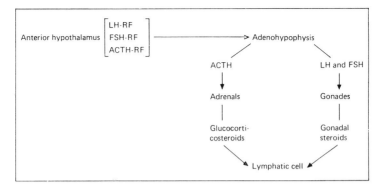

Fig. 5. Scheme of the relationship between the lymphatic cells, and the anterior hypothalamus, adenohypophysis, adrenals and gonades.

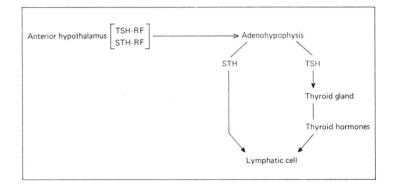

Fig. 6. Schematic presentation of the connection between the lymphatic cell, and the anterior hypothalamus, adenohypophysis and thyroid gland.

costeroids and gonadal steroids (fig. 5). In simple terms, electrolytic damage of the hypothalamus induces an increased secretion of luteinizing hormone-releasing factor (LH-RF), and hypothetical [29] follicle-stimulating hormone-releasing factor (FSH-RF) and adrenocorticotropic hormone-releasing factor (ACTH-RF) by the neighbouring non-lesioned cells. This may cause a hypersecretion of LH, FSH and ACTH by the adenohypophysis. The ACTH, through its action on adrenal glands, induces an increased production of glucocorticosteroids which then affect the lymphatic cell. On the other hand, gonadotropic hormones (LH and FSH) stimulate the synthesis of gonadal steroids which then influence the lymphatic cell. Specific effects of steroid binding to the rat thymus cells on glucose metabolism, and protein and RNA synthesis were described by MUNCK *et al.* [23].

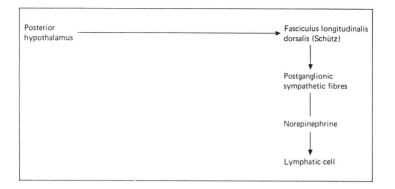

Fig. 7. Possible relationship between the lymphatic cell, and the posterior hypothalamus and adrenergic system.

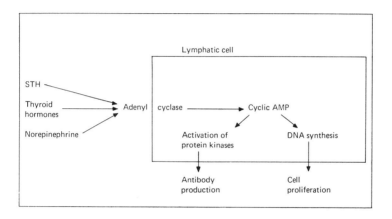

Fig. 8. Scheme illustrating the effect of somatotropic hormone (STH), thyroid hormones and norepinephrine on the formation of cyclic AMP in the lymphatic cell.

(b) The second possibility concerns the relationship between the lymphatic tissue and the anterior hypothalamus, somatotropic hormone (STH) and thyroid hormones (fig. 6). Electrolytic lesions of hypothalamic cells involved in the elaboration of hypothetical STH-releasing factor (STH-RF) induce via adenohypophysis a hyposecretion of the growth hormone and thus produce inadequate reactivity of the lymphatic cell. The same kind of brain lesions, by destroying cells which manufacture TSH-RF (thyroid stimulating hormone-releasing factor) in the hypothalamus, causes a decrease in the secretion of TSH. This would affect the thyroid gland and the synthesis of thyroxin and triiodothyronine. The final result would be the altered reactivity of the lymphatic cell.

(c) The third hypothesis takes into account the posterior hypothalamus and adrenergic system (fig. 7). Electrolytic disruption of hypothalamus and reticular formation areas affects the normal activity of the adrenergic system via the dorsal longitudinal fasciculus of Schütz and postganglionic sympathetic fibres, thus inducing a hyposecretion of norepinephrine. This neurohumoral change produces functional alterations in the lymphatic cell.

The hormones most probably exert their action on lymphatic cells through a common mediator, the cyclic AMP (cyclic-3′,5′-adenosine monophosphate) [31], and cyclic AMP may be involved in the chain of intracellular reactions leading to the formation of antibody [34]. Under normal conditions, the growth hormone, thyroid hormones and norepinephrine are capable of activating adenyl cyclase which catalyzes the formation of cyclic AMP from adenosine triphosphate in the lymphocyte [19]. However, the reduced secretion or absence of STH, thyroid hormones and norepinephrine, due to lesions in the hypothalamus and reticular formation, affects the activation of adenyl cyclase and subsequent formation of cyclic APM in the lymphatic cells. This will disturbe processes of protein kinase activation and DNA synthesis, and impair the synthesis of proteins (antibody) and cell proliferation (fig. 8).

All these mechanisms may be associated with the reticular formation, since this brain structure is connected with the hypothalamus by diffuse fibre systems [9], and is probably included in mediation of pituitary-adrenal response [3]. The electrolytic damage of the reticular formation most likely prevents the propagation of impulses from this structure to the hypothalamus and thus affects hypothalamic mechanisms related to the hypophysis and adrenergic system.

Since the causal evidence presented here is admittedly far from conclusive, the proposed three explanations provide the necessary background for further studies on the interconnections between neural, endocrine and lymphatic factors in immune response. Immunologists should certainly direct their interest and efforts to this fascinating and unexplored field of immunosciences.

Acknowledgments

We would like to thank Dr. Julius Ivanuš, Department of Neurophysiology, Institute for Biological Research, Belgrade, for his invaluable help in inducing brain lesions in rats.

References

1 BARONI, C.: Mouse thymus in hereditary pituitary dwarfism. Acta anat. *68:* 361–373 (1967).

2 BESREDKA, A.: Anaphylaxis and anti-anaphylaxis and their experimental foundations, p. 13 (Mosby, St. Louis 1919).

3 BOHUS, B.: Central nervous structures and the effect of ACTH and corticosteroids on avoidance behaviour: a study with intracerebral implantation of corticosteroids in the rat; in DE WIED and WEIJNEN Pituitary, adrenal and the brain. Progr. Brain Res., vol. 22, pp. 171–183 (1970).

4 DUMONDE, D. C.; KELLY, R. H., and WOLSTENCROFT, R. A.: Molecular pharmacology of cell-mediated immunity; in JANKOVIĆ and ISAKOVIĆ Microenvironmental aspects of immunity, pp. 705–711 (Plenum Press, New York 1973).

5 DUKOR, P. and DIETRICH, F. M.: Characteristic features of immunosuppression by steroids and cytotoxic drugs. Int. Arch. Allergy *34:* 32–48 (1968).

6 ELLIOTT, E. V. and SINCLAIR, N. R. S. C.: Effect of cortisone acetate on 19S and 7S haemolysin antibody. Immunology, Lond. *15:* 643–652 (1968).

7 FILIPP, G. and SZENTIVANYI, A.: Anaphylaxis and the nervous system. III. Ann. Allergy *16:* 306–311 (1958).

8 GISLER, R. H. and SCHENKEL-HULLIGER, L.: Hormonal regulation of the immune response. II. Influence of pituitary and adrenal activity on immune responsiveness *in vitro.* Cell. Immunol. *2:* 646–657 (1971).

9 HAUTA, W. J. H. and HAYMAKER, W.: Hypothalamic nuclei and fiber connections; in HAYMAKER, ANDERSON and HAUTA The hypothalamus, pp. 136–209 (Thomas, Springfield 1969).

10 JANKOVIĆ, B. D.: Biological activity of anti-brain antibody – an introduction to immunoneurology; in GAITO Macromolecules and behaviour, pp. 99–130 (Appleton Century Crofts, New York 1972).

11 JANKOVIĆ, B. D.: Structural correlates of immune microenvironment; in JANKOVIĆ and ISAKOVIĆ Microenvironmental aspects of immunity, pp. 1–4 (Plenum Press, New York 1973).

12 JANKOVIĆ, B. D.; ISAKOVIĆ, K.; IVANUŠ, J., and RAKIĆ, L.: Immune response in rats following electrolytic lesion of the hypothalamic area. Proc. yugoslav. Immunol. Soc. Abstract. *2:* 4–5 (1971).

13 JANKOVIĆ, B. D.; ISAKOVIĆ, K.; IVANUŠ, J., and RAKIĆ, L.: Immune response and lymphatic tissue reaction in brain-lesioned rats; in JANKOVIĆ and ISAKOVIĆ Microenvironmental aspects of immunity, pp. 661–666 (Plenum Press, New York 1973).

14 KALDEN, J. R.; EVANS, M. M., and IRVINE, W. J.: The effect of hypophysectomy on the immune response. Immunology, Lond. *18:* 671–679 (1970).

15 KHAI, L. M.; KOVALENKOVA, M. V.; KORNEVA, E. A., and SERANOVA, A. E.: Further study of the role of hypothalamic area in the regulation of immunogenesis (in Russian). J. Microbiol. Epidem. Immunobiol. *41:* 7–12 (1964).

16 KÖNIG, J. F. R. and KLIPPEL, R. A.: The rat brain. A stereotaxic atlas of the forebrain and lower parts of the brain stem (Williams & Wilkins, Baltimore 1963).

17 LUDIN, P. M.: Action of hypophysectomy on antibody formation in the rat. Acta path. microbiol. scand. *48:* 351–357 (1960).

18 LUPPARELLO, T. J.; STEIN, M., and PARK, C. D.: Effect of hypothalamic lesions on rat anaphylaxis. Amer. J. Physiol. *207:* 911–914 (1964).

19 MACMANUS, J. P.; WHITFIELD, J. F., and YOUDALE, T.: Stimulation by epinephrine of adenyl cyclase activity, cyclic AMP formation, DNA synthesis and cell proliferation in populations of rat thymic lymphocytes. J. cell. Comp. Physiol. *77:* 103–116 (1971).

20 MCMASTER, P. D. and FRANZL, R. E.: The effects of adrenocortical steroids upon antibody formation. Metabolism. *10:* 990–1005 (1961).

21 MÉTALNIKOV, S.: Rôle du système nerveux et des facteurs biologiques et psychiques dans l'immunité (Masson, Paris 1934).

22 MORGAN, J. A.: Influence of cortisone on survival of homografts in rabbits. Surgery *30:* 506–515 (1951).

23 MUNCK, A.; YOUNG, D. A.; MOSHER, K. M., and WIRA, C. R.: Specific metabolic interactions of glucocorticosteroids with rat thymus cells; in HAMBURGH and BARRINGTON Hormone in Development, pp. 191–201 (Appleton Century Crofts, New York 1971).

24 MUNROE, J. S.: Progesteroids as immunosuppressive agents. J. Reticuloendothel. Soc. *9:* 361–375 (1971).

25 PETRÁNYI, G.; BENCZUR, M., and ALFÖLDY, P.: The effect of single large dose hydrocortisone treatment on IgM and IgG antibody production, morphological distribution of antibody producing cells and immunological memory. Immunology, Lond. *21:* 151–158 (1971).

26 PIERPAOLI, W.; BARONI, C.; FABRIS, N., and SORKIN, E.: Hormones and the immunological capacity. II. Reconstitution of antibody production in hormonally deficient mice by somatotropic hormone, thyrotropic hormone and thyroxin. Immunology, Lond. *16:* 217–230 (1969).

27 PIERPAOLI, W.; FABRIS, N., and SORKIN, E.: The effects of hormones on the development of the immune capacity. 2nd Int. Convoc. Immunol., Buffalo 1970, pp. 25–30 (Karger, Basel 1971).

28 ROWLAND, V.: Stereotaxic techniques and the production of lesions; in MARTINI and GANONG Neuroendocrinology, vol. 1, pp. 107–132 (Academic Press, New York 1966).

29 SCHALLY, A. V.; KASTIN, A. J., and ARIMURA, A.: Hypothalamic follicle-stimulating hormone (FSH) and luteinizing hormone (LH)-regulating hormone: structure, physiology, and clinical studies. Fertil. Steril. *22:* 703–721 (1971).

30 SCHARRER, B.: General principles of neuroendocrine communication; in SCHMITT The neurosciences: second study program, pp. 519–529 (Rockefeller Univ. Press, New York 1970).

31 SUTHERLAND, E. W.: Studies on the mechanism of hormone action. Science *177:* 401–408 (1972).

32 SZENTIVANYI, A. and FILIPP, G.: Anaphylaxis and the nervous system. II. Ann. Allergy *16:* 143–151 (1958).

33 THRASHER, S. G.; BERNARDIS, L. L., and COHEN, S.: The immune response in hypothalamic-lesioned and hypophysectomized rats. Int. Arch. Allergy *41:* 813–820 (1971).

34 Watts, H. G.: The role of cyclic AMP in the immunocompetent cell. Transplantation *12:* 229–231 (1971).

35 Woodruff, M. F. A.: The effect of cortisone and other hormones on auto- and homografts of endocrine tissues in animals. Transplant. Bull. *1:* 10–11 (1956).

7

IN VITRO CROSS-REACTING ANTIBODIES FROM RABBIT ANTISERA TO RAT BRAIN SYNAPTIC MEMBRANES AND THYMOCYTES

B. D. Janković, J. Horvat, K. Mitrović, and M. Mostarica

Rabbit anti-rat brain synaptic membrane and anti-rat thymocyte antisera were used in cytotoxicity, immunofluorescence, and absorption assays to define the antigenic relationship between the rat brain and thymocytes, and the localizing properties of antibodies. Both antisera cross-reacted with brain tissue and thymocytes. However, anti-synaptic membrane and anti-thymocyte antisera also contained antibodies specific for neurons and thymocytes, respectively. Immunofluorescence showed that antibodies from anti-thymocyte antiserum reacted with antigenic determinants situated on the surface membrane of brain cells.

Heterologous antisera against whole brain tissue —that is, against a moiety of a large number of antigens—have been used to establish the antigenicity shared by the rat brain and thymocytes (3, 14, 18). We have recently used antisera from rabbits immunized with well-defined brain organelles (8) and brain proteins (9) in the study of the rat brain-lymphocyte antigen system. This report describes a previously unknown affinity of anti-rat thymocyte antibodies for membranes and fibrillar structures of the brain. In addition, antigenic correlation between rat brain synaptic membranes and thymocytes was demonstrated.

MATERIALS AND METHODS

Synaptic membranes (SM) were isolated as an 'M₂B' fraction (2) from the Wistar rat brain. Although electron microscopy showed that the SM preparation was homogeneous and composed of large and medium membrane sacs,

the complement fixation reaction, immunodiffusion in agarose, and immunofluorescence assay showed that the SM fraction contained a number of antigens, some of them cross-reacting with rat brain synaptic vesicles and rat superior cervical ganglion (7). The problem of purity of different fractions isolated from synaptic junctions has been reviewed by Morgan (12). Twenty mg of lyophilized SM was homogenized in 1 ml of saline, emulsified in complete Freund's adjuvant (vol/vol), and injected into the toe-pads of the rabbit hind legs. Subsequently, five injections of 18 mg of SM without adjuvant were given intraperitoneally and subcutaneously at monthly intervals. Serum samples were absorbed with rat erythrocytes, liver-cell membranes, and glutaraldehyde-treated IgM and IgG, as previously described (8). Anti-SM antiserum (ASMS) yielded antibody titers (512 to 2048) in the complement-fixation reaction (13) and developed two precipitin lines in Ouchterlony double diffusion. For the complement-fixation re-

Reprinted with permission from *Scand. J. Immunol* 6, 843–847. Copyright © 1977, Blackwell Scientific Publications Limited.

action, the optimal dilution of finely homog-enized SM contained 0.23 mg SM/ml saline. For double diffusion-in-gel, 60 mg SM/ml saline was used.

The thymuses were extirpated from Wistar rats perfused with saline. Thymocytes were isolated in medium 199 enriched to 10% with heat-inactivated absorbed normal rat serum, and purified on Isopaque-Ficoll. The viability of cells was determined by trypan blue. The production of anti-rat thymocyte antiserum (ATS) in rabbits was essentially the same as that described for the preparation of anti-chicken thymocyte antiserum (5).

ASMS and ATS were also absorbed with rat thymocytes and brain. For absorption with thymocyets, 1 ml of antiserum was mixed with 10^9 thymocytes, incubated for 2 h at room temperature and for 2 h at 4°C, and centrifuged at 35,000 g for 30 min. For absorption with brain, rat brains were homogenized in medium 199 (wt/wol), and after centrifugation at 1,600 g for 20 min, the supernatant fluid was removed, and 1 g of sediment was mixed with 1 ml of antiserum. The mixture was incubated and antiserum separated by centrifugation as described above.

The cytotoxicity tests (11) with rat thymocytes were carried out in duplicate and the cells counted independently by two observers. The indirect immunofluorescence assay was performed on sections of the rat brain by the method of Sainte-Marie (16) and on sus-

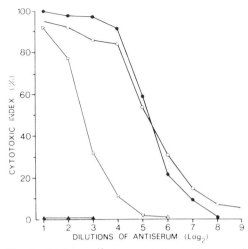

Fig. 1. Cytotoxic effects on rat thymocytes exerted by rabbit anti-synaptic membrane antiserum (ASMS) (○), anti-rat thymocyte antiserum (ATS) (●), ATS absorbed twice with rat brain homogenate (△), and ATS absorbed with 10^9 thymocytes (▲).

pensions of thymocytes (5, 9). Sheep fluorescein-conjugated anti-rabbit IgG (absorbed with rat erythrocytes, liver-cell membranes, brain homogenate, and thymocytes) was used for staining. Several controls were set up (5, 9), including the 'blocking' test and sections of the rat kidney treated with ASMS and conjugate. Each immunofluorescence assay with thymocytes and brain sections was repeated three times.

Table I. Number of fluorescent rat thymocytes after exposure to rabbit anti-synaptic membrane antiserum (ASMS) or anti-rat thymocyte antiserum (ATS) and fluorescein conjugate

Rabbit antiserum	Material used for absorption	Total of cells counted*	Total fluorescein-positive cells*	Percentage fluorescein-positive cells*
ASMS	None	1,203	1,037	86.2
	Thymocytes	1,137	4	0.3
	Brain	1,169	3	0.2
ATS	None	1,155	1,146	99.2
	Thymocytes	1,120	4	0.3
	Brain	1,078	968	89.7

* Mean of three experiments. Phase contrast microscopy and trypan blue test showed that stained lymphocytes remained viable.

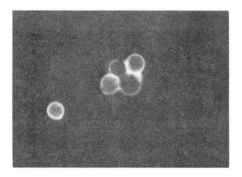

Fig. 2. Intense membrane fluorescence of rat thymocytes after exposure to rabbit anti-synaptic membrane antiserum and sheep anti-rabbit Ig fluorescein-conjugated serum. (Magnification, ×800.)

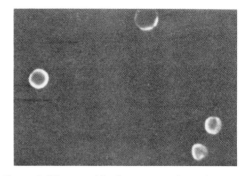

Fig. 3. Brilliant specific fluorescence of the ring type of rat thymocytes treated with rabbit anti-rat thymocyte antiserum and fluorescein conjugate. (Magnification, ×800.)

RESULTS

Rabbit ASMS and ATS exerted similar cytotoxic effects on rat thymocytes (Fig. 1). Absorption of ATS with 10^9 thymocytes completely eliminated the cytotoxicity for thymocytes, whereas two absorptions with rat brain homogenate only decreased this cytotoxicity. Serum samples from nonimmunized rabbits failed to kill thymocytes.

Results of indirect immunofluorescence assays performed on viable thymocytes are given in Table I. Stained thymocytes showed the ring type of fluorescence (Figs. 2 and 3). Absorption of ASMS and ATS with thymocytes rendered these antisera inactive for thymocytes. However, absorption of ATS with brain homogenate slightly affected the binding capacity of ATS for thymocytes (Table I).

The treatment of brain sections with ATS and conjugate resulted in a specific fluorescence (Fig. 4): neuronal membranes and fibrillar structures were stained but not the neuronal cytoplasm and nuclei. ATS absorbed with thymocytes (Fig. 5) or brain homogenate did

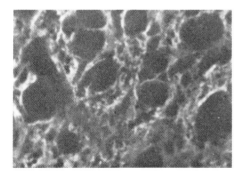

Fig. 4. Immunofluorescence photomicrograph of a section of the rat cerebrum stained with anti-rat thymocyte antiserum and fluorescein conjugate. Membrane and fibrillar structures exhibit specific fluorescence. Note round shadows of the nerve-cell bodies. (Magnification, ×500.)

Fig. 5. Immunofluorescence photomicrograph of a section of the rat cerebrum treated first with anti-rat thymocyte antiserum absorbed with 10^9 rat thymocytes and then with fluorescein conjugate. Note the complete absence of fluorescence. (Magnification, ×400.)

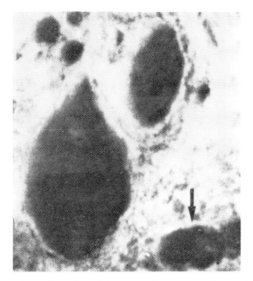

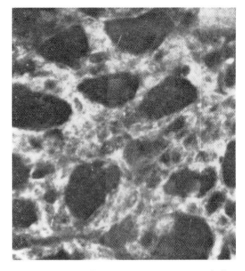

Fig. 6. A section of the rat cerebrum exposed to anti-synaptic membrane antiserum and fluorescein conjugate. Note the intense and confluent specific fluorescence of membranes and dense fibrillar network, and the absence of cytoplasmic and nuclear staining in the neurons. Arrow shows a large unstained blood vessel. (Magnification, ×600.)

Fig. 7. A section of the rat cerebrum treated first with anti-synaptic membrane antiserum absorbed with 10^9 rat thymocytes and then with fluorescein conjugate. Note less intense fluorescence compared with that shown in Fig. 6. Neuronal bodies remained unstained. (Magnification, ×500.)

not induce positive staining of the brain tissue.

Brain sections exposed to ASMS and conjugate displayed a brilliant and confluent specific fluorescence of neuronal membranes and a thick network of fibers (Fig. 6), whereas the nerve-cell bodies remained virtually unstained. This fluorescence decreased to some extent after absorption of ASMS with thymocytes (Fig. 7) and disappeared after two absorptions with brain homogenate. Control preparations of thymocytes and brain tissue were negative.

DISCUSSION

Absorption studies described here revealed that ASMS absorbed with thymocytes still contained antibodies for brain cells and, vice versa, that ATS absorbed with brain homogenate exhibited cytotoxic activity and binding capacity for thymocytes. Consequently, there were in ASMS and ATS antibodies that cross-reacted with brain and thymocytes (3, 8, 14, 18) and antibodies specific for brain cells or thymocytes. In other words, the thymocyte possessed a thymus-specific antigen not shared by brain, and the neuron contained an antigen not common to thymus. It should be mentioned here that alloantigen detected on thymocytes by antisera raised against brain tissue (15) has usually been referred to as theta or Thy-1 brain-associated antigen (3, 15, 18). However, this cross-reactivity is not the exclusive property of lymphocytes bearing theta markers. Indeed, brain and B lymphocytes of the mouse (17) and of the rat (Janković, Horvat & Mitrović, manuscript in preparation) have some antigens in common, and this points to the complexity of the brain-lymphocyte (BL) antigen system.

This experiment demonstrated that cross-reacting antibodies from ATS reacted preferentially with antigenic determinants situated on the surface membrane of brain cells. Similar localizing properties were exhibited by antibodies from ASMS. It has been shown, using anti-mouse whole brain antiserum produced in goats, that the mouse brain antigens that cross-reacted with mouse thymocytes were situated in the neuronal (myelin-depleted) fraction of the brain (4). A higher concentration of the mouse brain-thymus antigen was detected in gray matter than in white matter (1).

The relationship between the brain-specific membrane antigens (6) and antigens of various subcellular structures of the neuron still remains to be elucidated. Since fluorescence microscopy showed that antibodies from ASMS exhibited a pronounced binding capacity for the membrane of neuronal bodies, it would follow that some neuronal antigens are shared by the synaptic membrane and the neuronal surface membrane. That antibodies from ASMS do indeed combine with antigenic markers on the neuronal membrane was demonstrated in an immuno-neurological experiment dealing with bioelectrical activity of the rat sympathetic superior cervical ganglion (10): the living cervical ganglion explant was first exposed to rabbit ASMS immunoglobulin G and then to chicken anti-rabbit IgG. The reaction between rabbit IgG on the surface membrane of ganglion cells and chicken anti-rabbit IgG induced higher amplitudes of membrane potentials, as recorded by an electrode-stimulator-amplifier-oscilloscope assembly. It remains to be elucidated, however, whether anti-thymocyte antibody molecules are capable of affecting the bioelectrical pattern of the neuron. The shared antigenicity between the rat superior cervical ganglion and rat thymocytes will be presented elsewhere.

ACKNOWLEDGEMENT

This work was supported by grants from the Republic of Serbia Research Fund, Belgrade.

REFERENCES

1. Birnbaum, G. Studies on brain-thymus cross-reactivity antigens. *Brain Res. 84,* 111, 1975.
2. De Robertis, E. & Rodriguez De Lores Arnaiz, G. Structural components of the synaptic region. p. 365 in Lajtha, A. (ed.) *Handbook of Neuro-chemistry. Vol. 2.* Plenum Press, New York, 1969.
3. Golub, E. S. The distribution of brain-associated θ antigen cross-reactive with mouse in the brain of other species. *J. Immunol. 109,* 168, 1972.
4. Golub, E. S. & Day, E. D. Localization of brain-associated hematopoietic antigens in the neuronal fraction of brain. *Cell. Immunol. 16,* 427, 1975.
5. Isaković, K., Mitrović, K., Marković, B. M., Rajčević, M. & Janković, B. D. Preparation of specific anti-thymocyte and anti-bursacyte sera in rabbits. *J. immunol. Methods 7,* 359, 1975.
6. Jacque, C. M., Jørgensen, O. S., Baumann, N. A. & Bock, E. Brain-specific antigens in the quaking mouse during ontogeny. *J. Neurochem. 27,* 905, 1976.
7. Janković, B. D., Horvat, J. & Mitrović, K. Shared antigenicity between rat brain cells and rat superior cervical ganglion. *J. Neurochem.,* 1977. In press.
8. Janković, B. D., Horvat, J., Mitrović, K. & Mostarica, M. Antigenic determinants shared by rat thymocytes and rat brain subcellular fractions. *Keio J. Med. 24,* 355, 1975.
9. Janković, B. D., Horvat, J., Mitrović, K. & Mostarica, M. Rat brain-lymphocyte antigen: characterization by rabbit antisera to rat brain tubulin and S-100 protein. *Immunochemistry 14,* 75, 1977.
10. Janković, B. D., Savić, V. & Horvat, J. Bioelectrical changes induced by a reaction between rabbit Ig and anti-rabbit Ig on the surface of the rat cervical ganglion. *Experientia 31,* 1093, 1975.
11. Konda, S., Stockert, E. & Smith, R. T. Immunological patterns associated with various cell subpopulations. *Cell. Immunol. 7,* 275, 1973.
12. Morgan, I. G. Synaptosomes and cell separation. *Neuroscience 1,* 159, 1976.
13. Osler, A. G., Strauss, J. H. & Mayer, M. M. Diagnostic complement fixation. I. A method. *Amer. J. Syph. 36,* 140, 1952.
14. Peter, H. H., Clagett, J., Feldman, J. D. & Weigle, W. O. Rabbit antiserum to brain-associated thymus antigens of mouse and rat. I. Demonstration of antibodies cross-reacting to T cells of both species. *J. Immunol. 110,* 1077, 1973.
15. Reif, A. E. & Allen, J. M. V. The AKR thymic antigen and its distribution in leukemias and nervous tissue. *J. exp. Med. 120,* 413, 1964.
16. Sainte-Marie, G. A paraffin embedding technique for studies employing immunofluorescence. *J. Histochem. Cytochem. 10,* 250, 1962.
17. Santana, V. & Turk, J. L. Binding of heterologous anti-brain antibodies to mouse B cells. *Immunology 30,* 859, 1976.
18. Thiele, H.-G., Stark, R. & Keeser, D. Antigenic correlations between brain and thymus. I. Common antigenic structures in rat and mouse brain tissue and lymphocytes. *Europ. J. Immunol. 2,* 424, 1972.

8

HYPOTHALAMIC CHANGES DURING THE IMMUNE RESPONSE

H. Besedovsky, E. Sorkin, D. Felix, and H. Haas

The immune system is subject to an array of identified autoregulatory processes, but immunoregulation may also have a further basis in a network of immune-neuroendocrine interactions. Two antigens each produced an increase of more than 100 % in electrical activity of individual neurones in the ventromedial but not in the anterior nucleus of the rat hypothalamus. Animals that failed to respond to antigen manifested no increase in the firing rate. These findings constitute the first evidence for a flow of information from the activated immune system to the hypothalamus, suggesting that the brain is involved in the immune response.

1. Introduction

The immune system is subject to self-monitoring and self-regulating processes which are still incompletely understood [1]. In view of its critical importance in coping with threats of the environment this system is unlikely to function in a completely autonomous manner. As with most other systems it is presumably subject to regulation from the nervous and the endocrine systems. We have recently noted that after antigenic stimulation of rats there was a striking increase in the serum levels of corticosterone and a moderate decrease in thyroxine, coinciding in time with the elaboration of antibody-forming cells [2–4]. We regard this as an expression of the response of neuroendocrine structures to signals deriving originally from activated lymphoid cells. In order to obtain direct evidence for such a proposed afferent pathway, we looked for physiological changes manifested as electrical activity of individual neurones in the ventromedial nucleus of the hypothalamus of rats after immunization with two different antigens. This site is known to be involved in many autonomous and endocrine control mechanisms.

2. Materials and methods

2.1. Animals and antigens

A total of 98 female Holtzmann rats (Tierfarm Füllinsdorf, Switzerland) were used in this study. 49 rats were injected with antigen. Groups were immunized intraperitoneally with 5 x 10^9 sheep red blood cells (SRBC) or 250 µg trinitro-phenylated hemocyanin (TNP-HE) [5]. 44 rats received control injections of 1 ml of diluent (0.9 % NaCl) i.p. The animals were kept in individual cages at least one week before injection and until completion of the experiments. The kinetics of the immune response to these antigens was determined in numerous Holtzmann rats, using the Jerne technique for plaque formation in the spleen. Direct plaque formation to SRBC occurred from day 4 to day 7 with a peak at days 5–6 and to TNP-HE on day 1 to day 4 with a peak on day 3.

[I 1610]

2.2. Recording of hypothalamic activity

For measuring the rate of firing of unitary neurones in the ventromedial part of the hypothalamus the animals were anesthetized i.p. with 1350 mg/kg^-1 urethane. The animals were fixed in a Horsely-Clarke stereotactic apparatus, the electrode placed into the ventromedial nucleus. Action potentials were recorded extracellularly with monopolar platinum-iridium electrodes (tip diameter 1 µm, resistance 3 MΩ), or with glass micropipettes filled with 4 M NaCl or pontamine sky blue (2 % in 0.5 M sodium acetate). In several animals histological examination of electrode tracks of dye marks ejected from the electrode, confirmed the location of the recording sites. The recording electrodes were connected to a negative capacitance cathode follower. The spontaneous activity was displayed on an oscilloscope and plotted directly on a UV oscillograph. The rate of firing on each neurone was counted by a ratemeter and displayed continuously on the UV oscillograph. The discharge of each neurone was tested over a period of 200 sec. In addition to the chart recording, the mean frequency was enumerated by means of a programmable countertimer.

A total of 490 individual neurones were examined. Control and immunized animals were recorded alternately. After recording, the level of antibody formation in individual rats immunized with SRBC was also determined.

3. Results

3.1. Hypothalamic response after stimulation with SRBC

Typical data for 14 of 29 animals stimulated with SRBC are summarized in Fig. 1 a and b. On day 1 when no plaque-forming cells (PFC) are evident, no changes in firing frequency were demonstrable compared with controls. On day 5, at or near peak of PFC in spleen, there was a more than twofold increase in the firing rate of the ventromedial neurones (Control: 3.75 ± 0.28 spikes/sec.; SRBC: 8.82 ± 1.30 spikes/sec., p < 0.001). In several rats which were immunological nonresponders, no increase in firing rates occurred (not shown in Fig. 1). Furthermore, no changes in firing rates were observed in the anterior hypothalamic nucleus (Control: 5.77 ± 1.11; SRBC: 5.07 ± 0.96) on day 5 after SRBC injection.

This work was supported by the Swiss National Science Foundation, Grant Nr. 3.600.75 (H.B. and E.S.) and Nr. 3.534.0.75 (D.F.).

Reprinted from *Eur. J. Immunol.* **7** (No. 5), 323–325, 1977.

Abbreviations: SRBC: Sheep red blood cells **TNP-HE:** Trinitrophenylated hemocyanin **PFC:** Plaque-forming cell(s)

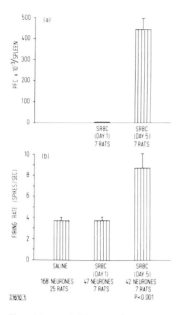

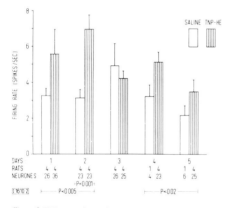

Figure 1. Increase in firing rates of neurones of ventromedial nuclei in the rat hypothalamus after antigenic stimulation. (a) Antibody-producing PFC in rat spleen; (b) Firing rates. Rats were injected intraperitoneally with 5 x 10⁹ SRBC.

Figure 2. Firing rates by rat hypothalamic neurones in the ventro-medial nuclei after intraperitoneal immunization with 250 µg TNP-HE.

3.2. Hypothalamic response following stimulation with TNP-HE

Hypothalamic responses to TNP-HE were studied in 20 rats on days 1 through 5 after injection. The results are depicted in Fig. 2. A significant increase in frequency of discharge was noted on days 1, 2, 4 and 5, the highest activation occurred on day 2, a time that precedes the peak of the direct PFC (Control: 3.23 ± 0.36 spikes/sec; TNP-HE: 6.84 ± 0.78 spikes/sec., $p < 0.001$). The reason why there is no change in firing rate on day 3 cannot be explained.

3.3. Hypothalamic response following wound healing and adrenalectomy

The corticosteroid blood levels increase during the immune response [2], and this increase might be one of the causes of the observed changes of firing rates in the ventromedial hypothalamic nucleus. In order to exclude this possibility, 8 rats were adrenalectomized and controls sham-operated. The firing rates of neurones of the ventromedial part of the hypothalamus were measured 5–10 days after surgery. The following results were obtained: adrenalectomized: 4.03 ± 0.62; sham-operated controls: 2.86 ± 0.41. It is concluded that the described increase in firing rates produced by the antigens can hardly be related to the increased corticosteroid levels.

The results with operated animals have an important bearing on the possible effects of wound healing, which include processes of inflammation and cell proliferation. No changes in firing rates in the ventromedial part of the hypothalamus were observed following the surgical procedure.

4. Discussion

The results of this study show that two separate, nontoxic, noninfectious antigens elicited apart from the conventional immune response and an endocrine response [2] a distinctive response in the hypothalamus. The only known common feature of these two agents is their immunogenicity, and it is considered most unlikely that these physiological alterations involve the antigen itself, but rather reflect events linked with the immune response which in turn evoke the changes in the hypothalamus.

The fact that on day 1 after SRBC injection, a time when no PFC are detectable, no increase in firing rates on the studied neurones occured, would seem to exclude factors of handling and stress as being involved in the neural alterations. Also body temperature was the same in controls and antigen-injected animals. It is of interest that in the case of TNP-HE the maximal hypothalamic response was found to be before the peak of the immune response.

The experiments dealing with adrenalectomy and its sham-operated controls provide strong evidence that the effects observed were not due to nonspecific factors. The surgical procedure has a major component of wound healing with attendant cell proliferation and inflammation, yet operated animals manifested no changes whatsoever in the firing rates during the succeeding 5–10 days, corresponding to the time elapsing between the administration of antigen and measurement in the hypothalamus. Thus, the above described increase of firing rates in the ventromedial hypothalamic nuclei is unlikely to be due simply to the increase of corticosteroid levels shown previously to occur during the immune response to SRBC and TNP-HE [2]. This is not surprising since it is known that only a small proportion of these neurones projects to the portal vessels.

It has been proved that electrolytic lesions in different parts of the brain can induce modifications in different immune response models [6–9]. We know of no previous suggestion that the immune response itself can produce changes in the hypothalamic activity. The present studies imply that after antigenic stimulation signals from lymphoid tissue reach the hypothalamus. Their nature is unknown, but there is no lack of candidates. The most likely would be the products of antigen-responsive cells (e.g. lymphokines). Other possibilities include immune complexes, or pharmacological mediators liberated during the immune response, or even electrical signals from nerve endings of lymphoid tissue. The nature of the pathway within the hypothalamus, the type of neurones and whether other brain structures are involved, remain to be determined.

The technical assistance of Ms. Ursula Frangi, Ms. Regula Kellerhals and Mr. A. Buhler is gratefully acknowledged.

5. References

1 Jerne, N.K., *The Harvey Lectures,* Series 70, 93 1974–1975. Academic Press, New York 1976.

2 Besedovsky, H.O., Sorkin, E., Keller, M. and Müller, J., *Proc. Soc. Exp. Biol. Med.* 1975. *150:* 466.

3 Besedovsky, H.O. and Sorkin, E., *Clin. Exp. Immunol.* 1977. *27:* 1.

4 Besedovsky, H.O. and Sorkin, E., *Proceedings of the V. International Congress of Endocrinology, Symposium "Hormones and Immunity",* Excerpta Medica, Amsterdam 1977, in press.

5 Rittenberg, M.B. and Amkraut, A.A., *J. Immunol.* 1966. *97:* 431.

6 Janković, B.D. and Isaković, K., *Int. Arch. Allergy Appl. Immunol.* 1973. *45:* 360.

7 Isaković, K. and Janković, B.D., *Int. Arch. Allergy Appl. Immunol.* 1973. *45:* 373.

8 Stein, M., Schiavi, R.C. and Camerino, M., *Science* 1976. *191:* 435.

9 Gestal, J. and Oehling, A., *Allergologia et Immunopathologia* 1974. *4:* 221.

9

IMMUNOREGULATION MEDIATED BY THE SYMPATHETIC NERVOUS SYSTEM

H. O. Besedovsky, A. del Rey, E. Sorkin, M. Da Prada, and H. H. Keller

A postulated immunoregulatory role for the autonomous nervous system was explored utilizing several *in vivo* and *in vitro* approaches. Local surgical denervation of the spleen in rats and general chemical sympathectomy by 6-hydroxydopamine combined with adrenalectomy yielded a similar removal of restraint expressed as enhancement in the number of PFC in response to immunization. Noradrenaline and the synthetic α-agonist clonidine which are, respectively, natural and artificial effector molecules of the sympathetic nervous system each strongly suppressed the *in vitro* induced immune response of murine spleen cells to SRBC. Further, radiometric-enzymatic assay of noradrenaline in the splenic pulp revealed a decrease in the content of this neurotransmitter just preceding the exponential phase of the immune response to SRBC (Days 3 and 4) in this site. Taken together, these findings point to a dynamic immunoregulatory relationship between the immune and sympathetic nervous system.

INTRODUCTION

With the progressive unraveling of the cellular and humoral elements of the immune system in recent years, the nature of its regulation has become a matter of major concern. It has long been evident that the immune system must be subject to internal regulatory mechanisms so as to maintain its homeostatic balance. Such regulation could be visualized as occurring at a number of levels, e.g., during differentiation in ontogeny as well as during the various stages of the response to antigen. Accordingly, considerable effort—both theoretical and experimental— has been committed to exploring a variety of regulatory mechanisms such as a lymphocyte network (1), the genetic control of immune responsiveness (2–3), and suppressor and helper lymphocytes and their mediators (4–7). Despite the incompleteness of our knowledge of these regulatory mechanisms there has developed a kind of consensus that the immune system is a self-monitoring, autoregulated system which in a purely operational sense, is rather analogous to other well-known self-regulated body systems.

With the primary role assigned to lymphocytes, antibody, and a few accessory cells, there was no particular reason to incorporate other higher, more integrative host systems into immunological thinking. In retrospect, this seems rather surprising, particularly as the autonomic nervous system represents one of the major integrative levels of *all* host regulation. Indeed, a number of the mediators of this system *do* affect immune processes, such as adrenaline, noradrenaline (NA),[1] and acetylcholine, its agonists and blockers. Lymphocytes express receptors for several neurotransmitters (8) which influence lymphoid cell proliferation and transformation (9–11), genetic expression (12, 13), rosette formation (14, 15), antibody formation (16), cytotoxicity (17–19), and intracellular cyclic nucleotide levels (8, 20, 21). Some of the reported data are contradictory, but on the whole, they indicate that neurotransmitters do in fact influence various parameters of the immune response, both *in vitro* and *in vivo*.

In addition, experimental evidence already exists that the immune system is under external regulation by the neuroendocrine system (22, 23). This evidence derives from experiments showing that hormones and neurotransmitters affect the functioning of the lymphoid system and reciprocally that the immune response causes changes in blood hormone levels (24) and in the electrical activity of neurons in certain hypothalamic areas (25).

The aim of the present work was to establish whether the sympathetic nervous system does in fact operate in immunoregulation. To this end, several experimental approaches were utilized:

(a) Surgical denervation of the spleen or chemical sympathectomy combined with adrenalectomy and subsequent measurement of the immune response.

(b) Quantitation of the NA content in the spleen pulp at various stages of an immune response.

(c) Study of the effect of NA and the synthetic α-adrenergic agonist clonidine on the immune response *in vitro*.

MATERIALS AND METHODS

Animals. *In vivo* experiments were performed with 2- to 3-month old female Holtzmann rats, while female C57Bl/6J mice, 2–3 months of age, were used for the *in vitro* experiments. Throughout the experiments, rats were housed individually.

Drugs. L-Noradrenaline hydrochloride (L-arterenol-hydrochloride) and 6-hydroxydopamine-hydrochloride (2,4,5-trihydroxy-phenylethylamine-hydrochloride, 6-OH-DA) were purchased from Fluka AG, Buchs, Switzerland. The synthetic α-agonist clonidine (2-(2,6-dichlorophenylamino)-2-imidazoline hydrochloride) was obtained from Boehringer, Ingelheim, Germany.

Denervation of spleen. Rats were anesthetized by intraperitoneal injection of 40 mg/kg pentobarbital sodium (Nembutal, Abbott, Zug, Switzerland). Denervation was performed by abdominal incision, exposure of the nerve vascular package, and dissection of artery, cutting the nerves before their bifurcation. Sham operations were also carried out in another group of rats following the same surgical procedure but without cutting the nerves.

Chemical sympathectomy. Newborn rats were injected daily ip with 150 mg/kg

---

[1] Abbreviations used: NA, noradrenaline; CA, catecholamine; PFC, plaque-forming cells; SRBC, sheep red blood cells; 6-OH-DA, 6-hydroxydopamine hydrochloride.

6-OH-DA during the first 5 days of life. According to Tranzer and Thoenen (26), this procedure results in a quite selective and permanent destruction of the peripheral adrenergic nerve terminals.

Adrenalectomy. Bilateral adrenalectomy was performed by two dorsolateral incisions. Operated animals were supplied with sodium chloride (0.9%) in addition to their regular water supply. Sham operations were carried out in another group of animals following the same surgical procedure but without removing the adrenals.

Measurement of the noradrenaline content of spleen pulp and heart. For measurement of NA the animals were killed by cervical dislocation and then exsanguinated either by aorta or heart perfusion with 200 ml cold 0.9% sodium chloride solution. Spleens were removed, weighed, and each divided into two parts. One portion was used for evaluation of the immune response, the other was decapsulated in order to measure parenchymal NA. Both spleen pulp and heart were stored at $-80°C$ until NA assay.

The radiometric-enzymatic assay for measuring femtomole (10^{-15}) quantities of CA as described by Da Prada and Zürcher (27) was applied to quantity NA in the spleen. The method consists essentially in conversion of the CA into its O-methylated analogue by catechol-O-methyltransferase in the presence of S-adenosyl[^{3}H]methionine and thereafter extraction in the presence of sodium tetraphenylborate. This extraction, together with an improved quick chromatographic separation and the oxidation of the labeled NA derivative to vanillin, yields extremely high sensitivity and specificity.

For determining the NA content of the heart, NA was extracted with 0.4 N $HClO_4$, absorbed onto Al_2O_3 at pH 7.7 to 8.0 using Tris base and eluted with 0.05 N $HClO_4$. Fluorimetric determination was carried out in a continuous flow system essentially as described by Waldmeier *et al.* (28).

Immunization. Sheep red blood cells (SRBC) were used as antigen in both *in vivo* and *in vitro* experiments. For the *in vivo* experiments SRBC were washed three times with 0.9% NaCl solution. SRBC (5×10^9) in 1 ml 0.9% NaCl solution were injected intraperitoneally into rats. Surgically treated animals were immunized 5 days after the performance of the operation. For the *in vitro* experiments SRBC were washed three times with sterile balanced salt solution (BSS) and resuspended in the culture medium.

Evaluation of the immune response. Plaque-forming cells (PFC) were determined according to the Jerne–Nordin technique (29) using splenic cells taken at various times after the injection of SRBC.

In vitro induction of immune response to SRBC. The Mishell and Dutton system, as modified by Schreier and Nordin (30) was used. Briefly, 10^7 adult female C57Bl/6J spleen cells were cultured together with 10^7 SRBC in RPMI-1640, containing 20% fetal calf serum (GIBCO), 1% glutamine, 5×10^{-5} M mercaptoethanol, 25 IU/ml penicillin, and 25 μg/ml streptomycin.

Cultures were maintained in a gas mixture, containing 10% CO_2, 7% O_2, and 83% N_2, gently rocked for 5 days, harvested, and plaque-forming cells were determined.

NA and clonidine effects on immune response in vitro. A range of NA and clonidine concentrations was added at the onset of the culture or 24 hr later. Three experiments were performed in triplicate and for each individual interaction mixture PFC were determined in triplicate.

RESULTS

Effect of Spleen Denervation on the Immune Response to SRBC

The spleen is known to have a relatively rich noradrenergic sympathetic innervation. Denervation would therefore be expected to result in a diminution of NA in spleen which in turn could affect the immune response. Denervated and sham-operated rats were injected ip with SRBC and the number of PFC were counted 5 days later. Figure 1 shows that an almost 70% increase in number of PFC/spleen was found in denervated animals as compared with sham-operated controls. These findings suggest that interruption of sympathetic nervous innervation removes an important suppressor of the immune response. Since splenic nerves are not entirely sympathetic, the basis for an increased number of PFC might not be due solely to the interruption of sympathetic fibers. To further clarify this point sympathectomy was performed by purely chemical means.

Effect of Chemical Sympathectomy on the Immune Response to SRBC

Chemical sympathectomy in newborn rats was produced by repeated 6-OH-DA administration. At 2 months of age animals were given an immunizing injection of 5 × 10⁹ SRBC ip and the number of PFC in the spleen determined 5 days later. Sympathectomized rats showed a tendency for increased PFC which was not statistically significant. It is known that following 6-OH-DA-induced sympathectomy there is a compensatory stimulation of the adrenals (31) so that normal and even high CA concentrations are present in the blood and therefore still acting on the spleen. Accordingly, in further experiments rats were first chemically sympathectomized and subsequently adrenalectomized as well. Three other groups served as controls: one injected with solvent and sham operated; another injected with 6-OH-DA and sham operated; and a third group injected with solvent and adrenalectomized. Figure 2 summarizes the results. Sham-operated rats treated

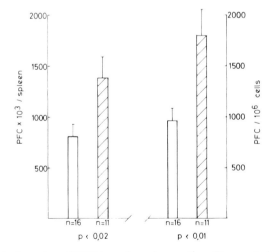

Fig. 1. Enhancement of number of PFC by spleen denervation. Denervated or sham-operated rats were injected ip with 5×10^9 SRBC and the number of PFC were measured 5 days later. Values are given as mean ± SEM. □, Sham-operated rats; ▨, denervated rats.

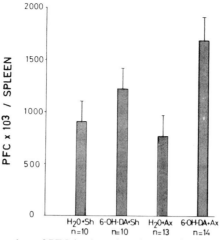

FIG. 2. Enhancement of number of PFC in the spleen by chemical sympathectomy combined with adrenalectomy. Group 1: Rats injected ip with 2 μl/g body wt solvent (H_2O) daily during the first 5 days of life and sham operated at 2 months of age. Group 2: Rats injected ip with 150 mg/kg 6-OH-DA and sham operated. Group 3: Rats injected with solvent and adrenalectomized. Group 4: Rats injected with 6-OH-DA and adrenalectomized. Group 2 showed a slight increase in the number of PFC when compared with control (Group 1). Adrenalectomy alone (Group 3) did not significantly change the magnitude of the immune response, whereas combined treatment of 6-OH-DA with adrenalectomy (Group 4) resulted in a 119% increase in number of PFC in the spleen ($P < 0.01$). Group 4 differed also significantly from Group 1 ($P < 0.01$).

with 6-OH-DA (Group 2) again showed a slight increase in number of PFC compared with controls (Group 1). Adrenalectomy alone (Group 3) did not exert any significant effect on numbers of PFC, affirming previous findings (22). In contrast, the combination of chemical sympathectomy via 6-OH-DA and adrenalectomy (Group 4) resulted in a 119% increase in the number of splenic PFC.

These experiments support the hypothesis that the sympathetic system exerts a significant influence on the immune response. To establish whether this influence reflects a means for physiological control over the immune system, the immune response itself should induce measurable changes in the sympathetic system. In the context of our concept this could take the form of changes in the level of neurotransmitter in lymphoid organs.

Accordingly, the content of NA in the spleen pulp during the immune response was examined.

Diminished NA Content in Spleen during the Immune Response

Groups of rats were immunized with 5×10^9 SRBC and the number of PFC and the NA content of the spleen pulp determined at various intervals. Figure 3 shows the results of one of the five experiments performed. The number of PFC followed the usual pattern, a low number on Day 3, very high on Day 4, a marked decrease on Days 6 and 8. The NA content of the spleen slightly decreased on Day 2, but a marked decrease was evident by Day 3, respectively, Day 4 compared with the controls ($P < 0.001$). By Day 8 when relatively few direct PFC were detectable, the

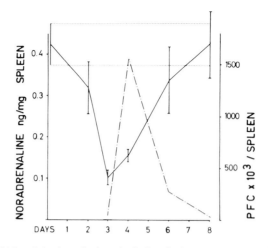

Fig. 3. Decreasing NA levels in the splenic pulp during the immune response. Rats were injected with 5×10^9 SRBC or physiological saline and the number of PFC and the NA content determined on Days 2, 3, 4, 6, and 8. Saline-injected controls showed no significant changes in splenic NA content and were used to define the normal control range (Day 0). Each point of the NA curve represents the mean value ± SEM obtained from determinations in spleens of four animals. NA, ——; PFC, –·–·–.

NA content had returned to normal. In all five experiments the decrease in NA content of spleen preceded the peak PFC. This reduction ranged from 40–70%. There was no significant change in spleen weight nor were the differences between immunized and control animals altered in terms of NA in total spleen. In two experiments, the NA content of a nonlymphoid organ, the heart, was also determined at various intervals following immunization. No changes in the NA level in this control organ are discerned during the immune response.

These data constitute the first discrete evidence that a physiologically meaningful change in the splenic content of NA occurs in the environment of antibody-forming cells. This is an event which we would expect to affect the performance of immunocompetent cells. In the experiments which follow, such actual effects of the sympathetic neurotransmitter NA and the synthetic α-adrenergic agonist clonidine on the *in vitro* induced immune response were in fact obtained.

NA and the Synthetic α-Adrenergic Agonist Clonidine Suppress the Immune Response in Vitro

It seemed especially important to affirm in an *in vitro* model the findings *in vivo* that surgical and chemical sympathectomy both led to diminution of the restraint on the immune response and a decrease in the NA content of a major antibody-forming organ upon immunization. Accordingly, experiments were designed in anticipation of a direct action by the neurotransmitter NA and its synthetic α-adrenergic agonist clonidine on the cells involved in a primary *in vitro* induced immune response. Few and contradictory results have been reported earlier (32, 33). In the present work, NA was added to mouse spleen cell cultures plus SRBC. A total of nine experiments were performed in which NA was added in concentrations of 10^{-4} to 10^{-8} M at zero time. In six of these experiments a suppression of the immune response occurred at all NA concentrations employed whereas in three other experiments the immune response was either not influenced or an increase was seen. This variation in results may be attributable to the instability (oxidized, metabolized) of NA in culture medium containing fetal calf serum.

Since NA stimulates predominantly α-adrenergic receptors, further experimentation *in vitro* was based on the synthetic α-agonist clonidine which is a stable compound resistant to monoamino oxidase and catechol-O-methyltransferase. As is shown graphically in Fig. 4, a strong suppression of the immune response was produced by clonidine at concentrations varying from 10^{-4} to 10^{-8} M. This immunosuppression was obtained irrespective of whether the agonist was added at the onset of the culture to the spleen cells together with the antigen or 24 hr later. It is noteworthy that addition after 24 hr induced an even more pronounced immunosuppressive effect. Clonidine in concentrations from 10^{-4} to 10^{-8} M did not manifest any discernible toxicity for spleen cells as determined by the trypan blue exclusion test. Indeed the number of recoverable cells was the same as in the controls after 5 days of culture.

DISCUSSION

During the past decade extensive study has shown that elements of the immune system itself function internally to achieve immunoregulation. Such regulatory control is evident at a variety of levels and by various means. The feature common to these elements is that they all involve control effected entirely within the immune system itself. In the present work an alternative, purely physiological means of effecting immunoregulation was explored.

The seemingly innocent act of administering an antigen foreign to the host is viewed by the immunologist as having purely immunobiologic consequences, i.e., antigen processing by macrophages, T- and B-lymphocyte triggering and their clonal expansion, release of soluble effector molecules including antibodies, and complex shifts within the lymphocyte network. However, those events might cause a significant perturbation of the *milieu interieur*. Autonomous mechanisms were

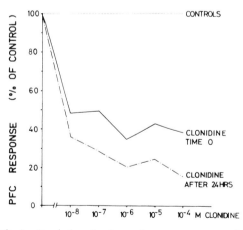

FIG. 4. Suppression of the *in vitro* induced primary immune response of mouse spleen cells by the α-adrenergic agonist clonidine. Clonidine was added at the indicated concentration either together with the antigen (SRBC) at the onset of the culture (——) or 24 hr later (–·–·–). Each curve represents the mean of three experiments. The response in the controls varied from 15,000 to 27,000 PFC per culture.

acquired in phylogeny, presumably to cope with external variability of the environment by imposing compensating responses on target organs. As a consequence of an immunologically perturbed *milieu interieur*, changes in the autonomic system may occur and be linked to immunoregulation.

Considerable evidence already exists that administration of hormones (22, 23, 34–36) and neurotransmitters *in vitro* and *in vivo* (9, 16), brain lesions or stimulation (37–41), extirpation of endocrine organs, and others, all affect the operation of the immune system. Findings such as these, while suggestive, do not support the inference that the immune system is necessarily under neuroendocrine control. To prove such immunoregulation dynamic neuroendocrine inputs reflected by hormone and neurotransmitter changes should be discernible at the right time and in appropriate sites, and be of such magnitude as to effect significant modulation in the amplitude and tempo of the immune response. The present communication provides the initial evidence for such a dynamic relationship between the sympathetic nervous system and the immune system. The observed decrease in the NA content of the spleen during an immune response, the immune consequences of chemical sympathectomy and surgical denervation, and the immunosuppressive effects of NA and the α-adrenergic agonist, clonidine, on antibody production *in vitro*, constitute primary evidence for immunoregulation by the sympathetic nervous system.

Local surgical denervation of the spleen or general chemical sympathectomy by 6-OH-DA combined with adrenalectomy produce a similar removal of restraint on the number of antibody-forming cells developed in spleen (Figs. 1 and 2). This suggests that the effect was caused by a decrement of splenic NA, thereby releasing cells involved in the immune response from the suppressive action of NA. That NA or the α-adrenergic agonist clonidine have indeed such direct suppressive action on splenic cells was attested by experiments *in vitro* (Fig. 4).

We considered that the decreased NA levels might enhance the number of PFC in the spleen by a change in traffic of lymphoid cells. However, Ernstrøm and Sandberg demonstrated in guinea pigs that chemical sympathectomy by 6-OH-DA does not change the splenic release of lymphocytes (42). Since these animals were not adrenalectomized, one cannot definitively exclude that more complete NA depletion would not also affect lymphoid cell traffic.

The strongest experimental evidence linking the immune system and the autonomic nervous system derives from the marked decrease of the NA level in spleen during the immune response in that major lymphoid organ (Fig. 3). It is highly significant that this NA decrease occurs in the immediate vicinity of antibody-forming cells. Changes such as these may well be restricted to lymphoid organs, since the content of NA in the heart (for example) remains unmodified during the immune response. The fact that the changes occur several days after administration of antigen seems to exclude any stress effects or for that matter any kind of direct effect by the antigen itself. Decreased NA levels might be attributed to its consumption by spleen cells or by other local factors. However, such explanations are viewed as unlikely. The relative constancy of NA content in organs during varying conditions is based on a feedback mechanism operating with a high degree of precision (43). Free NA influences NA synthesis at the rate-limiting step of tyrosine-hydroxylase activity (43). Consequently, unless it is assumed that activated lymphocytes release a specific enzymatic inhibitor, local NA changes will be rapidly compensated for via the aforementioned mechanisms.

Accordingly, it is proposed that changes in NA content during the immune response represent the efferent limb of a reflex mechanism triggered by antigen-stimulated cells. It seems to us that the changes in local concentration of neurotransmitters are most reasonably viewed as regulatory signals capable of modulating the ongoing immune response. Such changes may even be synchronized with appearance of receptors for catecholamine known to occur during activation of lymphoid cells (8).

The evidence for the proposed bidirectional network of interaction of the immune and neuroendocrine system (22) can be summarized as follows: (a) complex bidirectional interactions demonstrable between the endocrine and the immune system during early ontogeny (for review, see 22); (b) hormonal changes induced by the immune response itself (24); (c) changes in firing rates of neurons in discrete zones of the hypothalamus during the immune response (25); (d) diminution in NA content of the spleen during the immune response.

Knowledge of immune neuroendocrine interactions is still fragmentary, particularly pertaining to afferent signals. But the evidence thus far attests to efferent autonomic mechanisms capable of modulating the immune response. Thus, to the array of well-known regulatory mechanisms considered to control the immune response is now proposed still another basic mode for immunoregulation, one that is quite external to the immune system itself. It may well prove a formidable task to ascertain which among these immunoregulatory agencies is dominant, what determines when and how each is to participate in the overall pattern of regulation and control, and the interrelationship among them.

ACKNOWLEDGMENTS

We thank Drs. M. Landy and W. Haefely for careful readings of the manuscript and constructive criticism. We also thank Ms. Ursula Affolter, Mrs. Jytte Kerschbaumer, and Mr. Alois Bühler for excellent technical assistance, and Ms. Helen Kreuzer for typing of the manuscript.

This work was supported by Swiss National Science Foundation, Grant 3.213.0.77.

REFERENCES

1. Jerne, N. K., *Ann. Immunol. (Inst. Pasteur)* **125C**, 373, 1974.
2. McDevitt, H. O., and Landy, M. (Eds.), *In* "Genetic Control of Immune Responsiveness." Academic Press, New York/London, 1972.
3. Katz, D. H., and Benacerraf, B. (Eds.), *In* "The Role of Products of the Histocompatibility Gene Complex in Immune Responses." Academic Press, New York/San Francisco/London, 1976.
4. Waldmann, T. A., and Broder, S., *In* "Progress in Clinical Immunology" (R. S. Schwartz, Ed.), Vol. 3, pp. 155–199. Grune & Stratton, New York/San Francisco/London, 1977.
5. Gershon, R. K., *In* "Contemporary Topics in Immunobiology" (M. D. Cooper and N. L. Warner, Eds.), Vol. 3, pp. 1–40. Plenum, New York/London, 1974.
6. Waksman, B. H., and Namba, Y., *Cell. Immunol.* **21**, 161, 1976.
7. Katz, D. H., *In* "Lymphocyte Differentiation, Recognition, and Regulation" (D. H. Katz, Ed.), pp. 247–342. Academic Press, New York/San Francisco/London, 1977.
8. Bourne, H. R., Lichtenstein, L. M., Melmon, K. L., Henney, C. S., Weinstein, Y., and Shearer, G. M., *Science* **184**, 19, 1974.
9. Hadden, J. W., Hadden, E. M., and Middleton, E., Jr., *Cell. Immunol.* **1**, 583, 1970.
10. MacManus, J. P., Whitfield, J. F., and Youdale, T., *J. Cell Physiol.* **77**, 103, 1971.

11. Hadden, J. W., Johnson, E. M., Hadden, E. M., Coffey, R. G., and Johnson, L. D., *In* "Immune Recognition" (A. S. Rosenthal, Ed.), pp. 359–389. Academic Press, New York, 1975.
12. Hammerling, U., Chin, A. F., Abbott, J., and Scheid, M., *J. Immunol.* **115**, 1425, 1975.
13. Singh, U., and Owen, J. J. T., *Eur. J. Immunol.* **6**, 59, 1976.
14. Galant, S. P., and Remo, R. A., *J. Immunol.* **114**, 512, 1975.
15. Ito, M., Sless, F., and Parrott, D. M. V., *Nature (London)* **266**, 633, 1977.
16. Bourne, H. R., Melmon, K. L., Weinstein, Y., and Shearer, G. M., *In* "Cyclic AMP, Cell Growth, and the Immune Response" (W. Braun, L. M. Lichtenstein, and C. W. Parker, Eds.), pp. 99–113. Springer, Berlin/Heidelberg/New York, 1974.
17. Henney, C. S., Bourne, H. R., and Lichtenstein, L. M., *J. Immunol.* **108**, 1526, 1972.
18. Strom, T. B., Sytkowski, A. J., Carpenter, C. B., and Merrill, J. P., *In* "Lymphocyte Recognition and Effector Mechanisms" (K. Lindahl-Kiessling and D. Osoba, Eds.), pp. 509–513. Academic Press, New York/London, 1974.
19. Strom, T. B., Sytkowski, A. J., Carpenter, C. B., and Merrill, J. P., *Proc. Nat. Acad. Sci. USA* **71**, 1330, 1974.
20. Parker, C. W., *In* "Immune Recognition" (A. S. Rosenthal, Ed.), pp. 331–336. Academic Press, New York/San Francisco/London, 1975.
21. Strom, T. B., Lundin, A. P., III, and Carpenter, C. B., *In* "Progress in Clinical Immunology" (R. S. Schwartz, Ed.), Vol. 3, pp. 115–153. Grune & Stratton, New York, 1977.
22. Besedovsky, H. O., and Sorkin, E., *In* "Endocrinology" (V. H. T. James, Ed.), Vol. 2, pp. 504–513. Excerpta Medica, Amsterdam/Oxford, 1977.
23. Besedovsky, H. O., and Sorkin, E., *Clin. Exp. Immunol.* **27**, 1, 1977.
24. Besedovsky, H. O., Sorkin, E., Keller, M., and Müller, J., *Proc. Soc. Exp. Biol. Med.* **150**, 466, 1975.
25. Besedovsky, H. O., Sorkin, E., Felix, D., and Haas, H., *Eur. J. Immunol.* **7**, 325, 1977.
26. Tranzer, J. P., and Thoenen, H., *Experientia* **24**, 155, 1968.
27. Da Prada, M., and Zürcher, G., *Life Sci.* **19**, 1161, 1976.
28. Waldmeier, P., De Herdt, P., and Maître, L., *Clin. Chem.* **20**, 81, 1974.
29. Jerne, N. K., and Nordin, A. A., *Science* **140**, 405, 1963.
30. Schreier, M. H., and Nordin, A. A., *In* "B and T Cells in Immune Recognition" (F. Loor and G. E. Roelants, Eds.), pp. 127–152. Wiley, London/New York/Sidney/Toronto, 1977.
31. Thoenen, H., *In* "Handbook of Experimental Pharmacology" (O. Eichler, A. Rarah, H. Herken, and A. D. Welch, Eds.), Vol. XXXIII, pp. 813–844. Springer, Berlin/Heidelberg/New York, 1972.
32. Pearlman, D. S., *J. Allergy Clin. Immunol.* **47**, 109, 1971.
33. Makino, S., and Reed, C. E., *Fed. Proc.* **29**, 431, 1970.
34. Fabris, N., *In* "Comprehensive Immunology: Immunology and Aging" (T. Makinodan and Yunis, E., Eds.), Vol. 1, pp. 73–89. Plenum, New York/London, 1977.
35. Wolstenholme, G. E. W., and Knight, J. (Eds.), *In* "Hormones and the Immune Response," Ciba Foundation Study Group No. 36. Churchill, London, 1970.
36. Pierpaoli, W., Fabris, N., and Sorkin, E., *In* "Hormones and the Immune Response" (G. E. W. Wolstenholme and J. Knight, Eds.), pp. 126–153. Churchill, London, 1970.
37. Stein, M., Schiavi, P. C., and Camerino, M., *Science* **191**, 435, 1976.
38. Spector, N. H., *In* "Handbook of the Hypothalamus" (P. Morgane and J. Panksepp, Eds.), Dekker, New York, in press.
39. Jankovic, B. D., and Isakovic, K., *Int. Arch. Allergy* **45**, 360, 1973.
40. Isakovic, K., and Jankovic, B. D., *Int. Arch. Allergy* **45**, 373, 1973.
41. Korneva, E. A., Klimenko, V. M., and Shkhinek, E. K., *Sechenov Physiol. J. USSR* **60**, 556, 1974.
42. Ernstrøm, U., and Sandberg, G., *Scand. J. Haematol.* **11**, 275, 1973.
43. Euler, U. S., *In* "Handbook of Experimental Pharmacology" (O. Eichler, A. Rarah, H. Herken, and A. D. Welch, Eds.), Vol. XXXIII, pp. 186–230. Springer, Berlin/Heidelberg/New York, 1972.

10

INFLUENCE OF HORMONES ON LYMPHOID TISSUE STRUCTURE AND FUNCTION. THE ROLE OF THE PITUITARY ADRENOTROPHIC HORMONE IN THE REGULATION OF THE LYMPHOCYTES AND OTHER CELLULAR ELEMENTS OF THE BLOOD[1]

Thomas F. Dougherty and Abraham White

INTRODUCTION

THE WIDE VARIATIONS in the numbers of the blood cells in health and disease have not encouraged investigators to postulate a common regulatory mechanism controlling these elements. Yet the existence of numerical limits between which the blood cells fluctuate in the normal subject is remarkable in view of the proliferative capacity of the blood-forming tissues. It seems likely that mechanisms exist which restrain the degree to which the cellular products of these tissues accumulate. An influence of various endocrine glands on hematopoietic tissues has been suggested by several investigators on the basis of clinical observations. This subject has been reviewed by Drinker and Yoffey (1941).

It is the object of this paper to present experimental evidence that the pituitary adrenotrophic hormone is a factor in the regulation of the number of blood lymphocytes. This hormone may also be concerned with the regulation of certain bone marrow elements.

[1] A preliminary note has been published (Dougherty, T. F., and A. White. *Science*, 98: 367. 1943).

This investigation has been aided by grants from the Josiah Macy, Jr., Foundation, the International Cancer Research Foundation, and the Fluid Research Fund of Yale University School of Medicine.

Reprinted from *Endocrinology* 35 (No. 1), 1–14, 1944.

Mice and rats of both sexes were used in these studies. The mice were all of the Strong CBA strain and the rats of the Sprague-Dawley strain. The mice and rats were fed Purina Fox Chow. Adult rabbits and humans were also studied.

In so far as possible, the following conditions were standardized: diet, age of experimental animals, environmental temperature and experimental procedures. Most of the data have been obtained on mice 60 to 80 days old of a single strain (CBA Strong) because of their genetic uniformity and their availability in large numbers. However, supplementary observations have been made with rats (Sprague-Dawley) weighing 200 to 250 gms. and also with rabbits (weight approximately 2.5 kg.) of mixed parentage, and with adult humans. Food and water were available to the animals at all times during the studies. The human subjects were hospital patients on routine hospital diets.

Blood was taken from the tail vein of mice and rats for all determinations. Ear vein blood of rabbits and finger tip blood of humans were used. Total leucocyte and erythrocyte counts were done in the usual manner. Differential leucocyte counts were obtained by counting at least two hundred cells on blood smears stained with May-Grünwald Giemsa. Hemoglobin values were obtained by the alkaline hematin method, using the Evelyn photoelectric colorimeter (Evelyn, 1936). The specific gravity of whole blood was determined by the falling drop method (Kagan, 1941).

The adrenal glands were studied histologically for their lipid content and analyzed quantitatively for total cholesterol. Lipids were stained according to the Herzheimer technic using Sudan IV. Paired mouse adrenals were analyzed for total cholesterol by the method of Schoenheimer and Sperry as modified by Sperry (1938).

All materials were injected subcutaneously in aqueous solution, except where otherwise indicated. Descriptive information regarding the substances administered will be found in the section containing the data.

RESULTS

No effort was made to standardize the relationship between the amount of hormone administered and the body weight of the experimental species, owing to the quantity of hormone which would be necessary for the larger animals. Moreover, it was early observed that relatively small doses of hormone were effective even in the larger species.

Early in these investigations it was apparent that the secretion of the adrenal cortex has a profound influence on the level of certain blood cellular elements. Inasmuch as a variety of unrelated stimuli are known to affect adrenal cortical activity it was necessary to establish in a large number of normal animals the limits of variation of the numbers of blood cells under laboratory conditions. A possible diurnal variation in the blood picture has been checked by taking blood from different animals at various times during the day. Data on control animals are collected in table 1 and serve for comparison with values obtained in the various experiments. Experimental data for particular blood constituents are considered significant when the values exceed the limits of the average deviation obtained in the control animals.

It should be noted that although the segmented forms are referred to in the tables as polymorphonuclear cells, this is done as a matter of convenience in tabulating data for various species. These cells in the rabbit are pseudoeosinophils and in the rat and the mouse

TABLE 1. AVERAGE VALUES AND THEIR DEVIATION, FOR BLOOD CONSTITUENTS OF THE CONTROL MICE, RATS AND RABBITS

Species	No. of animals	Hemoglobin	R.B.C.	W.B.C.	Lymphocytes	Polymorphonuclear leucocytes	Specific gravity whole blood
		gm./%	millions/cu. mm.				
Mouse	99	15.3±1.06[1]	9.05±0.85[1]	12,814±3,632	9,584±3,047	3,257±1,304	1.060±0.0025[2]
One day adrenalectomized mouse	60	15.4±1.10[4]	8.65±1.39[4]	14,903±3,511	11,717±2,826	3,189±1,247	1.061±0.0016[3]
Rat	42	14.8±0.61[5]	8.88±0.91[5]	17,826±4,545	14,700±4,027	2,932±1,243	1.059±0.0008[6]
Rabbit	18	12.0±1.38[7]	5.67±0.77[7]	10,053±1,730	6,861±1,723	3,193±1,682	1.053±0.0009[8]

[1] 39 animals.   [2] 19 animals.   [3] 5 animals.   [4] 12 animals.   [5] 27 animals.   [6] 8 animals.   [7] 16 animals.   [8] 3 animals.

should probably be referred to as heterophils. Eosinophils are not grouped separately since they are few in number and apparently were unaffected by the experimental procedures.

Even under conditions standardized as carefully as possible, the alterations in blood picture produced by administration of the various agents used will depend upon (1) the normal blood picture of the species studied, (2) the quantity of agent administered, and (3) the route of administration.

Effect of Adrenotrophic Hormone Injection

Blood analyses were conducted at intervals after hormone injection, using different groups of mice at each time interval, rather than making successive determinations on the same animals.[3] Striking alterations occur in the numbers of blood cells of mice within the first few hours following a single subcutaneous injection of 1.0 mg. of purified pituitary adrenotrophic hormone (Sayers, White and Long, 1943) dissolved in 0.5 ml. of water. The blood picture obtained is characterized by a decrease in total leucocyte count, a decrease in absolute number of lymphocytes, and an increase in absolute number of polymorphonuclear cells. The alterations in the numbers of leucocytes are evident at one hour following hormone injection. The maximum lymphopenic effect is observed at 9 hours after injection. Shortly

---

[3] Initially in these studies it was considered inadvisable to conduct successive bleedings on the same mouse because of the possible influence of blood loss on the blood picture. However, 10 mice bled successively at 3 hour intervals over a 9 hour period showed no significant alterations from the initial blood picture. Similar results have been obtained with adrenalectomized mice. When larger animal species were studied the influence of bleeding was not considered.

thereafter the leucocyte picture tends to return to normal. These changes are depicted in figure 1.

The pattern of the changes illustrated in figure 1 is not invariably the same. The species of animal, and indeed the dose of hormone and method of administration within the same species, may affect the leucocyte picture. The degree and type of leucocyte changes and the time at which they are evident must depend on the rate at which the released adrenal cortical secretion reaches the lymphocytic elements.

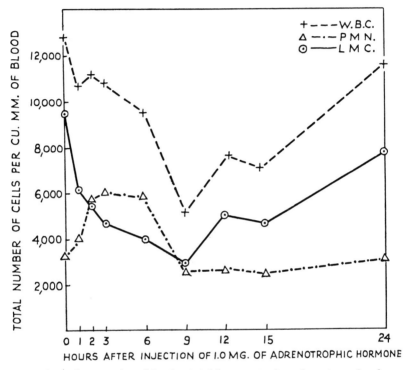

FIG. 1. Alterations produced in the total leucocyte, lymphocyte and polymorphonuclear blood counts of normal mice receiving, at zero time, a single, subcutaneous injection of 1.0 mg. of pituitary adrenotrophic hormone. The points on each curve at 0, 1, 2, 3, 6, 9, 12, 15 and 24 hours are, respectively, the averages of data for groups of 99, 3, 3, 5, 5, 7, 6, 7, and 7 animals.

Some of the species variations will be mentioned for each agent administered.

An initial increase in hemoglobin and red blood cells was generally observed within 3 to 6 hours after a single injection of adrenotrophic hormone. Subsequently, the hemoglobin concentration and the red blood cells fell to subnormal levels which persisted as long as 24 hours after the injection. The changes were not accompanied by significant alterations in the specific gravity of the whole blood. These data are shown in figure 2.

A marked decrease in total adrenal cholesterol occurs 3 hours after intraperitoneal injection of adrenotrophic hormone in the 21 day-old rat (Sayers, Sayers, White and Long, 1943; Sayers, Sayers, Fry, White and Long, 1944). This has been interpreted to be a criterion of adrenal cortical secretion. Since the most marked lymphopenia was observed in mice at approximately 9 hours following subcutaneous injection of adrenotrophic hormone, it was of interest to determine whether a correlation existed between the degree of lymphopenia and the extent of depletion of adrenal cholesterol and lipids.

For this study, mice were given single subcutaneous injections of 1.0 mg. of adrenotrophic hormone (in 0.5 ml. water) and sacrificed at 1, 2, 3, 6, 9 and 24 hours after injection. Groups of 3 animals were sacrificed at each interval. Total cholesterol analyses were conducted

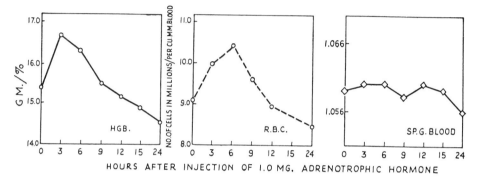

HOURS AFTER INJECTION OF 1.0 MG. ADRENOTROPHIC HORMONE

Fig. 2. Alterations produced in the total hemoglobin, total red cell count, and whole blood specific gravity of normal mice receiving, at zero time, a single, subcutaneous injection of 1.0 mg. pituitary adrenotrophic hormone. Each point on the curves is the average of data obtained for at least 5 animals.

on both adrenals from each of 2 animals; the adrenals of the third animal were fixed for Sudan staining. The cholesterol changes are shown in figure 3. As in the 21 day-old rat, adrenotrophic hormone injection in the mouse produces a distinct lowering of the level of total cholesterol in the adrenals. Depletion of adrenal sudanophilic material parallels cholesterol loss. Most striking is the similarity in the downward trends of both the adrenal cholesterol levels in figure 3 and the lymphocyte counts in figure 1.

In the rat, subcutaneous injection of 2.0 mg. of adrenotrophic hormone produces blood changes similar to those illustrated in figures 1 and 2 for mice. The level of blood lymphocytes was maintained at a lower value for a longer period of time following adrenotrophic hormone injection in the rat as compared to the mouse. Like mice, rats exhibited a definite polymorphonuclear leucocytosis. The hemoglobin concentration and red cell counts in rats given adrenotrophic hormone are also similar in trend to those observed in the mouse. The data are presented in table 2.

Rabbits show marked blood changes after the subcutaneous injection of 10 mg. of hormone. The maximum effect on the blood leucocytes occurs within 3 hours (table 2). The alterations in lymphocytes and polymorphonuclear cells are still evident in the rabbit 24 hours after hormone injection. Rats and rabbits, although receiving less hormone per unit of body weight, showed more profound and lasting effects than did the mouse.

Having established the effects of adrenotrophic hormone injection on the blood picture, the question arose as to whether all of the effect of this hormone was mediated through the adrenal cortex or whether a direct peripheral mechanism was also involved. The subcutaneous

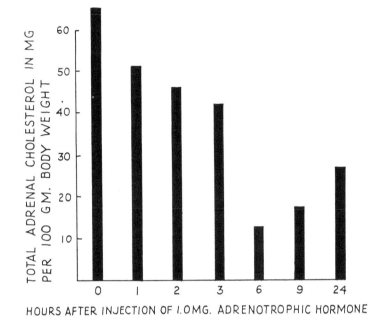

FIG. 3. Effect of a single injection of adrenotrophic hormone on the total adrenal cholesterol of normal mice.

injection of adrenotrophic hormone into mice one day after adrenalectomy does not produce leucopenia or lymphopenia. However, in the adrenalectomized animal adrenotrophic hormone produces an increase in the polymorphonuclear cells similar to that seen in the injected intact mouse.

The role of the pituitary adrenotrophic hormone in the control of ·blood lymphocyte levels is demonstrated further by the fact that the injection of 5.0 mgs. of this hormone into 2 hypophysectomized rats produced a decrease of approximately 5000 lymphocytes in each animal within 9 hours. This effect is similar to that seen in intact animals injected with adrenotrophic hormone and in adrenalectomized mice and rats given adrenal cortical extract.

Further evidence that adrenotrophic hormone affects blood constituents because of its hormonal action and not because of its protein nature is seen from the fact that 8 normal mice injected subcutaneously with 2.0 mg. of purified serum gamma globulin (human)[4] showed no lymphopenia when examined 3, 6 and 9 hours after injection. Also, 7 adrenalectomized mice injected with adrenotrophic hormone did not exhibit the lymphopenic effect. All of the evidence suggests that the blood changes reported are not due to the protein nature of the hormone.

TABLE 2. AVERAGE CHANGES IN BLOOD CONSTITUENTS RESULTING FROM A SINGLE, SUBCUTANEOUS INJECTION OF 5.0 MG. OF ADRENOTROPHIC HORMONE IN RATS AND 10.0 MG. OF HORMONE IN RABBITS

Number of animals	Time after injection	Hemoglobin	R.B.C.	W.B.C.	Lymphocytes	Polymorphonuclear leucocytes	Specific gravity whole blood
Rats	hours	gm./%	millions/ cu. mm.				
42	0	14.8[1]	8.88[1]	17,826	14,700	2,932	1.059[2]
12	3	15.3	9.48	7,634	4,016	3,240	1.058
12	6	15.1	8.43	9,712	3,873	5,884	1.059
8	9	14.6	8.76	10,551	3,386	7,111	1.061
12	24	13.0	7.36	11,819	7,782	3,776	1.055
Rabbits							
18	0	12.0[3]	5.67[3]	10,053	6,861	3,193	1.053[4]
4	3	11.5	5.69	7,175	2,562	4,597	1.054
4	6	11.3	5.94	10,338	2,196	8,149	1.061
4	9	11.2	5.26	11,925	3,877	8,051	1.057
2	12	11.2	7.42	13,775	3,724	10,051	1.055
3	24	—	—	11,961	5,066	6,895	—

[1] 27 animals.   [2] 19 animals.   [3] 16 animals.   [4] 3 animals.

Effect of Injection of Adrenal Cortical Hormone

Aqueous adrenal cortical extract (Wilson) was used in most of the experiments presented in this section. The subcutaneous injection of 0.5 ml. of this extract in mice produces an extreme lymphopenia within 3 hours (table 3). As in mice given adrenotrophic hormone, there is an accompanying polymorphonuclear leucocytosis. In animals receiving adrenal cortical extract, the lymphocytes return to normal levels within 6 hours after injection; elevated polymorphonuclear counts may persist at this time. The maximum blood alterations in mice given adrenal cortical extract occur earlier than in animals treated with adrenotrophic hormone. It should again be emphasized that these relationships are described for a particular dose of hormone administered subcutaneously in the mouse.

In adrenalectomized mice, subcutaneous injection of 0.5 ml. of adrenal cortical extract produces blood alterations which are indistinguishable from those seen in unoperated animals. The comparison is plotted in figure 4. The number of lymphocytes in animals one day after adrenalectomy is higher than in intact animals.

Intact mice given adrenal cortical extract showed decreases in

---

[4] Kindly prepared by Dr. L. S. Ciereszko of Sharp & Dohme, Inc.

hemoglobin and red cell counts similar to the animals receiving adrenotrophic hormone. However, with cortical extract no initial hemoglobin and red cell increases were observed (table 3). The data presented in this table also show that injection of aqueous adrenal cortical extract produced a lymphopenia in rats and in rabbits. The response to the hormone is similar in these species. It is interesting that adrenotrophic hormone has a more profound lymphopenic effect in the rabbit

TABLE 3. AVERAGE CHANGES IN BLOOD CONSTITUENTS RESULTING FROM A SINGLE, SUBCUTANEOUS INJECTION OF 0.5 ML. AQUEOUS CORTICAL EXTRACT IN MICE, 2.0 ML. IN RATS, AND 5.0 ML. IN RABBITS

Number of animals	Time after injection	Hemoglobin	R.B.C.	W.B.C.	Lymphocytes	Polymorphonuclear leucocytes	Specific gravity whole blood
	hours	gm./%	millions/cu. mm.	*Mice*			
99	0	15.3[1]	9.05[1]	12,814	9,584	3,257	1.060[2]
8	3	13.8	7.92	8,019	3,453	4,452	1.061
8	6	13.6	9.07	12,436	7,888	4,119	1.062
8	9	13.0	7.18	11,500	7,414	5,086	—
				Rats			
30	0	14.8[3]	8.88[3]	17,826	14,700	2,932	1.058[4]
4	3	15.3	9.52	6,203	3,574	2,629	1.058
4	6	14.3	8.88	9,340	3,999	5,341	1.057
4	24	13.6	8.07	9,588	6,341	3,247	1.056
				Rabbits			
18	0	12.0[5]	5.67[5]	10,053	6,861	3,193	—
2	1	—	—	8,650	4,315	4,335	—
4	3	11.3	5.93	10,650	4,715	5,935	—
4	6	11.8	6.38	14,382	5,506	8,857	—
4	9	11.9	5.64	15,740	9,682	6,043	—
4	24	11.3	5.30	10,462	7,189	3,278	—

[1] Average for 39 animals.   [2] Average for 19 animals.
[3] Average for 27 animals.   [4] Average for 8 animals.
[5] Average for 16 animals.

as compared to the response of this species to adrenal cortical extract. In the mouse, on the other hand, this difference in behavior to the types of hormone preparations was not seen.

Table 4 presents data obtained following subcutaneous injection of aqueous adrenal cortical extract in human beings.[5] The tendency toward a decrease in red cells, lymphocytes and hemoglobin resembles the alterations in blood picture seen in other species treated with hormone. With the dose of hormone employed, the blood changes in man were not as consistent, although the fall in total lymphocytes was relatively even more profound because of the lower initial lymphocyte level. A lymphopenia was not evident in all patients studied following every injection of hormone but was usually observed

[5] Acknowledgment is made to Dr. E. A. Lawrence and Dr. P. H. Lavietes for coöperating in the study of patients.

(unpublished results). Whether this less consistent response in man is a dose factor or individual variation cannot be decided at this time, since the data are too few. However, it is recognized that the dose of cortical extract used in the human studies is relatively small when compared on a body weight basis to doses used in the laboratory animals.

The effects of several adrenal cortical steroids on the blood picture of the mouse are presented in table 5. The injection of desoxycorti-

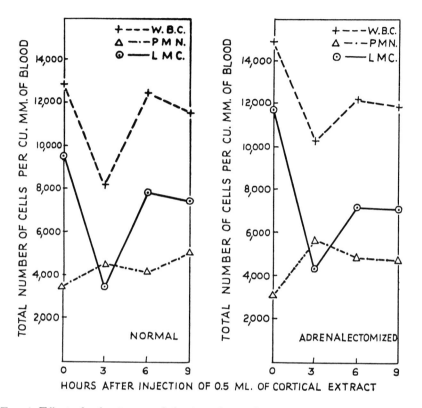

Fig. 4. Effect of subcutaneous injection of 0.5 ml. aqueous adrenal cortical extract on the white blood cell counts of normal and adrenalectomized mice. Each experimental point on the curves for normal animals represents the average of data obtained for a group of 8 mice. Groups of 6 animals were used to establish the experimental points on the curves for adrenalectomized mice.

costerone acetate (in sesame oil, Schering), even in relatively large doses produces no significant decrease in lymphocytes in normal or in adrenalectomized mice. An increase in polymorphonuclear leucocytes occurs after injections of desoxycorticosterone acetate. In contrast to the inability of this steroid to produce a lymphopenia, cortical steroids in oil (Upjohn),[6] corticosterone, or the adrenal cortical steroid called

[6] Grateful acknowledgment is made to Dr. E. Gifford Upjohn of The Upjohn Company for supplying this preparation.

Pa-tient	Diagnosis	Amt. hor-mone in-jected	Time after injec-tion	Hemo-globin	R.B.C.	W.B.C.	Lympho-cytes	Polymor-phonuclear leucocytes
		ml.	hours	gm./%	millions/ cu. mm.			
D.	lymphosar-coma	20	0	9.4	2.85	7,750	1,550	6,200
			3	8.6	3.25	8,300	587	7,713
			6	8.53	3.07	8,850	1,356	7,045
D.	lymphosar-coma	20	0	9.9	2.91	9,210	2,310	6,900
			3	8.6	2.51	7,050	987	6,063
			6	8.0	3.34	6,850	1,300	5,550
M.	lymphosar-coma	30	0	13.2	5.19	9,600	3,840	5,760
			3	14.0	3.83	7,000	2,032	4,970
			6	13.0	4.36	8,000	3,360	4,640
M.	lymphosar-coma	30	0	13.7	5.20	7,800	2,964	4,836
			3	13.7	3.95	5,300	2,014	3,286
			6	13.0	5.34	7,900	2,370	5,530
Q.	myxedema-lympho-sarcoma	25	0	—	—	6,300	3,275	3,025
			3	—	—	4,500	1,710	2,795

compound F by Wintersteiner,[7] all produce lymphopenia in adrenal-ectomized mice (table 5).

DISCUSSION

The numerical limits between which the blood cells fluctuate in normal animals suggests the existence of regulatory processes. These mechanisms may be concerned with (a) the production of the blood cells, and (b) the disposition of these cells. The dynamic balance which obtains at any particular time between these mechanisms determines the nature of the cellular picture of the blood. The data presented in this paper establish the pituitary adrenotrophic hormone as a prime factor in the regulation of the level of blood lymphocytes. This regulatory influence is exerted by the trophic action of this hormone on the adrenal cortex. Furthermore, the adrenotrophic hormone may also influence the number of circulating red cells.

The conclusion that the pituitary adrenotrophic hormone is concerned with blood lymphocyte levels is based upon the finding that the injection of this hormone or the products of its stimulatory action, i.e., adrenal cortical substances, into a variety of normal animal species produces a profound, absolute lymphopenia. The same result is ob-

[7] Compound F of Wintersteiner is the same substance as compound E of Kendall and compound Fa of Reichstein (Reichstein and Shoppee, 1943). Grateful acknowledgement is made for gifts to Dr. C. N. H. Long by Dr. Wintersteiner of the sample of compound F and by Dr. Kendall of the corticosterone.

TABLE 5. AVERAGE ALTERATIONS IN BLOOD CONSTITUENTS FOLLOWING SINGLE, SUBCUTANEOUS INJECTIONS OF ADRENAL CORTICAL STEROIDS IN NORMAL AND IN ADRENALECTOMIZED MICE

TABLE 5. AVERAGE ALTERATIONS IN BLOOD CONSTITUENTS FOLLOWING SINGLE, SUBCUTANEOUS INJECTIONS OF ADRENAL CORTICAL STEROIDS IN NORMAL AND IN ADRENALECTOMIZED MICE

Preparation and animal used	No. of animals	Dose	Time after injection	W.B.C.	Lymphocytes	Polymorphonuclear leucocytes
		mg.	hours			
Desoxycorticosterone acetate in sesame oil injected into normal mice	99	0.1	0	12,814	9,854	3,257
	5		3	13,680	7,929	5,751
	3		6	16,600	9,339	7,260
	3		9	17,667	9,266	8,400
Desoxycorticosterone acetate in sesame oil injected into normal mice	3	0.25	0	12,814	9,854	3,257
	3		3	26,700	13,269	13,431
	3		6	28,500	13,190	15,310
	3		9	15,050	8,995	6,065
Desoxycorticosterone acetate in sesame oil injected into adrenalectomized mice	60	0.1	0	14,903	11,717	3,189
	3		3	13,833	9,133	4,693
	3		6	10,700	8,640	2,060
	3		9	18,375	14,591	3,784
Desoxycorticosterone acetate in sesame oil injected into adrenalectomized mice	60	2.5	0	14,903	11,717	3,189
	3		3	16,033	10,357	5,676
	3		6	16,100	10,280	5,820
	3		9	13,517	10,277	3,263
Adrenal cortical steroids in oil injected into normal mice	99	0.1	0	12,814	9,854	3,257
	7		3	18,093	3,158	4,935
	3		6	18,933	10,088	8,845
	3		9	16,633	10,680	5,953
Adrenal cortical steroids in oil injected into adrenalectomized mice	60	0.1	0	14,903	11,717	3,189
	9		3	11,617	7,430	4,292
	3		6	13,617	12,157	1,460
	3		9	20,000	17,323	2,677
Compound F (Wintersteiner) injected into aqueous solution into adrenalectomized mice	60	0.25	0	14,903	11,717	3,189
	6		3	24,567	14,009	10,560
	6		6	14,767	6,733	8,034
	6		9	11,040	7,282	3,756
	3		24	14,488	10,030	4,387
Corticosterone injected in aqueous solution into adrenalectomized mice	60	0.25	0	14,903	11,717	3,189
	6		3	20,575	11,037	9,638
	6		6	15,400	8,050	7,356
	6		9	16,000	11,172	4,827
	3		24	16,767	10,560	6,207

served in the hypophysectomized rat given adrenotrophic hormone and in the adrenalectomized mouse treated with adrenal cortical extracts. Evidence that the adrenotrophic hormone is concerned with the disposition of lymphocytes is seen in the lymphocytosis resulting following adrenalectomy (Zwemer and Lyons, 1928; Corey and Britton, 1932), or hypophysectomy (unpublished results). The term "lymphocyte disposition" may have a two-fold interpretation. It may indicate either a peripheral removal of lymphocytes, or a decreased delivery of lymphocytes to the circulation. Either or both of these mechanisms would result in lymphopenia. Evidence available from histological studies (White and Dougherty, in press) suggests that the adrenotrophic hormone-induced lymphopenia is a result of a failure of delivery of adequate numbers of lymphocytes to the circulation.

The most profound lymphopenia occurs within a few hours following hormone injection. The tendency for the lymphocyte count to return to normal was observed in almost all animals within 24 hours after a single injection, although in the rat low lymphocyte levels were evident at this time. The effect of the hormone is an acute one, and delivery of the lymphocytes to the blood is rapidly restored to normal. Changes in blood lymphocytes are mirrored by the alterations in adrenal cholesterol concentration. Adrenal cholesterol levels have been shown to be lowered by stimulation of the adrenal cortex (Sayers, Sayers, White and Long, 1943; Sayers, Sayers, Fry, White and Long, 1944.

Although adrenotrophic hormone exerts a regulatory effect on the level of blood lymphocytes, it appears that the hormone does not directly influence the number of blood polymorphonuclear cells. A polymorphonuclear leucocytosis results from injection of adrenotrophic hormone into adrenalectomized animals, and therefore cannot be a specific hormonal effect in this case. A possible role of the adrenal cortex in regulation of blood polymorphonuclear cells is suggested by the work of Corey and Britton (1932) who found a markedly decreased number of these cells in adrenalectomized cats.

The injection of adrenotrophic hormone or adrenal cortical extract into normal mice produces an initial, transitory increase in red cells and hemoglobin followed by a decrease. In general, the red cell and hemoglobin values are distinctly below normal 24 hours following a single injection of hormone. The anemia observed cannot be attributed to changes in blood specific gravity.

The results which have been described for adrenotrophic hormone injection are a result of the specific physiological action of this hormone as a humoral agent and are not due to its protein nature. This is evident from the fact that serum gamma globulin injections in normal mice, and adrenotrophic hormone in adrenalectomized mice, did not influence the blood picture.

Injections of desoxycorticosterone acetate into normal or adrenalectomized animals did not reduce blood lymphocytes. In contrast, adrenal cortical compounds, e.g., adrenal cortical steroids in oil, compound F of Wintersteiner (compound E of Kendall), or corticosterone have a lymphopenic activity in adrenalectomized animals. It is significant that adrenal cortical steroids which have a glyconeogenic function (Long, Katzin and Fry, 1940) are also compounds which induce lymphopenia. Desoxycorticosterone, which does not affect carbohydrate formation from protein, does not decrease blood lymphocytes. The basis for the regulatory role of the adrenal cortex in glyconeogenesis may lie not primarily in its influence on the intermediary reactions of carbohydrate formation from protein, but in its capacity to supply protein to the blood (White and Dougherty, in press) and thus to the liver, from lymphoid tissue and perhaps other structures. Wells and Kendall (1940) have reported thymic involution with corticosterone and with a highly active concentrate of adrenal cortical steroids, but not with desoxycorticosterone. Data have been obtained (Dougherty and White, 1943) which demonstrate that the involution of thymic mass after adrenotrophic hormone injections is accompanied by an involution of other lymphoid tissue. This suggests that the effects of adrenotrophic hormone on numbers of blood lymphocytes and on lymphoid tissue are directly correlated. Many non-specific toxic agents which have been reported (Selye, 1937) to decrease thymic size would be expected to produce a lymphopenia, and vice versa. It is not unlikely that these non-specific factors cause some of their effects on lymphoid tissue through the pituitary adrenal cortex relationship, although large doses of toxic agents may have a direct action on lymphoid cells.

The fact that a continued lymphopenia may not be evident in conditions of chronic stimulation of the adrenal cortex would indicate that a balance exists between the proliferative capacity of the lymphoid tissue and the rate of removal of lymphocytes. The two processes, i.e., lymphocyte production and lymphocyte disposition, may be completely independent or related indirectly to one another. The evidence in this paper suggests a pituitary effect only on lymphocyte disposition. However, acceleration of this phenomenon might induce an exaggerated rate of production of lymphoid cells. Therefore, the blood lymphocyte picture and the lymphoid tissue structure may vary widely under normal and pathological conditions, depending on the relationship existing at a particular time between lymphoid cell production and disappearance.

The similarity of the lymphocyte pattern resulting from pituitary adrenal cortical stimulation to that seen in acute infectious processes, reactions to toxins (bacterial and otherwise) and to a variety of unrelated stimuli, indicates that the well known effect of these agents on the adrenal cortex (Sayers, Sayers, Fry, White and Long, 1944) may be the fundamental basis of the lymphocyte picture which has been described for these conditions. The data presented here may find application in the evaluation of adrenal cortical activity.

SUMMARY

Single injections of pituitary adrenotrophic hormone in mice, rats and rabbits produce within a few hours an absolute lymphopenia and an increase in polymorphonuclear leucocytes. The lymphopenia is a specific response to the hormone, because (a) it does not occur in adrenalectomized animals treated with adrenotrophic hormone, or

(b) in intact animals treated with a pure protein. The polymorpho-nuclear response is not specific in that it does occur in adrenalec-tomized animals given a variety of agents.

Single injections of adrenotrophic hormone or of adrenal cortical extract into intact mice and rats result in slight decreases in red cell and hemoglobin concentration.

Adrenal cortical extract, adrenal cortical steroids in oil, corticos-terone, or compound F (Wintersteiner) produce a lymphopenia in intact and adrenalectomized animals. On the other hand, desoxycor-ticosterone does not decrease the total number of blood lymphocytes in either normal or operated animals.

The regulation of the numbers of blood lymphocytes, and probably the red cells, is under pituitary control and is mediated by way of the adrenal cortex.

Acknowledgment is made to Miss Ruth E. Marck for technical as-sistance.

REFERENCES

COREY, E. L., AND S. W. BRITTON: *Am. J. Physiol.* 102: 699. 1932.
DOUGHERTY, T. F., AND A. WHITE: *Proc. Soc. Exper. Biol. & Med.* 53: 132. 1943.
DRINKER, C. K., AND J. M. YOFFEY: Lymphatics, lymph and lymphoid tissue. Harvard Univ. Press. Cambridge. 1941.
EVELYN, K. A.: *J. Biol. Chem.* 115: 63. 1936.
KAGAN, B. M.: *J. Lab. & Clin. Med.* 26: 1681. 1941.
LONG, C. N. H., B. KATZIN AND E. G. FRY: *Endocrinology* 26: 309. 1940.
REICHSTEIN, T., AND C. W. SHOPPEE: Vitamins & Hormones, Vol. 1, p. 346. Academic Press, New York, 1943.
SAYERS, G., M. A. SAYERS, E. G. FRY, A. WHITE AND C. N. H. LONG: *Yale J. Biol. & Med.* 16: 361. 1944.
SAYERS, G., M. A. SAYERS, A. WHITE AND C. N. H. LONG: *Proc. Soc. Exper. Biol. & Med.* 52: 200. 1943.
SAYERS, G., A. WHITE AND C. N. H. LONG: *J. Biol. Chem.* 149: 425. 1943.
SELYE, H.: *Endocrinology* 21: 169. 1937.
SPERRY, W. M.: *Am. J. Clin. Path.* 2: 91. 1938.
WELLS, B. B., AND E. C. KENDALL: *Proc. Staff Meet., Mayo Clin.* 15: 133. 1940.
WHITE, A., AND T. F. DOUGHERTY: *Proc. Soc. Exper. Biol. & Med.* 56: 26. 1944.
ZWEMER, R. L., AND C. LYONS: *Am. J. Physiol.* 86: 545. 1928.

11

THE QUANTITATIVE AND QUALITATIVE RESPONSES OF BLOOD LYMPHOCYTES TO STRESS STIMULI

Thomas F. Dougherty and Jules A. Frank

WHEN adrenalectomized animals are subjected to stressors, a lympho-cytosis occurs which is greater than that which characteristically fol-lows adrenalectomy alone.[1] The time of onset and the rate of increase of the number of circulating lymphocytes of such stressed adrenalectomized animals form a curve which is the inverse image of the lymphopenic response of in-tact animals known to be mediated by adrenocortical hormones[2] and, there-fore, has been termed the lymphocytotic response.

In addition to the changes in number of lymphocytes, microscopic examination of the blood films taken from adrenalectomized and stressed adrenalectomized mice revealed that many of the blood lymphocytes of these animals had undergone distinctive morphologic alterations as compared to the lymphocytes of intact nonstressed mice.

Experiments were designed by which the morphologic and numerical lymphocyte responses produced by stress could be compared.

MATERIALS AND METHODS

Twenty male CBA mice, twelve to sixteen weeks of age, whose body weights ranged between 26 and 28 Gm. were used. Epinephrine HCl (aqueous 1:1,000) was employed as a nonspecific stress stimulus and diluted so that 0.1 ml. contained 0.2 γ for intraperitoneal injection. Adrenalectomy was performed under ether anesthesia by the usual dorsal approach one hour prior to the experiment.

Tail blood samples for total leukocyte counts and differentials were taken prior to epinephrine injection (one hour after adrenalectomy) and at ten, thirty, sixty, one hundred and twenty, and two hundred and forty minutes after injection. Blood films were stained with May-Grünwald Giemsa, and differential leukocyte counts performed on a minimum of 200 cells with at least two observers contributing counts to each experimental group of animals. Lymphocytes were classified as normal lymphocytes and hyaline (or "stress" lymphocytes[3]).

The experimental procedures were performed on the following groups of animals: (1) Intact mice given 0.2 γ epinephrine intraperitoneally and (2) mice given 0.2 γ epinephrine intraperitoneally one hour after adrenalec-tomy. Control values consisted of total leukocyte counts and absolute

From the Department of Anatomy, University of Utah College of Medicine.

Aided by a grant from the Committee on Growth of the National Research Council acting for the American Cancer Society.

Reprinted from *J. Lab. Clin. Med.* **42** (No. 4), 1953.

TABLE I. Absolute Leukocyte Values in Thousands and Standard Errors of Normal, Intact Mice, Mice 60 Minutes After Adrenalectomy and Intact and Adrenalectomized Mice Given 0.2 γ Epinephrine I.P. 60 Minutes After Adrenalectomy

GROUPS	NO. OF MICE	TIME	W.B.C.		NORMAL LYMPHOCYTES		STRESS LYMPHOCYTES		TOTAL LYMPHOCYTES		POLYMORPHO-NUCLEARS		EOSINOPHILS	
			MEAN	S.E.	MEAN	S.E.	MEAN	S.E.	MEAN	S.E.	MEAN	S.E.	MEAN	S.E.
Control														
Normal intact	40	—	11.3	± 0.6	6.6	± 0.4	1.3	± 0.1	7.9	± 0.6	3.2	± 0.3	0.3	± 0.1
Adrenalectomized	25	60 min.	26.4	± 1.7	9.1	± 0.6	2.8	± 0.3	11.9	± 0.6	13.7	± 1.3	0.8	± 0.1
Experimental														
Intact mice 0.2 epinephrine i.p.	10	10 min.	14.8	± 1.3	6.5	± 0.6	2.2	± 0.2	8.7	± 0.5	5.8	± 1.5	3.8	± 1.1
	10	30 min.	15.5	± 3.1	2.6	± 0.5	1.7	± 0.3	4.3	± 0.6	11.0	± 2.6	2.4	± 0.7
	10	60 min.	19.3	± 1.7	4.7	± 0.7	1.5	± 0.3	6.2	± 0.7	12.8	± 1.8	2.7	± 0.7
	10	120 min.	21.1	± 3.5	4.4	± 1.1	1.3	± 0.2	5.7	± 1.2	15.3	± 2.3	1.8	± 0.6
	10	240 min.	40.7	± 3.7	5.2	± 0.9	4.2	± 0.8	9.4	± 1.7	31.0	± 2.8	1.5	± 0.8
Adrenalectomized mice 0.2 epineph- rine i.p.	10	10 min.	22.5	± 3.4	8.1	± 0.2	5.1	± 2.2	13.2	± 2.3	8.0	± 1.5	1.7	± 0.7
	10	30 min.	20.1	± 0.7	5.3	± 0.4	3.1	± 0.6	8.4	± 0.8	11.3	± 1.5	3.6	± 1.0
	10	60 min.	21.0	± 1.7	4.4	± 1.5	4.3	± 0.8	8.7	± 1.2	11.2	± 1.7	2.0	± 1.2
	10	120 min.	27.2	± 5.2	7.7	± 2.2	5.4	± 2.0	13.1	± 2.8	14.0	± 1.3	5.7	± 0.3
	10	240 min.	38.3	± 5.1	12.2	± 2.6	8.2	± 2.2	20.4	± 4.3	17.7	± 2.3	3.3	± 1.9

numbers of the various leukocytes determined on a group of 40 intact non-stressed mice and a group of 25 nonstressed adrenalectomized mice one hour after operation.

RESULTS

Total leukocyte counts and the absolute numbers of the different leukocytes of untreated-intact and untreated-adrenalectomized mice one hour after operation are presented in Table I. A significant lymphocytosis of both normal and stress lymphocytes occurred one hour following adrenalectomy.

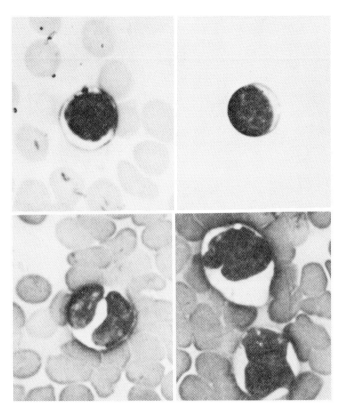

Plate I.—*A* and *B*, Normal mouse lymphocytes; *C*, stress lymphocytes with bilobed nucleus; *D*, stress lymphocytes.

A morphologic comparison of normal mouse lymphocytes and stress lymphocytes is presented in Plate I. The most constant morphologic alterations of stress lymphocytes as compared to normal cells were increased cytoplasmic-nuclear ratios and nuclear and cytoplasmic distortion. The large amount of cytoplasm was poorly basophilic and presented a hyaline appearance. Nuclei were round, polymorphous, or bilobed. The chromatin was found to be aggregated in small discrete clumps.

The curve of the lymphocytic response to stress stimuli may be divided into three phases (Fig. 1). Phase I is characterized by a lymphocytosis, and

Phase II by a lymphopenia (first demonstrated by Michael[4]). Reconstitution of the number of circulating lymphocytes to normal or greater than normal levels forms a third portion of the curve and is termed here Phase III. These categorizations provide a useful means for describing lymphocyte response curves.

A comparison of the lymphocyte responses of intact and adrenalectomized mice given 0.2 γ epinephrine is presented in terms of total lymphocytes, normal lymphocytes, and stress lymphocytes (Fig. 2). The bars represent the total numbers of lymphocytes, the stippled portion the number of stress lymphocytes, and the clear portion the number of normal lymphocytes. Standard errors are presented in Table I.

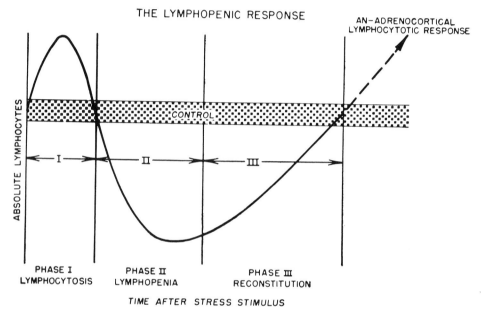

Fig. 1.—A diagrammatic representation of the lymphopenic response of intact animals following stress.

In the intact mice the lymphocytosis characteristic of Phase I did not occur. The lymphopenia of Phase II occurred at thirty minutes, and reconstitution (Phase III) by the end of the experimental period (two hundred and forty minutes). With the exception of a moderate rise in numbers of stress lymphocytes in Phase III there was no significant fluctuation in numbers of these cells at any other time. Both the lymphopenia and the reconstitution were entirely due to changes in numbers of normal lymphocytes.

In the adrenalectomized mice the curve of the total lymphocyte response was nearly identical in configuration to that of the intact mice. In terms of total lymphocytes, the lymphocytosis of Phase I was not significant; there was a relative lymphopenia in Phase II when compared to the adrenalectomized controls, although not a true lymphopenia if compared to the lymphocyte values for normal intact mice. Phase III was represented by a reconstitution and a lymphocytotic overshoot. During Phase II numbers of normal lymphocytes decreased significantly but returned to control values in Phase III. The most marked change was that of a gradual, significant increase in the numbers of stress lymphocytes throughout all phases.

Similar observations were noted when adrenalectomized mice were subjected to other types of stress stimuli, e.g., fasting, exposure to cold, anaphylaxis, histamine administration, and immunization to horse serum. Since the numerical and morphologic alterations occurring after these stress stimuli were similar to those described here, it is not deemed necessary to describe the results of each of these experiments.

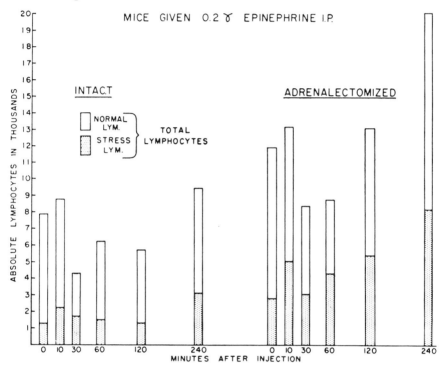

Fig. 2.—Comparison of the absolute numbers of lymphocytes of intact and adrenalectomized CBA mice following injection of 0.2 γ epinephrine intraperitoneally.

DISCUSSION

It is apparent from the data presented here that two morphologic types of lymphocytes exist in the normal intact mouse. The predominant form is the usual small, round lymphocyte exhibiting heavy nuclear chromatin and rimmed by a small amount of cytoplasm. Another type normally present in small numbers is a larger cell characterized principally by an increased amount of poorly basophilic cytoplasm. These cells have been termed stress lymphocytes since they are characteristically increased in number following stressors. It is evident from the data presented here that the total numerical lymphocyte response masks the differences of numerical response that exist between these two different types of lymphocytes, whether or not the response is adrenocortically mediated or nonadrenocortically mediated.

In these experiments, epinephrine was used as a nonspecific stressor, since it has been shown that epinephrine administration results in enhanced secretion of adrenocortical steroids.[5] Since the lymphopenia observed in Phase II in stressed intact mice did not occur in stressed adrenalectomized mice, this response is adrenocortically mediated and confirms the previous report of Gellhorn and Frank.[6] It should be emphasized as demonstrated here that the lymphopenia was due primarily to a decrease in numbers of normal lymphocytes, whereas the numbers of stress lymphocytes remained relatively constant. This finding suggests that normal lymphocytes are more susceptible to the well-known lymphocytolytic action of adrenocortical hormones than stress lymphocytes. This possibility is strengthened by the finding that administration of ACTH or cortisone to human subjects results in a lymphopenia of normal but not stress lymphocytes.[7]

Since circulating lymphocytes do not increase beyond a certain level following adrenalectomy,[1-8] a true lymphocytotic response is defined as an increase in numbers of lymphocytes to values significantly higher than those observed following adrenalectomy alone.[1]

The relative lymphopenia of Phase II (as compared to adrenalectomized control levels) in the stressed adrenalectomized mice was due to a decrease in the number of normal lymphocytes. Thus, although stress is not accompanied by a lymphopenia in adrenalectomized animals when the number of cells is compared to that of intact controls, it may be seen that a small decrease of lymphocytes does occur in Phase II even in the absence of the adrenal cortex. The outstanding characteristic of the lymphocyte response following epinephrine given to adrenalectomized mice was that of a marked lymphocytotic overshoot in Phase III, principally due to a significant increase in numbers of stress lymphocytes.

It is clearly demonstrated here that although adrenocortical secretions tend to decrease the number of circulating lymphocytes, absence of these hormones does not necessarily imply hyperactivity of those forces tending to increase the number of circulating lymphocytes. Kumagai and Dougherty[9] have found that the degree of the lymphocytotic response following a stress stimulus (histamine) in adrenalectomized mice was inversely proportional to the amount of cortisone given as prestress maintenance treatment.

In the intact animal stress stimuli effect two responses of lymphatic tissue: (1) the well-known lymphopenic response mediated by adrenocortical secretions, and (2) a nonadrenocortically mediated response (lymphocytotic) which tends to increase the number of lymphocytes. The results reported here contribute the additional evidence that following stress a lymphopenia is a result of destruction of normal lymphocytes and that the subsequent lymphocytosis is primarily the result of an increase in the numbers of stress lymphocytes. Therefore, it is felt that a normal distribution of blood lymphocytes reflects a balance between the adrenocortically mediated and nonadrenocortically mediated effects of stress on lymphatic tissue.

Histologic studies of lymph nodes of normal intact mice, mice which have been chronically treated with ACTH or cortisone[10] and stressed adrenalectomized mice[11] indicate that the lymphocytes of these lymphatic organs undergo similar alterations as do blood lymphocytes. The lymphatic tissue from hormone-treated mice reveals inhibition of mitosis and a monotony of small pycnotic lymphocytes.[10] The lymphatic tissue from stressed adrenalectomized mice is characterized by increased mitosis[1, 11] as compared to nonstressed adrenalectomized mice. It appears then that the lymphocytosis found in stressed adrenalectomized mice may be attributed partially to the concomittant increase in mitotic rate in the lymphatic tissue. The increase in number of stress lymphocytes could be due to a direct stress mediated effect on pre-existing normal lymphocytes or to a stimulation of development of this altered form from the reticuloendothelial lymphocyte precursors. Although this problem is still under investigation, the rapid increase in the stress lymphocytes following stressors indicates that at least some pre-existing normal lymphocytes were altered.

SUMMARY

Morphologic and numerical lymphocyte responses of stressed intact and adrenalectomized mice were studied.

Two morphologic types of lymphocytes exist in the normal intact mouse: (1) normal lymphocytes, and (2) stress lymphocytes which are large cells with increased amounts of poorly basophilic cytoplasm.

The lymphopenia induced by adrenocortical mediation of stress in intact mice was due to a decrease in numbers of normal lymphocytes, whereas the stress lymphocytes did not decrease or underwent an actual increase. It is thus apparent that stress lymphocytes are more resistant to the lytic effects of adrenocortical hormones than normal lymphocytes.

The lymphocytosis induced by stress in adrenolectomized mice was due primarily to an increase in numbers of stress lymphocytes.

The production of stress lymphocytes is due to nonadrenocortically mediated effects of stressors which bring factors into play which increase the number of lymphocytes and induce specific cytologic changes.

The authors wish to thank Miss Katherine Seymour for her excellent technical assistance.

REFERENCES

1. Dougherty, T. F., and Kumagai, L. F.: Influence of Stress-Stimuli On Lymphatic Tissue of Adrenalectomized Mice, Endocrinology 48: 691-699, 1951.
2. Dougherty, T. F., and White, A.: An Evaluation of Alterations Produced In Lymphoid Tissue by Pituitary-Adrenal Secretion, J. Lab. & Clin. Med. 32: 384-605, 1947.
3. Frank, J. A., and Dougherty, T. F.: Evaluation of Susceptibility to Stress Stimuli Determined by "Stress" Lymphocytes, Fed. Proc. 12: 45, 1953.
4. Michael, S. T.: Adaptation to Brief Stress, Yale J. Biol. & Med. 22: 71-92, 1949.
5. Dougherty, T. F.: The Relation of the Adrenal Cortical Hormones to the Hypersensitive State, Adrenal Cortex, Josiah Macy, Jr., Foundation, 88, 1950.
6. Gellhorn, E., and Frank, S.: Sensitivity of the Lymphopenic Reaction to Adrenalin, Proc. Soc. Exper. Biol. & Med. 69: 426, 1948.
7. Frank, J. A., and Dougherty, T. F.: Studies on Morphological Alterations of Human Lymphocytes, Western Soc. for Clin. Research, January, 1953.

8. Dougherty, Jean H., and Dougherty, T. F.: Acute Effect of 4-Aminopteroylglutamic Acid on Blood Lymphocytes and the Lymphatic Tissue of Intact and Adrenalectomized Mice, J. LAB. & CLIN. MED. **35**: 271-279, 1950.
9. Kumagai, L. F., and Dougherty, T. F.: Stress-Induced Lymphocytosis in Adrenalectomized Mice, Fed. Proc. **10**: Part 1, 1951.
10. Dougherty, T. F.: Studies of the Antiphlogistic and Antibody Suppressing Functions of the Pituitary Adrenocortical Secretions. Recent Progress in Hormone Research, **7**: 307-330, 1951.
11. Frank, J. A., Kumagai, L. F., and Dougherty, T. F.: Studies on the Rates of Involution and Reconstitution of Lymphatic Tissue, Endocrinology 1953. In Press.

12

THE EFFECTS OF ADRENOCORTICAL HORMONES, ADRENOCORTICOTROPHIC HORMONE AND PREGNANCY ON SKIN TRANSPLANTATION IMMUNITY IN MICE

*P. B. Medawar and Elizabeth M. Sparrow**

SUMMARY

The median survival time of skin homografts on A or CBA mice is prolonged 50 % by the injection of cortisone acetate 0·4 mg/day. Cortisol is as effective as cortisone; corticosterone, progesterone, testosterone, and oestradiol are ineffective, though corticosterone is more 'cortisone-like' in its action than the others. Deoxycorticosterone neither shortens the life of skin homografts nor interferes with the power of cortisone to prolong it. The injection of cortisone does not prevent a pre-existing state of transplantation immunity from taking effect. The action of corti-. sone is attributed partly to preventing the access of antigenic matter to regional lymph nodes and partly to an effect on the regional nodes themselves.

The injection of 1 mg/day adrenocorticotrophic hormone (ACTH) in a slow-absorption medium has effects indistinguishable from the injection of 0·4 mg/day cortisone acetate. ACTH is ineffective in adrenalectomized mice, not excepting females whose ovaries have been luteinized by prior administration of chorionic gonadotrophin, and is not less effective in ovariectomized female mice than in normal. Female mice are slightly less responsive to cortisone and ACTH than males. Adrenalectomy as such does not influence the survival time of homografts, but causes them to become more strongly united to the graft bed and to elicit a brisker mesenchymal reaction.

Transplantation immunity is not weakened by pregnancy in mice. Repeated heterospecific pregnancies neither elicit transplantation immunity nor weaken a state of immunity that is already in being. For reasons unconnected with pregnancy or parity, elderly female A-line mice react against homografts more feebly than CBA females of the same age.

Species differences in the responses of animals to cortisone and ACTH are interpreted in terms of the composition of cortical secretions and the sensitivity of tissues to their action.

In 1951 it was shown by Billingham, Krohn & Medawar, and, independently, by Morgan [1951], that the injection of rabbits with cortisone acetate greatly enfeebled their power to react upon and reject skin grafts transplanted from other rabbits.

The gist of our present knowledge about the action of steroid hormones on the skin homograft reaction is as follows. The subcutaneous injection of rabbits with 10 mg/day cortisone acetate prolongs the lifetime of skin homografts by a factor of three or four [Billingham *et al.* 1951a]; cortisol (hydrocortisone) is at least as effective as cortisone acetate, and the acetate is as effective as the free alcohol, but other steroid hormones—progesterone, corticosterone, or esters of deoxycorticosterone (DOC), testosterone or oestradiol—are ineffective in themselves and do not interfere with the action of cortisone [Krohn, 1954b]. Cortisone acetate can exercise its action when applied to homografts locally and intermittently, but it is powerless to protect homo-

* Working with a personal research grant from the Medical Research Council.

grafts against the pre-existing immunity caused by skin homografts which have been transplanted and rejected before the administration of cortisone begins [Billingham, et al., 1951b; see also Dempster, 1953]. It is true that the immune response can be weakened by the prolonged administration of cortisone after the disappearance of the first, immunizing, set of homografts and before the transplantation of the second; but, even so, the rabbit does not react upon its second homografts as if it had never been grafted before [Krohn, 1954c].

In guinea-pigs cortisone alcohol is about twice as effective as cortisone acetate in prolonging the life of homografts; but, compared with their action in rabbits, both are feeble, for about twice the absolute daily dosage of cortisone acetate is needed to produce half the effect [Sparrow, 1953, 1954]. Nor are monkeys 'good reactors' to cortisone: Krohn [1955] found that the survival time of skin homografts in male and female rhesus monkeys (*Macaca mulatta*) was prolonged to a barely appreciable degree, if at all, by the injection of 15 mg/day. Evidently there are big differences between the reactivities of members of different species; so far as the available evidence goes, man clearly belongs to the class of poor reactors: Woodruff [1953] found that the local application of cortisone acetate to skin homografts did not extend their normal lease of life.

The response of members of different species to ACTH is equally variable, but the activities of cortisone and ACTH do not go hand in hand. Krohn [1954a] showed that the daily injection of 25 mg ACTH in a slow-absorption medium sometimes prolonged the life of homografts in rabbits, but the results were irregular and unpredictable, and fell far short of what could be achieved by the injection of cortisone 10 mg/day. Nor did the preparatory treatment of female rabbits with chorionic gonadotrophin enhance the activity of ACTH. Guinea-pigs are better reactors, the injection of ACTH 12·5 mg/day in a slow absorption medium being about equivalent to the injection of cortisone acetate 25 mg/day [Sparrow, 1954]. In monkeys, the daily injection of 30 mg ACTH produced a trivial, but nevertheless recognizable effect [Krohn, 1955]; in man it is generally agreed that ACTH is ineffective [Ellison, Martin, Williams, Clatworthy, Hamwi & Zollinger, 1951; Baxter, Schiller, Whiteside, Lipshutz & Straith, 1951; McNichol, 1952].

What is known of the influence of pregnancy on the homograft reaction can be summarized more briefly. Heslop, Krohn & Sparrow [1954] showed that the unexpectedly prolonged survival of homografts on a pregnant rabbit reported by Billingham et al. [1951b] did not represent a vagary of sampling, for skin homografts transplanted to rabbits 20–24 days pregnant survived about twice as long as would otherwise have been the case; but, just as with cortisone-treated rabbits, pregnancy did not prevent a pre-existing immunity from taking effect. A variety of convincing but indirect evidence suggested that the effect of pregnancy was due to the enhanced secretion of cortisone-like steroids.

Unfortunately, experiments on pregnant rabbits of heterogeneous origin are open to the objection that the antigenic constitutions of mother and foetus cannot be varied at will. With inbred mice it is possible to draw a clear distinction between pregnancies of two extreme kinds: (a) *homospecific pregnancy*, i.e. pregnancy by a male containing no antigens not also present in the female. This is most easily achieved when male and female are members of the same highly inbred line, for when that is the case the parents and foetuses will be for most practical purposes isogenic; but it is also fulfilled when the female is a member of the F_1 generation of a cross between two such inbred lines, and the male is a member of either of the parental lines or of the F_1 or remoter (F_2, F_3, etc.) progeny of a cross between them. (b) *Heterospecific pregnancy*, which for the present purpose will be restricted to the limiting case in which the female is pregnant by a male having the same antigenic composition as the homograft donor, e.g. when a female of strain A, later to be grafted with CBA tissue, is pregnant by a CBA male. Any effect on the homograft reaction which is caused by pregnancy as such—and this must necessarily include all effects of endocrinological origin—will be apparent in homospecific pregnancies. Heterospecific pregnancies will serve to show up any complications attributable to the fact that, in pregnancies of this second kind, the foetus is an antigenically foreign body. Theoretically, the complications introduced by heterospecific pregnancies might be of two kinds: either an active immunization of the mother by antigens present in the foetus but absent from herself; or an absorption or inactivation by the foetus of any immune bodies which might have been formed as a consequence of an earlier immunization of the mother by homografts [Medawar, 1953].

The purpose of the work described in this paper was to investigate the influence of steroid hormones and of pregnancy on skin transplantation immunity in mice. Mice have many disadvantages for work of this kind, e.g. the short duration of pregnancy; but some of these disadvantages are outweighed by the benefits of exact genetic control.

METHODS

The technique of skin grafting in mice has been described by Billingham & Medawar [1951] and Billingham, Brent, Medawar & Sparrow [1954]. Its success depends upon the close apposition of the corium of the grafted skin (from which the fatty and muscular layers must be removed) to the undamaged panniculus carnosus of the graft bed. We are satisfied that no deviation from this practice is admissible, least of all when studying the behaviour of grafts under treatments which may impair their vascularization.

The mice were members of domestic sublines of three highly inbred strains (A, AU, CBA), the origins of which have been described by Billingham *et al.* [1954]. The median survival times (MST's), in days, of skin homografts transplanted between members of these three strains are as follows:

$$A \rightarrow CBA \quad 11 \cdot 0 \text{ (st. deviation } 1 \cdot 1; \text{ st. error } 0 \cdot 3)$$
$$CBA \rightarrow A \quad 10 \cdot 2 \text{ (st. deviation } 0 \cdot 9; \text{ st. error } 0 \cdot 3)$$
$$A \rightarrow AU \quad 9 \cdot 0 \text{ (st. deviation } 0 \cdot 9; \text{ st. error } 0 \cdot 3)$$
$$AU \rightarrow A \quad 9 \cdot 1 \text{ (st. deviation } 1 \cdot 4; \text{ st. error } 0 \cdot 4)$$

(The MST is the latest time, measured from the day of grafting, at which surviving epithelium is still present on the grafts borne by 50% of the experimental subjects.)

These figures apply to homografts on mice which are being grafted for the first time. The MST of 'second-stage homografts', on mice which have been immunized by an earlier homograft of the same origin transplanted 15–120 days beforehand, is less than 6 days [Billingham, Brent & Medawar, 1954]. Most experiments were done in the combination A→CBA or reciprocally; there is no important difference between the MST's of homografts transplanted in either direction, nor in the responses of the two strains of recipients to hormones administered under the regimens shortly to be described.

With rare exceptions, all hormones were administered by the subintegumentary route, different positions being chosen for each injection whenever daily administrations were required. ACTH (Armour, standard LA–1–A), in the form of a water-soluble 'lyophilized' powder, was injected in the slow-absorption medium of Bruce & Parkes [1952]. Cortisone acetate, cortisol acetate, deoxycorticosterone (DOC) acetate and trimethylacetate* and corticosterone were administered as fine crystals in watery suspension; deoxycorticosterone glucoside* and chorionic gonadotrophin were injected in watery solution, and progesterone, testosterone propionate and oestradiol dipropionate were injected in oily solution.

Adrenalectomy and ovariectomy were carried out by dorsal bilateral operations; most mice were protected during adrenalectomy, and during grafting operations carried out after adrenalectomy, by a single intraperitoneal injection of 0·1–0·5 mg cortisone acetate given 2–20 hr beforehand. A-line mice are more difficult to adrenalectomize than CBA or AU mice, because the right adrenal vessels are much shorter.

RESULTS

(A) Effects of hormones

(1) Action of cortisone acetate and cortisol acetate

(a) *Cortisone acetate* (strain combination CBA→A). Fifty-two sexually mature A-line mice, equally divided into males (mean weight 24½ g) and females (22 g) were grafted with skin from CBA donors and thereupon given the first of fifteen successive daily injections of 0·05–0·50 mg cortisone acetate. The mortality over this period was $5/52 = 9\frac{1}{2}\%$ and the mean loss of weight was 16 % for males and 19 % for females, but neither mortality nor loss of weight were noticeably correlated with dosage. The grafts were scored after 15 days for presence (1) or absence (0) of surviving epidermal epithelium, with the results set out in Table 1.

Table 1. *Survival* (1) *or non-survival* (0) *of skin homografts* 15 *days after their transplantation to mice receiving cortisone acetate* 0·05–0·50 *mg/day.* (*Bold entries refer to females.*)

No survival	Dosage (mg/day)	Survival
0 **0 0**	0·05	—
0 0 **0 0**	0·10	—
0 0 0 0 **0 0** 0 0 0 0	0·20	—
0 0 0 **0 0 0** 0	0·30	1 1 1
0 0 **0 0 0 0**	0·40	**1** 1 1 1 1
0 0 0	0·50	**1 1** 1 1 1 1 1

It is clear that the daily dosage which increases the MST (~ 10 days) by 50 % is about 0·4 mg/day, with more than a hint that the females are less responsive than the males, in spite of the slightly higher dosage they received weight for weight.

---

* Kindly supplied by Ciba Laboratories Ltd. For the experimental use of DOC-trimethyl acetate, see Gross & Tschopp [1952] and Gaunt, Leathem, Howell & Antonchak [1952].

Histologically and to outward appearance the grafts were very similar to those in rabbits receiving cortisone acetate 10 mg/day [Billingham *et al.* 1951 *a*]. The grafts were poorly vascularized; the corium, thin and sparsely populated with cells, was directly apposed to the graft bed, with no layer of newly formed fibrous tissue between. The epidermal epithelium was thin, mitotically indolent, and slow to re-differentiate: no graft gave any sign of the onset of a new cycle of hair growth. Outwardly, the grafts were flush with, or recessed below, the plane of the surrounding skin; they were so thin and translucent that the pathways of the major skin vessels could be seen through them. Attachment to the graft bed was so infirm that the grafts could be peeled away with ease.

Doses much higher than 0·5 mg/day are not tolerated: 75 % of mice injected with 1 mg/day died between the 10th and 15th days. Paradoxically, so high a dosage may reduce the survival time of homografts, for some grafts, being wholly unvascularized, survived in tissue-culture fashion for about 10 days and then slowly became mummified.

(*b*) *Cortisol acetate* (CBA→A). Ten adult A-line mice (5♂♂, mean weight 25 g; 5♀♀, 23½ g) were grafted with CBA skin and given the first of a daily series of injections of 0·5 mg cortisol acetate. At the 10th day the grafts showed no discernible immunological reaction; unfortunately, five mice died between the 10th and 15th days (the dosage, in this early experiment, was ill chosen) leaving five mice, of which four revealed a fully surviving epithelium at the 15th day. Cortisol is thus at least as effective as cortisone; outwardly and histologically the grafts had the appearance characteristic of cortisone treatment in an extreme form.

(*c*) *Ineffectiveness of cortisone in pre-immunized mice* (A→CBA). Ten CBA ♂♂ were grafted with skin from A-line donors. Two weeks later they were grafted for a second time from A-line donors, receiving thereupon the first of eight successive daily injections of 0·25 mg cortisone acetate. Inspection of the grafts as soon as 8 days after this second-stage operation revealed complete breakdown in 7/10 and all but complete breakdown in the remaining 3/10. The accelerated reaction against second-stage homografts was therefore not perceptibly impaired. The healing of these grafts, it should be observed, was so weak as to amount to little more than mere apposition. (It was for this reason that we thought it inadvisable to use a daily dosage higher than 0·25 mg.)

(2) *Other steroid hormones*

The hormones investigated were corticosterone, progesterone, testosterone and oestradiol. (The action of DOC is considered later.) All transplantations were carried out in the combination A→CBA; all hormones were administered daily from the day of grafting until the completion of the experiment 10 days later; no mouse died under experiment. It will be seen that all hormones were administered in dosages comparable, gravimetrically, with those of cortisone, but far in excess of what is necessary to produce a specific pharmacological action. This is specially true of oestradiol (0·5 mg/day), but all mice remained healthy under treatment with oestradiol, and the females gained weight.

The results, summarized in Table 2, show that none of these four hormones has the power to extend the life of homografts beyond normal expectation. In various small but clearly perceptible ways, however, the grafts on animals treated with corticosterone resembled those on animals receiving cortisone and cortisol. The grafts on the mice which received corticosterone were weakly healed, unswollen—indeed, slightly recessed below the general surface—and rather transparent; inflammation was subdued, and the contracture which normally brings the perimeter of a graft into

Table 2. *Effect of daily injections of corticosterone, progesterone, testosterone and oestradiol on the survival time of skin homografts*

Agent	Dose (mg/day)	Recipients		Weight change		Grafts with sur-viving epithelium at 10 days
		♂	♀	♂	♀	
Corticosterone	1·0	—	8	—	$-\frac{1}{2}$	5/8
Progesterone	1·0	3	5	+1	$+\frac{1}{2}$	1/8
Testosterone propionate	1·0	6	6	+1	+2	5/12
Oestradiol dipropionate	0·5	6	6	0	$+1\frac{1}{2}$	$\begin{cases} ♂4/6 \\ ♀0/6 \end{cases}$

exact union with the edges of the graft bed had not yet occurred. It is noteworthy that two of the five grafts scored in Expt. 1 as having some surviving epithelium did in fact show 100 % epithelial survival; in grafts of all other groups, survival was merely fractional.

(3) ACTH

(a) ACTH administered to normal mice. In this section it will be shown that the administration of ACTH prolongs the lifetime of skin homografts in mice. Thirty-eight A-line mice (19 ♂♂, mean weight $23\frac{1}{2}$ g; 19♀♀, $20\frac{1}{2}$ g) were grafted with skin from CBA donors and thereupon given the first of ten successive daily injections of a 10 mg/ml. or 20 mg/ml. suspension of ACTH. Each mouse received daily a quantity equivalent to 0·5 or 1·0 mg ACTH, LA–1–A standard. One mouse died (on the day after grafting, so that ACTH is not to be blamed); the mean weight losses in the remainder, over 1–10 days, were as follows: 0·5 mg/day, ♂♂ $3\frac{1}{2}$ %, ♀♀ 10 %; 1·0 mg./day, ♂♂ 10 %, ♀♀ 16 %.

The grafts were first examined on the 10th day postoperatively. In the twenty-seven mice of the 0·5 mg/day group, 25/27 grafts still showed epithelial survival, mainly with complete epithelial cover ('100 %'). In the 1 mg/day group, 10/10 grafts scored 100 % survival. Both outwardly and histologically they were entirely indistinguishable from grafts on animals which had received cortisone or cortisol in dosages of equivalent immunological effect (see Table 1).

Administration of ACTH was stopped on the 10th day, but the grafts on 19/27 of the 0·5 mg/day group and on all ten of the 1 mg/day group were followed daily until the completion of breakdown, with the results summarized in Tables 3 and 4 (which use the same notation as Table 1). The superiority of 1 mg/day over 0·5 mg/day is obvious; and although it happened that the mice carrying the most long-lived homografts were females (Table 4), the males were in general the more responsive to ACTH (as to cortisone: Table 1).

(b) ACTH administered to adrenalectomized and ovariectomized female mice (A → CBA). The experiments described in this section were done on virgin female CBA mice; they show that ACTH is quite ineffective in adrenalectomized female mice,

whether or not their ovaries have been luteinized by prior treatment with chorionic gonadotrophin; and, correspondingly, that ACTH is no less effective in ovariectomized mice than in normal.

Table 3. '*Life table*' *showing the survival* (1) *or non-survival* (0) *from* 10 *to* 13 *days of homografts on nineteen mice which had received* 0·5 *mg/day ACTH from day* 1 *to day* 10

Females		0	0	0	0
		1	0	0	0
		1	0	0	0
		1	1	0	0
		1	1	0	0
		1	1	1	0
		1	1	1	0
		1	1	1	0
		1	1	1	1
Males		0	0	0	0
		1	1	0	0
		1	1	1	0
		1	1	1	0
		1	1	1	0
		1	1	1	0
		1	1	1	0
		1	1	1	1
		1	1	1	1
		1	1	1	1
Days		10	11	12	13

Table 4. '*Life table*' *showing the survival* (1) *or non-survival* (0) *from* 10 *to* 16 *days of homografts on ten mice which had received* 1 *mg/day ACTH from day* 1 *to day* 10

Females	1	1	0	0	0	0	0
	1	1	0	0	0	0	0
	1	1	1	1	1	0	0
	1	1	1	1	1	1	0
	1	1	1	1	1	1	1
Males	1	1	1	1	1	0	0
	1	1	1	1	1	0	0
	1	1	1	1	1	0	0
	1	1	1	1	1	0	0
	1	1	1	1	1	0	0
Days	10	11	12	13	14	15	16

Several days before any other experimental treatment, all mice were injected with 2 mg DOC trimethylacetate, subdivided into four to six subintegumentary doses. In our experience, this single administration has proved entirely adequate to protect mice for at least a month from the salt depletion consequent upon adrenalectomy; they were accordingly maintained on a normal diet with ordinary drinking water.

In a first experiment nine mice were adrenalectomized, nine were ovariectomized, and three were left alone. Four days later all twenty-one were grafted with skin from A-line donors; they then received the first of ten daily injections of 1 mg ACTH. Ten days after their transplantation, the grafts were inspected and subdivided into three categories of epithelial survival, viz. complete (1), partial ($\frac{1}{2}$) and nil (0).

Mortality was unexpectedly high (1/9 in the ovariectomized mice, 3/9 in the adrenalectomized mice) leaving seventeen to score, with the following results:

Ovariectomy: 1 1 1 1 1 1 1 ½
Adrenalectomy: ½ 0 0 0 0 0
Controls: 1 1 ½

It is clear that ACTH was quite ineffective in the adrenalectomized mice; the ovariectomized mice were indistinguishable in their responses from mice with intact adrenals ('Controls' above, and see section 3a).

A second experiment was carried out on ten virgin female mice which had received ten daily doses of 5 i.u. chorionic gonadotrophin in watery solution, each dose being subdivided into equal morning and evening injections. (Observations on an independent group of mice showed that this regimen of injection causes extensive luteinization of the ovaries.) The mice were adrenalectomized 3 days before the last of the injections of chorionic gonadotrophin, and grafted with A-line skin 5 days later; they thereupon received the first of ten daily injections of 1·0 mg ACTH. Two mice died during the course of these treatments; the grafts on the remaining eight were inspected 10 days after their transplantation. By contrast to the theoretical expectation (if ACTH had been effective) of 8/8 grafts showing 100 % epithelial survival, only one graft showed 50 % survival, the remainder 25 % or less. In spite of the luteinization of their ovaries, ACTH was therefore ineffective in adrenalectomized mice.

(4) *The effect of adrenalectomy and of DOC*

The effect of adrenalectomy on the homograft reaction was studied (a) on animals maintained after the operation on drinking water containing 1 % NaCl in 5 % glucose, without hormone supplement; and (b) on adrenalectomized mice, which, against a single background dose of the slowly absorbed DOC-trimethylacetate, received daily or regular supplements of the water-soluble DOC glucoside. Mice of this latter group were given ordinary drinking water. The recipients were of strain AU or CBA; A-line mice are less satisfactory for the purpose (see Methods above). In both experiments, the operation of adrenalectomy itself, and the skin grafting operation which followed it, were done under the protection afforded by a single intraperitoneal dose of 0·1–0·5 mg cortisone acetate (the lower dosage is quite adequate).

(a) *Mice maintained on glucose saline.* A total of thirty-three male (mean weight $25\frac{1}{2}$ g) and thirty female ($22\frac{1}{2}$ g) mice, all but eleven of strain AU, were grafted with skin from A-line donors 5–10 (modally 5–7) days after bilateral adrenalectomy. The grafts were examined after 6 or 9 days when the recipients were of strain AU, and after 11 days when the recipients were CBA's. Mortality—excluding three mice which died within 24 hr of adrenalectomy—was disturbingly high, viz. 13/60, although the mean loss in weight over the whole period of the experiment, $2\frac{1}{2}$ g, was not excessive.

The survival scores summarized below are based upon the histological analysis of grafts taken from animals in which, with rare exceptions, the completeness of adrenalectomy was confirmed by their inability to subsist for more than a few days on a diet of mixed grain and plain water. The purely numerical scores reveal nothing which could be regarded as a significant departure from normality.

A→AU at 6 days (normal expectation: all grafts scoring $1 = 100\%$ epithelial survival): $1\ 1\ 1\ 1\ 1\ 1\ 1\ 1\ 1\ \frac{1}{2}\ \frac{1}{2}\ \frac{1}{2}\ \frac{1}{2}$. In the grafts scored '$\frac{1}{2}$', epithelial breakdown, though in progress, had only just begun.

A→AU at 9 days (normal expectation: 50% of grafts showing some degree of survival, i.e. 1 or $\frac{1}{2}$): $1\ \frac{1}{2}\ \frac{1}{2}\ \frac{1}{2}\ \frac{1}{2}\ 0\ 0\ 0\ 0\ 0\ 0$.

A→CBA at 11 days (normal expectation: 50% of grafts showing some degree of survival): $1\ \frac{1}{2}\ \frac{1}{2}\ \frac{1}{2}\ 0\ 0\ 0\ 0\ 0$.

The appearance and histological condition of the grafts is commented upon below.

(b) *Mice maintained on DOC* (see also section 5, below). In a first experiment, six CBA males (mean weight 26 g) and six CBA females (22 g) were grafted with A-line skin 4 days after adrenalectomy; 2 mg DOC-trimethylacetate had been administered in a divided subintegumentary dose before adrenalectomy, and 0·5 mg DOC glucoside was injected on the 2nd, 3rd, 4th, 6th and 8th days after grafting. During the experiment 3/12 mice died. At the end of the experiment, 10 days after grafting, the males had lost $3\frac{1}{2}$ g and the females $1\frac{1}{2}$ g in mean weight. Disregarding one mouse which had not been properly adrenalectomized, the 10-day survival scores of the remaining eight were as follows: males, $\frac{1}{2}\ \frac{1}{2}\ 0\ 0\ 0$; females, $\frac{1}{2}\ 0\ 0$—a score (3/8) which does not differ significantly from the normal expectation (4/8) if adrenalectomy had been without effect.

In a second experiment, seven adrenalectomized AU males (mean weight 27 g) which had been implanted beforehand with 2 mg DOC-trimethylacetate were grafted with A-line skin and subjected, during the 6 days' residence of the grafts, to injections of 1·0 mg DOC glucoside daily. After 6 days the seven grafts (quite indistinguishable from five concurrent controls) all showed 100% epithelial survival.

Although adrenalectomy with or without the injection of DOC did not sensibly curtail the survival time of homograft epithelium (the experiments of section 5 point to the same conclusion), it had a clear effect on the strength of healing of the grafts and on the nature of the mesenchymal reaction around and within them. After 10–11 days, union to the graft bed was so strong that the grafts could not be dislodged by grasping them at the edge with stout toothed forceps and attempting to strip them away. Correspondingly, the zone of new tissue between the original inner dermal surface of the graft and the panniculus carnosus of the graft bed was much thicker, more richly populated, and more highly collagenized than in normal grafts, and within this zone, particularly at the 6th day, plasma cells were sometimes abundant. With this evidence of a generally heightened activity of mesenchymal tissue, it is surprising that the immunological reaction in adrenalectomized mice was not appreciably quicker in onset than in normal mice. Perhaps it is so; our failure to reveal any acceleration of breakdown may have been due to use of strain combinations in which the homograft reaction is so violent as to leave little room to show up any slight intensification of its effect. The use of strain combinations yielding a median survival time of 15–20 days would have been preferable. Unfortunately no such combination was available to us.

(5) *Combination of DOC with cortisone or cortisol*

Although the survival time of homografts in adrenalectomized mice was not curtailed (section 4 above), irrespective of whether they were maintained on glucose saline or on DOC, it still remained possible [see Selye, 1955] that DOC might act antagonistically to cortisone or cortisol when both were administered to adrenalectomized mice simultaneously. Table 5 summarizes the results of four experiments in which DOC glucoside (0·25–0·5 mg/day) or DOC acetate (1·0 mg/day) were administered simultaneously with cortisone acetate or cortisol acetate (0·25–0·5 mg/day). All experiments were done in the strain combination A→CBA. The adrenalectomies were performed 4–6 days before grafting, and all inspections of grafts were carried out on the 10th day after transplantation. Expts. 2 and 3 of Table 5 made use of males only. The scoring of degree of survival follows the practice of sections 3 and 4. Mortality was high only in Expt. 4, that in which two of the three groups of mice received cortisol 0·5 mg/day, losing $3\frac{1}{2}$–$4\frac{1}{2}$ g in weight over the period of the experiment and revealing, by the utterly indolent condition of the grafts, a characteristic symptom of cortisone poisoning.

Table 5. *Complete survival* (1), *partial survival* ($\frac{1}{2}$) *or non-survival* (0) *of skin homografts* 10 *days after transplantation to mice receiving daily injections of DOC, cortisone* (*or cortisol*) *or both*

Expt.	Hormone dosage (mg/day)	Mortality	Survival scores
1	DOC-glucoside (0·25)	0/12	$\frac{1}{2}$ 0 0 0
	cortisone acetate (0·25)		$\frac{1}{2}$ $\frac{1}{2}$ 0 0
	both		1 1 0 0
2	DOC-glucoside (0·25)	1/10	0
	cortisone acetate (0·5)		1 1 1 1
	both		1 1 1 1
3	DOC-glucoside (0·5)	0/13	0 0 0 0 0
	cortisone acetate (0·5)		1 1 1 1
	both		1 1 1 1
4	DOC-acetate (1·0)	5/19	$\frac{1}{2}$ $\frac{1}{2}$ 0 0
	cortisol acetate (0·5)		1 1 1 1
	both		1 1 1 1 1 1

These four experiments make it clear that DOC, in the dosages administered, does not interfere with the action of cortisone or cortisol; homografts on mice which received cortisone or cortisol alone were quite indistinguishable from homografts on the mice which had received DOC as well.

(B) The effects of pregnancy and parity

In this section we report successively upon: (a) the effect of a first homospecific or heterospecific pregnancy upon the behaviour and survival time of skin homografts; (b) the behaviour of homografts on mice which have passed through a succession of homospecific or heterospecific pregnancies; and (c) the effect of pregnancy on a pre-existing state of immunity. The terms 'homospecific' and 'heterospecific' are defined in the introduction.

Tables 6 and 7 set out the survival scores, at what would normally be the median survival times, of homografts transplanted to mice at various stages of a first homospecific or heterospecific pregnancy respectively. In a purely quantitative sense the results hint at, but do not firmly establish, a slight *shortening* of the median expectation of survival. To outward appearance and histologically the grafts on pregnant mice are clearly distinguishable from those on males or non-pregnant females: vascularization is backward, so that the grafts tend to have a staring white rather than a pink coloration; the epidermis is mitotically inactive and the inflammatory and mesenchymal reaction is rather subdued.

It is clear that mice, with a gestation period of 18–20 days, are among the least suitable subjects for studying a phenomenon of 6–12 days' duration; only the requirements of genetical control obliged us to use them. We therefore turned to the study of homografts in mice which had passed through repeated homospecific or heterospecific pregnancies, whether or not they were again pregnant at the time of grafting. Here a clear difference between strains A and CBA was revealed.

Table 6. *Survival scores of skin homografts transplanted to mice at various stages of a first homospecific pregnancy*

Mouse no.	Strain combination	Day of pregnancy when grafted	Sex of donor	Survival score
1	A→CBA	$15\frac{1}{2}$	F.	0
6	CBA→A	$11\frac{1}{2}$	F.	1
9	A→CBA	$10\frac{1}{2}$	F.	Trace
11	A→CBA	$10\frac{1}{2}$	F.	0
23	A→CBA	$7\frac{1}{2}$	M.	0
26	A→CBA	$6\frac{1}{2}$	M.	0

Table 7. *Survival scores of skin homografts transplanted to mice at various stages of a first heterospecific pregnancy*

Mouse no.	Strain combination	Day of pregnancy when grafted	Sex of donor	Survival score
30	A→CBA	$9\frac{1}{2}$	M.	0
33	CBA→A	$10\frac{1}{2}$	M.	Trace
34	CBA→A	$10\frac{1}{2}$	M.	Trace
36	A→CBA	$6\frac{1}{2}$	M.	0
40	AU→A	$10\frac{1}{2}$	M.	Trace
42	A→CBA	$6\frac{1}{2}$	M.	0
43	A→CBA	$13\frac{1}{2}$	M.	0
44	AU→A	$12\frac{1}{2}$	M.	0
56	AU→A	$13\frac{1}{2}$	M.	$\frac{1}{2}$

(a) *Direction of grafting CBA→A.* Grafts from CBA donors were transplanted to twelve A-line females which had been through four to eight pregnancies by A-line males (9/12 had been through at least six such pregnancies); and to six strict A-line male controls—males which were inbred sibs of the females, reared in the same cages and operated upon at the same time as the females. Tables 8 and 9, set out as 'life tables', reveal a clearly significant difference between the survival times of homografts on old females and males. Table 10, however, shows the same prolongation or survival in old ($9\frac{1}{2}$–$10\frac{1}{2}$ months) virgin females as in multiparous females of the same age. Evidently the passage through repeated pregnancies has nothing to do with the weakening of the homograft reaction.

Table 11 is the corresponding life table for CBA homografts on A-line females which had been through four to seven *hetero*specific pregnancies, i.e. pregnancies by CBA males. It is a matter of some importance that here, too, as in A-line mice which had been through repeated homospecific pregnancies (Table 8), there was a clear *prolongation* of survival. Repeated heterospecific pregnancies cause no immunization of the mother of a kind that reveals itself by tissue transplantation immunity.

Tables 8–11. *Life tables showing the survival times of CBA homografts on A-line mice. (8) Female mice which had been through* 4–8 *homospecific pregnancies,* (9) *male controls,* (10) *elderly virgin females,* (11) *female mice which had been through* 4–7 *heterospecific pregnancies*

```
                  Table 8                          Table 9
        *
        *
        *   *
        *   *
        *   *   *
        *   *   *
        *   *   *                    *
        *   *   *                    *
        *   *   *                    *
        *   *   *   *                *
        *   *   *   *                *   *
        *   *   *   *                *   *   *   *
        9  10  11  12 days          8  10  11  12 days


                  Table 10                         Table 11
                                                  *
                                                  *
                                                  *
                                                  *
                                                  *   *
                                                  *   *
                                                  *   *
                                                  *   *   *
        *                                         *   *   *
        *                                         *   *   *   *
        *   *                                     *   *   *   *
        *   *                                     *   *   *   *
        *   *                                     *   *   *   *
        *   *                                     *   *   *   *   *   *
        *   *   *                                 *   *   *   *   *   *   *
        *   *   *   *                             *   *   *   *   *   *   *
        *   *   *   *   *   *   *                 *   *   *   *   *   *   *   *
        9  10  11  12  13  14  15 days           8  10  11  12  13  14  15  16 days
```

(b) *Direction of grafting A→CBA.* Grafts from A-line donors were transplanted to twelve CBA females which had been through five to eight (homospecific) pregnancies by CBA males, and, at the same time, to eight strict (see above) CBA male controls. There was no difference between the reactivities of males and females: in all mice, breakdown of the grafts was far advanced or complete by the 11th day after transplantation. Nor, equally, was there any prolongation of survival in A-line grafts transplanted to eight CBA females which had passed through four to seven (heterospecific) pregnancies by A-line males.

Nine of the twelve CBA mice belonging to the homospecific pregnancy group referred to above were pregnant at the time of operation; three were in the third to fifth day of pregnancy, and six in the 13th–14th. The grafts on these pregnant mice were less well vascularized and more indolent than grafts on the other multiparous mice, but this distinction was not reflected in any difference of epithelial survival time.

(c) *Effect of pregnancy on a pre-existing state of immunity.* The experiments just described show that passage through heterospecific pregnancies does not build up any perceptible state of sensitization towards homografts coming from the strain of the male. The reactivity of multiparous mice was just the same, whether the pregnancies they had been through were homospecific or heterospecific. The last test was designed to find out whether passage through a heterospecific pregnancy might not *lower* the sensitivity of a mouse which had already been immunized by a homograft coming from the strain of the male. In its simplest form, the argument in favour of such a possibility would be this: that the foetal tissue, containing the same antigens as the graft, might absorb antibodies (or other immune agents) circulating in the blood stream as a consequence of the earlier immunization.

In the outcome, nothing of the kind occurred. Five virgin CBA females were grafted with A-line skin. Each was then caused to pass through one or two pregnancies by an A-line male. Sixty days after the first operation the females were grafted for a second time from A-line donors. Six days later all the homografts had broken down completely, showing all the appearance characteristic of 'second-stage' homografts on sensitized mice. The immune state caused by the earlier grafting was therefore still in force, and not perceptibly impaired.

DISCUSSION

(a) *How does cortisone affect the homograft reaction?* Billingham *et al.* [1951*a*, *b*] argued that cortisone might influence transplantation immunity in one or more of the following ways: (*a*) by lowering the homograft's ability to elicit an immune reaction; (*b*) by enfeebling the host's systemic immunological response, presumably by an action upon lymph nodes or other lymphoid tissue; or (*c*) by preventing the fulfilment or local expression of the immune state—for example, by interfering with the inflammatory processes that accompany the breakdown of homografts. These three possibilities may be referred to for short as afferent, central and efferent inhibition, respectively.

It is as true of mice as of rabbits that cortisone has little power to prolong the life of homografts when an animal has already been immunized by an earlier grafting from the same donor. If immunity is present, it can take effect, and it follows that efferent inhibition (*c*) cannot be an important ingredient of the action of cortisone. Carefully designed experiments by Billingham *et al.* [1951*b*] nevertheless showed that some small part of the action of cortisone could only be attributed to an interference with the local fulfilment of the immune state.

The argument in favour of possibility (*b*), though very strong, is indirect. It is now a commonplace of endocrinology that the administration of cortisone or cortisol, in the high doses that are necessary when studying the homograft reaction, exercises a general inhibitory action on the growth and replacement of lymphoid tissue. In 1951 the 'possibility that the draining lymph nodes play an important part in the building up of immunity against homografts' was no more than a reasonable guess [Billingham *et al.* 1951*b*]. It is now certain that they do so [Mitchison, 1954; Billingham, Brent & Medawar, 1954; Scothorne & McGregor, 1955]. Moreover, it has repeatedly been shown—most recently, perhaps, by Berglund & Fagraeus [1956]—that the administration of cortisone retards at least the earlier stages of antibody formation. Given then that cortisone causes an involution of lymphoid tissue, that the regional lymph nodes are the anatomical seat of the homograft reaction, and that cortisone interferes with antibody formation in other, more orthodox immunological systems, it is difficult not to allow 'central inhibition' an important role in the reaction against homografts.

Nevertheless, it cannot now be doubted that some part of the action of cortisone in orthodox skin grafting in adults must be due to an interference with the liberation of antigens from the grafts or with their access to the regional nodes. Billingham *et al.* [1951*b*] were unable to refute this possibility in experiments expressly designed to weigh it up, but Scothorne [1956], in experiments of the same kind but of anatomically better design, has shown that the mere incapacitation of the regional nodes is not a sufficient explanation of how cortisone acts when it is locally applied. That some part, perhaps an important part, of the action of cortisone is due to afferent inhibition is not surprising: it retards and enfeebles all reparative processes, including vascularization and penetration by the lymphatics through which the antigens must be presumed to reach the regional nodes. A secondary consequence of the slowing down of vascularization is that grafts on cortisone-treated animals are mitotically indolent: it is therefore very much to the point that the antigens responsible for skin transplantation immunity are *nuclear* substances [Billingham, Brent & Medawar, unpublished work].

By whatsoever means cortisone and cortisol may act, their action is endocrinologically specific. Just as in Krohn's experiments with rabbits (see Introduction, p. 240), no other steroid hormone of the representative group we studied had any power to prolong the life of homografts in mice. All that can be said is that corticosterone was more 'cortisone-like' in its action than the others. The injection of DOC (ester or glucoside) did not perceptibly curtail the life of homografts nor interfere with the power of cortisone to prolong it.

Homografts on adrenalectomized mice were distinguished by healing of, in our experience, unexampled strength, and by an exuberant mesenchymal reaction in the graft dermis and graft bed. This was as true of adrenalectomized mice maintained on a salt-rich diet as of mice maintained by exogenous DOC; it is to be regarded, then, as a symptom of the absence of cortisone-like secretions rather than as evidence of any positive action on the part of DOC.

(*b*) *The action of ACTH.* Our experimental results accord with an entirely orthodox interpretation of the action of ACTH. ACTH acts upon the adrenal gland, producing results in no wise distinguishable from those produced by the injection of cortisol or cortisone. Having regard to the endocrinological specificity of the action of cortisol and cortisone, there is therefore no reason to doubt that ACTH acts by enhancing the endogenous secretion of cortisol or of some other compound exercising the same physiological effect.

The work of Clayton & Prunty [1951] had raised the possibility that the luteinized ovary might act as a target organ for ACTH. Our experiments gave no evidence that this was the case; nor did Krohn's (see p. 241). It should be remembered, however, that Clayton & Prunty's were 'acute' experiments and hardly comparable with our own.

(c) *Pregnancy.* In pregnant mice, unlike pregnant rabbits, homografts do not enjoy an abnormally long lease of life, and there were only minor symptoms of an interference with healing and vascularization that could be attributed to an enhanced secretion of cortisone-like steroids. This applies equally to first homospecific or heterospecific or to the last of a succession of pregnancies of either kind. Nor does passage through a heterospecific pregnancy—i.e. pregnancy by a male isogenic with the graft donor—either immunize a mouse against its homografts or interfere with the action of any immune state already in being. In an immunological sense the foetuses of a mouse are extraordinarily well insulated from their mothers. It was not, of course, to be expected that repeated heterospecific pregnancies should elicit the formation of immune iso-agglutinins, for the iso-antigens of red cells in mice have not matured by birth [Gorer, 1938; Mitchison, 1953]. According to unpublished observations by Billingham, Brent & Medawar, however, the iso-antigens of nucleated somatic tissue have matured before birth, and an iso-immunization against skin homografts might therefore be built up by the accidental leakage of, for example, foetal leucocytes into the maternal circulation. The fact that homografts on mice which have been through repeated heterospecific pregnancies do not fall short of their normal expectation of survival (on the contrary, their survival time in older female A-line mice is actually prolonged) is rather strong evidence that no such leakage occurs.

There is no means of deciding from present evidence whether the difference between the behaviour of homografts on pregnant mice and pregnant rabbits is due either (a) to different kinds of adrenal response in pregnancy, or (b) to responses of the same kind which exercise a weaker effect because of the generally lower sensitivity of mice to the cortisone-like steroids (see below), or (c) to the possibility that pregnancy in mice is too short for an enhanced secretion of cortical steroids to exercise an appreciable effect in our test system.

(d) *Species differences.* Our experiments have already revealed one clear difference of reactivity between members of different strains of mice: elderly female A-line mice, whether virgin or multiparous, react upon homografts more feebly than CBA females of the same age. Differences *between* species could hardly be less well pronounced, and the 'homograft reaction' does in fact show them up with particular distinctness. The following table summarizes the available evidence (see p. 241) on the sensitivity of homografts in different species to the action of cortisone acetate or free alcohol and ACTH (the figures roughly express the dosage, in mg/kg/day, needed to extend the median expectation of survival by at least 50 %):

Species	Cortisone	ACTH	References
Rabbits	≪2·5	≫10	Billingham *et al.* [1951a, b]; Krohn [1954a]
Guinea-pigs	15*	20	Sparrow [1953, 1954]
Monkeys	≫ 4	>10	Krohn [1955]
Mice	16	40	See above

* Free alcohol.

For one reason or another the tests upon which these figures are based were not fully comparable, but they serve as a general guide to the sensitivity of members of four different species to cortisone and ACTH. They show that rabbits are 'good reactors' to cortisone; that mice and guinea-pigs are 'bad reactors'; and that reactivity to ACTH varies out of step with reactivity to cortisone. The figures in the left-hand column reveal major differences between the net sensitivities of members of different species to the injection of cortisone by the subcutaneous or intramuscular route. It seems most unlikely that differences as great as these can be attributed merely to variations in the rates at which a local inoculum of cortisone acetate is de-esterified and systemically absorbed; there must, in addition, be a real quantitative difference of tissue responsiveness.

Following Krohn's argument closely [see Krohn, 1954a, b; 1955], it is clear on a priori grounds that the reactivity of an animal towards ACTH will depend upon at least four parameters: (a) the composition of the normal adrenal effluent [see Bush, 1953; Hechter & Pincus, 1954], (b) the total output per unit time of each ingredient, (c) the sensitivity of the tissues to adrenal steroids, and (d) the sensitivity and mode of response of the adrenal cortex to ACTH (whether to increase the total output or to alter its composition, etc.).

Krohn first reasoned that ACTH was ineffective in rabbits because they are predominantly secretors of a steroid, corticosterone, which does not influence the homograft reaction; on the other hand, they should be good reactors to cortisone because the reactivity of their tissues is adjusted to a low endogenous secretion of cortisol. Monkeys, on the other hand, are distinguished by a cortical secretion that is predominantly of cortisol: should not then ACTH prolong the life of skin homografts in monkeys? Krohn's experiments [1955] do not sustain this hypothesis, though they could hardly be said to refute it, and it may be that a monkey's tissues, being adjusted to a high rate of secretion of cortisol, are less sensitive than a rabbit's and therefore less responsive (as Krohn's findings show) to exogenous cortisone.

This argument, if pressed, might be thought to lead to the view that ACTH should never be able to prolong the life of homografts; for the animals whose tissues are highly sensitive to the action of cortisone will be predominantly endogenous secretors of corticosterone, and those whose tissues are relatively insensitive to cortisone will be predominantly endogenous secretors of cortisol; the effect of ACTH on the former will be to enhance the secretion of a (from our point of view) inactive steroid, and on the latter to produce an active steroid to which the tissues are relatively insensitive. But these are extremes: there must clearly be an intermediate state of affairs in which animals are slightly sensitive to cortisone and therefore slightly sensitive to ACTH; it may be that mice and guinea-pigs occupy this intermediate position, as the figures in the table suggest.

REFERENCES

Baxter, H., Schiller, C., Whiteside, J. H., Lipshutz, H. & Straith, R. E. [1951]. *Plast. reconstr. Surg.* **7**, 492.

Berglund, K. & Fagraeus, A. [1956]. *Nature, Lond.*, **177**, 233.

Billingham, R. E., Brent, L. & Medawar, P. B. [1954]. *Proc. Roy. Soc.* B, **143**, 58.

Billingham, R. E., Brent, L., Medawar, P. B. & Sparrow, E. M. [1954]. *Proc. Roy. Soc.* B, **143**, 43.

Billingham, R. E., Krohn, P. L. & Medawar, P. B. [1951a]. *Brit. med. J.* **1**, 1157.

Billingham, R. E., Krohn, P. L. & Medawar, P. B. [1951b]. *Brit. med. J.* **2**, 1049.

Billingham, R. E. & Medawar, P. B. [1951]. *Brit. J. exp. Biol.* **28**, 385.

Bruce, H. M. & Parkes, A. S. [1952]. *Lancet*, **1**, 71.

Bush, I. E. [1953]. *J. Endocrin.* **9**, 95.

Clayton, B. E. & Prunty, F. T. G. [1951]. *J. Endocrin.* **7**, 362.

Dempster, W. J. [1953]. *Arch. int. Pharmacodyn.* **95**, 253.

Ellison, E. H., Martin, B. C., Williams, R. D., Clatworthy, H. W., Hamwi, G. & Zollinger, R. M. [1951]. *Ann. Surg.* **134**, 495.

Gaunt, R., Leathem, J. H., Howell, C. & Antonchak, C. [1952]. *Endocrinology*, **50**, 521.

Gorer, P. A. [1938]. *J. Path. Bact.* **47**, 242.

Gross, F. & Tschopp, E. [1952]. *Experientia*, **8**, 75.

Hechter, O. & Pincus, G. [1954]. *Physiol. Rev.* **34**, 459.

Heslop, R. W., Krohn, P. L. & Sparrow, E. M. [1954]. *J. Endocrin.* **10**, 325.

Krohn, P. L. (1954a). *J. Endocrin.* **11**, 71.

Krohn, P. L. [1954b]. *J. Endocrin.* **11**, 78.

Krohn, P. L. [1954c]. *Brit. J. exp. Path.* **35**, 539.

Krohn, P. L. [1955]. *J. Endocrin.* **12**, 220.

McNichol, J. W. [1952]. *Plast. reconstr. Surg.* **9**, 437.

Medawar, P. B. [1953]. *Symp. Soc. exp. Biol.* **7**, 320.

Mitchison, N. A. [1953]. *J. Genet.* **51**, 406.

Mitchison, N. A. [1954]. *Proc. Roy. Soc.* B, **142**, 72.

Morgan, J. A. [1951]. *Surgery*, **30**, 506.

Scothorne, R. J. [1956]. *Transplantation Bull.* **3**, 13.

Scothorne, R. J. & McGregor, I. A. [1955]. *J. Anat., Lond.*, **89**, 283.

Selye, H. [1955]. *Experientia*, **11**, 35.

Sparrow, E. M. [1953]. *J. Endocrin.* **9**, 101.

Sparrow, E. M. [1954]. *J. Endocrin.* **11**, 57.

Woodruff, M. F. A. [1953]. *Transplantation Bull.* **1**, 10.

13

DEVELOPMENTAL HORMONES AND IMMUNOLOGICAL MATURATION

W. Pierpaoli, N. Fabris, and E. Sorkin

It has been reported in previous publications from our laboratory (Pierpaoli and Sorkin, 1967a, 1969a, b; Pierpaoli et al., 1969) and by others (Ambrose, 1964; Hollander, Takakura, and Yamada, 1968) that hormones influence the development and performance of the immune system. There is also abundant clinical evidence for the importance of hormones in immunity (Fisher, 1964). Immunologically competent lymphocytes are believed to derive from bone marrow cells which acquire immunological responsiveness through some action of the thymus. It is one of the main theses of this paper that processes of maturation and differentiation in the thymus and in thymus-derived tissues are under hormonal regulation and that the adenohypophysis controls these processes. Our present work is concerned with the action of some developmental hormones, such as somatotropin or growth hormone (STH) and thyroxine, on the maturation and expression of the immunological capacity. We shall discuss a number of experimental and hypothetical points about the significance of hormones in the ontogeny and maintenance of a functional immune system.

1. The Perinatal Thymus Is a Target Organ of the Adenohypophysis

There is evidence for the relationship between the thymus and the hypophysis. Pierpaoli and Sorkin (1967a, 1968) have described studies on the induction of wasting disease with thymus and spleen atrophy after treatment with rabbit anti-mouse-hypophysis serum or anti-bovine STH serum in young adult mice. On the other hand, if the thymus is a classical target organ of the adenohypophysis we should expect changes in the hypophysis such as are observed after extirpation of other target glands. We have demonstrated by both light microscopy (Pierpaoli and Sorkin, 1967b) and electron microscopy (Fig. 1) that a degranulation of the acidophilic, growth hormone-producing cells occurs in the adenohypophysis of mice after neonatal thymectomy. Figure 2 shows the increasing number of enlarged degranulated cells in the mouse anterior pituitary at increasing times after thymectomy at birth. These modifications in the number of acidophilic cells with confluent cisternae of the dilated endoplasmic reticulum ("thymotropic cells") are a manifestation of an increased demand for and output of the hormone from the cells after solubilization of the hormone granules in the Golgi apparatus. No such modifications were observed by optical microscopy in mice thymectomized as young adults (Pierpaoli and Sorkin, 1967b) or in neonatally splenectomized mice. These results demonstrate the interdependence between the perinatal thymus and STH-producing cells in the hypophysis.

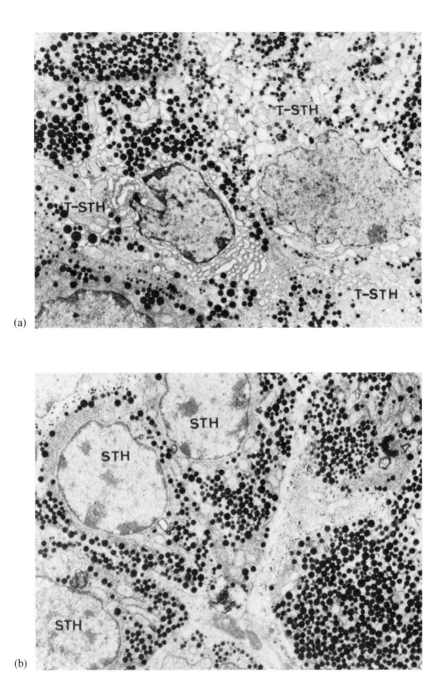

FIGURE 1. Electron micrograph of ''thymotropic'' acidophilic cells (T-STH) with dilatation of the cisternae of the endoplasmic reticulum in the adenohypophysis removed from neonatally thymectomized NMRI mice. (*a*) Adenohypophysis 33 days after neonatal thymectomy, showing thymotropic cells. × 4800. (*b*) Adenohypophysis of normal sham-operated littermate of same age, showing normal acidophilic cells (STH). × 4800. (*c*) Adenohypophysis 30 days after neonatal thymectomy. One thymotropic cell. × 10,000. (*d*) Adenohypophysis of normal sham-operated littermate of same age. One normal acidophilic cell. × 10,000. (Electron micrographs taken by Dr. Elena Bianchi, University of Pavia, Italy.)

(c)

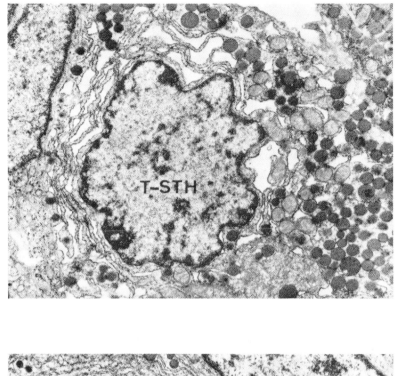

(d)

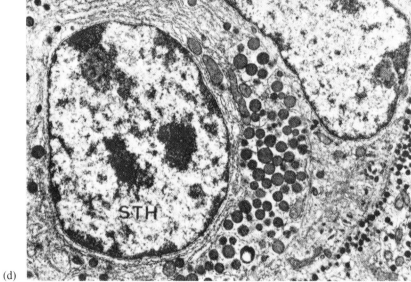

Figure 1. *Continued.*

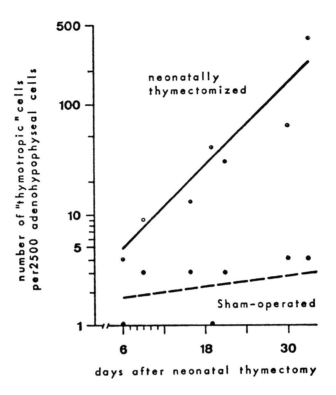

FIGURE 2. Number of "thymotropic" acidophilic cells in the adenohypophysis of neonatally thymecto-mized NMRI mice and sham-operated littermates at various times after operation.

Other recent evidence derives from experiments on autosomal recessive dwarf mice with a deficient pituitary. The thymus and lymph nodes of these mice are extremely depleted of lymphoid cells (Baroni, 1967; Pierpaoli et al., 1969, see section 2 below). This evidence supports the proposition that the thymus is a target organ of the adenohypophysis. It suggests but does not finally answer the question of whether somatotropic hormone is the thymotropic hormone.

2. Somatotropic Hormone Is a Thymotropic Hormone

The thymus is doubtless subjected to the influence of several endocrine glands (Comsa, 1961; Dougherty et al., 1964; Ernström and Larsson, 1965). Some of the evidence for a major role of STH during the development of the thymus-dependent immune system has been summarized above. The sensitivity of the thymus to STH has been tested by various means. Following the findings that anti-mouse hypophysis serum results in lymphocyte depletion of thymus and spleen, we prepared antisera to bovine STH (Raben type; mouse STH is not available) and injected them into mice (Pierpaoli and Sorkin, 1968). The recipients of these anti-STH sera showed similar lymphocyte depletion in the thymus cortex and in thymus-dependent areas of the spleen to that observed with anti-hypophysis sera.

In other experiments the Snell-Bagg hypopituitary dwarf mice served as a model. These mice produce only about a thousandth of the amount of STH produced by their normal littermates

(Garcia and Geschwind, 1968). Their thymuses and lymph nodes are practically devoid of lymphocytes (Baroni, 1967); they show normal immunoglobulin levels (Wilkinson, Singh, and Sorkin, 1970) and reject foreign skin grafts at between 20 and 40 days; that is, with a mean retardation of about 15 days (Fabris, Pierpaoli and Sorkin, 1970). They die within 45–150 days after birth, depending on their habitat. When 30-day-old Snell-Bagg dwarf mice were given STH, thyroxine, or STH and thyroxine together, their thymus and lymph nodes became fully repopulated with lymphoctyes (Pierpaoli et al., 1969). The production of antibodies to sheep red cells and homograft rejection, which were both delayed before hormone treatment, became normal.

These experiments are conclusive evidence that STH is a thymotropic hormone. It influences the cellularity of all lymphoid tissues. One open question concerns the purity of the STH preparations. It is conceivable that traces of other pituitary hormones are present in these bovine preparations. However, the clear finding that the acidophilic cells in the pituitary degranulate after thymectomy speaks in favour of our assumption (2). It does not exclude, however, the possibility that other hormones are acting on the thymus or that STH exerts its effect on the thymus indirectly through hormones of other target glands.

3. Immunological Maturation Depends on Endocrinological Function

This is the main and crucially important proposition. The parallelism of immunological and endocrinological immaturity in newborn and young rodents suggested to us the possibility of a causal relation between the two systems for the maturation of the immune capacity. Light microscopic examination of the adenohypophysis and the level of somatotropic hormone in the pituitary gland of rodents in the perinatal period (Siperstein et al., 1954; Daughaday et al. 1968), as well as previous findings on the dependence of thymo-lymphatic tissue development on some pituitary hormones, seem compatible with this assumption.

Although STH and other hormones most likely act on antibody-producing plasma cells, for example in polyribosomal synthesis, we assume that one of its main actions lies in the control of the development of a thymus-dependent lymphocyte population. This hormonal dependence of the onset of immunological reactivity during ontogenesis and perinatal life has been evaluated by testing the effect of hormones on donor cells in modifying the course of the graft-versus-host (GvH) reaction (Simonsen, 1962) and runt disease. Spleen cells or thymocytes from adult or newborn mice were inoculated together with hormones into normal or thymectomized newborn or mice a few days old of a histoincompatible strain or into the F_1 hybrid of the donor and recipient strain (Fig. 3).

a. Injection of Spleen Cells and Hormones into Newborn Histoincompatible Mice or Rats Influences the Course of Runt Disease

Spleen cells ($5–10 \times 10^6$) from young adult male C3H mice were injected intravenously into newborn Charles River (CR) recipients. Mice of the same litter were treated for seven or eight days with daily doses of 100 μg somatotropic hormone (STH) and 0.1–0.5 μg thyroxine. Mice treated with both hormones and cells developed an accelerated runt disease and died within 7 to 15 days of age (Fig. 4). Mice injected only with spleen cells developed runt disease a few days later, but some of them eventually recovered. Mice injected with hormone alone grew normally.

The same type of experiment was done using 4-week-old Long Evans rats as cell donors and as recipients, newborn Charles River rats. The newborn rats were injected intraperitoneally with 30×10^6 spleen cells, and some of them were treated with 200 μg STH and 0.5 μg thyroxine.

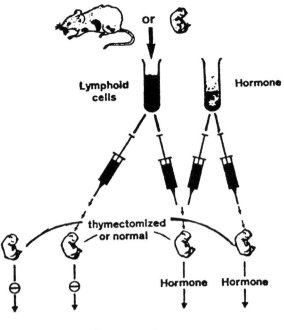

spleen indices

FIGURE 3. Diagram to illustrate the experimental model used to evaluate the effect of hormones on the immunocompetence of cells in the graft-versus-host assay.

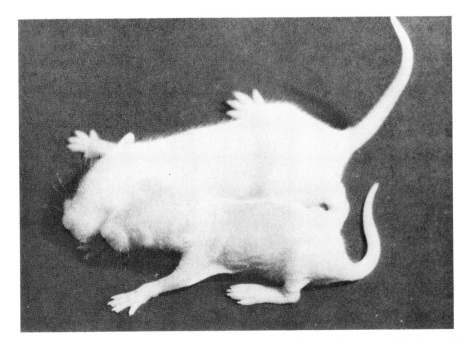

FIGURE 4. Eight-day-old Charles River mouse showing runting after one intravenous injection at birth of 5×10^6 spleen cells from an adult C3H donor; 100 μg STH and 0.1 μg thyroxine were injected for 7 days. Control littermate injected with cells only.

Some controls were treated with hormones alone. In this combination of strains the rats injected with only cells or hormones grew normally, while those treated with both spleen cells and hormones developed a runt disease. The pathological changes were those described in classical runt disease (Billingham, 1968). The above evidence suggests therefore that the graft-versus-host reaction has been influenced by STH and thyroxine and results in the development of runt disease.

b. STH Increases the Potential of Adult Allogeneic Mouse Spleen Cells to Induce a GvH Response in Newborns

The GVH test has been used to determine whether the effect of hormones in inducing runt disease was not due to a direct action of the hormone on the lymphatic tissues of the recipient. C3H mice were used as donors when newborn Charles River mice were the recipients. Adult CR or C3H mice were used as donors when (CR × C3H)F$_1$ hybrids were used as recipients. A striking increase of spleen size in mice injected with both spleen cells and STH was noted (Fig. 5). Whether STH influenced the immunocompetence of the injected allogeneic spleen cells or cells of one parental strain or whether it induced them to divide is unknown. The same type of experiment performed by injecting syngeneic cells did not show any specific STH-induced activation of the injected spleen cells.

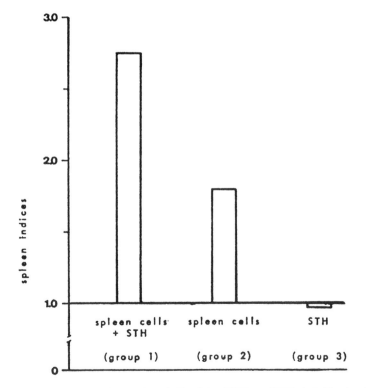

FIGURE 5. Graft-versus-host reaction (spleen indices) in (C3H × CR)F$_1$ hybrid mice injected once intraperitoneally, at birth, with 10×10^6 spleen cells from 4-week-old C3H donors. Daily doses of 100 µg STH were given for 9 days. Mice were killed on day 9.

c. STH Induces Immunocompetence in Thymocytes of Newborn and Adult Mice

While the experiments in (a) and (b) showed significant effects of STH on adult spleen cells they left open the crucial question of its action on cells of newborn, immunologically incompetent donors. In order to evaluate the effect of hormones on the maturation of thymus cells of newborn or adult mice, we injected cells from one parental strain of (C3H × CR)F$_1$ hybrids into newborn or a few days old (C3H × CR)F$_1$ hybrid recipients. The experimental conditions were similar to those in (b). As shown in Fig. 6A, STH strongly potentiates the weak capacity of thymocytes to induce a GVH response or even renders them capable of behaving as immunocompetent cells when their injection is followed by treatment with STH. The use of thymocytes from newborn donors makes it unlikely that the cell inocula contained immunocompetent cells from peripheral blood.

The capacity of certain developmental hormones to change immunologically non-reactive or weakly reactive cells of newborns into efficient effector cells in a graft-versus-host reaction suggested at first that these hormones act through the thymus of the recipient. However, neonatally thymectomized recipients behaved in an identical manner, as is shown below. It is therefore likely that these hormones act directly in some way on the transferred cells.

d. STH Induces Competence in Thymocytes from Newborn Donors in the Absence of the Recipient Thymus

The question of whether the effect of STH was exerted directly on the injected thymocytes without the need of the recipient thymus was evaluated as follows. F$_1$ hybrid recipients were

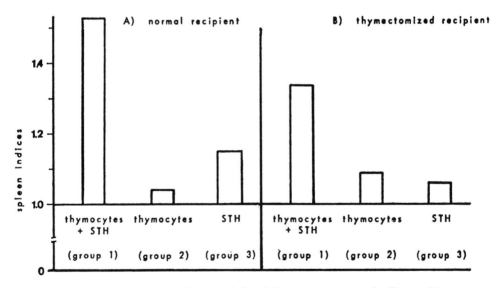

FIGURE 6. (A) (left). Somatotropic hormone-induced immunocompetence in Charles River mouse thymocytes. Assay: GvH response (spleen indices) in normal (C3H × CR)F$_1$ hybrid mice. Groups 1 and 2 were injected at 2 days after birth with 5 × 10^6 thymocytes from newborn Charles River donors. Groups 1 and 3 received 100 μg STH daily for 10 days. One group remained untreated. Mice were killed at day 12. (B) (right). STH-induced immunocompetence in Charles River mouse thymocytes. Assay: GvH response (spleen indices) in (C3H × CR)F$_1$ hybrid mice thymectomized at 4 days of age. Groups 1 and 2 were injected at day 5 with 5 × 10^6 thymocytes from newborn Charles River donors. Groups 1 and 3 received 100 μg STH daily for 10 days. One group remained untreated. Mice were killed at day 15.

thymectomized at 1–4 days of age, and at days 6–8 they were injected with $5–10 \times 10^6$ thymocytes from one of the newborn parental strains. Figure 6B indicates that the GvH response can be induced in thymectomized recipients just as well as in the normal ones, thus ruling out the participation of the host thymus in the process of differentiation or maturation of the injected cells by the hormone.

The historadioautographic technique with tritiated thymidine (Radiochemical Centre, Amersham, England: specific activity 10,000 µCi/mM) was used in similar experiments to evaluate the variation of mitotic activity in the spleen of the recipient mice injected with thymocytes alone, hormone alone, both cells and hormone, or of untreated controls. The results are illustrated in Fig. 7. The increased number of labelled spleen cells when both cells and hormone were injected indicate that the somatotropic hormone has enhanced the capacity of the injected thymocytes to induce a graft-versus-host reaction.

e. The Hormonal Reconstitution of Dwarf Mice Results in Long-Lasting Immunocompetence

It was found that after dwarf mice had been reconstituted with STH and thyroxine for 4 weeks, and after a rest period of 2 months, the 4-month-old mice could still reject a foreign skin graft in the normal time of 12–15 days. While many untreated dwarf mice died between 40–150 days, some of the reconstituted dwarf mice have in fact survived for over a year and one such mouse is now 450 days old. This may mean that these mice also have a high level of cellular and presumably humoral immunity. The evidence suggests that the hormones most probably created a long-lived lymphocyte population which out-lived the hormone action itself. The very low level of hormones produced by the dwarfs may suffice, however, to maintain the level of immunocompetent cells and to produce antibodies in adult life.

All the above experiments indicate that STH is a thymotropic hormone which is directly responsible, possibly with the cooperation of other hormones, for the transformation of

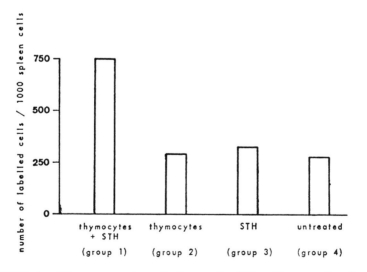

FIGURE 7. STH-induced immunocompetence in thymocytes. Historadioautography of spleen cells of neonatally thymectomized CR recipient mice. Groups 1 and 2 received at day 1, 5×10^6 thymocytes of adult C3H donors. Groups 1 and 3 received 100 µg STH daily. Group 4 was untreated. All mice were killed on day 4. [³H]thymidine, 0.8 µg/g body weight, was injected into all groups 1 hour before killing. Results evaluated as number of labelled cells per 1000 spleen cells counted.

Developmental Hormones and Maturation

thymocytes into immunocompetent cells which are active in cell-mediated immune reactions, such as the graft-versus-host response. Apparently no factors are needed from the recipient thymus for the development of cells active in such delayed-type immune reactions. Although the role of other hormones cannot be excluded, the experimental facts illustrate that the immunological function of the thymus cells and thymus-derived cells can be fully expressed only in the presence of somatotropic hormone. These data are in full agreement with our previous findings (Pierpaoli and Sorkin, 1969*a*, *b*) and views on the significance of the thymus-pituitary axis (Pierpaoli and Sorkin, 1967*a*).

A most salient point is the fact that thymocytes of a newborn animal under the influence of injected STH can evoke a cell-mediated immune reaction in another newborn animal. The recipient, being an F_1 hybrid, is incapable of reacting against these thymocytes. The presumable explanation for this is that the newborn recipient is endocrinologically and immunologically immature and cannot therefore react against the foreign thymocytes. Even if the injected hormone caused maturation in the recipient, as it presumably does of the donor cells, it would be incapable of mounting a host-versus-graft reaction, since it is a histocompatible hybrid. Since the newborn recipients were thymectomized these same experiments seem also to indicate that the STH-induced immunocompetence of the donor thymocytes is not mediated through the release of a hypothetical thymus factor by the recipients. It is possible that STH is acting on the thymocytes of the donor through thymosin (Goldstein *et al.*, 1970).

4. Significance of Interrelation of STH with Insulin and Thyroxine for Immunological Function

This problem has been previously investigated (Pierpaoli and Sorkin, 1969*a*; Pierpaoli *et al.*, 1969) by evaluating the effect of hormones on the lymphoid tissues or by the deficiencies produced by their absence or low levels. The known dependence of the activity of STH-producing cells on thyroid function (Purves and Griesback, 1946; Solomon and Greep, 1959; Daughaday *et al.*, 1968) was studied by using rabbit anti-bovine thyrotropic hormone serum. When this serum was repeatedly injected into young adult mice, it induced a striking involution of the spleen in spite of its own strong antigenicity, and antibody formation was reduced or absent (Pierpaoli and Sorkin, 1969*a*). STH treatment of these mice, whose thyroid function was impaired or reduced, produced a striking reconstitution of the peripheral lymphoid tissues, particularly in the perifollicular zones of the lymphoid follicles and in the thymus-dependent areas of the spleen.

Another experimental system was used to evaluate the dependence of STH on thyroxine and the role of STH in the immune response. Mice and rats were treated with propyl-thiouracil (PTU), which is known to block release of thyroxine. Treatment of these animals with PTU for 20 days produces a decrease in the relative spleen weight, while the relative thymus weight is not changed by comparison with the untreated controls. The primary immune response to sheep red blood cells is greatly impaired. A full reversal and recovery from these conditions can be obtained by injecting the PTU-treated animals with thyroxine or STH, the latter hormone giving an even more complete reconstitution in size and morphological appearance of the spleen and of the primary immune response to sheep red cells (Fig. 8). These actions of STH support the proposition that STH is the hormone responsible for the differentiation of lymphocytes into antibody-forming cells and/or for the actual performance of the latter.

The well-known interrelationship between STH and insulin has also been evaluated, as far as the delayed-type immune response is concerned, by using the graft-versus-host assay described in section (3). Injection of STH and insulin or of insulin alone, in combination with thymocytes or spleen cells, into (C3H $\times$ CR)F_1 hybrids induces a spleen enlargement which, however, does not seem specific for immunological function because it can be induced by the hormone alone. This shows that insulin, although strongly active in metabolic processes and in inducing enlargement of the spleen, does not influence the immunocompetence of the injected spleen cells or thymocytes.

5. The Most Critical Effect of Hormones is during the Development of the Immune System

Although developmental hormones are present and acting during the whole life of a mammal, we assume that their influence on immunological function is more essential at the time of its ontogenetic development than in the maintenance of an already fully developed immune system. Our assumption is based on the following facts.

(*a*) Anti-pituitary serum induces wasting disease only when given in the first weeks of life; when given later it does not produce any impairment of cellular immunity.

(*b*) Cellular and humoral immunity deficiencies can be observed in dwarf mice, whose hypopituitary condition is present already at birth. Reconstituted dwarf mice can survive many months without losing the immunological functions acquired by the hormonal treatment. Similarly, rats hypophysectomized as adults do not show any immunological deficiencies.

(*c*) Removal of some endocrine glands in rats gives different results depending on whether the operation is performed in adults or in 7-day-old animals. For example, thyroidectomy in

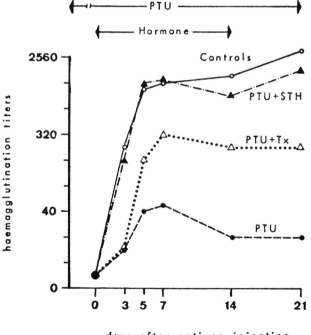

FIGURE 8. Reversal of depressed antibody production to sheep red cells in propyl-thiouracil (PTU)-treated young adult rats by STH or thyroxine. Thyroid function was blocked by 20 days' treatment with PTU. Hormones were given for 14 days, beginning at the time of antigenic challenge.

Developmental Hormones and Maturation 115

adult animals produces only a slight decrease in peripheral white blood cells, while the relative weight of the thymus and skin graft survival are unmodified (Fig. 9). If thyroidectomy is performed in 7-day-old animals, it produces a large decrease in relative thymus weight and in peripheral white blood cells and a significant delay of skin graft survival (Fig. 10).

(*d*) As is suggested by the experiments with the graft-versus-host model (see 3*c*), thymocytes of newborn animals need hormones to acquire their immune capacity.

It should be noted, however, that maturation and differentiation of immunocompetent cells takes place during the whole lifespan. This has been demonstrated by the appearance of immunological deficiencies many months after adult thymectomy or by the impairment of immunological recovery from X-irradiation by animals thymectomized in adult life (Miller, 1965; Metcalf, 1965; Taylor, 1965). In agreement with these observations, recent findings (Duquesnoy, Mariani and Good, 1969; our unpublished data) have shown that the immunological recovery of X-irradiated animals or animals given large doses of cortisol is dependent on the presence of certain endocrine glands. These facts provide further evidence that some hormones are needed for maturation and differentiation of immunocompetent cells, irrespective of the age at which such functional maturation takes place.

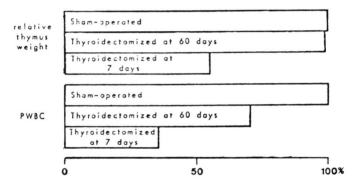

FIGURE 9. Effect of thyroidectomy on relative thymus weight and peripheral white blood cells (PWBC) in Charles River rats. The animals were operated at 7 or 60 days of age or sham-operated. Tests performed at 30 days after operation.

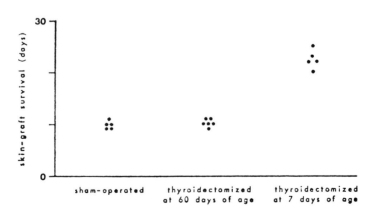

FIGURE 10. Effect of thyroidectomy on skin graft survival in Charles River rats. The animals were operated at 7 or 60 days of age or sham-operated. Skin from Long-Evans donor rats was grafted 30 days after the operation.

Neuroimmunomodulation

Discussion

The experimental data strengthen our view that some hormones, among them chiefly somatotropic hormone, strongly influence or even determine some maturational steps of the immunolymphatic tissue.

Virtually nothing is known yet about the hormone sensitivity of lymphoid cells at various stages of their development or is it clear whether these hormones are mainly promoting lymphocyte proliferation or cell differentiation. It is also conceivable that the regulation of the thymus and thymus-derived cells is subjected to a different hormonal control from other lymphoid cell populations. Evidence for this view comes from our previous work (Pierpaoli and Sorkin, 1968, 1969a; Pierpaoli et al., 1969), work by Mueller, Wolfe and Meyer (1960) and Warner and Burnet (1961) using testosterone in chickens, and by Sherman and Dameshek (1964) employing testosterone and estrogens in hamsters.

How far antigen modifies the hormone sensitivity of lymphoid cells needs also to be determined. Whether somatotropic hormone acts directly on lymphatic tissue or whether its action is mediated through other hormones is unknown.

The use of *in vivo* and *in vitro* systems, in which the specific stage of the hormone dependence of the precursors of antigen-sensitive cells could be established, might permit the identification of a cell population whose evolution needs the presence of some hormones at a certain stage of its differentiation. The debated question of morphological or anatomical cell compartmentation might then be solved on the basis of cellular hormone dependence.

The demonstration that STH strongly influences the development of lymphoid cells which determine delayed hypersensitivities, such as was shown in the reconstitution of dwarf mice, or the STH-induced maturation of newborn thymocytes, suggests new possibilities for the control of a mature immune system.

The ontogenetic approach—that is, the experimental possibility of influencing the functional capacity of lymphoid organs at an early stage of formation—combined with studies on the timing, sequence and mechanisms of action of hormones on the thymo-lymphatic immune system, should eventually permit the development of means to control the adult functional and mature immune system. It opens up a new unexploited means of influencing immunological reactions. Interfering with the processes of immunological maturation with anti-hormone sera, anti-pituitary sera or ideally with specific chemical inhibitors of hormones, might be a new approach to solving the problem of organ transplantation.

Summary

Several propositions have been made on the relation between endocrinological function and immunological maturation and expression of the immune capacity. The perinatal thymus is a target organ of the adenohypophysis. After neonatal thymectomy, thymotropic acidophilic cells in the anterior pituitary were detected by light and electron microscopy. Somatotropic hormone (STH) is a thymotropic hormone, as verified by the STH-sensitivity of the thymus. STH may act directly on thymus cells or by mediating the release of another factor (thymosin?) from these target cells in the manner of a classical hypophysis-target organ relationship. Immunological maturation seems to depend on endocrine function, as was shown by runt disease induced by STH and thyroxine and spleen cells in newborn mice and rats. STH when given together with thymocytes of newborn C3H or Charles River mice produces a graft-versus-host reaction in (C3H × CR)F$_1$ hybrids. The hormone presumably induced immunocompetence in the thymocytes of the newborn donors. Experiments using immunologically deficient hypopituitary dwarf mice suggest that after reconstitution with STH a long-lasting effective cellular immunity is established. Inhibition of thyroid function by antithyrotropic hormone or propyl-thiouracil results in changes in lymphoid tissues and impairment of the immune response. These effects can be reversed by STH or thyroxine. The most critical effect of hormones is at the time of ontogeny of the immune system, but developmental hormones presumably exercise their action throughout the entire mammalian life.

Acknowledgment

This work was supported by the Schweizerische Nationalfonds zur Förderung der wissenschaftlichen Forschung (Grant 3.246.69 SR).

References

Ambrose, C. T. (1964). *J. Exp. Med.* **119**, 1027–1049.

Baroni, C. (1967). *Experientia* **23**, 282–283.

Billingham, R. E. (1968). *Harvey Lect.* **62**, 21–78.

Comsa, J. (1961). *Pflügers Arch. Ges. Physiol.* **272**, 562–574.

Daughaday, W. H., Peake, G. T., Birge, C. A. and Mariz, I. K. (1968). In "Growth Hormone" pp. 238–252, ed. Pecile, A. and Müller, E. E. Amsterdam: Excerpta Medica Foundation. (International Congress Series No. 158.)

Dougherty, T. F., Berliner, M. L., Schneebeli, G. L. and Berliner, D. L. (1964). *Ann. N.Y. Acad. Sci.* **113**, 825–843.

Duquesnoy, R. J., Mariani, T. and Good, R. A. (1969). *Proc. Soc. Exp. Biol. Med.* **132**, 1176–1178.

Ernström, U. and Larsson, B. (1965). *Acta Physiol. Scand.* **64**, 426–433.

Fabris, N., Pierpaoli, W. and Sorkin, E. (1970) In "Developmental Aspects of Antibody Formation and Structure." Prague: Publishing House of the Czechoslovak Academy of Sciences. In press.

Fisher, E. R. (1964). In "The Thymus in Immunobiology" pp. 676–717, ed. Good, R. A. and Gabrielsen, A. E. New York: Harper.

Garcia, J. F. and Geschwind, I. I. (1968) In "Growth Hormone," pp. 267–291, ed. Pecile, A. and Müller, E. E. Amsterdam: Excerpta Medica Foundation. (International Congress Series No. 158.)

Goldstein, A. L., Asanuma, Y., Battisto, J. R., Hardy, M. A., Quint, J. and White, A. (1970). *J. Immun.* **104**, 359–366.

Hollander, V. P., Takakura, K. and Yamada, H. (1968). *Recent Prog. Horm. Res.* **24**, 81–131.

Metcalf, D. (1965). *Nature (London)* **208**, 1336–1337.

Miller, J. F. A. P. (1965). *Nature (London)* **208**, 1337–1338.

Mueller, A. P., Wolfe, H. R. and Meyer, R. K. (1960). *J. Immun.* **85**, 172–179.

Pierpaoli, W., Baroni, C., Fabris, N. and Sorkin, E. (1969). *Immunology* **16**, 217–230.

Pierpaoli, W. and Sorkin, E. (1967a). *Nature (London)* **215**, 834–837.

Pierpaoli, W. and Sorkin, E. (1967b). *Br. J. Exp. Path.* **48**, 627–631.

Pierpaoli, W. and Sorkin, E. (1968). *J. Immun.* **101**, 1036–1043.

Pierpaoli, W. and Sorkin, E. (1969a). In "The Immune Response and its Suppression (*Antibiotica Chemother.* **15**), pp. 122–134, ed. Sorkin, E. Basel: Karger.

Pierpaoli, W. and Sorkin, E. (1969b). In "The Lymphatic Tissue and Germinal Centers in Immune Response" (*Adv. Exp. Med. Biol.* **5**), pp. 397–401, ed. Fiore-Donati, L. and Hanna, M. G. New York: Plenum Press.

Purves, H. D. and Griesbach, W. E. (1946). *Br. J. exp. Path.* **27**, 170–179.

Sherman, J. D. and Dameshek, W. (1964). In "The Thymus in Immunobiology," pp. 542–548, ed. Good, R. A. and Gabrielsen, A. E. New York: Harper.

Simonsen, M. (1962). *Prog. Allergy* **6**, 349–466.

Siperstein, E. R., Nichols, G. W., Griesbach, W. E. and Chaikoff, I. L. (1954). *Anat. Rec.* **118**, 593–620.

Solomon, J. and Greep, R. O. (1959). *Endocrinology* **65**, 158–164.

Taylor, R. B. (1965). *Nature (London)* **208**, 1334–1335.

Warner, N. L. and Burnet, F. M. (1961). *Aust. J. Biol. Sci.* **14**, 580–587.

Wilkinson, P. C., Singh, H. and Sorkin, E. (1970). *Immunology* **18**, 437–441.

Reprinted from "Hormones and the Immune Response" (G.E.W. Wolstenholme and J. Knight, eds.), pp. 126–143. J. & A. Churchill, London, 1970.

14

HORMONAL REGULATION OF THE IMMUNE RESPONSE

I. Induction of an Immune Response *In Vitro* with Lymphoid Cells from Mice Exposed to Acute Systemic Stress

R. H. Gisler, A. E. Bussard, J. C. Mazié, and R. Hess

The effect of exposure of mice to stress, by acceleration and ether anesthesia, on *in vitro* immune responsiveness of their spleen or peritoneal cells, has been studied in different mouse strains. Stress 6, 16, or 24 hr prior to stimulation of explanted lymphoid cells with SRBC *in vitro* leads to suppression of immune reactivity, whereas a time interval of only 15 min resulted in impaired or normal or even enhanced production of PFC's.

By 72 hours, normal levels of immune responsiveness were reestablished. Similar findings were obtained with peritoneal and spleen cells from mice that had been freshly shipped to the laboratory and not given time to acclimatize. The onset and the degree of altered immune responsiveness were related to the mouse strain used and also to the experimental conditions. Histological examination showed a close relationship between depletion of small lymphocytes in the peripheral areas of the follicles and in the marginal zones of the spleen and diminished immune reactivity of the corresponding cell suspensions *in vitro*.

Introduction

While studying primary immune reactions of mouse peritoneal cells and spleen cell suspensions to sheep red blood cells (SRBC) *in vitro*, we observed that cells from recently shipped donors developed fewer plaque-forming cells (PFC) than those from animals that were well acclimatized to the laboratory environment. Situations of stress can induce various reactions that are thought to be mediated by the pituitary-adrenocortical system, such as involution of lymphoid tissue (1–4), leucopenia (5), and abnormal proliferation of plasmacytoid cells (6). It has in fact been suggested that adrenocortical hormones may take part in a homeostatic mechanism that exerts a moderating influence on lymphatic tissue during adult life (7, 8).

Modification of the immune response by stress is implied by a variety of findings. In mice exposed to various stressing procedures (shuttle box, physical restraint, high-intensity sound, electric-shock-avoidance learning) susceptibility to infection by viruses and parasites is increased (9–13). Furthermore, impaired elicitation of active and passive anaphylaxis (14, 15) and suppression of allograft rejection (16) have been reported in mice subjected to crowding or electric-shock-avoidance learning. The severity of delayed hypersensitivity in mice previously sensitized to 1-chloro-2,4,-dinitrobenzene was found to be diminished when the animals were

Reprinted from *Cell. Immunol.* **2**, 634–645, 1971.

exposed to a temperature of 37°C for 1 hr (17). On the other hand, exposure to cold did not appreciably affect the antibody response to various protein antigens in the rabbit (18). The following experiments were undertaken to determine the time-course of stress-induced immunological impairment in an *in vitro* model system. By studying the reactivity of cells taken from previously stressed donor mice it was possible to demonstrate definite changes in the response of spleen cells to SRBC *in vitro*. The spleens used for cell culture showed morphological changes that could be correlated with alterations in *in vitro* immune responsiveness.

Materials and Methods

Animals

Specific pathogen-free male and female mice of strains CBA/H, DBA/2, BD_2/F_1 = (C57Bl × DBA/2)F_1, and F_2D_2/F_1 = (Charles River × DBA/2)F_1, all 8–14 weeks old, were obtained from our animal breeding unit (Tierfarm AG, Sisseln). In preliminary experiments, germ-free CBA/H mice were included. All mice were fed a standardized diet (cubes) and water *ad libitum*.

Two types of stressing procedure were employed. In the first, mice were placed in 100-ml containers with their heads pointing towards the center of a radial centrifuge with an effective operating radius of 30 cm. They were exposed twice to 8 *g* for 10 min, with an interval of 30 min between the two centrifugations.

The second procedure consisted of superficial anesthesia (to the stage of the prenarcotic "etherrausch") performed in a closed vessel containing a cotton pad soaked with ether. At intervals of 15 min and 6, 16, 24, and 72 hr following either procedure the animals were decapitated and spleen cells removed for cell culture.

In Vitro Stimulation of Antibody Formation

The techniques used for the preparation of closed and open cultures of peritoneal cells were those described by Bussard and Lurie (19) and by Nossal *et al.* (20).

Spleen-cell suspensions were prepared and immunized *in vitro* according to the technique of Mishell and Dutton (21). The response of spleen cells to SRBC (direct plaques) was determined by a slide modification of the localized hemolysis-in-gel technique (22).

Organ Weights and Histology

Prior to the preparation of cell suspensions for culture, the wet weights of adrenals, thymus, and spleen were determined, sterile techniques being used for the spleens. Parallel series of spleens were fixed in Carnoy's fluid. From each spleen, 10 representative 7-μm sections were cut and stained with hematoxylin and eosin or with methyl green-pyronine. For planimetric analysis all the sections were projected on paper, and the outlines of the red and white pulp were traced. The delineated areas were cut out and weighed for each spleen. Moreover, in each section every clearly defined germinal center (accumulation of large blastoid cells in the follicular area of the white pulp, containing mitotic figures and tingible body macrophages) was counted.

Statistics

Standard deviations were estimated according to the method of Lord. The significance of the differences between the arithmetical means was determined by Student's *t*-test.

Neuroimmunomodulation

Results

Organ Weights and Histology

At different times after acceleration-stress, spleen, thymus, and adrenals were excised and the wet weights determined. The results are summarized in Table 1. The spleen weights were significantly ($p \leqq 0.01$) reduced 6 and 16 hr following stress. After 24 hr, recovery was practically complete. Significant ($p \leqq 0.01$) thymus involution was observed between 6 and 72 hr after stress. On the other hand, there was a slight increase in the adrenal weights. The organ-weight changes varied to some extent in the different strains of mice examined. The spleen weights of F_2D_2/F_1 mice, for instance, were increased immediately after stress, in contrast to those of the other strains.

As shown in Table 2, a corresponding, though more marked, change in the number of nucleated spleen cells took place. The comparatively lesser reduction in spleen weights may be due to the splenic congestion that was observed 6 and 16 hr after stress, which probably contributed to the organ weight.

Planimetric analysis of histological slides (Table 3) showed a gradually progressive reduction of the red pulp, which was already visible 15 min after cessation of acceleration stress. On the other hand, reduction of the white pulp only became evident after 6 hr.

A strikingly increased number of germinal centers was found early after stress (Fig. 1).

After 6 and 16 hr depletion of small lymphocytes in the peripheral areas of the follicles and in marginal zones was evident (Figs 2 and 3). In contrast, "thymus-dependent" periarteriolar lymphocyte sheaths were not depleted and failed to show any gross alterations. In addition, the sinusoids in the red pulp were dilated and densely packed with erythrocytes. Moveover, as compared with normal controls cellularity of the red pulp appeared to be augmented. This was mainly due to an increase in the number of erythroblastic foci (Fig. 3).

In Vitro Formation of Antibodies to SRBC

*a. Stress Due to Transportation.*In order to substantiate our initial observations, cell donors were transported over a distance of approximately 20 miles 1–2 hr before the experiments were set up. Table 4 illustrates the reactivity of peritoneal-cell preparations as well as spleen-cell suspensions from CBA/H mice that had been stressed under these conditions. The control animals had been left undisturbed after shipment for at least 1 week. The cells from three animals were pooled for each experiment. In most cultures from stressed donors, the number of PFC's was significantly lower than in controls. The considerable differences within the experimental groups presumably reflect varying sensitivity to stress of individual mice.

Although in each experiment peritoneal cells and spleen cells were obtained from the same three donors, there was no strict correlation with respect to the reactivity in the two culture systems. On the other hand, cells from germ-free animals behaved similarly to cells from specific pathogen-free mice.

b. Exposure to Acceleration Stress or Anesthesia. Figure 4 shows the reactivity of spleen-cell cultures prepared at different times after exposure of the cell donors to acceleration stress. In each case, hemolytic plaque assays were performed after the cells had been incubated with antigen for 4 days. Fifteen minutes after stress, the immune reactivity of spleen cells in culture was not impaired in any of the strains tested. On the contrary, F_2D_2/F_1 mice even showed plaque numbers almost twice as high as the nonstressed controls. In individual groups of the other mouse strains enhanced responses were rarely found. Cell cultures prepared 6, 16, and 24 hr after stress revealed a highly significant ($p \leqq 0.01$) reduction in the number of antibody-forming

TABLE 1. Relative Weights of Spleen, Thymus, and Adrenals at Different Times Following Acceleration Stress[a]

Organ	Mouse strain	Controls	Interval between exposure to stress and removal of the organs (hr)				
			0.25	6	16	24	72
Spleen	$F_2 D_2/F_1$	404 ± 32[b]	505 ± 42[c]	339 ± 12[c]	347 ± 25	416 ± 58	395 ± 36
	BD_2/F_1	368 ± 16	346 ± 18	283 ± 14[c]	276 ± 40[c]	324 ± 65	374 ± 28
	DBA/2	412 ± 26	437 ± 25	364 ± 11[c]	276 ± 56[c]	371 ± 62	408 ± 25
	CBA/11	396 ± 30	416 ± 38	317 ± 8[c]	277 ± 42[c]	352 ± 49	403 ± 21
Thymus	$F_2 D_2/F_1$	204 ± 8	208 ± 12	175 ± 18	173 ± 23[c]	173 ± 16[c]	175 ± 15[c]
	BD_2/F_1	204 ± 24	165 ± 35	151 ± 16[c]	143 ± 11[c]	131 ± 24[c]	156 ± 14[c]
	DBA/2	212 ± 36	207 ± 22	170 ± 24	124 ± 26[c]	159 ± 11[c]	163 ± 20
	CBA/11	164 ± 16	165 ± 20	125 ± 9[c]	107 ± 17[c]	138 ± 30	145 ± 33
Adrenals	$F_2 D_2/F_1$	22 ± 3	27 ± 4	24 ± 3	31 ± 4[c]	21 ± 3	23 ± 4
	BD_2/F_1	16 ± 3	21 ± 2	21 ± 1	22 ± 2[c]	16 ± 2	16 ± 2
	DBA/2	18 ± 2	21 ± 2	22 ± 3	20 ± 1	19 ± 2	19 ± 3
	CBA/11	22 ± 3	26 ± 3	28 ± 6	23 ± 1	24 ± 3	22 ± 3

[a]Between 20 and 45 animals were examined per group.
[b]Mean values (mg/100 g body weight) ± standard deviations.
[c]Significant difference from controls ($p < 0.01$).

TABLE 2. Comparison Between Spleen Weight and the Number of Nucleated Cells in F_2D_2/F_1 Mice at Different Times Following Acceleration Stress[a]

Intervals between stress and removal of the spleen (measurements) (hr)	Relative spleen weight (mg/100 g body weight) mean ± SD	n of nucleated cells × 10^6 per spleen mean ± SD
0[b]	420 ± 18	88 ± 14
0.25	483 ± 14[c]	123 ± 21[c]
6	307 ± 28[c]	47 ± 13[c]
16	320 ± 25[c]	64 ± 9[c]
24	372 ± 16[c]	70 ± 15
72	441 ± 20	84 ± 15

[a]Each group consists of 24 mice.
[b]Corresponding to normal control mice.
[c]Significant difference from controls ($p < 0.01$).

TABLE 3. Planimetric Analysis of the Spleen After Acceleration Stress (F_2D_2/F_1 Mice)

Time after exposure to stress (hr)	Red pulp area		White pulp area	
	Arbitrary units[a]	Changes in percentage of controls	Arbitrary units[a]	Changes in percentage of controls
0[b]	10666 ± 1803		3185 ± 325	
0.25	7723 ± 1360[c]	− 27.6	3386 ± 435	+ 6.3
6	6907 ± 695[c]	− 35.3	2127 ± 343[c]	− 33.3
16	5455 ± 819[c]	− 53.3	1238 ± 386[c]	− 61.2

[a]Milligrams paper (mean of 6 spleens; 10 slices per spleen).
[b]Corresponding to normal control mice.
[c]$p < 0.01$.

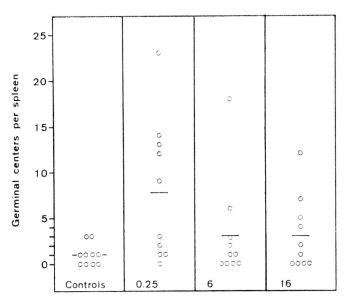

FIGURE 1. Scatterplot of the number of germinal centers in spleen follicles determined at different times following acceleration stress ($F_2D_2F_1$ mice). For each spleen 10 sections were counted. The time intervals in hours between termination of the stress procedure and explantation of the spleens are indicated in the lower left corner. The horizontal bars in each column represent mean values.

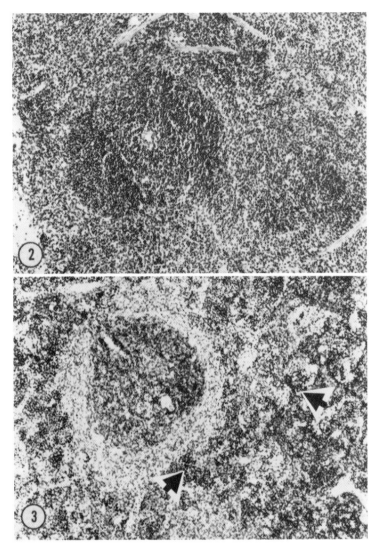

FIGURE 2. Spleen from a normal unstressed mouse. Densely arranged lymphocytes surrounding a central arteriole characterize the white pulp area. Haematoxylin and eosin. × 140.

FIGURE 3. Spleen from a mouse 16 hr after exposure to acceleration stress. Marked depletion of the peripheral follicular areas and the marginal zones. Note the difference between those areas and the spared periarteriolar lymphocyte sheaths. Clusters of erythroblasts in the red pulp are marked with arrows. Haematoxylin and eosin. × 140.

cells. Depending upon the mouse strain used, cell cultures from stressed animals gave 1.5 to 8.5 times fewer PFC's than the normal controls.

A different type of of stress, exposure to ether anesthesia, was applied in a further series of experiments with F_2D_2/F_1 mice. The results are summarized in Fig. 5. Here, impaired reactivity was already observed 15 min after stress. A still more pronounced reduction of PFC's occurred in cultures prepared after 6, 16, and 24 hr. As after acceleration stress, normal responsiveness

TABLE 4. *In Vitro* Response to SRBC of Peritoneal Cells and Spleen Cells from CBA/H Mice. Shipped 1–2 hr Prior to Cell Culture[a]

| | | Peritoneal cells (PFC/10^6) | | | | Spleen cells (96 hrs) (PFC/10^6) | | | |
| | | CMC closed system[b] (72 hrs) | | CMC open system[b] (24 hr) | | Stimulated with SRBC | | Controls without SRBC | |
Expt No	Animals	Control	Stressed	Control	Stressed	Control	Stressed	Control	Stressed
1	Germ free	145	13	630	452	258	62	10	16
2		n.d.[c]	n.d.	110	103	201	138	96	97
3		628	321	972	589	102	39	34	35
4		26	39	274	62	124	36	40	32
5		728	211	890	55	470	439	73	198
6		1107	699	1096	616	n.d.	n.d.	n.d.	n.d.
7	Specific pathogen free	297	46	890	432	122	52	12	28
8		n.d.	n.d.	89	55	278	66	21	35
9		198	26	1013	302	122	68	32	49
10		148	6	267	110	215	105	30	55
11		704	30	876	391	1005	999	163	88
12		1255	545	1431	521	n.d.	n.d.	n.d.	n.d.

[a]The cells from three mice were pooled for each experiment. Spleen cell and peritoneal cell donors are identical for each experimental group.
[b]CMC = carboxymethylcellulose (for local hemolysis in gum; Refs. (19, 20)).
[c]n.d. = Not done.

was restored by 72 hr. These results suggest that the onset and the degree of stress-mediated immune impairment may well depend upon the type of stress procedure used.

In order to determine whether generalized delayed cell death in cultures from stressed donor mice could explain the depressed immune responsiveness, cell recovery after 4 days of incubation was examined (Table 5). However, cultures from stressed donors failed to show a significantly lower degree of cell recovery than cultures from unstressed control mice.

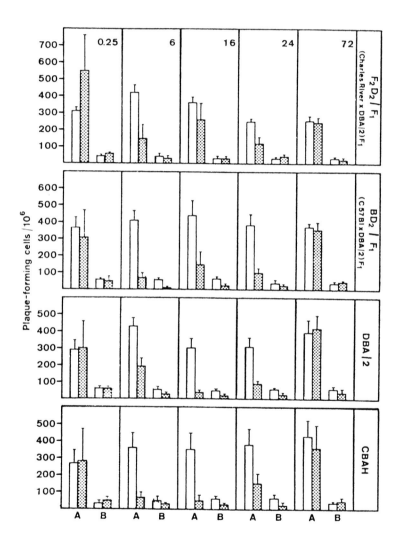

FIGURE 4. *In vitro* response to SRBC of spleen cells from mice exposed to acceleration stress at different times prior to cell culture. Time intervals in hours between termination of the stress procedure and explantation of the spleens for cell culture are indicated in the right upper corner. Each bar represents the mean of the PFC counts from at least 12 independent cell culture experiments. For each cell culture experiment the spleens from three animals were pooled. A, Stimulated with SRBC; B, controls without SRBC; unstressed controls, □; mice submitted to stress, ▨.

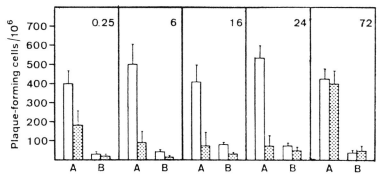

FIGURE 5. *In vitro* response to SRBC of spleen cells from mice exposed to ether anesthesia at different times prior to cell culture. Same legend as Fig. 4.

TABLE 5. Cell Recovery after 4 Days of Incubation with Antigen of Spleen Cell Cultures from Mice Exposed to Acceleration Stress[a]

Time after exposure to stress (hr)	Percentage of cell recovery of the inoculum mean ± SD
0[b]	34.2 ± 6.7
0.25	31.6 ± 6.2
6	28.9 ± 7.0
16	34.0 ± 7.5
24	29.9 ± 5.5
72	35.1 ± 8.0

[a]Between 25–65 cultures were counted per group.
[b]Corresponding to normal control mice.

Discussion

The present experiments indicate that short exposure of mice to acute stress situations significantly alters the immune reactivity *in vitro* of peritoneal cells and of spleen cells. The timing of stress exposure in relationship to stimulation in cell culture is critical. Stress by acceleration or anesthesia of donor animals 6, 16, and 24 hr prior to cell culture regularly leads to suppression of the immune response. Very early after stress, however, immune reactivity is either diminished or normal, or even found to be enhanced. After 72 hr, normal levels of responsiveness were reestablished in all strains examined. The onset and the degree of altered immune reactivity was found to differ between the individual mouse strains tested and also to depend upon the procedure used. The importance of strain differences in this context is demonstrated by the varied pattern of corticosterone response to electric-shock stress in different strains of mice (23).

The exact mechanism by which stress induced changes in immune reactivity of spleen and peritoneal cells is not known. As the number of cells incubated for *in vitro* stimulation is constant and cell recovery after 4 days of incubation was found to be within the range of control cultures from normal unstressed donors, an overall loss of viable cells *in vitro* can be excluded as the major cause of impaired reactivity.

Following stress, enlargement of the adrenals is observed. It would thus appear likely that stress-induced impairment is due to an enhanced adrenocortical secretion. Indeed, it has been shown (24) by other workers that acceleration stress leads to hypersecretion of corticosterone in the rat. According to our own findings, which will be reported in the next paper in this series (25), there is a striking correlation between stress-induced immunosuppression and augmentation of plasma corticosterone levels in the mouse. Moreover, both effects can be readily reproduced by a single injection of ACTH. Nevertheless, it should be noted that the immunosuppressive effect of corticosterone by itself is reported to be weak compared with that evoked by cortisone, cortisol or ACTH (26).

The action of adrenal corticosteroids may also explain some of our histological findings. Spleens from which poorly responding suspensions were harvested, revealed a transitory loss of small lymphocytes from the marginal zones of the red pulp and from the periphery of the follicular areas of the white pulp. These regions have been shown to contain mainly marrow-derived lymphocytes of extrathymic origin (27–30), i.e., cells that are considered to be concerned with antibody synthesis (31). On the other hand, no lymphoid depletion was evident in the periarteriolar lymphocyte sheaths, which contain predominantly thymus-derived lymphocytes (32). This regional cellular deficit may well be due to a selective loss of a steroid-sensitive lymphoid population or to interference with cellular traffic in these areas. Steroids are known to affect mainly short-lived lymphocytes (33–35) which abound in the follicular regions. Moreover, systemic administration of these hormones has been shown to selectively deplete the marginal zones and/or the follicular areas of peripheral lymphoid tissues (33, 35–37).

It is actually postulated that at least two different lymphocyte populations are required for the synthesis of antibodies to SRBC (38, 39). The possibility, therefore, exists that one of them was selectively depleted or metabolically blocked prior to the removal of lymphoid tissue for cell culture. Nevertheless, this interrelation may not apply to the peritoneal cell cultures. For these there is as yet no evidence that two types of cells are involved in the formation of antibodies.

Cell cultures from F_2D_2/F_1 mice that had been exposed to acceleration stress showed an enhanced reactivity to SRBC 15 min after the termination of the stress procedure (i.e., approximately 1 hr after its onset). At the same time, cellularity of the spleen was significantly increased. Moreover, there was an apparently much greater number of well-defined germinal centers in many of the spleens examined. The question, therefore, arises whether these changes constitute the morphological correlation of the enhanced immune responsiveness. Indeed, a decrease in the number of circulating lymphocytes immediately following stress or treatment with ACTH or corticosteroids has been ascribed to a temporary retention of (antigen-reactive?) lymphoid cell in lymphatic tissues (40).

Finally, one rather trivial point might be emphasized on the basis of these results. Animals used for immunological studies should certainly not be exposed to stressful situations before or during experimentation. A quarantine of at least 3 days would appear to constitute the minimum prerequisite for valid and reproducible responses in *in vitro* culture systems.

Acknowledgments

The excellent technical assistance of Miss M. Binkert, Mr. W. Brendlin, Mr. J. Page, Mr. A. Schöpfer, and Mr. E. Strub is gratefully acknowledged. Thanks are also due to Dr. P. Dukor, Dr. L. Schenkel, and Dr. P. Desaulles for helpful discussions.

References

1. Selye, H., *Nature (London)* **138**, 32, 1936.
2. Dougherty, T. F., and White, A., *J. Lab. Clin. Med.* **32**, 584, 1947.
3. Selye, H., "The Physiology and Pathology of Exposure to Stress," Acta, Montreal, 1950.
4. Dougherty, T. F., *Physiol. Rev.* **32**, 379, 1952.
5. Jensen, M. M., *RES J. Reticuloendothel. Soc.* **6**, 457, 1969.
6. Hirata-Hibi, M. *RES J. Reticuloendothel. Soc.* **4**, 370. 1967.
7. Dougherty, T. F., Berliner, M. L., Schneebeli, G. L., and Berliner, D. L., *Ann. N.Y. Acad. Sci.* **113**, 825, 1964.
8. Ernström, W., *Acta Pathol. Microbiol. Scand. Suppl.* **178**, 1965.
9. Shwartzman, G., Aronson, S. M., Teodoru, C. V., Adler, M., and Jahiel, R., *Ann N.Y. Acad. Sci.* **61**, 869, 1955.
10. Rasmussen, A. F., Jr., Marsh, J. T., and Brill, N. Q., *Proc. Soc. Exp. Biol. Med.* **96**, 183, 1957.
11. Davis, D. E., and Read, C. P., *Proc. Soc. Exp. Biol. Med.* **99**, 269, 1958.
12. Johnson, T., Lavender, J. F., and Marsh, J. T., *Fed. Proc. Fed Amer. Soc. Exp. Biol.* **18**, 575, 1959.
13. Jensen, M. M., and Rasmussen, A. F., Jr., *J. Immunol.* **90**, 21, 1963.
14. Rasmussen, A. F., Jr., Spencer, E. S., and Marsh, J. T., *Proc. Soc. Exp. Biol. Med.* **100**, 878, 1959.
15. Treadwell, P. E., and Rasmussen, A. F., Jr., *J. Immunol.* **87**, 492, 1961.
16. Wistar, R., and Hildemann, W. H., *Science* **131**, 159, 1960.
17. Pitkin, D. H., *Proc. Soc. Exp. Biol. Med.* **120**, 350, 1966.
18. Northey, W. T., *J. Immunol.* **94**, 649, 1965.
19. Bussard, A. E., and Lurie, M., *J. Exp. Med.* **125**, 873, 1967.
20. Nossal, G. J. V., Bussard, A. E., Lewis, H., and Mazié, J. C., *J. Exp. Med.* **131**, 894, 1970.
21. Mishell, R. I., and Dutton, R. W., *J. Exp. Med.* **126**, 423, 1967.
22. Berglund, K., *Nature (London)* **204**, 89, 1964.
23. Levine, S., and Treiman, D. M., *Endocrinology* **75**, 142, 1964.
24. Oyama, J., and Platt, W. T., *Endocrinology* **76**, 203, 1965.
25. Gisler, R. H., and Schenkel-Hulliger, L., *Cell. Immunol.* **2**, 646–657.
26. Medawar, P. B., and Sparrow, E. M., *J. Endocrinol.* **14**, 240, 1956.
27. Dukor, P., Bianco, C., and Nussenzweig, V., *Proc. Nat. Acad. Sci.* **67**, 991, 1970.
28. Dukor, P., Bianco, C., and Nussenzweig, V., **2**, *Europ. J. Immunol.* (In press).
29. Gutman, G., Weissmannn, I. L., *In* "Proceedings of the International Conference on Lymphatic Tissue and Germinal Centers, 3rd," Upsala, 1970. Plenum, New York (in press).
30. Parrott, D. M. V., and de Sousa, M. A. B., *Clin. Exp. Immunol.* **8**, 663, 1971.
31. Miller, J. F. A. P., and Mitchell, G. F., *Transplant. Rev.* **1**, 3, 1969.
32. Parrott, D. M. V., de Sousa, M. A. B., and East, J., *J. Exp. Med.* **123**, 191, 1966.
33. Craddock, C. G., Winkelstein, A., Matsuyuki, Y., and Lawrence, J. S., *J. Exp. Med.* **125**, 1149, 1967.
34. Miller, J. J., and Cole, L. J., *J. Exp. Med.* **126**, 109, 1967.
35. Esteban, J. N., *Anat. Rec.* **162**, 349, 1968.
36. Dukor, P., and Dietrich, F. M., *In* "Lymphatic Tissue and Germinal Centers in Immune Response" (L. Fiore-Donati and M. G. Hanna Jr., Eds.), p. 387. Plenum, New York, 1969.
37. Van den Broek, A. A., Kramer, M., and Wubbena, A., *In* "Proceedings of the International Conference on Lymphatic Tissue and Germinal Centers, 3rd," Upsala, 1970. Plenum, New York (in press).
38. Claman, H. N., Chaperon, E. A., and Triplett, R. F., *Proc. Soc. Exp. Biol. Med.* **122**, 1167, 1966.
39. Claman, H. N., and Chaperon, E. A., *Transpl. Rev.* **1**, 92, 1969.
40. Schnappauf, H., and Schnappauf, U., *Nouv., Rev. Fr. Hématol.* **8**, 555, 1968.

15

HORMONAL REGULATION OF THE IMMUNE RESPONSE

II. Influence of Pituitary and Adrenal Activity on Immune Responsiveness *In Vitro*

R. H. Gisler and Lotte Schenkel-Hulliger

Exposure of mice to acceleration stress, ether anesthesia or injection of adrenocorticotropic hormone (ACTH) resulted in a transitory increase of plasma corticosterone concentrations. Spleen cells explanted at the moment of increased levels of corticosteroids reacted poorly to antigen *in vitro*. Adrenalectomy of the cell donors did not affect the immune reactivity of spleen cell cultures, nor did ACTH show any effect in adrenalectomized mice. On the other hand, hypophysectomy of the cell donors led to a persistent depression of the immune response. Treatment of hypophysectomized animals with somatotropic hormone (STH) prior to cell culture resulted in an almost normal immune capacity. Moreover, subsequent ACTH treatment no longer impaired immune reactivity, although it effectively increased plasma corticosterone levels. It is concluded that recovery from corticosteroid-induced depression of immune reactivity is accelerated in the presence of somatotropic hormone. In hypophysectomized animals exogenous somatotropic hormone can interfere with the effect of increased endogenous corticosterone.

Introduction

Different hormonal systems are known to have a regulatory function on lymphoid tissues and to influence the maturation, magnitude, and quality of the immune response. Thus, adrenal cortical steroids as well as adrenocorticotropic hormone (ACTH) inhibit antibody synthesis and reduce ongoing production of antibody (1–3). On the other hand, somatotropic hormone (STH) seems to be essential for the immunological maturation and also for the expression of the immune capacity (4–6). Various noxious (stressful) stimuli activate the hypothalamic-pituitary-adrenal system, thus raising the level of plasma corticosteroids (7). In addition, the simultaneous release of STH under such conditions has been reported (8).

So far, hormonal influences on immunologic activity have been studied mainly in whole animals, in which complex homeostatic regulations tend to obscure the primary biological events. Therefore, an *in vitro* model was chosen in which immunologic reactivity of lymphoid cells explanted at various times after stress or treatment with ACTH could be determined under stable hormonal conditions. Impairment of the immune reactivity of spleen cell cultures due to previous exposure of the donor mice to stress has been described in the preceding paper (9). In the following communication we present the results of a more detailed study on the effect of

Reprinted from *Cell. Immunol.* **2**, 646–657, 1971.

stress or ACTH on the immune reactivity of spleen cells *in vitro*. Blood for plasma corticosterone determination was collected in donor animals at the time of spleen explantation. In addition, donor animals were adrenalectomized, hypophysectomized, and treated with ACTH and STH before harvesting cells for culture. Levels of plasma corticosterone concentration were inversely proportional to the impairment of immune responsiveness *in vitro*. Furthermore, evidence will be presented which indicates that the inhibitory action of corticosteroids is antagonized by STH.

Materials and Methods

Experimental Procedures in Animals

Specific pathogen-free male and female BD_2/F_1 = (C57Bl × DBA/2) F_1 mice, 8–14 weeks old, weighing 18–25 g, were obtained from our animal breeding unit. They were kept under standard housing conditions, fed a standardized diet, and given water *ad libitum*.

The sequence of experimental procedures for the different groups is summarized in Fig. 1. Stress was induced 15 min and 1, 6, and 16 hr prior to spleen explantation for culture. For groups A and B the stressing procedure consisted of exposure to acceleration or to ether anesthesia as described in detail in the previous paper (9), whereas for all the other groups a single subcutaneous injection of 0.3 mg/kg adrenocorticotropic hormone, ACTH (Tetracosactide, Synacthen, CIBA), was given. This dose was known to stimulate corticosterone production to a maximum level after approximately 1 hr in rats. The animals in groups D–G were adrenalectomized and/or hypophysectomized prior to the injection of ACTH. Based on our previous experience (9), time intervals of at least 3 days were allowed between the operation and ACTH injection to ensure complete recovery of the animals from surgical stress.

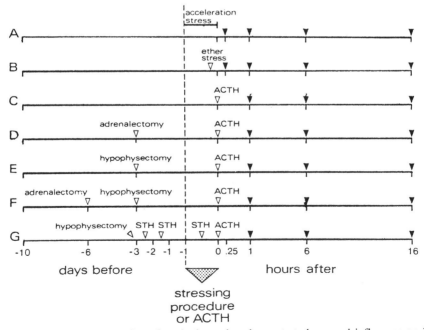

FIGURE 1. Schematic presentation of methods used to demonstrate hormonal influences on immune reactivity. At time 0 the stressing procedures were finished (groups A and B) or exogenous ACTH was injected (groups C–G). ▼ = time of spleen cell explantation for cell culture.

Adrenalectomy was performed under ether narcosis according to the standard procedures described for the rat (10). After the operation the animals were supplied with drinking water containing 1% saline. At autopsy completeness of adrenalectomy was checked. Incompletely adrenalectomized animals were excluded from the experiments.

Hypophysectomy was performed under ether narcosis according to the standard procedures described for the rat (11). Completeness of hypophysectomy was checked by necropsy inspection of the pituitary fossa. Detectable remnants of the hypophysis coincided with detectable amounts of corticosterone in the plasma; such animals were excluded from the experiments.

The mice of group G were injected intraperitoneally with bovine somatotropic hormone (NIH-GH-B4 and NIH-GH-B6, kindly donated by the Endocrinology Study Unit of the NIH, Bethesda, Md.) with either 3 mg/kg once or 15 mg/kg twice daily during the 3 days prior to ACTH injection.

The animals were decapitated and blood was collected for corticosterone determination. Since the adrenal activity of mice follows a circadian rhythm (12), the experiments were performed at the same hours of the day, in order to avoid additional variation in the corticosterone levels.

In Vitro Stimulation of Antibody Formation to Sheep Red Blood Cells (SRBC)

Spleen cell suspension cultures were prepared and immunized with SRBC in vitro according to the technique of Mishell and Dutton (13). The number of plaque-forming cells (PFC) against SRBC (direct plaques) was determined after 4 days of incubation by a modification of the localized hemolysis-in-gel technique (14).

Corticosterone Determination

Plasma corticosterone levels were determined in 20–50 μl of heparinized blood from individual mice by a fluorimetric method (15) or by a competitive protein-binding technique (16). With the fluorimetric method corticosterone concentrations as low as 0.005 μg per sample can be detected. As with other fluorimetric techniques a nonspecific background fluorescence due to the presence of other steroids (mainly cholesterol) is obtained. Thus, the sera of adrenalectomized and hypophysectomized animals, which are almost devoid of corticosterone, gave values of 0.12 (SE: 0.007) and 0.09 μg/ml (SE: 0.01), respectively.

The competitive protein-binding method detects as little as 0.0002 μg corticosterone per sample and is highly specific. Using this procedure, the plasma corticosterone levels of adrenalectomized and hypophysectomized animals were found to be 0.015 (SE: 0.004) and 0.014 μg/ml (SE: 0.007), respectively.

Results

The Effect of Stress or ACTH in Intact Animals

Mice were exposed to stress by acceleration or ether anesthesia, or injected with a single dose of ACTH. As indicated in Fig. 1 (A–C) spleen cells were taken for culture 15 min, 6 hr and 16 hr later and stimulated with SRBC in vitro.

Spleen cells from animals submitted to acceleration stress and cultured 6 or 16 hr after the termination of the stressing procedure revealed a clear-cut decrease in the number of plaque-forming cells (PFC). The plasma corticosterone levels of the donor mice were increased 15 min after termination of the stressing procedure (*i.e.*, 1 hr after its onset) and from then on declined only slowly (Fig. 2).

Ether anesthesia resulted in a similar, but slightly more pronounced, depressive effect (Fig. 3). Under these conditions, however, impairment of immune reactivity was already evident 15 min after the termination of stress. It was accompanied by a pronounced and early increase in the plasma corticosterone levels. In animals tested 16 hr after ether or acceleration stress the number of PFC's at the end of the culture period was still below the corresponding control values.

The injection of ACTH into cell donors resulted in a pronounced but shortlasting depression of immune reactivity, which coincided with a marked increase in corticosterone levels after 1 hr (Fig. 4). At 6 and 16 hr immune responsiveness as well as the concentrations of plasma corticosterone were within the same range as in the untreated controls.

Obviously there was an inverse relationship between corticosterone levels in the plasma of donor mice and the subsequent immune performance of their spleen cells *in vitro*. Upon comparison of the three types of adrenocortical stimulation (acceleration stress, ether anesthesia, and ACTH injection) some variation in the temporal course of immune reactivity and corticosterone levels could be observed.

The Effect of Adrenalectomy

To further substantiate the relationship between adrenalcortical function and immune reactivity, cell donor mice were adrenalectomized prior to the injection of ACTH (Fig. 1D). Under these conditions, ACTH had no effect on plasma corticosterone levels or antibody synthesis

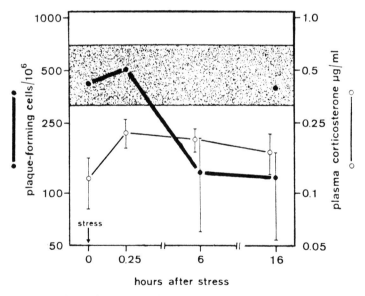

FIGURE 2. *In vitro* reactivity of spleen cells from mice exposed to acceleration stress (compare with Fig 1A) prior to cell collection; number of plaque-forming cells/10^6 spleen cells (—●—); concentration of plasma corticosterone in donor mice measured by the fluorimetric micromethod (15) at the time of spleen explantation for cell culture (—○—). The number of plaque-forming cells was determined after 4 days of incubation with SRBC. Each point represents the mean (± SD) of 10 independent cell culture experiments. The grey area delineates the range of plaque-forming cells in cultures from unstressed control mice.

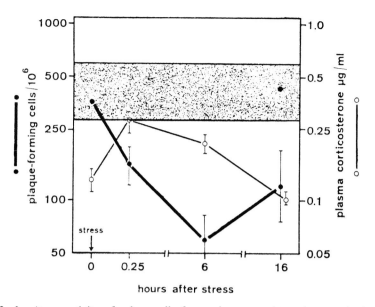

FIGURE 3. *In vitro* reactivity of spleen cells from mice exposed to ether anesthesia prior to cell collection (compare with Fig. 1B). Same legend as Fig. 2.

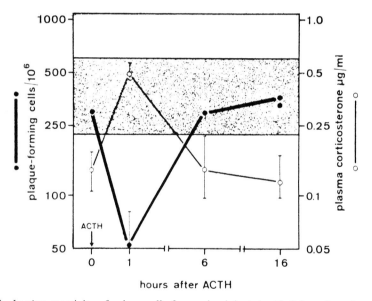

FIGURE 4. *In vitro* reactivity of spleen cells from mice injected with 0.3 mg/kg adrenocorticotropic hormone prior to cell collection (compare with Fig. 1D). Same legend as Fig. 2.

(Fig. 5). In fact, plasma corticosterone levels when determined by the competitive proteinbinding method were at the lower limit of detectability (0.016 µg; SE = 0.004).

In order to evaluate the long-term effect of adrenalectomy, spleen cell cultures from adrenalectomized animals were set up 1–16 days after the operation (Fig. 6). Decreased responsiveness was found only in cultures prepared 24 hr after adrenalectomy, which was most certainly due to surgical stress. Cultures prepared later responded like those from unoperated controls.

The Effect of Hypophysectomy on Normal and on Previously Adrenalectomized Animals

Hypophysectomy had a dramatic effect on the reactivity of spleen cells (Figs. 7a and 8). Mice hypophysectomized 3 days prior to cell culture (Fig. 1E) revealed a pronounced impairment of immune responsiveness *in vitro* (Fig. 8), although the donor animals had low plasma corticosterone levels (Table 1, top line). This finding was rather surprising as the animals should have recovered from the surgical stress by this time. Furthermore, markedly impaired immune responsiveness still persisted 16 hr after injection of saline or of ACTH (Figs. 7a and 9). In contrast, cultures from control animals receiving the same dose of ACTH responded normally by this time (Fig. 4). In addition, cell cultures from mice adrenalectomized prior to hypophysectomy (Fig. 1F) developed normal numbers of PFC (Fig. 7a).

We conclude from these experiments that the hypophysis plays an obligatory role in the recovery of the immune system from stress (corticosteroid)-induced impairment. Therefore, in a further series of experiments, the effect of treatment with STH following hypophysectomy on subsequent *in vitro* stimulation was investigated.

The Effect of STH on Hypophysectomized Animals

As before, mice were hypophysectomized 3 days prior to cell culture. During the time interval between the operation and spleen explantation for cell culture they were treated with either saline or with a total dose of 0.18 or 1.8 mg STH, which is well above physiological levels in mouse plasma. Considering the short half-life of STH, however, this dosage is close to the total amount of STH secreted per day. (Fig. 1G). This treatment resulted in a dose-dependent restoration of immune reactivity (Fig. 8). From the group pretreated with 0.18 mg STH only a few cultures produced normal numbers of PFC, whereas almost all cultures from mice pretreated with 1.8 mg STH were found to respond as control cultures. Animals pretreated

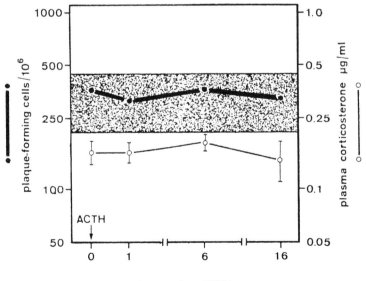

FIGURE 5. *In vitro* reactivity of spleen cells from adrenalectomized donor mice treated with 0.3 mg/kg adrenocorticotropic hormone prior to cell collection (compare with Fig. 1D). Same legend as Fig. 2.

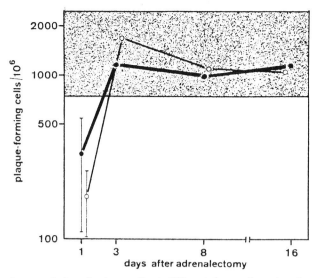

FIGURE 6. *In vitro* reactivity of spleen cells at different times after adrenalectomy of donor mice. —●— = adrenalectomized animals; —○— = sham-operated animals. The grey area delineates the range of plaque-forming cells in cultures from intact control mice after 4 days of incubation with SRBC.

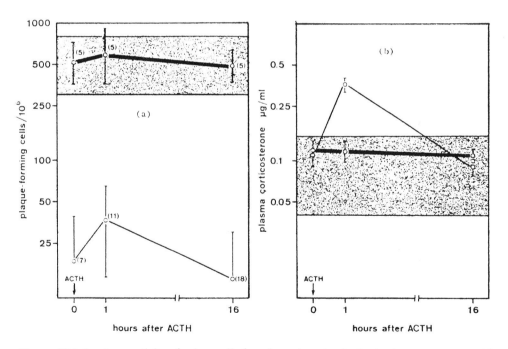

FIGURE 7(a) *In vitro* reactivity of spleen cells from hypophysectomized mice (—○—; compare with Fig. 1E) and from mice adrenalectomized prior to hypophysectomy (—●—; compare with Fig. 1F). Both groups of mice were injected with 0.3 mg/kg adrenocorticotropic hormone prior to cell culture. The grey area delineates the range of plaque-forming cells in cultures from corresponding untreated control mice. Near each point on the curve the number of independent cell culture experiments is indicated. (b) Plasma corticosterone levels of mice used for cell culture experiments shown in Fig. 7a measured by the fluorimetric micromethod (15). The grey area delineates the range of plasma corticosterone levels in intact untreated mice.

Hormonal Regulation of Immune Response 139

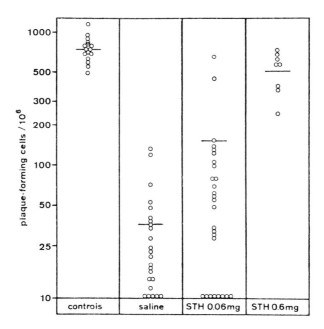

FIGURE 8. The effect of somatotropic hormone treatment of hypophysectomized cell donors (compare with Fig. 1G). Number of antibody-forming cells in 4-day-old spleen cell cultures stimulated with SRBC. The horizontal bars denote mean values. The groups treated with saline or STH are hypophysectomized.

TABLE 1. The Effect of Treatment with ACTH and STH on Corticosterone Levels in Hypophysectomized Donor Mice

Treatment	Spleen explantation; hours after ACTH injection	Plasma corticosterone (μg/ml)			
		Fluorometric determination		Protein binding assay	
		n	mean $\pm$ SE	n	mean $\pm$ SE
Saline		26	0.09 $\pm$ 0.01	9	0.014 $\pm$ 0.007
ACTH[a]	1	12	0.36 $\pm$ 0.03	3	0.147 $\pm$ 0.027
ACTH[a]	16	18	0.09 $\pm$ 0.01		n.d.[d]
STH[b]		29	0.08 $\pm$ 0.01	28	0.008 $\pm$ 0.002
STH[b] + ACTH[a]	1	5	0.22 $\pm$ 0.06	5	0.148 $\pm$ 0.060
STH[b] + ACTH[a]	16	17	0.10 $\pm$ 0.02		n.d.
Controls		20	0.14 $\pm$ 0.01		n.d.

[a]ACTH 0.3 mg/kg s.c.
[b]STH 3 mg/kg daily from day −3 to −1, day 0 being the day of spleen explantation.
[c]Intact untreated mice.
[d]n.d., not done.

with STH and injected thereafter with ACTH would be expected to show raised corticosterone levels and therefore a depressed immune responsiveness (Table 1, line 5). Surprisingly, the latter did not occur. Pretreatment with STH prevented the immunosuppressive effect of the subsequent injection of ACTH, although the usual rise in plasma corticosteroids could readily be induced (Fig. 9).

Neuroimmunomodulation

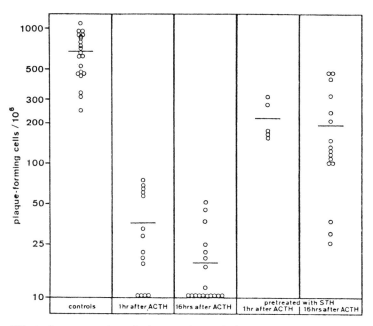

FIGURE 9. Effect of somatotropic and adrenocorticotropic hormone treatment in hypophysectomized cell-donor animals on the *in vitro* reactivity of spleen cells to SRBC (compare with Fig. 1G). *In vitro* reactivity of spleen cells to SRBC (number of antibody-forming cells in 4-day-old cultures). The horizontal bars denote mean values. The groups treated with ACTH or ACTH + STH are hypophysectomized.

Discussion

From the experiments reported in this communication it is evident that in the *in vitro* system used the number of antibody-forming spleen cells is inversely related to the plasma corticosterone level in donor mice. This conclusion is further supported by the observed effects of adrenalectomy in donor mice; the inhibitory effect of ACTH on immune reactivity is abolished by previous removal of the adrenals. Hypophysectomy, on the other hand, leads to a persistent depression of immune capacity. This may be explained by an initial secretion of ACTH due to ether anesthesia and surgical stress; however, in the absence of the hypophysis immunological recovery is absent or much delayed, whereas in its presence, the transitory depressant effect of stress or ACTH is apparently compensated after a relatively short time.

These results indicate that a pituitary factor is necessary for the reconstitution of immune reactivity after its depression by corticosteroids. In fact, repeated injections of STH could almost completely mimic the restorative effect of the hypophysis. We therefore assume that in the intact animal immunosuppression by corticosteroids is counterbalanced by STH.

The simultaneous release of STH and ACTH in various types of stress (17) may represent a regulatory mechanism. Furthermore, it has been demonstrated that increased levels of STH are induced by the injection of exogenous ACTH (18, 19). So far this has been investigated in man only. However, while the rate of secretion of ACTH appears to be fairly consistent, the release of STH seems to vary with different stimuli (17). This may explain the differences between recovery from acceleration stress, ether stress, or ACTH-induced impairment of immune reactivity which have been encountered in the present study.

Our findings on the effect of STH agree with an early report on its ability to antagonize the immunosuppressive properties of ACTH when the two substances are injected simultaneously (20). Furthermore, it has been demonstrated that cortisol-induced immunosuppression in adult mice can be reversed by treatment with STH prior to immunization (5). It has been suggested that a critical balance between the amount of cortisol injected and STH must be achieved to ensure complete restoration of immune reactivity. This is in agreement with the dose dependency of the STH effect found in our experiments. Further evidence indicating that a pituitary factor plays an important part has been obtained in young hypophysectomized rats, in which the recovery of antibody formation and allograft rejection after sublethal irradiation was defective (21).

In addition, the importance of somatotropic and luteotropic hormone during the ontogenic development of immune responsiveness has repeatedly been emphasized, and a functional relationship between the hypophysis and the development of the thymus has been postulated (6, 22). This was most clearly demonstrated for autosomal recessive pituitary dwarf mice (4, 23–25). Moreover, thymocytes of newborn mice pretreated *in vitro* with STH were shown to evoke a graft-versus-host reaction when injected into a histoincompatible newborn recipient (5).

Other workers, however, have described unchanged immune responsiveness to SRBC in young rats which had been hypophysectomized 5 days prior to immunization (26). The serum antibody titers were determined between 9 and 27 days after hypophysectomy, an interval which we have not covered in our experiments. We therefore cannot exclude the possibility that after hypophysectomy a slow restoration of immune capacity may still take place. Such a recovery might possibly be induced by small amounts of thyroxine excreted after hypophysectomy (27).

The cellular level at which corticosteroids and STH operate has not yet been clarified. The effect of corticosteroids may already be expressed in cell donors due to a selective elimination of a steroid-sensitive cell type required for the synthesis of antibody. In fact, some evidence for such a mechanism was provided by the histological studies of spleens from stressed mice as described in the preceding paper (9). On the other hand, cell-bound corticosteroids carried over from donor animals might continue to act on cell metabolism *in vitro*. As corticosteroids are known to interfere with the metabolism of most cells generally through a decrease in the turnover of glucose, amino acids, and nucleotides (28, 29), such an effect might be rather nonspecific.

The opposite seems to be true of STH, which presumably increases the uptake of glucose, amino acids, and nucleotides, as demonstrated for the rate of DNA synthesis in the spleen of immature rats treated with STH (30). This also agrees with our finding that treatment of hypophysectomized animals with 0.6 mg of STH results in a slight but significant ($p < .05$) increase in average spleen cell numbers. However, there was no correlation between cell numbers in the spleen and the immune performance of cell suspensions *in vitro*.

STH as well as corticosteroids may act on the same basic mechanism of cellular metabolism, though in an opposite way. The surprising ineffectiveness of ACTH in hypophysectomized animals pretreated with STH on spleen cells lasts considerably longer than one would expect from the short half-life of the injected STH.

All the evidence indicates that the secretion of STH in response to exogenous ACTH has a regulatory function in the maintenance of immune reactivity. However, further analysis of the mode of action of STH and corticosteroids is needed to elucidate the phenomena described.

Acknowledgments

The authors thank Miss M. Binkert, Mr. W. Brendlin, Miss W. Liebig, Mr. J. Page, Mrs. H. Schellenberg, and Mr. E. Strub for their expert technical assistance. The establishment of the art of hypophysectomy in mice is the merit of Mr. H. Hänni. Thanks are also due to Dr. P. A. Desaulles, Dr. F. M. Dietrich, and Dr. P. Dukor for helpful discussions.

References

1. Gabrielson, A. E., and Good, R. A., *Advan. Immunol.* **6,** 109, 1967.
2. Dukor, P., and Dietrich, F. M., *Int. Arch. Allergy Appl. Immunol.* **34,** 32, 1968.
3. Elliott, E. V., and Sinclair, N. R. St C., *Immunology* **15,** 643, 1968.
4. Pierpaoli, W., Baroni, C., Fabris, N., and Sorkin, E., *Immunology* **16,** 217, 1969.
5. Fabris, N., Pierpaoli, W., and Sorkin, E., *In* "Developmental Aspects of Antibody Formation and Structure" (J. Sterzl and I. Riha, Eds.), Vol. 1, pp. 79–95. Academia Publishing House of the Czechoslovak Academy of Sciences, Prague, 1970.
6. Pierpaoli, W., Fabris, N., and Sorkin, E., *In* "Hormones and the Immune Response" (G. E. Wolstenholme and J. Knight, Eds.), pp. 126–153. Churchill, London, 1970.
7. Sayers, G., and Sayers, M. A., *Endocrinology* **40,** 265, 1947.
8. Glick, S. M., Roth, J., Yalow, R. S., and Berson, S. A,. *Recent Progr. Horm. Res.* **21,** 241, 1965.
9. Gisler, R. H., Bussard, A. E., Mazié, J. C., and Hess, R., *Cell Immunol.* **2,** 000–000 1971.
10. Ingle, D. J., and Griffith, J. Q., *In* "The Rat in Laboratory Investigation" (E. J. Farris and J. Q. Griffith, Eds.), p. 444. Lippincott, Philadelphia, 1949.
11. Smith, P. G., *Amer. J. Anat.* **45,** 205, 1930.
12. Ungar, F., and Halberg, F., *Science* **137,** 1058, 1962.
13. Mishell, R. I., and Dutton, R. W., *J. Exp. Med.* **126,** 423, 1967.
14. Berglund, K., *Nature London* **204,** 89, 1964.
15. Glick, B., Redlich, D., and Levine, S., *Endocrinology* **74,** 653, 1964
16. Murphy, B. E. P., *J. Clin. Endocrinol. Metab.* **27,** 973, 1967.
17. Yalow, R. S., Varsano-Aharon, N., Echemendia, E., and Berson, S. A., *Horm. Metab. Res.* **1,** 3, 1969.
18. Zahnd, G. R., Nadeau, A., and von Mühledahl, K. E., *Lancet* **2,** 1278, 1969.
19. Strauch, G., Pandos, P., Luton, J. P., and Bricaire, H., *Ann. Endocrinol.,* in press.
20. Hayashida, T., and Li, C. H., *J. Exp. Med.* **105,** 93, 1957.
21. Duquesnoy, R. J., Mariani, T., and Good, R. A., *Proc. Soc. Exp. Biol. Med.* **131,** 1176, 1969.
22. Pierpaoli, W., and Sorkin, E., *Nature London* **215,** 834, 1967.
23. Baroni, C., *Experientia* **23,** 282, 1967.
24. Baroni, C., Fabris, N., and Bertoli, G., *Experientia* **23,** 1059, 1967.
25. Duquesnoy, R. J., Kalpaktsoglou, P. K., and Good, R. A., *Proc. Soc. Exp. Biol. Med.* **133,** 201, 1970.
26. Kalden, J. R., Evans, M. M., and Irvine, W. J., *Immunology* **18,** 671, 1970.
27. Rawson, R. W., Rall, J. E., and Sonenberg, M., *Hormones* **3,** 455, 1955.
28. Makman, M. H., Nakagawa, S., and White, A., *Recent Progr. Horm. Res.* **23,** 195, 1967.
29. Makman, M. H., Nakagawa, S., Dvorkin, B., and White, A., *J. Biol. Chem.* **245,** 2256, 1970.
30. Fast, D. K., Garland, M., Thomson M., and Richards, J. F., *Exp. Cell Res.* **62,** 441, 1970.

16

CHOLINERGIC AUGMENTATION OF LYMPHOCTYE-MEDIATED CYTOTOXICITY. A STUDY OF THE CHOLINERGIC RECEPTOR OF CYTOTOXIC T LYMPHOCYTES
(cGMP/Muscarinic Agents/Nicotinic Agents)

Terry B. Strom, Arthur J. Sytkowski, Charles B. Carpenter, and John P. Merrill

ABSTRACT Cholinergic agonists have previously been shown to augment the ability of sensitized lymphocytes to injure; cells bearing the sensitizing alloantigens. The cholinergic receptor of the attacking lymphocyte population has been studied with pharmacological manipulation of an *in vitro* system that quantitates the injury mediated by sensitized attacking cells upon target cells. The data reveal that muscarinic ligands are several orders of magnitude more potent than nicotinic agents in altering cytotoxicity.

Mice transplanted with histoincompatible grafts develop thymus-derived (T) lymphocytes which are selectively cytotoxic *in vitro* for cells bearing donor transplantation antigens (lymphocyte-mediated cytotoxicity or LMC) (1, 2). In a similar *in vitro* system, rats have been demonstrated to develop cytotoxic lymphocytes post-transplantation (3). Since the cytotoxic rat lymphoid cells do not adhere to glass bead columns (unpublished observation) or bear easily detectable surface immunoglobulin (4), it seems reasonable to assume that the effector cell is also a T lymphocyte. A variety of metabolic inhibitors (5–10) and increased intracellular levels of adenosine $3':5'$-cyclic monophosphate (cyclic AMP) (3, 4, 11, 12) inhibit the ability of sensitized T cells to injure appropriate histoincompatible target cells; however, cholinergic agonists (3, 4) and 8-bromo guanosine $3':5'$-cyclic monophosphate (8-bromo cyclic GMP) (4) have been found to enhance cytotoxicity. Since cholinergic stimulation of a variety of tissues (13–19), including lymphocytes, (18, 19) results in increased intracellular levels of cyclic GMP, these data indicate that the intracellular concentration of cyclic GMP, acting as a classical second messenger, is important in determining the extent of cytotoxicity, as is the level of cyclic AMP. The effect of cyclic GMP upon cytotoxicity has been shown to be upon the attacking lymphocyte population at the moment of initial attacking and target cell interaction (4).

Cholinergic receptors, classically designated muscarinic and nicotinic, have been differentiated by the use of agents which stimulate or block these receptors. It was previously shown that cholinergic augmentation of LMC was blocked by atropine (3). Although atropine is considered a muscarinic antagonist, several studies indicate that atropine can interact with nicotinic receptors (20–25), i.e., those found on skeletal muscle (20–24) and sympathetic neurons (25). In this study, the cholinergic receptor of the attacking lymphocyte (cyto-

toxic T lymphocytes) population has been studied using pharmacologic manipulation of LMC. The results reveal that both muscarinic and nicotinic antagonists inhibit cholinergic augmentation of LMC; however, muscarinic ligands are two to three orders of magnitude more potent.

MATERIALS AND METHODS

Carbamylcholine chloride, atropine sulfate, *d*-tubocurarine chloride, and hexamethonium bromide were purchased from Sigma Chemical Co., St. Louis, Mo.; tetramethylammonium chloride was purchased from Aldrich Chemical Co., Milwaukee, Wisc.; RPMI-1640 medium and fetal-calf serum were purchased from Grand Island Biological Co.; Grand Island, N.Y. α-Bungarotoxin (α-BGT) was purified and tested for biologic activity as described previously (23). Male Lewis, Brown Norway (BN) and Lewis × Brown Norway F_1 (LBN) rats were purchased from Microbiological Associates, Bethesda, Md. LMC was determined by a modification of the technique of Brunner *et al.* (26) as previously reported (3, 4). In brief, splenocytes were explanted from Lewis rats sensitized 7 days previously with an LBN skin allograft. The sensitized Lewis splenocytes were used as attacking cells, and ^{51}Cr-labeled BN thymocytes served as target cells. Cytotoxicity was quantitated by ^{51}Cr release from attacking cell and target cell mixtures after 4 hr of incubation at 37°. Pharmacologic agents diluted in *N*-2-hydroxyethylpiperazine-*N'*-2-ethanesulfonic acid (Hepes)-buffered RPMI-1640 medium just prior to use were interacted with the sensitized lymphocytes for a specified time interval at room temperature before introduction of the target cells. The pharmacologic agents, in the concentrations reported, did not injure either target or attacking cells as determined by ^{51}Cr release.

RESULTS

Carbamylcholine, a cholinergic agonist which can stimulate both muscarinic and nicotinic receptors (27), can augment LMC (3, 4); this effect is completely dependent upon a short period of preincubation of the attacking cells with the cholinergic agonist (4). The effect of muscarinic and nicotinic receptor antagonists upon carbamylcholine-induced augmentation of cytotoxicity was tested using four different cholinergic antagonists. In all experiments equimolar concentrations of atropine, a muscarinic antagonist (28), totally prevented the enhancement of LMC produced by carbamylcholine (Table 1), indicating that carbamylcholine augmented LMC, at least in part, by stimulating receptors capable of interacting with muscarinic ligands. Atropine alone at this

---

Abbreviations: T, thymus-derived; LMC, lymphocyte-mediated cytotoxicity; TMA, tetramethylammonium.

Reprinted from *Proc. Nat. Acad. Sci. U.S.* **71**, 1330–1333, 1974.

Lymphocyte-Mediated Cytotoxicity

TABLE 1. *The effect of atropine upon lymphocyte-mediated cytotoxicity and upon the cholinergic augmentation of cytotoxicity*

Concentration of				% Augmentation of specific lysis
Carbamyl-choline (pM)	Atropine (pM)	% Specific lysis	⁵¹Cr (cpm)	
			c (246–275)	
			ft (2204–2412)	
		42 (41–44)	u (1084–1142)	
	1	43 (42–44)	(1101–1149)	
1		64 (61–65)	(1503–1583)	52 (45–55)
1	1	43 (42–44)	(111–1149)	2 (0–4.7)
	1,000,000	49 (48–51)	(1223–1301)	17 (14–21)
	10,000,000	62 (60–63)	(1483–1537)	48 (43–50)

The range of triplicate samples is shown in parenthesis. c = spontaneous ⁵¹Cr release from target cells alone; ft = ⁵¹Cr release from freeze and thaw treated target cells; u = ⁵¹Cr release from sensitized mixtures of spleen and target cells that are not pharmacologically treated. In two additional experiments, atropine in concentrations equimolar to carbamylcholine (1–100 pM) virtually ablated cholinergic enhancement of LMC (46% and 53% augmentation was reduced to 3% and 1% respectively). Atropine treatment (10 μM) resulted in augmentation of cytotoxicity in three additional experiments (24%, 30%, and 38%, respectively).

concentration (1.0 pM) had no effect; however, in much higher concentrations (1–10 μM), atropine mimicked the effect of carbamylcholine in augmenting LMC.

d-Tubocurarine, a competitive blocking agent of nicotinic receptors at the myoneural junction and sympathetic ganglion (29), did not block the enhancement of LMC by carbamylcholine at equimolar concentrations; however, in three experiments, this agent did cause dose-dependent inhibition of carbamylcholine-induced augmentation of LMC at concentrations of 0.1–50 nM (Table 2). α-Bungarotoxin, a purified neurotoxin obtained from the venom of *Bungarus multicinctus*, binds to myoneural junction nicotinic receptors (30),

TABLE 2. *The effect of tubocurarine upon cholinergic augmentation of lymphocyte-mediated cytotoxicity*

Concentration of				% Augmentation of specific lysis
Carbamyl-choline (mM)	Tubo-curarine (nM)	% Specific Lysis	⁵¹Cr (cpm)	
			c (267–279)	
			ft (2308–2372)	
		46 (46–47)	u (1220–1244)	
0.1		60 (59–61)	(1494–1532)	30 (28–33)
0.1	0.1	60 (58–62)	(1484–1561)	30 (26–35)
0.1	1.0	53 (52–53)	(1351–1372)	15 (13–15)
0.1	50.0	49 (48–50)	(1264–1318)	7 (4–9)

The range of triplicate samples is shown in parenthesis, c, ft, and u are as indicated in Table 1. In two additional experiments a dose-dependent, subtotal inhibition of cholinergic augmentation of cytotoxicity was observed using tubocurarine treatment. Tubocurarine (50 nM) attenuated the enhanced cytotoxicity from 32% and 34% to 8% and 10%, respectively.

TABLE 3. *The effect of α-bungarotoxin upon lymphocyte-mediated cytotoxicity*

Concentration of				% Augmentation of specific lysis
Carbamyl-choline (nM)	α-Bunga-toxin (nM)	% Specific lysis	⁵¹Cr (cpm)	
			c (237–251)	
			ft (1786–1871)	
		41 (40–42)	u (877–909)	
0.1		59 (58–59)	(1166–1179)	44 (42–44)
0.1	0.1	60 (59–60)	(1172–1198)	46 (44–46)
0.1	1.0	47 (45–48)	(960–997)	15 (10–17)

The numbers listed in parenthesis are the range of triplicate samples c, ft, and u are as indicated in Table 1. In three additional experiments, 50–100 nM α-bungarotoxin completely prevented the augmentation of LMC induced by 0.1–0.01 nM carbamylcholine (32%, 36%, and 41% to 0%, 1%, and 1%, respectively) and 1 nM α-bungarotoxin inhibited cholinergic enhancement of LMC (from 32%, 36%, and 41% to 14%, 17%, and 18%, respectively).

acetylcholine receptors of brain (31), sympathetic neurons (25) and electroplax (32). α-Bungarotoxin was also ineffective in inhibiting the action of carbamylcholine at equimolar concentrations (Table 3); however, a 10-fold excess of α-bungarotoxin inhibited the enhancement of LMC produced by carbamylcholine and a 500-fold excess completely prevented cholinergic augmentation of cytotoxicity. Hexamethonium, an antagonist of nicotinic ganglionic receptors (33), was without effect at all concentrations tested (Table 4).

Tetramethylammonium (TMA), a predominantly nicotinic agonist (34), caused concentration and time dependent enhancement of LMC (Fig. 1). The augmentation of LMC produced by TMA is completely dependent upon a short period of preincubation of the attacking cells with this nicotinic agonist. Augmentation was not noted if the attacking cells were preincubated for more than 5 min prior to the introduction of the target cells, nor if the agonist was added at time of introduction of the target cells, or subsequent to the

TABLE 4. *The effect of hexamethonium upon the cholinergic augmentation of lymphocyte-mediated cytotoxicity*

Concentration of				% Augmentation of specific lysis
Carbamyl-choline (pM)	Hexa-methonium (pM)	% Specific lysis	⁵¹Cr (cpm)	
			c (238–247)	
			ft (1398–1503)	
		46 (45–48)	u (786–822)	
0.1		63 (62–66)	(991–1045)	37 (35–43)
0.1	0.1	63 (61–67)	(982–1053)	37 (33–45)
0.1	1000	63 (62–64)	(996–1015)	37 (35–39)
0.1	1,000,000	52 (61–64)	(979–1021)	35 (33–37)

The numbers listed in parenthesis are the range of triplicate samples. Hexamethonium was found to be ineffective in antagonizing the action of carbamylcholine in three additional experiments.

Neuroimmunomodulation

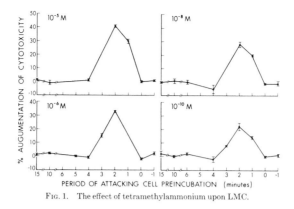

FIG. 1. The effect of tetramethylammonium upon LMC.

mixing of attacking and target cells. These findings are identical to the previously reported time-course studies with carbamylcholine (4), although a higher concentration of TMA than that of carbamylcholine is required for enhanced cytotoxicity.

DISCUSSION

Several lines of evidence indicate that T lymphocytes bear cholinergic receptors; cholinomimetic agents enhance LMC through an effect upon cytotoxic T lymphocytes (4); cholinergic agonists increase the release of migration inhibition factor from sensitized lymphocytes (19); cholinergic agonists increase lymphocyte proliferation noted in splenocytes explanted from animals undergoing the graft-versus-host reaction (35) and following phytohemagglutinin stimulation (19). The potential for modulation of *in vivo* immune responses by cholinergic stimulation is apparent. The pharmacologic properties of the lymphocyte cholinergic receptor(s) have now been studied in some detail. Antagonists of muscarinic (Table 1) or nicotinic receptors (Tables 2 and 3) inhibited the enhancement of LMC produced by carbamylcholine, a cholinomimetic agent capable of stimulation of both muscarinic and nicotinic receptors (27). Hexamethonium, an inhibitor of nicotinic ganglionic receptors (33) did not, however, abrogate cytotoxicity (Table 4). Furthermore, TMA, a nicotinic agonist (34) (Fig. 1), enhanced LMC, albeit at concentrations in great excess of the concentrations required for acetylcholine- or carbamylcholine- (3) induced augmentation of cytotoxicity. The TMA-induced enhancement of cytotoxicity was time dependent, requiring a brief period of attacking cell interaction prior to the addition of target cells. These findings are consistent with the previously reported time dependence of augmented LMC produced by carbamylcholine (4). The time dependence of the TMA effect suggests that the augmented cytotoxicity may be due to a transient metabolic change in attacking cells, perhaps a brief increase in cyclic GMP. The total dependence of augmented LMC upon a period of preincubation of cholinomimetics with attacking cells prior to introduction to target cells (Fig. 1), indicates that the action of the cholinergic agonists is upon the attacking and not the target cells.

The conceptually useful classic designation of acetylcholine receptors as either muscarinic or nicotinic (36) has been retained for 60 years (27). Several studies have demonstrated, however, that the muscarinic antagonist, atropine, in large doses inhibits stimulation of neuromuscular receptors (20–25). The iontophoretic stimulation of rat diaphragm (21) and cultured muscle cells (22) with acetylcholine has been blocked by atropine concentrations 2000 and 100 times, respectively, in excess of the inhibitory concentrations of *d*-tubocurarine; furthermore, atropine may bind to neuromuscular (23, 24) and ganglionic (25) receptors with sufficient avidity to competitively inhibit the binding of nicotinic antagonists when the concentration of atropine exceeds that of the nicotinic ligands by several orders of magnitude. Functional inhibition of "muscarinic" systems by α-bungarotoxin or nicotinic antagonists has not been previously reported, to our knowledge. The data reported herein reveal that muscarinic ligands are several orders of magnitude more potent than nicotinic agents in altering LMC. These data and the work of other investigators indicate that differences between receptors designated muscarinic and nicotinic (20–25) are not absolute, but may reflect the relative concentration-dependent efficiency of various ligands to stimulate or inhibit a given cholinergic receptor.

C.B.C. is an investigator of the Howard Hughes Medical Institute. Supported by NIH AM-15579 and by a grant from the Leukemia Research Foundation.

1. Cerottini, J. C., Nordin, A. A. & Brunner, K. T. (1970) "*In vitro* cytotoxic activity of thymus cells sensitized to alloantigens," *Nature* 227, 72–73.
2. Cerottini, J. C., Nordin, A. A. & Brunner, K. T. (1970) "Specific *in vitro* cytotoxic activity of thymus-derived lymphocytes sensitized to alloantigens," *Nature* 228, 1308–1309.
3. Strom, T. B., Deisseroth, A., Morganroth, J., Carpenter, C. B. & Merrill, J. P. (1972) "Alteration of the cytotoxic action of sensitized lymphocytes by cholinergic agents and activators of adenylate cyclase," *Proc. Nat. Acad. Sci. USA* 69, 2995–2999.
4. Strom, T. B., Carpenter, C. B., Garovoy, M. R., Austen, K. F., Merrill, J. P. & Kaliner, N. A. (1973) "The modulating influence of cyclic nucleotides upon lymphocyte mediated cytotoxicity," *J. Exp. Med.* 138, 381–393.
5. Brunner, K. T., Mauel, J., Cerottini, J. C. & Chapuis, B. (1968) "Quantitative assay of the lytic action of immune cells on ⁵¹Cr-labelled allogeneic target cells *in vitro*; inhibition by isoantibody and by drugs," *Immunology* 14, 181–196.
6. Ferluga, J., Asherson, G. L. & Becker, E. L. (1972) "The effect of organophosphorus inhibitors, *p*-nitrophenol and

cytochalasin B on cytotoxic killing of tumor cells by immune spleen cells and the effect of shaking," *Immunology* **23**, 577–590.

7. Mauel, J., Rudolf, H. Chapuis, B. & Brunner, K. T. (1970) "Studies of allograft immunity in mice. II. Mechanism of target cell inactivation *in vitro* by sensitized lymphocytes," *Immunology* **18**, 517–535.

8. Strom, T. B., Garovoy, M. R., Carpenter, C. B. & Merrill, J. P. (1970) "Microtubule function in immune and non-immune lymphocyte mediated cytotoxicity," *Science* **181**, 171–173.

9. Plaut, M., Lichtenstein, L. M. & Henney, C. S. (1973) "Studies on the mechanism of lymphocyte mediated cytolysis. III. The role of microfilaments and microtubules," *J. Immunol.* **110**, 771–780.

10. Cerottini, J. C. & Brunner, K. T. (1972) "Reversible inhibition of lymphocyte mediated cytotoxicity by cytochalasin B," *Nature New Biol.* **237**, 272–273.

11. Henney, C. S. & Lichtenstein, L. M. (1971) "The role of cyclic AMP in the cytolytic activity of lymphocytes," *J. Immunol.* **107**, 610–612.

12. Henney, C. S., Bourne, H. E. & Lichtenstein, L. M. (1972) "The role of cyclic 3′,5′-adenosine monophosphate in the specific cytolytic activity of lymphocytes," *J. Immunol.* **108**, 1526–1534.

13. George, W. J., Polson, J. B., O'Toole, A. G. & Goldberg, N. D. (1970) "Elevation of guanosine 3′,5′-cyclic phosphate in rat heart after perfusion with acetylcholine," *Proc. Nat. Acad. Sci. USA* **66**, 398–403.

14. Ferrendelli, J. A., Steiner, A. L., McDougal, D. R. & Kipnis, D. M. (1970) "The effect of oxotremorine and atropine on cGMP and cAMP levels in mouse cerebral cortex and cerebellum," *Biochem. Biophys. Res. Commun.* **41**, 1061–1067.

15. Schultz, G., Hardman, J. G., Davis, J. W., Schultz, K. & Sutherland, E. (1972) "Determination of cyclic GMP by a new enzymatic method," *Fed. Proc.* **31**, 440 abstr.

16. Yamashita, K. & Field, J. B. (1972) "Elevation of cyclic guanosine 3′,5′-monophosphate levels in dog thyroid slices caused by acetylcholine and sodium fluoride," *J. Biol. Chem.* **247**, 7062–7066.

17. Kuo, J., Lee, T., Reyes, P. L., Walton, K. G., Donnelly, Jr., T. E. & Greengard, P. (1972) "Cyclic nucleotide dependent protein kinases. An assay method for the measurement of guanosine 3′,5′-monophosphate in various biological materials and a study of agents regulating its level in heart and brain," *J. Biol. Chem.* **247**, 16–22.

18. Illiano, G., Tell, G. P. E., Siegel, M. I. & Cuatrecasas, P. (1973) "Guanosine 3′:5′-cyclic monophosphate and the action of insulin and acetylcholine," *Proc. Nat. Acad. Sci. USA* **70**, 2443–2447.

19. Hadden, J. W., Hadden, E. M., Meetz, G., Good, R. A., Haddox, M. K. & Goldberg, N. D. (1973) "Cyclic GMP in cholinergic and mitogenic modulation of lymphocyte metabolism and proliferation," *Fed. Proc.* **32**, 1022 abstr.

20. Botkin, S. (1862) "Über die physiologische Wirkung des schwefelsauren Atropins," *Virchows Arch. Anat. Physiol.* **24**, 83–92.

21. Beranek, R. & Vyskocil, F. (1967) "The action of tubocurarine and atropine on the normal and denervated rat diaphragm," *J. Physiol.* (London) **188**, 53–66.

22. Fischbach, G. D. & Cohen, S. A. (1973) "The distribution of acetylcholine sensitivity over uninnervated and innervated muscle fibers grown in cell culture," *Develop. Biol.* **31**, 147–162.

23. Vogel, A., Sytkowski, A. J. & Nirenberg, M. W. (1972) "Acetylcholine receptors of muscle grown *in vitro*," *Proc. Nat. Acad. Sci. USA* **69**, 3180–3184.

24. Sytkowski, A. & Vogel, A. (1973) "Characteristics of acetylcholine receptors on skeletal muscle grown *in vitro*," *Trans. Amer. Soc. Neuro-Chem.* **4**, 130 abstr.

25. Greene, L. A., Sytkowski, A. J., Vogel, Z. & Nirenberg, M. W. (1973) "α-Bungarotoxin used as a probe for acetylcholine receptors of cultured neurons," *Nature* **243**, 163–166.

26. Brunner, K. T., Mauel, J., Rudolf, H. L. & Chapuis, B., (1970) "Studies of allograft immunity in mice. I. Induction, development and *in vitro* assay of cellular immunity," *Immunology* **18**, 501–515.

27. Goth, A. (1972) in *Medical Pharmacology, Principles and Concepts* (C. V. Mosby Co., St. Louis), pp. 73–86.

28. Goth, A. (1972) in *Medical Pharmacology, Principles and Concepts* (C. V. Mosby Co., St. Louis), pp. 116–129.

29. Goth, A. (1972) in *Medical Pharmacology, Principles and Concepts* (C. V. Mosby Co., St. Louis), pp. 135–142.

30. Chang, C. C. & Lee, C. Y. (1963) "Isolation of neurotoxins from the venom of *Bungarus multicinctus* and their modes of neuromuscular blocking action," *Arch. Int. Pharmacodyn.* **144**, 241–257.

31. Bosmann, H. B. (1972) "Acetylcholine receptor. I. Identification and biochemical characteristics of a cholinergic receptor of guinea pig cerebral cortex," *J. Biol. Chem.*, **247**, 130–145.

32. Changeaux, J. P., Kasai, M. & Lee, C. Y. (1970) "Use of a snake venom toxin to characterize the cholinergic receptor protein," *Proc. Nat. Acad. Sci. USA* **67**, 1241–1247.

33. Paton, W. D. M. & Zaimis, E. J. (1949) "The pharmacological actions of polymethylene bistrimethylammonium salts," *Brit. J. Pharmacol.* **4**, 381–400.

34. Day, M. & Vane, J. R. (1963) "An analysis of the direct and indirect actions of drugs on isolated guinea pig ileum," *Brit. J. Pharmacol.* **20**, 150–170.

35. Strom, T. B., Hirsch, M. S., Black, P. H., Carpenter, C. B. & Merrill, J. P. (1973) "Modulation of lymphocyte blast transformation by cyclic mononucleotides," *J. Clin. Invest.* **52**, 83 abstr.

36. Dale, H. H. (1914) "The action of certain esters and ethers of choline and their relation to muscarine," *J. Pharmacol. Exp. Ther.* **69**, 147–190.

17

5-HYDROXYTRYPTOPHAN EFFECT ON THE DEVELOPMENT OF THE IMMUNE RESPONSE: IgM AND IgG ANTIBODIES AND ROSETTE FORMATION IN PRIMARY AND SECONDARY RESPONSES

Lidia Devoino, Ludmila Eliseeva, Olga Eremina, Galina Idova, and Margarita Cheido

In animals immunized with bovine serum albumin, 5-hydroxytryptophan prolonged the latent period of the IgM and IgG primary responses, decreased response intensity, delayed the response peak and suppressed IgG immunological memory.

In 5-hydroxytryptophan-treated mice, the number of rosette-forming cells (RFC) in the lymph node and spleen decreased during the primary and secondary responses. This effect was due to the decreased number of IgG RFC and to the later involvement of IgM RFC in the immune response. The absence of the secondary response was related to unprimed IgG memory cells.

5-hydroxytryptophan does not inhibit the primary and secondary responses after the connections between the hypothalamus and pituitary have been disrupted.

The participation of the n.raphe-hypothalaminc-pituitary system in immunoregulation and the putative mechanism underlying serotonin effect on the immune response are discussed.

1. Introduction

At present, it is becoming evident that although an administered antigen elicites the immune response and determines its magnitude, there exist other endogenous factors which are capable to exert a profound influence on the pattern of the immune response.

It has been reported that hormones of the adrenal cortex and hypophysis [1−3] have the ability of altering the immune response; furthermore, there is evidence indicating that highly active biogenic amines, serotonin in particular, may possess this ability [4−6]. This suggests the existence of systems which have a potential to participate directly in the physiological regulation of antibody production.

This work was undertaken to elucidate some of the changes of the primary and secondary IgM and IgG responses in animals, with the serotonin level increased by the administration of its precursor 5-hydroxytryptophan (5-HTP), and to establish the possible pathways through which these effects are exerted.

2. Materials and methods

2.1. Animals and immunization

The experiments were carried out on male BALB/c and CBA mice weighing 20−30 g and on male chinchilla rabbits, weighing 2.0−3.0 kg. Bovine serum albumin (BSA) was used for primary and secondary immunization. In assays of circulating antibodies mice were injected intraperitoneally and rabbits intramuscularly with 5 mg/kg body weight BSA in saline. While determining the rosette formation by isolated cells of the lymph node, spleen and thymus, immunization was effected by inoculation with 0.2 ml of complete Freund's adjuvant containing BSA (2 mg per mouse) and 0.1 ml was inoculated subcutaneously into each hind foot. Secondary immunization was carried out at 14, 35, 40 and 56 days after the first antigenic stimulus.

The mice (40 animals in a series) were bled from the retro-orbital sinus and the rabbits (10−15 animals in a series) from the marginal vein of the ear 4, 7, 10, 14, 21, 28, 32 and 40

Reprinted from *Eur. J. Immunol* **5**, 394–399, 1975.

days after the primary immunization and 2, 4, 7, 10, 14 and 21 days after the secondary immunization. Antibodies in mice were assayed in pooled sera from 10–15 mice.

2.2. Serological methods

IgM and IgG were fractionated through a column of Sephadex G-200 equilibrated with 0.02 M Tris-HCl buffer (pH 8.0) containing 0.28 M NaCl [7]. Protein estimations were made spectrophotometrically (spectrophotometer VSU-2P, GDR) at 280 nm.

Antibody activity in whole sera as well as samples of peak I and peak II, which were obtained after fractionation, were tested by passive hemagglutination. The fractions obtained were treated with 0.1 M 2-mercaptoethanol (2-ME) for 24 h at 37 °C. These treated fractions served as controls for fractionation.

2.3. Assays of rosette-forming cells (RFC)

RFC were determined by the method of Schwarzman [8] to detect rosettes in animals immunized with protein antigen. The regional lymph nodes, the thymus and the spleen were removed from 5–7 control animals and from the same number of 5-HTP-treated animals at different times after primary and secondary immunization and a suspension of single cells was prepared. The cells washed with saline were incubated with a 5 % suspension of sheep red blood cells which were conjugated to BSA with bisdiazotized benzidine. The mixtures were incubated at 37 °C for 15 min.

Phase contrast microscopy was used to study RFC. In each sample not less than 1000 cells were examined and the number of RFC calculated. The control tests demonstrated the specificity of this method. The number of RFC in nonimmunized animals was 0.4 ± 0.2. In CBA mice given a single immunization with BSA, the number of RFC on day 5 after immunization was 6.1 ± 1.1. By the pretreatment of the cellular suspension with antigen (1 mg/ml) for 1 h at room temperature the response was inhibited to 1.1 ± 0.18.

2.4. Determination of IgM and IgG RFC

To differentiate IgM and IgG RFC, pretreatment with 2-ME was used. The suspension of cells was divided into two portions. An equal volume of 2-ME was added to the first portion and phosphate buffer solution, pH 7.2, used to prepare the 2-ME solution, was added to the other portion. Both mixtures were incubated at 4 °C for 24 h. The number of IgG RFC was determined by the number of RFC in the 2-ME-containing portion. The number of IgM RFC was obtained by subtracting the number of IgG RFC from the total number of rosettes in the "cells + buffer solution" sample.

2.5. Drugs

To increase the level of endogenous serotonin, mice received 100 mg/kg 5-hydroxytryptophan (5-HTP, Reanal, Hungary) in incomplete Freund's adjuvant injected once on the first day, 30 min before immunization (0.1 ml in each side). Rabbits received 50 mg/kg 5-HTP in saline intraperitoneally for 7 days; the first injection was given 2 days before primary immunization.

2.6. Hypophysectomy or lesion of the pituitary stalk

Hypophysectomy or lesion of the pituitary stalk was performed electrolytically in rabbits under nembutal anesthesia. The electrodes were oriented according to the coordinates of the stalk pituitary position [9] and of the pituitary [10]. Lesions of the pituitary and its stalk were checked visually and histologically at the end of each experiment. The rabbits were immunized 7–10 days after the operation. In these experiments, intact rabbits, which had been immunized with BSA at the same dose and time as the operated animals, served as controls.

3. Results

3.1. Circulating antibodies

The analysis of the immune response in animals treated with the precursor of serotonin, 5-HTP, has shown that the synthesis of IgM and IgG antibodies is impaired both in primary and secondary immune responses.

This impairment was manifested in a decreased intensity of the antibody production of both types during the period of maximum response in control animals and in delayed peak titers. The prolongation of the latent period of antibody production, which is characteristic of both IgM and IgG antibodies, was marked in IgG antibodies (Fig. 1).

5-HTP administered during primary immunization also essentially altered the pattern and intensity of IgG antibody synthesis during secondary immune response, which suggested a weakly established immunological memory (Fig. 1). As far as IgM production after secondary immunization was concerned, the titer in 5-HTP-treated mice was found lower throughout almost the entire period of observation.

3.2. RFC

The determination of the number of RFC in the regional lymph nodes and spleen has demonstrated the dynamics of the increased number of RFC in immunized control animals to be of the primary response type reaching its maximum 5 days after immunization.

In the lymph nodes, starting from day 14, there was a second surge in the number of RFC (Fig. 2), their number remaining elevated during the entire observation period of 42 days.

In 5-HTP-treated animals, the first peak in the number of RFC in the lymph nodes and spleen as well was flattened, the number of RFC increasing slightly only on day 11, then decreasing and at last increasing slowly by day 42. The num-

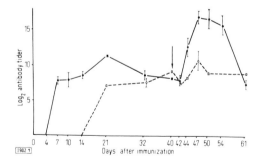

Figure 1. Inhibitory effect of 5-HTP on the production of IgG antibodies in BALB/c mice during primary and secondary immune responses. (●——●) IgG antibodies in immunized control animals; (○ – – –○) IgG antibodies in immunized 5-HTP-treated animals that received a single injection of 100 mg/kg drug in incomplete Freund's adjuvant on the day of primary immunization. (↓) Secondary immunization.

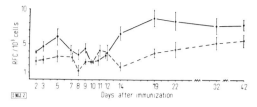

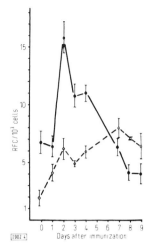

Figure 2. Effect of 5-HTP on the dynamics of changes in the number of RFC in CBA mice during primary response. (●———●) RFC in immunized control mice; (○ – – – ○) RFC in immunized 5-HTP-treated mice that received a single injection of 100 mg/kg drug in incomplete Freund's adjuvant on the day of primary immunization.

ber of RFC in the thymus did not exceed values normal for nonimmunized mice.

The analysis of the number of IgM and IgG RFC in the primary immune response (Fig. 3) has demonstrated that unlike control animals, in which IgM RFC predominated during the first days after immunization and IgG RFC started to prevail from day 7, there was no peak of IgM RFC in 5-HTP-treated animals. This gave a somewhat different shape to the curve depicted in Fig. 2. Up to day 14, there was also no appreciable increase of IgG RFC: IgM and IgG RFC increased in parallel.

The secondary immune response in control animals, which was elicited both in 14 days (Fig. 4) and in 40 days (Fig. 5) after primary immunization, was a typical anamnestic response. After secondary immunization in 5-HTP-treated mice the immune response was much less intense, developed more slowly and, thus, was similar to the primary response (Figs. 4 and 5).

The analysis of the participation of IgM and IgG RFC in the secondary immune response has shown that the time interval that elapses between primary and secondary immunization determines which type of RFC will prevail (Fig. 6).

In immunized control animals, prior to the secondary immunization, RFC populations were shown to be composed mainly of IgG cells. The secondary response 2 weeks later was provided chiefly by cells forming 2-ME-sensitive rosettes; when there was a 5-week interval, the rosettes were of IgM and IgG types and after an 8-week interval IgG RFC were detected only. In 5-HTP-treated animals, a typical secondary

Figure 4. Dynamics of RFC during secondary immune response elicited 14 days after primary immunization. (●———●) RFC in immunized control mice; (○ – – – ○) RFC in immunized mice that received a single injection of 100 mg/kg 5-HTP in incomplete Freund's adjuvant on the day of primary immunization.

immune response was observed only 5 weeks after the primary immunization and was represented by cells forming 2-ME-sensitive rosettes. We failed to establish immunological memory of IgG type in 5-HTP-treated animals.

3.3. Role of the hypothalamic-pituitary system in 5-HTP effect on the immune response

The idea that the hypothalamic-pituitary system may be involved in serotonin effect on the immune response was prompted by the observation that the destruction of midbrain raphe,

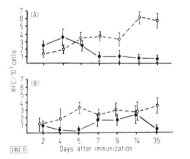

Figure 3. Pattern of primary IgM and IgG immune response. IgM (●———●) and IgG (○ – – – ○) RFC of lymph nodes in immunized control mice (A) and immunized mice treated with 100 mg/kg 5-HTP in incomplete Freund's adjuvant on the day of primary immunization (B).

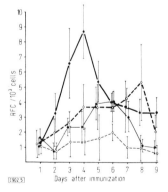

Figure 5. Dynamics of RFC of lymph nodes during primary and secondary immune response elicited day 40 after primary immunization. Immunized control mice during primary (●———●) and secondary (●———●) responses. Immunized 5-HTP-treated mice during primary (○ – – – ○) and secondary (○ – – – ○) response. 100 mg/kg 5-HTP in incomplete Freund's adjuvant was given in a single subcutaneous injection on the day of primary immunization.

IgM and IgG Immune Response and 5-Hydroxytryptophan

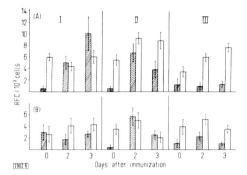

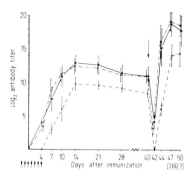

Figure 6. Secondary response of IgM and IgG RFC of the lymph nodes in immunized control mice (A) and mice that received a single subcutaneous injection of 100 mg/kg 5-HTP in incomplete Freund's adjuvant on the day of primary immunization (B).
▨ IgM RFC; ☐ IgG RFC; I secondary immunization after 2 weeks; II secondary immunization after 5 weeks; III secondary immunization after 8 weeks.

Figure 7. Production of humoral antibodies in immunized animals after hypophysectomy or lesion of the pituitary stalk under the effect of 5-HTP. (●——●) immunized control rabbits; (○ − − − −○) immunized rabbits that received intraperitoneally 50 mg/kg 5-HTP daily for 7 days starting from day 2 before primary immunization; (○ − · − · − ○) immunized rabbits after hypophysectomy or section of the pituitary stalk that received intraperitoneally 50 mg/kg 5-HTP daily for 7 days starting from day 2 before primary immunization.
(↓) Secondary immunization. (↑) Days of 5-HTP administration.

which contains serotoninergic neurons with axons terminating in the hypothalamus, stimulates the immune response [11]. In this connection, it is worthy to note that hypophysectomy or lesion of the pituitary stalk *per se* did not affect antibody production in rabbits (Table 1), which complies with the results of experimental hypophysectomy [12, 13].

Table 1. Production of humoral antibodies in rabbits after hypophysectomy or lesion of pituitary stalk

Days after immuniza-tion	Immunized animals				
	Unoperated (control)	Hypophysec-tomized	p[b]	Lesion of pituitary stalk	p
4	1.08 ± 0.8[a]	2.9 ± 1.7	> 0.2	1.8 ± 1.1	> 0.2
7	9.0 ± 0.9	10.5 ± 0.8	> 0.5	10.3 ± 0.6	> 0.5
10	12.1 ± 0.7	12.3 ± 0.9	> 0.5	11.5 ± 1.4	> 0.5
14	10.9 ± 1.1	10.9 ± 2.2	> 0.5	11.1 ± 1.0	> 0.5
21	10.1 ± 0.6	9.2 ± 0.5	> 0.5	9.9 ± 0.9	> 0.5
28	10.0 ± 0.6	8.9 ± 1.8	> 0.2	10.1 ± 1.6	> 0.5
40[c]	9.0 ± 0.3	8.3 ± 0.9	> 0.5	7.9 ± 1.4	> 0.5
42	0.6 ± 0.4	0.5 ± 0.6	> 0.5	0.8 ± 0.8	> 0.5
44	13.8 ± 0.8	13.6 ± 0.9	> 0.5	12.5 ± 0.9	> 0.5
47	16.0 ± 0.5	15.2 ± 1.2	> 0.5	15.8 ± 1.3	> 0.5
50	15.6 ± 0.8	14.9 ± 1.4	> 0.5	14.9 ± 2.1	> 0.5

a) Antibody titer in $\log_2$ (mean ± SE).
b) Significance of the difference from the control.
c) Secondary immunization.

However, hypophysectomy and lesion of the pituitary stalk prevented 5-HTP from exerting its effect on the immune response (Fig. 7). In lesioned animals 5-HTP did not inhibit the immune response and antibody titer and the kinetics of the response resembled those observed in control animals.

From the fact that similar results were obtained when the hypophysis was not destroyed and only the connections between hypothalamus and pituitary were disrupted (lesion of the pituitary stalk), it may be concluded that serotonin, whose level was raised by its precursor 5-HTP, acts on the development of the immune response via the hypothalamic-pituitary axis.

The enhancement of the immune response when serotonin level is lowered in the meso-hypothalamic regions of animals with lesioned n.raphe [11] as well as the abolition of 5-HTP effect on the immune response by section of the pituitary stalk proves that the serotoninergic n.raphe-hypothalamic-pituitary structures are, indeed, involved in the control of the immune response. Under physiological conditions serotonin may be assumed to play an important role in providing an adequate immune response to antigenic load.

4. Discussion

Our previous studies on the development of the immune response at altered levels of the biogenic amine serotonin as well as the pharmacological analysis (administration of serotonin and of its precursor 5-HTP, blockade of enzymic inactivation, impairment of monoamine binding, blockade of a specific hydroxylating enzyme) have led us to the conclusion that the elevation of the level of free active serotonin suppresses the immune response, which affects in equal measure the production of circulating antibodies and the immunological events related to cellular immunity [4–6].

The present study demonstrates that after the administration of 5-HTP, a drug known to increase serotonin level [14, 15], memory cells associated with IgG synthesis are not formed and cells providing the secondary IgM response appear later and in fewer number. If it is accepted that IgM and IgG memory is carried in separate cell populations [16, 17], it may be thought that cell populations involved in IgM and IgG rosette formation react differently to increased serotonin level.

As yet, it is difficult to determine the causes of the insufficient preparedness of memory cells. Based on the view that 5-HTP affects the formation of IgG immunological memory, which is known to be more dependent on the development of germinal centers and the prolonged presence of antigens in these centers [18–20] than IgM memory, it seems likely that the influence of the increased serotonin level by means of 5-HTP on the formation of memory cells is due to some changes in the processing, capturing and retaining of the antigen in the dendritic web of the reticular cells of germinal centers.

The analysis of the background of RFC prior to the secondary immunization has shown that in all cases, when the secondary immune response was clearly of IgM type (2–5 weeks interval between the primary and secondary immunization in control animals and 5 weeks in 5-HTP-treated animals), the background rosettes were, on the contrary, of the IgG type (Fig. 6). This suggests that either IgM memory cells are not capable of forming rosettes or that memory cells carry an IgG receptor only, irrespective of the type of the secondary response. The latter possibility does not appear tenable because it has been shown that T and B cells to which memory cells also belong [21] have mainly monomeric IgM molecules on their surface [22–24].

It is so far unclear what mechanisms induce the inhibitory effect of serotonin on the immune response. Since this study has indicated that the number of cells participating in the immune response decreases, it may be suggested that the inhibition of the immune response is based on weakened cell proliferation and differentiation. This suggestion is consistent with the observation that the administration of serotonin and monoamine oxidase inhibitors to rate inhibits cell proliferation in tumorous and embryonic tissues and suppresses almost completely the mitotic activity in corneal epithelium of adult rats [25].

However, the possibility cannot be excluded that altered cell proliferation and differentiation during the development of an immune response are secondary events, namely the consequence of impaired acceptance of antigenic information [26–28]. Thus, it has been reported that lesion of the posterior hypothalamus inhibits the immune response [29, 30] and that this inhibition is accompanied by a persisting antigen in the circulation and substantial decrease of the plasmocytic response in regional lymph nodes. It is difficult to say whether n.raphe-hypothalamic-pituitary serotoninergic structures are involved in the regulation of the proliferation and differentiation of cells or the acceptance of antigenic information or both.

5. References

1 Zdrodovsky, P., *Problems of Infection, Immunity and Allergy,* Medicine, Moscow 1969.

2 Pierpaoli, W., Baroni, C., Fabris, N. and Sorkin, E., *Immunology* 1969. *16*: 217.

3 Petranyi, C.Y., Benczur, M. and Alföldy, P., *Immunology* 1971. *21*: 151.

4 Devoino, L.V., *Proc. Acad. Sci. USSR* 1966. *169*: 1178.

5 Devoino, L.V., Korovina, L.S. and Ilyutchenok, R.Yu., *Eur. J. Pharmacol.* 1968. *4*: 441.

6 Devoino, L.V. and Ilyutchenok, R.Yu., *Eur. J. Pharmacol.* 1968. *4*: 449.

7 Nezlin, R.S. and Culpina, L.M., *Probl. Med. Chem.* 1964. *10*: 543.

8 Schwarzman, Ja.S., *Byull. Eksp. Biol. Med.* 1966. *62*, 12: 75.

9 Sawyer, C.H., Everett, J.M. and Green, J.D., *J. Comp. Neurol.* 1954. *101*: 801.

10 Kruk, B., *Acta Physiol. Polon.* 1964. *15*: 449.

11 Eremina, O.F. and Devoino, L.V., *Byull. Eksp. Biol. Med.* 1973. *74*, 2: 58.

12 Nagareda, C.S., *J. Immunol.* 1954. *73*: 88.

13 Kalden, J.R., Svans, M.M. and Irvin, W.J., *Immunology* 1970. *18*: 671.

14 Green, H. and Sawyer, J.L., *Progr. Brain Res.* 1964. *8*: 150.

15 Boggan, W.O. and Seiden, L.S., *Physiol. Behav.* 1973. *10*: 9.

16 Hamaoka, T., Kitagawa, M., Matsuoka, Y. and Yamamura, Y., *Immunology* 1969. *17*: 35.

17 L'Age-Stehr, J. and Herzenberg, L.A., *J. Exp. Med.* 1970. *131*: 1093.

18 Cooper, M.D. and Weller, E.M. in Fiore-Donati, L. and Hanna, M.G. (Eds) *Lymphatic Tissue and Germinal Centers in Immune Response,* Springer Verlag, New York 1969, p. 277.

19 Nettecheim, P. and Hammons, A.S., *Proc. Soc. Exp. Biol. Med.* 1970. *133*: 696.

20 Durkin, H.C. and Thorbecke, G.J., *J. Immunol.* 1971. *106*: 1079.

21 Storber, S. and Dilley, J., *J. Exp. Med.* 1973. *137*: 275.

22 Marchalonis, J.J., Cone, R.E. and Atwell, J.L., *J. Exp. Med.* 1972. *135*: 956.

23 Nossal, G.J.V., Warner, N.L., Lewis, N. and Sprent, J., *J. Exp. Med.* 1972. *135*: 405.

24 Goldscheider, I. and Cogen, R.B., *J. Exp. Med.* 1973. *138*: 163.

25 Puchalskaja, E. Ch. and Manco, Ju.K., *Byull. Eksp. Biol. Med.* 1964. *58*, 11: 107.

26 Mc Devitt, H.O., *J. Immunol.* 1968. *100*: 485.

27 Nossal, G.J.V., Abbot, A. and Mitchell, J., *J. Exp. Med.* 1968. *127*: 263.

28 Hanna, M.G., Nettesheim, P. and Francis, M.W., *J. Exp. Med.* 1969. *129*: 953.

29 Hai, L.M., Covalenkova, M.V., Korneva, E.A. and Seranova, A.E., *J. Microbiol. Epidemiol. Immunobiol. (USSR)* 1964. *10*: 7.

30 Saakov, B.A. , Poljak, A.I. and Zotova, V.V., *J. Microbiol. Epidemiol. Immunobiol. (USSR)* 1971. *1*: 103.

18

NETWORK OF IMMUNE-NEUROENDOCRINE INTERACTIONS

H. Besedovsky and E. Sorkin

In order to bring the self-regulated immune system into conformity with other body systems its functioning within the context of an immune-neuroendocrine network is proposed. This hypothesis is based on the existence of afferent-efferent pathways between immune and neuroendocrine structures. Major endocrine responses occur as a consequence of antigenic stimulation and changes in the electrical activity of the hypothalamus also take place; both of these alterations are temporally related to the immune response itself. This endocrine response has meaningful implications for immunoregulation and for immunospecificity. During ontogeny, there is also evidence for the operations of a complex network between the endocrine and immune system, a bidirectional interrelationship that may well affect each developmental stage of both functions. As sequels the functioning of the immune system and the outcome of this interrelation could be decisive in lymphoid cell homeostasis, self-tolerance, and could also have significant implications for pathology.

Introduction

The network of interactions of systems in higher organisms includes not only self-monitoring and self-regulatory processes, but also other integrative forms of regulation mediated by the nervous and endocrine system. The central function of the immune system is now believed to be the distinguishing of self from not-self (Burnet & Fenner, 1949). There are reasons for believing that the immune system to a large extent regulates its own functioning. The last decade has witnessed comprehensive progress in the various elements comprising immunoregulation (Jerne, 1977). As the immune system is also of critical importance for the host to cope with the threats and challenges of exceedingly complex internal and external environments, it is considered by us unlikely that it would function in the completely autonomous manner thus far proposed. That hormones exert distinctive effects on the immune system is generally appreciated. However, the operation of afferent and efferent pathways to and from the neuroendocrine structures has thus far not received any serious consideration in relation to the function of the immune system. Many kinds of neuroendocrine regulatory functions involve changes manifested in altered peripheral blood levels of certain hormones and in their hypothalamic activity. To conceive of neuroendocrine regulatory mechanisms in connection with immune responsiveness, it is first essential to ascertain that the immune response itself can elicit such hormonal changes.

In this laboratory it has recently been shown that in the course of the primary immune response to soluble antigens, or to nonreplicating foreign cells, there occur temporal endocrine

Reprinted from *Clin. Exp. Immunol.* **27**, 1–12, 1977.

changes of striking magnitude which parallel the elaboration of specific antibody-producing cells (Besedovsky *et al.*, 1975). Furthermore, there have concurrently been observed changes in electrical activity of neurons ('firing rate') in the ventromedial part of the rat hypothalamus after antigenic stimulation (Besedovsky, Sorkin Felix & Haes, 1976). Data such as these, attest to the existence of information transmitted to and from the neuroendocrine system during its response to antigenic stimulation. Also during early ontogeny, complex bidirectional interactions between the endocrine and the immune systems have been described.

In this communication we develop the proposition that during development and expression of immune functions there are permanent interrelations between the components of the immune and neuroendocrine systems. From such bidirectional interactions it would follow that the actual state of both systems at any given time is influenced by the integration of their functions. This communication briefly develops the concept of an immune-neuroendocrine network and identifies some of its implications for immunoregulation.

I. Mutual Influence of Endocrine and Immune Function in Ontogeny

The first point that bears emphasizing is the remarkable near-parallel development of the immune and endocrine systems in various mammalian species during early ontogeny. This can hardly be fortuitous.Thus, in species such as mice and rats which at birth have only marginal levels of immunoglobulins and in which immune responses are minimally effective during the first days of extrauterine life (Solomon 1971), many endocrine mechanisms are also underdeveloped at this time, notably sexual differentiation functioning of the hypophysis, thyroid and adrenal glands (Jost, 1969; Jost *et al.*, 1973). There are species, on the other hand, such as guinea pigs (Illingworth *et al.*, 1973; Pals, Reineke & Schaw, 1973; Moog & Ford, 1957), sheep (Alexander *et al.*, 1971; Bassett, Thorburn & Wallace, 1970; Bassett & Alexander, 1971; Dussault, Hobel & Fisher, 1971), cow (Dubois, 1971), and man (Jost, 1969), which to greater or lesser degree are more mature immunologically at birth; in these species the aforementioned endocrine mechanisms are likewise synchronized in a more advanced stage of development. The rabbit provides an example of a species intermediate between these extremes. In the aforementioned species, a similar time correlation has also been established between the effect of neonatal thymectomy on the development of the immune system and the endocrine status at birth.

In this report, it is intended to examine the proposition that there also exists a bidirectional influence (i.e. each affects the other) between the endocrine and the immune system. The evidence derives from experimental situations in which a disturbance of this interrelation at one level results in changes at other levels. Such a disturbance is found in conditions where the development of the immune system is impaired or alternatively where the endocrine environment is changed. In either case, the other parameters change in an essentially parallel fashion.

Four kinds of disturbances of the proposed bidirectionally interacting systems are given as examples.

1. The germ-free state, i.e., lack of antigenic challenge is manifested in a marked underdevelopment in the total mass of host lymphoid tissue and depressed immunoglobulin levels; it is also expressed in an altered endocrine state (Wostmann, 1968). There are reports of thyroid (Pleasants, 1968; Vought *et al.*, 1972), adrenal (Miyakawa & Ukai, 1970; Miyakawa, 1966) and testicular (Nomura *et al.*, 1973) insufficiency in germ-free mice and rats. In guinea pigs adrenal hyperfunction has been described (Chakhava, 1973).

2. Neonatally thymectomized mice and congenitally thymusless mice which have a T-lymphocyte deficiency, display a profoundly disturbed endocrine system. Absence of a thymus

in animals kept under conventional, specific-pathogen-free (SPF) or germ-free condition, results in a degranulation of STH-producing cells in the adenohypophysis (Bianchi, Pierpaoli & Sorkin, 1971), a delay of puberty in females (Besedovsky & Sorkin, 1974), persistence of the reticular zone of the adrenal gland (Pierpaoli & Sorkin, 1972), hypothyroidism (Pierpaoli & Sorkin, 1972; Pierpaoli & Besedovsky, 1975), and alterations in blood levels of gonadal hormones (Pierpaoli & Sorkin, 1972). A number of these parameters can be normalized *only* by early thymus implantation (Besedovsky & Sorkin, 1974). The passive transfer of lymphoid cells makes the recipients immunocompetent, but fails to normalize the aforementioned hormone-dependent parameters. Endocrine influences of the thymus on other endocrine glands are already expressed during perinatal life, especially with regard to female sexual function. This finding provides a strong indication that the thymus is involved in the programming of the neuroendocrine system (Besedovsky & Sorkin, 1974; Pierpaoli & Besedovsky, 1975).

3. Surgically bursectomized 62-hr-old chicken embryos show the following endocrine alterations later in embryonic life or at the time of hatching: degranulation of gonadotrophic cells in the hypophysis, underdeveloped oviduct, adrenal hypertrophy, low level of corticosterone in chorioallantoid fluid and high level of testosterone in this fluid in females (Besedovsky *et al.*, 1976, submitted for publication).

4. Changes in hormonal environment produce alterations in acquisition of immune capacity. Apart from thymic hormones there are numerous examples of hormonal influence on the development of the immune system (Pierpaoli, Fabris & Sorkin, 1970). An instructive model is the hypopituitary dwarf mouse with its deficiency in growth hormone and thyrotropin. Cell-mediated immunity as measured by transplantation criteria is defective; this deficit can be normalized by injection of STH and thyroxine (Fabris, Pierpaoli & Sorkin, 1971a, b).

The above-mentioned examples of interference at the level of antigenic challenge, development of central and peripheral lymphoid tissue, or at the level of endocrine functions attest to a complex network of interaction between the immune and the endocrine systems in ontogeny. Figure 1 illustrates in a diagrammatic way possible sequences of these interactions. It is rather predictable that the overall product of this interaction during different developmental stages could make for a situation which favored either tolerance to self components or immunity.

II. The Integration of the Immune and Endocrine Responses Following Antigenic Stimulation

The fact that hormones influence the immune system is well established. Such findings are entirely logical in view of the known role of hormonal influence on varied basic cellular functions such as protein synthesis, control of gene expression, cell replication and the allosteric arrangement of cell membranes, all of which are basic to physiological processes and have an essential function in the immune performance. Furthermore, some hormones operate via their capacity to influence the rate of formation of cyclic 3,5-adenosine monophosphate (cyclic 3,5-AMP), an intermediate which is also known to affect strongly lymphoid cells and antibody production (Bourne *et al.*, 1974).

In the past, investigations on the involvement of hormones in the immune response have been based on the administration of hormones or the ablation or blockade of endocrine glands. Depressed or stimulated immune responses resulted depending on the particular hormone involved, the dose and the timing of its administration. It is thus evident, that externally induced changes in the level of certain hormones can influence immune reactivity considerably. However, the possibility that the immune response itself could bring about changes in hormone levels has not been previously considered. We have shown that during the primary immune

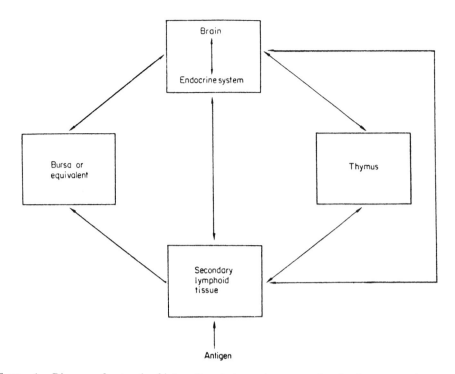

Figure 1. Diagram of network of interactions between immune and endocrine systems in ontogeny and in adult life.

response of rats to a particulate antigen, sheep red cells (SRBC), or to soluble antigen Trinitrophenyl-haemocyanin (TNP-Hae), and of mice to TNP-horse red blood cells (TNP-HRBC), corticosterone levels increased several-fold while there occurred temporal changes in thyroxine levels.

In Fig. 2b is shown a two- to threefold increase in serum corticosterone levels above normal at 5, 6, 7 or 8 days after injection of 4×10^9 SRBC into female rats. The fact that no significant changes in the serum corticosterone level occurred on days 1 and 3 after immunization attests to the fact that the animals were not stressed by handling or the injection of the cells.

A biphasic change in the serum thyroxine concentration was observed in animals treated with the higher dose of SRBC (Fig. 2c). After an initial increase on day 3, the serum thyroxine decreased by approximately 30% below normal on days 5–8. Rats injected with the same dose homologous red cells showed no changes in corticosterone and thyroxine levels at any time. Changes in blood hormone levels are known to be the main information for the neuroendocrine structures, e.g., the hypothalamus, and this organ regulates the blood hormone level. Accordingly, the observed changes, whatever their cause, can be considered as also involving a specific neuroendocrine response and attest to the existence of an afferent pathway from the activated immune system to the central regulatory structures involved in endocrine regulation.

It is not excluded that the almost infinite diversity of the process of immunization itself, i.e., the great spectrum of antigenic agents, the range of immunizing dosage and the route of administration, will all serve to make for diversity in the altered hormonal profiles which result. This would be a consequence of the qualitative and quantitative spectrum of lymphoid cells brought into play, their interactions and responses, and their consequences as manifested by elaboration of various classes of Ig, mediators, ag/ab complexes, etc. Moreover, dissimilar

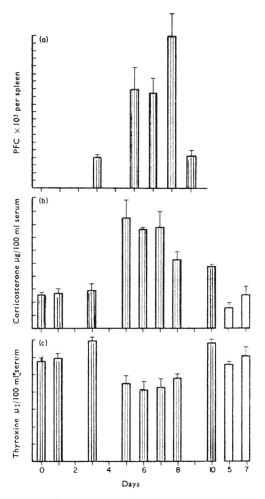

FIGURE 2. Changes in serum corticosterone and thyroxine levels during the immune response to sheep red blood cells (SRBC) in rats: (a) plaque-forming cells (PFC) $\times$ 10^3 per spleen; (b) corticosterone levels in serum; animals immunized with SRBC; control injected with rat red blood cells (RRBC); (c) thyroxine levels in serum; animals immunized with SRBC; $\square$ control immunized with RRBC.

neuroendocrine effects would be expected even in response to the same antigen differently administered, depending on whether the response it elicits involves primarily T cells, B cells, macrophages, etc.

III. Link between the Immune Response and the Hypothalamus

The described temporal endocrine changes which accompany the production of antibodies are in our view an expression of the response of neuroendocrine structures to signals which derive from activated lymphoid cells. To obtain direct proof of such a postulated afferent pathway, we looked for significant changes in the target organ, the hypothalamus. The experimental system utilized was the electrical activity of individual neurons in the ventromedial nuclei of the hypothalamus of rats after immunization with sheep red blood cells or TNP-hemocyanin.

The data for animals stimulated with SRBC are summarized in Fig. 3. On day 1 when PFC have not yet been produced, the firing frequency of neurons in the antigen-stimulated group was no different from that of saline controls. On day 5, which represents the peak of IgM PFC formation in spleen, there was seen a threefold increase in the firing rate of the neurons. Hypothalamic responses to the other antigen employed, 250 μg TNP-hemocyanin, were also observed. A greater than twofold increase in firing rate was noted.

Data such as these are tangible evidence for the operation of a flow of information from the activated immune system to the brain, showing that the immune system, just as a number of others, is linked with the CNS. Consequently, it seems a reasonable view that the hypothalamus is intimately linked to the process of immunoregulation in a manner external to the immune system.

Presumably, this neuroendocrine mechanism functions when a critical threshold of lymphoid tissue activation is reached, sufficient to elaborate products serving as a signal to the hypothalamus which in turn releases factors that via the hypophysis and its polypeptide hormones closes the circle by its effects on the immune system.

IV. Possible Nature of Link between Immune and Neuroendocrine Response

It is a rational assumption that the primary link between the immune and the neuroendocrine system is effected by one or another of the multiple events known to follow immunization. The afferent and efferent pathways to and from the hypothalamus could then be visualized as functioning in the following ways:

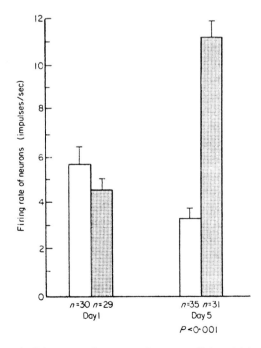

FIGURE 3. Increase in firing rates of neurons of ventromedial nuclei in the rat hypothalamus after i.p. injection of 5×10^9 sheep red blood cells (▨). Controls injected with saline (☐).

1. Antigen

While antigen is obviously the trigger of immune mechanisms, it has so far been unknown that the neuroendocrine system can be affected as well. It is most unlikely in our view that antigen itself is the direct cause of the altered blood hormone levels that ensue. For one thing, antigenic recognition by lymphocytes occurs well before the observed endocrine changes occur (see Fig. 2). For another thing, while the immune system has an enormous "library" of lymphocytes recognition sites for "reading" the almost infinite array of antigenic determinants, there is no evidence whatsoever that the neuroendocrine structure has an equally elaborate recognition counterpart for antigens.

2. Antibody

Since antibodies can cross the blood brain barrier, this specific humoral end product of antigenic stimulation must also be considered as possible messenger to the neuroendocrine system. However, no experimental data exist at present to suggest that antibodies to extrinsic antigen can influence the neuronal activity in the hypothalamus.

3. Electrical Signal from Peripheral Nerves

In contrast to the extensive knowledge on innervation of different organs or tissues to the best of our knowledge the significance of nerve endings in lymphoid structures is unknown. Accordingly, it is difficult at present to postulate an afferent or efferent neural pathway to and from the brain and to understanding the regulatory significance of the known pharmacological influence on the immune response by mediators of the autonomous nervous system, such as catecholamine (Hadden, Hadden & Middleton, 1970) and acetylcholine (Hadden *et al.*, 1975) and some reports of immunological alterations after neurotomy (Kesztyüs, 1967) or electrolytic lesions of the brain (Janković & Isaković, 1973; Isaković & Janković, 1973; Stein, Schiavi & Camerino, 1976). However, one cannot exclude entirely a bidirectional neural pathway between lymphoid tissue and the central nervous system contributing to immunoregulation.

4. Hormones

The immune response also elicits changes in peripheral hormone levels, which we believe can influence immune processes in an efferent way. Whether these hormonal changes are a direct consequence of the immune events on the endocrine target glands or secondary to effects of the neuroendocrine system on these targets is not known. Even if the former were the case, the hypothalamus-hypophysis axis would still represent the normal manner of controlling the endocrine system.

5. Mediators

Chemical mediators are released by activated T lymphocytes and by antibody-producing B cells during antigen induced proliferation. It is conceivable that one or another of these potent effector molecules may influence the endocrine target glands either directly or more likely via hypothalamus-hypophysis. An alternative possibility is that immune complexes via activation of plasma constituents or cells could initiate a similar sequence of events. It can hardly be a coincidence that histamine and serotonin, low mol. wt cell products also known to mediate the immune response, are present in high concentrations in the median eminence of the hypothalamus, the general pathway for all neuroendocrine processes (White, 1966; Crawford, 1958). There is also no blood–brain barrier for precursors of histamine and serotonin in the median eminence (Davison, 1958; Udenfriend, Weissbach & Bogdanski, 1957). Furthermore, it is now postulated that serotonin (Navmenko, 1973) and probably histamine as well (White, 1966) are linked (possibly via hypothalamic releasing factors) with ACTH release by the adenohypophysis; this sort of mechanism may be operative in effecting the increased corticosterone blood levels reported in Fig. 2b. There is no analogous information, at present, regarding the other major category of mediators of the immune response, the lymphokines.

V. Implications of the Bidirectional Relationships between Immune and Endocrine System

The previously discussed data and reasoning strongly support the idea of a complex network between two host systems, operative from early ontogeny into adult life. Further knowledge of the *profile* of hormonal responses and the neuroendocrine lymphoid tissue interrelationship will be required for a more definitive interpretation of the physiology and the biologic significance of this interaction. We are presently ignorant of the extent to which the endocrine changes consequent to the immune response affect, in turn, metabolic conditions and cellular activities and, consequently, the course of the immune response itself (efferent pathway). The information already at hand would seem sufficient to warrant some speculation on the ways in which hormonal control might be exerted over key situations such as immunospecificity, antigenic competition, tolerance, and macrophage function.

1. Immunospecificity

Specificity of the immune response has its basis in the interaction of antigen with specific receptors on lymphocytes. Following this primary event, a regulatory intervention by hormones could be exerted at many levels. The specificity of the response is due to high affinity cells, but antigen will also act on cells of lower affinity as well. Furthermore, nonspecific mediators released by activated cells can activate other cells, unrelated to the antigenic stimulus, and thereby induce a concommitant increase in nonspecificity. While the antigen provides the information for a highly specific response the activation of other cells would lead to a disturbance of the system, introducing background noise. Such an uneconomical event may be potentially harmful to the host to the extent of enhancing the probability of autoimmune reactions. Also an excessive expansion of lymphoid cell mass would in effect raise the concentration of soluble mediators to an undesirable or possibly even dangerous extent. One way of suppressing such untoward events would be through the action of corticosteroids and other steroids, which are well known to suppress or even delete lymphoid cells not stimulated by antigen as well as macrophage function and to inhibit lymphokines synthesis (Wahl, Altmann & Rosenstreich, 1975). Nonstimulated cells (before the onset of the immune response) are easily influenced by hormones, e.g., corticosteroid, but after the antigen administration the course of cellular events is much more difficult to modulate by the very same agent (Makinodan, Santos & Quinn, 1970; Claman, 1975). Indeed, the observed increase of corticosteroid during the immune response may well have this very function of suppressing a potentially harmful expansion of lymphoid tissue of low or no affinity for the antigen. This fits well with the observation that adrenalectomy leads to a pronounced increase in spleen weight in mice. Antigenic challenge of adrenalectomized mice results in a still further weight increase. Controls did not show any spleen weight increase when antigenically challenged (Kieffer & Ketchel, 1971). In our view, this is a consequence of prevention of antigen provoked corticosteroid increase, resulting in a deleted hormonal control.

This hormonally controlled mechanism could also be the key to the situation labelled as *antigenic competition,* where two or more antigens are injected simultaneously (or more often sequentially) and the resultant immune response to either antigen is less than when they are given singly. This phenomenon is actually an expression of the existence of a regulatory mechanism for suppressing unrelated cells. In our view, apart from suppressor cells, the hormonal changes following antigenic stimulation are also responsible for this suppression. The following experimental evidence strongly supports our contention.

When sheep red cells (SRBC) are injected into rats previously immunized with TNP-horse red cells, there occurs a marked depression of the response to SRBC. The first antigen had already evoked a severalfold increase in corticosterone blood levels at the time the second antigen (SRBC) was injected (Table 1). If this increase in corticosterone were responsible for the suppression of the SRBC response, prior adrenalectomy would be expected to counteract this suppression. The fact is that direct experimental test of this issue shows (Fig. 4) a twenty-fold increase in plaque-forming cells in adrenalectomized rats injected first with horse RBC and then with sheep RBC. In animals given only SRBC, adrenalectomy does not change the response appreciably.

In addition to those well-recognized factors that make for immunospecificity such as specific regulation by components of the system (e.g., suppressor T cells, antibodies), this can also be brought about by hormonal nonspecific regulation.

The maintenance of specificity by nonspecific intervention deserves special mention. Since there is no known means by which the wide range of antigenic determinants can be specifically recognized by hormones (nonspecific factors), we propose that hormones can enhance *specificity* by inhibiting or blocking unrelated or low affinity cells. Similar examples are found in the nervous system, another highly discriminative network. Lateral or afferent inhibition of sur-

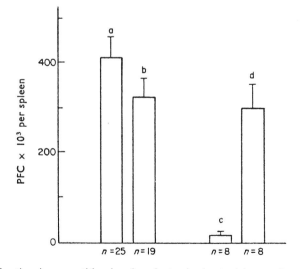

FIGURE 4. Prevention of antigenic competition in adrenalectomized rats; (a) normal rats immunized i.p. with 10^9 SRBC. Test on day 5; (b) adrenalectomized rats immunized with 10^9 SRBC. Test on day 5; (c) normal rats injected with 10^9 HRBC and 6 days later immunized with 10^9 SRBC. Test for PFC against SRBC on day 5 after SRBC; (d) adrenalectomized rats injected with 10^9 HRBC and 6 days later immunized with 10^9 SRBC. Test for PFC against SRBC on day 5 after SRBC.

TABLE 1. Increased Serum Corticosterone Levels during Antigenic Competition[a]

Antigen	Day of Sacrifice	Corticosterone μg/100 ml) serum
	0	5.81 ± 1.1
TNP/Horse RBC	6	28.7 ± 6.1
TNP/Horse RBC	11	11.9 ± 1.2
TNP/Horse RBC and on day 6 SRBC	11	28.4 ± 4.2
SRBC	5	30.4 ± 10.9

[a] Mean ± S.E. 10^9 TNP/Horse RBC resp. 10^9 SRBC were injected i.p. into adult female Holtzmann rats. The results show that there is an increase in serum corticosterone level 6 days after immunization with horse red cells, i.e., when the second antigen, SRBC, was injected. This maintains the high level of corticosterone and may influence the process of antigenic competition (see also Fig. 2).

rounding neurons is a well-known mechanism to eliminate background noise when an impulse is required to be highly discriminative.

Thus, we believe that hormonal regulation can augment or enhance immunospecificity of a response by suppression of low or nonspecific cellular events without disturbing the requisite clonal expansion of high affinity cells.

2. Endocrine Status and Tolerance

The decision whether an antigenic stimulus will drive the lymphocyte along the pathway of tolerance or immunity probably also involves the overall endocrine status. Since variation in hormone levels can augment or diminish the immune response, it is conceivable that the induction of the tolerant state would be affected by changes in hormonal levels in blood evoked by antigenic challenge. Such changes may be of different nature and duration at different stages of development.

Recognition of self and establishment of tolerance to self components develops during embryonic life at a time when the maximum number of new antigens are emerging. As already mentioned, there is a remarkable correspondence in the kinetics and pattern of the development of immune and endocrine function in various mammalian species during the embryonic period, and a mutual influence on both systems. Antigen interaction with "primitive" (not fully competent) lymphoid cells may well induce changes in hormonal levels which in turn would affect the endocrine status of the animal as observed during adult life. The outcome of the immune-neuroendocrine network of interactions during ontogeny can delete or inhibit the selfreacting cells. Regrettably, there is little known concerning the nature and profile of hormones during each stage of embryonic life. It is probable that early endocrine environment is highly unfavorable for the thymus (and bursa equivalent) to exert their maturational function on lymphocytes directly or by modifying the endocrine environment. Constant with such an interpretation is the finding that the thymus of, e.g., 14-day-old embryonic mice can establish immunocompetence in *adult* mice thymectomized at birth even though these embryos are themselves immunologically immature (Miller & Osoba, 1963).

Data have been obtained, suggesting that the foetal adrenal gland also plays some role in the generation of a hormonal environment in ontogeny which is unfavourable for thymus function. There is, for example, an inverse correlation between the time of acquisition of immunocompetence and involution of the fetal adrenal gland in diverse mammalian species (Besedovsky, 1971). Furthermore, engraftment of albino rat adrenal fetal gland, taken during the last week of gestation, effects prolongation of rat skin allograft survival. Later in ontogeny when ever fewer additional self-antigens are generated a reduction of the incidence of antigen interaction with primitive lymphoid cells would be expected with diminished consequences for the endocrine environment. The changes in these conditions would therefore make for a fuller expression of thymus and bursa function in immunological terms and in their endocrine interrelation with other glands. In such a sequence would be created a totally new and different endocrine and lymphoid cell environment which with emergence from the neonatal state increasingly favours the pathway to immunity rather than tolerance.

No less than five kinds of tolerance have been described by Medawar and many theories on mechanisms have been proposed (for review see: Howard & Mitchison, 1975; Katz & Benacerraf, 1974). The influence of hormones in the induction of adult tolerance has to be considered as a physiological component of that mechanism (Diener & Lee, 1974). It is here suggested that situations in which administration of antigen leads to tolerance will be found to be paralleled by concommitant endocrine changes evoked by that very same schedule of antigen. It will, therefore, be of particular interest to explore the *kinetics* of tolerance induction as it relates to hormone status. The present hypothesis would predict a certain parallelism between antigen-induced changes in hormonal responses, in particular of corticosteroids, concommitant with the acquisition of the state of tolerance.

3. Relevance of Endocrine Status for Monocyte/Macrophage Function

Corticosteroids can suppress the colloid clearance function of the reticuloendothelial system, prevent accumulation of macrophages in the delayed hypersensitivity reaction, depress their activation or decrease the number of circulating monocytes (for a summary, see: Baum, 1975; Claman, 1975). Since reactions of cell-mediated immunity and tumor-cell inhibition and killing involve an effector function for macrophages (Keller, 1973; Hibbs, Lambert & Remington, 1972; Evans & Alexander, 1972) and corticosteroid plasma levels are high in various forms of cancer (Mackay *et al.*, 1971), perhaps in part because of continuous antigenic challenge of the immune system, it is possible that the hosts macrophage/monocyte response is endocrinologically disturbed.

In contrast, estrogens are potent stimulators of reticuloendothelial phagocytic activity. Significantly, reticuloendothelial activity is higher in female than in male rats and mice and varies with the estrous cycle (reviewed in: Baum, 1971). In view of the aforementioned findings on the susceptibility of phagocytic monocytes to glucosteroids, it may be appropriate to now give consideration to the possibility that a changed endocrine environment induced by antigenic challenge could also affect macrophage function in its various immunologic manifestations.

4. Implications for Pathology

It is a rational expectation that as the described network of immune-neuroendocrine interactions has pervasive effects in both directions, this would have special implications for certain disease states. Thus, endocrine disorders have consequences for the immune system as in Cushing's disease (Britton, Thorén & Sjöberg, 1975). In the other direction, autoimmune mechanisms can produce several endocrine diseases (Irvine, 1974). There are also situations where both systems are simultaneously affected as in thymus- and bursaless animals, in which there is a parallel occurrence of immune and endocrine derangements (Besedovsky & Sorkin, 1974; Pierpaoli & Sorkin, 1972; Pierpaoli & Besedovsky, 1975; Besedovsky *et al.*, 1976). A further possibility is that multiple antigenic stimuli over a protracted period would lead to cumulative alterations in the coupled immune and neuroendocrine response. Such disruptions could include different kinds of hormonal or immune derangements, including for example uncontrolled proliferation of lymphoid tissue and accessory cells. Thus in lymphoproliferative diseases, viz. in the high leukaemia mouse strain AKR (Metcalf, 1960) and in SJL/J mice known to develop a high incidence of reticulum cell sarcoma and other neoplasms (Pierpaoli *et al.*, 1974), endocrine disorders are detected long before clinical disease syndromes are actually expressed. It is also a notable fact that some animals and humans bearing different kinds of tumours show very similar hormonal patterns, raised corticosteroid and depressed thyroxine levels, a pattern expressed briefly in our animals stimulated with conventional antigens (Shigeru *et al.*, 1966; Galton & Ingbar, 1966; Deshpande *et al.*, 1969; Marmorston, 1966; Deshpande, Hayward & Bulbrook, 1965; Ghosh, Lockwood & Pennington, 1973; Lancet, 1974; Jensen *et al.*, 1968; for similar changes in pre-illness respiratory infections, see Mason *et al.*, 1967). Such changes in endocrine pattern in blood and urine of cancer patients are already utilized for prognosis (Mackay *et al.*, 1971; Hayward & Bulbrook, 1968; Rao & Hewit, 1970). Also in patients with chronic lymphatic leukaemia (Gallagher *et al.*, 1962; Gallagher *et al.*, 1965), there is an increase in cortisol in blood.

The common feature of the endocrine changes observed in the above-mentioned diseases are in our view at least in part related to immune responses. These changed hormonal conditions might have a significant influence on the course of disease. Thus, it will be of interest to analyze the hormonal profile in patients with autoimmune disease, lymphoproliferative diseases and cancer in which we expect significant endocrine alterations.

Acknowledgments

This work was supported by the Schweizerischer Nationalfonds zur Förderung der wissenschaftlichen Forschung, grant no 3.600-0.75. We are grateful to Dr H. Laudy for helpful criticism.

The technical assistance of Miss Regula Kellerhals and Mr. A. Bühler is gratefully acknowledged.

References

Alexander, D. P., Britton H. G., Forsling, M. L., Nixon, D. A. & Ratcliffe, J. G. (1971). The concentrations of adrenocorticotrophin, vasopressin and oxytocin in the foetal and maternal plasma of the sheep in the latter half of gestation. *J. Endocr.* **49,** 179.

Bassett, J. M. & Alexander, G. (1971). Insulin, growth hormone and corticosterone in neonatal lambs. Normal concentration and the effect of cold. *Biol. Neonate,* **17,** 113.

Bassett, J. M., Thorburn, G. D. & Wallace, A. L. C. (1970). The plasma growth hormone concentration in the foetal lamb. *J. Endocr.* **48,** 251.

Baum, M. (1975). Effect of administered hormones on the immune reaction. *Host defence in breast cancer* (ed. by B. A. Stoll) p. 130. William Heinemann Medical Books Ltd, London.

Besedovsky, H. O. (1971). Delay in skin allograft rejection in rats grafted with fetal adrenal glands. *Experientia,* **27,** 697.

Besedovsky, H. O. & Sorkin, E. (1974). Thymus involvement in female sexual maturation. *Nature (Lond.),* **249,** 356.

Besedovsky, H. O., Sorkin, E., Keller, M. & Müller, J. (1975). Changes in blood hormone levels during the immune response. *Proc. Soc. exp. Biol. (N.Y.)* **150,** 466.

Besedovsky, H. O., Sorkin, E. Felix, D. & Haas, H. (1976). Hypothalamic changes during the immune response. Submitted for publication.

Besedovsky, H. O., Pedernera, E., Pagano, E. & Rossi Aloras, H. (1976). Involvement of bursa of fabricius in chicken endocrine development. Submitted.

Bianchi, E., Pierpaoli, W. & Sorkin, E. (1971). Cytological changes in the mouse anterior pituitary after neonatal thymectomy: a light and electron microscopical study. *J. Endocr.* **51,** 1.

Bourne, H. R., Melmon, K. L., Weinstein, Y. & Shearer, G. M. (1974) Pharmacologic regulation of antibody release *in vitro:* effects of vasoactive amines and cyclic AMP. *Cyclic AMP, Cell Growth, and the Immune Response* (ed. by Werner Braun, Lawrence M. Lichtenstein and Charles W. Parker), p. 99. Springer-Verlag, Berlin, Heidelberg, New York.

Britton, S., Thorén, M. & Sjøberg, H. E. (1975). The immunological hazard of Cushing's syndrome. *Brit. med. J.* iv, 678.

Burnet, F. M. & Fenner, F. (1949). *Production of antibodies.* Macmillan, Melbourne.

Chakhava, O. V. (1973). Ascorbic acid and glucocorticoid levels in relation to underdeveloped lymphatic tissue in germ-free guinea pigs. *Germfree Research. Biological Effect of Gnotobiotic Environment* (ed. by J. B. Heneghan), p. 507. Academic Press, New York-London.

Claman, H. N. (1975). How corticosteroids work. *J. Allergy clin. Immunol.* 55, 145.

Crawford, T. B. (1958). The distribution of 5-hydroxytryptamine in central nervous system of the dog. *5-Hydroxytryptamine* (ed. by G. P. Lewis), p. 20. Pergamon Press, Oxford.

Davison, A. N. (1958). Physiological role of monoaminoxidase. *Physiol. Rev.* **38**, 729.

Deshpande, N., Hayward, J. L. & Bulbrook, R. D. (1965). Plasma 17 hydroxcorticosteroids and 17 oxosteroids in patients with breast cancer and in normal women. *J. Endocr.* **32**, 167.

Deshpande, N., Jensen, V., Carson, P., Bulbrook, R. D. & Lewis, A. A. (1969). Some aspects of the measurement of cortisol production in patients with breast cancer. *J. Endocr.* **45**, 571.

Diener, E. & Lee, K.-C. (1974). B cell tolerance *in vitro.* The fate of the tolerant cell and its control by hormones. *Immunological Tolerance* (ed. by D. H. Katz and B. Benacerraf), p. 311. Academic Press, New York.

Dubois, M. P. (1971). Sur l'apparition des sécrétions hormonales dans hypophyse foetal dans bovins: mise en evidence par immunofluorescence des cellules gonadotrops thyréotrops. *C.R. Acad. Sci. D. (Paris)* **272**, 1793.

Dussault, J. H., Hobel, C. J. & Fisher, D. A. (1971). Maternal and fetal thyroxine secretion during pregnancy in the sheep. *Endocrinology,* **88**, 47.

Evans, R. & Alexander, P. (1972). Mechanism of immunologically specific killing of tumour cells by macrophages. *Nature (Lond.),* **236**, 168.

Fabris, N., Pierpaoli, W. & Sorkin, E. (1971a). Hormones and the immunological capacity. III. The immunodeficiency disease of the hypopituitary Snell-Bagg dwarf mice. *Clin. exp. Immunol.* **9**, 209.

Fabris, N., Pierpaoli, W. & Sorkin, E. (1971b). Hormones and the immunological capacity. IV. Restorative effects of developmental hormones or of lymphocytes on the immunodeficiency syndrome of the dwarf mouse. *Clin. exp. Immunol.* **9**, 227.

Gallagher, T. F., Bradlow, H. L., Miller, D. G., Zumoff, B. & Hellman, L. (1962). Steroid hormone metabolism in chronic lymphatic leukemia. *J. clin. Endocr. Metab.* **22**, 1049.

Gallagher, T. F., Hellman, L., Zumoff, B. & Miller, D. G. (1965). Steroid hormone metabolism in chronic myelogenous leukemia. *Blood,* **25**, 743.

Galton, V. A. & Ingbar, S. H. (1966). Effect of a malignant tumor on thyroxine metabolism and thyroid function in the rat. *Endocrinology,* **79**, 964.

Ghosh, P. C., Lockwood, E. & Pennington, G. W. (1973). Abnormal excretion of corticosteroid sulphates in patients with breast cancer. *Brit. med. J.* i, 328.

Hadden, J. W., Hadden E. M. & Middleton, E. (1970). Lymphocyte blast transformation. I. Demonstration of adrenergic receptors in human peripheral lymphocytes. *Cell. Immunol.* **1**, 583.

Hadden, J. W., Johnson, E. M., Hadden, E. M.,Coffey, R. G. & Johnson, L. D. (1975). Cyclic GMP and lymphocyte activation. *Immune Recognition* (ed. by A. S. Rosenthal), p. 359. Academic Press, New York.

Hayward, J. L. & Bulbrook, R. D. (1968). Urinary steroids and prognosis in breastcancer. *Prognostic Factors in Breast Cancer* (ed. by A. P. M. Forrest and P. B. Kunkler), p. 383. Livingstone, Edinburgh.

Hibbs, J. B., Lambert, L. H. & Remington, J. S. (1972). Possible role of macrophage mediated nonspecific cytotoxicity in tumour resistance. *Nature: New Biology,* **235**, 48.

Howard, J. G. & Mitchison, N. A. (1975). Immunological tolerance. *Progr. Allergy* **18**, 43.

Illingworth, D. V., Perry, J. S., Ackland, N. & Burton, A. M. (1973). The maintenance of pregnancy and parturition, in guinea pigs hypophysectomized within 4 days of mating. *J. Endocr.* **59**, 163.

Irvine, W. J. (1974). Autoimmune mechanisms in endocrine diseases. *Proc. roy. Soc. Med.* **67**, 449.

Isakovic, K. & Janković, B. D. (1973). Neuro-endocrine correlates of immune response. II. Changes in the lymphatic organs of brain-lesioned rats. *Int. Arch. Allergy,* **45**, 373.

Janković, B. D. & Isakivic, K. (1973). Neuro-endocrine correlates of immune response I. Effects of brain lesions on antibody production, Arthus reactivity and delayed hypersensitivity in the rat. *Int. Arch. Allergy,* **45**, 360.

Jensen, V., Deshpande, N., Bulbrook, R. D. & Doous, T. W. (1968). Adrenal function in breast cancer. Production and metabolic clearance of cortisol in patients with early or advanced breast cancer and in normal women. *J. Endocr.* **42,** 425.

Jerne, N. K. (1977). The immune system: a web of v-domains. *The Harvey Lectures.* (In press.) Academic Press, New York.

Jost, A. (1969). The extent of foetal endocrine autonomy. *Foetal autonomy.* Ciba Foundation Symposium (ed. by G. E. W. Wolstenhome and M. O'Connor), p. 79. Churchill, London.

Jost, A., Vigier, B., Prepin, J. & Perchellet, J. P. (1973). Studies on sex differentiation in mammals. *Recent Progress in Hormone Research,* Vol. 29 (ed. by R. O. Greep), p. 1. Academic Press, New York & London.

Katz, D. H. & Benacerraf, B. (1974). *Immunological Tolerance. Mechanisms and potential therapeutic applications.* Academic Press, New York, San Francisco, London.

Keller, R. (1973). Cytostatic elimination of syngeneic rat tumor cells *in vitro* by nonspecifically activated macrophages. *J. exp. Med.* **138,** 625.

Kesztyüs, L. (1967). *Immunität und Nervensystem.* Akadémiai Kiadó. Budapest.

Kieffer, D. J. & Ketchel, M. M. (1971). Effects of adrenalectomy and antigenic stimulation on spleen weight in mice. *Transplantation,* **11,** 45.

Lancet (1974). *Editorial.* The thyroid, prolactin and breast cancer, p. 908 and Immunological changes in women, p. 909.

Mackay, W. D., Edwards, M. H., Bulbrook, R. D. & Wang, D. Y. (1971). Relation between plasma-cortisol, plasma-androgen-sulphates, and immune response in women with breast cancer. *Lancet,* **ii,** 1001.

Makinodan, T., Santos, G. W. & Quinn, R. P. (1970). Immunosuppressive drugs. *Pharmacol. Rev.* **22,** 189.

Marmorston, J. (1966). Urinary hormone metabolite levels in patients with cancer of the breast, prostate and lung. *Ann. N.Y. Acad. Sci.* **125,** 959.

Mason, J. W., Buescher, E. L., Belfer, M. L., Mougey, E. H., Taylor, E. D., Wherry, F. E., Ricketts, P. T., Young, P. S., Wade, J., Early, D. C. & Kenion, C. C. (1967). Pre-illness hormonal changes in Army recruits with acute respiratory infections. *Psychosom. Med.* **29,** 545.

Metcalf, D. (1960). Adrenal control function in high and low leukemia strains of mice. *Cancer Res.* **20,** 1347.

Miller, J. F. A. P. & Osoba, D. (1963). The rôle of the thymus in the origin of immunological competence. *The immunologically competent cell,* Ciba Foundation Study Group No. 16 (ed. by G. E. W. Wolstenholme and Julie Knight), p. 62. J. & A. Churchill, London.

Miyakawa, M. (1966). The morphological characteristics of the germfree mammals, including the results of recent studies on the adrenal in the germfree rats at the department of pathology, Nagoya University. I. The morphological characteristics described for the cecum and the lymphatic tissue in the germfree mammals. *International Congress Microbiol. IX Symposia,* p. 291. Ivanorsky Inst. Virol. Moscow, Russia.

Miyakawa, M. & Ukai, M. (1970). Adrenal gland functions in germfree animals. *Jap. J. clin. Med.* **28,** 2178.

Moog, R. & Ford, E. (1957). Influence of exogenous ACTH on body weight, adrenal growth, duodenal phosphatase, and liver glycogen in the chick embryo. *Anat. Rec.* **128,** 592.

Navmenko, E. V. (1973). *Central regulation of the pituitary adrenal complex.* Studies in Soviet Science. Consultants Bureau, New York, London.

Nomura, T., Ohsawa, N., Kageyame, K., Saito, M. & Tajima, Y. (1973). Testicular functions of germfree mice. *Germfree Research* (ed by J. B. Heneghan), p. 515. Academic Press, New York, London.

Pals, A. J., Reineke, E. P. & Schaw, G. H. (1973). Serum thyroxine levels in the perinatal guinea pig. *Lab. Anim. Sci.* **23,** 511.

Pierpaoli, W. & Besedovsky, H. O. (1975). Role of the thymus in programming of neuroendocrine functions. *Clin. exp. Immunol.* **20,** 323.

Pierpaoli, W., Fabris, N. & Sorkin, E. (1970). Developmental hormones and immunological maturation. *Hormones and the immune response* (ed. by G. E. W. Wolstenholme and Julie Knight), p. 126. J. & A. Churchill, London.

Pierpaoli, W., Haran-Ghera, N., Bianchi, E., Müller, J., Meshorer, A. & Bree, M. (1974). Endocrine disorders as a contributory factor to neoplasia in SJL/J mice. *J. nat. Cancer Inst.* **53,** 731.

Pierpaoli, W. & Sorkin, E. (1972). Alterations of adrenal cortex and thyroid in mice with congenital absence of the thymus. *Nature: New Biology,* **238,** 282.

Pleasants, J. R. (1968). Characteristics of the germ-free animal. *The Germfree Animal in Research* (ed. by Marie E. Coates), p. 113. Academic Press, London, New York.

Rao, L. G. S. & Hewit, M. L. (1970). Prognostic significance of a steroid-discriminant function in patients with inoperable lung cancer. *Lancet,* **ii,** 1063.

Shigeru, S., Takeshi, T., Tsuguo, S., Takeshi, T., Yoshikasu, O., Keishi, M. & Tokuichiro, S. (1966). Blood corticosterone level of tumor-bearing rats. *Gann,* **57,** 307.

Solomon, J.B. (1971). Ontogeny of defined immunity in mammals. *Foetal and Neonatal Immunology* p. 234. North Holland Publishing Company, Amsterdam.

Stein, M., Schiavi, R. C. & Camerino, M. (1976). Influence of brain and behavior on the immune system. *Science,* **191,** 435.

Udenfriend, S., Weissbach, H. & Bogdanski, D. F. (1957). Increase in tissue serotonine following administration of its precursors. 5-hydroxytryptamine. *J. biol. Chem.* **224,** 803.

Vought, R. L., Brown, R. A., Sibinovie, K. H. & McDaniel, E. G. (1972). Effect of changing intestinal bacterial flora on thyroid function in the rat. *Horm. Metab. Res.* **4,** 43.

Wahl, S. M., Altmann, L. C. & Rosenstreich, D. L. (1975). Inhibition of *in vitro* lymphokine synthesis by glucocorticosteroids. *J. Immunol.* **115,** 476.

White, T. (1966). Histamine in the brain. *Handbook of Experimental Pharmacology, Vol. XVIII/1, Histamine and Anti-Histaminics Part 1.* p. 789. Springer-Verlag, Berlin, Heidelberg, New York.

Wostmann, B. S. (1968). Defence mechanisms in germfree animals. Part 1. Humoral defence mechanisms. *The Germfree Animals in Research* (ed. by Marie E. Coates), p. 197. Academic Press, London, New York.

19

INTERDEPENDENCE BETWEEN NEUROENDOCRINE PROGRAMMING AND THE GENERATION OF IMMUNE RECOGNITION IN ONTOGENY

W. Pierpaoli, Hans Georg Kopp, Jürg Müller, and Max Keller

Sequential, chronologically, and quantitatively critical inoculation of different allogeneic hybrid cells into mice during the neonatal and perinatal period results in an indefinite prolongation of the perinatal stage during which tolerance can be readily induced. Consequently, a permanent specific tolerance to the sequentially inoculated alloantigens and a parallel alteration and retardation in the maturation of the developing endocrine system which normally controls immune differentiation are observed. The endocrine and immune parameters are altered only when the successive presentation of alloantigens is begun at birth, as this is a critical stage of development at which both the neuroendocrine (hypothalamic-pituitary) and the thymo-lymphatic systems are still highly undifferentiated. The phylogenetically and ontogenetically interlocked and interdependent thymo-lymphatic and neuroendocrine networks thus constitute a basic homoeostatic regulatory system in which signals of both endocrine and antigenic nature are detected and elaborated with consequent proper response in a homeostatic fashion. On the basis of these considerations and the experimental findings that support them, the generation of tolerance and immunity (recognition of self and nonself components of the body) appears to be a part of the definitive brain programming for neuroendocrine and immune functions in early ontogeny. This would constitute an augmented interpretation of the concept of immune tolerance as "specific central failure of the mechanisms of response" originally put forth by Medawar (1956, *Proc. Roy. Soc.* 146B, 1).

Introduction

One of the main characteristics of embryogenesis is the rapid sequence of appearance of new molecular and cellular structures. The immunological expression of this is the emergence of new antigens. Also, the process of recognition of self is simultaneously developing during this early stage of life. The reason these rapidly arising new antigens are not perceived by the host as foreign structures continues to be a matter of speculation.

Self-recognition mechanisms are not compatible with a fully competent immune system, because, in early ontogeny, the end product of recognition processes is tolerance, not immunity. It is therefore conceivable that in early ontogeny the evolutionarily derived programming has already defined future immunological performance and has deleted any possible asynchronic differentiative step producing suicide mechanisms. On the contrary, after the time-linked programming period, any remaining embryogenic features are brought under control in a homeostatic fashion by immune surveillance mechanisms.

Reprinted by permission from *Cell. Immunol.* **29** 16–27. Copyright © 1977, Academic Press. Inc.

Hormones are known to profoundly influence immunological development, as evidenced by their capacity to delay or accelerate the proliferation and differentiation of the thymo-lymphatic system (1–7). The pituitary gland elaborates a group of protein hormone compounds which are impressively similar from cyclostome to mammal (8). As phylogenetically ancient, primordial molecules, the presence of hormones in evolution of the species has permitted their adaptation to more and more qualified functions.

In this regard, they can be considered to be essential, timely, and critical agents which render cells capable of modifying their intrinsic potential, especially by the ability to differentiate. These ordinate hormone-guided processes are operative and essentially similar, if not identical, in the whole phylogenetic development, representing a general primary mechanism in the course of evolution by which the inborn genetic pattern is progressively expressed and adapted to the actual requirements of body development, especially to the capacity to cope with challenges of the external environment.

It is conceivable that lymphoid cells, considered to be a population of morphologically similar or identical but functionally multipotential effectors (7, 9), are not under exclusive guide of the host's genetic pattern for their multiplication and differentiation. Nor are the newly arising foreign, antigenic molecules and structures necessarily the only factors which can shift their potential capacities toward a specific function. As expressed in previous work (1–6) and in the concept proposed here, relatively simple molecules, such as thyroxine and gonadal or adrenal steroids, or complex protein molecules, such as somatotropic hormone or prolactin, are probably among the essential catalysts and regulators of the immune system. It would therefore be conceivable that the processes of generation of new cells capable of either recognition or indifference (and therefore unreactive) to the presence of new antigenic structures are also under hormonal control. It then follows that the hormonal status during early embryogenesis would be responsible for timing the maturation of the immune system. *Conversely, this hormonal status might well depend on the rate and sequence of appearance of new cells or antigens. The decreasing rate of cell differentiation (less antigens) and proliferation (less cells) in the later stages of embryonic development might therefore influence the sequential neuroendocrine maturation,* as this same cell dynamics and developmental processes in late embryogenesis may also be under hormonal control. This later decrease in the *rate* of appearance of new antigens on existing or newly generated cells could therefore influence and change the hormonal environment, which, in turn, would allow the cells to acquire new functions directed toward active immunity. This interval most probably corresponds in mammals to the critical stage, at which the thymus is exerting its crucial endocrine action on the differentiation of the neuroendocrine centers in the brain (10). This concept of the *interdependence* between the development of the endocrine and immune systems in early ontogeny has been previously articulated, but in a less developed form (6, 7, see also 3 and 4).

The dramatic cellular and hormonal events in embryogenesis, leading to full acquisition of immunocompetence, are considered here as being very narrowly focused in time. Should this indeed be the case, it would be possible, by introducing new antigens sequentially, to prolong the fetal hormonal environment or to interfere with the postnatal endocrine development and thereby produce a permanent specific unresponsiveness in the immune system, in the sense of "specific central failure of the mechanisms of response" as originally envisaged by Medawar (11).

This concept as formulated predicts that the introduction of antigens or of immunologically incompatible cells (allogeneic cells) at this state of fetal life induces a temporary arrest, delay, or impairment of the hormonal development. As a consequence of this temporary arrest of the differentiative action of hormones at a critical stage of development, cell differentiation toward immunity is impeded, thus leading to tolerance or unresponsiveness. In this condition of delayed development of immune responsiveness of general, i.e., *nonspecific character*, introduction of any antigen will result in *specific tolerance*.

Experimental Approach

The experimental approach to the concept was based on the well-known model developed by Billingham *et al.* (12–14) in mice which has provided an experimental support to the clonal selection theory of Burnet (15). It appeared to be possible that presentation of new antigens by introduction of allogeneic cells into newborn, immunologically immature mammals would mimic and prolong artificially embryologic development and retard neuroendocrine maturation. In fact, both cell proliferation and differentiation during embryogenesis could be mimicked and magnified by introducing into a newborn mouse viable *syngeneic* (proliferation) or *allogeneic* (differentiation) cells. The expected consequence would have been that the mice, periodically confronted with massive quantities of different and new allogeneic cells in sequence in the neonatal and postnatal time, would maintain a condition of *immune* and *endocrine* immaturity, permitting the inducement of tolerance at a postnatal time when, normally, the animals have already acquired the capacity to recognize allogeneic cells and mount a normal cell-mediated immune reaction. It was also expected that a parallel, specific and well-defined retardation and impairment of certain endocrine functions would occur as a consequence of sequential presentation of allogeneic cells. Therefore, in trying to mimic, prolong, and delay the process of embryogenesis, both the immune and the endocrine parameters were evaluated (Fig. 1).

The critical modalities for the accomplishment of the experiments were achieved after several attempts by which it was possible to establish appropriate conditions for obtaining full immune tolerance with the strain combinations used. The whole series of experiments was repeated five times.

Material and Methods

Animals

Male and female histoincompatible inbred BALB/c (Melchers), CBA/J, C57BL/6J, and DBA/J mice and their F_1 hybrids were used. Recipients of allogeneic or syngeneic cells were newborn (day of birth), 4-, and 8-day-old male and female BALB/c mice. Donors of spleen cells were adult (4–6 months old) male or female F_1 hybrid CBA/J × BALB/c, C57BL/6J × BALB/c, and DBA/J × BALB/c mice (allogeneic cells) or BALB/c male or female adult mice (syngeneic cells).

Induction and Testing of Tolerance

In all experiments, the number of spleen cells was adjusted to 20×10^6 cells in 0.05 ml of phosphate-buffered solution (PBS), pH 7.4, when the mice were injected on day of birth or in 0.1 ml of PBS when + or 8-day-old mice were used. Spleen cell suspensions were prepared by gently teasing the spleens in cooled PBS with a loose-fitting Teflon pestle. They were washed six to eight times and filtered two to three times through gauze. The cells were injected intravenously (iv) into the orbital branch of the anterior facial vein when the mice were newborn and intraperitoneally (ip) when the recipients were + or 8-day-old mice. The hole of the

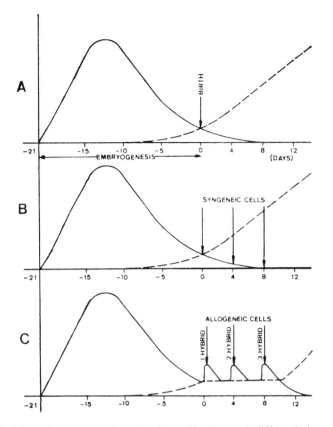

FIGURE 1. (A) Schematic representation of cell proliferation and differentiation with concomitant maturation of the autonomous endocrine system during embryogenesis and postnatal interval.—, Theoretical rate of cell proliferation and generation of new self antigens; ----, differentiation of the autonomous endocrine system. (B) Inoculation of syngeneic cells does not affect maturation of the developing neuroendocrine system. (C) The sequential and timely critical (4-day interval) inoculation of different allogeneic hybrid cells (2×10^7 spleen cells each inoculation) into mice during the neonatal and perinatal periods results in a prolongation of the perinatal stage, during which tolerance can be induced. Parallel alteration and retardation in the maturation of that section of the endocrine system which normally controls immune differentiation are observed.

injection was sealed with 4% collodium to prevent leakage. Donors of skin for transplantation were mice from the parental strains (see above). Recipients of skin grafts were BALB/c mice (groups of 10–15 mice of each sex), untreated or injected neonatally or perinatally with syngeneic or allogeneic cells (Table 1). In all experiments, the mice were skin-grafted between 40 and 60 days of age. Skin transplantation was performed according to the standard technique (16). The mice were liberated from the corset after 8 days and the viability of the grafts was followed daily. The recipients of skin grafts from allogeneic donors were considered to be tolerant when the graft was *permanently* accepted and fluent hairs were growing on the accepted skin.

TABLE 1. Experimental Plan for Administration of Allogeneic Cells Postnatally to Prolong Tolerance to Allogeneic Antigens in Mice and to Induce Concomitant Impairment and Retardation of Endocrine Maturation[a]

BALB/c recipients (designation of groups)	Number of transplanted mice	Birth (C57BL/6J × BALB/c)	Day 4 (DBA/J × BALB/c)	Day 8 (CBA/J × BALB/c)	Number of accepted allogeneic skin grafts (BALB/c recipients)
		Sequential injections of allogeneic cells (F$_1$ hybrid donors)			
A	32	+	−	−	C57BL/6J (30)
B	40	+	+	−	C57BL/6J (35) DBA/J (33)
C	52	+	+	+	C57BL/6J (46) DBA/J (41) CBA/J (40)
D	22	−	+	+	None
E	15	−	−	+	None
F	10	−	−	−	None

[a]Newborn, 4-, and 8-day-old BALB/c mice were injected intravenously (newborns) or intraperitoneally (4 and 8 days old) with 2×10^7 syngeneic (BALB/c) or allogeneic (C57BL/6J × BALB/c, DBA/J × BALB/c, CBA/J × BALB/c) spleen cells. Many of the mice were exsanguinated on Day 12 and levels of hormones were determined in serum (see Table 2). The skin-grafted adult BALB/c mice included an equal number of males and females. The BALB/c mice of all groups (A–F) were first tested for tolerance to C57BL/6J donors. Each single BALB/c mouse of groups A–C which was tolerant to skin from C57BL/6J donors (111/124, or 89%, of the mice showed no sign of rejection after 60 days) was successively transplanted with skin from the other allogeneic donors from the parental hybrid strains (BDA/J and CBA/J) after removal of the first or second accepted graft. The BALB/c mice of groups B and C were considered to be tolerant to DBA/J and CBA/J only when the grafts were accepted permanently. The graftings were repeated when they were technically defective or doubtful.

Determinations of Hormones

To collect serum for hormone determinations, the mice were exsanguinated under strictly standardized conditions, between 10:00 and 12:00 AM, by recision of the neck vessels or from the retroorbital venous plexus. Sera from male and female mice (at least 12 mice each group and sex) were kept separate, pooled, divided into aliquots, and maintained frozen at $-20°C$ until hormone determinations were performed. The mice were bled at 12 days of age, after inoculation of the allogeneic or syngeneic spleen cells, according to the scheme reported in Table 2. Serum was also obtained from large groups (40–80 mice) of normal untreated male and female, newborn or 12-day-old BALB/c mice. Serum levels of the following hormones were determined: thyroxine (T-4), corticosterone, 17-β-estradiol, progesterone, testosterone, luteotropic hormone (LH), follicle-stimulating hormone (FSH), growth hormone (GH), and prolactin (PRL). The rat kits for radioimmunoassay of protein hormones were a generous gift from the National Institute of Arthritis, Metabolism, and Digestive Diseases, Rat Pituitary Hormone Distribution Program, Bethesda, Maryland (NIAMD Rat LH-I-3, Rat FSH-I-3, Rat GH-I-2, and Rat Prolactin-I-1). All hormone determinations were performed on duplicate samples of coded sera and repeated when the internal variability on repeated assays exceeded 10%. The values of protein hormones correspond to the average radioimmunoassayable hormone content of one serum pool from the different groups (A to G, see Table 2). The hormone values given in Table 2 derive from two identical experiments of a total of five experiments. They represent the hormonal level in BALB/c mice in our experimental conditions.

The hormone values obtained when another recipient strain was used reflected the hormone levels which are a characteristic attribute of that strain; however, the qualitative and quantitative variations were quite similar to those indicated in Table 2. Therefore, the phenomenon is repeatable when other strain combinations are used, provided they are incompatible at the main H-2 histocompatibility locus.

Results

Induction and Prolongation of Tolerance

Table 1 illustrates the experimental plan for induction of tolerance in BALB/c mice inoculated at birth and/or during the first 8 days of life with different allogeneic spleen cells from F_1 hybrids. No tolerance could be achieved in many attempts when the time interval between the inoculation was 5 instead of 4 days and the same sequence and number of F_1 hybrid spleen cells (2×10^7) were maintained. Beyond 4 days, even a difference of a few hours interfered with the induction of tolerance. Under these experimental conditions, 4 days seems to be the longest interval within which presentation of 2×10^7 new allogeneic cells effects a further prolongation of immunological immaturity and extends the time during which tolerance can be induced. Shorter or longer intervals for maintenance of tolerance can probably be achieved with different strain combinations or increments of cells. In no case could full tolerance or even a prolongation of the rejection time be achieved unless mice were inoculated on the day of birth. No cross-reactivity was observed in any of all possible interstrain skin grafts. The induced tolerance persisted, as manifested by successful grafting at 4–5 months of age or later in life. The unresponsive state was consistently specific, being limited to the parental strain donors of the allogeneic cells.

Hormonal Changes

Impairment and dissociation of development of the endocrine parameters were observed when the mice were inoculated with allogeneic cells starting on the day of birth. This impairment was measured by comparing serum levels of hormones and appeared to be confined to the adrenal and gonadal steroids (Table 2, groups A–C). Values for thyroxine were not altered or were there significant changes in protein hormones. In mice injected with allogeneic cells *starting on the day of birth,* the levels of corticosterone, 17-β-estradiol, and testosterone were quite dissimilar (much higher or lower) from those in mice injected with syngeneic cells (Table 2, groups A–C). These differences were absent or eventually the opposite effect was observed when mice were injected with the allogeneic cells, with the first inoculation given at the age of 4 and/or 8 days (Table 2, groups D and E). The following three main different situations must be considered.

(a) Passive transfer of 2×10^7 syngeneic cells from adult donors into newborn, immunologically immature mice induces per se an obvious anticipation and acceleration of immune maturation with possible effects on the hormonal status of the animals in the first days of life. In fact, Table 2 shows that passive transfer of syngeneic spleen cells produces changes in

TABLE 2. Delay and Impairment of Maturation of Adrenal and Sexual Functions Expressed through Changes in Levels of Adrenal and Gonadal Steroids in Postnatal Mice Injected Sequentially with Different Allogeneic Spleen Cells

Newborn BALB/c recipients (identification of groups)	Injection[a]			Hormone levels at 12 days of age								
	Birth (BALB/c × C57BL/6J)	Day 4 (BALB/c × DBA/J)	Day 8 (BALB/c × CBA/J)	Thyroxine (µg/100 ml)	Corticosterone (µg/100 ml)	Testosterone (ng/100 ml)	17-β-Estradiol (n M/liter)	Progesterone (ng/100 ml)	GH (ng/ml)	LH (ng/ml)	FSH (ng/ml)	PRL (ng/ml)
(A)Male	+	–	–	–	–	398 ± 12	–	–	–	–	104	–
controls[b]	+	–	–	–	5.8 ± 0.2	153 ± 10	–	–	–	–	125	–
(A)Female	+	–	–	–	3.4 ± 0.4	–	0.119 ± 0.003	116 ± 4	44	–	–	nd
controls	+	–	–	–	5.7 ± 0.3	–	0.157 ± 0.011	155 ± 6	33	–	–	nd
(B)Male	+	+	–	–	–	491 ± 5	–	–	–	–	–	–
controls	+	+	–	–	–	119 ± 17	–	–	–	–	–	–
(B)Female	+	+	–	–	–	–	0.183 ± 0.011	232 ± 12	–	–	–	–
controls	+	+	–	–	–	–	0.189 ± 0.010	197 ± 14	–	–	–	–
(C)Male	+	+	+	11.3	6.6 ± 0.2	214 ± 22	–	–	40	33	145	nd
controls	+	+	+	10.3	4.5 ± 0.2	433 ± 34	–	–	36	34	230	nd
(C)Female	+	+	+	10.3	21.8 ± 0.7	–	0.110 ± 0.004	212 ± 10	34	66	580	nd
controls	+	+	+	12.1	4.5 ± 0.5	–	0.221 ± 0.012	237 ± 17	46	43	595	<0.5
(D)Male	–	+	+	–	7.1 ± 0.2	355 ± 18	–	–	16	38	–	–
controls	–	+	+	–	10.8 ± 0.2	452 ± 45	–	–	25	58	–	–
(D)Female	–	+	+	–	10.3 ± 0.3	–	0.185 ± 0.018	284 ± 16	–	49	–	–
controls	–	+	+	–	10.2 ± 0.4	–	0.147 ± 0.016	245 ± 20	–	29	–	–
(E)Male	–	–	+	–	3.6 ± 0.1	118 ± 10	–	–	–	63	–	–
controls	–	–	+	–	6.8 ± 0.3	600 ± 24	–	–	–	71	–	–
(E)Female	–	–	+	–	5.6 ± 0.3	–	0.192 ± 0.011	287 ± 7	48	52	620	nd
controls	–	–	+	–	6.2 ± 0.2	–	0.222 ± 0.020	175 ± 10	42	37	560	nd
(F)Male	–	–	–	11.5	6.2 ± 0.3	222 ± 15	–	–	23	32	292	<0.5
females	–	–	–	11.9	4.3 ± 0.4	–	0.175 ± 0.016	230 ± 12	26	41	550	nd
(G)Males	Bled on day of birth			–	8.6 ± 0.2	119 ± 6	–	–	–	33	–	–
(G)Females	Bled on day of birth			–	10.0 ± 0.3	–	0.174 ± 0.011	111 ± 4	–	48	–	–

[a]Allogeneic or syngeneic (controls) spleen cells (2 × 10^7).
[b]Control mice of all groups (A–E) were also injected with syngeneic cells at the given schedule. nd, not detectable.

levels of corticosterone, testosterone, and, to a lesser extent, estradiol and progesterone (Table 2, groups A–E). This may explain the differences in hormone levels when compared with uninjected, 12-day-old mice (group F).

(b) Passive transfer of allogeneic spleen cells induces changes of the hormonal status (adrenal and gonadal steroids) which are *opposite* to those obtained with syngeneic cells. As the only difference between the syngeneic and the allogeneic cells is the presence in the latter ones of antigens to the host, this indicates that it is the *antigenicity* of the cells which modifies the hormonal status of the mice, especially with regard to adrenal and gonadal steroids (Table 2, groups A–C).

(c) Passive transfer of allogeneic spleen cells into 4-day-old (group D) and 8-day-old (group E) mice can be considered to be the immunization of as yet incompletely mature but, nonetheless, more mature animals. Therefore, the hormonal status might reflect the effect of immunization on the endocrine system. This status is in contrast to that of animals maintained in a condition of tolerance by inoculation of allogeneic spleen cells starting on day of birth (groups A–C). Therefore, the general tendency of mice sequentially injected with allogeneic cells, starting on the day of birth, was clearly that of maintaining or approaching the levels of corticosterone, testosterone, and estradiol which are characteristic of mice during the first day of life (group G), i.e., *the mimicking of the perinatal hormonal status* (17–24). This aberration could only be achieved when inoculation of the alloantigens was started on the day of birth. The considerable differences in values between male and female mice reflect the great basic hormonal diversity of perinatal hormone levels in the two sexes. In fact, sexual development and differentiation obey a completely chronologically asymmetrical pattern in male and female mice (25, 26).

Discussion

The findings developed in this investigation show that the sequential confrontation of mice with different alloantigens during the neonatal and perinatal periods *induces*, in parallel: (a) changes of hormone levels in blood which resemble a retardation and impairment of maturation of the endocrine system, especially with regard to adrenal and gonadal functions, and (b) specific unresponsiveness or "tolerance" to the alloantigens with which the mice have been sequentially confronted. With the dose and the three different combinations of allogeneic hybrid cells used in the present work, a prolongation of the "tolerogenic" time is obtained as long as 4 and 8 days after the inoculation of the cells. It is implicit that the experimental conditions (dose and types of cells, number of hybrids, and others) could be further elaborated so as to obtain an extended prolongation of the tolerogenic postnatal time or adapted to a variety of experimental conditions under which the genesis of immunocompetence and tolerance is explored.

These findings are consonant with the proposition (3, see Discussion) that *the evolutionary development of the immune and endocrine systems in mammals takes place in a closely interlocked synchronic and interdependent manner*. The signals of both hormonal and antigenic nature are participating in the formation of fully developed immune recognition mechanisms and in the continuation of such mechanisms in adult life. The mimicking and prolongation of embryogenesis by the introduction in massive amounts of "foreign" cell antigens serve to impede the development and maturation of that aspect of the endocrine system which is specifically devoted to immune differentiation of T and B cells, the vehicles of the recognition mechanisms. The consequences of this artificially induced alteration in the "timing" of development of the immune and endocrine systems are a protracted postnatal incapacity of the animal to recognize foreign structures as "nonself" and, consequently, to accept permanently allogeneic skin grafts.

This model does not demonstrate a direct link between antigen presentation and endocrine derangements during perinatal time in mice. However, in accordance with the concepts expressed in this work, it has been previously shown that, in fact, inoculation of certain hormones (e.g., GH) into the endocrinologically and immunologically immature newborn mice changes the immune reactivity of thymus cells and increases that of spleen cells in a modified graft-versus-host assay (3, 5).

It is not surprising that the neuroendocrine system, through its hypothalamic-hypophysis feed back mechanisms, acts on the generation of immunocompetent cells and that these cells, conversely, give signals to neuroendocrine regulation. The most striking example of this kind of evolutionary symbiosis is the thymus, the function of which in mammals is clearly that of generating precursors of immunocompetent cells and of participating, *at the same time* and through its endocrine action, in the formation of an environment in which these thymus-derived cells mature to immunocytes (10, 27–29). The close ontogenetic interdependence in the development of the endocrine and thymolymphatic systems is supported by findings indicating, for example that there is a genetic association between the H-2 gene and testosterone metabolism in mice (30). It is therefore credible, as shown in our model, that introduction of alloantigens into immature mice *retards* the expression of these strain-specific H-2-linked genes, thus influencing the development of gonadal steroid-dependent organs, affecting selectively the maturation and differentiation of the cell population of the thymolymphatic tissues, and prolonging the tolerogenic perinatal time.

A question that is still unanswered is whether or not lymphocytes from an immunologically mature animal, upon interacting with antigens, function as *messengers to the central nervous system* by modulating the immune response (antibody production and cell-mediated immunity) via elaboration of lymphokines or of other soluble mediators. This would be expected on the basis of their embryological derivation from an endocrine organ, the thymus. Conversely, corticosteroids have been shown to inhibit synthesis of lymphokines (31).

The generation of immunological tolerance, unresponsiveness, or nonrecognition of self components of the body can therefore be regarded as a part of the definitive brain programming at the hypothalamic-hypophysis levels. The antigenic stimuli occurring during embryogenesis delete the immune response to the self components and prevents, already at the level of the central nervous system, the sequence of reactions which are otherwise performed through the automatic, intergrating, and homoestatic neuroendocrine regulation of the immune response in mature animals. In a condition of specific unresponsiveness, antigens cannot possibly evoke any corresponding neuroendocrine chain reaction bringing control and possibly elimination of antigenic or foreign intrusion into the body by formation of antibodies or by other immune mechanisms. This concept coincides and provides an explanation for Medawar's (11) idea that tolerance represents a *"specific central failure of the mechanisms of response."* This alternative interpretation of the ontogenic development of tolerance and self-recognition mechanisms is also in basic harmony with Medawar's (32) recent comments that tolerance can still be considered to be *essential nonreactivity* of the immune system, in the sense that certain cells reacting to antigenic stimuli *have not been generated.* This concept of the generation of immunocompetent cells in strict synchrony with the development of endocrine functions and organization of the hypothalamic brain centers makes for a more comprehensive interpretation of the well-known natural models, such as that of the athymic nude mouse in which transplantation immune reactions are absent (28, 33). This model and the evidence provided here show that asynchrony and improper timing of cellular (antigens) and humoral (hormones) events lead to an inability to generate competent cells and an inability to recognize foreign molecular structures. There seems, therefore, to be a critical phase in immune development in which the proper timing and proper combination of cells and hormones produce a plus or minus status, as exemplified by the model of the nude mouse (10, 28).

It is now fully accepted that the development and expression of immune responsiveness are under genetic control (34). In connection with what was mentioned above, it must also be stressed that the genetically determined pattern of hormonal status and, consequently, of the postnatal environmental shaping the different species and strains of the experimental animals might explain the differences in immune reactivity and responsiveness as well as the onset, acceleration, or prevention of autoimmune disorders. It is therefore conceivable that the characteristics (initiation, amplitude, duration, etc.) of an immune response are largely dependent on the genetically built-in endocrine status of the host and on its strain- and species-specific capacity to react with a different hormonal response to the same antigenic stimulus. This might hold also for all of the studies with germ-free animals in which lack of stimulation from the interestinal flora and from the environmental antigens might produce a retardation of endocrine and, consequently, immune development. It is clear that, in the early stages of immune and endocrine differentiation, asynchrony and inappropriate timing can produce irreversible consequences which are subsequently expressed as defects in the immune parameters. Natural models could well be the athymic nude mouse (28) and the New Zealand Black (NZB) mouse, in which the wrong, delayed [nude mouse (10, 28)], or anticipated (NZB mouse) endocrine maturation does not, in the former, permit the generation of immunocompetent cells or, in the latter, allows premature generation of "recognizing" cells which react to self antigens. The latter suggestion that the origin of autoimmune clones in NZB mice depends on the aberrant perinatal environment still awaits experimental affirmation.

Thus, the basic genetically determined hormonal status might well underlie various phenomena related to proliferation and performance of immune-reacting cells, activation of macrophagic functions, and liberation of biochemical signals or mediators.

The implications of these findings are particularly relevant to comprehending the physiological processes of immune differentiation and the generation of immune diversity. In fact, this model offers a means for identifying the hormones which promote differentiation of immunocompetent cells or suppress immune reactions. The plasticity and receptivity of the maturing central nervous system to immunological messages seem to be a normal evolutionary developmental condition in which the integrating activity is performed by the hypothalamic-pituitary axis and hormones are the versatile multifunctional vehicles. Once more the aphorism of P. B. Medawar (35) is apt: "It is not hormones which have evolved but the uses to which they are put."

Acknowledgments

The authors are deeply grateful to Hoffmann-La Roche AG, Animal Farm Füllinsdorf, for free supply of most of the animals used in this work. With exclusion of the work connected with determinations of hormones (H. G. Kopp, J. Müller, and M. Keller), this project was supported by the Swiss National Fund for Scientific Research, Grant No. 3.8750.72.

References

1. Pierpaoli, W., and Sorkin, E., *J. Immunol.* **101**, 1036, 1968.
2. Pierpaoli, W., Baroni, C., Fabris, N., and Sorkin, E., *Immunology* **16**, 217, 1969.
3. Pierpaoli, W., Fabris, N., and Sorkin, E., *In* "Hormones and the Immune Response," Ciba Foundation Study Group No. 36 (G. E. W. Wolstenholme and Julie Knight, Eds.), p. **126**. Churchill, London, 1970.
4. Fabris, N., Pierpaoli, W., and Sorkin, E., *In* "Developmental Aspects of Antibody Formation and Structure" (J. Sterzl and I. Riha, Eds.), p. 79. Czechoslovak Academy of Science, Prague, 1970.
5. Pierpaoli, W., Fabris, N., and Sorkin, E., *In* "Cellular Interactions in the Immune Response" (S. Cohen, C. Cudkowicz, and R. T. McCluskey, Eds.), p. 25. Karger Verlag, Basel, 1971.
6. Pierpaoli, W., and Sorkin, E., *Nature New Biol.* **238**, 282, 1972.
7. Pierpaoli, W., and Sorkin, E., *Experientia* **28**, 1385, 1972.
8. Hoar, W. S., *In* "The Pituitary Gland" (G. W. Harris and B. T. Donovan, Eds.), Vol. 1, p. 242. Butterworths, London, 1966.
9. Fabris, N., Pierpaoli, W., and Sorkin, E., *Nature (London)* **240**, 557, 1972.
10. Pierpaoli, W., and Besedovsky, H. O., *Clin. Exp. Immunol.* **20**, 323, 1975.
11. Medawar, P. B., *Proc. Roy. Soc.* **146B**, 1, 1956.
12. Billingham, R. E., Brent, L., and Medawar, P. B., *Phil. Trans. Roy. Soc.* **239**, 357, 1956.
13. Billingham, R. E., Brent, L., and Medawar, P. B., *Transplant. Bull.* **3**, 84, 1956.
14. Billingham, R. E., Brent, L., and Medawar, P. B., *Nature (London)* **178**, 514, 1956.
15. Burnet, F. M., "The Clonal Selection Theory of Acquired Immunity." Cambridge University Press, 1959.
16. Billingham, R. E., and Silvers, W. K., "Transplantation of Tissues and Cells." The Wistar Institute Press, Philadelphia, 1961.
17. Levine, S., and Treiman, L. J., *In* "Foetal Autonomy" (G. E. W. Wolstenholme and M. O'Connor, Eds.), p. 271. Churchill, London, 1969.
18. Dähler, K. D., and Wuttke, W., *Endocrinology* **94**, 1003, 1974.
19. Resko, J. A., Feder, H. H., and Goy, R. W., *J. Endocrinol.* **40**, 485, 1968.
20. Dullart, J., Kent, J., and Ryle, M., *J. Reprod. Fert.* **43**, 189, 1975.
21. Ojeda, S. R., and McCann, S. M., *Endocrinology* **95**, 1499, 1974.
22. Cheng, H. C., and Johnson, D. C., *Neuroendocrinology* **13**, 357, 1974.
23. Goldman, B. D., Grazia, Y. R., Kamberi, I. A., and Porter, J. C., *Endocrinology* **88**, 771, 1971.
24. Stiff, M. E., Bronson, F. H., and Stetson, M. H., *Endocrinology* **94**, 492, 1974.
25. Harris, G. W., *Endocrinology* **75**, 627, 1964.
26. Jost, A., Vigier, B., Prepin, J., and Perchellet, J. P., *Rec. Progr. Horm. Res.* **29**, 1, 1973.
27. Pierpaoli, W., and Besedovsky, H. O., *Brit. J. Exp. Pathol.* **56**, 180, 1975.
28. Pierpaoli, W., *Immunology* **29**, 465, 1975.
29. Pierpaoli, W., Kopp, H. G., and Bianchi, E., *Clin. Exp. Immunol.* **24**, 501, 1976.
30. Ivanyi, P., Hampl, R., Starka, L., and Mickova, M., *Nature New Biol.* **238**, 280, 1972.
31. Wahl, S. J., Altmann, L. C., and Rosenstreich, D. L., *J. Immunol.* **115**, 476, 1975.
32. Medawar, P. B., *Transplant. Proc.* **5**, 7, 1973.
33. Rygaard, J., *In* "Thymus and Self. Immunobiology of the Mouse Mutant Nude," p. 111. FADL, Copenhagen, 1973.
34. McDevitt, H. O., and Landy, M., "Genetic Control of Immune Responsiveness." Academic Press, New York, 1972.
35. Medawar, P. B., *In* "The Pituitary Gland," Anterior Pituitary (G. W. Harris and B. T. Donovan, Eds.), Vol. 1, p. 283. Butterworths, London, 1966.

20

PHARMACOLOGICAL CONTROL OF THE IMMUNE RESPONSE BY BLOCKADE OF THE EARLY HORMONAL CHANGES FOLLOWING ANTIGEN INJECTION

Walter Pierpaoli and Georges J. M. Maestroni

Antigen injection into mice induces a rapid increase in blood levels of gonadotropins. Suppression of these hormonal changes by a combination of drugs acting on the neuroendocrine regulation as well as on cell membrane receptors results in a blockade of antibody synthesis and specific "tolerance." In addition, remarkable suppression of transplantation immunity is achieved.

Introduction

Much experimental work of the last decade attests to the modulation of the immune response by several hormones (1–3). These early data gave rise to the concept that, during ontogeny, the neuroendocrine and the immune systems are interdependent, thus influencing and conditioning each other (1–5). That work in turn led to the identification of some hormonal factors which are involved in the differentiation of the thymolymphatic system to the mature, adult status. This approach is consistent with the recent identification of the mammalian thymus as an endocrine organ required in early ontogeny for the final, functional organization of the hypothalamus (6, 7) and for the development of a proper, chronologically critical hormonal environment in which the bone marrow-derived (B) and thymus-derived (T) lymphocytes can differentiate to immunocompetent cells, i.e., become capable of reacting to antigens and to initiate an immune response (7–9).

The present study was based on the hypothesis that an interaction of an antigen with immunoreactive lymphocytes, known to induce the synthesis of lymphokines, might induce very rapid changes in the host hormonal status and cause, in turn, a hormone-dependent alteration of the initially antigen-activated cells. That such feedback mechanisms do indeed modulate the immune response is shown in this communication. The experimental results reported here demonstrate that injection of allogeneic lymph node cells into mice evokes prompt changes in the levels of two gonadotropins, i.e., luteotropic hormone (LH) and follicle-stimulating hormone (FSH).

These very early hormonal events occurring after antigen challenge suggested the possibility that blocking the initial message to the hypothalamic–pituitary centers consequent to the interaction of antigen with antigen-sensitive cells, or preventing the immediate hormonal changes

Reprinted by permission from *Cell Immunol.* **31**, 355–363. Copyright © 1977, Academic Press, Inc.

which follow, might inhibit the subsequent stages of the immune response and so induce a specific unresponsiveness to the antigen.

For this purpose, drugs were tested which inhibit or delay neuroendocrine functions for gonadotropins or interfere with synthesis or release of gonadotropin-releasing factors (LH-FSH-RF) in the hypothalamus or block their activity on the target cells in the adenohypophysis. Also, the effect of these drugs on peripheral endocrine glands and on the adrenergic receptors on lymphocytes was considered (10–17). Two of the drugs considered had been shown to be immunosuppressive when tested singly at high dosage (18, 19). These drugs were tested either singly or in combination in mice for their capacity to block or suppress primary and secondary immune responses to SRBC. Their capacity was also tested to inhibit or block allogeneic skin graft rejection in adult mice and runt disease in newborn albino recipient mice.

The findings show indeed that the simultaneous administration of antigen and a combination of drugs known to act both on the central neuroendocrine regulation and on certain cell membrane receptors (adrenergic receptors) results in the induction of a specific unresponsiveness, essentially complete in the case of the humoral and less so of the cell-mediated response.

Materials and Methods

Animals

Adult (+ to 5-month-old) male and female inbred C3H/HeJ and C57BL/6J mice and outbred newborn and adult male and female Swiss albino mice were used. The mice were maintained in air-conditioned animal rooms under conventional conditions. They received water and food *ad libitum*.

Preparation of Cell Suspensions

Suspensions of spleen cells or lymph node cells were prepared by teasing the tissues in cooled Gey's solution using a Teflon pestle and a loose-fitting tube. The cells were washed four to five times, filtered through gauze, and finally adjusted to the desired volume and concentration. Cells from mesenteric, axillary, inguinal, and submaxillary lymph nodes were pooled.

Determinations of Hormones

The mice were exsanguinated under strictly standardized conditions. Sera from the different groups were pooled and divided into aliquots. Radioimmunoassay (RIA) of the protein hormones luteotropic hormone (LH), follicle-stimulating hormone (FSH), growth hormone (GH), and prolactin (PR) was performed by using the rat kits supplied as a gift from the National Institute of Arthritis, Metabolism, and Digestive Diseases, Rat Pituitary Hormone Distribution Program, Bethesda, Maryland (NIAMD-Rat LH-I-3, FSH-I-3, Rat GH-I-2, and Rat Prolactin-I-1). The hormone determinations were performed on duplicate samples of coded sera. The values were corrected by using reference samples of mouse pituitary hormones.

Drugs

The α-blocker phentolamine (mesylate salt, pure substance) was kindly presented by Ciba-Geigy AG, Basel, Switzerland. The neuroleptic drug haloperidol was a gift from Janssen

Pharmaceutica, Beerse, Belgium. L-5-Hydroxytryptophan was purchased from Calbiochem, San Diego, California. The drugs were either dissolved in 0.5% citric acid and incorporated into Freund's incomplete adjuvant or given as a suspension in saline. They were administered subcutaneously (sc).

Hormones

Adrenocorticotropic hormone (ACTH) was purchased from Ciba-Geigy AG, Basel, Switzerland (Synacthen). LH and FSH were received as a gift from the Endocrinology Study Section of the National Institutes of Health, Bethesda, Maryland (NIH-LH-B9 and NIH-FSH-B1). They were dissolved in distilled water and injected sc.

Skin Transplantation

The mice were transplanted by the conventional technique. The corset was removed after 8 days. The grafts were considered as rejected when the first signs of rejection appeared (edema, infiltration). Defective or doubtful transplants were repeated. Some mice were transplanted repeatedly in order to confirm the length of the rejection time, when this was prolonged over 20 days.

Immunological Tests

The conventional hemolytic plaque assay was used. Nucleated spleen cells from individual mice were counted and their number was adjusted to 1×10^6 nucleated cells in 0.1 ml of medium (Gey's solution).

Test for the Early Endocrine Changes after Injection of Allogeneic Cells

Groups of male C3H/HeJ mice (three 5-month-old mice per group) were inoculated intravenously (iv) with 5×10^7 lymph node lymphocytes from untreated or alloimmunized C57BL/6J mice (injected 4 weeks earlier with spleen cells from C3H/HeJ mice). Control groups were inoculated with the same number of syngeneic cells (C3H/HeJ) or with the suspension medium (Gey's solution). Groups of mice were rapidly exsanguinated at 0.5, 1, 2, 3, 4, 5, 6, 7, or 8 hr, respectively, after inoculation of the cells. The sera from each group were pooled separately, divided into aliquots, and used for radioimmunoassay of the protein hormones (LH, FSH, GH, and prolactin).

Results

Administration of Allogeneic Cells Induces Rapid Hormonal Changes in Blood

The levels of LH increased sharply between 1 and 2 hr after injection of allogeneic cells (Fig. 1), most rapidly when lymph node cells were from alloimmunized donors. Similar but less marked increases in levels of FSH were also observed (from 52 to 120 ng of FSH/ml 2 hr after inoculation of allogenic cells).

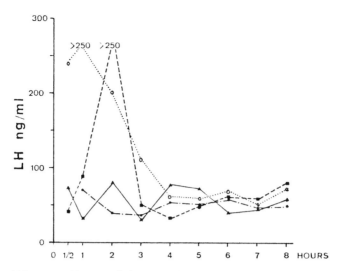

FIGURE 1. Rapid increase of luteotropic hormone (LH) in blood of mice after inoculation of allogeneic cells. Groups of three 5-month-old male C3H/HeJ mice were injected iv with 5×10^7 lymph node cells from untreated C57BL/6J mice (■———■), alloimmunized (with spleen cells from C3H/HeJ mice 4 weeks before), C57BL/6J mice (○———○), or syngeneic C3H/HeJ mice (▲———▲). One group was injected with the medium used for the cell suspensions (●———●). At the time given, the mice were rapidly exsanguinated, and the serum from each group and time was pooled and frozen until determination of LH.

Pharmacological Blockade of the Immune Response

Antibody production to SRBC was completely prevented by the following combination of drugs: L-5-hydroxytryptophan (5HTP), phentolamine, and haloperidol. 5HTP is the main metabolic precursor of 5-hydroxytryptamine (serotonin), an important hypothalamic neurotransmitter; phentolamine blocks α-adrenergic receptors for catecholamines; haloperidol blocks dopaminergic receptors. The probable final effect of the combination of these drugs on secretion of hormones at the pituitary level is summarized in the tabulation below (10–17).

Hormone	Effect on hormone levels
LH and FSH (LH-FSH-RF)	Marked decrease or block
ACTH (CRF)	Decrease
TSH (TRF)	Decrease
Growth hormone (GHRF-SRIF)	No effect or slight decrease
Prolactin (PRF-PIF)	Increase

(A) These three drugs in combination produced complete inhibition of the primary and secondary response to SRBC, measured in terms of direct (IgM-producing) plaque-forming cells (PFC) (Table 1). This inhibition could be prevented by prior or simultaneous administration of LH, FSH, and ACTH (adrenocorticotropic hormone, Table 2) as predicted from the hormonal changes observed shortly after antigenic stimulation. It is notable that the drug-induced inhibition of antibody formation was counteracted only when the hormones were given

TABLE 1. Immunological Unresponsiveness to Sheep Red Cells (SRBC) in Mice Induced by a Combination of Three Drugs[a]

Treatment	Primary response			Memory response		
	Number of mice	Nucleated cells/spleen ($\times 10^6$)	PFC/10^6 spleen cells	Number of mice	Nucleated cells/spleen ($\times 10^6$)	PFC/10^6 spleen cells
SRBC + drugs	16	123 ± 45	5 ± 5	16	231 ± 43	12 ± 12
SRBC	18	208 ± 43	636 ± 165	6	269 ± 32	520 ± 290

[a]Adult (4- to 5-month-old) female C3H/HeJ mice were injected intraperitoneally (ip) with 4×10^8 SRBC. The number of direct plaque-forming cells (PFC) was estimated 4 days after antigen injection. In some groups (memory response). 4×10^8 SRBC were reinjected at Day 12 after the first inoculation, and the number of direct PFC was measured 2 days later. One to two hours before the first antigen injection, and then once a day for 3 successive days, a mixture of three drugs was administered subcutaneously (sc) at the following doses: L-5-hydroxytryptophan, 40 mg/kg body weight; haloperidol, 12 mg/kg body weight; phentolamine, 12 mg/kg body weight. The drugs were dissolved in 0.5% citric acid and incorporated into incomplete Freund's adjuvant (FIA).

prior to treatment with drugs and antigen. This implies that hormones are involved in the differentiation of the antigen-sensitive cells to antibody-forming cells (Table 2). The hormones mixture did not counteract the action of the drugs when it was given after drugs–antigen administration (Table 2). It must be stressed that formation of indirect plaques (IgG-producing cells) was also prevented by the same procedure, and the same mice, still "unresponsive" to SRBC 40 days after the last injection of drugs, were able to respond normally to a second antigen (*Brucella abortus* antigens).

(B) An impressive prolongation of the rejection time for allogeneic grafts was obtained in outbred albino mice transplanted with skin from inbred C57BL/6J mice (Table 3). In this case, dopamine (40 mg/kg body weight) was added to the drug combination in order to block or strongly diminish release of growth hormone (GH) since the combined action of dopamine and an α-blocker (phentolamine) is considered to block release of GH (10, 19). This was done because GH has been shown to be needed for the differentiation of T-derived cells to im-

TABLE 2. Protection from and Prevention of Drug-Induced Blockade of Antibody Response to SRBC in Mice by Hormones[a]

Inoculation sequence	Number of mice	Nucleated cells/spleen ($\times 10^6$)	PFC/10^6 spleen cells
SRBC	10	270 ± 41	554 ± 95
Drugs-SRBC	10	130 ± 37	7 ± 5
SRBC-drugs	4	115 ± 74	49 ± 34
Drugs-hormones-SRBC-hormones	8	141 ± 25	69 ± 21
Hormones-SRBC-hormones-drugs	7	211 ± 40	386 ± 112

[a]Hormones (LH, 200 μg/day; FSH, 200 μg/day; ACTH, 5 μg/day) were injected ip in three aliquots on Day 0 and in two aliquots on Days 1, 2, and 3 at the given sequence. The drugs (same doses as in Table 1) were given sc on Day 0 and for the 3 successive days at the sequence given above. Direct plaque-forming cells (PFC) were estimated 4 days after antigen inoculation.

TABLE 3. Delay of First Set Allogeneic Skin Graft Rejection in Mice Induced by a Combination of Four Drugs[a]

	Number of mice	Numbers and percentages of viable grafts					
		10 Days[b]	15 Days	20 Days	25 Days	30 Days	35 Days
Normal	15	10 (66%)	0	—	—	—	—
Drug treated	50	50 (100%)	45 (90%)	34 (68%)	21 (42%)	15 (30%)	0

[a]Outbred Swiss albino mice were grafted with full-thickness skin from inbred C57BL/6J mice by the conventional technique. The protective corset was removed after 8–10 days. The graft was considered viable only until no signs of rejection (infiltration, edema, or ischemia) were present. Most of the drug-treated mice were inoculated daily sc on day of grafting (1 to 2 hr before transplantation) and for 2 successive days with 40 mg/kg body weight of L-5-hydroxytryptophan, 12 mg/kg body weight of haloperidol, 12 mg/kg body weight of phentolamine, and 40 mg/kg body weight of dopamine. Half this dose was then injected for a further 5–7 successive days.
[b]Days after grafting.

munocompetent cells (1–3, 20, 21). These cells are needed for a normal function of transplantation immunity. Our criterion for a complete "take" of the graft was absence of any sign of ischemia and infiltration. Most of the grafts showing some signs of ischemia were in fact retained for as long as 40 to 50 days, showing that the mechanisms of rejection are greatly weakened. The rejection time for a second graft from C57BL/6J donors in the same animals 6 months after the first grafting was similar to the first, indicating that no recovery of immune responsiveness to the same antigens had occurred. However, the same mice were able to reject skin grafts from DBA/J mice within a normal time (12–14 days).

(C) A very pronounced suppression of the runting syndrome was obtained in newborn albino mice inoculated with spleen cells from C57BL/6J mice which had been previously made unresponsive to albino mouse alloantigens by inoculation of albino mouse spleen cells and drug treatment. Most of the animals in this group survived large doses of incompatible cells (2 × 10^7) which regularly killed most of the newborn recipients in the other groups (Table 4).

TABLE 4. Prevention of Runt Disease in Newborn Albino Mice by Drug-Induced Tolerance in Allogeneic Donor Mice[a]

Spleen cell donors: C57BL/6J mice	Number of injected newborn mice	Percentages and numbers of surviving mice			
		7 Days[b]	15 Days	21 Days	27 Days
Untreated	31	93% (29)	64% (20)	32% (10)	10% (3)
Alloimmunized	10	100% (10)	60% (6)	30% (3)	10% (1)
Alloimmunized and drug treated	38	100% (38)	100% (38)	94% (37)	60% (23)
Drug treated	23	91% (21)	82% (19)	56% (13)	13% (3)
Controls, no injection	26	100% (26)	100% (26)	100% (26)	100% (26)

[a]Outbred newborn Swiss albino mice were injected ip on the day of birth with 2 × 10^7 spleen cells from C57BL/6J donors which were untreated or alloimmunized (with spleen cells from albino mice 4 weeks beforehand). Groups of donors of each kind were also treated with the drug combination so as to render them "unresponsive." Dosage of drugs in the donor mice was as indicated in Table 3. No runting disease occurred after 4 weeks of age.
[b]Days after cell injection.

Moreover, the surviving mice showed no or only very mild symptoms of the GvH reaction–runt disease (exfoliative dermatitis, diarrhea). These results show the remarkable inability of cells from unresponsive or "blocked" C57BL/6J donors to induce GvH–runting disease in the newborn recipients, thereby allowing them to escape the disease and to mature to immunocompetent adults.

Discussion

Our findings show that pharmacologic control of the immune response can be achieved by interfering with those endocrine changes consequent to antigen challenge. Both immediate (antibody production) and delayed-type (transplantation immunity) immune reactions are

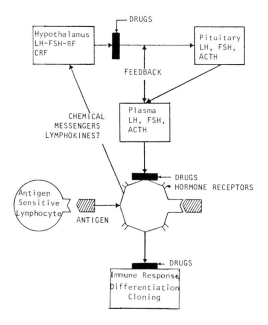

FIGURE 2. Conceptual scheme for mechanism by which haloperidol, 5HTP, and phentolamine block the immune response and induce immune tolerance. Binding of antigen to antigen-sensitive lymphocytes leads to the uncovering of receptors for hormones (LH, FSH, ACTH, and possibly GH) on their membranes and/or synthesis and release of lymphokines (chemical messengers) to the hypothalamus-pituitary system. This provokes a decrease of circulating gonadotropins with consequent stimulation of releasing factors for LH, FSH, and ACTH (LH-FSH-RF; CRF) due to a feedback mechanism and/or direct action of lymphokines. The α-blocker, phentolamine, blocks the α-adrenergic receptors at both the central (hypothalamus) and peripheral levels (cell membranes). Catecholamines, whose level is increased by haloperidol, a neuroleptic drug which blocks dopaminergic receptors, act on the free β-adrenergic receptors, provoking intracellular increase of cyclic AMP in the antigen-stimulated lymphocytes and inhibition of gonadotropins and ACTH release. The inhibition is completed by L-5-hydroxytryptophan (5HTP), the precursor of serotonin, which is a neurotransmitter inhibiting LH-FSH-RF and CRF. The blocking drugs and the hormones appear to act in a competitive fashion (Table 2). Differentiation and cloning of the antigen-sensitive lymphocytes is thus specifically and irreversibly blocked, leading to persistent immune unresponsiveness.

strongly delayed or prevented by a combination of three or four drugs. Since these drugs are essentially ineffective individually in inducing a complete and long-lasting unresponsiveness to antigens, either they must each act at different levels or there is a remarkable synergy. Whether they prevent the initiation of the hormone-dependent differentiation of immunoreactive cells before or after the contact of the cells with the antigen remains to be clarified. This pharmacologic intervention also seems to block the specific antigen-reactive cells at some stage following receipt of the antigenic signal. Consequently, tolerance to the antigens is established, at least as far as T-dependent antigens are concerned. However, we still do not know whether the animals remain permanently unresponsive or "tolerant" to the antigens or if a recovery of immune reactivity to those antigens occurs months or years after the immune blockade has been achieved. This is presently being investigated. A possible mechanism of action of the drugs and their potential targets are shown schematically in Fig. 2.

The drugs might act on the endocrine system, on hormone receptors of antigen-reactive cells, on differentiation of antibody-forming cells, on formation of cytotoxic lymphocytes, or on the elaboration of lymphokines. It is known that haloperidol increases plasma catecholamines. It is therefore possible that catecholamines play a role in blocking the immune response by a mechanism involving adrenergic receptors and lymphocyte cyclic AMP (13–17, 22–24). It is probable that the drugs used in our experiments act on the central nervous system by affecting secretion of hormones, but a peripheral mechanism on other glands or on hormone receptors on unstimulated or antigen-activated T- or B-derived lymphocytes is not excluded (10–17, 22–24) (Fig. 2). Two components of the combination, e.g., haloperidol and phentolamine, might bind competitively to those receptors on the membrane of the antigen-sensitive lymphocytes, which are the targets for the hormones involved in the initiation of the immune response. However, both central and peripheral mechanisms are most probably involved simultaneously to account for the suppression achieved (Fig. 2). Intravenous inoculation of SRBC into mice induces a sudden elevation of prostaglandins in the spleen (25). This increase does not occur in T-deficient athymic mice (25). These findings suggest that a correlation might exist between secretion of mediators from T lymphocytes, synthesis of prostaglandins, and the increase of gonadotropins after inoculation of antigens. However, the role of prostaglandins in synthesis or release of gonadotropins is still controversial (26–31).

Although preliminary, these findings suggest a radically different basis for therapeutic and experimental manipulation and control of acquired immunity, which could have practical application in transplantation and possibly in autoimmune disease. Immunosuppressive agents include antimitotic and cytotoxic drugs, corticosteroids, and antilymphocytic serum. They are extensively used but their limitations and shortcomings are well known. In contrast, although the dose levels used exceed those normally used therapeutically, the present approach offers the advantages of brevity of treatment and of selective suppression of the immune response to the antigens administered.

Acknowledgments

We thank Dr. H. G. Kopp for his help in the determinations of LH and Miss K. Naumann for technical assistance. The authors are deeply grateful to Dr. Maurice Landy for his constant inspiring encouragements and suggestions, to Professor Ernst Sorkin for his criticism, and to Professor John Humphrey for his comments, criticism, and revision of this manuscript. This work was supported by the Swiss National Fund for Scientific Research, Grant Nos. 3.8750.72 and 3.600.75.

References

1. Pierpaoli, W., Fabris, N., and Sorkin, E., *In* "Hormones and the Immune Response" (G. E. M. Wolstenholme and Julie Knight, Eds.), p. 126. Ciba Foundation Study Group No. 36. Churchill, London, 1970.
2. Fabris, N., Pierpaoli, W., and Sorkin, E., *In* "Developmental Aspects of Antibody Formation and Structure" (J. Sterzl and I. Riha, Eds.), Vol. 1, p. 79. Czechoslovak Academy of Science, Prague, 1970.
3. Pierpaoli, W., Fabris, N., and Sorkin E., *In* "Cellular Interactions in the Immune Responses" (S. Cohen, G. Cudkowicz, and R. T. McCluskey, Eds.), p. 25, Karger, Basel, 1971.
4. Pierpaoli, W., and Sorkin, E., *Experientia* **28**, 1385, 1972.
5. Pierpaoli, W., and Sorkin, E., *Nature New Biol.* **238**, 282, 1972.
6. Pierpaoli, W., and Besedovsky, H. O., *Clin. Exp. Immunol.* **20**, 323, 1975.
7. Pierpaoli, W., Kopp, H. G., and Bianchi, E., *Clin. Exp. Immumol.* **24**, 501, 1976.
8. Pierpaoli, W., *Immunology* **29**, 465, 1975.
9. Pierpaoli, W., Kopp, H. G., Müller, J., and Keller, M., *Cell. Immunol.* **29**, 16, 1977.
10. Frohman, L. A., *Hosp. Pract.* **10**, 54, 1975.
11. Kamberi, I. A., *In* "Frontiers in Catecholamines Research" (E. Usdin and S. H. Snyder, Eds.), p. 849. Pergamon Press, New York, 1973.
12. Fuxe, K., Schubert, J., Hökfelt, T., and Jonsson, G. *In* "Advances in Biochemical Psychopharmocology" (E. Costa, G. L. Gessa, and M. Sandler, Eds.), Vol. 10, p. 67. Raven Press, New York, 1974.
13. Braun, W., and Rega, M. J., *Immunol. Commun.* **1**, 523, 1972.
14. Henney, C. S., *In* "Cyclic AMP, Cell Growth and the Immune Response" (W. Braun, L. M. Lichtenstein, and C. W. Parker, Eds.), p. 195. Springer, Berlin, 1974.
15. Bourne, H. R., Melmon, K. L., Weinstein, Y., and Shearer, G. M., *In* "Cyclic AMP, Cell Growth and the Immune Response" (W. Braun, L. M. Lichtenstein, and C. W. Parker, Eds.), p. 99. Springer, Berlin, 1974.
16. Singh, U., and Owen, J. J. T., *Eur. J. Immunol.* **6**, 59, 1976.
17. Ganong, W. F., *In* "Frontiers in Catecholamines Research" (E. Usdin and S. H. Snyder, Eds.), p. 819. Pergamon Press, New York, 1973.
18. Devoino, L., Eliseeva, L., Eremina, O., Idova, G., and Cheido, M., *Eur. J. Immunol.* **5**, 394, 1975.
19. Levy, J. A., and Munson, A. E., *Fed. Proc.* **35**, 333, 1976 (abstract).
20. Pandian, M. R., and Talwar, G. P., *J. Exp. Med.* **134**, 1095, 1971.
21. Arrenbrecht, S., *Nature (London)* **252**, 255, 1974.
22. Watson, J., Epstein, R., and Cohn, M., *Nature (London)* **246**, 405, 1973.
23. Garovoy, M. R., Strom, T. B., Kaliner, M., and Carpenter, C. B., *Cell Immunol.* **20**, 197, 1975.
24. Bösing-Schneider, R., and Haug, M., *Cell Immunol.* **27**, 121, 1976.
25. Webb, D. R., and Osheroff, P. L., *Proc. Nat. Acad. Sci. USA* **73**, 1300, 1976.
26. Kragt, C. L., and Bergstrom, K. K., *Prostaglandins* **10**, 833, 1975.
27. Deis, R. P., and Vermouth, N. T., *J. Reprod. Fert.* **45**, 383, 1975.
28. Kuhl, H., Frey, W., Rosniatowski, C., Dericks-Tan, J. S., and Taubert, H. D., *Acta Endocrinol. (Copenhagen)* **82**, 15, 1976.
29. Drouin, J., Ferland, L., Bernard, J., and Labrie, F., *Prostaglandins* **11**, 367, 1976.
30. Convey, E. M., Beal, W. E., Seguin, B. E., Tannen, K. J., and Lin, Y. C., *Proc. Soc. Exp. Biol. Med.* **151**, 84, 1976.
31. Warberg, J., Eskay, R. L., and Porter, J. C., *Endocrinology* **98**, 1135, 1976.

II

BEHAVIOR AND IMMUNE FUNCTION

A. Exposure to Experimental Stressors

Chapters 21 through 33

B. Conditioning and Immunity

Chapters 34 through 36

C. Human Behavior and Immunity

C1. Psychosocial Influences on Immunity in Humans

Chapters 37 through 43

C2. Mental Illness and Immunity

Chapters 44 through 51

21

EFFECT OF STRESS ON SKIN TRANSPLANTATION IMMUNITY IN MICE

R. Wistar, Jr. and W. H. Hildemann

Abstract. Chronic avoidance-learning stress was found to depress the immune reaction responsible for skin homograft rejection to a modest but significant degree. This effect was observed in a genetically uniform as well as a heterogeneous line of mice.

Although diverse types of systemic stress have long been known to modify the immunological responses of mammals (*1*), precise experimental investigations have recently elucidated the effect of such stress on particular immune reactions. Thus, mice subjected to a standardized avoidance-learning type of stress show an increased susceptibility to *Herpes simplex* virus infection (*2*) as well as a decreased susceptibility to passive anaphylaxis (*3*) and a depressed colloid-clearing capacity of the reticuloendothelial system.

The study discussed here was undertaken to determine the effect of controlled stress on skin-homograft rejection. The immunologic basis of the homograft reaction has been well established and shows the characteristics of a typical hypersensitivity of the delayed type (*4*).

The stressing procedure employed has been described in detail by Rasmussen *et al.* (*2*). The apparatus makes use of a shuttle box with wired floor each half of which is alternately electrified with a 20- to 30-volt current painful to the mouse. Alteration of current from one side to the other is preceded by signals from a light and buzzer. Mice soon learn to avoid the shocking current, which occurs at about 5-minute intervals. The animals are subjected to this stress 6 hours per day, 6 days per week. Such stress regularly engenders significant changes in the weights of organs: the weights of the thymus and spleen decrease, whereas those of the liver and adrenal increase. Moreover, a progressive leukopenia occurs as the stress is continued over several weeks. Randomly bred Swiss-Webster BRVS mice for which the stress parameters have been determined (*2*) were employed, along with highly inbred C57B1 and A-line mice. Single, orthotopic skin homografts were made by the technique of Billingham and Medawar (*5*) in two donor-recipient combinations—A→ C57B1 and C57B1→Swiss. Thus, both inbred and genetically diverse recipients were tested. The Swiss recipients were all virgin females, whereas both sexes were represented in the C57B1's.

Mice about 5 weeks old were exposed to the standardized stress experience for 2 weeks before grafting. On the day after grafting, the mice were again subjected to stress until homograft rejection was complete. The control mice received grafts in the same manner but were not exposed to experimental stress. Protective bandages were removed for the initial inspection on the 8th day, and graft survival was scored daily thereafter. Intermediate stages of breakdown were estimated by gross inspection and confirmed in several instances by histologic examination of biopsy sections stained with hematoxylin and eosin. Zero survival end points were assessed on the basis of no surviving graft epithelium. Median survival times as well as tests for parallelism and reaction-time ratios, with their 95-percent confidence limits, were computed by the method of Litchfield (*6*).

The cumulative percentage of homografts destroyed in each experiment is plotted against days after grafting in Fig. 1. While it is apparent that the

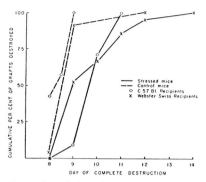

Fig. 1. Cumulative time-mortality curves for skin homografts in stressed and non-stressed mice.

time-mortality distributions of grafts in the comparable groups of control mice and stressed mice are distinctive, the prolongation of skin homograft survival in the stressed mice was not extensive. Also, the figure reveals that the uniform C57B1 recipients showed a narrow range of graft-survival times, whereas the Swiss mice showed the broad distribution characteristic of genetically diverse recipients. The results are summarized in Table 1. When the data were subjected to the parallelism and reaction-time ratio tests of significance, the difference between stressed and control mice in both combinations is significant at the 95-percent level of probability.

Although the stress applied is known to induce profound physiological changes in mice, it appears probable that the observed inhibition of transplantation immunity in stressed mice is affected primarily by hypersecretion of adrenal corticosteroids. Indeed, the decrease in weight of the spleen and the progressive leukopenia in stressed mice can be duplicated by administration of cortisone. Since homograft immunity, like other delayed types of hypersensitivity, is clearly mediated by lymphoid

cells, a substantial depression of such cells by corticosteroids would be expected to allow a prolongation of skin homograft survival. Nevertheless, the endocrine situation is complex. While the normal mouse secretes principally corticosterone and little if any cortisone and hydrocortisone (7), Medawar and Sparrow (8) have shown that injection of the latter compounds but not of corticosterone will prolong homograft survival time in mice. An analysis of the endogenous corticosteroid levels in stressed mice now under way in this laboratory should indicate whether such mice preferentially secrete the hormones known to prolong homograft survival. The possibility remains, of course, that the stress-induced inhibition of the homograft reaction is mediated mainly through channels other than the adrenal corticoids. In this connection, studies with rats (9) have revealed that adrenal corticoid output may actually decrease below normal levels during prolonged stress.

It should be noted that our control mice were unfortunately exposed to the periodic noise of building reconstruction and thus were moderately stressed. Some additional stress may also have resulted from caging the animals singly. Hence, the difference between experimental and control groups might be more striking under ideal conditions.

Even though the physiological pathways of action are still poorly defined, it is clear that chronic, avoidance-learning stress induces a prolongation of homograft survival times to a small but significant degree in genetically homogeneous as well as in heterogeneous lines of mice (10).

Table 1. Summary of results.

Group	Donor-recipient combination	No. of mice	Median survival times (days) with 95% confidence limits
Control	A→C57B1	7	8.2 (7.2–9.3)
Stressed	A→C57B1	11	9.6 (9.3–9.9)
Control	C57B1→Swiss	23	8.5 (8.3–8.7)
Stressed	C57B1→Swiss	21	9.2 (8.6–9.9)

References and Notes

1. H. Selye, Science 122, 625 (1955).
2. A. F. Rasmussen, Jr., J. T. Marsh, N. Q. Brill, Proc. Soc. Exptl. Biol. Med. 96, 183 (1957).
3. A. F. Rasmussen, Jr., E. S. Spencer, J. T. Marsh, ibid. 100, 878 (1959).
4. L. Brent, J. Brown, P. B. Medawar, Lancet 2, 561 (1958).
5. R. E. Billingham and P. B. Medawar, J. Exptl. Biol. 28, 385 (1951).
6. J. T. Litchfield, Jr., J. Pharmacol. Exptl. Therap. 97, 399 (1949).
7. F. Halberg, R. E. Peterson, R. H. Silber, Endocrinology 64, 222 (1959).
8. P. B. Medawar and E. R. Sparrow, J. Endocrinol. 14, 240 (1956).
9. K. M. Knigge, C. H. Penrod, W. J. Schindler, Am. J. Physiol. 196, 579 (1959).
10. This work was supported by research grants (E835 and C4027) from the National Institutes of Health, U.S. Public Health Service, Bethesda, Md.
* U.S. Public Health Service post-sophomore fellow.

Behavior and Immune Function

22

STRESS AND SUSCEPTIBILITY TO VIRAL INFECTION

I. Response of Adrenals, Liver, Thymus, Spleen and Peripheral Leukocyte Counts to Sound Stress[1]

Marcus M. Jensen and A. F. Rasmussen

The influence of experimentally induced emotional stress in increasing host susceptibility to viral infections has been demonstrated by Rasmussen *et al.* (1) and Johnsson *et al.* (2). These investigators found that mice subjected daily to either avoidance-learning stress in a shuttle box or physical restraint in screen envelopes were more susceptible to herpes simplex and Coxsackie B1 viruses than were normal mice.

Electrical shock and forced activity of the avoidance-learning system, or immobilization in restraint, might directly influence resistance by means other than central nervous system (CNS) mediated response. To avoid these possibilities we selected high intensity sound as the stressor. It minimizes physical stress, is applicable to large numbers of animals, and can be applied uniformly.

The responses of the pituitary-adrenal, thymicolymphatic and blood leukocytic systems to all forms of stress (3), and specifically to sound, have been reported (4-6). As these systems are closely associated with host defense mechanisms, any stress-induced alteration in the function of these tissues might influence susceptibility to infection. We are concerned here with the determination of the efficacy of sound as a nonspecific stressor as determined by adrenal hypertrophy, lymphatic atrophy and changes in circulatory leukocyte counts.

MATERIALS AND METHODS

All animals employed were female Swiss albino mice, Webster strain, 6 to 7 weeks of age. The mice were housed in groups of seven in stainless steel nesting boxes containing wood shavings and were maintained in quiet air-conditioned rooms. Commercial mouse ration (Purina Laboratory Chow) and water were available *ad libitum,* except during the periods of stress, when water was removed.

Stressing procedure. The stress cages were 40- by 15- by 20-cm wire cages subdivided into ten 7.5- by 8- by 20-cm compartments. All construction was of open mesh wire to allow unobstructed passage of sound waves to all areas of the cages. One mouse was placed in each compartment. Four cages were then placed in a heavy cardboard cylindrical chamber 40 cm in diameter and 3 m long.

Sound was produced by a 35-cm loudspeaker installed across one end of the cylinder. The power source was a 10-watt audio amplifier in combination with a signal oscillator producing a pure sine wave signal. Sound intensity levels were measured with a standard type decibel meter. An 800 cps sound tone at an intensity level of 123 db was employed.

During the stress period, the open end of the chamber was sealed with a 50-cm thick fiber glass wedge and a 2.5-cm thick plywood cover. Fresh air was continuously supplied from an air-conditioning unit to maintain room temperature. A Plexiglas window was installed for observational purposes. Unless otherwise stated, a 3-hr per day exposure to this stressor was employed.

The experimental animals were removed from the home boxes only during the stress period. The control mice remained in the home boxes at all times.

Organ weight determination. Animals were individually weighed before and after each period of stress. After the 1st, 2nd, 4th and 6th daily stress periods groups of mice were ether anesthetized

[1] Supported by grants from the National Institutes of Allergy and Infectious Diseases and of Mental Health, USPHS.

[2] Predoctoral trainee, Mental Health Training Program, USPHS. 2M-6415.

Reprinted from *J. Immunol.* **90** (No. 1), 17–20, 1963.

and sacrificed by exsanguination. The adrenals, thymus, spleen and liver were immediately removed, weighed and expressed as milligrams per gram of total body weight based on the daily prestress weight. Weights for nonstressed control mice were simultaneously evaluated.

Passive anaphylaxis. The mice were tested for resistance to passive anaphylaxis after the 1st and 2nd days of stress by the method of Treadwell *et al.* (7). Increased resistance suggests stimulation of the pituitary-adrenal axis.

Leukocyte counts. At intervals on given days of stress, six control and six stressed mice were ether anesthetized, their tails amputated about 3 cm from the base with a sharp scalpel and the first four drops of blood discarded. A sample was then collected and white blood cells (WBC) were counted by standard methods. Differential counts were made on cover slips stained by the May-Gruenwald technique.

RESULTS

Organ weights. No significant weight changes were observed in the liver, spleen and thymus.

A progressive hypertrophy of the adrenal glands was induced by this form of stress. The differences in control and stressed adrenal weights were highly significant after the 4th day of stress (Table I).

Passive anaphylaxis. After the first period of stress mice were not significantly more resistant to passive anaphylaxis than controls; 12 of 16

TABLE I

Adrenal weights in milligrams per gram of total body weight after given periods of stress

Day of Stress	Group	No. of Mice	Mean	Range
1	Stress	17	0.32	0.26–0.39[a]
	Control	18	0.29	0.25–0.34
2	Stress	17	0.33	0.25–0.42[a]
	Control	14	0.30	0.20–0.37
4	Stress	6	0.36	0.32–0.47[b]
	Control	6	0.26	0.22–0.30
6	Stress	4	0.35	0.32–0.38[b]
	Control	5	0.29	0.26–0.30

[a] P value between 0.05 and 0.1 by Mann-Whitney U Test.
[b] P value >0.001 by Mann-Whitney U Test.

stressed and 15 of 16 control mice developed fatal anaphylaxis ($X^2 = 0.94$, $P = 0.35$). After the second stress period 10 of 29 stressed and 23 of 29 control mice died, showing a significant increase in resistance ($X^2 = 10.3$, $P = 0.002$).

Leukocyte counts. All control mice gave approximately the same values. Counts made between 0800 and 0900 hours ranged from 11,000 to 15,000 cells/cu mm (mean about 13,000). By 1200 hr the mean value was about 10,000 cells/cu mm and remained approximately at this level up to the last daily sampling at 2100 hr.

The mean deviations in the leukocyte counts of the stressed mice during and after the stress periods are shown in Figure 1. The control values are reported as zero, and the experimental values represent their deviations from the norm. Thus, when the stressed group has a value of +5000, this represents 5000 cells/cu mm above the comparable control group bled at the same time and not 5000 above the average control value.

The same basic pattern was manifested on each day. Shortly after the onset of stress, there was a significant decrease in the total peripheral WBC. The lowest level was recorded after 1½ hr of continuous stress. The differential values at this time were 72% lymphocytes and 24% polymorphonuclear leukocytes. The leukocyte concentration then increased steadily, returning to the control level at approximately 1½ hr after the termination of stress and reaching a peak significantly above the control level 2 to 3 hr later. The differential values obtained during this leukocytosis were 82% lymphocytes and 15% polymorphonuclear leukocytes. The extent and duration of the leukocytosis varied somewhat. For example, on the 1st and 2nd days of stress, the counts returned to the control level, or slightly below, 6 hr after stress and remained at this level or slightly above until the last reading. A similar pattern (not recorded) was observed on the 7th day. On the 3rd day the leukocytosis persisted much longer. Limited counts taken on days 4–6, 10, 11 and 25 of stress indicated the same general biphasic pattern. This response has not been studied beyond 25 days.

Various investigators (8–10) have demonstrated that stress-induced leukopenia is a result of an increased secretion of adrenal hormones. To determine the influence of adrenal function in this system, total WBC counts were determined in adrenalectomized mice during and shortly

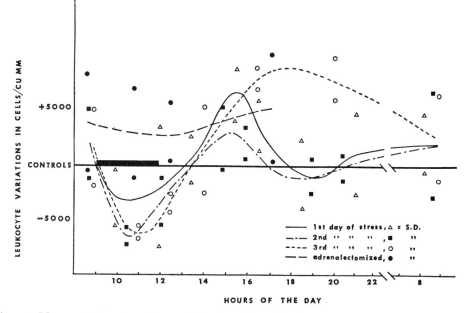

Figure 1. Mean variations from the control values (center line) and standard deviations (S.D.) in peripheral leukocyte counts of intact and adrenalectomized mice during and after the first, second and third daily exposures to sound stress. Counts from adrenalectomized mice for the 3 days are combined. The bar indicates the 3-hr stress period.

after the stress period. These results (Fig. 1) clearly demonstrate the absence of the characteristic stress-induced leukopenia in adrenalectomized animals.

At no time were audiogenic convulsions induced. Since stress caused by handling the mice was found to be insignificant, control animals were not subjected to simulated experimental procedures.

DISCUSSION

Marsh and Rasmussen (11) used the changes in adrenal, thymus and spleen weights, and blood leukocytes, as criteria for measuring stress responses in mice. Significant changes were observed in the adrenal weights after 3 days, and in the spleen and thymus mass after 14 days of stress. Anthony *et al.* (5) observed adrenal hypertrophy and signs of increased adrenocortical action in mice subjected to high intensity, low frequency sound for 15 min daily for 4 weeks. No corresponding atrophy was found in organs or tissues influenced by adrenal secretions. Sackler *et al.* (4) noted adrenal hyperplasia and reduction in weight of liver, spleen and thymus in rats

subjected to daily auditory stimulus (5 min) for several weeks.

We found no significant weight decrease in the thymicolymphatic tissues after several daily exposures to sound stress. The adrenal hypertrophy and increased resistance to passive anaphylaxis suggested an early increased response of these glands. A biphasic secretion of corticosteroids following various stressors was shown by Knigge *et al.* (12), and during sound stress by Henken and Knigge (13).

Various investigators have studied the leukocytic, and in particular the eosinophilic, response to stress (4, 6, 11, 14–16). When one surveys these reports, a variation in results is seen. This may be due, in part, to differences in the species of animals or experimental procedures employed. Since only one or two samplings were taken at fixed intervals on given days in most of these studies, diurnal or stress-induced phasic variation may have been overlooked. Several investigators (3, 17) have warned against errors due to fixed periods of sampling.

By making a serial analysis of the WBC counts we were able to demonstrate a marked biphasic variation in the peripheral concentration of these cells in response to a stressful stimulus. The failure of the adrenalectomized mice to develop a leukopenia when exposed to sound stress indicates the role of adrenal glands in this particular response.

We did not observe changes in the thymicolymphatic tissues that might lower host resistance to infection. The stress-induced biphasic variation in leukocytes suggests a similar response in other physiologic systems which might influence susceptibility.

Our findings emphasize the necessity of obtaining serial readings to determine the presence of and to characterize any possible phasic responses when exploring stress-induced responses.

Acknowledgment. The authors wish to acknowledge the assistance of Dr. Robert W. Leonard, Department of Physics, in designing the sound stressing chamber.

SUMMARY

Daily 3-hr exposures to high intensity sound induced adrenal hypertrophy in mice. Peripheral leukocyte counts responded biphasically to this stressor, exhibiting a leukopenia during and a leukocytosis following the stress period on each day. Leukopenia was not seen in stressed-adrenalectomized animals.

REFERENCES

1. RASMUSSEN, A. F., JR., MARSH, J. T. AND BRILL, N. Q., Proc. Soc. Exper. Biol. & Med., **96**: 183, 1957.
2. JOHNSSON, T., LAVENDER, J. F. AND MARSH, J. T., Fed. Proc., **18**: 575, 1959.
3. SELYE, H., *Stress*, Acta, Inc., Montreal, 1950.
4. SACKLER, A. M., WELTMAN, A. S., BRADSHAW, M. AND JURTSHUK, P., JR., Acta Endocrinol., **31**: 405, 1959.
5. ANTHONY, A. E., ACKERMAN, E. AND LLOYD, J. A., J. Acoust. Soc. Am., **31**: 1430, 1959.
6. BIRO, J., SZOKOLAI, V. AND KAVACH, A. G. B., Acta Endocrinol., **31**: 542, 1959.
7. TREADWELL, P. E., WISTAR, R. AND RASMUSSEN, A. F., JR., J. Immunol., **84**: 539, 1959.
8. ELMADJJAN, F. AND PINCUS, G., Endocrinol., **37**: 47, 1945.
9. GELLHORN, E. AND FRANK, S., Proc. Soc. Exper. Biol. & Med., **69**: 426, 1949.
10. SPEIRS, R. S. AND MEYER, R. K., Endocrinol., **45**: 403, 1949.
11. MARSH, J. T. AND RASMUSSEN, A. F., JR., Proc. Soc. Exper. Biol. & Med., **104**: 180, 1960.
12. KNIGGE, K. M., PENROD, C. H. AND SCHINDLER, W. J., Am. J. Physiol., **196**: 579, 1959.
13. HENKEN, R. I. AND KNIGGE, K. M., Acta Endocrinol. (Suppl.), **51**: 39, 1960.
14. HARLOW, C. M. AND SELYE, H., Proc. Soc. Exper. Biol. & Med., **36**: 141, 1937.
15. CHANCELLOR, L. AND GLICK, B., Am. J. Physiol., **198**: 1347, 1960.
16. ANTHONY, A., J. Acoust. Soc. Am., **27**: 1150, 1955.
17. HALBERG, F., HALBERG, E., BARNUM, C. P. AND BITTNER, J. J., *Photoperiodism and Related Phenomena in Plants and Animals*, pp. 803, Edited by R. B. Withrow, Am. A. Adv. Sc., Washington, D. C., 1959.

23

THE INFLUENCE OF AVOIDANCE-LEARNING STRESS ON RESISTANCE TO COXSACKIE B VIRUS IN MICE[1]

Torsten Johnsson,[2] John F. Lavender,[3] Eskil Hultin, and A. F. Rasmussen, Jr.

In a study of the role of emotional stress in the pathogenesis of infectious diseases, Rasmussen, Marsh and Brill, (1) have reported that mice subjected to avoidance-learning stress in a shuttlebox 6 hr daily for 2 to 4 weeks were more susceptible to infection with the virus of herpes simplex than were unstressed controls. It became of interest, then, to determine whether the stress-induced susceptibility to herpes simplex was an isolated phenomenon or whether other viral infections might also be more severe in stressed mice. In considering viruses for further study, Coxsackie virus infection in mice was suggested as a suitable host-virus system because of the striking changes in resistance, from marked susceptibility to relative refractoriness, which occur within a period of 1 to 3 weeks after birth (2). After this age, there is not, however, solid resistance; adult mice infected with Coxsackie B virus may develop an acute and chronic pancreatitis manifested by loss of weight, although they seldom die (2, 3).

MATERIALS AND METHODS

Mice. Albino mice from an inbred colony originally derived from the Salmonella resistant Webster Swiss strain were used. The mice were fed a commercial mouse ration.

Virus. The Conn. 5 strain of Coxsackie B1 virus, originally obtained from Dr. J. L. Melnick and maintained by serial infant mouse carcass passage, was transferred through 10 passages in 3- to 6-week-old mice in the form of 10% pancreas suspension. Pancreas was harvested 48 hr after intraperitoneal inoculation, ground in a mortar and diluted to 10% in saline containing 500 units of penicillin and 1.0 mg of streptomycin/ml. After clarification by light centrifugation, the supernatant was stored at $-40°C$. The virus stock, titrated in suckling mice 24 to 48 hr old by i.p. inoculation of serial dilutions, had a titer of $10^{8.5}$/ml. An inoculum of 10^9 infant mouse LD_{50} doses was used in the stress experiments.

The stressing method. Mice were exposed to avoidance-learning stress in the shuttlebox situation previously described (1) which utilized a double-grill box with the two sections of grid flooring separated by a barrier. A low voltage A.C., usually 30 v, could be connected to the grid flooring on either side and to parallel wires $\frac{1}{8}$ in. above the top of the barrier to discourage barrier sitting. The current was controlled by an electronic programming apparatus. Five seconds before one side of the grid flooring was electrified, a buzzer and a light were turned on. Every 5 min the conditioned stimulus was repeated and the current was switched to the other side. Mice were subjected to this stressor for 6 hr daily for 3 to 4 weeks. They rapidly learned to avoid shock by jumping during the light-buzzer signal, so that by the end of 7 days 80 to 90% of the animals avoided shock. The stressful element in such situations is thought to be the anticipation of pain which in turn produced fear (4–6). The electric shock employed was harmless so far as could be determined except when mice chewed the grid wire and current passed through the head with occasionally fatal results.

Selection, measurement of weights and observation of mice in the stress experiments. Randomly mixed mice 3 to 4 weeks old, weighing from 10 to 15 g, were used. Age varied from 1 to 3 days

[1] Supported by Research Grant in Aid, National Institute of Allergy and Infectious Diseases, and Training Grant 2M 6415, USPHS.

[2] Partially supported by Training Grant from Swedish State Medical Research Fund. Present Address, State Bacteriological Laboratory, Stockholm, Sweden.

[3] Trainee, Mental Health Training Program, USPHS 2M 6415.

Reprinted from *J. Immunol.* **91**, 569–579, 1963.

within experiments. Animals were weighed before stress, before inoculation, thereafter every 2nd or 3rd day the 1st weeks and every 2nd week up to 2 months after inoculation.

Mice were observed daily or every 2nd day during the first weeks after inoculation for the characteristic signs of infection which consisted of hunching, swollen eyes and rough fur.

Evaluation of weight response. The means of weight changes and the standard deviation of weight changes about the average were calculated for the various groups and the groups compared to each other. First, a comparison of the standard deviations of the weight changes in the two treatment groups was achieved with the F test. The hypothesis being tested was that a group receiving additional treatment did not have greater variance than the group with which it was compared. Stress and viruses are causes for variation in addition to normal biologic variation. Therefore, the upper 5%, 1%, etc., points of the F distribution as given in regular F tables were used for a test at the 5%, 1%, etc., level of significance. The standard deviation in most cases was significantly different for differently treated groups. Hence, a comparison of the means of two treatment groups was achieved by a modified t test (7). Thus, the quotients between the differences in mean values and the combined standard errors were compared to the weighted mean of the two values in the t table corresponding to the degrees of freedom for the two groups compared. The value for interaction between influences of stress and of virus was also computed according to the same method. It may be mentioned here that it was observed in these computations that the F test and the t test can be used only for groups whose values have a reasonably normal distribution. Hence, extreme values were removed according to Dixon's method (8) which will be discussed later in this paper.

Preparation and titration of tissues. Five mice were sacrificed daily during the first 5 days after inoculation. Blood, pancreas, liver, heart, muscle, fat and brain were collected aseptically and pooled by organs for virus titrations. One hind limb from each mouse of a group was taken for skeletal muscle. Blood was collected from the severed brachial artery and pooled, 0.5 ml from each mouse. Organs and muscle tissue were pooled and ground in a mortar with sterile saline

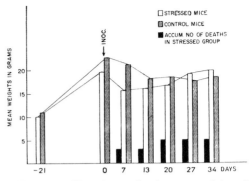

Figure 1 (Experiment 1). Average weight of stressed and control mice before stress period, after stress period but before inoculation of Coxsackie virus B1, and after inoculation of virus.

making 10% suspensions, which were clarified by centrifugation at 2000 g for 30 min. The supernatant fluid was titrated by 10-fold dilutions in saline. Suckling mice, 24 to 48 hr of age, were pooled and distributed in groups of six mice per dilution tested. The mice were observed for 12 days, and deaths occurring in the first 48 hr were considered nonspecific. Titration end points (LD_{50}) were calculated by the method of Reed and Muench.

EXPERIMENTAL

Experiment 1 (Fig. 1). In the first preliminary experiment 3-week-old mice were used with sexes mixed at random. Two groups were employed, one stressed and one unstressed. Both were inoculated with virus 3 weeks after the onset of the stress period.

Experiment 2 (Tables I and II). Three-week-old mice were divided into 4 groups. Two groups were stressed for 3 weeks; the other two groups were not stressed. One of the stressed groups and one of the unstressed groups were inoculated with virus; the stress was continued for 2 days after inoculation.

Experiment 3 (Tables III and IV). In this series two groups of 4-week-old mice were used. One group was stressed for 4 weeks and the other was not stressed. Both were inoculated with virus. There was no stress after inoculation. Five mice were harvested in each group daily from the 1st to the 5th day after inoculation. Pools of organs were titrated for presence of virus as described above.

TABLE I

Comparison of initial weights to weights at intervals after inoculation in Experiment 2

Period for Comparison: Days after Inoculation	Experimental Groups[a]	No. of Animals	Mean Weight Increase or Decrease	Standard Error of Mean Weight Increase or Decrease	Standard Deviation of Weight Changes about the Average Change	Significance Level for Weight Increase or Decrease
			g			
7 *vs.* 0	0	10	1.15	0.40	1.27	$0.05 > P > 0.01$
	S	8	0.94	0.51	1.43	$0.1 > P\ 0.05$
	V	27	−0.31	0.44	2.26	$P > 0.1$
	SV	23	−2.20	0.36	1.74	$P < 0.001$
16 *vs.* 0	0	10	1.85	0.22	0.71	$P < 0.001$
	S	8[b]	1.00	0.32	0.89	$0.05 > P > 0.01$
	V	27	−0.41	0.60	3.10	$P > 0.1$
	SV	23	−0.63	0.78	3.75	$P > 0.1$
36 *vs.* 0	0	10	4.05	0.20	0.64	$P < 0.001$
	S	7	4.86	0.67	1.77	$P < 0.001$
	V[c]	22	4.14	0.24	1.13	$P < 0.001$
	V[d]	27	3.57	0.64	3.34	
	SV[c]	20	3.70	0.73	3.25	$P < 0.001$
	SV[d]	23	1.98	1.14	5.47	

[a] S = stressed but not inoculated with virus; V = inoculated with virus, but not stressed; SV = stressed and thereafter inoculated with virus; 0 = neither stress nor inoculated with virus.

[b] One mouse later lost by accident.

[c] The main group; *cf.* Figure 2.

[d] The whole group; the distribution differs significantly from a single normal distribution and hence it is considered heterogeneous, and consequently no computation of significance was made.

TABLE II

The change in weights in the various groups of mice in Experiment 2

Period for Comparison: Days after Inoculation	Comparisons of Groups[a]	Differences in Mean Values for Gain or Loss of Weight			Differences in Standard Deviation of Weight Changes about the Average Change	
		Difference	Standard error of difference	Significance level[b]	Variance ratio	Significance level
7 *vs.* 0	S *vs.* 0	−0.21	0.65	$P > 0.1$	1.27	$P > 0.1$
	V *vs.* 0	−1.46	0.59	$0.05 > P > 0.01$	3.17	$0.05 > P > 0.01$
	SV *vs.* 0	−3.35	0.54	$P < 0.001$	1.88	$P > 0.1$
	SV *vs.* V	−1.89	0.57	$0.01 > P > 0.001$	0.59	$P > 0.1$
	SV *vs.* S	−3.14	0.62	$P < 0.001$	1.48	$P > 0.1$
16 *vs.* 0	S *vs.* 0	−0.85	0.39	$0.1 > P > 0.05$	1.57	$P > 0.1$
	V *vs.* 0	−2.26	0.64	$0.01 > P > 0.001$	19.1	$P < 0.001$
	SV *vs.* 0	−2.48	0.81	$0.01 > P > 0.001$	27.9	$P < 0.001$
	SV *vs.* V	−0.22	0.98	$P > 0.1$	1.46	$P > 0.1$
	SV *vs.* S	−1.63	0.84	$0.1 > P > 0.05$	17.8	$P < 0.001$
38 *vs.* 0	S *vs.* 0	0.81	0.70	$P > 0.1$	7.65	$0.01 > P > 0.001$
	V[c] *vs.* 0	0.09	0.31	$P > 0.1$	3.12	$0.05 > P > 0.01$
	SV[c] *vs.* 0	−0.35	0.76	$P > 0.1$	25.8	$P < 0.001$
	SV[c] *vs.* V[c]	−0.44	0.77	$P > 0.1$	8.27	$P < 0.001$
	SV[c] *vs.* S	−1.16	0.99	$P > 0.1$	3.37	$0.1 > P > 0.05$

[a] S = stressed but not inoculated with virus; V = inoculated with virus, but not stressed; SV = stressed and thereafter inoculated with virus; 0 = neither stressed nor inoculated with virus.

[b] Computed according to Cochran and Cox (7).

[c] The main group (*cf.* Fig. 2).

TABLE III (Experiment 3)

Virus titers[a] of organs from stressed (S) and unstressed (U) mice 1 to 5 days after inoculation of coxsackie B virus

Organ (Pools of 5)	Days after Inoculation				
	1	2	3	4	5
Blood	S: 4.5[a] U: 4.7	S: 3.5 U: 2.3	S: <1 U: <1	S: <1 U: <1	S: <1 U: <1
Pancreas	S: 8.6 U: 7.6	S: 6.8 U: 5.3	S: 6.4 U: 6.5	S: 4.9 U: 3.5	S: <1 U: <1
Liver	S: 6.2 U: 5.4	S: 5.7 U: 4.3	S: 3.6 U: 3.7	S: 3.6 U: 2.0	S: <1 U: <1
Heart	S: 4.5 U: 3.6	S: 3.7 U: 3.5	S: 4.7 U: 1.7	S: 2.3 U: <1	S: <1 U: <1
Muscle	S: 5.3 U: 3.7	S: ≥4.5 U: 3.5	S: 3.6 U: 2.0	S: 2.6 U: 2.3	S: 2.0 U: <1
Fat	S: n.d. U: n.d.	S: 4.8 U: 4.7	S: 4.7 U: 3.5	S: 5.0 U: 5.5	S: ≥5.5 U: 1.5
Brain	S: 2.2 U: 2.0	S: 2.5 U: 1.0	S: 1.2 U: 1.7	S: 1.4 U: 1.0	S: 3.7 U: ≥1.5

[a] Titer/0.1 ml, expressed as the negative logarithm of the dilution, which will kill 50% as calculated according to Reed and Muench.

TABLE IV (Experiment 3)

Analysis of variance: the influence of stress on virus titers at various times in pancreas, liver, heart and muscle[a]

Source of Variation	Degrees of Freedom	Reduced Sum of Squares	Variance	F
Two treatments.............................	1	9.570	9.57	23.7[b]
Four days.................................	3	35.216	11.74	29.1[b]
Four organs...............................	3	45.471	15.16	37.6[b]
Interaction day-organ.......................	9	4.925		
Interaction organ-treatment.................	3	0.469		
Interaction treatment-day...................	3	0.124		
Interaction treatment-day-organ.............	9	4.162		
Sum.....................................	31	99.937		
Combined interaction (error)................	24	9.680		

[a] Sequence of days not taken into account.
[b] $P < 0.001$.

RESULTS

Signs of Coxsackie B infection were much more pronounced in stressed than in unstressed mice. Stressed, infected mice regularly exhibited the typical syndrome of Coxsackie B infection, whereas unstressed, infected mice did so irregularly.

In Experiment 1 the stressed, infected mice lost significantly more weight than the unstressed, infected mice during the 1st week following injection. During the latter part of this week three mice died, and two more died later. In four of these five mice weight had decreased noticeably. Consequently, the mean weight of survivors became larger than it would have been if all mice had survived.

Experiment 2 was first analyzed for sex differences. No such differences were found, and hence the results for the two sexes were pooled.

During the 1st week there was little difference in the changes of weight. After about 2 weeks, however, a few stressed and unstressed mice inoculated with virus began to lose weight somewhat more than the others. This was very pronounced 38 days after inoculation in both stressed and unstressed, infected groups (Fig. 2). At this time extreme deviations in changes of weight from the main group occurred as follows: a) three stressed, infected animals had persistent severe weight losses, and one of these mice died; b) four unstressed, infected mice had weight losses; c) one unstressed, infected mouse had an extreme weight gain. These three groups were investigated according to Dixon and Massey's d) method for processing data for extreme values. With this method it was found that these animals responded in a significantly different manner. Thus, they were excluded from the main groups.

Statistical comparison of the four experimental groups was made: in the acute stage 7 days after the inoculation, in the subacute stage after 16 days, and, finally, in a more chronic stage after

38 days, the significantly extreme values being removed as discussed above. A consequence of such an exclusion is that results regarding low average gain of weight or wide dispersion show a lower degree of significance than if the extreme values had been included. However, a comparison using t and F tests can only be done if the experimental values do not differ significantly from the normal distribution. No mice died during the period registered in Tables I and II, but during the following months two mice in the stressed, infected group died.

In Table I the weights of the remaining mice at the indicated intervals after infection are compared to the weights before inoculation. It can be seen that a) unstressed, uninfected mice gained weight throughout; b) stressed, uninfected mice also gained weight throughout; c) unstressed, infected mice showed no significant weight change after 7 and 16 days but gained weight thereafter; and d) stressed, infected mice showed a weight loss in the first 7 days, but regained weight later.

In Table II the groups are compared with each other at different times after inoculation. The stressed and the unstressed groups of uninfected mice show no significant difference 7 days after inoculation. After 16 days there is a slight difference in mean values between the two groups. Later a difference is obvious, not in mean values, but in dispersion. As regards unstressed mice, the infected group and the uninfected group show a slight difference both in mean

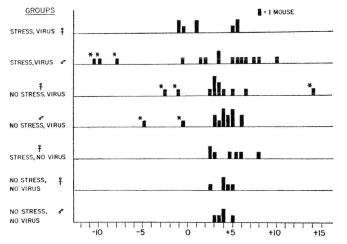

Figure 2 (Experiment 2). Individual changes in weight 38 days after the time of inoculation.

* Mice significantly different in weight from the main group.

values and in dispersion after 7 days. After 16 days these differences have a high significance level, but 38 days after the inoculation only a small difference in dispersion remains.

When the group of stressed, infected mice is compared to the group of unstressed, uninfected mice, a significant difference in mean values is demonstrable at 7 and 16 days, but disappears later. A significant difference in dispersion was not found at 7 days but appeared at 16 days and persisted 38 days after the inoculations. Regarding infected mice, a difference between the stressed group and the unstressed group can be demonstrated on the 7th but not on the 16th day. However, 38 days after the inoculation there is a significant difference in dispersion of the deviation of individual weight losses (or gains) from the mean value. Finally, the infected stressed and the uninfected stressed mice differed significantly in mean value at 7 days, but this difference had disappeared at 16 days. Highly significant differences in dispersion appeared at 16 days, but these differences were later reduced to become almost insignificant.

It might be mentioned that the few mice with extremely low weight in the infected unstressed group 38 days after inoculation but not included in the statistical comparison had recovered 2 months later, whereas the corresponding mice in the infected, stressed groups died or did not recover later on. This late outcome of the mice with extremely low weights supports the result from the main group that stressed mice respond to infection with greater loss of weight and larger dispersion than unstressed mice.

Some computations were done in order to show whether or not there is an interaction between stress and viral infection. The difference from the comparison "S vs. O" was compared to the difference from the comparison "SV vs. V." The largest difference occurred 7 days after inoculation and was positive. However, the level of significance was low $(0.1 > P > 0.05)$. No significant difference was observed 16 and 38 days after inoculation.

The results from Experiment 3, in which stressed and unstressed mice were compared as to the virus titers of internal organs, are listed in Table III.

It is evident from Table III—particularly if the values are plotted in graphs—that, considering the period during which virus in easily measurable quantities was found in various organs, three groups can be distinguished. In the first group, in which only blood is included, the virus titer decreased so rapidly that no reliable measurements could be carried out on samples taken later than 2 days after inoculation. In another group, consisting of pancreas, liver, heart, and muscle, there was a clear tendency for the virus titer to decrease for about 5 days to a value too small to be measured. In a third group consisting of fat and brain, there was no obvious tendency for decrease or increase in titer values during a period of 5 days. This formation of groups was supported by a statistical analysis of the regression lines.

The measurements of blood titer values were not sufficient to permit any conclusions about the influence of stress.

For pancreas, liver, heart[5] and muscle, the t test, when applied to each of these organs, showed that the titer values for stressed mice and for unstressed mice differed, although with low significance $(0.1 > P > 0.05)$, whereas the t test, applied to the organs as a group, showed a highly significant increase in virus titer for the stressed mice $(P < 0.001)$. An analysis of variance was also carried out (Table IV) and gave the same result.

For fat and brain the t test showed no significant difference in titer values between stressed and unstressed mice $(P > 0.1)$.

DISCUSSION

In previous stress experiments on mice, increased susceptibility to herpes simplex virus was observed as increase in death rates (1). In the present experiments, using Coxsackie B1 virus, failure to gain weight and even loss of weight after the inoculation appear as a sensitive index. Inoculation with Coxsackie B1 virus thus provided a simple means for following continuously the course of the experimental disease. Furthermore, by this refined technique, not only the influence of stress and the influence of virus infection can be studied but also the occurrence of possible interaction.

In most instances the mice appear to recover more or less completely from stress and/or Coxsackie B1 infection. It is apparent, however, that there is a time relationship in recovery with the stressed, infected group being the last to gain weight. This time relationship can also be

[5] The value for unstressed mice on the 4th day was assumed to be 0.5.

traced in the standard deviations of weight changes about the average changes which are listed in Table I and compared to each other in Table II.

The increased variation in individual response among those mice subjected to stress may be related to the variation in emotional disturbance from mouse to mouse, which may also be combined with some damage which resulted from failure to avoid the current. So far, however, we have not been able to demonstrate individual variations in the frequency of avoidance. The role of the current is difficult to evaluate, but in some preliminary experiments there was no correlation between mortality and the amount of shock sustained. Furthermore, confinement stress, which involves no shock, gave results similar to those with avoidance-learning stress in decreasing resistance to herpes virus infection.

The mechanism of the stress-induced susceptibility is not apparent from these experiments. It has been shown that the stress employed causes changes associated with increased adrenal cortical activity including atrophy of the spleen and thymus and leukopenia (9). These changes are in agreement with the general experience that increased adrenal cortical activity or administration of corticoids produce a general impairment of the defensive functions of the reticuloendothelial system including specific antibody response. One of the more striking features of the experimental infection in stressed mice as compared to the controls was the significant increase in virus levels in most of the organs tested the first days after inoculation. Those observations indirectly suggest that it is not interference with antibody response that makes the stressed mice more susceptible but rather the well known antiphlogistic effect of corticoids. The recent findings of inhibition by cortisone of the synthesis and action of interferon might also play some role (10).

The lower virus level in the stressed mice may be caused by lack of some nonspecific substance such as properdin. In a preliminary study it was, however, shown that the heat-labile anti-viral activity of the serum in stressed mice was within normal ranges

Although the artificial nature of the stressor and Coxsackie B1 infection for mice require caution in relating these results to natural infection in man, the facts indicated that centrally mediated responses to environmental stress may contribute significantly to the pathogenesis of infectious diseases, particularly in converting latent or mild infections into clinical disease. The adverse influence of stress alone is barely detectable as a failure to gain weight at the normal rate, and the viral infection in unstressed mice is manifest only as a transitory loss in weight. In contrast, the combination of stress and Coxsackie B1 infection result in more severe disease ranging from a delay in recovery in some mice to nutritional impairment and even death in others.

SUMMARY

Coxsackie virus B1 infections were induced in mice subjected to avoidance-learning stress and in unstressed controls. Infected, stressed mice were more susceptible than infected, unstressed mice as manifested by weight loss and deaths during the 1st week after inoculation, and as an increased dispersion in weight changes about 5 weeks after inoculation.

A significantly higher virus titer could be demonstrated in the pancreas, liver, heart and muscle of stressed mice as compared to unstressed mice.

REFERENCES

1. RASMUSSEN, A. F., JR., MARSH, J. T. AND BRILL, N. Q., Proc. Soc. Exper. Biol. & Med., **96**: 183, 1957.
2. PAPPENHEIMER, A. M., KUNG, L. J. AND RICHARDSON, S., J. Exper. Med., **94**: 45, 1951.
3. DALLDORF, G. AND GIFFORD, R., J. Exper. Med., **96**: 491, 1952.
4. MILLER, N. E., J. Exper. Psychol., **38**: 89, 1948.
5. ADLER, R. AND CLINK, D. W., J. Pharmacol. & Exper. Therap., **121**: 144, 1957.
6. MILLER, R. E., MURPHY, J. V. AND MIRSKY, I. A. T., Pharmacol. and Exper. Therap., **120**: 379, 1957.
7. COCHRAN, W. G. AND COX, GERTRUDE M., *Experimental Designs*, p. 92, John Wiley and Sons, Inc., New York, 1950.
8. DIXON AND MASSEY, *Introduction to Statistical Analysis*, 2nd Ed., p. 275, McGraw-Hill Co., New York, 1957.
9. MARSH, J. T. AND RASMUSSEN, A. F., JR., Fed. Proc., **18**: 583, 1959.
10. KILBOURNE, E. D., SMART, K. M. AND Pokorny, B. A., Nature, **190**: 650, 1961.

24

POLIOMYELITIS IN MONKEYS: DECREASED SUSCEPTIBILITY AFTER AVOIDANCE STRESS

James T. Marsh, John F. Lavender, Shueh-Shen Chang, and A. F. Rasmussen

Abstract. *Eleven monkeys were subjected to avoidance stress for 24 hours followed immediately by intravenous inoculation with type I poliovirus. Twelve control monkeys not so stressed were similarly inoculated. Seven of 11 stressed animals survived the infection while only one of the controls lived and their average incubation period was significantly longer than the average for controls. The number of circulating lymphocytes decreased significantly in experimental animals during and immediately after exposure to stress.*

Changes in resistance to herpes simplex virus and to anaphylactic shock in mice exposed to the stress of confinement or avoidance in a shuttlebox have been reported (1–3).

We now summarize effects of stress on resistance to poliovirus infection in cynomolgus monkeys.

In these experiments the Sidman avoidance procedure was used (4). Animals learned to press a telegraph key at a steady rate to avoid a shock to the tail which would be delivered once every 10 seconds if the lever was not pressed. Monkeys learn this procedure well and when fully trained receive few shocks during long periods of exposure. Despite this fact, the avoidance procedure is stressful for monkeys. During prolonged periodic exposure increased amounts of 17-hydroxycorticosteroids are found in blood and urine (5), and fatal gastrointestinal disorders develop (6).

The experiment was repeated five times with a total of 23 adult male monkeys. Throughout each experiment the animals lived in chairs (7) in which they were held loosely at the neck and waist. All 11 experimental animals and 7 of the 12 controls were trained to make the avoidance response; five controls were not trained. At the end of training all animals were permitted to rest for at least 9 days during which three blood samples were taken for base line total and differential white blood cell counts. Experimental animals were then exposed to the avoidance situation continuously for 24 hours, with a 10-minute interruption for feeding midway. Control animals remained in adjacent chairs but were not subjected to stress. In two experiments blood samples were taken at 3-hour intervals during the stress period to determine changes in white blood counts. At the conclusion of the 24-hour period of stress blood samples were taken, and experimental and control monkeys were inoculated intravenously with 100 tissue culture ID_{50} (50 percent infectious dose) of Brunhilde strain of type I poliovirus. Thereafter, blood samples were taken daily and the animals were observed for the development of fever and paralytic disease.

Exposure to the stressful avoidance situation results in a marked decrease in susceptibility to poliovirus infection. Whereas 7 of 11 stressed animals survived the infection and recovered, only 1 of the 12 controls lived. This difference in survival rates is significant at the .01 level (Fisher exact test). Three of the stressed animals showed little or no residual paralysis. The other four survivors, while appearing healthy, showed some residual leg, arm, or facial paralysis. Except for a higher incidence of quadriplegia and bulbar involvement in controls, paralytic patterns did not differ in the two groups. Prolonged incubation is also evidence of the protective effect of exposure to avoidance stress (Table 1). On the average, stressed animals developed symptoms 2 days later than controls (6.8 days as against 4.8). This difference tested by *t*-test is significant at the .001 level.

The number of circulating lymphocytes decreased in experimental animals during exposure to stress. Values for

Reprinted from Science, June 28, 1963, Vol. 140, No. 3574, pages 1414-1415

Table 1. Effects of avoidance stress on susceptibility to poliomyelitis. Signs of experimental infection were tremor and paralysis with difficulty in breathing and swallowing. Four monkeys, two stressed and two controls, died overnight without developing detectable paralysis; all four showed tremor a day before death. The remaining animals that died all exhibited paralysis before death.

Mortality ratios		Mean incubation (days)	Number of monkeys developing poliomyelitis at times after inoculation					
Total	Died		Day 4	Day 5	Day 6	Day 7	Day 8	Day 9
			Stressed monkeys					
11	4	6.8	0	2	3	2	1	2
			Control monkeys					
12	11	4.8	5	4	1	1	0	0

stressed animals were significantly lowered at the end of the 24-hour avoidance period, as well as 4 hours after its termination. In those instances where blood samples were taken at 3-hour intervals during exposure to stress, mean lymphocyte values were significantly lower for experimental animals than for controls after 3 hours of avoidance stress. Significantly lowered values were observed for control monkeys on the 4th and 5th days after inoculation. Presumably these values reflect a response to the developing stress of infection which occurred earlier in controls.

These results contrast sharply with previous findings on reduced resistance to virus infection in mice subjected to shuttle box stress (*1*, *2*). They also contrast with observations of increased susceptibility to poliovirus in hamsters and mice treated with cortisone before inoculation (*8*, *9*). One factor which may be important in accounting for the directional difference in susceptibility is the schedule of exposure to stress. In experiments with mice an intermittent "chronic" stress schedule was used in which the animal was exposed for 6 hours daily with 18 hours of rest between exposures for a period of weeks, whereas, in the monkey, exposure was to a single "acute" 24-hour period of avoidance stress. A period of at least 14 days of intermittent exposure to stress was the minimum for producing decreased resistance to virus infection in the mouse in contrast to the 24-hour period which proved effective for increasing resistance in the monkey. In earlier work on the mouse (*10*) it was demonstrated that physiological changes, presumably related to pituitary adrenal function, occurred very early in exposure to intermittent stress, as did increased resistance to anaphylactic shock. Resistance decreased along with thymus and spleen involution only after 14 or more days of exposure to stress.

Seven of the 12 control monkeys received the original avoidance training because of the possibility that it and the stress associated with it might influence subsequent response to stress during the experiment. This did not prove to be true as all of the trained controls succumbed to polio while 7 of the 11 trained stressed animals did not. Similarly, the duration of the rest period (ranging from 9 to 480 days) between original training and the experiment did not affect results.

The effects of shock per se on resistance might be questioned since controls received no shocks. If shock was a crucial factor, some correlation between the number sustained by stressed animals and resistance to poliovirus might be expected. The total number of shocks sustained in the 24-hour period ranged from a minimum of 155 to 6042 in one animal. (The latter resulted from apparatus failure.) The four that died ranked fourth, sixth, eighth, and tenth among the 11 stressed monkeys in terms of the number of shocks. The number clustered about the mean for the group. Similarly there was no correlation between the number of shocks and the length of incubation period (see *11*).

References and Notes

1. A. F. Rasmussen, J. T. Marsh, N. Q. Brill, *Proc. Soc. Exptl. Biol. Med.* **96**, 183 (1957).
2. T. Johnsson, J. Lavender, J. Marsh, *Federation Proc.* **18**, 575 (1959).
3. A. F. Rasmussen, E. S. Spencer, J. T. Marsh, *Proc. Soc. Exptl. Biol. Med.* **100**, 878 (1959).
4. M. Sidman, *Science* **118**, 157 (1953).
5. R. W. Porter, J. V. Brady, D. Conrad, J. W. Mason, R. Galambos, D. M. Rioch, *Psychosomat. Med.* **20**, 379 (1958).
6. J. W. Mason, J. V. Brady, E. Polish, J. A. Bauer, J. Robinson, R. M. Rose, E. D. Taylor, *Science* **133**, 1596 (1961).
7. J. W. Mason, *J. Appl. Physiol.* **12**, 130 (1958).
8. G. Schwartzman, *Proc. Soc. Exptl. Biol. Med.* **75**, 835 (1950).
9. G. M. Findlay and E. M. Howard, *J. Pharm. Pharmacol.* **4**, 37 (1952).
10. J. T. Marsh and A. F. Rasmussen, *Proc. Soc. Exptl. Biol. Med.* **104**, 180 (1960).
11. Supported in part by grant 2M-6415 from U.S. Public Health Service and research grant FD-GR-60-2 from the Army Chemical Corps. One of us (S.S.C.) had a grant from the International Cooperation Administration under the Visiting Research Scientists Program administered by the National Academy of Sciences.

25

EFFECTS OF GROUPING ON LEVELS OF CIRCULATING ANTIBODIES IN MICE

Stephen H. Vessey (Introduced by J. J. Christian)

The purpose of this work was primarily to investigate the effects of grouping on antibody titer, and secondarily, to study the effects of social rank on antibody titer. Since under some circumstances adrenocortical hormones inhibit antibody responses, and since various stressors, such as grouping, may increase the output of these hormones, grouped mice should respond to a particular antigen with a lower titer of antibody than should isolated mice.

Adrenocortical hormones affect host resistance through several mechanisms. Antibody responses to various antigens were inhibited by cortisone in rabbits(1), guinea pigs(2), rats(3), and mice(4). Inflammatory responses were diminished or delayed in rabbits(5) and guinea pigs(6).

Indirect evidence that various stressors increase the output of adrenocortical hormones is considerable. For example, grouped mice had heavier adrenals(7) and lower numbers of circulating eosinophils(8) than did isolated mice. A more indirect case is that grouped mice were less resistant to infestation by *Trichinella spiralis* than were isolated mice (9). Also, mice stressed in shuttle boxes were protected against anaphylactic shock(10).

Direct evidence shows that grouping increases adrenocortical steroid output. Rats kept in colonies had higher levels of plasma corticosterone than those in groups of four (11). Also, groups of 20 had higher levels than did singly caged animals(12).

Available evidence, then, indicates that adrenocortical steroids may inhibit the antibody response, that various stressors cause increased production of adrenocorticoids, and that grouping often is a sufficient stressor to cause such an increase. It follows that grouping may inhibit the circulating-antibody response if the quantitative relations are adequate. Also, since social rank of mice shows an inverse relationship to adrenal weight(13) and a direct relationship to number of circulating eosinophils(8), it may be that a rela-tionship exists between social rank and antibody titer.

Methods. Mice used in these experiments were C3H males. They were weaned at 20 days of age and placed in separate one-gallon jars; dry dog food pellets and water were supplied *ad lib*. Cardboard was placed between the jars so that the mice were visually as well as physically isolated. Mice used in experiments ranged in age from 9 to 15 weeks.

Mice to be grouped were individually marked, then placed in a metal can 3 feet in diameter for 4 hours per day for duration of the experiment. Experiment I involved 6 grouped mice and 6 isolated controls. Also, 5 mice were placed together in an $18 \times 12 \times 5$ inch plastic cage for duration of the experiment. Experiment II consisted of 2 groups of 6 mice each and 5 isolated controls. All mice in these 2 experiments were injected with antigen. Experiment III involved 6 grouped mice and 5 isolated controls; mice in this experiment were not injected.

Grouped mice were observed for 20 minutes each day. The number of fights each mouse won or lost was recorded, as was the number of times he chased or was chased by another mouse. A mouse was ranked above another if he dominated in more than half of their interactions.

Mice to be tested for antibody response were injected i.p. with 0.5 ml of a 1:5 dilution of beef serum on the fifth day of grouping. Blood samples were taken from all injected mice before injection, and 4, 8, 11, 18 and 28 days after injection. Four or 5 drops of blood were obtained for each sample from behind the eye with a drawn-out piece of heparinized, 5 mm glass tubing. Each sample of blood was centrifuged, the plasma drawn off and placed in a precipitin tube along with an equal volume of saline, coded, and frozen for later use. A total of 204 plasma samples was collected.

TABLE I. Mean Logarithms of Antibody Titers.

Exp	Grouped	Mice	0 M	4 M	4 S.E.	4 P	8 M	8 S.E.	8 P	11 M	11 S.E.	11 P	18 M	18 S.E.	18 P	28 M
I	Yes	6	0	0	—	n.s.	.87	.27	n.s.	.98	.22	<.05	.50	.22	<.02	0
	No	6	0	.50	.25	n.s.	1.30	.13	n.s.	1.55	.05	<.01	1.20	.10	<.05	0
	Yes*	5	0	.40	.22		.86	.22		.66	.27		.60	.25		0
II	Yes	6	0	.55	.25	<.01	1.05	.07	<.001	1.10	.06	<.01	.33	.29	<.05	0
	No	5	0	1.15	.07	<.001	1.45	.07	<.02	1.45	.07	<.01	1.05	.06	<.01	0
	Yes	6	0	.17	.17		.88	.18		1.15	.07		.33	.21		0

Days after injection†

* Grouped continuously rather than only 4 hr per day.
† A mean of zero indicates that all titers were below 10.

S.E. is standard error of mean.

Antibody titers were determined by the ring precipitin test of Hanks(14), except that tests were incubated at room temperature for one hour, stored in the refrigerator overnight and then read.

At conclusion of each experiment both adrenal glands were removed from all mice, preserved in 10% formalin and later weighed wet on a Roller Smith 25 mg torsion balance. Results are expressed without regard to body weight since no correlation between body weight and adrenal weight was found for the 16 isolated mice used in these experiments.

Results. Antibody titers of both grouped and isolated mice (Exp. I) generally increased to the 11th day following injection, then declined (Table I). The mean logarithm of the antibody titer for each of the 2 groups was compared with that of the 6 isolated mice for each day samples were collected by the "t" test. Mean titers of the isolated mice were found to be significantly higher than those of either of the groups (P less than .05) for days 11 and 18. No significant differences were found for days 4 and 8. On day 28 the titers of all mice were below 10, which was the lowest dilution used.

To test this approach again, 2 additional groups of 6 mice each were grouped 4 hours per day, and 5 mice were kept isolated (Exp. II). Titers of both grouped and isolated mice generally increased to the 11th day following injection, then declined (Table I); "t" tests showed that the mean logarithm of the titers of the 5 isolated mice for each day

samples were collected was significantly higher than those of the 2 groups (P less than .05) for days 4, 8, 11 and 18. Titers of all mice were below 10 by day 28.

Social rank, as determined by number of wins and losses in fights between individual mice of a group, was compared with antibody titer. In most cases it was not possible to rank all of the mice in a particular group; generally only the 2 or 3 top-ranking mice were determined. Inspection of the values of antibody titers indicated no correlation with position in the hierarchy except for the top-ranking mice. The mean logarithm of the titers of the 4 dominant mice from the above experiments was plotted with the mean values for the other 20 mice in these experiments for each day samples were taken (Fig. 1). Analysis of variance showed that the mean logarithms of the titers of the dominant mice were significantly higher than the mean values for the other mice (P less than .05)

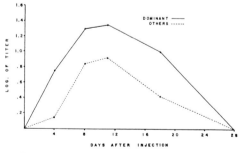

FIG. 1. Mean antibody titers of dominant mice and other mice from the 4 groups of Exp. I and II.

Behavior and Immune Function

TABLE II. Mean Body Weights and Mean Adrenal Weights.

Exp	Grouped	Duration (days)	Injected	Mice	Mean body wt (g)		Adrenal wt (g)	
					Before	After	Mean	S.E.
I	Yes	38	Yes	6	22.8	22.2	3.89	.14
	" *	38	"	5	27.4	30.6	4.29	.49
	No	38	"	6	24.3	30.2	2.95	.10
II	Yes	28	"	6	23.2	22.0	4.34	.36
	"	28	"	6	31.8	31.8	5.01	.37
	No	28	"	5	27.4	31.8	3.35	.17
III	Yes	38	No	6	22.7	25.3	4.20	.10
	No	38	"	5	24.8	33.4	3.12	.25

* Grouped continuously rather than only 4 hr per day.

for days 4, 8, 11 and 18.

Mean weights of the adrenals of the mice in groups were compared with those of the isolated mice within each experiment by the "t" test (Table II). In all cases the adrenals of the grouped mice were significantly heavier than those of the isolated mice (P less than .05).

Effects of injecting antigen and taking blood samples on adrenal weight were tested by comparing adrenal weights of grouped and isolated mice that had not been injected or bled with those that had. The mean adrenal weight of 5 isolated mice that were neither injected nor bled was not significantly different from the means of the isolated mice in the 2 experiments in which mice were injected and bled. Similarly, the mean for the 6 grouped mice that were neither injected nor bled was not significantly different from any of the means of the groups in the 2 experiments in which mice were injected and bled. Thus this small test does not indicate that the procedure itself altered the adrenal weight.

Discussion. Examination of Table I indicates that the duration of detectable antibody titers of grouped mice is almost identical to that of isolated mice. The primary difference is one of magnitude. Thus, it can be concluded that grouping is sufficient to cause a significantly lower level of circulating antibody to a beef serum antigen in grouped mice than in isolated mice.

Also we conclude that dominant mice respond to an antigen with a higher titer than do the other mice in their group. This result was expected since dominant mice have lighter adrenals than their subordinates and presumably are producing smaller amounts of adrenocorticoids(13).

In previous work Christian(7) found that the adrenal weights of mice grouped for 7 days were significantly higher than those of isolated mice. Evidence is given here that grouping mice for 28 and 38 days gives similar results. Grouping mice continuously has been shown to increase adrenal weights to the same degree as grouping them 4 hours per day for a 10 day period(13). Our evidence is that mice grouped continuously for 38 days also show an increase which is about the same as that of mice grouped 4 hours per day.

Summary. The effects of grouping and social rank on circulating-antibody titer were studied using C3H mice. Previously isolated mice were placed together in groups of 6 each for 4 hours per day and injected with beef serum on the fifth day of grouping. Antibody titers were determined from blood samples by the ring precipitin test. Grouped mice were found to have significantly lower titers of circulating antibody than did isolated mice. Dominant mice had significantly higher titers than the other mice in their groups. The adrenal glands of grouped mice, taken after 28 and 38 days of grouping, were significantly heavier than those of isolated mice.

1. Malkiel, S., Hargis, B., *J. Immunol.* 1952, v69, 217.

2. Germuth, F. G., Ottinger, B., Oyama, J., Proc. Soc. Exp. Biol. and Med., 1952, v80, 188.

3. Eisen, H. N., Mayer, M. M., Moore, D. H., Tarr, R. R., Stoerk, H. C., *ibid.*, 1947, v65, 301.

4. Hayes, S. P., Dougherty, T. F., *Fed. Proc.,* 1952, v11, 67.

5. Michael, M., Whorton, C. M., Proc. Soc. Exp. Biol. and Med., 1951, v76, 754.

6. Schricker, R. L., Hanson, L. E., *Am. J. Vet. Res.,* 1961, v22, 580.

7. Christian, J. J., *Am. J. Physiol.,* 1955, v182, 292.

8. Vandenbergh, J. G., *Animal Behaviour,* 1960, v8, 13.

9. Davis, D. E., Read, C. P., Proc. Soc. Exp. Biol. and Med., 1958, v99, 269.

10. Treadwell, P. E., Rasmussen, A. F., *J. Immunol.,* 1961, v87, 492.

11. Eechaute, W., Demeester, G., LaCroix, E., Leusen, I., *Arch. Int. Pharmacodyn.,* 1962, v136, 161.

12. Barrett, A. M., Stockham, M. A., *J. Endocrinol.,* 1963, v26, 97.

13. Davis, D. E., Christian, J. J., Proc. Soc. Exp. Biol. and Med., 1957, v94, 728.

14. Hanks, J. H., *J. Immunol.,* 1935, v28, 95.

Reprinted from *Proc. Soc. Exp. Biol. Med.* **115**, 252–255, 1964.

Behavior and Immune Function

26

PSYCHOLOGICAL STRESS, EARLY RESPONSE TO FOREIGN PROTEIN, AND BLOOD CORTISOL IN VERVETS

Charles W. Hill, William E. Greer, and Oscar Felsenfeld

In this study, the focus of attention was the biological response of vervet monkeys (*Cercopithecus aethiops*) under psychological stress to a well-defined protein, bovine serum albumin, with plasma cortisol as an indicator of alterations in the pituitary-adrenocortical system. The term "psychological" was used simply to indicate that the stress aspects of the experimental situation were considered to have their impact upon the animals primarily by way of the sensory systems, rather than through direct physical or physiological trauma. After immunization, 5 animals were subjected to irregular noise, light, and vertical movement, while 5 controls remained undisturbed except for periodic blood collections. The stress group showed delayed antibody formation, and the antibodies rose to a lower level than in the control group. The serum cortisol values were markedly elevated during the initial period of the experiment in the group exposed to stress.

THE RESPONSE of mice to psychological stress has been studied by Marsh and Rasmussen.[1] The weight of the adrenals increased, but the number of white blood cells decreased during the early phases of the experiments. Involution of the thymus and spleen were noted later. Two or 3 weeks after termination of the stress, these organs and the white blood count returned to normal. The susceptibility of mice to herpes simplex, Coxsackie B1 virus, and anaphylactogenic stimuli, as well as homograft reaction and delayed hypersensitivity had already decreased after a few sessions of exposure to stress. These observations are in accord with the studies of Selye,[2] who documented the influence of stress on the pituitary-adrenocortical, thymicolymphatic, and leukopoietic systems. Mason *et al.*[3] recorded increased serum corticosteroid levels in monkeys under stress. Florica and Muehl[4] demonstrated the same phenomenon in man. Our group noted that vervet monkeys under stress developed agglutinating and precipitating antibodies against a specific lipopolysaccharide at a later time and to a lesser extent than did the control animals.[5]

In the above and other studies, the term "stress" has been applied to a variety of factors and situations. The

From the Tulane University Delta Regional Primate Research Center, Covington, La.

Received for publication Apr. 25, 1966.

Reprinted from *Psychosom. Med.* **29,** 279–283, 1967.

common feature within this diversity is believed to be that of disturbance in behavior, physiological functioning, or both. In other words, stress has been a stimulus or stimulus-complex which produces a relatively intense and diffuse reaction in the organism. In the present study, the focus of attention was the biological response of vervets under psychological stress to a well-defined protein, with plasma cortisol as an indicator of alterations in the pituitary-adrenocortical system. Here the adjective "psychological" was used simply to indicate that the stress aspects of the experimental situation were considered to have their impact upon the animals, initially at least, by way of the sensory systems, rather than through direct physical or physiological trauma.

Experimental Data

Bovine serum albumin (BSA)* gave a single, sharp precipitation line with rabbit anti-BSA serum* in the Preer and in the Ouchterlony tests.[6] Its electro-

phoretic mobility on Sepharaphore III strips* was in accordance with calculations and gave a single band when stained with Ponceau S. It was injected into the experimental primates, first subcutaneously with Freund's complete adjuvant,† then after 1 week's interval, intravenously, in 20-mg. aliquots per animal, in physiological saline solution, weekly for 3 weeks. The injections were given on the first day of each week. The subcutaneous BSA administration took place at 0 in Fig. 1, the intravenous injections at 1, 2, and 3 weeks (Fig. 1).

Vervets (African green monkeys, *Cercopithecus aethiops*) were selected for the study. The animals were approximately 2 years old, weighed 2–2.5 kg., were in good physical health, and were under constant supervision by a qualified veterinarian. The sexes were equally represented in each group. The vervets were kept in the primate colony under identical conditions prior to the experiment. Their blood tests, basic biochemistry, and repeat bacteriological and parasitological examinations showed no

---

*Nutritional Biochemicals Corp., Cleveland, Ohio.

*Gelman Instrument Co., Ann Arbor, Mich.
†Difco Laboratories, Detroit, Mich.

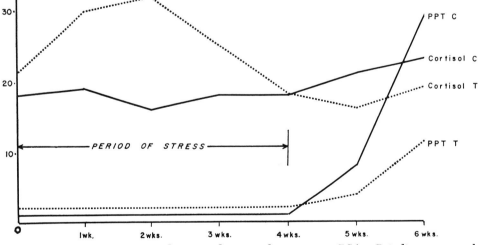

FIG. 1. Response of *Cercopithecus aethiops* under stress to BSA. *C* indicates controls (solid lines); *T*, test animals (dotted lines), and *PPT*, reciprocal titer $\times 10^{-2}$.

Behavior and Immune Function

deviations from values considered normal; nor were they found to harbor pathogenic microorganisms.

The monkeys were divided into 2 groups of 5 animals each. One group was exposed to stress; the other served as control.

Stress

The stress situation imposed upon the experimental group was more sophisticated than that described for an earlier study,[5] with the emphasis still upon the psychological end of the stress continuum. The animals were housed for the duration of the study in individual cages, 12 in. wide, 12 in. deep, and 24 in. high, and were removed only for blood drawings and inoculations.

A program of systematic disturbance was initiated the day before the first inoculation and continued, with several short interruptions, for 30 days thereafter. One part of this program was automated, consisting of a 21-min. cycle of noise, lights, and silence as follows: bells and buzzers on, 2 min.; silence, 5 min.; lights on, 2 min.; silence, 5 min.; lights and bells, 2 min.; silence, 5 min. The bells and buzzers were of the household door type; the lights were three 150-watt floodlights. All were mounted on the cage rack with the lights facing into the cages.

Another part of the disturbance program consisted of a gradual elevation and sudden dropping of all 5 cages simultaneously through a 6-in. distance by means of a hand-cranked mechanism. This operation was performed 1–4 times a day at irregular intervals during normal working hours only, through the 30-day period.

The experimental animals were fed the standard Purina chow either once or twice a day at irregular times. It was believed that the effects of the complete situation (small cages, interrupted noise and lights, aperiodic vertical movements, and irregular feeding) were primarily psychological in nature, as defined above.

The control animals were housed individually in large cages, 24 in. wide, 36 in. deep, and 46 in. high. They were fed at the normal hours, and were otherwise undisturbed except for the blood drawings and inoculations pertaining to this study.

Clinical observations consisted of weekly physical examinations, as well as food-intake and body-weight determinations.

All laboratory tests were carried out in triplicate.

Blood Tests

Blood specimens were collected before, and each week after the initiation of the experiments. Serum or plasma were separated as soon as possible to prevent changes in the steroids, and kept at $-20°$ C. The time of drawing blood was between 8 and 11 A.M., to avoid the influence of diurnal fluctuations.

Precipitation tests were carried out with the Ouchterlony and Preer micromethods[6] using Ionagar* as the supporting gel. When results were positive, tube tests with serial serum dilutions were set up, the end titers determined, and the amount of precipitated nitrogen estimated after nesslerization[7] to check the completeness of the reaction. The BSA solution used for injecting the animals served as the antigen also in these tests.

Pituitary Adrenocortical Function

Cortisol was chosen as a marker of pituitary-adrenocortical function. It was determined according to the method described by van der Vies[8] that is considered to measure cortisol independently from other corticosteroids.

This procedure consists of the extraction of the serum or plasma with methylene chloride, carbon tetrachloride, and

---

*Oxoid, London, England.

a mixture of sulfuric acid and ethyl alcohol. Instead of UV fluorescence, thin layer chromatography on silica gel G was used for the final determinations.*

Results

The appetite, weight, and excretion of stools and urine did not show statistically significant changes during the experiments.

Table 1 and Figure 1 show the geometrical means and the standard deviations of the results of the serum examinations.

Precipitating antibodies appeared in the serums of the 5 control animals in 5 weeks, and in the experimental animals 6 weeks after the commencement of the experiments. The initial levels were 1:780 ± 80 after 5 weeks, and 1:2,900 ± 180 after 6 weeks in the control group, whereas the experimental group showed 1:300 ± 50 after 5, and 1:1,100 ± 100 after 6 weeks.

The cortisol levels remained fairly standard in the control group throughout the experiment, fluctuating between 16 ± 2 and 22 ± 3 μg. The group exposed

*The reference standards were purchased from the Sigma Chemical Corp., St. Louis, Mo.

to stress showed a marked initial increase, from 21 ± 2 to 30 ± 4 μg. 1 week after exposure to stress was started. The level remained high, 32 ± 4 μg. during the second week but decreased to 25 ± 3 and 18 ± 2 μg. in the third and fourth weeks, respectively, of the tests. After that, the cortisol levels remained within normal limits.

Discussion and Conclusions

Under the conditions of this experiment, psychological stress altered the output of cortisol, a marker of several pituitary-adrenocortical functions, as well as the response to foreign body protein (BSA), by retarding as well as depressing the antibody production against a parenterally administered protein. It would be premature to make a firm statement at this time concerning the mechanism involved. Little is known about the correlation between the pituitary-adrenocortical system and antibody formation. Modern theories[9] pinpoint the lymph gland-splenic system as the factory of antibodies, but the relationship of the latter to the pituitary-adrenocortical system has not yet been studied sufficiently from the point of view of immunochemistry. While present studies

TABLE 1. Cortisol and Precipitin Levels in Vervets Exposed to Stress

Time	Cortisol levels (μg.%)			Precipitin levels (reciprocal titers)		
	Under stress	No stress (controls)	P*	Under stress	No stress (controls)	P*
Before immunization	21 ± 2†	18 ± 2	.33	< 20	< 20	
After immunization (wk.)						
First	30 ± 4	19 ± 2	.07	< 20	< 20	
Second	32 ± 4	16 ± 3	.03	< 20	< 20	
Third	25 ± 3	18 ± 2	.11	< 20	< 20	
Fourth	18 ± 2	18 ± 2		< 20	< 20	
Fifth	16 ± 3	22 ± 2	.17	300 ± 50†	780 ± 80	.02
Sixth	20 ± 2	23 ± 3	.47	1100 ± 100	2900 ± 180	.03

*Probability, Student's t test.
†Geometric means and standard deviations.

focused on adrenocortical hormones, other hormones might also be involved in the mediation of the effect of stressful conditions on antibody formation. Further research is therefore indicated to elucidate this question.

The decrease in cortisol levels in the experimental animals while the stress situation was still in effect was probably due to adaptation. This problem has been discussed elsewhere,[5] and attempts were continued in the present study to preserve uncertainty through irregularity throughout the 4 weeks of the test. However, irregularity of timing might not be sufficient over so long a period, and qualitative changes in the stimuli will be tried in subsequent experiments of this type.

Summary

Ten vervets were immunized with bovine serum albumin. Five of them were exposed to psychological stress, the others served as controls and were not disturbed except for periodic blood collections. The group under stress showed delayed antibody formation and the antibodies rose to a lower level than in the control group. The serum cortisol values were markedly elevated during the initial period of the experiment in the group exposed to stress.

References

1. MARSH, J. T., and RASMUSSEN, A. F. JR. Response of adrenals, thymus, spleen and leucocytes to shuttle box and confinement stress. *Proc Soc Exp Biol Med* 104:180, 1960.

2. SELYE, H. *Stress*. Acta, Montreal, 1950.

3. MASON, J. W., MANGAN, G. JR., BRADY, V. J., CONRAD, D., and RIOCH, D. McK. Concurrent plasma epinephrine, norepinephrine and 17-hydroxycorticosteroid levels during conditioned emotional disturbances in monkeys. *Psychosom Med* 23:344, 1961.

4. FLORICA, V., and MUEHL, S. Relationship between plasma levels of 17-hydroxycorticosteroids (17-OH-CS) and psychological measure of manifest anxiety. *Psychosom Med* 24:596, 1962.

5. FELSENFELD, O., HILL, C. W., and GREER, W. E. Response of *Cercopithecus aethiops* to cholera vibrio lipopolysaccharide and psychological stress. *Proc Roy Soc Trop Med Hyg* In press.

6. CROWLE, A. J. *Immunodiffusion*. Academic, New York, 1961.

7. CAMPBELL, D. H., GARVEY, J. S., CREMER, N. E., and SUSSDORF, D. H. *Methods in Immunology*. Benjamin, New York, 1964.

8. VAN DER VIES, J. Individual determination of cortisol and corticosterone in a single sample of peripheral blood. *Acta Endocr (Kbh)* 38:399, 1961.

9. COHEN, S., and PORTER, R. R. Structure and biological activity of immunoglobulins. *Advance Immunol* 4:287, 1964.

27

EARLY EXPERIENCE AND IMMUNITY

George F. Solomon, Seymour Levine, and John Kersten Kraft

MANY physiological and behavioural variables in adult life have been related to infantile experience. There have, however, been no large scale studies of the effects of infantile stimulation on the immunological system—influences on which might have important implications in host resistance to infectious disease, to cancer (in view of growing evidence that resistance to many tumours is immunological in nature[1,2]) and possibly to auto-immune diseases, which may have an association with states of immunological insufficiency[3]. Emotions and stress have been related to the onset and course of infections, cancer and auto-immune diseases[4], and we have now studied differential immunological responses to flagellin in rats handled and not handled before weaning.

Previous work showed that rats treated in infancy either by simply being picked up once daily and placed briefly in a different environment or by being given electric shocks for 3 min once daily until weaning at 21 days as adults explored a new environment more freely, defaecated less and seemed to show "more adaptive behaviour" by learning avoidance conditioning more rapidly[5,6]. Animals manipulated before weaning showed less change in adrenal weight under chronic stress[7] but greater adrenal cortical hormone response to electric shock[8]. It seemed possible that one of the chief consequences of infantile stimulation is to endow the organism with the capacity to make fine discriminations concerning the relevant aspects of the environment[9]. This view seems to be supported by evidence that manipulated animals showed less adrenal response to a new situation and quicker habituation[10]. Adaptive physiological as well as behavioural consequences of early experience have been noted, although the adequacy of a unitary concept of emotional reactivity for describing the effects of early stimulation has been questioned[11]. Rats handled in infancy showed less physical change and lighter adrenal weight after immobilization and survived longer under severe deprivation of food and water, though the pre-weaning and post-weaning experiences of different experiments might not be comparable[12-14].

The only previous work on early experience and antibody response was a pilot study in which non-manipulated

Reprinted by permission of *Nature* 220 (No. 5169), pp. 821–822. Copyright © 1968, Macmillian Journals Limited.

rats showed greater production of haemolysin after injection with 2 per cent sheep red cells but less antibody response when 0·5 per cent sheep cells were used[9]. On the other hand, changes in susceptibility to encephalomyocarditis virus or murine leukaemia virus (Rauscher agent) were not found on the basis of differential early experience[15]. Somewhat conflicting results are found in the few studies of the effects of early experience on the growth of tumours. Rats which were held and stroked for 10 min daily after weaning (from mean age 22 days to 45 days) and implanted with Walker carcinoma 256 2 days after cessation of handling survived significantly longer and had smaller adrenals than did non-handled littermate controls[16]. In another study, daily handling in the pre-weaning but not in the post-weaning period decreased the rate of growth of Walker 256 carcinoma, but electric shock had no effect[17]. Mice handled for the first 24 days of life showed shorter survival after transplantation of lymphoid leukaemia as adults[18]. Animals "gentled" in early infancy lost more hair secondary to skin painting with the carcinogen methylcholanthrene than did controls or animals subjected to neonatal stress[19].

We used pregnant inbred Fisher rats, obtained commercially. From parturition each pup in the handled group was picked up, removed from the nest, placed in a 3 inch square box for 3 min, and then returned. Control (non-handled) animals were undisturbed. This procedure was continued daily for 21 days (until weaning). Handled and unhandled animals were then housed in separate cages, with two or three animals in each cage. At 9 weeks all animals were injected intraperitoneally with 100 ng of flagellin polymer, at which low dosage we have produced consistent and vigorous antibody response in the Fisher rat. Flagellin is prepared from the flagella of *Salmonella adelaide* and is a novel antigen to the rat, giving a true primary response (personal communication from G. J. V. Nossal). We and others have found no pre-immunization antibody[20]. Animals were bled from the tail at 4, 7, 14, 21 and 28 days after primary immunization. On day 28 a booster of 100 ng of flagellin was given. Blood was drawn 7, 14 and 21 days after secondary immunization.

The experiment was conducted twice in order to replicate initial findings. The first experiment involved twenty-three handled and twenty-eight unhandled rats; the second, thirty-one handled and twenty-six unhandled. In so far as the replications did not differ statistically, the data were combined, except that only the second groups were titrated 21 days after the primary immunization. Titrations were done "blind" without the experimental group being known. Assay was regularly checked on sera of known titre to assure reliability. Serial dilutions of 0·25 ml. volume were added to 0·25 ml. of a 10^8 organisms/ml. concentration of living *Salmonella adelaide* in broth culture, which was freshly prepared each day. Antibody titre is expressed as the dilution of serum affecting immobilization of the swimming bacteria (geometric progression), and as the serial dilution tube number at which immobilization took place (arithmetic progression). The first tube contained a 1 : 5 dilution of serum, tube 2, 1 : 10 dilution, tube 3, 1 : 20, and so on. Four, 7 and 14 days after primary immunization, titration was performed with and without the addition of mercaptoethanol, which destroys the 19S component (essentially IgM), and results at these points are expressed as total antibody and IgM.

Statistical analysis was by a non-parametric method using only the rank order of the titres. All titres were ranked for each day and a Kruskal–Wallis test was used to test the significance of the differences among the groups. Then the daily rank of each subject was averaged during primary response (days 4–28) and during secondary response (booster + 4 − booster + 14). These average ranks were then ranked and a Kruskal–Wallis test used again. (This method avoids problems of geometric progression that might give misleadingly great differences at high titres and of distribution with the possibility of non-uniform errors.)

Antibody response in male and female animals was calculated separately; there were no significant differences, so these data are not included. Only three handled and three unhandled animals did not show antibody at the fourth day after primary immunization.

Table 1 shows that the serum antibody titre was higher in every case after primary and secondary immunization in handled than in unhandled animals. The initial 19S response of handled animals was double that of unhandled. The secondary response titre dropped off more quickly in unhandled animals. Both overall primary response ($P < 0.001$) and overall secondary response ($P < 0.02$) were significantly greater in handled than in unhandled animals, the primary response differing more impressively.

Thus the immunological responsivity of the adult seems to be modified by early experience. We can only speculate about possible mechanisms. Environmentally responsive hormones may affect thymic function, which plays a part in the establishment of immunological competence[21]. Our data might be interpreted as supporting evidence that the hypothalamus has a regulating role in immunity[22,23] because other physiological parameters modified by early experience are thought to have hypothalamic mediation[9].

We thank Professor G. J. V. Nossal and Dr Gordon Ada of the Walter and Eliza Hall Institute of Medical Research, Melbourne, for their help and advice, and for providing the flagellin; Dr Alfred Amkraut for consultation in immunology; Dr Helena Kraemer for statistical

Table 1. ANTIBODY RESPONSE IN HANDLED AND UNHANDLED RATS

	Primary response											Secondary response		
Day	4		7		14		21	28				Booster +4	Booster +7	Booster +14
	Total antibody	19S antibody	Total	19S	Tota	19S								
Handled														
No. of animals	53	47/50	52	42	54	47	31	53				54	53	50
Mean titre	1:44	1:10	1:384	1:11	1:2816	1:5·5	1:9728	1:1152				1:3840	1:3072	1:1280
Mean dilution number	4·1	2·0	7·2	2·1	10·1	1·1	11·9	8·8				10·5	10·2	9·0
Unhandled														
No. of animals	54	40/43	54	49	52	44	26	54				51	51	54
Mean titre	1:24	1:5	1:272	1:8	1:1152	1:6	1:3840	1:768				1:3072	1:1408	1:832
Mean dilution number	3·2	1·0	6·7	1·6	8·8	1·2	10·5	8·2				10·2	9·1	8·3

consultation; and Suzanne Donohue for technical assistance. This work was supported by the Veterans Administration Hospital and a grant from the US Public Health Service. S. L. holds a US Public Health Service research scientist award.

[1] Prehn, R. T., *Conceptual Advances in Immunology and Oncology* (Paul B. Hoeber, Inc., Medical Book Dept of Harper and Row Publishers, Inc., New York, 1963).

[2] Habel, K., *Conceptual Advances in Immunology and Oncology* (Paul B. Hoeber, Inc., Medical Book Dept of Harper and Row Publishers, Inc., New York, 1963).

[3] Fudenberg, H. H., *Hosp. Prac.*, **3**, 43 (1968).

[4] Solomon, G. F., and Moos, R. H., *Arch. Gen. Psychiat.*, **11**, 657 (1964).

[5] Levine, S., Chevalier, J. A., and Korchin, S. J., *J. Pers.*, **24**, 477 (1956).

[6] Levine, S., *J. Pers.*, **25**, 70 (1956).

[7] Levine, S., *Science*, **126**, 405 (1957).

[8] Levine, S., *Science*, **135**, 795 (1962).

[9] Levine, S., *Endocrines and the Central Nervous System* (edit. by Levine, R.) (Williams and Wilkins Co., Baltimore, 1966); (*Res. Publ. Assoc. Res. Nerv. Ment. Dis.*, **43**, chap. 13, 280; 1966).

[10] Levine, S., and Broadhurst, P. L., *J. Comp. Physiol. Psychol.*, **56**, 423 (1963).

[11] Henderson, M. D., *Psychosom. Med.*, **30**, 62 (1968).

[12] Weininger, O., *J. Comp. Physiol. Psychol.*, **49**, 1 (1956).

[13] Weininger, O., *Canad. J. Psychol.*, **7**, 111 (1953).

[14] Levine, S., and Otis, L. S., *Canad. J. Psychol.*, **12**, 103 (1958).

[15] Friedman, S. B., and Glasgow, L. A., *Pediat. Clin. N. Amer.*, **13**, 315 (1966).

[16] Newton, G., Bly, C. G., and McCrary, C., *J. Nerv. Ment. Dis.*, **134**, 522 (1962).

[17] Denenberg, V. H., *Psychol. Rep.*, **5**, 357 (1959).

[18] Levine, S., and Cohen, C., *Proc. Soc. Exp. Biol. and Med.*, **102**, 53 (1959).

[19] Winokur, G., Stern, J. A., and Graham, D. T., *J. Psychosom. Res.*, **2**, 266 (1958).

[20] Diener, E., *J. Immunol.* (in the press).

[21] Miller, J. F. A. P., *The Biological Basis of Medicine* (edit. by Bettar, E. E.), (Academic Press, London, in the press).

[22] Korneva, E. A., and Khai, L. M., *Fizio. Zh. SSSR Sechenov*, **49**, 42 (1963).

[23] Korneva, E. A., *Fizio. Zh. SSSR Sechenov*, **53**, 42 (1967).

28

STRESS AND ANTIBODY RESPONSE IN RATS

G. F. Solomon

Introduction

Though there are considerable data to link personality factors, stress, and, particularly, failure of psychologic defenses or adaptations to the onset and course of infection [1], cancer [2], the resistance to which may be immunologic in nature [3], and autoimmune diseases [4], which seem to be associated with states of relative immunologic incompetence [5], there are few experimental studies relating stress to infectious processes and fewer correlating stress and immunologic parameters. Demonstration of stress-induced suppression of antibody synthesis has been rare [6, 7], and no studies have correlated primary and secondary immunologic response with different stresses. RAS-MUSSEN and co-workers at the University of California at Los Angeles have pioneered in this work but have been unable to document any influence of various types of stress on antibody production [8]. They report that both avoidance-learning in a shuttle-box and restraint increased susceptibility to herpes simplex virus in mice [9]. Disappearance of vesicular stomatitis from the site of inoculation was enhanced in mice subjected to shuttle-box stress after injection, but no differences were noted in serum neutralizing antibody levels [10]. Stress increased susceptibility to Coxsackie B virus in normally resistant mice [11, 12]. Apprehension-electric shock stress subsequent to inoculation increased mortality from parainfluenza infection in mice [13]. Environmental stress events, adrenal hypertrophy and susceptibility to paralytic poliomyelitis were correlated in hamsters [14]. Stress relationships to infection may be complex. Monkeys subjected to avoidance stress for 24 h prior to inoculation showed *decreased* susceptibility to poliomye-

Reprinted from *Intern. Arch. Allergy Appl. Immunol.* 35, 97–104, 1969.

litis [15]. A single episode of high intensity sound stress prior or subsequent to inoculation decreased resistance of mice to vesicular stomatitis virus; likewise, chronic stress subsequent to inoculation decreased resistance; whereas, sustained stress prior to inoculation increased resistance [16, 17]. Resistance to virus infection is based in part on interferon, a non-specific protein. We found that apprehension-electric shock stress for 5 h prior to intravenous injection of Newcastle disease virus significantly *enhanced* interferon production in mice, while such stress during interferon production did not alter response [18].

This study relates primary and secondary antibody response in inbred rats to four stresses administered prior to and following inoculation with the potent bacterial antigen flagellin.

Methods

Male inbred Fisher rats of 9–12 weeks of age were utilized in all experiments.

Stress. Four stress parameters were utilized. In all cases stress was begun a week prior to immunization and continued throughout the course of immunologic observation in order to maximize the possibility of observing stress effects. (Differential effects of stress prior to and subsequent to immunization will be evaluated later). One stress was low-voltage electric shock delivered to the feet by a grid, with alternate electrification of components to prevent avoidance, for 15 sec preceded for 15 sec by a warning buzzer. Amperage was gradually increased over the course of the experiment to reduce habituation. Apprehension-shock was administered 5 times per hour at randomized intervals with automated programming for 8–10 h per day. The second stress was overcrowding. Animals previously housed 2/cage were housed 5–6/cage. (Little aggression and no physical damage were observed.) The last two stresses were designed to evaluate the effect of rapid eye movement sleep deprivation on immunity [19]. Rats were placed either on small or large platforms (flower pot bases) in a large pan of water. Animals on small platforms are REM deprived because they must maintain muscle tone to remain on the platform, and the muscle relaxation that accompanies REM sleep would result in immersion. The large platform served as a stress control. To assure survival, platform stress was intermittent. Animals remained on the pots 2 days prior and 2 days subsequent to primary and secondary immunization. On the other occasions, 4 days of platform stress preceded each bleeding.

Immunologic techniques. Rats were immunized intraperitoneally with 100 ng (0.01 mg) of flagellin polymer, a potent antigen novel to the rat derived from the flagellae of Salmonella adelaide [20]. (We and others find no pre-immunization antibody to flagellin in the rat.) We had determined this immunizing dose to give consistent responses in Fisher rats. Secondary immunization was with the same dose as the primary, given 28 days later. Animals were bled from the tail 4, 7, 14, and 21 days after primary immunization and 4, 7 and 14 days after booster (unfortunately except for 4 and 21 day intervals in overcrowded animals). Two-fold serial dilutions of serum of 0.25 ml volume were added to 0.25 ml of a fresh suspension of Salmonella adelaide in a concentration of 10^8 organisms/ml. Antibody titer is expressed as that dilution of serum which served to immobilize the swimming bacteria observed microscopically (an exponential function). The serial dilution figure is expressed as the tube in which immobilization took place (arithmetic progression). The first tube contained a 1:5

dilution of serum; the second a 1:10 dilution; third, 1:20, etc. Assay was checked regularly on sera of known titer to assure reliability. Titrations were done 'blind' without awareness of experimental group.

Statistical procedure. Statistical analysis was by a non-parametric method using only the rank order of the titers. All titers are ranked for each day and a Kruskal-Wallis test used to test the significance of the differences among the groups. Then the daily rank of each subject was averaged during primary response (days 4–28) and during secondary response (booster + 4 — booster + 14). These average ranks are then ranked and a Kruskal-Wallis test used again. (This method avoids problems of geometric progression that might give misleadingly great differences at high titers and of distribution with the possibility of non-uniform errors.)

Results

As can be seen in the accompanying table, there was no difference between controls and animals subjected to apprehension-electric shock stress in primary or secondary response. However, a reduced antibody response occurred at each titration interval in animals subjected to overcrowding. Secondary response was virtually eliminated by overcrowding. Both overall primary and secondary responses were comparably very significantly lower (p much <0.001) in overcrowded animals than in controls (or shock-stressed animals). There were no differences in antibody response between animals stressed by remaining on large platforms or small (rapid eye movement sleep deprived), and these two groups were combined for statistical analysis. The platform-stress group, however, showed lower antibody levels in every instance than controls, but only overall primary response was significantly different statistically (p <0.001) from controls, while overall secondary response showed no significant difference.

Peak antibody titer of overcrowded stressed animals was significantly lower than peak titer of controls (p <0.001), but peak titer of animals subjected to apprehension-electric shock was significantly higher than that of controls (p <0.01) as well as of the overcrowded stress group (p <0.001).

Discussion

It is clear that some but not all forms of stress can be immuno-suppressive. Overcrowding stress in rats prior to and subsequent to immunization was particularly effective in reducing primary and secondary response to a potent natural antigen, possibly of relevance to population control in nature. The lack of difference in antibody response in animals stressed by being placed on small platforms (REM deprived) or

Table. Antibody response and stress

Primary response Day	4 total	7 total	14 total	21 total	28 total	Secondary response B+4	B+7	B+14
Controls No. of Animals	16	18	18	17	18	18	17	16
Mean titer	1:60	1:224	1:1664	1:1408	1:1408	1:3328	1:7168	1:1664
Mean dilution number	4.5	6.4	9.3	9.1	9.1	10.6	11.8	9.3
Overcrowding stress No. of animals	–	10	10	–	10	10	10	10
Mean titer	–	1:72	1:416	–	1:176	1:576	1:80	1:68
Mean dilution number	–	4.8	7.3	–	6.1	7.8	5.0	4.7
Shock stress No. of animals	8	8	8	8	8	8	8	8
Mean titer	1:30	1:256	1:1216	1:2560	1:1280	1:9728	1:18.432	1:7168
Mean dilution number	3.5	6.6	8.9	10.0	9.0	11.9	12.8	11.4
Platform stress No. of animals	8	8	8	7	7	8	8	8
Mean titer	1:38	1:128	1:224	1:176	1:576	1:1920	1:6144	1:4352
Mean dilution number	3.9	5.6	6.4	6.1	7.8	9.5	11.2	10.7

larger platforms may be accounted for by the total sleep loss that occurs during the first few days even on larger platforms, and REM compensation may be incomplete in the subsequent 3 days [20]. Apparently, primary response, which was altered by platform stress, is more sensitive to stress influence than is secondary, perhaps reflecting a greater sensitivity of cells responsible for primary response to stress-responsive hormones. Episodic stress, even if frequent for a significant portion of the day, evidently does not activate immunosuppressive mechanisms either as a result of brief transient effects or habituation. In this regard, comparative blood 17-OH corticosteroid levels under different chronic stress situations would be informative, though it is by no means clear that stress-induced immunosuppression is completely adrenally mediated as experiments with adrenalectomized animals should reveal.

McMaster's and Franzl's review of the extensive literature in the area points out that the effects of adrenocortical steroids upon antibody are complex [21]. We observed that many animal studies employed non-physiologic doses of steroids or non-naturally occurring compounds, and there are few studies of prolonged administration. Inhibition of antibody formation of corticoids is dependent upon the dose of the antigen, the nature and dose of the hormone, and the time of administration of the hormone in relation to the injection of the antigen. There is considerable evidence that ACTH and adrenocortical steroids given prior to and accompanying injection of antigen suppress circulating antibody.

The central nervous system might play a role in control of immune response. Electrical stimulation of the lateral hypothalamus alters gamma-globulin levels in rats [22]. Soviet workers claim that a destructive lesion of the dorsal hypothalamus leads to a complete suppression of the production of complement-fixing antibodies and to a prolonged retention of antigen in the blood and that electrical stimulation of the same region enhances antibody production [23, 24].

Whether the stress is artificial or 'naturalistic' as overcrowding may be significant.

Christian and Davis feel that behavioral-endocrine feedback mechanisms play an important role in the regulation of population in many species including rodents [25]. They noted adrenal hypertrophy and sex organ atrophy in overcrowded mice. They speculated that naturally occurring epizootics may be the result of reduced immunity secondary to overcrowding. Morning and afternoon plasma 17-OH corticosteroid levels are significantly higher in monkeys moved from individual to group cages [26]. Wild mice housed in groups show increased susceptibility to trichinosis over singly housed animals [27]. Male mice crowded before or after inoculation with a low dose of tubercle bacilli show less resistance to chronic infection, while female mice under the same conditions show increased resistance [28]. Male and female mice crowded before and housed singly after a large inoculum of bacilli are more resistant to acute tuberculosis than mice housed singly before and crowded after infection. Overcrowding stress and ACTH both were noted to reactivate rabies virus in guinea pigs [29, 30]. Previously isolated mice were placed in groups of 6 for 4 hours a day and were injected with beef serum on the 5th day of stress [6]. Grouped mice developed significantly less precipitating antibody and had heavier adrenals.

Grouped male mice of some strains develop and succumb to amyloidosis, which can be retarded by castration or administration of reserpine or estrogen, the behavioral effect of these manipulations being considered the important influence [31].

In recent work, HILL and co-workers subjected monkeys to various 'psychological' stresses such as noise, light, loss of support after immunization with bovine serum albumin [7]. The stress group, the serum cortisol levels of which were markedly elevated in the initial period of the experiment, showed delayed antibody formation, and the antibodies rose to a lower level than in the control group.

That some stresses can be immunosuppressive in animals seems clear. Mediating mechanisms, immune dynamics and significance for human diseases associated with immunologic deficiency remain to be clarified.

Acknowledgments

SUZANNE DONAHUE and J. KERSTEN KRAFT provided technical assistance. Professor G. J. V. NOSSAL and GORDON ADA, Ph. D. of the Walter and Eliza Hall Institute of Medical Research, Melbourne, Australia, gave valuable advice and encouragement as well as providing the antigen. ALFRED A. AMKRAUT, Ph. D., gave critical comment. HELENA KRAEMER, Ph. D., was statistical consultant. The research was conducted in part with research funds of the Veterans Administration.

Summary

Overcrowding stress but not the stress of apprehension-electric shock administered for a week prior to immunization with a potent bacterial antigen, flagellin, and continued during the course of observation significantly reduced both primary and secondary antibody response in inbred male rats. The stress of remaining on a small platform (with rapid eye-movement sleep deprivation) or medium sized platform (without REM deprivation) over a pan of water significantly reduced primary but not secondary response.

References

1. Friedman, S. B. and Glasgow, L. A.: Psychological factors and resistance to infectious disease. Ped. Clin. N. Amer. *13:* 315 (1966).
2. Leshan, L. L. and Worthington, R. E.: Personality as factor in pathogenesis of cancer; review of literature. Brit. J. Med. Psychol. *29:* 49 (1956).
3. Prehn, R. T.: Role of immune mechanisms in biology of chemically and physically induced tumors; in Hoeber's Conceptual advances in immunology and oncology (Harper & Row, New York 1963).
4. Solomon, G. F. and Moos, R. H.: Emotions, immunity and disease: a speculative theoretical integration. Arch. gen. Psychiat. *11:* 657 (1964).
5. Fudenberg, H. H.: Are autoimmune diseases immunologic deficiency states? Hosp. Prac. *3:* 43 (1968).
6. Vessey, S. H.: Effects of grouping on levels of circulating antibodies in mice. Proc. Soc. exp. Biol., N.Y. *115:* 252 (1964).
7. Hill, C. W.; Greer, W. E. and Felsenfeld, O.: Psychological stress, early response to foreign protein, and blood cortisol in monkeys. Psychosom. Med. *29:* 279 (1967).
8. Personal communication.
9. Rasmussen, A. F., Jr.; Spencer, E. S. and Marsh, J. T.: Increased susceptibility to herpes simplex in mice subjected to avoidance-learning stress or restraint. Proc. Soc. exp. Biol., N.Y. *96:* 183 (1957).
10. Yamada, A.; Jensen, M. M. and Rasmussen, A. F., Jr.: Stress and susceptibility to viral infections. III. Antibody response and viral retention during avoidance-learning stress. Proc. Soc. exp. Biol., N.Y. *116:* 677 (1964).
11. Friedman, S. B.; Ader, R. and Glasgow, L. A.: Effects of psychological stress in adult mice inoculated with Coxsackie B virus. Psychosom. Med. *27:* 361 (1965).
12. Johnson, T.; Lavender, J. F.; Hultin, E. and Rasmussen, A. F., Jr.: The influence of avoidance-learning stress on resistance to Coxsackie B virus in mice. J. Immunol. *91:* 569 (1963).
13. Kawasaki, S. *et al.:* The influence of conditioned emotional stress on parainfluenza infection in mice. Fukuoka Acta Med. *56:* 969 (1965).
14. Teodoru, C. V. and Shwartzman, G.: Endocrine factors in pathogenesis of experimental poliomyelitis in hamsters; role of inoculatory and environmental stress. Proc. Soc. exp. Biol. *91:* 181 (1956).
15. Marsh, J. T.; Lavender, J. F.; Chang, S. and Rasmussen, A. F., Jr.: Poliomyelitis in monkeys; decreased susceptibility after avoidance-stress. Science *140:* 1414 (1963).
16. Jensen, M. M. and Rasmussen, A. F., Jr.: Stress and susceptibility to viral infection. I. Response of adrenals, liver, thymus, spleen, and peripheral leucocyte counts to sound stress. J. Immunol. *90:* 17 (1963).
17. Jensen, M. M. and Rasmussen, A. F., Jr.: Stress and suceptibility to viral infections. II. Sound stress and susceptibility to vesicular stomatitis virus. J. Immunol. *90:* 21 (1963).
18. Solomon, G. F.; Merigan, T. C. and Levine, S.: Variation in adrenal cortical homones with physiologic ranges, stress and interferon production in mice. Proc. Soc. exp. Biol., N Y. *126:* 74 (1967).
19. Morden, B.; Mitchell, G. and Dement, W.: Selective REM sleep deprivation and compensation phenomena in the rat. Brain Res. *5:* 339 (1967).

20. COHEN, H.: Personal communication.
21. McMASTER, P. D. and FRANZL, R. E.: The effects of adrenocortical steroids upon antibody formation. Metabolism *10:* 990 (1961).
22. FESSEL, W. J. and FORSYTH, R. P.: Hypothalamic role in control of gamma-globulin levels (Abstract). Arth. Rheum. *6:* 770 (1963).
23. KORNEVA, E. A. and KHAI, L. M.: Effect of destruction of hypothalamic areas on immunogenesis. Fizio. Zh. SSSR Sechenov. *49:* 42 (1963).
24. KORNEVA, E. A.: The effect of stimulating different mesencephalic structures on protective immune response patterns. Fizio. Zh. SSSR. Sechenov. *53:* 42 (1967).
25. CHRISTIAN, J. J. and DAVIS, D. E.: Endocrines, behavior and population. Science *146:* 1550 (1964).
26. MASON, J. W. and BRADY, J. W.: The sensitivity of psychoendocrine system to social and physical environment; in LEIDERMAN and SHAPIRO Physiological approaches to social behavior (Stanford Univ. Press, Stanford 1964).
27. DAVIS, D. E. and READ, C. P.: Effect of behavior on development of resistance in trichinosis. Proc. Soc. exp. Biol., N.Y. *99:* 269 (1958).
28. TOBACH, E. and BLOCH, H.: Effect of stress by crowding prior to and following tuberculosis infection. Amer. J. Physiol. *187:* 399 (1956).
29. SOAVE, O. A.: Reactivation of rabies virus infection in a guinea pig with ACTH. J. infect. Dis. *110:* 129 (1962).
30. SOAVE, O. A.: Reactivation of rabies virus infection in the guinea pig due to the stress of crowding. Amer. J. vet. Res. *25:* 268 (1964).
31. EBBESEN, P.: Spontaneous amyloidosis in differently grouped and treated DBA/2, BALB/c and CBA mice and thymus fibrosis in estrogen-treated BALB/c males. J. exp. Med. *127:* 387 (1968).

29

EXTEROCEPTIVE STIMULATION AS A CONTINGENT FACTOR IN THE INDUCTION AND ELICITATION OF DELAYED-TYPE HYPERSENSITIVITY REACTIONS TO 1-CHLORO-, 2-4, DINITROBENZENE IN GUINEA PIGS

Peter J. G. Mettrop and Piet Visser

ABSTRACT

This study attempted to determine whether a prior period of "stress" would elicit the sensitization reaction of the skin to topically applied chemical agents. A subthreshold concentration of 1-chloro-, 2-4, dinitrobenzene (DNCB) was applied to the skin of 40 guinea-pigs, 20 of which had been subjected to repetitive electrical shocks throughout the previous 15 minutes. They were examined 24 hours later, and were retested with DNCB at another site after 9 days for signs of delayed sensitization. The stressed animals exhibited a more severe contact-reaction ($p < .01$) after the induction test and also after the delayed test.

DESCRIPTORS: Exteroceptive stimulation, Delayed-type hypersensitivity of skin, 1-chloro-, 2-4, dinitrobenzene, Psychosomatics, Guinea-pig. (P. J. G. Mettrop and P. Visser).

The proposition often is made that conflict-inducing situations can elicit allergic and sensitization reactions. The "delayed hypersensitivity" of the skin of guinea-pigs was chosen as a model for the present investigation, although according to Spector (1967) the term delayed hypersensitivity is not an ideal one, since it refers to an operational element in a complex situation. It should be pointed out that De Weck and Frey (1966), in discussing tolerance for allergens of simple chemical structure, deny the direct influence of the nervous system on induction and elicitation of delayed-type hypersensitivity skin-reactions. Nevertheless the authors refer to an earlier publication (Guy, 1952), which reports that interference with the sleep cycle of animal subjects changed the overt behavior and increased the response of their skin to repeated contacts with sensitizing agents. The outcome of recent research leads to the conclusion that

The authors want to express their thanks to the Dutch Foundation "De Drie Lichten" for financial support, and to Prof. Dr. J. R. Prakken, Prof. Dr. J. T. Barendregt, Prof. Dr. R. L. Zielhuis, and Dr. H. Musaph for their valuable discussion and enthusiastic support during the study. They also want to acknowledge their high appreciation for the technical skill and devotion of Mr. J. Alkema and Mr. J. H. A. Kleyn.

Reprinted by permission from *Psychophysiology* 5 (No. 4), 385–388. Copyright © 1969, The Society for Psychophysiological Research.

we must accept the contingency of connections between hormonal and/or constitutional factors and sensitization (Miller, 1963; White, 1963; Monaonkov, 1965; Coons, 1965; Russell, 1965). We have started from the assumption that stimulation and/or "stress" of experimental animals can lead to a lower threshold for external contacts and influences. In our experiment we followed the line of earlier experiments by Frey and Wenk (1956). These authors point out that a concentration of a "contactant" which under normal conditions is ineffective, will upon later testing produce a sensitization of skin-reactions.

Specifically, we predicted that exteroceptive stimulation of experimental animals in a period directly prior to a first application of 1-chloro-, 2-4, dinitro-benzene (DNCB) (induction dose) would produce a reaction to a test-dose administered after 9 days (delayed-type hypersensitivity) different from the reaction of experimental animals who did not undergo extra exteroceptive stimulation. According to Willoughby, Walters and Spector (1965) the histo-logical appearance of lesions occurring in guinea-pigs in response to DNCB contact showed no obvious difference from that seen in tuberculin reactions.

METHOD

Subjects were 40 white female guinea-pigs of the same breed, weight $\pm$ 500 gms. These were randomly divided into 2 groups of 20, one of which was used as a control group.

The right side of the body of all animals was shaven. The experimental group was then submitted to the electrical stimulation. Shocks were given via bars in the bottom of circular containers having a diameter of 50 cm. Stimulus strength was 110 V, 1 mA in the mean, given by a voltage-stimulator. The duration of each shock was 0.2 sec, frequency 2.5 per sec, with a total stimulation period of 15 minutes. Directly afterwards 0.09 % DNCB (111 μ μ M DNCB/2 cm²) was applied. The control group underwent the same treatment, but without prior stimulation.

Afterwards the animals were placed in cages in pairs, because "solitary confinement" may have a stressful effect upon the guinea-pig (Conger, Sawrey, & Turrell, 1958).

The reactions were read after 24 hours.

After a period of 9 days, the left side of the body was shaven, and two test doses, one of 0.09 % DNCB (111 μ μ M DNCB/2 cm²) and one of 0.06 % DNCB (74 μ μ M DNCB/2 cm²) were applied.

The reaction was again read after 24 hours. Photographs were taken with several techniques (infra-red; positive/negative black and white; positive- and dia-colourfilm; highspeed Ektachrome and AGEP-black and white film, magn. ½), in an attempt to obtain sufficiently clear pictures of the reactions to enable further study and quantification of the reactions.

RESULTS AND DISCUSSION

Since the photographs proved inadaquate for scoring, all judgments were made à vue. Every guinea-pig was given a score of 0, 1, or 2, depending on whether neither, one, or both observers ascertained a "contact-reaction." The

TABLE 1

Reactions of control animals (N = 20) and experimental animals (N = 20) to induction dose and elicitation (test) dose as recorded by two observers

Subjects	After the Induction Dose (0.09% DNCB)		After the Elicitation Dose				Score*
	Observer No. 1	Observer No. 2	Obs. No. 1		Obs. No. 2		
			0.09	0.06	0.09	0.06	
Control Group:							
1	0**	0	0	0	0	0	0
2	+***	+	+	0	0	0	1
3	0	0	0	0	0	0	0
4	+	+	0	0	0	0	0
5	0	0	+	0	+	0	2
6	0	0	0	0	0	0	0
7	0	0	+	0	0	+	2
8	0	+	0	0	0	0	0
9	0	0	0	0	0	0	0
10	0	0	+	0	+	0	2
11	+	0	0	0	0	0	0
12	0	0	+	0	0	0	1
13	0	0	0	0	0	0	0
14	0	+	0	0	0	0	0
15	0	0	+	+	+	0	2
16	+	+	0	0	0	0	0
17	0	0	+	+	+	+	2
18	0	0	+	0	+	0	2
19	0	0	0	0	0	0	0
20	0	0	+	0	+	0	2
Experimental Group:							
1	0	0	+	0	+	0	2
2	0	+	+	+	+	+	2
3	+	+	0	0	0	0	0
4	+	+	+	+	+	+	2
5	+	+	+	+	+	+	2
6	+	+	+	+	+	+	2
7	0	+	+	+	+	+	2
8	+	+	+	+	+	+	2
9	+	+	0	0	+	0	1
10	+	+	+	0	0	+	2
11	+	+	dead	—	—	—	—
12	+	+	+	+	+	+	2
13	+	+	+	+	+	+	2
14	+	+	+	+	+	+	2
15	0	0	+	+	+	+	2
16	+	+	+	+	0	+	2
17	0	0	+	0	+	0	2
18	+	+	0	0	0	0	0
19	0	0	+	0	+	0	2
20	+	+	+	0	+	0	2

* Every guinea pig was given a score of 0, 1, or 2, depending upon whether neither, one or both the observers reported reaction.

** 0 = no reaction.

*** + = reaction.

Stress and Antibody Response

observers consisted of the first author (obs. 1) and a person not connected with the experiment (obs. 2). Results are shown in Table 1.

It is seen that prior exposure to exteroceptive stimulation aggravates the response to an immediate sensitizing dose and also to a test dose applied 9 days later. These differences were significant at the 0.01 level, using the Wilcoxon test.

The observations à vue show a definite influence of exteroceptive stimulation on the emergence of the chosen form of contact-reaction when the applied concentration of DNCB is below the sensitization threshold. The results support the hypothesis, regarding the contingent sensitizing influences from the environment.

For the time being without histological data, we only have used the operational term sensitization. The contingent influences on both toxicity (first-contact response; hypersusceptibility) and on allergy (repeated-contact response; delayed-hypersensitivity) are sofar not specified.

REFERENCES

Applezweig, M. H. Neuroendocrine aspects of stress. In B. E. Flaherty (Ed.), *Psychophysiological aspects of space flight*. New York: Columbia University Press, 1961. Pp. 139–157.

Conger, J. J., Sawrey, W. L., & Turrell, E. S. The role of social experience in the production of gastric ulcers in hooded rats placed in a conflict situation. *Journal of Abnormal & Social Psychology*, 1958, *57*, 214–220.

Coons, A. H. Discussion: Remarks on cortisone and antibody formation. In J. Sterzl (Ed.), *Symposium on molecular and cellular basis of antibody formation*. Praha, Czechoslovakia: Publishing House CS. Academic Sciences, 1965. Pp. 417–611.

De Weck, A. L., & Frey, J. R. *Immunotolerance to simple chemicals*. Basel, Switzerland: S. Karger, 1966. P. 41.

Frey, J. R., & Wenk, P. Experimentelle Untersuchungen zur Pathogenese des Kontaktekzems. (Experimental researches into the pathogenesis of contact dermatitis.) *Dermatologica*, 1956, *112*, 265.

Guy, W. B. Neurogenic factors in contact dermatitis. *Archives of Dermatology and Syphilology*, 1952, *66*, 1–8.

Mikhail, A. A., & Holland, B. X. A simplified method of inducing ulcers. *Journal of Psychosomatic Research*, 1966, *9*, 343–347.

Miller, J. F. A. P. Origins of immunological competence. *British Medical Bulletin*, 1963, *19*, 214–218.

Monaonkov, A. M. Discussion paper on individuality: Factors in cytomorphologic properties of antibody formation. In J. Sterzl (Ed.), *Symposium on molecular and cellular basis of antibody formation*. Praha, Czechoslovakia: Publishing House CS. Academic Sciences, 1965. Pp. 606–608, 611.

Russell, J. A. The adrenals. In Ruch & H. D. Patton (Eds.), *Physiology and biophysics*. (19th ed.) New York: W. B. Saunders, 1965. Pp. 1134–1136.

Spector, W. G. Histology of allergic inflammation. *British Medical Bulletin*, 1967, *23*, 35–38.

White, R. G. Factors affecting the antibody response. *British Medical Bulletin*, 1963, *19*, 207–213.

Willoughby, D. A., Walters, M. N. I., & Spector, W. G. Lymph node permeability factor in the Dinitrochlorobenzene skin hypersensitivity reaction in guinea pigs. *Immunology*, 1965, *8*, 78–84.

EFFECTS OF THE SPACE FLIGHT ENVIRONMENT ON MAN'S IMMUNE SYSTEM.
II. LYMPHOCYTE COUNTS AND REACTIVITY

Craig L. Fischer, Jerry C. Daniels, William C. Levin, Stephen L. Kimzey, Elaine K. Cobb, and Stephen E. Ritzmann

FISCHER, C. L., J. C. DANIELS, W. C. LEVIN, S. L. KIMZEY, E. K. COBB and S. E. RITZMANN. *Effects of the space flight environment on man's immune system: II. Lymphocyte counts and reactivity.* Aerospace Med. 43(10):1122-1125, 1972.

The present studies were undertaken to assess the effects of the environment of space flights on the cellular division of the human immune system. Peripheral blood absolute lymphocyte counts were determined at various preflight and postflight intervals for the 21 crewmen of Apollo Missions 7-13.

Mean lymphocyte numbers tended to exhibit a delayed significant but fluctuating increase shortly after recovery, although a variety of responses was seen in individual astronauts. The in vitro reactivity of lymphocytes, reflected by RNA and DNA synthesis rates by unstimulated and PHA-stimulated lymphocytes tissue-cultured preflight and postflight from the same participants, was found to remain within previously established normal ranges. These results indicate that functional integrity of cellular immune potential as reflected by in vitro techniques is maintained during this spaceflight experience.

K NOWLEDGE OF THE EFFECTS of the environment of space flights on man's immunological functions is essential for the determination of human capacity to attain a normal immune response within the framework of present and future space explorations. In a preceding report[7] we have described the effects of space flight upon the serum immunoglobulins G, A, M, the C-3 complement component, the transport proteins transferrin, ceruloplasmin and haptoglobin and the antiproteases α_1-antitrypsin, and α_2M-globulin, as well as α_1-glycoprotein. Here we describe the effects of the environment of space flights on the numerical aspects of lymphocytes and their antigenic response patterns as a measure of their functional capacity.

The cellular aspects of immunity reside primarily in circulating small lymphocytes (thymus-dependent T-cells). Cellular immune functions are responsible for viral, tuberculous and fungal immunity and probably represent a surveillance system against the proliferation of "nonself" antigenic compositions, whether of exogenous or endogenous origin, thereby possessing an intimate relationship to susceptibility to autoimmune disorders and to neoplasia. Techniques for the *in vitro* assessing of cellular immunity evaluate the ability of small lymphocytes to undergo morphologic changes in response to antigenic stimulation. These morphological alterations are accompanied by characteristic patterns of biochemical changes which provide a useful measure of cellular immunocompetence. The present studies represent the application of such methods to lymphocytes obtained from Apollo astronauts in an attempt to evaluate the effects of the environment of space flights on cellular immunity.

MATERIALS AND METHODS

Individuals Studied—The 21 Apollo crewman participating in Apollo Missions 7 through 13 were compared in respect to the parameters measured with 19 normal individuals who served as a control population.

Lymphocyte Counts—Peripheral blood lymphocyte counts were obtained by standard hemocytometric techniques and expressed as lymphocytes/mm³.

Antigenic Responsiveness—Lymphocytes from astronauts and control subjects were analyzed for *in vitro* antigenic responsiveness by quantitating the rates of synthesis of RNA and DNA both in the presence and absence of the mitogen phytohemagglutinin (PHA). The details of this technique have been previously described.[1] Essentially, lymphocytes separated from heparinized venous blood by a nylon reticulum column were cultured, with or without PHA, in appropriate me-

J. C. Daniels is a J. W. McLaughlin Clinical Fellow.

Supported by NAS Contracts 9-6811, 9-8122, 9-8258, 9-11088 and 9-11161.

Reprinted from *Aerospace Med.* **43**, 1122–1125, 1972.

dia. At the times of maximal RNA and DNA synthesis, 24 and 72 hours respectively, cultures were pulsed for one hour with either H³-uridine or H³-thymidine. The radioactivity incorporated into washed lymphocytes was measured by liquid scintillation spectrometry. Lymphocyte viability at the time of harvest was assessed by supravital fluorescent staining, and the results calculated as H³ disintegrations per minute (DPM) per million viable cells by correcting for quench and counting efficiency. This technique, with appropriate modifications for maintaining cellular functional capacity, has been demonstrated to yield valid data in the face of the various modes of transport over considerable distances necessary for collecting lymphocyte samples.[2] All cultures contained >90% viable lymphocytes.

RESULTS

Lymphocyte Counts—Absolute lymphocyte counts were determined for each of the 21 astronauts at 30 days preflight (designated F-30), 15 days preflight (F-15), 5 days preflight (F-5), as soon as possible after recovery (designated A.S.A.P.), and various days after recovery (R + 1, R + 6, R + 16). Figure 1 illustrates a scattergram of individual lymphocyte counts, and the mean absolute lymphocyte counts computed for the 21 Apollo crewmen at these sampling times. A different fluctuating increase in lymphocyte numbers occurs very soon after recovery, in the individual astronauts, although the mean counts at recovery (A.S.A.P.) for the astronauts as a group do not differ significantly from preflight levels, but the degree of delayed postflight lymphocytosis at R + 1 (mean: 3124 ± 1200/mm³) was significantly higher than preflight counts (mean: 2677 ± 649/mm³) at a p level of <0.01. Figure 1 summarizes these data.

The lymphocyte counts of individual astronauts, however, fluctuated rather widely. In 15 individuals there was an increase of lymphocytes above the normal mean (i.e., >2400/mm³) postflight, but only in 2 astronauts an increase of lymphocytes above the normal upper limits (i.e., >4000/mm³) were observed; in 3 individuals

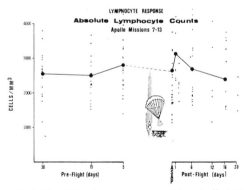

Fig. 1. Absolute lymphocyte counts per mm³ from Apollo 7-13 astronauts (mean levels: solid line) determined at preflight and postflight intervals (A.S.A.P. = point of determination as soon as possible after recovery).

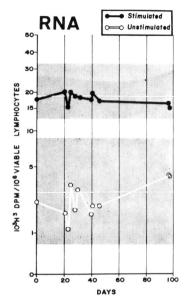

Fig. 2. Serial determinations of RNA synthesis (as H³ DPM/ 10⁶ viable lymphocytes) by normal lymphocytes, unstimulated (lower) and PHA-stimulated (upper). Shaded regions denote 90th percentile normal values for our laboratory (n = 19). (Reproduced from Aerospace Med. 41:1298, 1970).

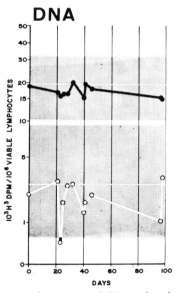

Fig. 3. Serial determinations of DNA synthesis by normal lymphocytes. Conventions are the same as for Figure 2. (Reproduced from Aerospace Med. 41:1298, 1970).

there was a postflight decrease in lymphocyte counts (between 1100–1400/mg%) and in the remainder of the group there was no significant postflight change in lymphocyte numbers.

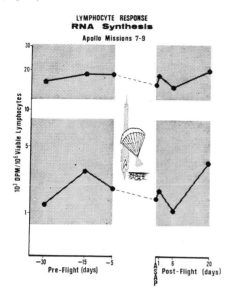

Fig. 4. Preflight and postflight RNA synthesis by lymphocytes from Apollo astronauts, as DPM/10⁶ viable lymphocytes.

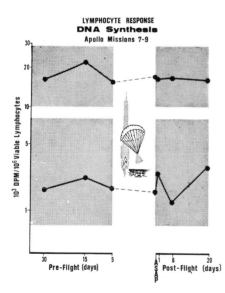

Fig. 5. Preflight and postflight DNA synthesis by lymphocytes from Apollo astronauts, as DPM/10⁶ viable lymphocytes.

Nucleic Acid Synthesis—Normal *in vitro* lymphocyte synthesis of nucleic acids, in both the basal unstimulated state and in response to the stimulating agent phytohemagglutinin (PHA), tends to remain well confined within relatively narrow ranges of variability, irrespective of the lymphocyte counts in the individual astronauts. Figure 2 illustrates serial determinations of RNA synthesis, by both stimulated and unstimulated lymphocytes from 19 normal control individuals. The shaded areas demarcate the 90th percentile normal ranges for our laboratory. Figure 3 illustrates, in the same manner, these data for DNA synthesis by normal lymphocytes. Figures 4 and 5 indicate, again with shaded areas representing the normal ranges, the RNA and DNA synthesis rates for lymphocytes cultured preflight and postflight from the 21 Apollo astronauts. These synthesis rates are seen to remain well within the normal 90th percentile ranges.

DISCUSSION

Based on phylogenetic and ontogenetic evidence, two related divisions of the immune system have been recognized: the cellular system and the humoral system. The thymus-associated cellular system, mediated primarily by the small lymphocyte (T-cells), protects against diseases such as tuberculosis, fungal and certain viral infections. It confers transplantation immunity and delayed skin hypersensitivity, and may represent a sur-

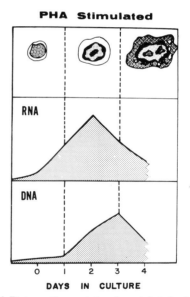

Fig. 6. Diagrammatic presentation of morphological and functional response patterns of normal blood lymphocytes cultured with PHA. (Reproduced with permission from: Ritzmann, S. E. and Daniels, J. C.—Chapter 7A—In Textbook of Laboratory Medicine, G. J. Race, M.D., (Ed.) Publisher. Hoeber Medical Division of Harper and Rowe, New York, New York; In Press, 1972).

veillance system against autoimmunity, neoplastic transformation and oncogenesis.[3,4] Integrity of cellular immunity is central to the stated medical objectives[5,6] of the Apollo program: a search for possible aberrations imposed by the space flight environment, the provision of baseline data for future manned space flight and the development of predictive techniques for such entities as inflammation and radiation effects.

While well-developed *in vitro* assay techniques have permitted quantitative evaluation of the serum immunoglobulins, complement factors and other proteins during space flight,[7] the methodology pertinent to cellular immunity is more subject to biological and technical variations. However, at least two meaningful parameters have been measured at various preflight and postflight intervals in the crew members of Apollo Missions 7-13.

The first parameter examined was peripheral blood *absolute lymphocyte counts.* While individual astronauts exhibited variability of lymphocyte patterns preflight and postflight, the majority exhibited a significant but fluctuating increase in lymphocyte numbers shortly after, but not coincident with, recovery. The mean lymphocyte count for all 21 Apollo astronauts, however, reflects a value which remains within the normal range. Based on a normal human peripheral blood lymphocyte mean count of 2400/mm³ and a range[8,9] of approximately 1500-4000/mm³ 15 of the 21 astronauts exhibited early postflight increases above the normal mean, and 2 of the 21 above the upper limit of the normal range, whereas 3 astronauts experienced lymphocyte counts below the normal range.

The significance of this lymphocyte pattern is unknown. Several factors must be considered in the context of the normal environment during space flights. These include demargination and mobilization of lymphocytes from sequestered pools, adrenal corticosteroid influences, possible effects of radiation, impaired recirculation pathways, etc. Clearly, further studies are needed to clarify the observed responses.

The second parameter studied was the ability of small lymphocytes to respond to antigenic stimulation by the kidney bean extract phytohemagglutinin (PHA) with increased synthesis of RNA and DNA. This phenomenon, associated with characteristic morphologic changes, is generally accepted as an *in vitro* indicator of *in vivo* immunocompetence of T-cells. Normal values for such synthesis rates have been established in previous studies.[1,2]

A diagrammatic presentation of these events is pictured in Figure 6, reflecting the blastoid transformation of small blood lymphocytes cultured with PHA during a 3-day period. These morphologic alterations are paralleled by functional changes, such as increased RNA and increased DNA synthesis rates. The rates of spontaneous unstimulated and PHA-stimulated synthesis of both RNA and DNA by lymphocytes cultured preflight

and postflight from the 21 Apollo astronauts remained within the 90th percentile normal ranges for these categories. The most meaningful mode of data presentation for such determinations, which are based on liquid scintillation counting of radiolabeled nucleotide precursor incorporation, is absolute radioactivity per million viable lymphocytes.[10,11]

Thus, while lymphocyte numbers fluctuate significantly shortly after return from space flight, tending to exhibit a delayed increase, the immunocompetence of these cells, as judged by *in vitro* stimulation techniques, remains stable throughout the preflight and postflight observation periods. This finding is of significance in engendering confidence that the human immune system, particularly such vulnerable components as circulating antigen-sensitive small lymphocutes, can maintain functional integrity in the environments of space flights of the duration of the Apollo flights (10-12 days). The influence of longer duration space flights (such as Skylab) awaits further investigation.

REFERENCES

1. DANIELS, J. C., H. SAKAI, E. K. COBB, A. R. REMMERS, JR., H. E. SARLES, J. C. FISH, W. C. LEVIN, and S. E. RITZMANN: Altered nucleic acid synthesis patterns in lymphocytes from patients with chronic uremia. *Amer. J. Med. Sci.* 259:214-227, 1970.
2. DANIELS, J. C., E. K. COBB, C. FISCHER, W. C. LEVIN and S. E. RITZMANN: Lymphocyte cultures under varied logistical conditions: stability of nucleic acid synthesis. *Aerospace Med.* 41:1298-1301, 1970.
3. RITZMANN, S. E., and J. C. DANIELS: Current concepts of immunology: summation. *In* Laboratory Medicine, G. J. Race (Ed.), Hoeber Medical Division of Harper & Row, New York. In press.
4. DANIELS, J. C., S. E. RITZMANN and W. C. LEVIN: Lymphocytes: morphological, developmental and functional characteristics in health, diseases and experimental study—an analytical review. *Tex. Rep. Biol. Med.* 26:5-92, 1968.
5. BERRY, C. A.: Preliminary clinical report of the medical aspects of Apollos VII and VIII. *Aerospace Med.* 40:245-254, 1969.
6. BERRY, C. A.: Summary of medical experience in the Apollo 7 through 11 manned spaceflights, *Aerospace Med.* 41:500-519, 1970.
7. FISCHER, C. L., C. GILL, J. C. DANIELS, E. K. COBB, C. A. BERRY and S. E. RITZMANN: Effects of the space flight environment on Man's immune system: I. Serum proteins and immunoglobulins. *Aerospace Med.* 43:856, 1972.
8. WINTROBE, M. M.: *Clinical Hematology.* Lea & Febiger, Philadelphia, 1961, 5th Edition, p. 249.
9. ORFANAKIS, B. A., R. E. OSTLUND, C. R. BISHOP and J. W. ATHENS: Normal blood leukocyte concentration values *Amer. J. Clin. Path.* 53:647-651, 1970.
10. DANIELS, J. C., H. SAKAI, E. K. COBB, A. R. REMMERS, JR., H. E. SARLES, J. C. FISH, W. C. LEVIN and S. E. RITZMANN: Interpretation of nucleic acid synthesis studies of renal-failure lymphocytes. *J. of Renticuloendothelial Society* 8:240-247, 1970.
11. DANIELS, J. C., H. SAKAI, A. R. REMMERS, JR., H. E. SARLES, J. C. FISH, E. K. COBB, W. C. LEVIN and S. E. RITZMANN: In vitro reactivity of human lymphocytes in chronic vraemia: Analysis and interpretation. *Clin. Exper. Immunol.* 8:213, 1971.

Behavior and Immune Function

31

IMMUNOSUPPRESSIVE EFFECTS OF PREDATOR INDUCED STRESS IN MICE WITH ACQUIRED IMMUNITY TO *HYMENOLEPIS NANA**

D. R. Hamilton

Abstract—Mice were given an immunizing infection with the eggs of the cestode *Hymenolepis nana*. Subsequently, they were exposed to either a cat or an empty stress chamber for 10 min of each hour for 1, 2, 4 or 8 periods per day. A challenge egg infection was administered 96 hr before euthanasia on the 17th day. Increasing frequency of exposure to the cat produced proportional increases in adrenal weights, decreases in seminal vesicle and spleen weights and retarded normal body weight gain in mice. Plasma corticosterone levels were proportionally higher at all exposure levels in cat-stressed mice than in mice exposed to an empty chamber. Reinfection rates indicated that the well-established acquired immunity of cat-stressed animals was significantly depressed in proportion to the frequency of exposure. Animals exposed to an empty chamber maintained uniform immunity.

THE DEGREE to which emotional stress modifies the pathological and etiological manifestations of disease is currently receiving long overdue attention. The genesis of recent studies [1] implicates altered immunological competence as fundamental to the pathogenesis of allergy, infectious disease, autoimmune disease and cancer. However, there is a distinct paucity of studies relating emotional stress to the immunological parameters of parasitism.

Noble [2] reported that fighting among ground squirrels stimulated increased numbers of cecal trichomonads. Grouped wild mice developed more severe clinical symptoms of trichiniasis than individually housed controls [3]. Weinmann and Rothman [4] demonstrated that when intense fighting occurred among male mice during the immune induction period, resistance to *Hymenolepis nana* was depressed.

A problem common to previous studies has been the use of stressors involving either physical trauma or situations unnatural to the animal. The use of purely symbolic threats of a predator was suggested by the observations of earlier workers who noted the "unusual" behavior displayed by rodents exposed to a cat. Small [5] described this behavior, which was subsequently termed "freezing" by Curti [6]. Näätänen and Jänäklä [7] reported increases in adrenal weights when rats were exposed to a cat, but the rats were reported to have fought with each other. Henry *et al.* [8] used cats to produce prolonged systolic hypertension in mice.

The present study utilizes a unique helminth life cycle to demonstrate the effect of threatening exposure to a natural predator on a well established host–parasite relationship. The life cycle of *Hymenolepis nana* is novel in that it may or may not exhibit a parenteral phase as well as a lumen phase in mice. Herin [9] demonstrated that an infection induced by ova produced a tissue stage and host resistance to reinfection

* Florida Agricultural Experiment Station Journal Series No. 5226.

was acquired, whereas infections caused by cysticercoids resulted in a lumen stage only and resistance to reinfection was not conferred. It has been shown by Hearin [9] and confirmed by Heyneman [10] that an extremely rapid and lifelong immunity occurs with the initial egg infection. This immunity was discernible as quickly as 9 hr after infection, marked a 12 hr, and apparently absolute after 24 hr. A challenge egg infection given after this time was usually completely blocked.

Immunosuppression in the present study was defined as the ability of immune mice to accept a challenge ova infection. Adrenal response was evaluated by plasma corticosterone determination, body weight changes, and organ tissue and weight changes.

METHODS

Three hundred male weanling littermates from a worm-free FDP/SW colony were ultimately formed into 60 groups of 5 animals each. Groups in which fighting was observed were replaced with compatible groups. Ova from the cestode *Hymenolepis nana* were recovered from infected mouse feces using a modification of the Stoll hookworm egg dilution method. An immunizing infection of 1000 ova was administered *per os* to each animal on the day it began its experimental schedule at 60–70 days old and 29–31 g in weight.

The experimental schedule, adopted from Bronson and Eleftheriou [11] consisted of exposing 30 groups of mice to a cat in a specially designed stress chamber (stressed mice). An additional 30 groups of mice were designated "handled mice" and received identical treatment except that their chamber never contained a cat. Exposures to these two situations occurred at the rate of 0, 1, 2, 4 or 8 times per day for 17 consecutive days. Since 2 treatments, 0 exposure to a cat and 0 exposure to an empty chamber, were identical, the 60 animals involved constituted control animals. Each exposure lasted 10 min. When more than one exposure per day was scheduled, the mice were returned to the colony and left undisturbed for 45 min between exposures. The daily schedule was begun before 8:00 a.m. and both stressed groups and their handled counterparts always received their exposures at the same time.

The stress chamber consisted of a modified fiberglass fume hood mounted over a compartmentalized box with a layer of wire mesh separating the upper cat chamber from the three lower mouse chambers. Openings in the wire mesh measured 1.0×1.25 in, which permitted the cat to reach for the mice with most of the foreleg. The distance from the floor of the mouse chamber to the wire mesh was adjusted to prevent actual contact.

A challenge infection of 1000 ova was administered to all mice 96 hr before euthanasia on the 17th day of their stress schedule. Mice were weighed and began their final day at an hour chosen to permit the full schedule of exposures. Euthanasia always took place between 8:00 and 11:00 a.m. to avoid the influence of diurnal variation in adrenocortical response noted by other workers [12]. After the final exposure, mice were returned to the animal colony for 30 min before being killed by decapitation.

Animals were removed from their home cage, decapitated, and exsanguinated in less than 20 sec. Arteriovenous trunk blood was collected directly into heparinized vacutainers and pooled for the group. After being centrifuged, the plasma was pipetted into shell vials and frozen immediately.

Paired adrenal glands were removed, trimmed and blotted in a consistent manner, and weighed on a Mettler balance. The spleen, paired testes, and seminal vesicles were removed and weighed in a similar fashion. The entire small intestine, from the pylorus to the cecum was removed, split open, and the presence of adult worms verified. Cysticeroid examination was made by the method of Hunninen [13]. The stomach and duodenum were examined for ulceration and hemorrhage.

Peripheral plasma levels of corticosterone, the predominant adrenocortical steroid in the mouse, [14] were determined using the method of Mattingly, [15] as modified by St. Bartholomew's Hospital, London, and Vanderbilt University Hospital, Nashville, Tennessee.

The method relies upon the principle that unconjugated plasma corticosteroids may be extracted in dichloromethane and an aliquot of the subsequent extract will fluoresce when mixed with ethanolic-sulfuric acid. The threshold sensitivity of this method is between 2 and 4 μg when the plasma sample gives a reading which is at least double the reagent blank. The mean difference between duplicates of 36 plasma samples ranging from 3 to 64 μg was 0.44 ± 0.12 (SE) μg%. On the day of assay, instrument standards of 5, 15 and 25 μg% in water were made up in triplicate from a stock solution previously validated by its ultraviolet absorption spectra and assayed along with the experimental plasma and triplicate water blanks. The fluorescence was allowed to develop for 30 min before reading and the samples were read on an Aminco–Bowman spectrophotofluorometer equipped with a xenon

Behavior and Immune Function

lamp and a blank subtracting photomultiplier microphotometer. The excitation wavelength was 475 μm and the emission wavelength was 520 μm.

Experimental results were evaluated with a type III analysis of variance using Tukey's A procedure to convert F-values to probabilities.

RESULTS

Mice placed in the stress chamber with a cat assumed typical freezing postures. Their normal exploratory patterns were completely interrupted, and they usually remained crouched in the same place at which they were deposited on the chamber floor. They exhibited a high startle response although no vocalization was noted. Defecation and urination were inhibited completely during these periods, but were subsequently restored as mice lost their freezing behaviors.

This behavior eventually vanished in stressed mice receiving exposures at the rate of eight per day but remained throughout the experiment in the mice exposed at the rate of one and two exposures per day. Mice which had lost their freezing response tended to remain huddled in the chamber corners. Handled mice never exhibited freezing or huddling, and their normal exploratory patterns remained uninhibited.

The experimental procedure resulted in definite alternation of weight gain (Fig. 1). The average weight gain during the 17-day period of control mice was 3 g, handled mice 2·5 g and stressed mice gained only 0·75 g. The weight gains of stressed mice declined with the increasing frequency of ex-

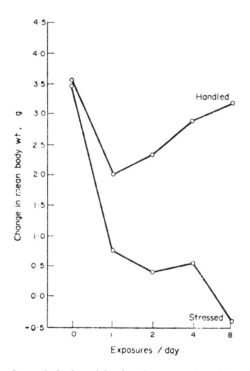

FIG. 1.—Average change in body weights in mice exposed to either a cat or an empty stress chamber for 17 days. Each point represents a group of 30 mice.

posures until the average weight change was a negative value at the 8 exposure per day level. A t-test showed significant differences ($p = 0·001$) between handled and stressed groups at all exposure levels.

The mean paired adrenal weights of stressed mice were significantly ($p = 0·001$) greater than those of handled mice at the 2, 4 and 8 exposure per day level (Fig. 2). As the daily frequency of exposures to a cat or an empty chamber increased, adrenal weights also increased. Histological examination verified cortical hypertrophy.

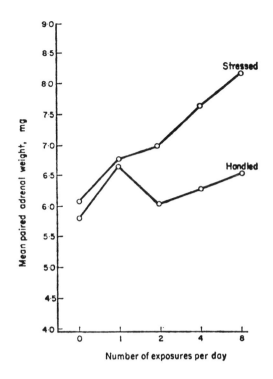

Fig. 2.—Mean paired adrenal gland weights of mice exposed to either a cat or an empty stress chamber for 17 days. Each point represents a group of 30 mice.

Similar but inconsistently significant weight changes were noted in other organs, particularly in stressed mice receiving 8 exposures per day. The mean seminal vesicle and mean paired testis weights of these animals decreased from control weights of 310 and 222·4 mg, respectively, to 258 and 213·5 mg, respectively. Involution of lymphoid tissue was apparent since mean spleen weights declined from control values of 190·7–144·9 mg in these mice. Marked atrophy of the corpuscular germinal centers was noted.

A 30-min interval between the last stress period and euthanasia was verified to be that period when corticosterone levels were the most elevated above baseline values. Figure 3 shows the difference in mean plasma corticosterone levels between stressed and handled mice. An analysis of these differences using the T ratio demonstrated significance ($p = <0·001$) at all exposure levels beyond the zero exposure per day controls. Both stressed and handled mice exhibited the highest corticosterone levels when exposed at the rate of once per day, and declining values for two and four exposures per day. At the eight exposure per day level, a sizeable divergence occurred between the two groups. Stressed animals exhibited a plasma corticosterone peak of 9·54 µg% compared to 3·42 µg% for handled animals which represents a value lower than controls.

Stressed animals at all exposure levels were much more frequently reinfected than handled animals, with the highest reinfection rate occurring at the eight per day level (Fig. 4). The highest reinfection rate among control mice was 10·7 per cent, among handled mice 30 per cent, and 76 per cent among stressed mice. Furthermore, handled mice exhibited a rather uniform reinfection rate (30 per cent) at all exposure levels, but stressed mice responded to increasing frequency of exposure with a stepwise increase in reinfection rate. No gastric hemorrhages were noted. Both handled and stressed mice at all exposure levels were entirely free of intestinal ulceration.

Analysis of variance confirmed that the indices of stress (measures) differed significantly ($p = <0·001$) between the handled group and the stressed group in a duration by group comparison.

Behavior and Immune Function

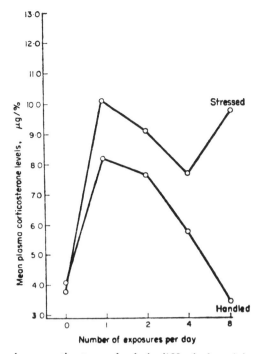

FIG. 3.—Mean plasma corticosterone levels (μg/100 ml plasma) in mice exposed to either a cat or an empty stress chamber for 17 days. Each point represents a group of 30 mice.

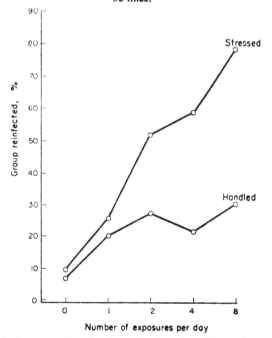

FIG. 4.—Re-infection rates in mice immunized against *Hymenolepis nana* following exposure to either a cat or an empty stress chamber. Each point represents a group of 30 mice.

DISCUSSION AND CONCLUSIONS

The absence of gastrointestinal ulceration in mice in this study is not surprising. Douglas and Lavern [16] showed that below a given level of stress in the guinea pig, ulceration was rare. Rosenberg [17] reported that rats required 12 hr of combined electroshock and cold stress before ulceration appeared. Brady's [18] classical report on ulcers in "executive" monkeys indicated that the development of stress ulcers required a critical sequence of stress and rest periods.

Although all mice began the experiment as young robust males, matched in age and weight, both handling and stressing produced definite alterations of weight gain. Decreasing body weight gains in proportion to increasing frequency of episodic stress has been noted by other workers [11]. Although mild weight losses were noted in handled animals, both control mice and animals handled eight times per day showed a 10 per cent body weight gain during the 17 day period.

Consistent hypertrophy of the adrenal cortex approximated the stress response described by other workers [19], Weinmann and Rothman [4] reported that the average paired adrenal weights increased from 5·6 to 7·5 mg following stress by repeated exposure to new group associations. Comparable results were noted in the present study since average adrenal weights increased from 6·0 to 8·0 mg in the most frequently stressed groups.

The corticosterone levels appeared to indicate that maximal stress occurred at the one exposure per day level in both stressed and handled groups. Animals receiving only one exposure per day did not habituate to either procedure and it is probable that each exposure remained a novel experience. The general decline between one and four exposures per day may indicate resistance to the stress in both groups of animals. Beyond the four exposure per day level, the corticosterone curve for handled animals rapidly descended to a value lower than baseline control levels. This is interpreted as complete adaptation. Stressed animals, however, developed another corticosterone peak which approached maximal values. This terminal peak at the eight exposure per day level may indicate imminent exhaustion on the adrenocortical system. Mean plasma corticosterone levels were in general, somewhat lower in the present study than in previous reports. Loach and Higgenbotham [20] reported control values of $9·3 \mu g/100$ ml plasma in controls and $11·9 \mu g/100$ ml plasma in dominant and subordinate members respectively, of mouse groups. Differences in methods of assay might easily explain such disparity.

Re-infection rates among 60 control mice averaged 7–10 per cent which compares with Heyneman's [10] report of 8 per cent re-infection when mice were challenged 48 hr after immunization. Both exposure to a cat and handling during the immune induction period resulted in a significant degree of immunosuppression. The reinfection rate among predator exposed animals increased from 10 to 76 per cent in proportion to increasing frequency of exposure. Mere handling of mice eight times per day was immunosuppressive since the reinfection rate increased 3-fold. Weinmann [4] produced an average reinfection rate of 12 per cent after 7–19 days of intense fighting among male mice. Only the dominant mouse showed development of acquired immunity comparable to that occurring in nonstressed controls. Subordinate mice ranking lowest in the fighting group were significantly more susceptible to challenge infection than were any of the non-immune controls. The same workers reported severe debilitation due to wounding consequent to the fighting.

Predator-induced stress is a particularly valuable model for use in psychosocial stress studies. The purely symbolic threats of a predator as perceived by the mouse, elicits a very characteristic manifestation of fear. Besides producing both the alarm and the chronic response, episodic exposure must closely approximate field conditions for the majority of rodents. Observed physiologic responses are due entirely to emotional trauma rather than somatic insult, physical activity, or food deprivation. Predator avoidance may also be implicated in the behavioral–endocrine feedback system postulated by Christian and Davis [21] as fundamental to the regulation of mammalian population growth. These workers suggested that increased population density stimulated pituitary–adrenocortical activity and inhibition of reproductive function. Increased mortality would be the sequent as a result of lowered resistance to disease, parasitism, and adverse environmental conditions.

SUMMARY

Three hundred mice were immunized with the eggs of *Hymenolepis nana*. After 17 days of brief exposures to either a cat or an empty chamber at the rate of 0, 1, 2, 4 or 8 times per day, a challenge infection was given. Predator stressed groups showed a high level of reinfection, high plasma corticosterone levels, increased adrenal gland weights, and decreased body weight gains in proportion to increasing frequency of exposure. Animals handled in a similar way, naive of the cat, showed a slight increase in reinfection rate, moderate corticosterone levels and adrenal gland weights, and normal body weight gains.

Acknowledgements—The author extends his sincerest appreciation to Dr. Mary C. Dunn, for her patience and encouragement and to Dr. Robert Prytula for his statistical evaluation of voluminous results. Mr. Wendell Nicholson of the Plasma Fluorogenics Laboratory, Vanderbilt Medical School, provided access to methods and instrumentation otherwise unavailable to the author. The technical expertise of Mr. Fain Hubbard is also gratefully acknowledged.

REFERENCES

1. SOLOMON G. F. and MOOS R. H. Emotions, immunity and disease: A speculative theoretical integration. *Archs gen. Psychiat.* **11**, 657 (1964).
2. NOBLE G. A. Stress and parasitism—II. Effect of crowding and fighting among ground squirrels on their coccidia and trichomonads. *Exp. Parasitol.* **12**, 368 (1962).
3. DAVIS D. E. and READ C. P. Effect of behavior on development of resistance in trichinosis. *Proc. Soc. exp. Biol. N.Y.* **99**, 269 (1958).
4. WEINMANN C. J. and ROTHMAN A. H. Effects of stress upon acquired immunity to the dwarf tapeworm *Hymenolepis nana.* *Exp. Parasitol.* **21**, 61 (1967).
5. SMALL W. S. Notes on the psychic development of the young white rat. *Am. J. Psychol.* **11**, (1899).
6. CURTI M. W. Native fear responses of white rats in the presence of cats. *Psychol. Monographs* **46**, 78 (1935).
7. NÄÄTÄNEN N. and JÄNKÄLÄ D. Adrenal weight increases in rats stimulated by fear. *Ann. Med. exp. Biol. Fenniae* **32**, 410 (1954).
8. HENRY J. P., MEEHAN J. P. and STEPHENS P. M. The use of psychosocial stimuli to induce prolonged systolic hypertension in mice. *Psychosom. Med.* **29**, 408 (1967).
9. HEARIN J. T. Studies on the acquired immunity to the dwarf tapeworm *Hymenolepis nana* var *fraterna*, in the mouse host. *Am. J. Hyg.* **33**, 71 (1941).
10. HEYNEMAN D. Studies on helminth immunity—I. Comparison between lumenal and tissue phases of infection in the white mouse by *Hymenolepis nana.* *Am. J. Trop. Med. Hyg.* **11**, 46 (1962).
11. BRONSON F. H. and ELETHERIOU R. E. Chronic physiological effects of fighting in mice. *Gen. Comp. Endocrin* **4**, 9 (1964).
12. GUILLEMIN R., DEAR W. E. and LIEBELT R. E. Nycthermal variations in plasma free corticosterone levels of the rat. *Proc. Soc. exp. Biol. N.Y.* **101**, 394 (1959).
13. HUNNINEN A. V. A method of demonstrating cysticercoids of *Hymenolepis nana* in the intestinal villi of mice. *J. Parasitol.* **21**, 124 (1935).
14. BUSH I. E. Species differences in adrenocortical secretion. *J. Endocrinol.* **9**, 95 (1953).

15. Mattingly D. A simple fluorometric method for the estimation of free 11-hydroxycorticoids in human plasma. *J. Clin. Pathol.* **15**, 374 (1962).
16. Douglas H. O. and LeVern H. H. Stress ulcers. *Archs Surg.* **100**, 178 (1970)
17. Rosenberg A. B. Production of gastric lesions in rats by combined cold and electroshock. *Am. J. Dig. Dis.* **12**, 1140 (1967).
18. Brady J. V. Ulcers in executive monkey. *Scientific Am.* **199**, 95 (1958).
19. Selye H. Stress. *Montreal. Acta. Inc.* 1950.
20. Loach C. D. and Higginbotham M. The relation between social rank and plasma corticosterone levels in mice. *Gen. Comp. Endocrinol.* **8**, 441 (1967).
21. Christian J. J. and Davis D. E. Endocrines, behavior and population. *Science* **146**, 1550 (1964).

32

STRESSOR EXPOSURE AND IMMUNOLOGICAL RESPONSE IN MAN: INTERFERON-PRODUCING CAPACITY AND PHAGOCYTOSIS

Jan Palmblad, Kari Cantell, Hans Strander, Jan Fröberg, Claes-Göran Karlsson, Lennart Levi, Marta Granström, and Peter Unger

THE ASSUMPTION that stressful events may increase a person's susceptibility to or aggravate the course of infectious diseases has been based to a large extent on speculation and anecdotes. It is only recently that some statistical evidence has been presented of a positive association between the degree of exposure to psychosocial stressors and the morbidity in various diseases, including infections (for a review, see [1, 2]).

The hypothesis that psychosocial stimuli may affect resistance to infections and immunological mechanisms [3] rests on a few experimental studies on *animals* subjected to various stressors. Thus, it has been shown that stressor exposure can increase morbidity or mortality in experimental viral infections [4]. Possible mechanisms in this type of response may be both humoral (e.g. diminished antibody synthesis [5, 6]) and cell-mediated (e.g. interferon production [7] and function of the reticuloendothelial system, RES [8]).

Although these studies provide a useful basis for speculation, almost nothing is known about *human* immunological reactions to various stressor exposures, e.g. phagocytic capacity and ability to produce interferon. Such responses, if indeed evoked, might play a role in modifying the human organism's resistance to infection. This report concerns the results of an experiment part of which aimed at determining whether the production of interferon in circulating lymphocytes and the phagocytic rate of blood polymorphonuclear leucocytes (PMN) and monocytes were affected in healthy human volunteers by exposure to a moderately stressful 77-hr vigil.

MATERIAL AND METHODS

Subjects, experimental procedure

The larger study, of which this investigation formed a part, will be published elsewhere.

The present subjects were eight healthy female volunteers (informed consent), aged 23–44 yr, mean 33. Due to technical problems, N is occasionally <8 but always >5. The study was approved by the Ethical Committee of the Karolinska Institutet.

The experiment, a vigil, started on a Tuesday morning and ended 77 hr later, on a Friday afternoon. Control periods were superimposed the day before the start and five days after the end of the exposure proper. The stressor procedure included performance on a specially designed shooting-range, "firing" an electronic rifle at small targets (tanks) fitted with photo diodes. An authentic battle noise from a tape recorder was amplified to a level of 95 dB-C. After an unabated $2\frac{3}{4}$-hr of such "military" activity and exposure, there followed a concentrated 15-min period for answering questionnaires, ingestion of a standard meal, voiding urine for analysis and attendance to other toilet functions. In this manner

Reprinted with permission from *J. Psychosom. Res.* **20**, 193–199. Copyright © 1976, Pergamon Press, Ltd.

the experiment was continued for three days without any rest or sleep. No activity but the experimental one was allowed. The subjects were required to sit on their chairs all the time except when voiding or giving blood samples for analysis. No stimulants or smoking were allowed. During the control periods the same procedure was followed except for the experimental stimuli. The subjects' menstrual cycles were found to be randomly dispersed in the various phases. For further details of the experimental design, see Levi [9].

Blood samples were obtained on four occasions, always at 12.30, on the day before the start of the vigil, on the second day of the vigil, on its last day and five days after the end of the experiment.

Methods

Interferon production. Interferon production was induced in the blood samples by adding 100 hemagglutination units of Sendai virus per ml as described previously [10]. After incubation for 24 hr at 37°C in a roller, the sera were separated, dialyzed against pH2 and assayed for interferon by the VSV plaque reduction method [11]. Titers were expressed in terms of the unit assigned to the standard research preparation 69/19 (International Symposium on Standardization of Interferon and Interferon Inducers, London, 1969) and given per ml of serum. The number of interferon units obtained was related to the number of lymphocytes present in the blood samples. The results would have been essentially the same if the calculations had included the polymorphonuclear cells.

Phagocytosis. The rate of phagocytosis was determined according to Unger [12]. The buffy coat of heparinized blood was incubated with a fixed amount of heat-killed Staphylococcus albus. Smears

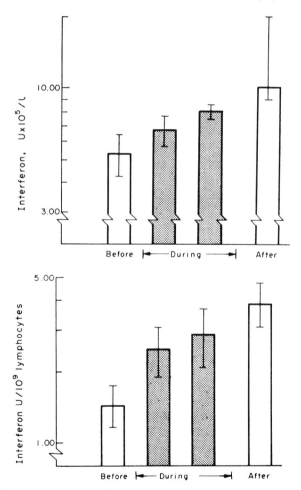

FIG. 1.—Total interferon producing ability per ml blood (a) and per 10⁶ lymphocytes (b) before, during and after stressor exposure. Mean and standard error of mean.

were made after 60 min, and the degree of phagocytosis was estimated by microscopic examination of 200 cells. The number of cells which had phagocytized any amount of bacteria was expressed as a percentage of the total number. The error of the method is 5–7%. Routine total white-cell counts and differential counts timed as indicated above were also performed. Statistical analyzes were performed with Student's t-test.

EXPERIMENTAL FINDINGS

The *interferon*-producing ability of the blood samples rose in absolute values during and after the vigil (Fig. 1a). The increase in interferon production per lymphocite (Fig. 1b) was even more marked ($p < 0.01$) (Fig. 1a, b).

Phagocytosis. As shown in Fig. 2, the leukocyte phagocytic activity decreased during the vigil, but was elevated on the second control day, i.e. five days after the end of the exposure. The changes between the first control day and the second day of the vigil, and between the latter and the second control day are both significant ($p < 0.05$). The number of circulating PMN and monocytes did not

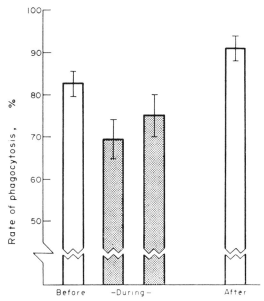

FIG. 2.—Rate of phagocytosis before, during and after stressor exposure (samples obtained at 12.30 pm). Mean and standard error of mean.

TABLE 1.—PERIPHERAL PMN, MONOCYTE AND LYMPHOCYTE COUNTS × 10⁹/1. MEAN AND STANDARD ERRORS OF MEAN

Variable	before	during		after
		2nd day	last day	
B-PMN and monocyte counts	4.7±0.8	3.9±0.6	3.9±0.4	2.6±0.8
B-lymphocyte counts	3.4±0.3	3.0±0.2	3.2±0.4	2.8±0.3

change significantly during exposure in relation to pre-exposure values (see Table 1). The differential counts did not shift over the period in question.The lymphocyte counts exhibited a non-significant decrease during and after the vigil (Table 1).

DISCUSSION

Briefly, then, the exposure to a 77-hr vigil was accompanied by significant changes in phagocytosis and interferon producing capacity. The mechanisms behind these reactions are not known.

Changes in the interferon system, which is known to play a part in the anti-viral defence process, have been reported in animals exposed to various stressors. Interferon levels fell transiently when mouse interferon production was stimulated *during* a stressor exposure [13, 14] but the interferon titer did not change at other timing schedules. Mouse interferon formation was enhanced, on the other hand, when stimulation took place five hours *after* stressor exposure [7]. As these studies were concerned with whole-body interferon production, it is conceivable that the results could be accounted for, at least in part, by changes in the cell quantities producing the interferon.

Further, animal experiments on interferon production in response to psychosocial stimuli have concerned relatively short periods [4]. The exposure to psychosocial stimuli has usually lasted only a few hours, though it has been repeated in some experiments. As everyday exposure to such stimuli often lasts considerably longer, an experimental design permitting exposure for several days would be closer to real life conditions.

In the animal studies attempts have been made to correlate the hormonal changes evoked by the psychosocial stimulation with a synchronous change in interferon production. Solomon *et al.* hypothesize that the increased adrenal cortical activity during a stressor exposure may "exhaust" [7] the adrenal cortex, leading to increased interferon production after the exposure. They also compared the enhanced post-stress interferon production with the increased production seen in adrenalectomized mice.

Studies concerning the influence of vasoactive amines on the elaboration of interferon in mice [15] showed that the interferon response fell after high doses of adrenaline, whereas low doses caused an increased response. The lowered response could be counteracted with alpha-adrenergic blocking agents.

In vitro it has been shown that both adrenal corticosteroids and catecholamines can influence granulocyte function, either by inhibiting the uptake of particles [16], altering the hexose monophosphate shunt [17] or inhibiting the intracellular bactericidal activity [18, 19]. No studies have been published concerning effects of stressor exposure on peripheral blood cell phagocytosis, either in animals or in man.

Briefly, then, studies have demonstrated that interferon producing capacity as well as phagocytosis might be influenced by adrenal cortical and medullary hormones.

Earlier studies (for a review, see Kagan and Levi [20]) have demonstrated increases in these very hormones under conditions similar to those of the present study. Some parameters of the endocrine reactions were included in the study reported here. Thus, the excretion of adrenaline and noradrenaline in urine samples collected between 8.00 and 11.00 am was higher during exposure than during the post-exposure control period five days afterwards (Fig. 3). Serum cortisol levels were markedly higher before

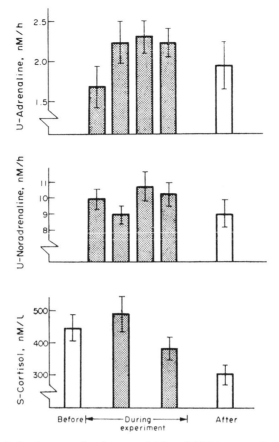

FIG. 3.—Urinary catecholamine excretion between 8.00 and 11.00 am on four consecutive days of sleep deprivation and between the same hours five days after the end of exposure (top). Cortisol in serum before, during and after stressor exposure (bottom).

and during exposure than after. The relatively high values during the first control period were possibly due to pre-exposure anticipation (Fig. 3) [21].

In the present investigation, the rise in interferon-producing ability during the vigil could not be attributed to an increased sympathetic activity, because the interferon levels were highest on the post-stress control day, when catecholamine excretion was lowest.

The highest interferon production (well above the pre-stress values, which were within the normal range) was observed when serum cortisol had reached the lowest level after the vigil. This level is considered to reflect a basic level. As time spacing differs between the studies, it is only possible to conclude that both the animal and the human studies reveal an increased propensity of the organism, or part of it, to react with augmented interferon production after stressor exposure.

The changes found in the levels of catecholamines and cortisol are relatively similar to that in the rate of phagocytosis and could, but need not, be of importance in mediating the latter.

So far, the discussion has focused on the relationship between each of a number of hormones and phagocytosis and interferon production. Nothing is known about possible complex interactions of various endocrine systems in relation to such effects, i.e. reactions provoked by various *patterns* of endocrine activity, or the *in vivo* reactions of phagocytes.

Phagocytic activity is further known to be related to opsonin activity. The present study gives no direct information on changes in the latter. However, other types of stressor exposure (surgery and other traumata) have been found to decrease the clearance of particles by the reticuloendothelial system, possibly due to depression of opsonin activity [22]. It is noteworthy that this initial depression is followed by a gradual increase in phagocytosis by the RES [8], a course that is similar to the present one, i.e. a decrease of phagocytosis during exposure and an increase above pre-exposure values some days afterwards.

SUMMARY

Exposure of 8 healthy human females to a moderately stressful 77-hr vigil under strictly controlled conditions was accompanied by changes in adrenal cortical and medullary hormones compatible with a stress reaction. The ability of the lymphocytes to produce interferon in response to the addition of Sendai virus to blood samples rose during the stressor exposure and was highest after this. Phagocytosis by peripheral blood phagocytes showed a decrease during the vigil and was followed in post-exposure samples by a rise to levels above pre-exposure values.

Acknowledgements—Professor Lars Engstedt, Department of Internal Medicine IV, South Hospital, Stockholm, contributed very constructive criticism during the planning and presentation of this study. Mrs. I. Olsson and Mr. J. Magnusson were of great help in undertaking some of the technical aspects. The study was made possible by a grant from the Swedish Delegation for Applied Medical Defence Research, which is gratefully acknowledged.

REFERENCES

1. RAHE R. H. Subjects' recent life changes and their near-future illness susceptibility. *Adv. Psychosom. Med.* **8,** 2 (1972).
2. JACOBS M. A., SPILKEN A. and NORMAN M. Relationship of life change, maladaptive aggression, and upper respiratory infection in male college students. *Psychosom. Med.* **31,** 31 (1969).
3. SOLOMON G. F., AMKRAUT A. A. and KASPER P. Immunity, emotions and stress. In *Mechanisms in Symptom Formation, Proc. 2nd Congr. Int. College Psychosom. Med.* (Edited by MUSAPH H.). Basel, Karger, 209 (1974).
4. RASMUSEN JR. A. F. Emotions and immunity. *Ann. N.Y. Acad. Sci.* **164,** 458 (1969).
5. SOLOMON G. F. Stress and antibody response in rats. *Int. Arch. Allergy* **35,** 97 (1969).
6. HILL C. W., GRER W. E. and FELSENFELD O. Psychosocial stress, early response to foreign protein, and blood cortisol in vervets. *Psychosom. Med.* **29,** 279 (1967).
7. SOLOMON G. F., MERIGAN T. C. and LEVINE S. Variations in adrenal cortical hormones within physiologic ranges, stress and interferon production in mice. *Proc. Soc. Exp. Biol. Med.* **126,** 74 (1967).
8. SCHILDT B. E. Fluctuation of the RES after thermal and mechanical trauma in mice. *Acta Chir. Scand.* **136,** 359 (1970).
9. LEVI L. Stress and distress in response to psychosocial stimuli. *Acta Med. Scand. Suppl.* 528 (1972).
10. STRANDER H., CANTELL K., LEISTI J. and NIKKILÄ E. Interferon response of lymphocytes in disorders with decreased resistance to infection. *Clin. Exp. Immunol.* **6,** 263 (1970).
11. STRANDER H. and CANTELL K. Further studies on the production of interferon by human leukocytes *in vitro. Ann. Med. Exp. Fenn.* **45,** 20 (1967).
12. UNGER P. A study of phagocytosis. *Proc. 10th Congr. Europ. Soc. Haematol. Strassbourg.* **II,** 443 (1965).
13. CHANG S. S. and RASMUSSEN A. F. Stress-induced suppression of interferon production in virus-infected mice. *Nature (London)* **205,** 623 (1965).
14. JENSEN M. M. Transitory impairment of interferon production in stressed mice. *J. Infec. Dis.* **118,** 230 (1968).

15. JENSEN M. M. The influence of vasoactive amines on interferon production in mice. *Proc. Soc. Exp. Biol. Med.* **130,** 34 (1969).
16. WIENER E., MARMARY Y. and CURELARU Z. The *in vitro* effect of hydro-cortisone on the uptake and intracellular digestion of particulate matter by macrophages in culture. *Lab. Invest.* **26,** 220 (1972).
17. COOPER M. R., DECHATELET L. R. and McCALL C. E. The *in vitro* effect of steroids on polymorphonuclear leukocyte metabolism. *Proc. Soc. Exp. Biol. Med.* **141,** 986 (1972).
18. QUALLIOTINE D., DECHATELET L. R., McCALL C. E. and COOPER M. R. Effect of catecholamines on bactericidal activity of polymorphonuclear leukocytes. *Infec. Immunity* **6,** 211 (1972).
19. MANDELL G. L., RUBIN W. and HOOK E. W. The effect of an NADH oxidase inhibitor (hydro-cortisone) on polymorphonuclear leukocyte bactericidal activity. *J. Clin. Invest.* **49,** 1381 (1970).
20. KAGAN A. R. and LEVI L. Health and environment—psychosocial stimuli: a review. *Soc. Sci. Med.* **8,** 225 (1974).
21. MASON J. W. A review of psychoendocrine research on the pituitary adrenal cortical system. *Psychosom. Med.* **30,** 576 (1968).
22. SABA T. M. Mechanism mediating reticuloendothelial system depression after surgery. *Proc. Soc. Exp. Biol. Med.* **133,** 1132 (1970).

33

STRESS-INDUCED MODULATION OF THE IMMUNE RESPONSE

Andrew A. Monjan and Michael I. Collector

After mice were exposed to a daily auditory stressor for varying lengths of time, the responses of their splenic lymphoid cells *in vitro* were assessed. Both the blastogenic activity of concanavalin A or lipopolysaccharide and the ability of immune lymphocytes to lyse P815 target cells showed the same patterns of immunosuppression and enhancement.

While the immunosuppressive properties of short-term exposures to various stressors have been well established (*1*), the effects of long-term stress on the immune response are less clear (*2*). To further elucidate the latter interaction, we have assessed *in vitro* the responses of lymphoid cells obtained from mice subjected to various periods of environmental stress. The immunoresponsiveness of splenic lymphocytes was evaluated by determining their blastogenic activity following mitogen stimulation (*3*), and by the ability of splenic lymphocytes obtained from mice immunized *in vivo* to kill P815 target cells (*4*).

Male mice (7 to 12 weeks old) of the AKR or C57/Bl$_6$ strains were used. The mice (four per cage) were subjected to a broad band noise at about 100 db daily for 5 seconds every minute during a 1- or 3-hour period around midnight, at the height of the diurnal activity cycle. Unstimulated controls were exposed only to the normal activity of the animal room. The controls and experimental mice were killed at the same time. Their spleens were removed, and suspensions of splenocytes were prepared. Erythrocytes were lysed with 0.83% NH$_4$Cl buffered to pH 7.5 with tris for 10 minutes and then washed in Hanks balanced salt solution. Cells were resuspended and maintained in RPMI 1640 and 10% heat-inactivated fetal calf serum.

Both assays of immunologic reactivity, one nonspecific and the other specific, showed the same temporal pattern of hypo- and hyperresponsiveness (Fig. 1), the data having been confirmed in further replications. The activities of both B and T cells (derived from bone marrow and thymus, respectively) appeared to be affected similarly: B cell function as reflected by stimulation with lipopolysaccharide (LPS), and T cell function as reflected both by stimulation with concanavalin A (Con A) and by the specific lysis of P815 target cells.

The clearest demonstration of the stress-induced modulation of immune function is found in Fig. 1B. Short-term exposure of the animals to the sound stressor (initiated during the week preceding or following immunization with a T-dependent antigen) clearly depressed the lymphocyte-mediated cytotoxic response, while enhancement occurred with longer exposures to sound stress.

Assays of plasma cortisol (*5*) in similarly stressed C57/Bl$_6$ mice (Fig. 2A) show that there is an increase in the circulating levels of this adrenal corticosteroid corresponding to the depression of the immunologic function, and not apparently associated with the enhancement. Daily

Reprinted with permission from *Science* **196**, 307–308. Copyright © 1977, the American Association for the Advancement of Science.

exposure to the sound stress for more than 10 days produces an adaptation which brings cortisol to base-line levels. However, acute stress increases the blood cortisol to concentrations that are able to suppress the immunologic response to antigens introduced during this period. Coincident with the heightened steroid level is a decrease in the number of viable nucleated cells recovered per spleen from the mice subjected to short-term stress compared to the number recovered from the nonstressed controls (Fig. 2B). This result corresponds to similar decreases in lymphocyte cytotoxicity and spleen index after the administration of exogenous hydrocortisone, as reported by Fernandes *et al.* (6). Such depletion of lymphoid cells could occur as a result of either cortisone-induced toxicity or changes in lymphocyte migration patterns (7). It is interesting that there is a comparable decrease of cells during the period of immunopotentiation when cortisol levels are normal.

The ability of environmental stimuli to enhance as well as to depress immunoreactivity has not been fully appreciated. Certainly, the available evidence supports the view that the stress-

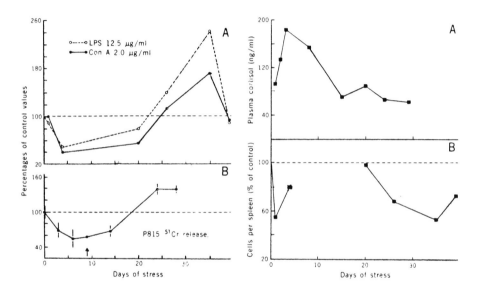

FIGURE 1 (left). Stress-induced modulation of immune function. (A) Response of splenic lymphocytes *in vitro* to mitogens LPS or Con A following stimulation (*in vivo*) of mice with sound stress for 1 hour per day for up to 39 days. Each point represents the mean of triplicate replications from a pool of two spleens per datum. For control animals, the mean number of counts per minute were 9078 for LPS and 59,368 for Con A. The [³H]thymidine uptake for cells not treated with mitogens ranged from 128 to 400 count/min. (B) Ability of immune lymphocytes to kill target cells *in vitro* following stimulation (*in vivo*) of mice with sound stress for 3 hours per day for up to 28 days. Each point represents the mean of triplicate replications from each of two individual spleens. Vertical bars show the range of values. Only one spleen was used at day 9. Arrow indicates that mice were immunized with P815 cells 9 days before they were killed. Some animals had their daily sound stress periods initiated prior to immunization (represented by points to the right of the arrow) while others had their stress sessions started after immunization (represented by points to the left of the arrow). All animals were killed at the same time and the lytic activities of their splenic lymphocytes were assessed simultaneously. The mean lysis in control experiments was 23 percent.

FIGURE 2 (right). Humoral and splenic changes induced by long-term exposure to sound stress. (A) Plasma cortisol levels of mice subjected to sound stress for 3 hours per day for up to 28 days. (B) Viable nucleated splenocytes recovered per spleen from mice subjected to sound stress for 1 hour per day for up to 39 days. Each point represents the average of two mice.

Behavior and Immune Function

induced immunosuppression is mediated through the action of cortisone upon lymphocytes. What of the potentiation of the immune response? That it has not been well documented may be a reflection of differences in assay systems and sampling intervals, as well as in the qualitative and quantitative parameters of stress. For example, stimulation of suckling mice significantly shortens the time they survive after receiving a transplantable lymphoid leukemia (8), while the same type of neonatal stress in handled rats significantly increased the amount of antibody produced in response to an injection of nonreplicating antigen (9). On the other hand, rats stressed by overcrowding for 1 week prior to immunization by that same nonreplicating flagellar antigen have significantly lower antibody levels than uncrowded animals (10), while splenic lymphocytes from rats crowded for 5 weeks prior to immunization with human thyroglobulin showed, in vitro, an increased incorporation of [^{3}H]thymidine when they were stimulated with that antigen (11).

Gisler and Schenkel-Hulliger (12) have shown that an intact pituitary is necessary for the recovery from adrenocorticotropic hormone (ACTH)-stimulated depression of plaque-forming cells in vitro following immunization with sheep erythrocytes in vivo. A hypophysectomized mouse would not regain normal immune responsiveness unless the administration of ACTH was preceded by receipt of somatotropic hormone (STH). This hormone is but one of the many humoral factors whose concentrations are increased by long-term exposure to environmental stressors (13). Therefore, we propose that the enhancement phenomenon reported herein may be due to the elevation of one or more such circulating factors which stimulate lymphocyte reactivity through activation of guanosine 3',5'-monophosphate, a cyclic nucleotide that is involved in lymphocyte proliferation, and which can be induced by any of a number of neurohumors (14).

In summary, we have shown that environmental stressors not only can depress immune responsiveness, but can also enhance it. Both suppression and potentiation appear to be associated with a decrease in the number of viable nucleated splenocytes. Whether this loss is due to the cells' interacting with humoral factors, or to humoral factors causing a change in migration patterns, remains to be elucidated. Levels of cortisol in plasma appear to be temporally related to immunological hyporeactivity but not to hyperreactivity. The mechanism for this latter phenomenon is now open for inquiry.

References and Notes

1. A. F. Rasmussen, Jr., E. S. Spencer, J. T. Marsh, *Proc. Soc. Exp. Biol. Med.* 100, 878 (1959); R. H. Gisler, A. E. Bussard, J. C. Mazie, R. Hess, *Cell. Immunol.* **2**, 634 (1971); R. J. Hudson, *Can. J. Zool.* **51**, 479 (1973); H. Folch and B. Y. Waksman, *J. Immunol.* **113**, 127 (1974).
2. A. Yamada *et al.*, *Proc. Soc. Exp. Biol. Med.* **116**, 677 (1964); C. W. Hill, W. E. Greer, O. Felsenfeld, *Psychosom. Med.* **29**, 279 (1967).
3. For the mitogen stimulation experiments, viable nucleated cells (2 × 10^6 cells per milliliter) from AKR mice were placed (0.2 ml per well) in a 96-well microtiter plate (Linbro) to which had been added optimal doses of the mitogens lipopolysaccharide (LPS) of *Escherichia coli* 055:B5 (Difco) or Con A (Sigma), bringing the volume per well to 0.25 ml. After 3 days of incubation at 36°C in a 5% CO_2 atmosphere, 1 μC of [^{3}H]thymidine was added to each well for 4 hours at which time the cells were harvested with a Biomedical Research Institute cell harvester, and the residual radioactivity counted in a Packard liquid scintillation counter after addition of Brays solution.
4. For the lymphocyte cytotoxicity assay, spleen cell suspensions from C57/Bl$_6$ mice were prepared as previously described. However, 9 days before they were killed, the animals received 3 × 10^7 DBA/2 mastocytoma (P815) cells, intraperitoneally. Immune or nonimmune splenocytes were incubated with 10 × 10^3 ^{51}Cr-labeled P815 target cells at a ratio of 100 : 1 for 16 hours at 37°C in a 5% CO_2 atmosphere. The amount of ^{51}Cr released into the media was determined in a Packard gammaspectrometer and the percentage of specific lysis was calculated from [(counts released by immune cells minus counts released by the nonimmune cells) divided by (total input counts of ^{51}Cr)] × 100.

5. Plasma cortisol levels were determined by radioimmunoassay with materials and procedures supplied with the ^{3}H-labeled cortisol (RIA Pak, New England Nuclear).
6. G. Fernandes, E. J. Yunis, R. A. Good, *Clin. Immunol. Immunopathol.* **4**, 304 (1975).
7. F. Elmadjian and G. Pincus, *Endocrinology* **37**, 47 (1945); M. F. Greaves, J. J. T. Owen, M. C. Raff, *T and B Lymphocytes* (American Elsevier, New York, 1974); A. S. Fauci, *Transplant. Proc.* **7**, 37 (1975).
8. S. Levine and C. Cohen, *Proc. Soc. Exp. Biol. Med.* **102**, 53 (1959).
9. G. F. Solomon, S. Levine, J. K. Kraft, *Nature (London)* **220**, 821 (1968).
10. G. F. Solomon, *Int. Arch. Allergy Appl. Immunol.* **35**, 97 (1969).
11. A. Joasso and J. M. McKenzie, *ibid.* **50**, 659 (1976).
12. R. H. Gisler and L. Schenkel-Hulliger, *Cell. Immunol.* **2**, 646 (1971).
13. H. Selye, *Stress in Health and Disease* (Butterworths, Boston, 1975).
14. N. D. Goldberg, R. F. O'Dea, M. K. Haddox, *Adv. Cyclic Nucleotide Res.* **3**, 155 (1973).

Supported by PHS grant HD 08490.

34

THE ROLE OF CONDITIONED REFLEXES IN IMMUNITY*

S. Metal'nikov and V. Chorine

The importance of the study of *conditioned reflexes* has been brought to light due to the remarkable works of J. Pavlov and his students. These reflexes can be described as follows.

After Glinsky succeeded, at Pavlov's laboratory, in creating fistulas on the ducts of salivary glands, it became possible to examine closely the functioning of these glands.

Wolfson was one of the first to show the influence of the psychic centers on the secretion of saliva. Subsequently, a systematic and detailed study of these interesting phenomena was undertaken at Pavlov's laboratory.

Tolochinov and Babkin established that the mere smell or sight of food are sufficient to provoke a flow of saliva in dogs, which is in no way different from the saliva secreted during meals.

While studying the physiology of the salivary glands, Boldirev was the first to show that each external stimulus which is applied simultaneously with direct gustatory stimuli, can subsequently become an independent reflex and provoke, by itself, a flow of saliva.

Thus, for example, if during stimulation of the gustatory centers of the dog, he is made to listen at the same time to an identical sound, or if his skin is scratched at the same time in the same spot, it will be sufficient, after a series of events in which these two types of stimuli coincide, to scratch the dog's skin or to produce the same sound as before, in order to determine the flow of saliva.

Thus, auditory or mechanical stimuli which have nothing in common with the salivary glands and which never affected the latter in any way, become capable of determining the flow of saliva, after they have been combined several times with direct gustatory stimuli. Pavlov called stimuli of this nature *conditioned stimuli*, and the reflexes provoked them by, *conditioned reflexes*.

Boldirev, Vartanov, Zeliony, Orbeli, and Tsitovitch obtained similar conditioned reflexes using sounds, smells, beams of light, the local cooling or heating of the skin to 50°, etc. (*1*).

We have attempted to apply Pavlov's method to the study of immunity. In a series of operations we demonstrated that the basis of immunity is formed by defensive reactions of the various cells of the organism.

Defensive reactions may occur either on the outside of the organism (on the mucosa of the nose, the eyes, the throat, etc.), or on the inside of the organism (in the blood, the body cavities or the organs). Not only do the free cells of the blood react, but all of the other cells do so as well: connective and reticuloendothelial cells, vessels, hematopoietic glands, nerves, etc. The

*Translated from the original French (*Ann. Pasteur Inst.* **40**, 893–900, 1926), by Ria Olsen, for Language Consultants, Wellesley Hills, Massachusetts.

formation and the secretion of various antibodies are also manifestations of these defensive reactions of the cells (2).

Since these reactions are involuntary, we can state that they are highly complicated, internal reflexes. These defense reflexes may vary greatly under the influence of different stimuli, i.e., different microbes, toxins, or foreign bodies which have been introduced into the organism.

Thus, by injecting a given microbe emulsion into the peritoneum of a guinea pig we can always provoke a typical reaction. The duration and the strength of these reactions depend upon the quantity and the quality of the injected substances. We may repeat these injections several times and we will always obtain the same typical reflex.

One question presents itself: Wouldn't it be possible, by repeating these injections 10 to 20 times in a row and by associating them with external stimuli, to create a reflex similar to Pavlov's *conditioned reflexes?* To solve this question, we undertook a series of experiments on 24 guinea pigs.

The peritoneum of each guinea was injected daily with a small dose of tapioca, B-anthracoids or a staphylococcus filtrate. This injection was always associated with an external stimulus—the skin was scratched at the same spot, or it was brought into contact with a heated metal plate (3). After 15 to 20 injections and external stimuli of this type we let the guinea pigs rest for 12–15 days, until the exudate of their peritoneal cavity returned to normal. On that day, we would apply the external stimulus (scratching or heating) several times, without injecting anything into the peritoneum. Afterward, the peritoneal exudate was examined several times, over a period of 24 to 48 hours.

We should point out that in a normal animal which has not been injected, the peritoneal exudate is transparent and contains only few elements, in particular, lymphocytes and monocytes.

Almost immediately after the injection of a foreign substance in the peritoneum, the leukocytes appear in large numbers, which continue to increase hour after hour.

The polynuclears, in particular, start to react during the first hours following the injection. Toward the end of the first and of the second day, the number of polynuclears diminishes rapidly. The monocytes then start appearing in large quantities, to reach their highest numbers around the third and the fourth day after injection.

Finally the lymphocytes show up; they are most numerous around the fifth and the seventh day (4).

For further clarification, the results of some experiments are shown below:

Experiment I. Cell reaction in the peritoneum of guinea pig No. 42, which received a tapioca emulsion (2 cc.).

	Leukocytic formula			Cell quantity
	Polynuclears	Monocytes	Lymphocytes	
Before the injection	0	35	65	+
30 Minutes after the injection	4	16	80	+ +
2 Hours after the injection	26	14	60	+ +
5 Hours after the injection	90	8	2	+ + +
24 Hours after the injection	82	16	2	+ + + +
48 Hours after the injection	47	35	8	+ + + +
3 Days after the injection	29	50	21	+ + + +
5 Days after the injection	12	37	51	+ + +

Experiment II. Guinea pig No. 42 has received 21 tapioca injections. Before each injection, the skin was brought into contact with a heated metal plate; thirteen days after the last injection, the same skin area was heated several times.

	Leukocytic formula			Cell quantity
	Polynuclears	Monocytes	Lymphocytes	
Before the stimulus	0.6	29	69.6	+
2 Hours after the stimulus	9.3	78.2	12.5	+ +
5 Hours after the stimulus	62	32	6	+ + +
24 Hours after the stimulus	24.5	53	22	+ +

Experiment III. Guinea pig No. 16 received 18 injections of a B-anthracoid emulsion associated with an external stimulus (heating of the skin). Fifteen days after the last injection, the same skin area was heated several times.

	Leukocytic formula				Cell quantity
	Polynuclears	Monocytes	Lymphocytes	Eosinophils	
Before the stimulus	0	35	54.5	10.5	6,300
3½ Hours after the stimulus	41.6	26.6	20.4	10.8	8,650
24 Hours after the stimulus	1.5	30.5	58	15.5	13,300
48 Hours after the stimulus	0.4	46.9	45.8	7.3	9,500
3 Days after the stimulus	0.5	50.9	38.8	9.5	11,920

Experiment IV. Guinea pig No. 98 was injected 25 times in the peritoneum with a B-anthracoid emulsion associated with an external stimulus (scratching of the skin on the right-hand side); 15 days after the last injection, the same skin area was scratched several times. The scratching was repeated the following day.

	Leukocytic formula				Cell quantity
	Polynuclears	Monocytes	Lymphocytes	Eosinophils	
Before the experiment	0	36.6	62.8	0.6	5,000
3½ Hours after the stimulus	5.2	50.5	44.1	1.0	9,500
25 Hours after the stimulus	0.8	54.6	43.6	0.9	8,560
48 Hours after the stimulus	16.1	52.6	27.7	1.1	8,560
3 Days after the stimulus	7.0	41	50	2	8,560
4 Days after the stimulus	1.1	12.4	82.3	4.2	8,560

Upon examination of the results of experiments II, III, and IV we notice that guinea pigs 42, 98, and 16, which received nothing in the peritoneum but which were stimulated externally, yielded the same leukocyte reaction in the peritoneum.

This reaction is weaker and of shorter duration than the reaction in the animals which received the emulsion in the peritoneum, but it is highly conclusive. While in a normal guinea pig the monocyte reaction always occurs at a later time (after 2 to 4 days), in guinea pigs with conditioned reflexes the monocytes often react faster than the polynuclears (see Experiment II).

If the external conditioned stimuli are capable of provoking an internal defense reaction, would it not be possible to use these stimuli as a means of defense against a deadly infection?

To answer this question, we undertook a series of experiments.

Experiment V. Two guinea pigs, Nos. 95 and 96, were injected 12 times in the peritoneum with a staphylococcus filtrate associated with an external stimulus (scratching of the skin); 10 days after the last injection, the same skin area was scratched several times.

The following day, both guinea pigs, as well as a control animal (guinea pig No. 85) were injected in the peritoneum with deadly doses of cholera vibrios (1.25 of culture in agar).

While the control animal, No. 85, died within 6 hours, the two guinea pigs with conditioned reflexes lived.

Experiment VI. Two guinea pigs, Nos. 20 and 75, were injected 25 times in the peritoneum with B-anthracoids associated with an external stimulus (scratching). Fifteen days after the last injection, the same skin area of guinea pig No. 20 was scratched. The following day, guinea pigs Nos. 20 and 75, as well as the control animal No. 48, received a deadly dose of cholera (1.20 of culture in agar). The control animal No. 48 died after 7 or 8 hours.

No. 75, which had not been stimulated, died after 6 hours.

No. 20 died after 36 hours (the dose was too strong).

Experiment VII. Two guinea pigs, Nos. 21 and 16, were injected 18 times in the peritoneum with B-anthracoids associated with an external stimulus. Seventeen days after the last injection, both guinea pigs were scratched several times.

The following day, guinea pigs Nos. 21 and 16, as well as the control animal no. 69, received a deadly cholera dose. While the control animal died, guinea pigs Nos. 21 and 16 lived.

Experiment VIII. Both guinea pigs, Nos. 21 and 16, are retested (one month after the last cholera injection). Only guinea pig No. 16 is exposed to conditioned stimuli, guinea pig No. 21 is not. The following day, both guinea pigs Nos. 16 and 21, as well as both control animals Nos. 10 and 11, receive deadly doses of virulent streptococci. The two control animals Nos. 10 and 11, and guinea pig No. 21, die; guinea pig No. 16 lives.

Of the 24 guinea pigs which were subjected to these experiments, 10 died from causes outside the experiments; of the 14 remaining, 10 presented typical defense reactions, while the last 4 did not.

All of these experiments show that in guinea pigs with conditioned reflexes, the influence of a corresponding stimulus may produce defense reactions which, in certain cases, may offer protection against a deadly infection.

Recently, we had the opportunity of reading the work of Dr. Krilov, from Professor Pavlov's laboratory (5), which confirms and completes our results. Krilov succeeded in demonstrating the existence of conditioned reflexes in poisoning phenomena. While studying the effect of morphine on dogs, he noticed that even when the morphine injections are repeated several times, no attenuation of, or tolerance to, this poison occurs. On the contrary, the poisoning phenomena appear much faster and with greater intensity. This fact remained incomprehensible until he noticed at one point that the poisoning phenomena often appeared even before the injection of the morphine, i.e., when he was preparing the needles. The idea occurred to him that this phenomenon might be explained by the existence of conditioned reflexes. The following experiment fully confirmed this idea.

He took a dog and injected it every day underneath the skin of the left leg with a morphine dose which always caused the typical symptoms: vomiting, defecation, sleep, etc.

After eight to ten days, he injected the dog with physiological water instead of morphine, and noticed that the same poisoning phenomena occurred. He continued these experiments for several more days and succeeded in provoking poisoning phenomena by introducing a needle underneath the skin of the leg, by making noises with the needles, etc. Often, the arrival of the experimenter in the room produced the same effect on the dog.

All of these experiments show that conditioned reflexes may play a very important role, not only in immunity reactions but also in various diseases. Everything surrounding the patient may act as a conditioned stimulus, provoking the same illness as the original cause. From that point of view, sensations of pain or discomfort may occur not only as the result of a natural cause (virus, intoxication, etc.), but also through the action of various stimuli which have become accidentally associated during the illness. It is possible that in many chronic and nervous illnesses (asthma, heart trouble, neuroses, etc.), attacks and outbursts occur as the result of conditioned stimuli which have nothing in common with the real cause of the illness. For this reason, similar patients should not be treated by means of some remedy, but by suppressing conditioned stimuli which develop in the course of the illness. A simple change in living conditions (i.e. the suppression of some conditioned reflexes) is often sufficient to produce a favorable effect on the patient. On the other hand, during the period of convalescence and immunization, conditioned reflexes are formed also which are very useful because they provoke defense reactions. As we saw in our experiments, these conditioned reflexes are often capable of protecting the organism against a deadly infection and they have a favorable effect.

(1) Tsitovitch, Origine et formation des réflexes conditionnels [Origin and development of conditioned reflexes], *Thesis*, *Mil. Med. Academy*, St. Petersburg; J. Pavlov, Réflexes conditionnels. Contributions à l'étude de la fonction du système nerveux des animaux supérieurs [Conditioned reflexes. Contributions to the study of the function of the nervous system in the higher animals], Petrograd, 1923.

(2) S. Metalnikov and Toumanov. *Ann. Pasteur Inst.* Nos. 39 and 40.

(3) According to Professor Pavlov's guidelines, the conditioned stimuli have to precede the normal stimuli. For this reason, in our experiments, we always gave the injections after the external stimuli.

(4) S. Metalnikov and Toumanov, Réactions des cellules et phagocytose chez le cobaye normal et immunisé [Cell reaction and phagocytosis in a normal, immunized guinea pig]. *Ann. Pasteur Inst.*, 1925.

(5) Memoirs published for Professor Pavlov's Jubilee, Petrograd, 1924.

35

NEW EXPERIMENTAL DATA ON THE CONDITIONED REFLEX REPRODUCTION AND SUPPRESSION OF IMMUNE AND ALLERGIC REACTIONS*

A. O. Dolin, V. N. Krylov, V. I. Luk'ianenko, and B. A. Flerov

The neuroreflex regulation of defensive functions and particularly of immunological reactions is at the present time receiving considerable attention from investigators. Particular attention has been attracted by the possibility of the conditioned reflex reproduction and, more recently, the conditioned reflex suppression of immunological reactions.

Among our recent laboratory findings, experiments carried out by V. I. Luk'ianenko and B. A. Flerov at the Tabakhmel'skii Biological Combine on ten experimental bullocks, used for the production of anti-pasteurella serum, are of decided interest. It was established that when the immunological activity of the blood serum was maintained at a high level for a considerable time by conditioned reflex reproduction, the content of γ-globulins in the total blood protein (nephelometry and electrophoresis) was maintained at a high level over a period of 6 months.

In these experiments the globulin fraction of the protein was maintained at a high level for a prolonged time by conditioned reflex means despite the fact that the unconditioned reinforcement (living *Pasteurella* culture) was not used at any time during the period.

In many respects these experiments are in agreement with the facts established earlier by Dzhmukhadze, Dzheiranishvili and Dosychev [3], who carried out similar investigations on the same experimental animals, but over longer periods.

After publication of the first experimental findings (Metal'nikov [15], Dolin and Krylov [6]), the number of papers and publications proving the fundamental possibility of the involvement of conditioned reflex mechanisms in the regulation of immunological reactions increased considerably. Positive results obtained in a number of laboratories by use of a wide range of antigenic stimuli (bacterial, serous, cellular, viral, anatoxic) and, on a large number of animals of different species do not leave any doubt as to the factual side of the question.

Some microbiologists still, however, deny the possibility of any cortical regulation of immunological reactions from the higher divisions of the central nervous system. Nor is there any unanimity of opinion on this problem even among immunologists. For example, Zhukov-Verezhnikov [7] considers that "it is proved absolutely that the entire operation of the Mechnikov phagocytic system (inflammation and phagocytosis, the production of specific antibodies) is subject to conditioned reflex in the same wasy as it is to unconditioned reflex influences," but Zil'ber [10] holds that conditioned reflex regulation is only possible for the cell factors in natural

*From *Zh. vyssh. nervn. deyatel.* **10**: No. 6, 832–841 (Engl. version, pp. 889–899), 1960. Translated by R. Crawford.

immunity, as phylogenetically older defensive reactions. Zdrodovskii [8] categorically denies all possibility of cortical regulation of immunity reactions. Confining himself to the experimental findings of his own laboratory (A. A. Klimentova, G. V. Shumakova, K. T. Khalyapina), Zdrodovskii [9] continues to maintain his former views. Notwithstanding the fact that many who have investigated this problem have presented experimental proofs of the conditioned reflex regulation of cell and humoral factors in natural and artificial immunity (cell reactions involving leukocytes, phagocytosis, lysozyme, complement, agglutinins, precipitins hemolysins, antitoxins), Zdrodovskii and Zil'ber still assert that most investigators have not obtained conditioned reflex reproduction of immune reactions.

Our critical analysis (Dolin [4], [5], Krylov [12], Luk'ianenko [13], Luk'ianenko and Flerov [14]) of investigations in which negative results were obtained and the experimental checking of the main experiments carried out by Zdrodovskii's co-workers have shown that there were generally serious methodological deficiencies in the actual arrangement of experiments in these complex physiological investigations, carried out without the cooperation or advice of physiologists. For example, the regular use from "experiment to experiment" of intravenous injections of glucose with ascorbic acid and also the use of a chamber with a raised oxygen content as "indifferent" conditioned stimuli actually constitute complexes of stimuli of defensive significance, which undoubtedly restricted closure of the cortical connection in these experiments. In addition to the insufficient attention given to the selection of adequate conditioned stimuli, the smoothing effect of the time factor must also be considered a serious defect. This concerns the duration of the action of the conditioned stimulus alone, the duration of the coincidence in time of the conditioned and unconditioned stimuli, points which are particularly important in model immunological experiments in which the unconditioned reflex itself and the conditioned reflex formed on its basis occur in the form of slow processes occurring over a considerable time.

Apart from the many departures from methodological rules, arrival at the true position in relation to this problem was rendered difficult, as we have indicated earlier (Dolin, Ninth Meeting of the Academy of Medical Sciences) by the fact that, as the combinations of antigen injection with the conditioned stimulus continued, no account was taken of the state of functional tension in the immunogenic system or of the need to ensure that the interval between the course of vaccinations and testing of the conditioned stimulus should, as was essential, fall in the period of greatest immunological activity.

In view of the exceptional theoretical importance of the question of nervous regulation of immunological processes for general physiology and the physiology of higher nervous activity, for experimental and practical immunology and also for furthering our knowledge of the reciprocal connections between processes of immunochemical nature and nervous processes, we have undertaken further investigation of the regulating functions of the higher parts of the central nervous system on immunological and allergic models. For this purpose we have in the course of the last 6 years carried out new experiments for investigation of the importance of systemization in the activity of the higher parts of the brain in the immune reactions of the organism, in relation to change in its sensitivity to bacterial and serum antigenic stimuli.

In this connection attention should be given to the form of our experiments, in which we used the mechanism of the dynamic stereotype in order to reproduce the complex nervous phenomenon described in the physiology of higher nervous activity as the "reflex to the relationship between stimuli" as a model for immunological reactions. A firmly established stereotype was created in rabbits to injections of two stimuli differing in immunological activity, given in strict alternation at 4-day intervals, namely the specific stimulus-injection of Gärtner vaccine (10^9 bacterial cells/ml) and, 4 days later, the nonspecific stimulus—isogenic serum (1 ml). When the stereotype was consolidated, there was complete reproduction of the reaction, firmly established in the higher parts of the animal's brain, to the order of succession and to the relationship between the immunological strengths of the antigen when the two different stimuli were suddenly replaced by isogenic serum alone (Fig. 1, tests 1 and 3).

The relationship between the strengths of the immunological effects was also retained when the order of succession of the stimuli was changed, rabbit serum being injected in place of the Gärtner vaccine and, after 4 days, the vaccine being injected in place of the rabbit serum (Fig. 1, test 2). In these experiments the unconditioned immunological reactions afforded clear evidence of the persistence of the reaction to the relationship between the stimuli, consolidated earlier by means of a dynamic stereotype mechanism. The physiological basis of this phenomenon should be recognised as a reflex to the relationship between conditioned stimuli, as studied in the Pavlov School in relation to secretory and motor unconditioned and conditioned reflexes.

In another form of experiment (Krylov), tending in the same direction and important from the standpoint of the evaluation of the role of a "new" stimulus reproducing the latent and veiled reaction, rabbits were given regular subcutaneous injections of a combination of three sera, horse, sheep and guinea pig (1 ml of each). An 8.5-month interval followed consolidation of this stereotype. Precipitin titre examinations after the interval showed that the immunological reaction was completely extinguished. Under these conditions the injection into the rabbits of a "new" stimulus, never used previously, namely human blood serum, resulted in "revival" of the immunological reaction to the compound stimulus used a long time previously, namely the combination of horse, sheep and guinea pig serum (Fig. 2, rabbits No. 26, 24, 25). Yet at that time precipitins for the new protein stimulus (human blood serum) could only be detected in very low dilutions (1:50 to 1:100). There are reasonable grounds for thinking that, in revealing the latent reactions of the nervous system in the reproduction of "anamnestic" immunological reactions, in the same way as was demonstrated earlier by us on experimental pathological model we were dealing with general phenomena which indicate that trace reaction already created and retained in latent form (Speranskii [16]), were reproduced in the completely integrated, consolidated form by virtue of the provocative effect of the "new" stimulus.

These experiments on immunological models thus emphasized the importance of the dynamic stereotype as a unified and consolidated system of cortical and subcortical reflexes, reproduced by the action of stimuli of specific and non-specific nature, even to the point of "revival" of a latent immunological reaction by new stimuli. The great variety and complexity of the

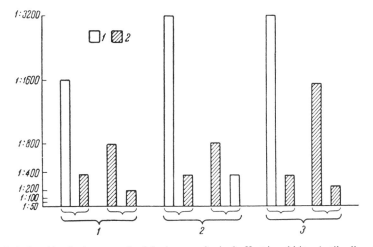

FIGURE 1. Relationships in the strength of the immunological effect in rabbits. Antibodies: (1) Vaccine. (2) Serum.

Conditioned Reflex Suppression of Immune/Allergic Reactions 271

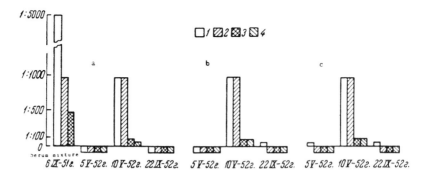

FIGURE 2. (a) Rabbit No. 26. (b) Rabbit No. 25. (c) Rabbit No. 24. Sera: (1) horse, (2) sheep, (3) guinea pig, (4) man.

model experiments makes it clearly evident that in this case the regulation of the immunological reactions was effected in complete accordance with and on the basis of the physiological patterns of the systematized activity of the higher divisions of the central nervous system, elucidated in the Pavlov School on the classical conditioned and unconditioned reflex models.

The part played by dynamic stereotype mechanisms in the retardation or even complete inhibition of reaction to antigenic stimuli of various physiological strengths becomes of particular importance in connection with the problem of the nervous control of immunological reactions.

In this connection we have undertaken new forms of experiments (V. I. Luk'ianenko) with other antigens and on other laboratory animals. Under stereotype conditions 1 ml saline was regularly injected subcutaneously into guinea pigs. In the 16th experiment, all other experimental conditions being the same, the saline was replaced by horse serum (1 ml of 1:100 dilution). The injections of saline were continued during the next 10 days. The titers of precipitins for the protein stimulus injected earlier were examined on the 26th experimental day. No precipitins could be demonstrated in 8 of the 15 experimental animals (No. 4, 5, 6, 7, 8, 10, 11, 14) and in the remaining 7 the precipitin titer was extremely low and did not exceed 1: 10–1: 20. Precipitins were demonstrated in 8 of 10 control animals: in 6 of these guinea pigs precipitins were noted in dilutions of 1:80–1: 40 (No. 3, 6, 7, 1, 4, 9); in the remaining animals the precipitin titers were very low or absent altogether.

The reaction of the organism to an antigenic stimulus in threshold dose was thus sharply attenuated or, in a considerable number of cases, completely suppressed in these experiments on guinea pigs. The selection of the guinea pig, a weaker producer of antibodies than the rabbit, as the experimental animals and the employment of the protein stimulus in threshold dose were determined by our desire to investigate this phenomenon in conditions as close to physiological as possible.

In another series of experiments on rabbits (Luk'ianenko) subcutaneous saline injections (2 ml) were given regularly for 60 days and the indifferent stimulus (saline) was then replaced by and E. coli vaccine (dose 2×10^9 bacterial cells). Reaction to the first injection of antigen was completely inhibited in all the experimental animals (No. 1, 2, 3, 4, 5, 6, 7), whereas definite antibody production was noted in control animals (No. 1, 2, 3). Thereafter, these experimental rabbits continued to receive saline injections as before for a further 21 days. During this period both the experimental and control rabbits received two injections of antigen in the same dose as

Behavior and Immune Function

before. Some of the experimental animals remained areactive to the antigen (No. 2, 3, 5, 7) and in others the reaction took the form of a sluggish and inconsiderable increase of antibodies to 1:25–1:50 (No. 1, 4, 6); in the case of the control animals the antibody titers reached were 1:800 in rabbit No. 1, 1:1600 in rabbit No. 2 and 1:800 in rabbit No. 3.

Comparison of these investigations with the preceding experiments brought out clearly the importance of the degree of stability of the experimentally created dynamic stereotype (consolidation of the stereotype by twice the number of experiments) and of the strength of the antigenic stimulus (*E. coli* is an antigen with weak immunogenic properties in comparison with paratyphoid and dysentery antigens) in determining the intensity of the inhibition of immunological reactions by dynamic stereotype mechanisms.

Experiments carried out by Flerov, also on rabbits, showed that fatal results from the injection of lethal doses of tetanus toxin could be delayed or, in some cases, completely averted by dynamic stereotype mechanisms, an observation which confirmed the earlier results of Karpov *et al.* [11]. In these experiments the animals were given daily intramuscular injections of 4 ml 25% magnesium sulfate solution under stereotype conditions. After 26 such injections a lethal dose of tetanus toxin in a volume of 4 ml was injected instead of the magnesium sulfate. Although toxin was injected, the development of a pathological process was considerably reduced: two of the four animals survived and in the other two the development of the tetanus toxemia was markedly retarded, the average survival period of these animals being 249 hr, whereas all three rabbits of the control group died after an average period of 90 hr (Fig. 3). Three rabbits also died (with an average survival period of 128 hr) in a second experimental group of animals, the experiments on which were carried out with intentional variation of the conditions attaching to the experimental setting (time of day, methods of fixing the animal, etc.) for the purpose of preventing the formation of a dynamic stereotype.

These findings indicate that the physiological strength of and the part played by the dynamic stereotype in changing the resistance of the organism are determined by the combination of the entire complex of external and internal stimuli into a united system.

We also thought it important that the central mechanisms and conditions contributing to inhibition of the reaction of the organism to protein stimuli in allergic states should be in-

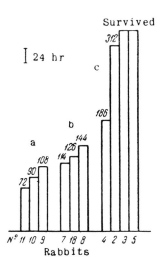

FIGURE 3. Comparative survival periods of rabbits. (A) Control. (B) Experimental, second group. (C) Experimental, first group.

vestigated. This was even more important in that the allergic state is in fact the reverse aspect of immunity. Existing reports of investigations on mechanisms for the nervous regulation of allergic reactions do not touch at all on the applicability in these cases of the dynamic stereotype patterns, although study of these problems as manifestations of increased resistance to unusual stimuli of various origins is a task of first-rate importance.

For the experimental treatment of this problem we selected the model of a local manifestation of an allergic reaction (Arthus-Sakharov phenomenon) and its generalized form (anaphylactic reaction). One series of investigations (Luk'ianenko and Flerov) demonstrated, in experiments on rabbits, that the Arthus-Sakharov phenomenon could be suppressed by the mechanisms of a consolidated stereotype of reactions to the injection of isotonic sodium chloride solution. In these experiments consolidation of the stereotype to the subcutaneous injection of saline (20 injections) was followed immediately by six subcutaneous injections of horse serum 5 ml at intervals of 5 to 6 days. The stereotype of saline injections was maintained in the intervals between the injections of serum. Under these conditions the protein injections lost their characteristic allergic effect entirely. When repeated injections of horse serum (5 ml every 5–6 days) were given to control rabbits, there was development of an exudative, necrotic, hemorrhagic inflammation with subsequent separation of the necrosed area of skin.

Another series of experiments, carried out by Luk'ianenko, proved that the anaphylactic reaction to the injection of a precipitating dose of protein could be considerably attenuated or inhibited if the horse serum were injected on the background of a firmly established stereotype produced by regular saline injections.

Under strictly standardized experimental conditions, the experimental guinea pigs were given regular subcutaneous injections of 1 ml saline. After 15 injections a sensitizing dose of protein (1 ml of 1:100 dilution) was injected subcutaneously under the same experimental conditions. The saline injections were continued thereafter for 25 days under stereotype experimental conditions, and a provocative dose of protein (1 ml of 40–80% horse serum) was given in the 41st experiment with strict observation of all the experimental conditions. Figure 4 shows the degree of prominence of the reaction in response to the injection of anaphylactogen in this series of experiments. Fifteen of the 25 guinea pigs were experimental animals and ten controls. A first group of controls (No. 42, 43, 44, 45, 46) served as clean controls for production of the anaphylactic reaction apart from any additional interference; the animals in the second control group (No. 47, 48, 49, 50, 51) were given daily saline injections, but with deliberate variation of the experimental conditions (different experimental setting, differences in

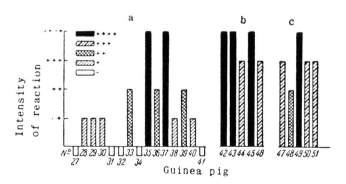

FIGURE 4. Effect of a dynamic stereotype on the prominence of the anaphylactic reaction. (a) Experimental group. (b) Control, first group. (c) Control, second group.

time of day, site of injection and the method of fixing the animal), the purpose of which was to prevent the formation of a dynamic stereotype.

Five (No. 27, 31, 32, 34, 41) of the 15 experimental animals reacted to the injection of the provocative dose by acute general inhibition, with loss of unconditioned (orienting, alimentary) and conditioned natural alimentary reflexes. Slight forms (+) of anaphylactic shock were seen in guinea pigs No. 28, 29, 30, 38, and 40. Three (No. 33, 36, 39) exhibited moderate degrees (+ +) of shock and guinea pigs No. 35 and 37 died (+ + + +). Grave states of shock, terminating fatally, developed in animals of both control groups (No. 42, 43, and 45 of the first control group and No. 49 of the second). The results obtained with the second control group show how important meticulous observation of standardized experimental conditions in the formation of the dynamic stereotype is in these complicated and prolonged experiments. The experiments also showed that regular injections of saline did not act as a desensitizing factor.

The intensity of the inhibitory effect of dynamic stereotype mechanisms in relation to sensitization of the animal was also studied as part of an investigation on the role of a dynamic stereotype in the suppression of anaphylactic shock in a model of passive anaphylaxis (experiments of Luk'ianenko). Forty guinea pigs (20 experimental and 20 control) were sensitized to rabbit serum precipitating equine protein in dilution of 1:10,000. In the case of 20 guinea pigs the sensitizing dose of serum was injected after consolidation of a dynamic stereotype elaborated over a period of 70 days to subcutaneous injections of saline. Simultaneously, the other 20 guinea pigs (control group) were given the sensitizing injection of serum without the preliminary elaboration of a stereotype to saline injections. After 24 hr both experimental and control animals were given intracardiac injections of 0.05–0.1 ml whole horse serum as a provocative dose.

The result was that 12 of the 20 experimental animals survived and 8 died, shock reactions of various intensities being noted in nine of the surviving guinea pigs and pronounced general inhibition in the remaining three. Seventeen of the 20 guinea pigs in the control group died with signs of acute shock. The mortality of the control animals was thus twice that of the control group. In addition, death was significantly delayed in the case of some of the experimental animals: the experimental animals died after 8 to 16 hr whereas the corresponding period in the control group was 2–5 min.

These findings indicate that, while there was considerable attenuation of the effect of the provocative dose of protein, the process of sensitization was not, under these particular experimental conditions, subject to the inhibitory effect of dynamic stereotype mechanisms. This should possibly be connected with the particular conditions attaching to the arrangement of the experiment, in which the sensitizing effect of serum had only a short period (not more than a few days) in which to develop, and with the inadequacy of the time parameters for development of the retarding effect of the stereotype in relation to the sensitizing process. The mechanisms engendered by systematized, regular action could thus attenuate or completely inhibit both the local allergic reaction (Arthus-Sakharov phenomenon) and the generalized allergic reaction.

There was then another series of experiments (V. I. Luk'ianenko) on the development of the complement reactions as one of the components of natural immunity. Under standardized experimental conditions, guinea pigs were given regular subcutaneous saline injections (1 ml). At the time for the 16th injection all the experimental animals were given a sensitizing dose of 1 ml whole horse serum diluted 1:100. The saline injections were then continued for a further 25 days. When the number of injections had reached 40 the saline was suddenly replaced by the injection of 1 ml horse serum diluted 1:1. Figure 5 shows that the complement titers were reduced in only two (No. 6, 13) of the 15 experimental animals, to 0.20 and 0.22, as against initial values of 0.08 and 0.10, respectively. The complement titers in the remaining 13 animals were almost unchanged. All ten control guinea pigs reacted to the same dose of protein by a

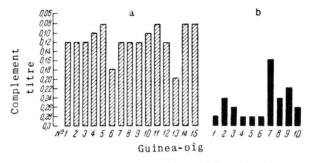

FIGURE 5. (a) Experimental guinea pigs. (b) Control guinea pigs.

pronounced decline in the level of complement (to 0.22–0.28). These experiments showed that the dynamic stereotype mechanisms could prevent reduction in the complement titer when provocative doses of horse serum, producing subacute or chronic shock, were injected into sensitized animals. Proof is thus afforded of the nervous control of such an important factor in natural immunity as complement. These facts are in agreement with observations made in L. A. Zil'ber's laboratory on the conditioned reflex regulation of another component of natural immunity, namely lysozyme.

The experimental results described in this paper, demonstrating the part played by and the importance of mechanisms associated with systematized action in the regulation of the defensive functions of the organism, are in accord with findings obtained by other investigators in relation to tetanus toxemia (Karpov et al [11]), foot and mouth disease (Gar'yan [1]), phagocytic activity (Kiutukchiev et al., 1954), leukocytic reactions (Gel'dyeva [2]) and also antibody formation (Yakovlev, 1955; Sakanian and Kostanian, 1957), all proving that the effects of unconditioned antigenic and toxic stimuli were determined in considerable degree by experimentally produced readjustment of the nervous system. The results of our investigations along with other published findings on the role of the dynamic stereotype as a composite, united system of unconditioned and conditioned reflexes, in immune and allergic processes serve to emphasize the fact that all manifestations of these intimate body reactions are controlled by the higher divisions of the brain.

An ultimate understanding of all the multiform manifestations of the higher regulating mechanisms for defensive functions, an understanding which is essential for the development of theoretical and practical immunology, will be successfully acquired if physiologists, immunologists and neurochemists combine their productive efforts. These investigations require that there should be wide use of the latest physiological, serological, and biochemical methods.

REFERENCES

1. Gar'yan, B. V., O roli nervnoi sistemy v patogeneze yashura. (The Nervous System in the Pathogenesis of Foot and Mouth Disease.) Moscow, 1955.
2. Gel'dyeva, A. G., Izv. Akad. Nauk Turkm. SSR No. 2, 1955.
3. Dzhmukhadze, A. P., Dzheiranishvili, V. V. and Dosychev, A. I., Zh. vyssh. nervn. deiatel. **10:** No. 4, 1960.
4. Dolin, A. O., Arkh. biol. nauk **56:** No. 3, 1941; Tez. dokl. VII Vses. s''ezda fiziol., biokhim. i farmakol. (Proceedings of Seventh All-Union Congress of Physiologists, Biochemists and Pharmacologists.) **1:** 147, 1947; Trud. Nevropatol. L-da **2:** 94, 1949.

5. Dolin A. O., Tez. dokl. VIII Vses. s''ezda fiziol., biokhim. i farmakol. (Proceedings of Eighth All-Union Congress of Physiologists, Biochemists and Pharmacologists.) **1:** 1955.

6. Dolin, A. O. and Krylov, V. N., Zh. vyssh. nervn. deyatel. **2:** No. 4, 1952.

7. Zhukov-Verezhnikov, N. N., Zh. vyssh. nervn. deyatel. **2:** No. 1, 1952.

8. Zdrodovskii, O. F., Sovremennoe sostoyanie eksperimental'noi immunologii i ee blizhaishie zadachi. (Present State of Experimental Immunology and its Immediate Tasks.) Moscow, 1956.

9. Zdrodovskii, P. F., Vestn. Akad. Med. Nauk SSSR No.1, 1958.

10. Zil'ber, L. A., Osnovy immunologii. (Fundamentals of Immunology.) Moscow, 1958.

11. Karpov, M. K., Lebedinskii, V. A. and Minaev, A. V., Zh. mikrobiol., epidemiol. i immunol. No. 5, 1955.

12. Krylov, V. N., Zh. mikrobiol., epidemiol. i immunol. No. 5, 1956; *ibid.* No. 10, 1959.

13. Luk'ianenko, V. I., Zh. mikrobiol., epidemiol. i immunol. No. 10, 1959.

14. Luk'ianenko, V. I., Tez. II Vses. nauchn. konfer. stud. biol., posvyashch. pamyati. J. Lamarck i C. Darwin. (Proceedings of Second All-Union Conference of Student-Biologists, Dedicated to the Memory of J. Lamarck and C. Darwin.) Moscow, 1959.

15. Metal'nikov, S. I., Dokl. na Mezhdunar. knogr. zoologov v Lissabone. (Proceedings of International Congress of Zoologists at Lisbon.) 1935/1936.

16. Speranskii, A. D., Elementy postroeniya teorii v meditsiny. (Elements for the Construction of a Theory of Medicine.) Moscow and Leningrad, 1935.

36

BEHAVIORALLY CONDITIONED IMMUNOSUPPRESSION

Robert Ader and Nicholas Cohen

An illness-induced taste aversion was conditioned in rats by pairing saccharin with cyclophosphamide, an immunosuppressive agent. Three days after conditioning, all animals were injected with sheep erythrocytes. Hemagglutinating antibody titers measured 6 days after antigen administration were high in placebo-treated rats. High titers were also observed in nonconditioned animals and in conditioned animals that were not subsequently exposed to saccharin. No agglutinating antibody was detected in conditioned animals treated with cyclophosphamide at the time of antigen administration. Conditioned animals exposed to saccharin at the time of or following the injection of antigen were significantly immunosuppressed. An illness-induced taste aversion was also conditioned using LiCl, a nonimmunosuppressive agent. In this instance, however, there was no attenuation of hemagglutinating antibody titers in response to injection with antigen.

INTRODUCTION

The hypothesis that immunosuppression might be behaviorally conditioned was invoked to explain certain incidental observations made in a study of illness-induced taste aversion [1]. In the illness-induced taste aversion paradigm [2–4] an animal is given a distinctively flavored drinking solution such as saccharin, which is followed by a toxic agent capable of eliciting temporary gastrointestinal upset. Lithium chloride, apomorphine, and cyclophosphamide are but a few of the toxins that are effective in inducing a taste aversion after a single trial in which the toxin (the unconditioned stimulus or US) is paired with a novel drinking solution (the conditioned stimulus or CS). By pairing different volumes of a preferred saccharin solution with a single intraperitoneal (ip) injection of 50 mg/kg cyclophosphamide (CY), rats acquired an aversion to the saccharin solution; the magnitude of the reduction in saccharin intake and the resistance to extinction of this aversion were directly related to the volume of saccharin consumed on the day of conditioning. It was also observed that some of the cyclophosphamide-treated animals died and that mortality rate tended to vary directly with the volume of saccharin originally consumed.

In order to account for this observation, it was hypothesized that the pairing of a neutral stimulus (saccharin) with cyclophosphamide, an immunosuppressive agent [5], resulted in the conditioning of immunosuppression. If the conditioned animals that were exposed to saccharin every 2 days over a period of 2 months responded to this conditioned stimulus by becoming immunologically impaired,

From the Departments of Psychiatry and Microbiology, University of Rochester School of Medicine and Dentistry, Rochester, New York 14642.

Presented at the Annual Meeting, American Psychosomatic Society, March 23, 1975, New Orleans.

This research was supported by Grants K5-MH-06318 to RA and K4-AI-70736 and 9R01-HDA1-07901 to NC from the United States Public Health Service and by funds generously provided by Mr. Arthur M. Lowenthal of Rochester, New York.

Reprinted from *Psychosom. Med.* **37** (No. 4), 333–340.

they would have been more vulnerable to the superimposition of latent pathogens that may have existed in the environment.

We report here our initial documentation of behaviorally conditioned immunosuppression.

METHODS

Ninety-six male Charles River (CD) rats, approximately 3 months old, were individually caged under a 12 hr light-dark cycle (light from 5 AM to 5 PM) and provided with food and water ad libitum. During a period of adaptation the daily provision of tap water was slowly reduced until all animals were provided with and consumed their total daily allotment during a single 15 min period (between 9 and 10 AM). This regimen was maintained throughout the experiment. The first 5 days under this regimen provided data on the baseline intake of water under these conditions.

On the day of conditioning (Day 0), animals were randomly distributed into conditioned, nonconditioned, and placebo groups. Conditioned animals received a 0.1% saccharin chloride solution of tap water during their 15 min drinking period and 30 min later were given ip injections of CY (50 mg/kg in a volume of 1.5 ml/kg).[1] Nonconditioned animals were, as usual, provided with plain tap water and 30 min after drinking were similarly injected with CY. Placebo animals received plain water and ip injections of an equal volume of vehicle (distilled water). On the following two days all animals were provided with plain water during their 15 min drinking period.

Three days after conditioning all animals were injected ip with antigen, 2 ml/kg of a 1% thrice washed suspension of sheep red blood cells (SRBC; approximately 3×10^8 cells/ml). Thirty minutes later randomly selected subgroups of conditioned and nonconditioned animals were provided with saccharin or plain water and/or received ip injections of CY or saline according to the treatment schedule outlined in Table 1.

One group of conditioned animals received a single drinking bottle containing the saccharin solution and drinking was followed by a saline injection; these animals constituted an experimental group. Two additional groups of conditioned animals received plain water; one of these groups was subsequently injected with CY (in order to define the unconditioned response produced by the immunosup-

---

[1]Cyclophosphamide was generoulsy supplied by the Mead Johnson Research Center, Evansville, Indiana.

TABLE 1. Experimental Treatments

Group	Day 0		Subgroup	N	Day 3		Day 6	
	Drnk. Soln.	Inj.			Drnk. Soln.	Inj.	Drnk. Soln.	Inj.
Conditioned (N= 67)	Saach.	CY	CS₁	11	Sacch	Sal	H₂O	—
				9	H₂O	—	Sacch	Sal
			CS₀	10	H₂O	Sal	H₂O	—
				9	H₂O	—	H₂O	Sal
			US	10	H₂O	CY	H₂O	—
				9	H₂O	—	H₂O	CY
			CS₂	9	Sacch	Sal	Saach	—
Nonconditioned (N=19)	H₂O	CY	NC	10	Sacch	Sal	H₂O	—
				9	H₂O	—	Sacch	Sal
Placebo (N=10)	H₂O	Placebo	P	10	H₂O	—	H₂O	—

pressive drug) while the second received saline (as a control for taste aversion conditioning, per se). Following antigen administration a nonconditioned group was provided with saccharin and injected with saline. These animals provided a control for the effects of saccharin consumption and the ip injections. Placebo animals remained unmanipulated and received plain water during the 15 min drinking period. On Day 6 of the experiment, conditioned and nonconditioned animals that had received antigen but had not been manipulated on Day 3 were first treated as described for Day 3, i.e., one conditioned group received the saccharin drinking solution, one conditioned group received water and CY, and one conditioned group received neither saccharin nor CY; a nonconditioned group also received saccharin. In addition, there was one experimental sample of conditioned animals that was provided with saccharin on Days 3 and 6. All animals remained unmanipulated on Days 7 and 8. Throughout this period the volume of plain water or saccharin consumed was measured daily.

On Day 9 (6 days after injection with SRBC), all animals were sacrificed. Trunk blood was collected in heparinized tubes for subsequent analysis of plasma corticosterone (8) and in nonheparinized tubes for the collection of sera to be used in the hemagglutinating antibody assay. Serum from each rat was heat inactivated (56°C for 30 min) and divided into aliquots some of which were stored at -70°C and others of which were refrigerated and assayed for hemagglutinating antibody activity within 24 hr of collection. Antibody titrations were performed according to standard procedures in microtiter trays and hemagglutination was assessed under the microscope. Titers were recorded as reciprocals of the endpoint dilutions expressed as powers of the base$_2$.

The provision of plain water or saccharin and the injections of CY or placebo were conducted from coded data sheets. Similarly, antibody titrations and plasma corticosterone determinations were conducted without knowledge of the group to which an animal belonged.

RESULTS AND DISCUSSION

Cyclophosphamide treatment administered 30 min after the ingestion of a novel saccharin drinking solution resulted in an aversion to the saccharin solution (Fig 1).

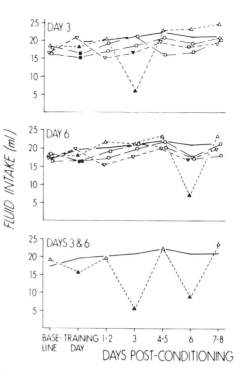

Fig. 1. Mean intake of plain water (open symbols) and saccharin (filled symbols) for placebo (———) and nonconditioned (▼) animals, and conditioned animals that received saccharin (Δ), cyclophosphamide (□), or neither (○) on Day 3, Day 6, or Days 3 and 6. As a point of reference, the placebo-treated animals are shown in each panel.

Conditioned animals provided with saccharin on Day 3, on Day 6, or on Days 3 and 6 showed a reduced intake of the distinctively flavored solution on those days.

With regard to antibody responses, the following pattern of results was predicted. Sera from placebo-treated animals were expected to be relatively high titered. Nonconditioned animals, although subsequently presented with a saccharin drinking solution, were also expected to show high antibody levels. However, it was anticipated that the titers of sera from nonconditioned animals might be somewhat lower than those of placebo animals as a result of the CY administered 3 days before injection with SRBS (6,7). Sera from conditioned animals that were given antigen but never again exposed to either saccharin or CY were expected to have antibody titers equivalent to those of unconditioned animals. Conditioned animals that were given a second injection of CY, an unconditioned stimulus for immunosuppression, were expected to show a minimum antibody response to SRBC. The critical groups for testing the hypothesis that immunosuppression can be behaviorally conditioned were the conditioned animals that were given one or two exposures to saccharin, the conditioned stimulus, following exposure to SRBC. Evidence in support of the hypothesis would be provided by an attenuation of the antibody response in these animals.

Antibody titers from the several groups are shown in Fig. 2. Conditioned animals exposed to saccharin on Day 3 or Day 6 did not differ and were combined to form a single conditioned group (group CS) that received only one exposure to the conditioned stimulus, saccharin. Similarly, the conditioned animals that remained unmanipulated (group CS0), the conditioned groups treated with CY on Day 3 or 6 (group US), and the nonconditioned animals given saccharin on Day 3 or 6 (group NC) were combined into single groups.

The results were as we had predicted. Placebo-treated animals showed the highest antibody titers. Conditioned animals that received neither saccharin nor CY and nonconditioned animals that were subsequently exposed to saccharin after antigen

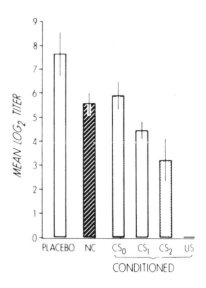

Fig. 2. Hemagglutination titers (means ± SE) obtained 6 days after ip injection of antigen (SRBC). NC = nonconditioned animals provided with saccharin on Day 3 or Day 6; CS_0 = conditioned animals that did not receive saccharin following antigen treatment; CS_1 = conditioned animals given one exposure to saccharin on Day 3 or Day 6; CS_2 = conditioned animals exposed to saccharin on Days 3 and 6; US = conditioned animals injected with cyclophosphamide following treatment with antigen.

treatment showed similar hemagglutination titers that were also relatively high, although significantly lower than the titers of immune sera from placebo animals in the case of both unconditioned ($t = 2.07, P < 0.05$) and conditioned ($t = 1.71, P < 0.10$) animals.[2] As expected, the hemagglutination tests revealed that administration of CY after SRBC caused complete

[2]The significance levels reported in the text are based on two-tailed t-tests. Based on the specific differences that were predicted, however, it would be appropriate to report one-tailed probabilities and the reader may wish to interpret the results in this light.

Behavior and Immune Function

immunosuppression. Conditioned animals that experience a single exposure to saccharin following antigen treatment (group CS$_1$) showed an antibody response that was significantly lower than that of placebo as well as nonconditioned animals ($t = 1.96, P < 0.05$) and conditioned animals that were not exposed to saccharin ($t = 2.14, P < 0.05$). The conditioned animals that experience two exposures to saccharin also showed an attentuated antibody response that was significantly below all other groups with the exception of the conditioned animals that received only one exposure to the conditioned stimulus.

Relative to placebo-treated animals, the reduction in hemagglutinating antibody titers shown by nonconditioned animals (group NC) and conditioned animals that were not given either saccharin or CY after antigen treatment (group CS$_0$) is most simply explained as resulting from some residual effect of CY administered on the day of conditioning (3 days prior to injection with SRBC) (9). These groups, then, become the relevant control condition against which to assess the antibody responses of the conditioned animals exposed to saccharin following antigen treatment. This latter condition did not result in complete suppression of the immune response, but conditioned animals exposed to saccharin did show a significant attentuation of the antibody response relative to these control groups. The attentuation would not appear to have resulted from saccharin, per se, since a comparable exposure to saccharin in association with and following antigen treatment was experienced by the nonconditioned animals for whom saccharin was not a conditioned stimulus. Also, behavioral conditioning, per se, did not result in antibody titers that differed from those of nonconditioned animals. The results, then, support the notion that the association of saccharin with CY enabled saccharin to elicit a conditioned immunosuppressive response.

The present study yielded little additional data that would be of direct importance in suggesting an explanation for this phenomenon. There were no differences among the several groups in body weight measured prior to the adaptation period, on the day before conditioning, or at the time that animals were sacrificed. Also, in conditioned animals exposed to saccharin there were nonsignificant correlations ranging from -0.34 to 0.16 between hemagglutination titer and volume of saccharin consumed. The correlation between plasma corticosterone level sampled at the time that animals were sacrificed and antibody titer was virtually zero, and there were no group differences in steroid levels at this time.

Consistent with the known immunosuppressive properties of adrenocortical steroids and despite the failure to observe differences in plasma corticosterone levels *at the time of sacrifice*, it could be postulated that the attentuated antibody response observed in conditioned animals is a reflection of a nonspecific "stress" response to the conditioning procedures, or, perhaps, of a behaviorally conditioned elevation in steroid level in response to saccharin. Further support for such an explanation might be derived from the relationship between immune processes and physical and socioenvironmental "stress" or emotional responses (11–19) which, presumably, act through the hypothalamus, and from the several studies (e.g., 20,21) that suggest that hypothalamic lesions may influence some immune responses.

In order to evaluate the possibility that

an elevation in adrenocortical steroids was responsible for the attentuation of antibody titers in conditioned animals, a second study used lithium chloride instead of cyclophosphamide as the US in inducing a taste aversion. Whereas lithium chloride also produces noxious gastrointestinal effects, it is not immunosuppressive. In this study, antigen was injected 5 days after conditioning, and the population of conditioned animals that was subsequently provided with the saccharin drinking solution (Group CS, N = 10) was exposed to the CS three times: at the time of injection with SRBC, and 2 and 4 days later. As in the first experiment, all animals were sacrificed 6 days after treatment with antigen.

The association of LiCl with saccharin was effective in inducing an aversion to the saccharin solution. Conditioned animals showed a 66% reduction in consumption of the saccharin solution on the initial test day relative to the intake measured on the day of conditioning. This corresponds closely to the 61%–68% reductions shown by animals conditioned with cyclophosphamide. Antibody titers for the conditioned animals and for the several control groups are shown in Fig. 3. As indicated by the high titers found in animals injected with LiCl at the time of injection with SRBC, LiCl is not an unconditioned stimulus for suppression of the immune response. Although conditioning was effective in inducing an avoidance of the CS solution, antibody titers were similar in all groups.

It is not unreasonable to assume that an elevation in steroid levels might accompany the conditioning of a taste aversion. Nevertheless, the present data provide no support for the hypothesis that such an elevation in steroid levels could have been solely responsible for the attentuated im-

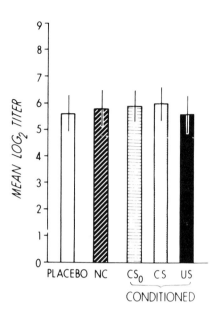

Fig. 3. Hemagglutination titers (means ± SE) obtained 6 days after ip injection of SRBC in animals conditioned with LiCl as the US. NC = nonconditioned animals; CS_0 = conditioned animals that did not receive saccharin following antigen treatment; CS = conditioned animals given three exposures to saccharin; US = conditioned animals injected with LiCl following treatment with antigen.

mune response that was observed when conditioned animals were exposed to a CS previously associated with the administration of an immunosuppressive agent. The probability of an interaction between the magnitude and/or duration of an elevation in steroid level and the residual effects of cyclophosphamide, however, remains as a viable hypothesis.

The present results suggest, again, that there may be an intimate and virtually unexplored relationship between the central nervous system and immunologic processes and that the application of behavioral conditioning techniques provides a means for studying this relationship in the intact animal. Confirmation of the capacity of behavioral conditioning procedures to suppress (or elicit) immune responses would raise innumerable issues regarding the normal operation and modifiability of the immune system in particular and the mediation of individual differences in the body's natural armamentarium for adaptation and survival in general. Such data also suggest a mechanism that may be involved in the complex pathogenesis of psychosomatic disease and bear eloquent witness to the principle of a very basic integration of biologic and psychologic function.

SUMMARY

The present study was designed to examine the possibility that behavioral conditioning techniques could be used to modify immune processes.

An illness-induced taste aversion was conditioned in rats by pairing saccharin (CS) with cyclophosphamide (CY), an immunosuppressive agent (US). Three days after conditioning, animals received ip injections of SRBC; 30 min later, subgroups of conditioned animals were (a) supplied with the CS solution, (b) provided with water but injected with the US, or (c) given neither CS nor US. A nonconditioned group was provided with the saccharin drinking solution, and a placebo group was injected with antigen but was otherwise unmanipulated.

The association of saccharin and CY was effective in inducing an aversion to the CS when it was presented 3 days after conditioning (at the time of antigen administration). Hemagglutinating antibody titers measured 6 days after injection of SRBC were high in placebo-treated rats. Relatively high titers were also observed in nonconditioned animals and in conditioned animals that were not subsequently exposed to the CS. No agglutinating antibody was detected in conditioned animals treated with CY at the time of antigen administration. In contrast, conditioned animals exposed to the CS when injected with SRBC (and /or 3 days later in additional samples of conditioned animals) were significantly immunosuppressed.

Similar procedures were used in a second experiment in which LiCl, a nonimmunosuppressive agent, was used as the US. While LiCl was effective in inducing a taste aversion, conditioned animals showed no attentuation of hemagglutinating antibody titers.

The results are interpreted as providing evidence for behaviorally conditioned immunosuppression. Further, it is suggested that this phenomenon is not mediated directly by nonspecific elevations in adrenocortical steroids that may be presumed to accompany an illness-induced taste aversion.

The authors acknowledge with gratitude the technical assistance of Elsje Schotman, Sumico Nagai, Darbbie Mahany, and Betty Rizen.

REFERENCES

1. Ader R: Letter to the editor. Psychosom Med 36:183–184, 1974
2. Garcia J, Ervin RF, Koelling RA: Learning with prolonged delay of reinforcement. Psychon Sci 5:121–122, 1966

3. Garcia J, Kimmeldorf R, Koelling R: Conditioned aversion to saccharin resulting from exposure to gamma radiation. Science 122:157–158, 1955

4. Garcia J, McGowan BK, Ervin RF, Koelling RA: Cues: Their relative effectiveness as a function of the reinforcer. Science 160:794–795, 1968

5. Gershwin ME, Goetzl EJ, Steinberg AD: Cyclophosphamide: Use in practice. Ann Intern Med 80:531–540, 1974

6. Santos GW, Owens HA, Jr: A comparison of selected cytotoxic agents on the primary agglutinin response in rats injected with sheep erythrocytes. Bull Johns Hopkins Hosp 114:384–401, 1964

7. Makinodan T, Santos GW, Quinn RP: Immunosuppressive drugs. Pharmacol Rev 22:198–247, 1970

8. Friedman SB, Ader R, Grota LJ, Larson T: Plasma corticosterone response to parameters of electric shock stimulation in the rat. Psychosom Med 29:323–329, 1967

9. Miller TE, North JDK: Host response in urinary tract infections. Kidney Int 5:179–185, 1974

10. Zurier RB, Weissman G: Anti-immunologic and anti-inflammatory effects of steroid therapy. Med Clin North Am 57:1295–1307, 1973

11. Brayton AR Brain PF: Studies on the effects of differential housing on some measures of disease resistance in male and female laboratory mice. J Endocrinol 61:xlviii–xlix, 1974

12. Fessel WJ: Mental stress, blood proteins, and the hypothalamus. Arch Gen Psychiatry 7:427–435, 1962

13. Gisler RH: Stress and the hormonal regulation of the immune response in mice. Psychother Psychosom 23:197–208, 1974

14. Hamilton DR: Immunosuppressive effects of predator induced stress in mice with acquired immunity to *Hymenolepis nana*. J Psychosom Res 18:143–153, 1974

15. Hill OW, Greer WE, Felsenfeld O: Psychological stress, early response to foreign protein, and blood cortisol in vervets. Psychosom Med 29:279–283, 1967

16. Solomon GF, Amkraut AA, Kasper P: Immunity, emotions and stress. Psychother Psychosom 23:209–217, 1974

17. Solomon GF, Moos RH: Emotions, immunity, and disease. Arch Gen Psychiatry 11:657–674, 1964

18. Vessey SH: Effects of grouping on levels of circulating antibodies in mice. Proc Soc Exp Biol Med 115:252–255, 1964

19. Wistar R, Hildemann WH: Effect of stress on skin transplantation immunity in mice. Science 131:159–160, 1960

20. Korneva EA, Kahl LM: Effect of destruction of hypothalamic areas on immunogenesis. Fed Proc 23:T88–T92, 1964

37

THE INFLUENCE OF PSYCHIC ACTS ON THE PROGRESS OF PULMONARY TUBERCULOSIS[1]

Tohru Ishigami

Recently a relation between physiological activities and psychical changes has been established by actual experimentation in several instances. Pawlow (1902) and his pupils noted such a relationship in the study of gastric secretion. Cannon (1910–1911) and his pupils have recorded an increase in the adrenal secretion and an increase in the blood sugar associated with psychical excitation. It has long been recognized that the mental state of a patient has a great deal to do with his reaction to disease. I have noted this relationship in the treatment of tuberculosis. It thus became of interest to study the relation between various mental states and the opsonin production in tuberculous patients. Attracted by the observations of Cannon, I have attempted to ascertain whether the change in sugar metabolism and secretion of adrenaline have any association with the change in the opsonic index. To determine this both animal and test tube experiments have been performed.

Clinical Observations

Since 1906, I have conducted a series of opsonin examinations in a large number of tuberculous patients. In general it has been found that the opsonic index of patients with advanced tuberculosis is lower than in the less advanced cases, and that the proper treatment with the injection of antigen and immune serum gradually raises the index until an index of 1 or 2.5 is reached. Patients gain in weight simultaneously. In untreated cases, the index is generally higher in those with a more favorable prognosis. When the index fluctuates constantly, with occasional high index but usually low, prognosis is invariably unfavorable. These observations have been reported previously.

Sudden lowering of the opsonic index is frequently the result either of improper administration of tuberculin and other injected materials or to excessive exertion on the part of the patients (auto-inoculation). A high febrile condition invariably sets in, and subsides to normal in the course of a few days. In cases where neither one of the above factors can be traced as causing the lowering of the opsonic index, high fever usually does not occur, and the opsonic index returns to normal in 2 or 3 days.

The conditions leading to this latter phenomenon have been found to be associated with mental excitation. The cause of this mental change may have been a letter from home or a

[1]Translated by Goichi Asami, Washington University School of Medicine, Saint Louis, Missouri.

Reprinted with permission from *Amer. Rev. Tuberculosis* **2**, 470–484. Copyright © 1918–1919, American Review of Respiratory Disease.

conversation with visitors which caused the patient to worry and lie awake the night before examination. The depressed opsonic index lasts only a few days as usual, but, if circumstances causing such mental states are prolonged, the return to the normal index is correspondingly delayed, giving rise to what Wright terms the "cumulative negative phase." The course of the disease is made gradually worse, with loss of appetite, insomnia, and high fever. Local symptoms increase, and the opsonic index is kept low. The personal history usually reveals failure in business, lack of harmony in the family, or jealousy of some sort. Nervous individuals are especially prone to attacks of this type, and the prognosis is generally bad.

On the other hand, patients with extensive local manifestations and with sputum rich in microorganisms may have a comparatively high opsonic index and the disease follow a favorable course. These patients are found to be optimistic and not easily worried.

Again, in chronic cases, patients may go on apparently well without any subjective knowledge of symptoms, with a relatively high opsonic index until some misfortune happens. This immediately alters the course of the disease. Patients beyond the secondary stage may appear well while nursing their consumptive mother, wife, child, or some such close relatives. However, should their dear ones happen to die, with the subsequent despair comes a sudden appearance of severe symptoms with a lowered opsonic index. These cases may die.

The above are only a few instances of my clinical observations extending over a period of 10 years. Since any number of clinicians will substantiate these statements, I shall avoid the cumbersome task of citing further cases.

The significant point in my observations lies in the determinations of the relationship existing between clinical symptoms and opsonic indices which are influenced by psychic states.

To determine whether or not an actual increase of the sugar in the blood is produced by psychic excitations, a urine analysis was made weekly or, in cases deemed necessary, daily in 140 cases. Of these, 30% or 42 patients showed glycosuria, as follows:

Number of patients examined for glycosuria	140
Number of patients showing glycosuria	42 or 30%
Number of patients who had glycosuria previous to admission to the Institute	2
Number of patients showing transient glycosuria	40

Of these cases, 26, or 65%, had advanced tuberculosis, and 14, or 35%, were less advanced cases. They were all nervous individuals, being easily excited by trivial things. The opsonic index was low in each case. Urine analysis was made by combined Trommer and Nielander methods in the uncertain cases. The phenylhydrazine method, the polariscope, and fermentation methods were also used.

It is interesting to note that out of 140 cases, 7 were fatal during the last 4 months and all of these had a glycosuria. It is true that all consumptive patients may excrete sugar either transiently or continuously prior to death.

Animal Experimentation

The influence of adrenaline and glucose upon the opsonin reaction was determined by examination of phagocytosis after intraperitoneal injection of a mixture of these substances and emulsions of tubercle bacilli in one series, and by intraperitoneal injections of bacillary emulsion into animals which were previously inoculated subcutaneously with adrenaline and glucose.

Several loop-fulls of young cultures of tubercle bacilli of known virulence were freed from moisture with filter paper, ground in a mortar, and suspended in a definite quantity of isotonic sodium chloride solution. The emulsion was filtered through paper and the filtrate was centrifugalized. A supernatant fluid portion was used which, upon examination, presented from 10 to 15 organisms per optical field.

An alcohol and ether mixture was used in fixing the specimens. Ziehl-Gabett solution was used for staining. Dilute methyl orange was used as counterstain. One hundred phagocytes, chiefly polymorphonuclears, were examined for the number of organisms engulfed in each. Organisms engulfed in a lump were counted as one, and a cell containing over six organisms was considered as containing five organisms.

Series 1

In this series mixtures of a suspension of tubercle bacilli with adrenaline and glucose were injected intraperitoneally into healthy guinea pigs. After a given period of time the peritoneal fluid was drawn out and examined. Rabbits, white rats, and guinea pigs were used as control animals. Data obtained for guinea pigs alone are recorded as controls because of the cumbersomeness of tabulation.

The percentage of phagocytosis was determined by averaging ten counts. The weight of the guinea pigs was from 300 to 500 gm. The results of this series may be tabulated as follows:

Time (minutes)	Control 5 mm^3 tubercle bacilli suspension	Glucose (2% of suspension) + 5 mm^3 tubercle bacilli suspension	Adrenaline (1 to 1000) (0.5 mm^3) + 5 mm^3 tubercle bacilli suspension
15	Leukocytes scanty; phagocytosis not found; opsonic index 2.10	Same as control	Same as control
30	Phagocytes increased; phagocytosis active; index 2.10	Same as 15 minutes	Phagocytosis has occurred 0.41
40	2.15	0.40	0.55
60	2.50	0.42	0.89
90	2.50		
120	1.62	0.98	1.11
180	1.32	0.60	0.75

From the above data it is seen that both glucose and adrenaline have strong inhibitory action upon phagocytosis. The action of adrenaline is not, however, as pronounced as that of glucose.

Series 2

In this series the natural process was simulated as closely as possible by injecting glucose and adrenaline subcutaneously 2 or 3 hours previous to intraperitoneal injection of bacilli. At different intervals after the injection of bacilli, a sample of peritoneal fluid was taken out and examined for phagocytosis as in series 1. Subcutaneous injection of sugar and adrenaline was followed in 2 or 3 hours by an elimination of sugar in the urine of the animal.

1. The quantities injected were 0.1 gm (glucose) and 0.1 mm^3 (adrenaline 1:1000) per 100 gm weight of the animal.

2. Tubercle bacilli emulsions were injected in quantities varying from 3 to 5 mm^3 according to the size of the animal (for guinea pig and rabbit) and 2 to 3 mm^3 for various sizes of white rats.

3. Phagocytotic indices were determined thirty minutes and two hours after intraperitoneal injection of bacilli. Figures were taken from the average of six readings for guinea pigs and rabbits, and two readings for white rats, with the following results:

	Guinea pig	Rabbit	White rat
Control	2.17	1.51	2.35
Glucose	0.60	0.49	0.63
Adrenaline	1.74	0.87	1.56

In this experiment the inhibition of phagocytosis by glucose injection is considerable; and a similar but weaker inhibition is exerted by adrenaline injection. In the case of adrenaline, the inhibition may be considered due to the sugar increase in the blood caused by the adrenaline injection.

Series 3

Relation of the quantities of adrenaline and glucose injected and the extent of phagocytosis.

In the animal body the extent of phagocytosis varies with species, individuals, age, differences in the rapidity of leukocytosis, and in the strength of the opsonin reaction due to emotional states. For this reason, an accurate quantitative determination of the inhibitory actions exerted by glucose and adrenaline cannot be made by animal experimentation. In this series, therefore, only a rough estimate of the general quantitative relationship is to be expected.

It was found that glucose, mixed with tubercle bacilli emulsion to a 3% concentration or over, inhibits phagocytosis when injected intraperitoneally, for several hours. As the concentration of sugar is decreased, this inhibitory action gradually decreases until with 0.1% or lower this effect becomes almost negligible. The same relationship holds in the case of adrenaline; with 0.005% phagocytosis is prevented entirely, and with 0.001% the inhibition is greatly enfeebled.

Test Tube Experiments

A. By the experiments described above, the presence of the inhibitory action of glucose and adrenaline upon phagocytosis in the peritoneal cavity was proved. In this present experiment, Wright's method was employed for the quantitative determination of the opsonic index, using dead bacilli as indicators.

As a control, normal human serum was used. It was taken from a person having a negative von Pirquet reaction and no physical signs of disease. It is customary to employ normal human leukocytes, but for convenience, white cells of guinea pigs were used as phagocytes.

Indices were computed from the averages of eight counts, discarding two doubtful results from the total ten counts.

Control: A mixture of equal volumes of normal human serum, emulsion of guinea pig leukocytes, and tubercle bacilli emulsion was examined for phagocytosis and the amount of phagocytosis determined was taken as the standard in computing the opsonic index for each of the following tests.

Test 1

For the first test mixtures containing equal volumes of normal human serum, guinea pig leukocytes, tubercle bacilli emulsion and solutions of glucose (8, 4, 2, 1, and 0.4%) were prepared. The percentage of glucose in these solutions was reduced by the mixing to 2, 1, 0.5, and 0.25% and 0.1%, respectively.

Test 2

For the second test normal human serum, guinea pig leukocytes, tubercle bacilli emulsion, and adrenaline solution were added in equal parts. The actual concentration of adrenaline in each experiment is noted in the table.
These two tests resulted as follows:

	Concentration of added reagents (%)	Phagocytotic indices
Glucose	2.00	0.26
	1.00	0.50
	0.50	0.55
	0.25	0.70
	0.10	0.72
Adrenaline	2.0 (0.002)	0.33
	1.0 (0.001)	0.47
	0.5 (0.0005)	0.53
	0.25 (0.00025)	0.79
	0.10 (0.0001)	0.83

Thus, it is seen that both glucose and adrenaline exert inhibitory influences upon opsonic reaction, their activity decreasing in direct proportion to the decrease in concentration. As dilute a solution as 0.1% glucose or 0.0001% adrenaline still show some inhibitory action.

B. In this series the inhibition by glucose and adrenaline upon the opsonic reaction in the blood of consumptive patients was the aim of the experimentation. To approach the natural conditions as closely as possible, both opsonin and phagocytes were taken out of the patient, and the organisms were used alive. The leukocytes were by previous examination found to contain no bacilli in their cell bodies.

Method of Observation

Three series of test tubes were set up as follows:

Tube 1. 1 mm^3 tubercle bacilli suspension in isotonic salt solution.
Tube 2. 1 mm^3 tubercle bacilli suspension in isotonic salt solution + 1% adrenaline (1:1000).
Tube 3. 1 mm^3 tubercle bacilli suspension in isotonic salt solution + 1% glucose solution.

These were heated to 38°C in a water bath, after which 5 drops of patient's blood, drawn out by means of a hypodermic syringe from a vein, were added to each tube. Tubes were again heated for 45 minutes at 38°C. The blood cells sank to the bottom and thus the contents of the tubes divided themselves into two layers. By means of a capillary pipette, the fluid at the junction of the two layers was removed. Cover glass preparations were made and fixed carefully with a mixture of equal parts of alcohol and ether. After staining with Ziehl solution, the red blood cells were removed from the vision by means of acetic acid and decolorization with sulfuric acid. The preparations were finally counterstained with dilute methylene blue. Blood was taken from the patients always at 10 AM or 3 PM to avoid complication with meals. The syringe needle used was ⅓ mm in diameter, 1000 drops of blood corresponding to 1 mm³, and 130 drops of salt solution to 1 mm³.

The following are the tabulated results of the above test with 60 patients (see Table 1):

TABLE 1. With Consumptive Patients Without Glycosuria

Case No.	Sex	Age	Lesion in	Number of tubercle bacilli in	Degree of symptoms	Phagocytosis		
						Tube I	Tube II	Tube III
1	Male	37	Right superior lobe (lung)	Sputum 6	Medium	108	70	43
2	Male	34	Right superior lobe + left apex (lungs)	Sputum 3	Medium	138	78	114
3	Female	25	Both lungs and colon	Sputum 7 Stool 1	Advanced	96	49	35
4	Male	32	Entire right lung	Sputum 7	Medium	121	85	91
5	Male	34	Entire right lung	Sputum 7	Advanced	87	23	20
6	Female	37	Right superior and intermediate lobes	Sputum 3	Medium	101	47	68
7	Female	22	Right superior, intermediate + left superior lobes	Sputum 10	Advanced	77	56	62
8	Female	51	Entire left lung	Sputum 3	Medium	55	47	44
9	Male	25	Right intermediate and inferior lobes	Sputum 3	Medium	72	33	23
10	Female	26	Superior lobes in both lungs	Sputum 3	Medium	88	64	55
11	Male	19	Superior lobes in both lungs	Sputum 5	Medium	75	35	34
12	Female	37	Superior lobes in both lungs, and colon	Sputum 7 Stool 2	Advanced	62	29	4
13	Female	19	Right superior lobe and left pleurisy	Sputum 3	Slight	105	48	40
14	Male	22	Right superior lobe and larynx	Sputum 7	Advanced	62	21	52
15	Male	25	Both lungs, larynx, and colon	Sputum 7	Advanced	35	31	8
16	Male	18	Right superior lobe	Sputum 6	Medium	168	75	111
17	Male	58	Right superior lobe + left apex	Sputum 6	Medium	191	127	105
18	Male	26	Entire right lung and left apex	Sputum 7	Medium	159	90	74

Continued

Behavior and Immune Function

TABLE 1. *Continued*

Case No.	Sex	Age	Lesion in	Number of tubercle bacilli in	Degree of symptoms	Phagocytosis		
						Tube I	Tube II	Tube III
19	Female	21	Right superior and inferior lobes and left apex	Sputum 5	Medium	204	116	87
20	Male	38	Right superior lobe	Sputum 3	Medium	164	77	75
21	Female		Right superior and middle lobes	Sputum 1	Medium	95	39	30
22	Male		Entire right lung	Sputum 6	Advanced	113	36	27
23	Female		Superior lobes in both lungs	Sputum 10	Advanced	129	49	44
24	Male		Superior lobes in both lungs	Sputum 7	Advanced	74	57	34
25	Male		Entire right lung	Sputum 7	Medium	81	69	51
26	Female		Left superior lobe	Sputum 7	Medium	87	9	10
27	Male		Superior portions of both lungs	Sputum 3	Medium	77	42	43
28	Female		Entire left lung and right superior lobe	Sputum 5	Advanced	92	35	26
29	Female		Entire left lung + right superior lobe	Sputum 7	Advanced	63	61	51
30	Male	43	Superior portions of both lungs	Sputum 5	Medium	65	61	34
31	Female	25	Entire left lung	Sputum 5	Advanced	73	47	33
32	Male	27	Entire right lung + left superior lobe	Sputum 5	Advanced	81	33	23
33	Male	31	Superior lobes of both lungs	Sputum 5	Advanced	69	22	13
34	Female	15	Right superior and intermediate lobes	Sputum 3	Medium	94	39	36
35	Male	42	Superior portion of left lung, and right pneumonia	Sputum 2	Medium	78	51	39
36	Male	25	Entire right lung + left pneumonia	Sputum 3	Medium	91	51	33
37	Male	44	Right pleuro-pneumonia	Sputum 1	Light	81	64	33
38	Male	16	Left superior lobe	Sputum 1	Light	70	39	31
39	Female	33	Superior portion of right lung and left pneumonia	Sputum 1	Light	70	42	13
40	Male	26	Right superior intermediate lobe	Sputum 1	Light	99	66	60
Average						96.175	52.825	45.200
Control (healthy individual)						229.00	51.00	49.00

These data show that (1) adrenaline and glucose have a marked inhibitory influence upon phagocytosis in the blood of consumptive patients, and (2) phagocytosis is, in general, more marked in the less severe cases than in the more advanced ones.

Occasionally advanced cases show a relatively high opsonic index and the less severe cases a comparatively low index. These variations are apparently only coincidences of the time when the examination is made—temporary arrest of unfavorable symptoms in the advanced cases, causing an increased phagocytosis, and a temporary acute symptom in the lighter cases depressing it. Treated advanced cases show a relatively higher opsonic index than the untreated mild cases.

In addition to the two facts previously noted in Table 1, it is shown that at the time glycosuria is present on account of emotional excitement, phagocytosis is decreased, and that an addition of adrenaline or glucose to the test tube mixture still further decreases the reaction.

In cases 9 and 13, remarkable divergence from the general tendency is obtained, the addition of glucose and adrenaline increasing phagocytosis. No explanation for this phenomenon is as yet available.

TABLE 2. A Study of Twenty Consumptive Patients with Glycosuria*

Case No.	Sex	Lesions in	Number of tubercle bacilli in	Urinary sugar	Degree of symptoms	Phagocytosis		
						Tube I	Tube II	Tube III
1	Male	Entire right lung + left superior lobe	Sputum 8	0.247	Advanced	132 42	97 24	50 25
2	Male	Right superior and intermediate lobes	Sputum 8	0.476	Light	36 13	8 10	39 12
3	Female	Right superior lobe + left apex	Sputum 8	1.120	Advanced	60 22	53 8	66 0
4	Female	Entire left lung + peritonitis	Sputum 8	0.767	Advanced	84 18	79 8	52 9
5	Male	Entire right lung + left inferior lobe	Sputum 8	1.269	Advanced	66 4	39 4	33 3
6	Male	Left superior lobe	Sputum 8	0.192	Medium	44 12	33 0	39 0
7	Male	Both lungs (entire)	Sputum 8	0.350	Advanced	62 22	40 0	31 0
8	Male	Upper left half + entire right lung	Sputum 8	0.100	Advanced	43 27	20 28	27 23
9	Male	Entire both lungs	Sputum 8	0.277	Advanced	57 0	42 0	117 0
10	Female	Entire right lung + left superior lobe	Sputum 8	0.363	Advanced	48 0	60 13	71 18
11	Female	Entire both lungs and colon	Sputum 8	0.308	Advanced	152 47	42 28	11 34
12	Male	Entire left lung + larynx, + right apex	Sputum 8	0.755	Advanced	182 22	76 20	90 28
13	Female	Entire right lung + peritonitis	Sputum 8	0.416	Medium	60 18	130 0	126 0
14	Male	Left superior lobe	Sputum 8	0.290	Light	72 18	44 5	28 0
15	Female	Superior portion of left lung, and larynx and colon	Sputum 8	0.324	Advanced	48 17	22 0	30 8

Continued

TABLE 2. *Continued*

Case No.	Sex	Lesions in	Number of tubercle bacilli in	Urinary sugar	Degree of symptoms	Phagocytosis		
						Tube I	Tube II	Tube III
16	Male	Entire right lung and left pneumonia	Sputum 8	0.300	Advanced	64 23	25 16	44 18
17	Male	Right superior and intermed-iate lobes	Sputum 4	0.100	Medium	68 35	35 30	30 22
18	Male	Right superior and intermed-iate lobes	Sputum 1	0.588	Light	103 36	41 18	45 21
19	Male	Entire right lung + left apex + larynx	Sputum 6	1.250	Advanced	68 22	23 18	18 2
20	Male	Entire left lung, right superior lobe, larynx	Sputum 7	0.542	Advanced	53 27	27 12	30 5
Average		....				75.10 22.25	46.80 12.20	53.75 11.40

*In the above table in the column labelled phagocytosis, the upper figures show the number of organisms engulfed at the usual time, and the lower show the amount of phagocytosis at a time glycosuria had occurred after emotional excitement. The amount of urinary sugar is that determined shortly before the opsonic examination was made.

Discussion

Previous to the work of Pawlow, Biedl and Schmidt (1852) had noted a pronounced influence exerted by various psychic acts upon the secretory activities of the digestive glands.

Bickel and Sasaki in 1905 had confirmed Pawlow's work. Later Oechsler (1914) demonstrated the existence of a similar relationship between emotional states and pancreatic and biliary secretions. Furthermore, the same was found to hold for the mechanical movement of the digestive organs by Le Conte (1900), Bickel and Sasaki (1905), Fommel (1903), Cannon (1902), Auer (1907), and others. Richet (1878), Hornborg (1904), Cade et Latarjet (1905), Bogen (1907), Lavenson (1901), and Mueller (1907) clinically demonstrated similar relationships in man.

The period of this reaction of the digestive organs to psychic influences has been known to extend beyond the period of stimulation. Jacobi (1891), Bickel (1897), Dreyer (1898–1899), Tacheboksaroff (1910), Asher (1912), Joseph and Meltzer (1912), Elliott (1912), and Cannon and Lyman (1913), showed that the innervation of the suprarenal glands was derived from the splanchnic nerves. Stimulation of these nerves causes an increase in adrenaline secretion, giving rise to heightened blood pressure and pupillary dilatation. Again in 1910–1911 Cannon and de la Paz showed that pupillary dilation in cats was associated with impaired digestion. The cardiac acceleration, and the erection of hair in the back and tail which is associated with fear, may be reproduced by sympathetic stimulation. And after artificial stimulation of the sympathetic nerve which supplies the suprarenal glands, these investigators experimentally demonstrated that the adrenaline secretion is similarly increased by various psychic acts.

In 1901 Blum showed that an injection into an animal of an extract of suprarenal gland brings about an increase in blood sugar and causes glycosuria. Later in that year Takamine, and independently of him Aldrich (1901–1905), isolated the active principle of suprarenal gland and named it adrenaline. With the isolation of adrenaline Straub and Ritzman (1907–1909) showed that this substance, when injected, gives rise to an increase in the sugar content of the blood, and glycosuria. The adrenaline stimulates a decomposition of glycogen in muscle and liver into glycose and, therefore, the condition is similar to the diabetes of sympathetic nervous origin. Subcutaneous injection of 1 to 2 mg of adrenaline into rabbits brings about a glycosuria after 30 minutes of 3 hours, the condition lasting from 3 hours to a day.

In observations recorded in this paper, it was shown that advanced consumptives, especially nervous individuals frequently show transient glycosuria. Cannon proved experimentally the capacity of adrenaline to remove muscle fatigue and also to hasten the coagulation of blood, and considered an adrenaline increase as a beneficial compensatory mechanism. By an increase in the adrenaline secretion the splanchnic and cutaneous vessels are constricted, blood pressure raised, and the blood accumulates in the brain, lungs, heart, and muscles of the limbs, preparing the individual for emergencies such as a sudden attack by an enemy. Removal of muscle fatigue and an increase in the coagulability of blood also are designed for such an emergency. On the other hand, when this increased amount of adrenaline and sugar remains unutilized in the blood it acts injuriously, as pointed out previously, by lowering the opsonic index and thus increasing the symptoms of the disease. Psychic excitations in the tuberculous patients, corresponds to the latter condition. The adrenaline increase and an increase in the blood sugar are caused by various mental activities. These substances impair the phagocytotic action of the blood. What Cannon terms a compensatory mechanism is apparently designed as a temporary means for combating certain situations. The factor calling forth such a compensatory mechanism is itself injurious to individuals, especially when it exceeds a certain limit. Adrenaline and particularly sugar in the blood are inhibitory to phagocytosis, as seen in the experimental and clinical data presented. I am inclined to conclude that the injurious effect exerted upon consumptive patients by psychic excitations is due to the lowering of the opsonic index caused by an increase in adrenaline in secretion and the subsequent increase in blood sugar.

This conclusion is supported not only by the experiments described above but also by the time honored clinical observations of the subnormal resistance shown by diabetic patients towards infections such as tuberculosis and furunculosis. Glycosuria is observed in those tuberculous patients which are advancing and which have a bad prognosis.

It must be borne in mind, however, that the lowered opsonic index is not the sole cause of the decided impairment in the course of the disease. Depression of digestive function by psychic acts, causing the loss of appetite and emaciation, must be considered as an important factor.

The relationships above brought out must hold in cases of healthy individuals as well as in the sick, emotional acts predisposing them to tuberculous and other infections. Hence the problem is important not only to therapy but also to preventive medicine.

According to the statistical returns of our country the individuals of ages between fifteen and thirty-five constitute one-third of the total number of fatal cases of pulmonary tuberculosis. In England (1914) ages between thirty-five and fifty show greatest mortality. In the United States 25 states reported in the same year the highest mortality between the ages of twenty and twenty-five.

In Japan the occupational classification shows the greatest percentage of mortality from consumption among primary school teachers. The relative number of young individuals suffering from consumption is greatest in Japan. According to the recent investigations by Roemer and Freymuth (1912) the pulmonary tuberculosis seen in early adult life is the reappearance at puberty of the previous infection which had occurred in childhood and was subsequently held in check. This phenomenon was called by them auto-inoculation. Although the accuracy of the statement is open to question, a high percentage of positive von Pirquet tests among the children of our city schools indicates that the infection is acquired in some way similar to the one suggested by these investigators.

Thus it appears that the high death rate from pulmonary tuberculosis among the young individuals in our country is attributable to inadequacy in prophylactic measures against tuberculosis during the school age, the heavy strain on the children by our didactic method of teaching and our peculiar linguistic difficulties, and especially the incomparably severe entrance examinations to higher schools which are necessitated by the insufficiency in the school accommodations. A large number of students become neurasthenic, and some of these neurasthenic youths are virtually forced, upon graduation, to face the high cost of living and low salaries, as school teachers. Thus they fall victims to tuberculosis and then very probably infect the children under their care. An improvement in the educational system and in the treatment of teachers is radically necessary in combating tuberculosis.

Conclusions

1. Psychic acts frequently influence the course of pulmonary tuberculosis unfavorably and render the treatment difficult.

2. The psychic influences upon the disease are accompanied by a lowering of the opsonic index.

3. Psychic acts often cause transient glycosuria.

4. Sugar and adrenaline both inhibit opsonic reaction.

5. Lowering of the opsonic index in emotional excitement is caused by an increase in the amount of sugar and adrenaline in the blood.

6. Impairment in the progress of the disease is caused both by a decrease in the opsonic reaction and in the digestive function.

7. Overtaxation of the mind of our youths by our unsatisfactory educational system seems to be the cause of the high mortality of young consumptives in our country.

8. The high mortality of our youths from tuberculosis is also partly due to the infection from tuberculous teachers, who in turn are the victims of excessive mental strain.

9. Prevention of excessive mental strain by an improvement in our educational system is one effective means of preventing the spread of consumption among our youths.

Acknowledgments

The author takes this opportunity to pay his respects to his teacher, Professor Kitasato.

38

CONVALESCENCE FROM INFLUENZA

A Study of the Psychological and Clinical Determinants

John B. Imboden, Arthur Canter,
and Leighton E. Cluff

In a recent study[1] of convalescence from acute brucellosis the findings strongly supported the view that delay or failure in symptomatic recovery from that disorder is critically dependent upon the emotional state or attitude of the person. While no objective clinical or laboratory findings differentiated those persons who recovered quickly and completely from those who retained symptoms for a long period of time (chronic brucellosis), there were striking differences between these two groups in terms of psychological adjustment and life situation concurrent with the acute phase of the infection. The evidence pointed to the importance of depression particularly in retarding symptomatic recovery from the illness.

The study of convalescence of patients with brucellosis was done retrospectively in that the persons were investigated medically and psychologically some time after the acute illness had been contracted. We felt reasonably assured that certain features of the study enabled us to differentiate between primary psychological characteristics of the patients and responses secondary to the infection. The present investigation was conducted to obtain psychological information on persons prior to acute infection to evaluate its relationship to convalescence from the illness.

In view of the observations made in the study of brucellosis showing a close relationship between depression and delay in convalescence, an attempt was made to determine if depression propensity, as detected by preillness testing, could be correlated with the rate of recovery from an infection. In August of 1957, a nationwide epidemic of Asian influenza was anticipated, and we obtained psychological data on a group of persons in the expectation that the recovery patterns of those in this group who contracted Asian influenza could be observed.

Method

In August , 1957, a total of 600 employees (540 men and 60 women) at Fort Detrick were administered the Minnesota Multiphasic Personality Inventory (MMPI), the Cornell Medical

Supported by a contract with the Army Chemical Corps, Fort Detrick, Frederick, MD.

Reprinted from *Arch. Internal Med.* **108**, 393–399. Copyright © 1961, American Medical Association.

Index Health Questionnaire (CMI), and a brief social questionnaire.[2,3] The MMPI requires the subject to respond to a large nember of questions pertaining to feelings, attitudes, reaction tendencies, and experiences as being either true or false of himself. It was originally standardized on an empirical basis, i.e., in persons who had been psychiatrically studied and diagnosed and in subjects who were considered normal. In this way it was found that the items of the MMPI could be separated into groups, or "diagnostic keys," corresponding to various clinical categories. There were thus developed the hypochondriasis (Hs), depression (D), psychasthenia (Pt), and hysteria (Hy) keys used in this study. In addition, a key called the Morale-Loss index,[4] which was developed from the MMPI, was used. The scores from these tests are derived in an objective manner and are not influenced by bias of the examiner.

Full cooperation of the personnel was readily obtained, and the great majority of the employees agreed to participate in the study. It was made clear to all persons that the test results, in terms of individual identity, would be kept confidential within the team of investigators and would have no bearing on employment status.

All employees involved in this study are required to report to the dispensary in the event of any kind of illness even if the person does not regard his symptoms as related to his occupation. This situation was admirably suited to this study, for it facilitated medical follow-up of the personnel without the necessity of making any significant changes in the existing routine. All of those persons who reported to the dispensary in the winter of 1957–1958 with apparent influenza were requested to return to the dispensary 3 to 6 weeks after the beginning of their illness. At this return visit, it was ascertained whether or not each person was symptomatically recovered, the nature of persisting symptoms if any, and the approximate duration of illness.

A history was taken and physical examination was performed on each patient when first seen with symptoms of influenza. Follow-up evaluation was done on all patients and on some during the course of the infection. All subjects had been previously followed and studied in this same dispensary by periodic examinations, various serological studies, and chest x-ray.

Serological Tests

Serum was obtained from blood collected by venipuncture during the acute and convalescent periods of the infection. Hemagglutination-inhibition tests were performed with serial dilutions of the sera pretreated with periodate to remove nonspecific inhibitors. The virus used for hemagglutination was the A Japan 305 57 strain.

Virus Isolation

In a few patients virus isolation was attempted by inoculation of pharyngeal washings into embryonated eggs, and the harvested allantoic fluid was analyzed for hemagglutination activity, and hemagglutination-inhibition was performed using a standard reference serum for positive identification of the influenza virus.

Results

Twenty-six persons among the 600 subjects reported to the dispensary during the winter of 1957–1958 with an influenza-like syndrome, representing an attack rate of about 5%. This corresponds with the incidence of Asian influenza in Maryland during that period. Not all patients were seen on the first day of illness. The average interval between time of onset of symptoms and first visit to the clinic was a little more than 1 day with a range from 1 to 7 days, there having been one patient who waited 7 days before seeking medical care.

Upon returning to the dispensary 3 to 6 weeks after the initial visit, 14 persons reported that they were completely recovered from their illness, and the other 12 persons stated that they still had symptoms. The first group we have called the Recovered group and the second, the Symptomatic group. The average age was 38.0 years for the Symptomatic group and 30.6 years for the Recovered group. All of the patients were male except for one woman in the Symptomatic group (Table 1). The mean duration of illness of the Recovered group was 7.9 days, with a range from 3 days (2 patients) to 14 days (2 patients). The duration of symptoms in the Symptomatic group exceeded 3 weeks in every case, but no effort was made to determine the time needed for symptomatic recovery of these patients (Fig. 1).

The symptoms presented by the 26 persons with acute influenza in this study were fever, myalgia, cough, headache, "chills," rhinitis, sore throat, arthralgia, malaise, and anorexia. The Symptomatic and Recovered groups did not significantly differ in the character of the symptoms associated with their acute illness (Table 2). Serological tests and/or virus isolation confirmed the diagnosis of Asian influenza in 19 patients. It is of interest that in one patient in whom the convalescent serological test was negative, the Asian influenza virus was isolated during the acute infection. The clinical symptoms of the 7 patients in whom the diagnosis was not confirmed by serological tests or virus isolation did not differ from those of the remaining 19; 3 of the unconfirmed cases were in the Symptomatic group and 4 in the Recovered group.

One patient in the Symptomatic group had a history of brucellosis 7 years previously, another had a distant past history of ulceroglandular tularemia, and a third had a long-standing history of nondisabling chronic bronchitis. Other than these 3, none of the patients had histories of disease that might be contributory to delayed convalescence from influenza.

Most patients did not develop specific complications during the course of their influenza. However, 2 persons did develop transient signs of pneumonitis; one of these was in the Symptomatic group and the other was in the Recovered group. One individual in the Recovered group

TABLE 1. Data on 26 Patients with Influenza

	No. of persons	Duration of illness	Age (yr.)	M	F
Symptomatic group	12	3 weeks (or longer)	38.0*	11	1
Recovered group	14	7.9 days*	30.6*	14	0

*These entries are the mean values.

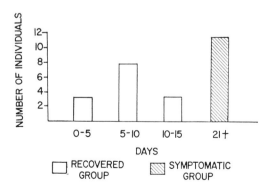

FIGURE 1. Distribution of patients according to duration of symptoms following onset of influenza.

Convalescence from Influenza

TABLE 2. Symptoms and Signs of the Acute Illness

	Recovered group, no. persons	Symptomatic group, no. persons
Fever 99–100°F	5	5
Fever 100–103°F	8	7
Myalgia	13	10
Cough	8	10
Headache	8	7
"Chills"	9	5
Rhinitis	7	6
Sore throat	7	6
Arthralgia	6	6
Malaise	6	5
Anorexia	3	4

developed sinusitis and another acute otitis media; in both instances, clinical recovery was rapid and evidently complete.

From the clinical data, there were no apparent differences in symptoms, physical signs, laboratory findings, or complications of the acute infection between those who recovered slowly as opposed to those who recovered promptly from influenza.

As seen in Table 3, the patients in the Symptomatic group complained of a variety of residual symptoms 3 weeks or more after the acute infection. The most common was tiredness or weakness. Other persisting symptoms included cough, insomnia, headache, anorexia. Two patients complained of feeling depressed. Five persons had 3 or more residual symptoms, 5 had 2, and 2 persons in this group had only 1 complaint.

As noted above, the CMI and MMPI were administered 3 to 6 months in advance of the occurrence of influenza. When the scores obtained on these tests by the Recovered group were compared with those of the Symptomatic group, certain rather consistent differences appeared. As shown in Table 4, the median total CMI score was 16.0 for the Symptomatic group as compared with 9.0 for the Recovered group. This difference was significant at $P = 0.05$. Similarly when the sections M-R of the CMI, which deal particularly with overt clinical

TABLE 3. Persisting Complaints of the Symptomatic Group

	No. Persons
Tired and/or weak	10
Cough	5
Insomnia	3
Headache	3
Anorexia	3
Feeling "blue"	2
Draining sinusitis	1
Aching	1
Nausea	1
Chronic rhinitis	1

TABLE 4. Summary of Cornell Medical Index Health Questionnaire Scores

	Total CMI scores*		Section M-R (psychological)*	
	Median	Range	Median	Range
Symptomatic group	16.0	4–30	3.5	0–13
Recovered group	9.0	0–44	1.3	0– 5

*The differences between the symptomatic and recovered groups on both sets of scores are significant as determined by the Mann-Whitney U test at $P = 0.05$.

manifestations of emotional disturbance, were examined, the median score of the Symptomatic group was significantly higher than that of the Recovered group ($P = 0.05$).

The MMPI test results were consistent with those of the CMI. The mean scores of the Symptomatic group were higher in 7 of the 9 scales than were those of the Recovered group. The indices of depressive tendency as determined by the D and ML scores of the MMPI were of particular interest in this study. As may be seen in Table 5, both D and ML scores of the Symptomatic group were significantly higher than those of the Recovered group. None of the other observed differences in the MMPI scales was significant. In addition, the D score dominated the profiles of MMPI scores of 9 of the 12 members of the Symptomatic group in contrast to only 3 of the 14 recovered subjects.

Comment

The severity of the acute influenza, height of fever, complications, and serological response did not serve to differentiate those persons who were symptomatically recovered from the infection from those who still had symptoms at the time of the follow-up examination. The latter patients complained most commonly of persisting tiredness or weakness, and in this respect they

TABLE 5. Scores on Preillness MMPI

Scale	I Symptomatic group ($N = 12$) Mean T-score	II Recovered group ($N = 14$ Mean T-score
Hs	53.8	57.8
D	61.0*	51.5*
Hy	61.0	59.7
Pd	59.3	57.9
Mf	59.3	57.4
Pa	55.1	50.0
Pt	58.0	53.5
Se	56.3	52.6
Ma	50.8	54.6
M-L (Raw Scores)	7.2†	2.7†

*Significant at $P = .025$ as determined by t.
†Significant at $P < 0.01$ as determined by t.

resembled those persons with delayed recovery following acute brucellosis.[1] It is to be noted, however, that the 2 convalescent groups delineated in this study of influenza do not represent the same extremes in recovery patterns as were manifested in the brucellosis study where the chronic subjective syndrome had endured for several years and was often severe.

The psychological test data, on the other hand, did serve to differentiate those persons who recovered relatively quickly following influenza from those whose symptoms persisted. The Depression and Morale-Loss index scores, derived from the MMPI, and the total Cornell Medical Index scores of the Symptomatic group were significantly higher than were those of the Recovered group. As shown in Table 6, these observed differences in the D and ML scores between the two convalescent influenza groups are virtually identical with those differences observed between the corresponding convalescent groups of the brucellosis study. In the present investigation, however, the psychological evaluation was obtained well in advance of the acute illness. Thus the observed differences on the psychological tests are not secondary to the occurrence of influenza.

It was noted that the Symptomatic group tended to be somewhat older than the more rapidly recovered persons. The possibility arose that the higher D scores of the former group were merely a reflection of this age difference. However, inspection of the data revealed no significant correlation between level of D score and age. Furthermore, when we randomly selected 3 groups of 50 persons each (drawn from the original group of 600 subjects) whose ages ranged from 20 to 29, 30 to 39, and 40 to 76, respectively, no significant differences between the D scores of these groups were obtained. It thus appears likely that the variables represented by age and D score in this group of subjects are relatively independent of each other. It would therefore seem reasonable to assume that slower recovery following influenza is associated with the somewhat older age of the Symptomatic group as well as with their psychological characteristics.

It is pertinent to note that many references to the relationship between the psychological and emotional state of the patient and recovery from illness have been made in the medical and nonmedical literature. In a study of 50 soldiers during World War II with a history of proven acute schistosomiasis, Frank[5] observed that many patients showed a degree and persistence of invalidism out of proportion to any objective evidence of disease. He noted that the most common persisting symptoms were weakness or fatigue. While a number of morale-undermining factors were discernible in this group, Frank felt that the aura of strangeness and uncertainty associated with schistosomiasis was particularly important in the development of emotional reactions that tended to impede recovery. In a thorough clinical and psychological investigation of 50 soldiers with recurrent malaria, Tumulty et al.[6] noted that "weakness" (described as loss of strength, lack of energy, or easy fatigability) was the most common chronic symptom that remained more or less constantly present between acute attacks of the disease.

TABLE 6. Comparison of MMPI Scores in 2 Convalescent Studies

Groups		Mean D score	Mean M-L score
Recovered	Influenza*	51.5	2.7
	Brucellosis†	51.0	2.7
Symptomatic	Influenza*	61.0	7.2
	Brucellosis†	63.7	7.4

*Tests administered prior to illness.
†Tests administered after illness.

Behavior and Immune Function

While it was felt that the malarial infection was the prime contributor to the fatigability it was also observed that the adjustment of the person and his concurrent situation were significant factors particularly in their influence on the severity of symptoms.

In 1947, Brodman et al.[7] published their study of the relationship between personality disturbance and duration of convalescence from acute respiratory infections that occurred in the military and which required hospitalization. The Cornell Service Index (a precursor of the CMI), administered soon *after* subsidence of acute symptoms, was used as a measure of personality disturbance and the duration of hospitalization as the measure of convalescence. These investigators concluded that the average duration of hospitalization was significantly prolonged in those patients whose Cornell Service Index scores indicated personality disturbance. They also interpreted their data as showing that ''a higher percentage of patients on respiratory wards had personality disturbances than did troops in the population from which these patients were drawn.'' Although this interpretation may be valid, it seems equally likely that scores on the Cornell Service Index, when administered to hospitalized persons recovering from acute respiratory infections, would be higher than when administered to nonhospitalized troops on active duty simply as a reflection of the former's convalescent status. To conclude that a difference in scores under these circumstances reflects a difference in incidence of ''personality disturbance'' would seem questionable.

Greenfield, Roessler, and Crosley[8] recently reported their observations apparently showing a correlation between ''ego strength,'' as measured by the Barron Ego Strength Scale and the Meeker LH·4 Scale, and length of recovery from infectious mononucleosis. Since their psychological tests were administered about 6 months after recovery from the disease it seems unlikely that the test results were contaminated by the illness itself. Their study is of particular interest since the duration of illness was defined in terms of objective hematological criteria. In contrast, this report and the other studies cited here, dealing with the recovery from various illnesses, have been concerned primarily with prolongation of subjective symptoms.

The present study, dealing with Asian influenza, essentially confirms previous work pointing to an apparent association between certain indices of personality or emotional ''disturbance'' and the persistence of subjective symptoms following acute infectious disease. It differs from previous studies principally in that psychological data were obtained in advance of the illness under scrutiny.

We are inclined to speculate that the psychological data primarily reflect a greater degree of *propensity* to become depressed, rather than actual clinical depression, in the group who remained symptomatic longer following acute influenza. It seems likely that depression-vulnerable persons are more apt to respond with some degree of depression-like symptoms to an acute infection than those persons who do not have this vulnerability. In any event, the clinical symptoms of depression, such as fatigue, lack of energy or interest, or other vague somatic complaints, whether arising in response to the somatic illness or already present, would tend to be merged with the weakness or fatigability that is normally present immediately following an acute infectious disease. This intermingling of symptoms in the convalescent period obscures the end-point of the infectious illness from the views of both patient and physician. As Frank[5] remarked, referring to his patients with delayed recovery following schistosomiasis: ''One did not know how to be sure a patient was cured, or what part of the symptoms of a given patient at a given time were due to the parasite, what part to the treatment, and what part to his emotional reactions.'' To this we would only add that most convalescent patients are apt to attribute their persistent lack of well-being to persistence of the ''physical'' disease. As shown in the brucellosis study, this interpretation carries the least threat to the patient's sense of self-esteem.

Summary and Conclusions

In August of 1957, a total of 600 subjects were administered the MMPI and the CMI. In the winter of 1957–1958, 26 of these persons reported to the dispensary with an acute illness that was diagnosed as influenza. In 19 of these cases, the diagnosis of Asian influenza was confirmed by ser0logical tests or virus isolation.

The 26 persons with influenza were divided into two groups: (1) Recovered group, 14 persons, who became asymptomatic 3–14 days with an average of 7.9 days after the onset of the illness and (2) Symptomatic group, 12 persons, who retained symptoms beyond 3 weeks.

These two groups did not differ from each other with respect to clinical characteristics of their acute illness. Significant differences were observed, however, in the psychological test results and are in accord with the prediction, derived from a previously reported study of recovery patterns following acute brucellosis, that delayed recovery following acute self-limited illness occurs in persons who respond to psychological tests in patterns characteristic of depression-prone patients. Since the psychological data in this study were obtained prior to the illness, the evidence supports the view that this emotional state or attitude is not secondary to the illness, existed prior to it, and in significant measure was a determining factor in delaying symptomatic recovery from acute illness. In addition, it is probable that the somewhat older age of the Symptomatic group also contributed to their slower recovery following influenza.

Acknowledgment

We wish to express our gratitude to Dr. Paul Kadull and Dr. Richard Reynolds who assisted materially in this study.

References

1. Imboden, J.; Canter, A.; Cluff, L., and Trever, R.: Brucellosis: III. Psychologic Aspects of Delayed Convalescence. *A.M.A. Arch. Intern. Med.* **103,** 406–414 (March) 1959.
2. Hathaway, S. R., and McKinley, J. C.: Minnesota Multiphasic Personality Inventory Manual, Ed. 2. New York: Psychology Corporation, 1951.
3. Brodman, K.; Erdman, A. J., and Wolff, H. G.: The Cornell Medical Index Health Questionnaire, New York, Cornell University Medical College, Manual, 1956.
4. Canter, A.: The Efficacy of a Short Form of the MMPI to Evaluate Depression and Morale Loss. *J. Consult. Psychol.* **24,** 14–17 (Feb.) 1960.
5. Frank, J. D.: Emotional Reactions of American Soldiers to an Unfamiliar Disease. *Amer. J. Psychiat.* **102,** 631 (March) 1946.
6. Tumulty, P. A.; Nichols, E.; Singewald, M., and Lidz, T.: An Investigation of the Effects of Recurrent Malaria. *Medicine* **25,** 17–75 (Feb.) 1946.
7. Brodman, K.; Mittelmann, B.; Wechsler, D.; Weider, A., and Wolff, H.: The Relation of Personality Disturbances to Duration of Convalescence from Acute Respiratory Infections. *Psychosom. Med.* **9,** 37–44 (Jan.-Feb.) 1947.
8. Greenfield, N.; Roessler, R., and Crosley, A., Jr.: Ego Strength and Length of Recovery from Infectious Mononucleosis. *J. Nerv. Ment. Dis.* **128,** 125–128 (Feb.) 1959.

39

STREPTOCOCCAL INFECTIONS IN FAMILIES
Factors Altering Individual Susceptibility

Roger J. Meyer and Robert J. Haggerty
With Technical Assistance of Nancy Lombardi and Robert Perkins

THERE IS LITTLE precise data to explain why one person becomes ill with an infecting agent and another not. Stress, in the form of immersion in cold water, many years ago, by Pasteur,[1] was shown to increase the susceptibility of chickens to anthrax. In humans such experimental data is difficult to obtain, but it is clear that for many common infections (such as those with beta hemolytic streptococci) commensalism, or peaceful-coexistence between this organism and its human host, is the rule, while disease is the exception. Cornfeld *et al.*[2,3] found that as many as 29.8% of well school children harbored this agent, but Mozziconacci *et al.*[4] showed that the risk of being colonized by streptococci was not a random one, for in some individuals the rate was higher than expected. Despite intimate exposure between husbands and wives, both rarely carry the same organism at the same time.[5]

Once an individual is colonized with streptococci, his risk of developing illness varies, widely, being reported as high as 43%[6] to a low as 20%.[2] Breese and Disney,[7] Brimblecombe *et al.*,[8] and others have also shown that susceptible individuals vary in their rate of acquisition and illness when exposed to other persons carrying hemolytic streptococci.

The present study was designed to study some of the factors responsible for this variability in individual susceptibility to beta hemolytic streptococcal acquisition and illness.

METHODS

Sixteen lower-middle class families, comprising 100 persons who were being followed in a comprehensive family health care program, were systematically investigated for a 12-month period from April, 1960, through March, 1961. They were selected if they had two or more children and would co-operate in the study. All but one family had at least one child of school age. In the hope of obtaining wide variation in the rates of infection, two groups of eight families each were chosen on the basis of their previous history of frequent or infrequent respiratory infections.

Throat cultures were made on all family members every 3 weeks and at times of acute illness, by vigorous swabbing of both tonsils or tonsillar fossae. These swabs were promptly inoculated on the surface of 5% defibrinated horse-blood agar plates, and a stab was made through the streaked material to study hemolysin production by subsurface colony growth. After incubation at 37°C for 18 to 24 hours, representative beta-hemolytic colonies were isolated in pure subculture on 5% defibrinated sheep-blood agar, and identified by Gram-stained smear, grouped by the bacitracin disk method[9] and grouped and typed by Lancefield's method.[10] Specific typing sera against 39 different serologic types were supplied by the Communicable Disease Center of the United States Public Health Service at Chamblee, Georgia. Sera for anti-streptolysin 0 titers were drawn approximately every

Supported by grants from the Barnstable Chapter of the Massachusetts Heart Association and the Commonwealth Fund. Dr. Meyer's research was supported by Grant 2M-6420 from the National Institute of Mental Health.

Presented at meeting of The Society for Pediatric Research, Atlantic City, May 4, 1961.

4 months and measured by standard methods.[11] A difference of 2 dilution increments was considered a significant increase.

Acquisition was defined as the detection of a new type of Group A beta-hemolytic streptococcus or the reappearance of the same type after at least 8 weeks with negative cultures. *Streptococcal illness* was defined as the appearance, in association with a positive culture for beta-hemolytic streptococcus, of one or more of the following: a red, sore throat with or without exudate or cervical adenopathy; coryza; epistaxis; moderate or marked pharyngeal exudate; cough; otitis media; and scarlatina-form rash.

Diagnosis and treatment of respiratory infections deemed serious enough by the parents to warrant a call to their physician were carried out as usual by the family's assigned pediatric house officer or medical student under the supervision of the authors. Diagnoses were made on the basis of anatomic findings, symptoms, or both, and conformed to the usually accepted diagnostic terms.

Serial interviews were conducted by the authors with the families about past and current medical and social factors that might influence the incidence of illness; each family kept, in addition, a diary of illness, therapy, and life events. Since this was an exploratory study, attempts were made to record many factors considered by other authors or by the families to be responsible for the development of infections, with the goal of a detailed study of a few families for fruitful leads, rather than a definitive study of only a few variables. The independent variables recorded were streptococcal acquisition and illness rates, prolonged carrier states (defined as over one month), and antistreptolysin O titer rises. Table I indicates the dependent variables studied, grouped under host, agent, and environmental categories.

RESULTS

Of the 1,639 cultures obtained, 248 (20.6%) were positive for beta-hemolytic

TABLE I

BETA-STREPTOCOCCAL INFECTIONS IN FAMILIES:*
FACTORS STUDIED

Host	*Agent*
Age	Colony count
Sex	Group-type
Family history	
Antibody response	
Tonsillectomy	

Environmental Factors	
Season	Sleeping arrangements
Weather	Acute stress
Housing	Chronic stress
Family size	Therapy

* 100 persons, 16 families, 12 months.

streptococci (Table II), 22.4% of which did not belong to Group A. Twenty-four per cent of *all* recorded illnesses in the families were associated with an isolation of beta-hemolytic streptococci, but 52.5% of all acquisitions were not associated with any illness. The over-all streptococcal illness rate was 0.9 per person year.

Agent Factors

Surprisingly, no significant differences were found between illness rates associated with the acquisition of Group A as compared to non-Group A streptococci (Table III), nor with the various specific types of Group A streptococci. Of the Group A strains nontypable ones were isolated 99 times (40%), A-1 and A-12 31 times each (each 12%); types 4, 5, 13, and 28 accounted for all the others (48%) seen. Persons with greater numbers of streptococci on a blood agar plate also were no more likely to be ill than those who had small numbers of colonies (Table IV).

While quantitation of the number of colonies per blood agar plate is not an infallible method of determining the number of organisms in patients, carefully standardized techniques of swabbing, culturing, and reading by the same experienced technician were carried out to minimize these variations.

This lack of correlation between illness

TABLE II

BETA-STREPTOCOCCAL INFECTIONS IN FAMILIES*

Age (yr)	Persons (no.)	Person-months	Cultures (no.)	Positive Cultures (no.)	Positive Cultures per Person-month
<2	16	192	228	11	0.057
2–5	28	360	563	98	0.272
2–15	22	252	386	99	0.392
16+	34	396	462	40	0.103
	100	1,200	1,639	248	0.206

* 12 months, 16 families.

and the two agent factors—streptococcal group and type, and number of colonies—may have been because most of the illnesses recorded were not caused by the streptococci isolated.

The low rate of antistreptolysin O increase observed following beta-hemolytic streptococcal acquisitions (28%) may be partially explained by the predominance of younger patients less likely to develop antibodies in response to streptococcal infection; a number of young children sustained quite elevated titers during the study, however. Another factor may be that the interval between samples was prolonged, although Rantz et al.[12] reported persistence of elevated titers over a considerable period of time, varying with age, reinfection and other factors. The relatively high rate of reinfection in the present study tends to diminish the disadvantage of the prolonged interval between antistreptolysin O titers, despite the desirability of a shorter interval. Even in those illnesses in association with beta-hemolytic streptococci and fol-

lowed by antistreptolysin O increase, there was no significant difference between antibody increase associated with non-Group A (21.9%) and Group A (29.0%) strains. When more than half the colonies in the original agar plate were streptococci, 38% of these patients had a subsequent antibody increase, while only 21% with plates with under 50% streptococci developed such an increase (p less than 0.01).

Thus, differences in the group and type of streptococci, and the number of colonies isolated, while undoubtedly of some importance in the pathogenesis of illness, did not seem to play a crucial role in determining acquisition, illness rates, or immune response. Increased predominance of streptococci on culture was associated with a significantly higher frequency of antibody increases, but neither were consistent indicators of clinical disease.

Host Factors

Age was certainly one important factor responsible for differences in colonization

TABLE III

BETA-HEMOLYTIC-STREPTOCOCCAL INFECTIONS IN FAMILIES: RELATION OF ILLNESS TO STREPTOCOCCAL GROUP

Group	Cultures				Acquisitions			
	Ill		Not Ill		Ill		Not Ill	
	No.	%	No.	%	No.	%	No.	%
A	68	34.4	129	65.6	48	43.2	63	56.8
Non-A	21	36.8	36	63.2	8	38.0	13	62.0

TABLE IV

Beta-streptococcal Infections in Families: Relation of Number of Colonies to Illness

Quantity of Colonies	Positive Cultures (%)	
	Ill	Not Ill
<25%	23.5	27.6
25–50%	42.4	38.3
>50%	28.2	31.1
Unknown	5.9	2.9
	100.0	99.9

rates, with school children having the highest, 2-to-5-year-olds the second highest, adults the next, and infants under 2 years old the lowest rates of acquisition (Table II). Once colonized, the chance of an individual becoming ill varied little between different age groups (Table V), but the type of illness was quite different in these different age groups (Table VI), a point clearly documented by Rantz et al.[13] and others. In spite of these differences in the symptoms and signs of infection, there was little difference in severity by age.

Only 28% of all streptococcal acquisitions were followed by an anti-streptolysin O elevation. This was far more likely to occur after an illness (49%) than after an asymptomatic colonization (16%), and it occurred more frequently in school-age groups than in either younger children or adults (al-

though the numbers for each group are too small to permit significance testing).

There was no significant association of streptococcal illness or antibody increase with sex, family history of repeated respiratory infections, strong personal allergic history, or the presence or absence of tonsils. There was a slightly higher chronic carrier rate among individuals still possessing their tonsils. Mothers were more likely to become colonized and ill than fathers.

Environmental Factors

PHYSICAL ENVIRONMENT: The largest number of cultures positive for beta-hemolytic streptococci occurred in March and April, but a great deal of variation in both colonization and illness was observed from month to month, with several other months almost equalling the spring months. The late summer and fall months were characterized by the isolation of a much higher proportion of non-Group A strains, however. In spite of this general correlation with the seasons, no consistent relation of colonization or illness rates to specific weather characteristics could be determined; no relation could be found between the rates of streptococcal acquisition or illness and humidity, temperature level and change, or type or amount of precipitation. Housing was generally adequate for all these families, and there was no correlation between acquisition or illness rates and

TABLE V

Beta-streptococcal Infections in Families*

Age (yr)	Persons in Study (no.)	Persons with Positive Culture during Year (no.)	Individual Beta-streptococcal Acquisitions	
			Total Number	With Illness
<2	16	7	9	4
2–5	28	26	53	31
6–15	22	20	48	25
16+	34	19	29	13
Individuals	100	72	139	73
Total Family Episodes	..	..	47	33

* All 16 families were positive at sometime during the 12 months observation.

TABLE VI

BETA-STREPTOCOCCAL INFECTIONS IN FAMILIES

Age (yr)	Persons (no.)	Illness Rates Per Person-year (associated with beta-streptococci)			
		Undifferentiated Upper Respiratory	Pharyngitis & Tonsillitis	Otitis Media	All Other
<2	16	1.68 (0.31)	0.31 (0)	0.69 (0.18)	0.56 (0)
2–5	28	2.52 (0.53)	0.68 (0.43)	0.43 (0.14)	1.80 (0.14)
6–15	22	2.18 (0.81)	0.46 (0.27)	0.05 (0)	1.41 (0.31)
16+	34	0.97 (0.17)	0.56 (0.24)	0 (0)	0.76 (0.12)

* Beta streptococcal illness rate per person-year, 0.9; 24.1% of all illness associated with beta streptococci 52.5% of all acquisitions not associated with illness.

number of rooms, type of heating, or type of house.

Surprisingly, there was also no consistent relation between family size and number of acquisitions or illness. For example, the greatest number of individual acquisitions occurred in a family of only two children, while another family with seven children had one of the lowest rates. All families had about the same potential contact with streptococci, as judged by the number of school age children, the degree of neighborhood crowding, and other types of non-home contacts, including the fathers' working environment.

Family sleeping patterns appeared to be the only physical factor related to acquisition or illness; when one family member acquired a beta-hemolytic streptococcus he was twice as likely to spread it to another family member occupying the same bedroom as to the other family members sleeping in separate rooms.

HUMAN ENVIRONMENT: Throughout the year parents frequently commented on the relation of acute family crises to the onset of illness. Figure 1 illustrates such an example in a family who otherwise had no streptococcal acquisitions during the entire year. As far as can be determined, exposure of all family members to beta-hemolytic streptococcus occurred on May 1, but only the child who was subjected to increasing pressure during the week to learn her catechism before confirmation, became colonized and ill. This was not an isolated coincidence; similar circumstances were seen in other families. By means of the interview and diaries, life events that disrupted family or personal life and caused excess anxiety, and other evidences of disorganization were independently recorded.

About one quarter of the streptococcal acquisitions and illnesses followed such acute family crises, and there was an even clearer relation between both acquisitions and illness and these acute crises when the period 2 weeks before and 2 weeks after acquisitions or illness was compared. Table VII documents this relation and shows that streptococcal acquisition and illness, as well as non-streptococcal respiratory infections, were about four times as likely to be preceded as to be followed by acute stress. While this difference is statistically quite significant, the causal role and the precise mechanisms are far from clear. The types of acute crises seen in the 29 episodes occurring in the 2 weeks before acquisition of streptococci are listed in Table VIII. Exposure of children to wet and cold often occurred during the study but was rarely associated with such acquisitions unless fatigue was also present.

An equally useful dependent variable was the level of chronic stress found in

TABLE VII

RESPIRATORY INFECTIONS IN FAMILIES: RELATION TO ACUTE STRESS

Type Episode	Episodes of Acute Stress (no.)		Infections	
	Two Weeks before	Two Weeks after	Total Number	Associated with Stress (%)
Beta-strep illness	17	3	56	35.7
Beta-strep acquisitions without illness	12	3	76	19.5
Non-strep respiratory infections	17	4	201	10.5
Totals	46	10	333	17.0

each family. The level of chronic stress was determined by a rating scale based upon four general indices of family functioning as judged independently by two observers (physician and bacteriology technician) and occasionally by other members of the health team (Table IX). This rating scale was designed to measure family functioning as described by Bell and Vogel[14] and others. Total scores could range from 0 to 16, with higher numbers indicating greater degrees of disorganization and chronic stress.

When all four independent variables (acquisition rates, prolonged carrier states, streptococcal illness rates, and antistreptolysin O responses) were compared, there is a definite increase of all these variables as chronic stress scores increased (Fig. 2). Table X indicates the number of streptococcal acquisitions followed by an increase of antibodies in the low compared to the moderate and high stress families. After an acquisition of streptococci, antistreptolysin O increases were seen in only 21% of the patients in the low-stress families, compared to 49% of those patients in the moderate-high stress families, a statistically significant difference (p = 0.01).

As part of the initial interview with these families, they were asked which of their children was most likely to become ill. All had a ready answer, sometimes modifying this by saying that although one was more likely to become ill, another was more likely

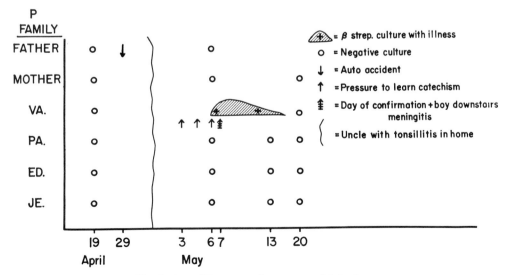

FIG. 1. Acute life stress and streptococcal infection.

TABLE VIII

ACUTE FAMILY STRESS AND RESPIRATORY INFECTIONS

Type of Stress	Episodes (no.)
Loss of family member	6
Death of grandmother (3)	
Serious illness in family	3
Pneumonia, amputation, nephritis	
Minor illness: serious implications	6
Broken leg, birth, breast lump removal	
Family crisis: non-medical	8
Aunt divorced, burned out, confirmation, father lost job, all tired and wet	
Non-family crisis: impact on members	4
Witness to violent death	
Multiple family stresses	2
Total	29

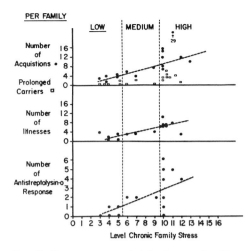

FIG. 2. Beta-streptococcal infections in families—relation to chronic stress. The dotted line represents a visual mean for each of the independent variables.

TABLE IX

RESPIRATORY INFECTIONS IN FAMILIES: CHRONIC FAMILY STRESS RATING SCALE

Family Function	Scale		
	Smoothly Functioning	→	Disorganized
External relations	0	→	4
Arrangement for outside activity			
Ability to use non-family members in emergency			
Ability to use community resources			
Network of relations-friends and neighbors			
Relation to legal institutions			
Internal relations	0	→	4
Child-rearing values consistent with children's needs			
Parental and family responsibility for each other			
Realistic care of ill member			
Parents' relations to each other			
Emotional adjustment of family members			
Medical care	0	→	4
Plan for preventive services			
Realistic ability to detect and seek help for individual ills			
Capacity to relate to medical resources			
History of handling of previous medical stresses			
Environmental and economic	0	→	4
Suitability and organization of home			
Income adequacy-cost in parents' energy			
Ability to meet medical and other needs			
Total	0	→	16

TABLE X

BETA-STREPTOCOCCAL INFECTIONS IN FAMILIES*

| Level of Chronic Family Stress | Antistreptolysin O Response† | | | No Strep Acquisitions |
| | Episodes Group A Acquisition | | | |
	ASO Rise	No Rise	Total	
Low	3	11	14	19
Moderate-high	34	36	70	9

* 100 persons, 16 families, 12 months.
† Two or more tubes.   (P<0.05.)

to become seriously ill if he became sick at all. It is interesting that the parents were able to predict correctly which child was more likely to become ill in 11 of the 16 families.

Therapy

Adequate penicillin therapy for streptococcal infections has been shown to eradicate the organism[15,16] and also to suppress antibody responses[17,18] in the majority of instances. As seen in Table XI patients adequately treated with penicillin were less likely to have an antibody increase following acquisition of a beta-hemolytic streptococcus than those not treated. A larger number of patients would be required before antibody response could be correlated significantly with the time therapy was begun, however.

Adequate treatment was followed by reappearance of the same type of streptococcus in a few families, confirming previous

TABLE XI

BETA-STREPTOCOCCAL INFECTIONS IN FAMILIES*

| Therapy | Antistreptolysin O Response† to Separate Acquisitions | | |
	Rise	No Rise	Total
Penicillin	11	33	44
No therapy	22	12	34
	33	45	78

* 100 persons, 16 families, 12 months.
† Two or more tubes.

reports.[17] In three families these recurrences ceased only after prolonged carrier states had been allowed to exist until antistreptolysin O rises occurred.

Thirty per cent of acquisitions treated with penicillin were followed by the appearance of penicillin resistant staphylococci in the throat, compared to only 19% in those patients who received no therapy. In two patients the presence of these penicillinase-producing organisms was associated with failure of penicillin treatment to eradicate the streptococcus.

COMMENT

It is clear that there are few solid data to explain why one child becomes sick or colonized, while another does not, with such a common organism as the beta-hemolytic streptococcus. From the clinician's point of view it has become exceedingly difficult to decide who should be treated, a paradoxical situation since there are few other infections for which such safe and effective therapy is available. The clinical diagnosis of streptococcal infection cannot be expected to be much better than 75% correct[19] even if "syndromes of symptoms and signs" are used[20] rather than single findings. On the other hand, streptococci are so often found in healthy children that their presence in children with acute respiratory infections does not, *per se*, indicate a significant streptococcal infection. Thus throat cultures, while helpful, cannot be used alone to decide which person requires therapy. Since therapy does not reduce the duration of acute symptoms[21] or lower the carrier rate in schools,[2, 22] there are only two general reasons to treat streptococcal disease: (1) the presence of suppurative complications, or (2) the risk of non-suppurative complications. The patient with suppurative complications presents only a minor problem; all would agree that he must be treated. But not until more satisfactory criteria are available for deciding who is most likely to develop the non-suppurative complications can more rational treatment be given. The fact that adequate penicillin therapy will reduce the antistreptolysin O response to a given infection has been shown before[17, 18] and is confirmed in our data. Such treatment for illness does not depress the individual's eventual production of antibodies, which may well be the response to a large number of asymptomatic infections ultimately giving rise to antibody responses, as shown by Breese et al.[23] Although type-specific streptococcal immunity does not prevent colonization, it does inhibit type-specific illness, which bears out the importance of such acquired immunity.[24] If, as seems likely, it is useful for an individual to develop antibodies, the least risk of non-suppurative complications probably follows such asymptomatic infections. Thus, in general, carrier states may be left untreated with very little risk.

Indeed, in occasional patients penicillin therapy seems to exert an adverse influence either by supressing the formation of protective antibody or by promoting the growth of penicillinase producing staphylococci that may interfere with the action of penicillin against streptococci.

The purpose of this investigation was to study the factors that predispose to respiratory infections, with the ultimate hope that one might gain some clinically useful data as to which individuals in family groups would be more likely to acquire such infections. The agent factors investigated did not yield much useful information; neither group, type nor number of colonies were very reliable indicators of

who had significant infection. Although only Group A streptococci are generally credited with responsibility for non-suppurative complications, Packer et al.[25] also reported that non-Group A organisms were capable of producing both illness and antibody response.

Age was an important factor in host susceptibility to streptococcal illness. (School-aged children were most susceptible, followed by 2-to-5-year-olds.) Weather played only a minor seasonal role, for while infection increased during the late winter and spring, precise types of weather or weather changes could not be shown to be associated with higher rates of infection in this small study group, as had previously been shown for influenza.[26] Close contact with other family members ill with proven streptococcal disease, particularly through sharing a bedroom, increased the likelihood of significant disease.

When acute life stress or chronic family disorganization is considered in addition to these other factors, there seems to be an additional criterion for selecting the more susceptible individual or family. Not only are higher acquisition and illness rates associated with acute and chronic stress situations, but also the proportion of persons in whom there is a significant rise of antistreptolysin O following the acquisition of streptococci increases with increasing stress. While this does not prove that such persons are more likely to have non-suppurative complications—only a very large study could show this—it does suggest that this may be one explanation for the well-known increased risk of rheumatic fever among lower socio economic groups.[27, 28] It remains to be determined whether stress is higher or significantly different in lower socioeconomic groups.

Certain emotional states have been shown to be associated with the onset of certain illnesses[29] and with the occurrence of beta-hemolytic streptococcal colonization.[30] Neither the precise emotional states that might predispose to increased rates of infection, nor the pathophysiologic mechanisms by which such changes could be mediated are known.

Stress is generally credited with increasing the output of adrenal corticosteroids, but beyond isolated examples in patients with tuberculosis[31, 32] and varicella,[33] few data exist to support such a mechanism as being responsible for increased risk in acute infections. While a great many studies have been performed in animals in an attempt to elucidate some of these factors responsible for resistance and susceptibility[34-39] it is difficult to translate these findings to man. Studies aimed at linking changes in the host's internal environment as measured by hormones, antibodies and leukocytes, with external environmental changes of weather, housing, nutrition, family living, fatigue, medical therapy, and life stress are clearly the next step. Only in this way can meaningful relations with sound therapeutic and preventive implications be found. From our data it seems likely that no one cause will be found, for beta-hemolytic streptococcal infections seem to be another example of "multiple causation" of disease.

SUMMARY

Sixteen lower-middle-class families, comprising 100 persons, were intensively studied for one year, with systematic throat cultures for beta-hemolytic streptococci, periodic measurements of antistreptolysin O titer, and clinical evaluation of all illnesses; the results of those observations were compared to certain dependent variables of host, agent, and environment. The factors that seemed to play an important part in determining whether a given person acquired a streptococcus, became ill with this acquisition, or developed a subsequent increase in antistreptolysin O were age, season, closeness of contact with an infected person as measured by sleeping arrangements, acute or chronic family stress, and penicillin treatment. No relationship was found between streptococcal episodes and the number or type of streptococci present, sex of the patient, the presence or absence of tonsils, an allergic history, changes in weather, type of housing, or family size. Further evidence for the multiple causation of beta-hemolytic streptococcal disease has been obtained, although the mechanisms through which these factors exert their influence are not clear.

REFERENCES

1. Pasteur, L., Joubert, J., and Chamberland: Le charbon des poules. Compt. Rend. Acad. Sci., **87**:47, 1878 (Cited by Perla, D., and Marmorston, J., in Natural Resistance and Clinical Medicine, Boston, Little, Brown & Co., 1941).

2. Cornfeld, D., and Hubbard, J. P.: A four-year study of the occurrence of beta-hemolytic streptococci in 64 school children. New Engl. J. Med., **264**:211, 1961.

3. Cornfeld, D., et. al.: Epidemiologic studies of streptococcal infection in school children. Amer. J. Pub. Health, **51**:242, 1961.

4. Mozziconacci, et al.: A study of group A hemolytic streptococcus carriers among school children: II. Significance of the findings. Acta Pediat., **50**:33, 1961.

5. Harvey, H. S., and Dunlap, M. D.: Upper respiratory flora of husbands and wives: a comparison. New Engl. J. Med., **262**:976, 1960.

6. James, W. E. S., Badger, G. F., and Dingle, J. H.: A study of illness in a group of Cleveland families: XIX. The epidemiology of the acquisition of group A streptococci and of associated illness. New Engl. J. Med., **262**: 687, 1960.

7. Breese, B. B., and Disney, F. A.: The spread of streptococcal infections in family groups. PEDIATRICS, **17**:834, 1956.

8. Brimblecombe, F. S. W., et al.: Family Studies of respiratory infections. Brit. Med. J., **1**:119, 1958.

9. Maxted, W. R.: The use of bacitracin for identifying group A hemolytic streptococci. J. Clin. Path., **6**:224, 1953.

10. Swift, H. F., Wilson, A. T., and Lancefield, R. C.: Typing group A streptococci by micro precipitation in capillary pipettes. J. Exp. Med., **78**:127, 1943.

11. Hodge, B. E., and Swift, H. F.: Varying hemolytic and constant combining capacity of streptolysins: influence on testing for antistreptolysins. (Massell, B.: Modification of this method). J. Exp. Med., **58**:277, 1933.

12. Rantz, L. A., Maroney, M., and DiCaprio, J. M.: Antistreptolysin O response following hemolytic streptococcus infection in early childhood. Arch. Int. Med., **87**:360, 1951.

13. Rantz, L. A. Maroney, M., and DiCaprio,

J. M.: Hemolytic streptococcal infection in childhood. PEDIATRICS, 12:498, 1953.

14. Bell, N. W., and Vogel, E. F. (Editors): Introductory Essays, *in* a Modern Introduction to The Family. Glencoe, Free Press, 1960.

15. Chamovitz, R., *et al.*: Prevention of rheumatic fever by treatment of previous streptococcal infections. New Engl. J. Med., 251:466, 1954.

16. Breese, B. B., and Disney, F. A.: Penicillin in the treatment of streptococcal infections: a comparison of effectiveness of five different oral and one parenteral form. New Engl. J. Med., 259:57, 1958.

17. Brock, L. L., and Siegel, A. C.: Studies on prevention of rheumatic fever: effect of time of initiation of treatment of streptococcal infections on immune response of host. J. Clin. Invest., 32:630, 1953.

18. Lancefield, R. C.: Persistence of type specific antibodies in man following infection with group A streptococci. J. Exp. Med., 110:271, 1959.

19. Breese, B. B., and Disney, F. A.: The accuracy of diagnosis of beta streptococcal infections on clinical grounds. J. Pediat., 44:670, 1954.

20. Stillerman, M., and Bernstein, S. H.: Streptococcal pharyngitis: evaluation of clinical syndromes in diagnosis. J. Dis. Child., 101:476, 1961.

21. Brumfitt, W., O'Grady, F., and Slater, J. D. H.: Benign streptococcal sore throat. Lancet, 2:419, 1959.

22. Phibbs, B., *et al.*: The Casper Project—an enforced mass-culture streptococci control program. J. A. M. A., 166:1113, 1958.

23. Breese, B. B., Disney, F. A., and Talpey, W. B.: The prevention of type specific immunity to streptococcal infections due to the therapeutic use of penicillin. J. Dis. Child., 100:353, 1960.

24. Wannamaker, L. W., *et al.*: Studies on immunity to streptococcal infection in man. Amer. J. Dis. Child., 86:347, 1953.

25. Packer, H., Arnoult, M. B., and Sprunt, D. H.: A study of hemolytic streptococcal infections in relation to antistreptolysin O titer changes in orphange children. J. Pediat., 48:545, 1956.

26. Kingdon, K. H.: Relative humidity and airborne infections. Amer. Rev. Resp. Infect., 81:504, 1960.

27. Knownelden, J.: Mortality from rheumatic heart disease in children and young adults in England and Wales. Brit. J. Soc. Prev. Med., 3:29, 1949.

28. Quinn, R. W., and Quinn, J. P.: Mortality due to rheumatic heart disease in the socio-economic districts of New Haven, Connecticut. Yale J. Biol. Med., 24:15, 1951.

29. Schmale, A. H., Jr.: Relationship of separation and depression to disease: a report on a hospitalized medical population. Psychosom. Med., 20:259, 1958.

30. Kaplan, S. M., Gottshalk, L. A., and Fleming, D. E.: Modifications of oropharyngeal bacteria with changes in the psychodynamic state. Arch. Neurol. Psychiat., 78:656, 1957.

31. Lurie, M. B.: The reticuloendothelial system: cortisone and thyroid function: their relation to native resistance and to infection. Ann. N.Y. Acad. Sci., 88:83, 1960.

32. Holmes, T. H., *et al.*: Psychosocial and Psychophysiologic studies of tuberculosis. Psychosom. Med., 19:134, 1957.

33. Haggerty, R. J., and Eley, R. C.: Varicella and Cortisone. PEDIATRICS, 18:160, 1956.

34. Dubos, R. J., and Schaedler, R. W.: Nutrition and infection. J. Pediat., 55:1, 1959.

35. Evans, D. G., Miles, A. H., and Niven, J. S. F.: The enhancement of bacterial infections by adrenaline. Brit. J. Exp. Path., 29:20, 1948.

36. Hayashida, T.: Effect of pituitaryadrenocorticotropic and growth hormone on the resistance of rats infected with pasteurella pestis. J. Exp. Med., 106:127, 1957.

37. Teodoru, C. V., and Shwartzman, G.: Endocrine factors in pathogenesis of experimental poliomyelitis in hamsters: role of inoculatory and environmental stress. Proc. Soc. Exp. Biol. Med., 91:181, 1956.

38. Sprunt, D. H., and Flanigan, C. C.: The effect of malnutrition on the susceptibility of the host to viral infection. J. Exp. Med., 104:687, 1956.

39. Rasmussen, A. F., Jr., Marsh, J. T., and Brill, N. Q.: Increased susceptibility to herpes simplex in mice subjected to avoidance–learning stress or restraint. Proc. Soc. Exp. Biol. Med., 96:183, 1957.

Acknowledgment

The authors wish to express their appreciation for the professional advice of Dr. Benedict Massell in carrying out this study, and to the families whose co-operation made the study possible.

40

INHIBITION OF MANTOUX REACTION BY
DIRECT SUGGESTION UNDER HYPNOSIS

Stephen Black, J. H. Humphrey, and Janet S. F. Niven

Experimental inhibition of immediate-type hyper-sensitivity responses by direct suggestion under hypnosis (D.S.U.H.) has already been reported (Black, 1963a, 1963b). The results are presented below of a study of the effect of D.S.U.H. on the delayed-type hyper-sensitivity response to tuberculin. Four Mantoux-positive subjects were tested by intracutaneous injection of purified protein derivative of tuberculin (P.P.D.) in one arm ; the tests were then repeated in the other arm after a period of daily treatment by D.S.U.H. not to react to the injection. Records were made of the reactions in terms of the areas of firm swelling and erythema. Since the essential elements of the tuberculin reaction are characterized by cellular infiltration, full-thickness skin biopsy specimens were also taken for histological comparison.

Methods and Materials

Subjects.—Since skin biopsies were required, only male subjects were accepted, and because these investigations concerned a psycho-physiological phenomenon and not a therapeutic process the subjects were selected as being individuals thought likely to inhibit an allergic reaction following D.S.U.H., for reasons explained elsewhere (Black, 1963a). Twenty-eight male hypnotic subjects were screened by hypnosis and preliminary Mantoux-testing in the selection of the four found suitable for the experiment. Two of those chosen were deep-trance subjects, amnesic of the period of the hypnotic trance and capable of being psychologically regressed to childhood states, and two were medium-trance subjects, deeply hypnotizable, but neither amnesic nor regressable. A fifth Mantoux-negative medium-trance subject was also examined.

Experimental Procedure

The experiment was divided into six parts : (1) intra-dermal marking of the experimental areas ; (2) pre-liminary assessment of tuberculin sensitivity ; (3) clinical assessment, recording, and biopsy of the response area *before* D.S.U.H. not to react to P.P.D. ; (4) treatment by D.S.U.H. not to react to P.P.D. ; (5) clinical assessment, recording, and biopsy of the response area *after* D.S.U.H. ; and (6) histological study of the results.

To limit any effects due to variations in technique each procedure was carried out by the same operator throughout the experiment : the inoculations with P.P.D. were given by Dr. T. S. L. Beswick, then of the Division of Immunological Products Control, M.R.C. Labora-tories, Hampstead, London ; the biopsy specimens were taken by Mr. I. F. K. Muir, consultant in the Mount Vernon Centre for Plastic Surgery, Northwood, Middle-sex ; and all other procedures were divided between us as indicated with initials in the text.

1. *Intradermal Marking of Experimental Areas.*—To facilitate histological examination of the biopsy material the skin of each subject was marked by intradermal inoculation with Pelikan black ink in volumes of 0.01 ml. at two sites on each forearm, 8 and 18 cm. below the level of the medial epicondyle of the humerus (S. B.). As with all inoculations throughout the experiment, the needle was inserted into the skin from distal to proximal, thus limiting the region of trauma involved to the distal portion of the specimen. After marking in this way, a period of not less than eight weeks was allowed in every case for any temporary effect of the ink to subside completely.

2. *Preliminary Assessment of Tuberculin Sensitivity.*—To facilitate comparison between one subject and

another it was aimed to administer to each subject a quantity of P.P.D. sufficient to elicit a response with an area of firm swelling of diameter 1 cm. This degree of response was chosen as being a clear-cut positive of moderate intensity. The sensitivity of each subject was therefore determined three days before the first experimental test in each case. Into an area of the skin of the right forearm, 6 cm. lateral to the marked sites, intracutaneous injections were made of 0.1 ml. of P.P.D. solution diluted with Hanks's solution, equivalent to 10, 1, and 0.1 T.U. The responses at 48 hours were then recorded and that dilution selected which gave a response of the right order in each individual (S. B.). Throughout the experiment all areas of swelling and erythema were recorded by tracing directly on to "sellotape," and the areas were subsequently measured by planimetry, as already described (Black, 1963b).

3. *Clinical Assessment, Recording, and Biopsy of Response Area before D.S.U.H.*—Tests of the response before treatment by D.S.U.H. were carried out in each case at the distal marked site on the right arm ; the proximal marked site on the same arm was used as a control area into which an inoculation of an equal volume of Hanks's solution was given. The intra-cutaneous inoculation with the selected dilution of P.P.D. at the distal site was given in a volume of 0.1 ml., using a 1-ml. tuberculin syringe and a No. 26 needle. The point of the needle was aimed to deliver the fluid in the skin just distal to the actual mark, so that the resulting bleb was in each case precisely under the mark. With a similar syringe and needle, 0.1 of Hanks's solution was then injected into the proximal site. At 48 hours an independent clinical assessment of the Mantoux reaction was made (J. H. H.) and the areas of weal and erythema were recorded (S. B.). Full-thickness skin biopsies were then taken from both sites under general anaesthesia. The biopsy areas were out-lined so as to include 1 cm. of normal skin proximally and distally, the distal end being marked before incision with a silk suture tag to facilitate gentle handling. In addition 3 mm. of normal skin was included medial and lateral to the area of the response, so that the eventual specimen was a lozenge-shaped strip of skin approximately 3 cm. long and 1.6 cm. wide at its widest part. At the proximal control site a strip of skin with similar dimensions was outlined around the intradermal mark and the distal end identified in the same way with a suture. Histological preparation was begun immediately after removal (J. S. F. N.).

4. *Treatment by D.S.U.H. Not to React to P.P.D.*—Forty-eight hours after the first biopsies were taken each subject started a 12-day course of daily treatment by D.S.U.H. in which forceful suggestions were given to the effect that there would be no reaction to any further inoculations with P.P.D. (S. B.). The subject lay on a couch and was hypnotized into a deep trance by use of a code word and a deepening technique already described (Black, 1963a). The principal suggestions were given in a standardized form with the words: "You are now different—you will no longer react to the injection as you did before: there will be no redness, no swelling, no heat, no itching, no pain—the skin will remain perfectly normal on both sites of your left arm after the next injections—your skin is now different, your left arm is now different, you are now different...." This was repeated no fewer than five times at each session together with any other suggestions judged by the hypnotist as likely to be effective according to the

subject's personality and history. As additional rein-forcement, both under hypnosis and in the waking state, all subjects were encouraged to relate any subjective experience associated with the suggestions and to discuss the experiment. Material obtained in this was then fed back to the individual concerned in the form of further suggestions. After five days each subject was also instructed that he would dream about the experi-ment, and the next day the dream material resulting from these suggestions was elicited under hypnosis and similarly used for reinforcement. Daily treatment in this way was continued until the biopsies were taken.

5. *Clinical Assessment, Recording, and Biopsy of Response Area after D.S.U.H.*—The second inoculation with P.P.D. was carried out while D.S.U.H. not to react was being given. The procedure was otherwise identical with procedure No. 3 in each case, except that the inoculations were given in the left arm. At 48 hours an independent clinical assessment of the Mantoux reaction was made (J. H. H.), the areas of swelling and erythema were recorded (S. B.), and full-thickness skin biopsies were taken and prepared for histological examination in the same way (J. S. F. N.).

6. *Histological Study of Results.*—Each specimen taken at operation was immediately pinned out in such a way as to prevent distortion during fixation, but also to allow free access of the fixative, which was a solution of saturated corrosive sublimate containing 4% glacial acetic acid. Cuts were later made transversely to the surface of a short axis so that penetration of the fixative would be as complete as possible. The wedges of tissue thus obtained consisted of (1) a central block within the limits of the marker spot area, 2.3 mm. in thickness ; (2) an adjoining block containing the proximal zone of the marker spot, approximately 2.5–3 mm. in thickness ; and (3) a distal adjoining block, which in this instance included, as well as the peripheral part of the marker spot, the site of the needle puncture. All these wedges of tissue were sectioned serially at 6μ in their entirety. The two remaining pieces of tissue, proximal and distal, were also cut transversely. These were then sectioned serially only to beyond the limits of pathological change. In the specimens taken from the areas of skin into which Hanks's solution alone had been injected, only the central blocks required to be cut serially in their entirety. The staining methods used included haema-toxylin and eosin, orcein for elastic tissue, the periodic-acid Schiff procedure, and various trichrome methods for collagen and for fibrin.

Results

The results are discussed in terms of (1) assessment and measurement of the areas of swelling and erythema, (2) histology, and (3) subjective experience. The four experimental subjects are here designated A, B, C, and D ; the control Mantoux-negative subject, E.

Assessment and Measurement of Areas of Swelling and Erythema

Before treatment all four subjects (A–D) gave definite positive tuberculin responses. The tuberculin-negative subject (E) gave no measurable response to 10 times the maximum amount of P.P.D. used in the other subjects. After treatment by D.S.U.H. not to react to P.P.D., the individual responses in A, B, and C were negative. A slight response was still evident in subject D, but was small enough to be described as Mantoux-negative. There was also no measurable swelling in

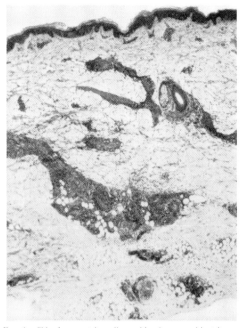

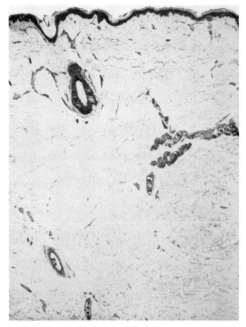

FIG. 1.—Skin from a tuberculin-sensitive human subject inoculated 48 hours previously with 10 units P.P.D. Hair follicles and sweat and sebaceous glands are embedded in a dense infiltrate of mononuclear cells of lymphocytic type. Similar cells are present also in the hypodermis and are abundant in the fat and around blood-vessels. (×35.)

FIG. 2.—Skin from tuberculin-negative human subject inoculated 48 hours previously with 100 units P.P.D. The skin is essentially normal and shows the usual distribution of accessory skin structures and blood-vessels. (×30.)

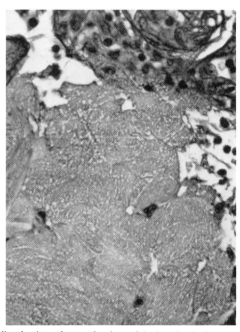

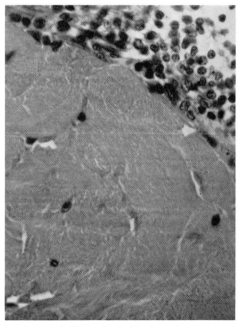

FIG. 3.—Area of connective tissue of the hypodermis close to a blood-vessel showing the loose reticular structure of the collagen in the normal uninhibited response. (×645.)

FIG. 4.—Area similar to that in Fig. 3 showing the compact character of the collagen in the inhibited response after treatment by D.S.U.H. (×645.)

Hypnotic Inhibition of Mantoux Reaction

subjects A, B, and C, and in D the area was reduced from 308 to 10 sq. mm. The area of erythema was reduced in all subjects but absent only in subject C. A summary of these results is given in the Table.

Mantoux Reaction: Effects of D.S.U.H. Not to React

Subjects: Hypnotic trance state:	A Medium	B Deep	C Medium	D Deep	E Medium
Normal Response					
Dose (T.U.)	10	0·1	10	1·0	100
Clinical assessment ..	Pos.	Pos.	Pos.	Pos.	Neg.
Area of firm swelling (sq. mm.)	78	28	42	308	0
Area of erythema (sq. mm.)	289	154	218	770	0
Response after D.S.U.H. Not to React					
Dose (T.U.)	10	0·1	10	1·0	Not tested
Clinical assessment ..	Neg.	Neg.	Neg.	Neg.	
Area of firm swelling (sq. mm.)	0	0	0	10	
Area of erythema (sq. mm.)	48	83	. 0	319	

Histology

Despite the clear naked-eye differences between the normal uninhibited response and that following treatment by D.S.U.H. the cellular pattern was found to be indistinguishable in both instances. As would be expected in a 48-hour tuberculin response (Special Plate, Fig. 1), extensive lymphocytic infiltration in relation to blood-vessels was the outstanding feature, and many of the capillaries and venules were packed with lymphocytes. In the central zone, where the reactions were most intense, lymphocytes were also found in the connective tissue at some distance from the blood-vessels, either in small groups or in rows separating collagen bundles. They were also abundant in the interstices of the fatty tissue at the lower margins of the specimen. Polymorphs were scanty and confined mainly to capillary channels. A representative section from the Mantoux-negative subject (E) is shown in Fig. 2 (Special Plate).

The explanation of any difference between the responses before and after D.S.U.H. must therefore reside in non-cellular factors of the response, and of these the microscopically visible local oedema and erythema are the most obviously relevant. Staining for fibrin was negative except in the normal uninhibited response of D, where there was a small haemorrhage ; and here the fibrin was present only in the haemorrhagic area. However, it was noted consistently under standard conditions that the collagen in the control specimens and in the inhibited response stained more intensely than the collagen of the normal uninhibited response and that the fibril bundles themselves were more compact. With the periodic-acid Schiff procedure and trichrome methods used it was possible to define in the normal uninhibited response a distinct separation between the fibrillar material and ground substance in the collagen (Special Plate, Fig. 3). In the control material (no P.P.D.) and in the inhibited response (Special Plate, Fig. 4) the individual fibrils were not separated by obvious interfibrillar material in this way. It must be assumed, therefore, that this appearance is due to the accumulation of fluid between the fibrillar components of the collagen.

Distinction was less easy in respect of the erythema. At the microscopical level it was not possible on structural findings to divide the material into two groups as was the case when using collagen appearance as a method of differentiation. Beyond the area of lymphocytic infiltration the capillaries in the third plexus just below the epidermis regularly appeared more conspicuous and congested than in the controls, but areas could also be found in the inhibited series in which the dilatation and congestion were of the same order.

Subjective Experience

All subjects reported paraesthesiae associated with the left arm after the sessions when treatment was given by D.S.U.H. not to react to P.P.D. As stated, the inoculations with P.P.D. were given under hypnosis, and all four subjects reported afterwards that they were unaware of the injection, although no specific instructions concerning anaesthesia had been given. When seen at 24 hours for further treatment by D.S.U.H. all subjects reported that there was " no reaction " and that they had felt no itching, no pain, and no subjective evidence of inflammation of any kind. At 48 hours, when subjects A and B showed small areas of erythema and subject D a very small area of swelling as well, all four still maintained that they felt " nothing like the reaction before."

Discussion

The experiments described above were designed so far as possible to exclude any variations in the intensity of the successive tuberculin reactions in a given subject apart from such as might be due to hypnotic suggestion. Thus the subjects were well sensitized to tuberculin, and a small test dose was sufficient to elicit a reaction which was quite definite, though of only weak-to-moderate intensity. It is unlikely that either the preliminary injections or the tests themselves would have affected the subsequent reactions ; in so far as any desensitization might have occurred it would have been most likely to affect the first test, which was that carried out before any suggestion under hypnosis had been made. The solutions were prepared and the intracutaneous injections were performed by persons not connected with the investigation, and the subsequent assessments of the macroscopic responses were made independently by two observers.

Although the findings relate to only four test subjects they indicate that there was a clear-cut diminution in the macroscopic response to tuberculin after D.S.U.H. not to react. This was evident in the size of the central firm swelling and of the surrounding area of erythema. Despite the absence of any obvious swelling in three of the subjects a palpable area of induration was present at the sites injected with tuberculin.

When examined histologically after 48 hours all the reaction sites showed extensive mononuclear-cell infiltration typical of a tuberculin response ; such changes were absent from control sites injected with diluent alone, or from sites in a Mantoux-negative control subject injected with much larger amounts of tuberculin. Thus, although the macroscopic reactions were not intense, the underlying cellular changes indicated that an extensive specific reaction had occurred. There were *no* detectable differences in the degree of mononuclear-cell infiltration in reactions elicited before and after treatment by D.S.U.H., and in this respect the reactions were not affected by the treatment. However, the naked-eye differences were confirmed at the histological level by the observation that the fibrillar components of the collagen bundles, as compared with those of normal skin, were conspicuously separated from one another in the reactions studied before treatment with D.S.U.H., whereas after treatment this feature was virtually absent. Even in subject D, in whom a slight degree of firm swelling was recorded, specimens taken before and after D.S.U.H. could be readily distinguished. The detailed histological observations will form the subject of a separate publication by one of us (J. S. F. N.).

Tuberculin-reactive humans almost invariably have circulating antibodies against components of the tubercle bacillus, especially against carbohydrate constituents, and traces of the latter are found in nearly all preparations of tuberculin, including P.P.D. (see, for example, Long, 1958). Consequently tuberculin reactions carried out in man almost inevitably show, in addition to the mononuclear-cell infiltration typically associated with a delayed-type response, characteristics associated with Arthus-type hypersensitivity. These, in experimental animals, are represented by vascular damage, oedema, and a marked degree of polymorphonuclear migration ; they are maximal after 6 to 18 hours, but may persist for 48 hours, although by then the polymorphonuclear leucocytes will largely have become pyknotic or will have been destroyed. It is difficult to be certain whether the oedema seen in the human tuberculin reaction represents the residue of an Arthus-type response or is truly associated with the delayed-type response. Nevertheless our findings suggest that it was the exudation of fluid in the response that was affected by D.S.U.H. not to react, while the cellular infiltration characteristic of the delayed-type response was essentially unchanged. This evidence would therefore seem to indicate that the mechanism of inhibition by D.S.U.H. involves a vascular constituent and that the process is probably similar to the inhibition by D.S.U.H. of the immediate-type hypersensitivity weal and erythema response already reported (Black, 1963a, 1963b).

Conclusions

It is concluded that the tuberculin reaction as observed clinically in the Mantoux test can be inhibited by D.S.U.H. in suitable subjects, although histologically there may be no observable change in the degree of cellular infiltration. In the normal uninhibited response, however, the connective tissue was demonstrated to be consistently less compact than in the inhibited response and control material, and this is assumed to be due to an accumulation of fluid between the fibrillar components of the collagen. On this evidence it is thus further concluded that such inhibition of the Mantoux reaction by D.S.U.H. probably involves control of the fluid exudation normally present and that therefore in the mechanism of inhibition a vascular constituent is likely to be involved.

Summary

The effect of direct suggestion under hypnosis (D.S.U.H.) on the delayed-type hypersensitivity response to tuberculin in the Mantoux test was studied in four hypnotic subjects and full-thickness skin biopsies were taken for histological examination. The results showed that the tuberculin reaction as observed clinically in the Mantoux test was inhibited by D.S.U.H., and that while histologically there was no observable change in the degree of cellular infiltration, there was evidence that the exudation of fluid had been inhibited. It is concluded that the Mantoux-positive reaction can be inhibited by D.S.U.H. to give a Mantoux-negative result and that a vascular constituent of the reaction is probably involved in the mechanism of inhibition.

REFERENCES

Black, S. (1963a). *Brit. med. J.*, **1**, 925.
—— (1963b)   Ibid., **1**, 990.
Long, E. R. (1958). *The Chemistry and Chemotherapy of Tuberculosis.* Baillière, Tindall and Cox, London.

41

THE RELATIONSHIP OF PERSONALITY TO THE PRESENCE OF RHEUMATOID FACTOR IN ASYMPTOMATIC RELATIVES OF PATIENTS WITH RHEUMATOID ARTHRITIS

George F. Solomon and Rudolf H. Moos

Two groups of asymptomatic female relatives of patients with rheumatoid arthritis were compared psychologically by means of the Minnesota Multiphasic Personality Inventory. The results indicated a greater incidence of emotional decompensation in those relatives lacking rheumatoid factor. It is speculated that emotional disturbance in conjunction with rheumatoid factor may lead to rheumatoid disease.

As Moos has pointed out,[1] the retrospective correlation of personality patterns or emotional conflicts with an organic disease inevitably leads to questions of whether the illness, especially when a chronic one, might induce personality change; whether the observed factors might only reflect what the

From the Department of Psychiatry, Stanford University School of Medicine, Palo Alto, Calif.

Supported in part by grants from the Northern California Chapter of the Arthritis and Rheumatism Foundation and the National Foundation. The work was carried out in conjunction with family studies by the Rheumatic Disease Group, University of California Medical Center, San Francisco. We are greatly indebted to Dr. Ephraim P. Engleman, who made the subjects available, to Dr. Wallace V. Epstein, in whose laboratory the serological determinations were performed, and to Mrs. Eleanor Vaughn, who was of great help throughout the study.

Reprinted from *Psychosom. Med.* 27, 350–360, 1965.

patient says about himself in test or interview, thus possibly representing only a change in response tendency; and, of course, whether such personality characteristics are "specific" to the disease in question. Other considerations limiting the applicability of results of studies of personality factors associated with psychosomatic disorders have been: (1) gross lack of information about patient characteristics, (2) considerably differing methods and theoretical orientations among studies, (3) almost universal lack of adequate control groups, and (4) gross over-emphasis of "negative" personality evaluations.

Provided that there is an awareness of pertinent variables, a clear definition of theoretical assumptions, and careful controls, many of the aforementioned difficulties can be best overcome by predictive studies to determine in what sorts of individuals and/or in the context of what situations psychosomatic disease ensues. Another prospective approach is to attempt to correlate personality variables with a physiologic variable that is predictive of, rather than indicative of, disease. We have been concerned with the problem of personal and social factors in relation to the onset and course of rheumatoid arthritis. In the study reported here we attempted to correlate personality characteristics with the presence of rheumatoid factor,* also referred to as "FII," in asymptomatic female relatives of patients with rheumatoid arthritis. Although the issue remains controversial, Lawrence[2] has stated that current evidence makes it appear that the presence of rheumatoid factor in the serum may predispose a person to arthritis. Thus, any emotional correlates of this serologic abnormality may have predictive significance.

Predictive studies have been carried out in certain other illnesses for which "psychosomatic" pathogenic mechanisms have been postulated. Lebovits and co-workers[3] administered the Minnesota Multiphasic Personality Inventory (MMPI) to a large group of middle-aged men; 5 years later they retested 75 of these men in whom coronary heart disease had developed and 75 matched healthy men. They found that differences between original and new MMPI scores (as a result of increases in "neuroticism") were greater in those who suffered myocardial infarction than in healthy men or those with angina pectoris only. Although retrospective conclusions about differences between the mean scores of patients with angina and those in comparison groups would have accurately reflected differences observed prospectively, this would not have been the case between scores of those with infarct and scores of comparison (healthy

and angina) groups. They conclude that it is erroneous to infer from data of this type that a particular constellation of personality factors existed before the onset of major illness in an individual case; in some instances, however, conclusions from prospective and retrospective data will be similar if based on means derived from relatively large samples.

Harris and co-workers[4] correlated psychologic variables with a predictive physiologic variable in the absence of manifest disease. Because of the higher-than-average actuarial probability of later hypertension among young adults with at least transiently elevated blood pressure, Harris et al. selected a group of college women with elevated blood pressure on matriculation physical examination. These "prehypertensives" and matched controls were exposed to emotion-provoking, stressful psychodramas. The prehypertensives were found to be less well-controlled, more impulsive, more egocentric, less adaptable, and apparently more vulnerable to psychologic stress than controls. In a study of the same women 4 years later, Kalis et al.[5] found the prehypertensives to be experiencing unusual difficulties in establishing appropriate life roles, and their behavior seemed likely to provoke stressful interactions with other people. The personality characteristics of these prehypertensives were like those observed in older women with essential hypertension.

Weiner and co-workers[6] were able to differentiate hyper- from hypopepsinogen secretors on the basis of psychologic tests. Although they found duodenal ulcers developing only in persons with high serum pepsinogen levels, the results of their study indicated that a combination of a high rate of gastric secretion, a particular personality constellation centering around persistent, unresolved conflict about dependency and oral gratification, and exposure to social situations

---

*A macromolecular anti-gamma globulin autoantibody that is itself a gamma globulin.

noxious to the individual were apparently all necessary to precipitate an active ulcer.

Ziff[7] summarized the current knowledge of the clinical aspects of rheumatoid factors as follows. Titer tends to be: (1) relatively fixed with time, (2) characteristic of the patient, (3) established early in the course of the disease, (4) not related to "activity" of disease, (5) correlated with the destructive features of the disease (especially vascular) and with sustained disease, and (6) absent or low in children with juvenile (Still's) disease. Somatic mutations,[8] chronic antigenic stimulation,[9] or in vivo alteration of gamma globulin[10]—as may occur in antigen-antibody reactions[11] or secondary to proteolytic enzyme activity (which is increased under conditions of stress)[12]—have all been suggested as leading to the formation of rheumatoid factor. The actual clinical significance of the rheumatoid factors and even their prevalence, especially in relatives of rheumatoid patients, remain somewhat unclear, and in large-scale prospective studies investigators are currently attempting clarification. Lawrence and Ball[13] found a fourfold increase in incidence of clinical, radiologic, and serologic rheumatoid arthritis in relatives of patients suffering from serologically positive rheumatoid arthritis and no increase in serologic abnormalities in relatives of propositi who had clinical disease without serologic abnormality. Data on the incidence of rheumatoid factor are not comparable in most studies (none of which has included normals, rheumatoids, and relatives), since the sensitivity of the test for rheumatoid factor varies greatly according to technique. Most patients with rheumatoid arthritis have rheumatoid factor (approximately 85% of patients with active disease according to the American Rheumatism Association).[14] Since we cannot state the general prevalence of rheumatoid factor in asymptomatic relatives of rheumatoid patients because of inconsistency and incomparability of methods among studies, we can only cite the fact that approximately 25% of the first-degree relatives in our sample were FII-positive. Rheumatoid factor,[15] like other autoantibodies,[16] occurs with greater frequency in the elderly (persons over 55 years of age).

In his review of data on familial predisposition to rheumatoid disease, Holman[17] found that current data indicate that there is an unusually high incidence of rheumatic disease and immunologic abnormalities within certain families and that many asymptomatic members of these families will possess serologic abnormalities. He feels that the serologic factors themselves are not pathogenic but, rather, are by-products of altered immunologic reactivity. He favors the contention that some form of susceptibility to rheumatic disease is influenced by hereditary factors. In a recent investigation of five sets of monozygotic female twins discordant for rheumatoid arthritis, Meyerowitz et al.[18] found that although personality patterns were similar in both twins and were like those described for patients with rheumatoid arthritis (e.g., presence of hypermotility and tendency to do for others), the affected twin had been involved in conflictual interpersonal relationships. They concluded that precipitation of manifest illness in a predisposed individual appears to be determined by factors mediated in the course of psychologic stress. Schmidt and Slatis'[19] evidence of an incidence of clinical and serologic abnormalities in the spouses of patients with rheumatoid arthritis higher than that in spouses of control patients may be interpreted as being in agreement with the conclusions of Cobb,[20] who states that rheumatoid arthritis may be "transmitted" interpersonally. Perhaps mates with personality factors associated with serologic abnormality may be selected by persons with rheumatoid arthritis. Cobb[21] suggests that psychosocial factors account for the familial aggregation of rheumatoid arthritis, a position analogous to that of Jackson,[22] who criticized the evidence for genetic transmission of schizophrenia. The genetic hypothesis in rheumatoid arthritis is challenged by the absence of familial aggregation of rheumatoid disease or serologic abnormalities found by Burch and others[23] in a tribe of American Indians.

Method

Subjects

Thirty-six healthy female adult or adolescent relatives of female clinic patients suffering from rheumatoid arthritis were included in this study. The health of the subjects was determined by history, physical examination and joint X-ray. The patients to whom the subjects were related were classified as having "definite" (fulfilling five or six of the criteria established by the American Rheumatism Association for active rheumatoid arthritis[14]) or "classical" (fulfilling seven or eight of the criteria) rheumatoid arthritis. One of these criteria is the presence of rheumatoid factor. About 85% of the patients to whom our subjects are related are FII-positive.

Fourteen FII-positive female relatives were studied and the results compared with those obtained on 21 FII-negative female relatives of comparable mean age and socioeconomic status; the average age and years of education in the FII-positive group was 47.9 and 10.2 years, respectively, and in the FII-negative group, 49.0 and 11.0 years, respectively. The subjects were distributed according to marital status as shown below.

FII	Single	Married	Widowed, divorced or separated*
Pos.	3	5	6
Neg.	1	14	6

The distribution of the subjects according to number of children and occupational class is as follows:

---

*Includes subjects who have remarried.

Children (No.)	FII positive	FII negative
0	5	2
1	3	2
2	2	6
3	4	7
>3	0	4
Occupational class*		
I	0	0
II	1	3
III	10	16
IV	3	2
V	0	0

Seven of the 21 FII negative and 6 of the 14 FII positive relatives in this study had been studied previously.[24, 25]

The Fraction II hemagglutination test, which measures rheumatoid factor by the agglutination of washed sheep red cells coated with Fraction II of human plasma,[26] was used to measure rheumatoid factor. In this test the dilution of serum (titer) at which agglutination of the coated cells still occurs, the number of the three separate, presumably identical tubes at a given titer showing agglutination, and the amount of agglutination in each tube are all taken into account in determining positivity. Thus, at lower titers a given result may be judged either positive or negative on the basis of consideration of all criteria. The hemagglutination test tends to be more sensitive in detecting rheumatoid factor than the commonly used latex fixation test. In order to obtain a sufficient sample for statistical purposes, a few individuals on whom only one test was done were included in the study Serologic data are summarized in Tables 1 and 2.

Procedure

Relatives were asked to complete the MMPI as part of a general family study

*Group I, professional; Group II, semiprofessional and managerial; Group III, clerical, skilled tradesmen, and owners of retail businesses; Group IV, semiskilled occupations, minor clerical positions, and minor businesses; and Group V, trades and occupations requiring little education or ability. Subjects not employed are classified according to occupation of person on whom they are dependent for support.

TABLE 1. Serologic Data on FII Positive Group

Subject	*Titer*								
	0	1:28	1:56	1:112	1:224	1:448	1:896	1:1792	1:14,000
1						++			
2			−		+	+			
3						+			+
4	−		+	+					
5							+	+	
6						+	+		
7					+				
8						+			
9			−		+	+			
10					+	+			
11					+	+			
12				+					
13							+		
14					++				

Minus (−) indicates FII-negative; plus (+), FII-positive. Each symbol represents a single determination.

which also included medical history, questionnaires, physical examination, and X-ray and laboratory tests. Responses on 88 MMPI scales,[27] including the 12 basic scales and a variety of special scales derived from many different research reports, were analyzed by computer. A one-tailed statistical test based on our previous prediction of direction of response in the FII-positive vs. FII-negative relatives, was used to determine differences between the 2 groups.

Results

The responses of the subjects on 16 of the 88 MMPI scales showed statistically significant (P < .05) differences between the 2 groups. The FII-positive relatives scored significantly higher on scales reflecting inhibition of aggression (impulse control), concern about the social desirability of actions and about socioeconomic status, and ego strength (indicative of capacity for successful psychologic defense, coping, mastery, and integration). They also scored higher on an ulcer scale, the items of which reflect compliance, shyness, conscientiousness, religiosity, and moralism.

The FII-negative relatives scored higher on the standard "psychesthenia" scale, essentially indicative of the obsessive-compulsive syndrome consisting of rumination and rituals, abnormal fears, worrying, difficulties in concentrating, guilt feelings, excessive vacillation in making decisions, excessively high personal standards, self-critical feelings, and aloofness. Interestingly, the FII-negative relatives had more somatic complaints; showed more psychoneuroticism and less ego mastery, with defective inhibition of impulses; and tended more readily to admit psychiatric symptoms, to lack self-acceptance, and to feel both self and social alienation. Self concept and ideal self are seen as relatively disparate in the FII-negative group. The FII-negative group also tended more frequently to dissimulate, to attempt deliberately to appear less healthy. This group more often demonstrated evidence of failure of psychologic defenses, as reflected in scores on the judged-anxiety scale and inner-maladjustment scales, indices of emotional illness. The responses to the inner-maladjustment scale showed the greatest differences between the 2 groups

TABLE 2. SEROLOGIC DATA ON FII-NEGATIVE GROUP

Subject	Titer 0	1:28	1:56	1:112
1	--			
2	--			
3	-		-	
4	--	-		
5	---			
6	---			
7	-			
8			-	
9	---			
10	---			
11	---			
12	-		-	
13	--			
14	-			--
15	---			
16	---			
17	-			
18	---			
19				-
20	-	-		
21	-			

Minus (−) indicates FII-negative; plus (+), FII-positive. Each symbol represents a single determination.

(mean of 40 for FII-negatives vs. mean of 26 for FII-positives). Consistent with these elevations, the FII-negative group had higher dependency scores. Their relative elevation on the ethnocentrism scale implies rigidity and inflexibility of emotional attitudes, which may be related to poor prognosis in psychotherapy. It should be recalled that the ego strength scale, the criterion for the development of which was response to psychotherapy, was higher in the FII-positive group. The FII-negative group also scored higher on the paranoid schizophrenia scale, which serves well in separating new schizophrenics from other general psychiatric cases and which, as might be expected, contains a great number of unfavorable items.

Specific MMPI items answered *true* significantly more frequently (P < .05) by the FII-positive relatives are listed below.

I seldom or never have dizzy spells.
I find it hard to make talk when I meet new people.
I have few or no pains.
I am often inclined to go out of my way to win a point with someone who has opposed me.

The FII-negative relatives checked the following items *true* significantly more frequently:

My hardest battles are with myself.
Some people are so bossy that I feel like doing the opposite of what they request, even though I know they are right.
Most people are honest chiefly through fear of being caught.
I have often lost out on things because I couldn't make up my mind soon enough.
I like to know some important people because it makes me feel important.
I dream frequently about things that are best kept to myself.
I often feel as if things are not real.
People often disappoint me.
I worry quite a bit over possible misfortunes.
I used to have imaginary companions.
I am quite often not in on the gossip and talk of the group I belong to.
I often memorize numbers that are not important (such as automobile licenses, etc.).
I have a habit of counting things that are not important (such as bulbs on electric signs, etc.).
Sometimes some unimportant thought will run through my mind and bother me for days.

It can be seen from both scale score and specific item differences that apparently healthy relatives of rheumatoid arthritic patients who have rheumatoid factor in their sera tended to have well-functioning psychologic defenses and to be essentially psychiatrically asymptomatic. On the other hand, psychoneurosis and even more serious mental disturbances with failure of psychic homeostasis—anxiety, alienation, lack of control, fear, guilt, low self-esteem—were relatively much more common in those relatives lacking rheumatoid factor. In the latter group it was as if various defenses including somatizing and projection were being used in relatively unsuccessful attempts to ward off conflict and painful affect.

It must be emphasized that the *magnitude* of the scale elevations differentiating the FII-negative from the FII-positive group generally was not great quantitatively. The differences are consonant with the FII-positive group reflecting a generally emotionally healthy population and with the FII-negative group containing a somewhat higher than expected incidence of a variety of psychopathologic states.

Discussion

A survey of the literature[1] in this area comprising data on over 5000 patients disclosed that investigators generally agreed that patients with rheumatoid arthritis, when compared to various control groups, tended to be self-sacrificing, masochistic, conforming, self-conscious, shy, inhibited, perfectionistic, over-reactive to their illness, and interested in sports and games. In a study comparing 16 female patients with rheumatoid arthritis and their same-sexed, nearest-aged, healthy siblings by means of personality tests and interviews,[24, 25] the patients showed more compliance-subservience, nervousness-restlessness, depression, conservatism-security seeking, and sensitivity (to anger) than the controls. Patients tended to describe themselves as nervous, tense, worried, struggling, depressed, moody, high-strung, and easily upset, whereas their siblings tended to describe themselves as liking people, as active and constantly busy, as easy to get acquainted with, and as good, hard, conscientious, productive workers. Patients were bothered more by perceived rejection by their mothers and strictness from their fathers. Patients also showed a good deal more masochism, self-sacrifice, and denial of hostility. No differences were found between the 2 groups in either the extent of their physical activity or in the extent to which they manifested dependency. A MMPI study[28] of a large number of females with rheumatoid arthritis and their healthy family members gave similar results. Scales differentiating patients from relatives reflected: (1) physical symptoms; (2) depression, apathy, and lack of motivation; (3) general "neurotic" symptoms such as anxiety, masochism, self-alienation, and over-compliance; (4) psychologic rigidity; and, (5) similarity to other psychosomatic conditions. In addition, comparisons of patients showed that those whose disease progressed rapidly[29] and those whose functional incapacity was greater than expected for the stage of their illness[30] showed more evidence of emotional decompensation such as self-alienation, isolation from others, anxiety, hostility, and problems in controlling their impulses. Similar findings have been reported in rheumatoid arthritic patients who respond poorly, in contrast to those who respond well, to medical treatment.[31]

How can we relate this greater degree of "neuroticism" in rheumatoid arthritics as compared to healthy siblings and other relatives and the evidence of failure of psychologic defense in those arthritics who do poorly (as contrasted to those with a benign course) to the intact ego-functioning in healthy relatives of rheumatoid arthritics with rheumatoid factor in their sera in contrast to a greater frequency of psychiatric symptoms in physically well relatives lacking rheumatoid factor?

The findings suggest that influences involved in the production of rheumatoid factor may well differ from those involved in the production of rheumatoid disease. The relationship of rheumatoid factor to the pathogenesis of rheumatoid arthritis remains unclear, since some individuals with rheumatoid arthritis have no rheumatoid factor in their sera.[16] The functional significance of the presence of rheumatoid factor is further confused by the observation that, while rheumatoid factor is relatively commonly found in the sera of psychotic patients,[32] actual rheumatoid arthritis appears to be exceedingly rare in conjunction with mental illness.[33, 34, 35] Thus, our data imply a basic difference in the significance of rheumatoid factor in persons without rheumatoid arthritis between those from a general and those from a psychotic population. Neurotic symptoms appear rare in conjunction with rheumatoid factor in our sample of physically healthy persons; but, rheumatoid factor, like other autoimmune globulins,[36] is common in conjunction with overt mental illness. Our data suggest that a psychologic comparison between psychotic patients with and without rheumatoid factor would be worthwhile. Possibly explanatory is Cobb's[37] recent suggestion (based on differences in heat stability and in agglutination of uncoated latex particles) that the "rheumatoid factor" in schizophrenic patients' sera is different from the rheumatoid factor found in arthritic patients.

A reasonable hypothesis based upon the present data would seem to be that, given a genetic or constitutional predisposition to rheumatoid disease, expressed in some individuals by the presence of rheumatoid factor, only those individuals with significant emotional conflict and psychologic distress go on to the development of disease, the rate of progression of which may be related to the degree of psychic turmoil.[28] Thus, individuals with rheumatoid factor but without manifest rheumatoid disease must be in good psychological equilibrium; if they were not, they might be expected to become physically ill. On the other hand, persons lacking rheumatoid factor on such an organic basis might well have significant emotional conflict in the absence of physical disease.

Although the presence of rheumatoid factor in a healthy individual seems to be related to well-functioning psychologic defenses, it is possible that the *kind* of adaptations of FII-positive relatives are similar to those in persons with rheumatoid arthritis, but that they are working better, either as a result of greater ego strength or of less environmental stress. The inhibition of aggression, concern about appearances, and similarity to another psychosomatic group seen in the FII-positive relatives have been found in *patients* with rheumatoid arthritis when compared with a group of healthy relatives without regard to their FII status. Thus, a propensity to formation of rheumatoid factor might be linked to psychologic mechanisms but still needs to be coupled with some degree of emotional decompensation to lead to disease. The possible physiologic mechanism for emotional influence on production of rheumatoid factor, especially if not tied to the concept of psychologic distress, which elsewhere[38] we have tried to relate to dysfunction of the immunologic system, is unclear. Genetic or constitutional factors might be integrated with a psychologic theory by the assumptions that the biological *capacity for* production of rheumatoid factor is present in some or all individuals; that actual rheumatoid factor production is triggered in some cases by the physiologic consequences of certain types of psychologic conditions and is accompanied by *disease* in the presence of other or more intense psychologic factors.

Romano[39] has said, "Health and disease are not static entities but are phases of life, dependent at any time on the balance maintained by devices, genetically and experientially determined, intent on fulfilling needs and adapting to and mastering stresses as they may arise from within the organism or from without." Engel[40] comments, "Disease corresponds to failures or disturbances in the growth, development, function, and adjustments of the organism as a whole or of any of its systems."

Salk[41] points out that the central nervous system and immunologic system may be intimately interrelated. There may be embryologic connections and histologic resemblances between CNS cells and cells of the reticuloendothelial system. Both CNS and immunologic systems relate the organism to the outside world; both have the property of memory; both are modified by experience; both possess functions of defense in the service of homeostasis; even the concepts of tolerance and self vs. nonself may be applied to both. Maladaptive or excessive defenses can produce physical (e.g., allergic) or emotional (e.g., hysteric) disease. West[42] raises the possibility that the balance between adaptive and maladaptive, between successfully operating and decompensating immunologic and psychologic defenses, may relate to the presence of psychiatric symptoms and/or physical disease in association with immunologic abnormality.

It is important to note the limitations of this study. The relatively small number of subjects and limited degree of personality difference between the relatives who possessed rheumatoid factor and those who did not should be kept in mind in evaluating these findings. Our results indicate that relatives of patients with rheumatoid arthritis are far from a homogeneous group. It is possible that there could be two groups of relatives of arthritic patients as different from each other as either is from a group of patients. This finding has important implications for research which attempts to identify personality factors related to arthritic disease. If a control group of FII-positive family members was compared with an experimental group of arthritic patients, a wide variety of personality differences would be shown between the two groups. If, in contrast, a control group of FII-negative family members was compared with the same group of arthritic patients, then fewer personality differences would be shown. On the other hand, some personality variables (e.g., similarity to other psychosomatic conditions, inhibition of aggression) might be more similar between the FII-positive relative group and a patient group. In general, the proportion in any comparison of FII-positive to FII-negative family members would be directly related to the number of significant differences between the family members and an experimental group of rheumatoid arthritic patients. This consideration demonstrates the importance of specifying the FII titers of relatives used in personality comparisons with arthritic patients.

An attempt to replicate this work is in order. In this connection, separate comparisons between FII-positive patients and their FII-positive and FII-negative relatives as well as between FII-negative patients and their FII-positive and FII-negative relatives might be informative. It is tempting from the point of view of preventive medicine to raise the question of whether emotional disturbances in a person who already has rheumatoid factor might lead to development of rheumatoid arthritis. Screening of relatives of arthritic patients for serologic abnormality in conjunction with early psychiatric treatment when indicated conceivably might abort disease. Only further research, especially prospective studies on the development of rheumatoid disease in family members of arthritic patients, will tell.

Summary

Two groups of asymptomatic female relatives of female patients with rheumatoid arthritis were compared psychologically by means of the Minnesota Multiphasic Personality Inventory. The first group of 14 relatives had rheumatoid factor in their sera, whereas the second group of 21 relatives had no rheumatoid factor. There were significant differences between the 2 groups. The relatives lacking rheumatoid factor scored higher on scales reflecting somatic complaints, the admission of psychiatric symptoms, social and self-alienation, lack of self-acceptance, anxiety, and rigidity. The relatives with rheumatoid factor, on the other hand, scored higher on scales reflecting inhibition of aggression (impulse control), concern about the social desirability of their responses and about socioeconomic status, and ego strength (indicative of capacity for successful psychologic defense, coping, mastery, and integration).

Possible explanations for these findings and implications for preventive medicine are discussed. It is speculated that emotional disturbance in conjunction with rheumatoid factor may lead to rheumatoid disease.

References

1. Moos, R. H. Personality factors associated with rheumatoid arthritis: a review. *J. Chron. Dis.* 17:41, 1964.
2. Lawrence, J. S. Epidemiology of rheumatoid arthritis. *Arth. & Rheumat.* 6: 166, 1963.
3. Lebovits, B. Z., Shekelle, R. B., Ostfeld, A. M., and Oglesby, P. Prospective and retrospective psychological studies of coronary heart disease. American Psychosomatic Society meeting, San Francisco, Apr. 4, 1964.
4. Harris, R. E., Sokolow, M., Carpenter, L. G., Freedman, M., and Hunt, S. P. Response to psychologic stress in persons who are potentially hypertensive. *Circulation* 7:874, 1953.
5. Kalis, B. L., Harris, R. E., Bennett, L. F., and Sokolow, M. Personality and life history factors in persons who are potentially hypertensive. *J. Nerv. & Ment. Dis.* 132:457, 1961.
6. Weiner, H., Thaler, M., Reiser, M. F., and Mirsky, I. A. Etiology of duodenal ulcer. 1. Relation of specific psychological characteristics to rate of gastric secretion (serum pepsinogen). *Psychosom. Med.* 19:1, 1957.
7. Ziff, M. Possible clinical and pathological associations of rheumatoid factor. *Arth. & Rheumat.* 6:481, 1963.
8. Burch, P. R. J. Autoimmunity: some aetiological aspects. Inflammatory polyarthritis and rheumatoid arthritis. *Lancet 1:*1253, 1963.
9. Dresner, E., and Trombly, P. The latex fixation reaction in non-rheumatic diseases. *New England J. Med. 261:* 981, 1959.
10. Milgrom, F. Response to altered analogous antigens. In *Autoimmunity—Experimental and Clinical Aspects.* Proceedings N. Y. Acad. Sci. In press.
11. Aho, K., and Simons, K. Studies of the nature of the rheumatoid factor: reaction of the rheumatoid factor with human specific precipitates and with native human gamma globulin. *Arth. & Rheumat. 6:*676, 1963.
12. Latner, A. I. Anxiety as a cause of fibrinolysis. *Lancet 1:*194, 1947.
13. Lawrence, J. S., and Ball, J. Genetic studies on rheumatoid arthritis. *Ann. Rheumat. Dis.* 17:160, 1958.
14. Committee of the American Rheumatism Association. Primer on the Rheumatic Diseases. *J.A.M.A.* 171:1205, 1345, and 1680, 1959.
15. Litwin, S. D., and Singer, J. M. In Proceedings of the Tenth Interim Session of the American Rheumatism Association. *Bull. Rheumat. Dis.* 14:341, 1964.
16. Goodman, M., Rosenblatt, M., Gottlieb, J. S., Miller, J., and Chen, C. H. Effect of age, sex, and schizophrenia on thyroid autoantibody production. *Arch. Gen. Psychiat.* 8:518, 1963.
17. Holman, H. R. Clinical and immunological evidence for a predisposition to rheumatoid disease in certain families. *Prog. Med. Genetics* 2:210, 1962.
18. Meyerowitz, S., Jacox, R. F., and Hess, D. W. An investigation of monozygotic twins discordant for rheuma-

toid arthritis. Amer. Psychosom. Soc. meeting, San Francisco, Apr. 4, 1964.

19. SCHMID, F. R., and SLATIS, H. Incidence of serum and clinical abnormalities in spouses of patients with rheumatoid arthritis (Abstract). *Arth. & Rheumat.* 5:319, 1962.

20. COBB, S. Interpersonal transmission of rheumatoid arthritis. (Abstract) *Arth. & Rheumat.* 3:437, 1960.

21. COBB, S. Intrafamilial transmission of rheumatoid arthritis. Unpublished.

22. JACKSON, D. D. A critique of the literature on the genetics of schizophrenia. In *The Etiology of Schizophrenia*, ED. by Jackson, D. D., Basic Books, New York, 1960.

23. BURCH, T. A., O'BRIEN, W. M., and BUNIM, J. J. Occurrence of rheumatoid arthritis and rheumatoid factor in families of Blackfeet Indians. (Abstract) *Arth. & Rheumat.* 5:640, 1962.

24. MOOS, R. H., and SOLOMON, G. F. Psychological comparisons between rheumatoid arthritics and their siblings: I. Personality test and interview rating data. *Psychosom. Med.* In press.

25. MOOS, R. H., and SOLOMON, G. F. Psychological comparisons between rheumatoid arthritics and their siblings: II. Content analysis of interviews. *Psychosom. Med.* In press.

26. KAMMERER, W. H. The hemagglutination test for rheumatoid arthritis. II. The influence of human plasma Fraction II (gamma globulin) on the reaction. *J. Immunol.* 72:66, 1954.

27. DAHLSTROM, W., and WELSH, G. S. *An MMPI Handbook. A Guide to Use in Clinical Practice and Research.* University of Minnesota Press, Minneapolis, 1960.

28. MOOS, R. H., and SOLOMON, G. F. Minnesota Multiphasic Personality Inventory response patterns in patients with rheumatoid arthritis. *J. Psychosom. Res.* 8:17, 1964.

29. MOOS, R. H., and SOLOMON, G. F. Personality correlates of the rapidity of

progression of rheumatoid arthritis. *Ann. Rheumat. Dis.* 23:145, 1964.

30. MOOS, R. H., and SOLOMON, G. F. Personality correlates of the degree of functional incapacity of patients with physical disease. *J. Chron. Dis.* In press.

31. MOOS, R. H., and SOLOMON, G. F. Personality correlates of rheumatoid arthritic patients' response to treatment. (Abstract) *Arth. & Rheumat.* 7:331, 1964.

32. FESSEL, W. J. Disturbed serum proteins in chronic psychosis. *Arch. Gen. Psychiat.* 4:154, 1961.

33. TREVETHAN, R. D., and TATUM, J. C. Rarity of occurrence of psychosis and rheumatoid arthritis in individual patients. *J. Nerv. & Ment. Dis.* 120:83, 1954.

34. PILKINGTON, T. L. The coincidence of rheumatoid arthritis and schizophrenia. *J. Nerv. & Ment. Dis.* 124:604, 1956.

35. ROTHERMICH, M. O., and PHILLIPS, V. K. Rheumatoid arthritis in criminal and mentally ill populations. *Arth. & Rheumat.* 6:639, 1963.

36. FESSEL, W. J. Blood proteins in functional psychoses; a review of the literature and unifying hypothesis. *Arch. Gen. Psychiat.* 6:132, 1962.

37. COBB, S. Personal communication.

38. SOLOMON, G. F., and MOOS, R. H. Emotions, immunity and disease: a speculative theoretical integration. *Arch. Gen. Psychiat.* 11:657, 1964.

39. ROMANO, J. Basic orientation and education of the medical student. *J.A.M.A.* 143:409, 1950.

40. ENGEL, G. A unified concept of health and disease. *Perspectives Biol. and Med.* 3:459, 1960.

41. SALK, J. Personal communications and: Biological basis of disease and behavior. *Perspectives Biol. and Med.* 5:198, 1962.

42. WEST, L. J. Personal communication. May 30, 1964.

42

DEPRESSED LYMPHOCYTE FUNCTION AFTER BEREAVEMENT

R. W. Bartrop, L. Lazarus, E. Luckhurst, L. G. Kiloh, and R. Penny

Summary During 1975 twenty-six bereaved spouses took part in a detailed prospective investigation of the effects of severe stress on the immune system. T and B cell numbers and function, and hormone concentrations were studied approximately 2 weeks after bereavement and 6 weeks thereafter. The response to phytohæmagglutinin was significantly depressed in the bereaved group on the second occasion, as was the response to concanavalin A at 6 weeks. There was no difference in T and B cell numbers, protein concentrations, the presence of autoantibodies and delayed hypersensitivity, and in cortisol, prolactin, growth hormone, and thyroid hormone assays between the bereaved group and the controls. This is the first time severe psychological stress has been shown to produce a measurable abnormality in immune function which is not obviously caused by hormonal changes.

INTRODUCTION

CELL and tissue changes are known to be part of a non-specific response to stressful stimuli.[1] Stressful physical stimuli in rodents increased their susceptibility to infection.[2] These findings implied modification of the immune response, and were attributed to the effects of adrenal corticosteroids. Recent work extending these studies to other species has implicated the action of other hormones,[3] possibly mediated via lymphocyte receptors.[4]

The experiments in the NASA Skylab Programme,[5] which demonstrated depression of lymphocyte transformation and rosette formation on the day of splashdown, appear to be the only prospective studies of the effects of stress on the immune system of healthy people. Retrospective investigations of bereavement and other severely stressful situations have been claimed to show an association between stress and many diseases,[6] including diabetes mellitus, coronary-artery disease, ulcerative colitis, rheumatoid arthritis, lupus erythematosus, and schizophrenia. Claims for an increased mortality after conjugal bereavement are controversial. Bereavement is a life event resulting in great distress or the need for considerable adaptation.[7] We determined prospectively the behavioural, endocrinological, and immunological consequences of bereavement.[8]

Reprinted from *Lancet* 1, 834–836, 1977.

Subjects.—Arrangements were made in our group of hospitals for one of us (R. B.) to provide a counselling service for the surviving spouses of patients either fatally injured or who had died from illness. Twenty-six people between the ages of 20 and 65 years[9] were interviewed for the study.

Control group.—This group consisted of twenty-six hospital staff members (not bereaved within the previous 24 months) who were matched for age, sex, and race with a bereaved spouse.

Design of study.—The service and the study were explained to the spouse on the first visit. Further contact was maintained with all families either directly or through ministers of religion or social workers. The first blood-samples were taken 1–3 weeks after bereavement (sample 1) and the second samples obtained 6 weeks later (sample 2). Control subjects had blood-samples taken at the same times for identical laboratory testing.

Physical health.—Each individual received a standardised questionnaire and was excluded if there was a history of recent infection, allergic diathesis, or blood dyscrasia.

Stimulation with mitogens.—Peripheral-blood mononuclear cells were isolated on 'Ficoll-Hypaque'[10] and lymphocyte transformation tests were performed as described elsewhere.[11] Response to phytohæmagglutinin (P.H.A.) was assessed at doses of 10, 20, 100, 200 μg/ml, and to concanavalin A at doses of 1, 5, and 50 μg/ml.

Lymphocyte markers.—E and EAC rosette-forming lymphocytes were detected by methods previously reported.[11]

Serum-protein concentrations.—Serum protein electrophoresis was performed with a Beckman microzone system. Radial immunodiffusion methods were used to measure serum IgG, IgA, IgM, and α_2-macroglobulin.

Autoantibodies.—Sera were tested for antinuclear factor, mitochondrial, and smooth-muscle antibodies by immunofluorescence techniques. The R.A. latex test was performed for rheumatoid factor.

Delayed skin hypersensitivity.—Twelve bereaved spouses and fourteen control subjects had skin tests with dermatophyton O, streptokinase-streptodornase, mumps antigen, and purified protein derivative of tuberculin.

Hormone assays.—The following were measured by standard radioimmunoassays: thyroxine and triiodothyronine, growth hormone, and cortisol; and prolactin was assayed by a modification of the standard radioimmunoassay with reagents provided by N.I.H. (U.S.A.).

Statistical analysis.—Results of tests of cell-mediated immunity were expressed as the geometric mean ($\pm$ S.E.M.) values as reported elsewhere.[12] Statistical analysis was carried out by means of the Wilcoxon rank sum test (Mann-Whitney).

RESULTS

Lymphocyte transformation test.—The results of the lymphocyte transformation tests on samples 1 and 2 with P.H.A. and concanavalin A are shown in the accompanying figure. Responses to doses of 10 and 20 μg/ml P.H.A. in sample 2 were strikingly different in the bereaved and control groups (P<0·05). In addition, there was a significant difference between samples 1 and 2 of the spouse group at a dose of 100 μg/ml P.H.A. At 6 weeks (sample 2) responsiveness to doses of 5 and 50 μg/ml P.H.A. At 6 weeks (sample 2) responsiveness to doses of 5 and 50 μg/ml of concanavalin A in the bereaved group was significantly less than in the control group (P<0·05). In addition, the responsiveness of lymphocytes in samples 1 and 2 of the bereaved group was significantly different at doses of 5 and 50 μg/ml concanavalin A.

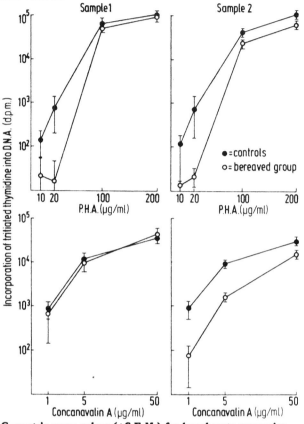

Geometric mean values (±S.E.M.) for lymphocyte responsiveness to P.H.A. and concanavalin A in control and bereaved groups.

Other measures of T and B cell function.—There was no significant difference between the bereaved and control groups in terms of T and B cell numbers, serum protein electrophoresis, immunoglobulins, α_2-macroglobulin concentrations, the presence of autoantibodies, and delayed hypersensitivity.

Hormone assays.—Mean serum concentrations of thyroxine, triiodothyronine, cortisol, prolactin, and growth hormone were no different in the bereaved and control groups.

DISCUSSION

This is the first prospective study of immunological function in healthy people under great psychological stress. We demonstrated that T-cell function was significantly depressed after bereavement (sample 2) in the absence of a change in T-cell numbers as tested by E rosetting. We have not demonstrated abnormal B-cell function, as measured by IgG, IgA, and IgM concentrations, after bereavement, nor any differences in B-cell numbers between the bereaved and control groups, as tested by the EAC rosetting scheme.

Hamburg et al. reported that concentrations of adrenocortical, adrenomedullary, and thyroid hormones were raised for weeks or months at times of great stress and seemed to correlate directly with the degree of distress and inversely with the ability to cope.[3] We did not demonstrate any significant difference in hormone concentrations between the two groups in either sample 1 or sample 2. This would tend to exclude these hormones as mediators of the T-cell functional abnormality that we demonstrated.

A detailed endocrinological analysis was not attempted in the bereaved group, a single blood-sample being used for hormone assays. An extended study will include a more detailed investigation of hormonal responses rather than isolated blood estimations and this will be particularly pertinent in the case of cortisol, but we also intend to continue investigation of other hormones.

For the first time, we have shown prospectively that severe psychological stress can produce a measurable abnormality in immune function. The origin of the defect in T-cell function is being investigated and a more extensive analysis of B-cell function is required. This may give a clue to the genesis of suggested stress-related diseases which have an immunological basis.

REFERENCES

1. Selye, H. *A. Rev. Med.* 1951, **2**, 327.
2. Gisler, R. H., Bussard, A. E., Mazie, J. C., Hess, R. *Cell Immun.* 1971, **2**.
3. Hamburg, D. A., Hamburg, B. A., Barchas, J. D. *in* Emotions: Their Parameters and Measurement (edited by L. Levi); p.232. New York, 1974.
4. Bourne, H. R., Lichtenstein, L. M., Melmon, K. L., Henney, C. S., Weinstein, Y., Shearer, G. M. *Science*, 1974, **184**, 19.
5. Kimzey, S. L. *Acta Astronautica*, 1974, **127**, 1.
6. Solomon, G. F., Amkraut, A. A. *Front. Radiat. Ther. Onc.* 1972, **7**, 84.
7. Tennant, C., Andrews, G. *Aust. N.Z. J. Psychiat.* 1976, **10**, 27.
8. Amkraut, A. A., Solomon, G. F. *Int. J. Psychiat. Med.* 1974, **5**, 541.
9. Foad, B. S. I., Adams, L. E., Yamauchi, Y., Litwin, A. *Clin.exp. Immun.* 1974, **17**, 657.
10. Boyum, A. *Scan. J. clin. Lab. Invest.* 1968, **21**, suppl. 97, p. 51.
11. Cooper, D. A., Petts, V., Luckhurst, E., Biggs, J. C., Penny, R. *Br. J. Cancer*, 1975, **31**, 550.
12. Ziegler, J. B., Hansen, P., Penny, R. *Clin. Immun. Immunopath.* 1975, **3**, 451.

43

PSYCHOSOCIAL RISK FACTORS IN THE DEVELOPMENT OF INFECTIOUS MONONUCLEOSIS*

Stanislav V. Kasl, Alfred S. Evans, and James C. Niederman

In a 4-year prospective seroepidemiological study of infectious mononucleosis (IM) of one class of some 1400 cadets at the West Point Military Academy, susceptibles and immunes were identified by the absence or presence of antibody to Epstein-Barr virus (EBV), the causative agent, and new infections by the appearance of antibody (seroconversion). On entry, about ⅓ lacked EBV antibody, of whom some 20% became infected (seroconverted); about ¼ of seroconverters developed definite, clinical and recognized IM. Psychosocial factors that significantly increased the risk of clinical IM among seroconverters included: 1) having fathers who were "overachievers"; 2) having a high level of motivation; 3) doing relatively poorly academically. The combination of high motivation and poor academic performance interacted in predicting clinical IM. Additional data on presence of elevated titers among seroconverters with inapparent disease and on length of hospitalization among cases of clinical IM revealed that these two additional indices of infection or illness could also be predicted from the same set of psychosocial risk factors.

INTRODUCTION

A quick overview of the social science and medicine literature concerned with psychological and social risk factors in illness (1−5) readily reveals that most of the studies are concerned with chronic conditions, and that relatively few examine acute illness episodes or *infectious diseases*; the older work on tuberculosis (e.g., 6, 7) appears to be the one exception to this generalization. For example, a recent review of "onset conditions for psychosomatic symptoms" (8) covers 53 studies, but only 3 of them deal with acute illness. Among the studies that are concerned with acute conditions, such as respiratory illness, there are those which confound illness with illness behavior. Thus the work of Jacobs and his colleagues (9, 10) contrasts college students who have and have not sought medical care for respiratory difficulties, and it is extremely difficult to separate factors that influence medical care seeking from factors that contribute to onset of illness. This is especially true for symptoms that are usually regarded as not very serious (11). There are other studies, particularly those using the stressful life events approach (12−14), in which the outcome variables are "illness rates" or some broad health indicator. And even though acute or infectious conditions are the dominant component of such indices, it is not possible to specifically isolate the role of the psychosocial risk factors on the infectious conditions only. Moreover, it is possible

*Based on a paper presented at the Annual Meeting of the American Psychosomatic Society, March 31, 1978, Washington, D.C.

From the Department of Epidemiology and Public Health, Yale University School of Medicine, New Haven, Connecticut.

that infectious conditions are less sensitive to the psychosocial risk factors than are the chronic conditions (15).

Some of the older reviews of the psychosocial literature on immunity or *resistance* to infectious disease (e.g., 16, 17) reveal a good deal of the material to be speculative, at least in its application to humans. For example, the evidence from animal stress studies is combined with other relevant laboratory findings, such as those regarding the influence of adrenocortical hormones on antibody levels and interferon production, and one then extrapolates to role of stress in immunity in humans. The more recent reviews (18–21) document the progress in the field, but also reveal the great complexity of relationships. This complexity involves, among others: the immune system itself as a complicated network, the relation between psychological "stress" and immunosuppression (vs. enhancement of the immune response), the issue of time and timing of the "stress" in relation to host characteristics, and the relation of changes in the various immune components to illness development.

Studies of acute illness development in humans tend to be done under limited laboratory conditions, involving experimentally induced infections, and various narrowly defined manipulations of stress or psychosocial stimuli (16–25). However, more broadly designed field studies reveal the possible greater complexity of the relationships. For example, in a study of recurrent herpes labialis (RHL) and moods (26), it was found that the general unhappiness factor on the Clyde Mood Scale predicted the frequency of RHL during a one-year follow-up. However, in a daily follow-up of mood fluctuations, the onset of RHL was totally unrelated to any kinds of mood changes. It appears, then, that subjects (nursing students) whose overall stable perception of themselves is as relatively unhappy are at greater risk of RHL; but actual fluctuations in unhappiness were not associated with onset of RHL, which was just as likely to take place when they were relatively happy as unhappy. Another recent field study (27) failed to find any association between various psychosocial variables (life events, depression, anxiety, repressed hostility) and postimmunization antibody levels among subjects who received the A/NJ/76 ("swine") flu vaccine. The authors speculate that perhaps the major impact of stress and emotions is on the cellular as opposed to the humoral immune system. Two recent reports from field studies (28, 29) have noted that an elevation of catecholamine activity tended to occur within 3 days prior to onset of symptoms of acute respiratory illness; however, neither study measured "stress" per se and the numbers of subjects involved were rather small.

It would seem that part of the problem in designing an effective epidemiological or field study of psychosocial factors in infectious disease is our inability to separate out the four major ways in which psychosocial factors can exert an influence: 1) On the initial immunity status of the cohort at the start of the study; 2) On the exposure to infection among susceptibles; 3) On the clinical expression of the disease and its course among susceptibles who are infected; and 4) On the treatment-seeking behavior and response to treatment among those with symptoms.

There are probably two major types of reasons why a particular study design cannot pinpoint the role of psychosocial factors. The first concerns failure to obtain all the necessary initial and/or follow-up data on immunity, exposure to infection, disease status, and medical care. The second reflects the fact that the particular disease under study may not fit exactly the model presupposed by the previous paragraph. For example, the concept of long-term immunity may not be applicable or, if applicable, one may not know how to assess it. Similarly, the notion of exposure to infection may not be relevant, since such exposure may be typically continuous for that particular disease; and there may be no way of assessing if there is some threshold level of exposure to infection and/or if vulnerability to clinical disease has increased. Nevertheless, if the above model of disease is appropriate and if the necessary data can be collected, then the investigator has an unusually good opportunity to examine the role of psychosocial factors.

The recent advances in the study of infectious mononucleosis (IM) make this a highly appropriate infectious disease in which to examine the role of psychosocial factors. The above paradigm of four separate psychosocial influences, idealized for many infectious conditions, becomes a realistic blueprint for the study of IM. Below, we give a brief outline of the accumulated evidence concerning IM; the reader is referred to lengthier reviews (30, 31) for a more detailed documentation and summary.

THE ETIOLOGY OF INFECTIOUS MONONUCLEOSIS

Epstein-Barr virus (EBV), a member of the herpes group of viruses, is the cause of heterophile-positive IM, of some heterophile-negative cases, and of occasional cases of tonsillitis and pharyngitis in childhood. Furthermore, EBV is strongly implicated in the development of African Burkitt lymphoma (in a developmental sequence together with malaria)

and of nasopharyngeal carcinoma in the Chinese.

The causation of heterophile-positive IM by EBV has been established beyond reasonable doubt in some eleven prospective seroepidemiological studies. These studies have repeatedly shown that antibody to EBV of the IgG type has been consistently absent in sera taken prior to the onset of IM, regularly appears during the illness, and persists for years thereafter. The presence of this antibody indicates immunity to clinical IM and its absence indicates susceptibility to the disease. No other virus has been found that induces a similar antibody and no other viral antibody has been demonstrated during heterophile-positive IM.

The EBV-specific antibody of the IgM class has been demonstrated during acute IM, but found to disappear during convalescence, thus indicating that this is a primary response to EBV infection. Because of its transient nature, the IgM-type antibody can be used as a serological tool only for incidence data, i.e., during the acute illness and as an essential diagnostic feature.

The prevalence of antibody to EBV has been determined in many countries and for many age groups (31). In tropical areas and developing countries, most children will have been infected by age six. On the other hand, in developed countries and among adolescents from upper social strata, as few as 25% may have the antibody. The incidence of clinical IM is estimated between 45 and 200 per 100,000; for college students, the estimate is 840 per 100,000. Hospitalization rates for IM in the armed forces are about 150 to 250 per 100,000 and represent the fifth commonest infectious disease. The "mono syndrome" is primarily a disease of older children and young adults (30, 31).

Aside from the repeatedly observed finding of higher EBV infection and lower clinical IM among low socioeconomic groups, little is known about psychosocial factors in clinical IM. One early study (32) showed that college students who took longer to recover from IM were lower on ego strength. A later study (33) revealed that students admitted to the infirmary with the diagnosis of IM reported somewhat fewer stressful life events than control students; this difference was contrary to prediction. Clinical observations and psychiatric sequelae in a few cases of IM have also been published (34, 35).

METHODS

The present study represents an *opportunistic* merging of two available data sets in order to explore the psychosocial risk factors in IM. One set of data comes from a prospective epidemiologic surveillance of the class of 1973 of cadets at the U.S. Military Academy at West Point. The cadets were first bled on arrival at the Academy in July 1969, and then followed for 4 years. The seroepidemiologic and clinical IM data have already been fully reported (36). The other data set consists of various background, academic, and psychosocial data made available to us by the Academy for the purpose of exploring some rather esoteric notions regarding the possible association between serum uric acid and achievement (37). All of the psychosocial data, except academic performance at West Point, were obtained during the extensive testing when the cadets first arrived on campus and coincided with the first bleeding.

Table 1 summarizes the major findings from the earlier report (36). Criteria of diagnosis of definite IM included: 1) a clinical picture of sore throat, fever, and cervical lymphadenopathy; 2) a total lymphocyte and monocyte count of 50% or more with at least 10% atypical lymphocytes; 3) elevated heterophile antibody titer ($\geq$ 1:40) after guinea pig absorption or beef hemolysin titer ($\geq$ 1:80); and 4) the development of EBV antibody between pre- and postillness sera. Clinical surveillance was based on carefully following all cadets for the occurrence of febrile illness suggestive of IM. All cases of suspected IM were seen and/or their records reviewed; this included examination of outpatient visits as well as hospitalizations. The hospital at the Academy, which is the only source of medical care

TABLE 1. Immunity, EBV Infection Rates, and Clinical IM in Class of 1973 in U.S. Military Academy (26)

1327 Cadets: 890 (67.1%) with EBV antibody at matriculation (immune)	
First Year	*437* without EBV antibody at matriculation (susceptible)
	383 without EBV antibody at end of year (not infected)
	54 with EBV antibody at end of year (infected; seroconverters)
	15 Definite clinical IM
	39 Subclinical, or without known illness
Second Year	*356* without EBV antibody at start of year (susceptible)
	269 without EBV antibody at end of year (not infected)
	87 with EBV antibody at end of year (infected; seroconverters)
	21 Definite clinical IM
	66 Subclinical or without known illness
Third & Fourth	
Years	*60* additional seroconverters
	17 Definite clinical IM
	43 Subclinical or without known illness
Summary	2/3 arrive immune
	1/5 of susceptibles infected (per year)
	1/4 of infected get clinical IM (per year)

for all cadets, participated fully in this prospective study from its inception.

Table 1 reveals that some 67% of the cadets arrive at West Point with EBV antibody. Of the initially susceptible cadets, a total of 46% became infected over almost 4 years of serologic observation. Among the cadets infected with EBV over this period, some 26% satisfied the criteria for definite clinical IM. On an annual basis, about 1/5 of susceptibles become infected, and about 1/4 of those infected get clinical IM.

Psychosocial data made available to us for record linkage and analysis include: socio-demographic data on parents; ability and achievement test data, and high school rank; academic performance at West Point, for all semesters; and diverse perceptions, evaluations and expectations about the Academy and military career, obtained as part of the initial assessment of all incoming cadets. Additional details about these measures will be offered as the results are presented.

Additional group data were available from a pamphlet entitled "A Comparison of New Cadets at U.S.M.A. with Entering Freshmen at Other Colleges, Class of 1973." This permits a comparison of the incoming cadets with national data on male students entering all 4-year colleges, technical institutions, and public and private universities. This comparison reveals that: 1) On participation in high school sports and in leadership positions held in student organizations, the cadets surpass all other types of freshmen. 2) On religious background, high school scholastic performance, educational plans beyond college, and probable major field of study, the cadets resemble closely freshmen entering technical institutions. 3) On parental socio-demographic data, the cadets are like freshmen entering public universities. Other data reveal the cadets as more conservative, more certain of their plans for the future, and with a greater sense of civic responsibility. This, then, is a capsule summary of the study population.

The primary objective of this article is to explore the psychosocial variables that distinguish the seroconverters who go on to develop clinical IM from the seroconverters who remained without known illness and/or with only subclinical manifestations. Variables distinguishing these two groups may be seen as risk factors for clinical IM *among those who could develop the disease.* Cadets who were initially immune, or who never became infected, could not develop clinical IM and are naturally left out of this primary analysis. However, for the purpose of presenting as complete a picture of psychosocial factors in clinical IM as possible, we shall also note any variables that are associated with initial immunity status and with subsequent infection.

We wish to emphasize again that this article represents an opportunistic data analysis, which brings together two available data sets. Among the shortcomings of such opportunism are: 1) Inability to include variables currently considered important by the field of psychosocial etiology of illness; 2) Inevitable reliance on post hoc and ad hoc interpretations of variables and associations; 3) Detection of epidemiological associations without being able to suggest convincing intervening mechanisms of influence.

RESULTS AND DISCUSSION

Variables Associated with Initial Immunity Status

We shall first consider briefly selected variables that may discriminate cadets who possessed EBV antibody on entry (immune) from those who lacked such antibody (susceptible). The results are summarized in Table 2 for 728 immune and 432 susceptible cadets; omitted from analysis are some additional 235 cadets who dropped out during the first year prior to any serological follow-up on them. The group means are given in standard scores to permit the reader an estimate of the magnitude of the association. All 1395 cadets on whom some data were available were used in this standardization. Because the first year dropouts were sometimes different from the 1160 cadets used in Table 2 (e.g., they were considerably lower on motivation for, or certainty about, a military career), the weighted averages of the pairs of means in Table 2 do not necessarily equal 0.0.

Variables reflecting the social status of family of origin reveal the already noted (31) social class gradient: absence of EBV antibody in adolescence is associated

TABLE 2. Relationship of Selected Psychosocial Variables to Immunity–Susceptibility Status at Matriculation

	Mean Scores[a] for Cadets Who at Matriculation Were		Significance of Difference (p)
	Immune (EBV antibody present)	Susceptible (EBV antibody absent)	
Father's education	−0.06	0.16	<0.001
Mother's education	−0.03	0.15	<0.001
Father's occupation	−0.03	0.03	n.s.
Family income	−0.01	0.09	n.s.
High school rank	0.00	0.07	n.s.
SAT scores (verbal & math)	−0.12	0.25	<0.001
No. of sports in high school	0.06	−0.09	<0.01
Body index (weight/height²)	0.07	−0.15	<0.001
Data Obtained on Arrival at Academy			
Importance of graduating from college (5 pt. scale, 5 = very important)	0.04	0.06	n.s.
Certainty about continuing in a military career (9 pt. scale, 9 = very certain)	0.01	0.18	<0.001
Commitment to a military career (100 pt. scale, 100 = strong commitment)	−0.03	0.17	<0.001
Commitment to graduating from the academy (100 pt. scale, 100 = strong commitment)	0.03	0.09	n.s.
Certainty of wanting a military career (9 pt. scale, 9 = very certain)	0.01	0.11	0.05
N	728	432	

[a] In standard scores (mean = 0.0, standard deviation = 1.0) using data on all 1395 cadets.

with higher social status. However, Table 2 reveals that parental education is the primary component that accounts for this association. If transfer of infected saliva on fingers, toys, and other inanimate objects in settings of somewhat poorer hygiene in the home of the child is seen as the primary mechanism of acquisition of early immunity (31), then these results simply suggest that education, more than occupation or income, influences such standards of hygiene.

The remainder of the significant associations in Table 2 reveals the susceptibles to be: higher on aptitude, less likely to have participated in high school sports, somewhat thinner, and with greater motivation for and commitment to a military career. None of these variables is strongly related to parental social status (for example, the highest correlation is between SAT scores and father's education, r = 0.18) and thus they represent *additional* correlates of immunity−susceptibility status. Since the major route of transmission of EBV infections in adolescence is probably through intimate oral contact in kissing (30, 31), one can only speculate that the above cluster of variables— aptitude, body build, participation in sports, and motivation toward a military career—reflects broad differences in adolescent lifestyle in which kissing is also one component.

Variables Associated with Exposure to Infection Among Susceptibles

The 728 initially immune cadets are of no further interest to this report. The 432 susceptibles can be subdivided into 3 groups: 1) 141 cadets who were not infected during the 4 years at West Point; EBV antibody was absent through the last serological follow-up and they remained susceptible. 2) 194 cadets who became infected; in these seroconverters, EBV antibody was present at some point in the serological follow-up and they were at risk for developing clinical IM while at West Point. 3) 97 cadets who dropped out of the academy during the second or later years and on whom complete follow-up was not possible.

Table 3 reveals that the characteristics which differentiate cadets who remained susceptible from the seroconverters are pretty much those which, in Table 2, differentiated the initially susceptible ones from the immune ones. Those not acquiring EBV antibody had higher academic standing in high school, participated in fewer sports, and are of thinner body build. These cadets are also more motivated toward their military career and

TABLE 3. Relationship of Selected Psychosocial Variables to Seroconversion at the Academy

	Mean Scores[a] for Initially Susceptible Cadets Who During the 4 Years at the Academy		
	Were not Infected and remained susceptible (EBV antibody absent)	Were infected and seroconverted (acquired EBV antibody)	Significance (p)
Father's education	0.21	0.18	n.s.
Mother's education	0.10	0.06	n.s.
Father's occupation	0.15	0.00	n.s.
Family income	0.14	0.02	n.s.
High school rank	0.25	−0.01	<0.01
SAT scores (verbal & math)	0.27	0.14	n.s.
No. of sports in high school	−0.22	0.04	<0.05
Body index (weight/height^2)	−0.23	0.04	<0.01
Data Obtained on Arrival at Academy			
Importance of graduating from college	0.01	0.11	n.s.
Certainty about continuing in a military career	0.29	0.03	<0.01
Commitment to a military career	0.29	0.08	<0.05
Commitment to graduating from the academy	0.12	0.05	n.s.
Certainty of wanting a military career	0.30	−0.04	<0.001
Academic Performance			
Grade point average (GPA)	0.33	0.09	<0.01
GPA adjusted for SAT	0.22	−0.03	<0.01
N	141	194	

[a] In standard scores (mean = 0.0, standard deviation = 1.0) using data on all 1395 cadets.

have a better academic performance at West Point. In general, the data in Table 3 show that cadets who are pursuing more vigorously purely academic goals are less likely to become infected. This would not be inconsistent with the assumption that seroconversion during the 4 years at West Point is more related to specific opportunities for infection (e.g., kissing) than to general hygienic practices.

All of the variables in Table 3 are assessed prospectively in relation to seroconversion status except the last two. Regarding these, it could be argued that the 48 cadets who among the seroconverters developed clinical IM and were hospitalized, should be removed from analysis, since the illness could have adversely affected their GPA. However, this is not the case and the recomputed means are virtually identical (0.08 for GPA, −0.04 for SAT-adjusted GPA).

Variables Associated with Development of Clinical IM Among Seroconverters

We are now ready to zero in on the seroconverters and consider the variables that may distinguish the 48 cadets who developed clinical IM from the 146 cadets who experienced only subclinical infection. Social status indicators on parents revealed no significant differences on family income, father's and mother's education, and mother's occupation (listed for about a third of the mother's). However, fathers of cadets who developed clinical IM had significantly higher occupational status than fathers of cadets who did not develop IM. Since these status indicators are substantially correlated, this pattern of results suggested that one particular form of status inconsistency in parents (38) was unduly frequently present among the cadets who developed clinical IM: father's occupational attainment exceeding his own education or wife's education or occupation. In order to explore this further, we constructed 3 related indices of what we call in this report father's occupational "overachievement": father's occupational status (as measured by the Duncan code) in relation to: 1) his educational attainment, 2) his wife's (i.e., the cadet's mother) educational attainment, and 3) his wife's occupational status for mothers working outside the home. The first two indices are constructed by predicting in a linear regression occupational level from educational level and then subtracting the predicted occupational status from actual status. The third variable was computed by converting the occupational status scores into standard scores, separately for fathers and mothers, and then subtracting the mother's score from the father's. The basic findings are presented in Table 4.

The top of the table reveals that on all 3 indices of father's occupational "overachievement," the cadets who developed clinical IM had significantly higher scores than did the seroconverters who developed only mild or inapparent disease. The bottom of the table presents the same data in the form usual to prospective epidemiologic studies: percents developing the disease by different levels of the presumed risk factor.

Previous work (39) suggests that an occupationally "overachieving" father imparts stronger values about achievement to the son, with the result that the son is more strongly motivated to achieve and more strongly committed to succeed in the chosen career path. Our very tentative interpretation is that in the special setting of the U.S. Military Academy, a stronger motivation to achieve and to succeed in one's chosen career path may be, among

TABLE 4. Father's Occupational "Overachievement" as a Risk Factor for Clinical IM

Index of Father's Occupational "Overachievement"	Mean Scores[a] for Seroconverters who		
	Developed clinical IM	Did not develop clinical IM	Significance of difference (p)
Fa. occup. status > Fa. educ. level	0.20 (N=42)	−0.24 (N=120)	<0.005
Fa. occup. status > Mo. educ. level	0.29 (N=42)	−0.16 (N=121)	<0.01
Fa. occup. status > Mo. occup. status	0.50 (N=15)	−0.23 (N=30)	<0.025

		Percent Developing Clinical IM Among All Seroconverters					
		Fa. Occ. > Fa. Educ.		Fa. Occ. > Mo. Educ.		Fa. Occ. > Mo. Occ.	
		N	%	N	%	N	%
Score on Father's Occupational "Overachievement"	Low	37	10.8	15	6.7	9	0.0
	Moderate	73	23.3	99	22.2	27	37.0
	High	52	40.4	49	38.8	9	55.6
	Total	162	25.9	163	25.8	45	33.3
		gamma = .47 p < 0.001		gamma = .45 p < 0.005		gamma = .69 p < 0.025	

[a] In standard scores using data on all cadets.

the seroconverters, a risk factor for developing clinical IM. This speculation becomes somewhat more compelling as we present additional results on this theme.

The data in Table 4 were broken down by year at the academy during which seroconversion took place, but no significant variations in the overall association were found.

The 3 variables indicative of father's occupational "overachievement" were also examined in relation to immunity—susceptibility status at matriculation and to acquisition of EBV antibody versus continued susceptibility during the 4 years at the Academy. No significant associations were observed.

The next variable to be examined is a more direct indicator of motivation, Commitment to a Military Career. It was obtained on the initial testing done prior to the start of the first year, and derives from the question "To what degree are you now *certain* that you will continue an active military career until mandatory retirement?" Along with the question, there was a separate sheet with a rating scale, going from 0 to 100 and having some 13 anchor points verbally reflecting various degrees of certainty. On the basis of the tentative interpretation of the results in Table 4, we would expect the cadets developing IM to have initially stronger commitment (motivation) than the seroconverters who did not. This proved to be the case: the mean (in standard scores) for the former was 0.38, compared to −0.02 for the latter (p < 0.005 for the difference). Table 5 presents the same data as percent of seroconverters developing

TABLE 5. Strength of Commitment to a Military Career as a Risk Factor for Clinical IM

		Percent Developing Clinical IM among All Seroconverters		
		N	%	
	Low	28	10.7	
Commitment to a military career	Moderate	145	22.8	gamma = .58 $p < 0.005$
	High	21	57.1	
	Total	194	24.7	

the disease, stratified by level of motivation. A more detailed analysis of this association by year at the academy during which seroconversion took place revealed no significant variation, but there was some evidence of a weaker association during the later years.

It is interesting to note that the initially susceptible cadets who never acquired EBV antibody tend to be also high on Commitment to a Military Career (see Table 3). Thus one and the same variable predicts lower chances of infection among susceptibles (without which clinical IM cannot develop) and higher chances of clinical IM, if infection does take place. The implication is that had one followed prospectively the whole group of initially susceptible cadets, but did not also monitor their seroconversion, one would be forced to combine 2 motivationally heterogeneous subgroups, neither of whom developed clinical IM: the never-infected (higher scores) and the seroconverters with inapparent disease (lower scores). This would certainly obscure the role of this psychosocial variable in the etiology of IM.

There are 3 other similar motivational variables that are fairly strongly related (average r = 0.56) to the Commitment to a Military Career: Certainty About Continuing in a Military Career, Commitment to Graduating from the Academy, and Certainty of Wanting a Military Career (see Tables 2 and 3). They also discriminate the cadets who went on to develop clinical IM from those who did not, but the associations are somewhat weaker. The average difference in the pairs of means (in standard scores) is 0.25, compared to the difference of 0.40 noted above for the Commitment to a Military Career. It is also interesting to note that on the variable Importance of Graduating from College, the 2 groups of cadets have identical means. This suggests that the specific content of the motivational variables which are a risk for clinical IM will be specific to the setting in which the subjects are studied—in this instance, cadets in a military academy.

Table 6 presents the results with two other variables that may be interpreted as reflecting the strength of motivation for a successful career at West Point and in the military. The first one is based on a single item in the questionnaire: "How important was the quality of the leadership training provided [here] to your decision to accept an appointment at U.S.M.A.?" Precoded answers provided 5 points of scaled importance. Since one of the Academy's most highly publicized aspects is leadership training, we assume that those who consider leadership training as personally very important consider, in effect, their overall training and career at the Academy as important. The results in Table 6 show that high importance is a risk factor for clinical IM, but only during the first year. During subsequent years, it no longer shows an association with clinical IM; the difference in the associations during the first and subsequent years is

TABLE 6. Other Motivational Variables as Risk Factors for Clinical IM

		Mean Scores[a] for Seroconverters who		Significance of Difference Between Clinical Groups (p)	Significance of Interaction with Year at Academy
		Developed clinical IM	Did not develop clinical IM		
Personal importance of leadership training to be provided at U.S.M.A.	First year only	0.58 (N = 13)	−0.35 (N = 38)	<0.005	<0.01
	Later years	0.12 (N = 32)	0.17 (N = 103)	n.s.	
Associating "military career" with "fame, personal status, power"	First year only	0.34 (N = 14)	−0.30 (N = 39)	<0.025	<0.025
	Later years	−0.08 (N = 34)	0.09 (N = 105)	n.s.	

[a] In standard scores, using data on all cadets.

also reliable (i.e., a significant interaction).

The second variable derives from a part of the questionnaire called "Military Association Scale." The instructions were: "The following is a list of words and phrases which have been associated with the military career. Indicate the degree to which you like the association." There followed about 20 words or phrases, each of which was rated on a 3-point scale. A separate factor analysis revealed one cluster which consisted of "fame," "personal status," and "power." Since in our society these are highly positive and highly valued general goals or attributes, we assumed that those cadets who link the military career closely with these valued attributes have a stronger motivation for a military career, including their career at West Point. The results in Table 6 reveal that this variable is a risk factor for clinical IM, but only during the first year; the difference in the associations during the first and subsequent years is significant (i.e., a significant interaction).

We do not know why the two variables in Table 6 are a risk factor for clinical IM only during the first year. There are at least 2 possible reasons: 1) The answers to the question (obtained at initial testing) reflect a stable motivational disposition, but such a disposition ceases to be a risk factor after the first year; this change could be due to unmeasured processes of adaptation or due to changes in the psychosocial setting of the academic setting. 2) The motivational disposition remains a risk factor throughout the 4 years, but the answers to the question reflect this disposition accurately for a more limited time period, since it is subject to change; repeated reassessments of this disposition would be needed to demonstrate its status as a risk factor during the later years at the Academy. With the limited data at hand we cannot choose between the two alternatives.

The epidemiological associations described in Tables 4−6 suggest that variables indicative of high levels of motivation, specific to the particular study setting, increase susceptibility to clinical IM among those who are infected; such higher levels of motivation may represent a source of pressure or index a higher level of arousal. If we invoke McGrath's (40) definition of stress as "a perceived substantial imbalance between demand and response capability, under conditions where failure to meet demand has important (perceived) consequences" (p. 20), we can see that in looking at the motivational variables we examined only contributors to stress that affect the importance of outcome, but do not influence the probability of failure. We shall now turn to a factor that bears on the issue of probability of failure in meeting demands, academic performance at West Point.

There were two considerations which influenced the way we analyzed the academic performance data. First, in order to preserve the prospective nature of our inquiry, data on grades for one year were related to the development of clinical IM among seroconverters during the next year; in this way we avoided any possibility of "reverse causation," the experience of illness affecting academic performance. Secondly, we wished to treat grades as an indicator of the success—failure dimension. However, a sense of success or failure is an individual reaction in which actual grades are evaluated in relation to expectations or aspirations. In the absence of any direct measures of the latter, we settled on the following two procedures: 1) Within a particular year, those whose second semester grades are better than first semester grades are classified as doing relatively well, while those whose second semester grades are worse are assumed to be doing relatively poorly. 2) Within a particular year, those whose second semester grades are better than predicted from background data (SAT scores, high

school rank, and achievement test scores) are assumed to be doing relatively well, while those whose grades are below those predicted are presumed to be doing relatively poorly. (The average correlation between the combined background data and semester grades was 0.61.) These two indicators of academic "success—failure" in any given year are moderately correlated ($r = 0.41$).

The prediction that is being tested is that relatively poor academic performance at West Point for a given year places the cadet who is a seroconverter in the next year at greater risk for clinical IM. (The first year seroconverters are omitted from analysis, since they have no West Point grades from previous year.) The results supported the hypothesis strongly for the last two years, but not for year 2. On both measures, seroconverters developing clinical IM in years 3 or 4 had poorer performance ($p < 0.005$) than seroconverters with inapparent illness; during year 2, the two groups of seroconverters were quite similar. The interaction term, reflecting the differing associations in years 3 and 4 versus year 2, was also significant for both measures ($p < 0.05$).

Table 7 summarizes these findings, using a classification of relative academic performance that combines both of the measures. The difference in the association between the risk factor and clinical IM for the second versus third and fourth years is consistent with the intuitive notion that relatively poor academic performance may be more distressing and threatening if it happens late in the four years of college studies, since cumulatively more effort had been invested by then and time is running out for any opportunity to reverse the trend.

The data in Tables 5 and 7 suggest the additional hypothesis that high commit-

TABLE 7. Relative Academic Performance During a Year as Risk Factor for Clinical IM in Subsequent Year

		Percent Developing Clinical IM among All Seroconverters			
		2nd Year		3rd & 4th Year	
		N	%	N	%
Relative academic performance during year prior to seroconversion (see text for details)	Relatively poor	34	20.6	16	50.0
	Average	20	30.0	21	23.8
	Relatively good	30	23.3	18	5.6
		gamma = 0.06 n.s.		gamma = −0.69 $p < 0.005$	

ment to a military career should be a risk factor for clinical IM, particularly among seroconverters who are doing relatively poorly academically, since high levels of motivation in the face of poorer grades may be presumed to be more "stressful" than in the face of academic success. Stated another way, one would expect that good grades would nullify the pressure that comes from high levels of motivation. The relevant data are given in Table 8. The measure of motivation combines the last 3 variables listed in Table 2: commitment to a military career, to graduating from the Academy, and certainty of wanting a military career. The measure of academic performance is simply the grade point average for the semester prior to the year of seroconversion; for first year seroconverters (who are included), the measure is based on high school grades. Both measures are dichotomized. The hypothesized interaction is evident: the combination of high level of motivation and relatively poor performance is associated with highest rates of clinical IM. Additional analyses

by year of seroconversion reveal a stronger effect during years 3 and 4: among seroconverters who were high on motivation and low on performance, 60% developed clinical IM, compared to 12.5% in the other 3 cells. The corresponding figures for years 1 and 2 were 35.5% and 21.7%, a significantly smaller difference in percentages ($p < 0.05$).

Support for the hypothesis tested in

TABLE 8. Interaction of Motivation and Academic Performance as Risk Factors for Clinical IM

		Percent Developing Clinical IM among All Seroconverters[a]	
		Level of motivation	
		Low	High
Academic performance	Poor	15.1% (N = 53)	43.5% (N = 46)
	Good	26.2% (N = 42)	17.6% (N = 51)

[a] Interaction $p < 0.005$

Table 8 proved replicable when examined with the use of different measures of performance and motivation. For example, pairing the two academic performance indices (which are used in Table 7) with Commitment to a Military Career (Table 5) produced interactions of a similar magnitude as that seen in Table 8. Consequently, we feel there is some robustness to the finding of an interaction or synergism of the influence of high motivation and poor academic performance on the development of clinical IM among seroconverters.

Distinguishing Illness from Illness Behavior

At this point we wish to take up the issue of the significance of the dichotomous classification of seroconverters into those who developed clinical IM versus those who had only a mild infection or inapparent disease. Essentially, we wish to argue that this dichotomy, based on the presence or absence of hospitalization for clinical IM, reflects an underlying dimension of severity of disease. Conversely we wish to show that two rival interpretations are less likely: 1) the dichotomy reflects differences in medical care seeking behavior rather than severity of illness; 2) inadequate monitoring missed the episodes of clinical IM occurring in the group called inapparent or mild disease.

We readily acknowledge that the discrete, dichotomous classification is dictated by the fact of hospitalization. It is imposed on an underlying continuum severity of disease and thus the dichotomy represents only an arbitrary cut-off point on this continuum. Furthermore, it is likely that a "true" index of severity of disease—if we had one—would reveal some misclassification around the cut-off:

some cases of clinical IM having a milder disease than some cases of more severe infection who were not hospitalized. These limitations of the dichotomous classification must be acknowledged.

Part of the evidence describing the differences between the subclinical and clinical seroconverters has been presented in an earlier report of the serological follow-up of the two groups (41). The presence of heterophile antibody is roughly correlated with the severity of the infection; it is often absent or in low titer in milder cases and in childhood infections. The horse red cell absorbed test is a sensitive indicator of heterophile antibody and elevated titers persist for 7−9 months or more (41). Using this test on cadets who showed EBV seroconversion without recognized clinical IM, 48.4% showed a diagnostic level of heterophile antibody ($\geq$ 1:40) and 47.5% had a demonstrable antibody rise (41). The geometric mean antibody titer of 1:216 in this group was much lower than that of 1:2560 found in cadets with clinically recognized IM, thus affirming a correlation with severity. The heterophile antibody thus provided a clue for possible missed clinical cases as well as another indicator of the severity of the host response independent from clinical symptoms.

The follow-up study (41) included an intensive search for missed episodes of IM among the 129 seroconverters with inapparent illness, both through individual questionnaires and a careful review of the hospital and clinic records of all of them. Of the 65 cadets with a significant rise in titer of heterophile antibody on any one of the 3 tests, only 8 had some evidence suggestive of a missed diagnosis, 4 others had episodes of pharyngitis or tonsilitis that might have represented mild IM, and

3 others had an upper respiratory infection; in the remaining 50 cadets, no known illness was identified. Of the 64 cadets who had an EBV seroconversion without demonstrable rises in titer of heterophile antibody on any of the 3 tests, 3 had suggestive symptoms of IM, 2 had upper respiratory illness, and 1 had pharyngitis/tonsilitis. These results suggest that no more than 9 to 12% of seroconverters classified as inapparent disease could have actually had clinical IM. Presumably, they failed to be hospitalized either because of the very mild nature of their illness and/or because of a strong disinclination to seek medical care.

The above data strongly suggest that neither inadequate monitoring of cases of clinical IM nor differences in the readiness to seek medical care could be seriously compromising the dichotomous classification, clinical IM versus inapparent disease, as an indicator of the severity of the disease. However, because of the crucial importance of separating illness from illness behavior or sick role behavior, we shall offer additional data and discussion on this issue.

One line of argument deals with the nature of the disease and the study setting. Essentially, IM is not a mild illness, such as a cold, where a good deal of discretion regarding medical care seeking is possible. Low readiness to seek treatment would mean "ignoring" the disease, which is perhaps possible in other college settings, where the strategy of a very low level of activity can be adopted (e.g., attend classes but otherwise rest and sleep). However, at West Point, with its daily rigorous physical demands, "ignoring" IM is nearly impossible and would likely lead to more severe manifestations of the disease, including the possibility of such medical disasters as a ruptured spleen. On the opposite side of the coin, we could have cadets with a very high readiness to seek medical treatment or a high inclination to adopt the sick role. Such a readiness may lead them to be hospitalized in the face of mild symptoms, but in the absence of IM they will fail to meet the diagnostic criteria for IM; their sick role behavior alone will not bring them into the classification of clinical IM.

Another line of evidence involves the analysis of additional data, number of *days of hospitalization* among the cases of clinical IM. The argument is as follows: High readiness for medical care, or a strong inclination to adopt the sick role, means that cadets with even mild disease are hospitalized; their hospital stay should be brief. Conversely, low readiness means that hospitalization occurs only when the disease is relatively severe; their hospital stay should be long. In short, length of hospitalization should be negatively associated with indicators of readiness for medical care. Now, if the results in Tables 4 to 8 are to be interpreted as reflecting an association with readiness for medical care rather than with severity of illness—because the classification of inapparent illness versus clinical IM is seriously contaminated by the readiness variable—then we would predict that the risk factors in Tables 4 to 8 will be themselves negatively associated with length of hospitalization. Absence of such a negative association would suggest that readiness for medical care is an unlikely alternate explanation of the results in Tables 4 to 8. Of course, a positive association between length of hospitalization and the risk factors would further strengthen the interpretation that the classification of inapparent illness versus clinical IM reflects a severity gradient of disease, since the variables predicting the development of clinical IM among seroconverters also predict longer hospitalization among those with clinical IM.

The relevant data are presented in Table 9. Abstracts of hospital records were made available to us for the cases of clinical IM for the first two years. All but 3 of these records contained information on date and length of hospitalization and on date of onset of symptoms. The average length of hospitalization was 17.4 days (SD = 9.8). The first variable Father's Occupational "Overachievement" is an average of two of the indices listed in Table 4, Fa. Occup. Status > Fa. Educ. Level and Fa. Occup. Status > Mo. Educ. Level; the third index, involving mother's occupation, is omitted because of missing data. The second variable is the motivational indicator used in Table 5, while the third variable is a combined measure averaging the two indices displayed in Table 6. In the case of this last variable, data only on the 14 first year cases of clinical IM are presented because it is only during this year that the motivational variable is a risk factor for clinical IM among the seroconverters. Data on relative academic performance, seen in Table 7, are omitted from analysis in Table 9, because this variable is a risk factor for clinical IM only during 3rd and 4th years, for which data on length of hospitalization were not available to us.

There is no question that the results in Table 9 are strongly consistent with the interpretation that these are risk factors for severity of disease, whether this is reflected by the classification of inapparent illness versus clinical IM among seroconverters or by length of hospital stay among cases of clinical IM. Conversely, the results permit a strong rejection of the rival hypothesis involving readiness for medical care.

TABLE 9. Predictors of Length of Hospitalization among Cadets Who Developed Clinical IM During the First Two Years

| | | Father's Occupational "Overachievement"[a] | |
		Low	High
Days of hospital stay	≤ 10	6	0
	11–20	6	6
	≥ 21	2	6

| | | Strength of Commitment to a Military Career[b] | |
		Low	High
Days of hospital stay	≤ 10	6	2
	11–20	10	3
	≥ 21	2	8

| | | Personal Importance of Leadership and Associations to "Military Career"[c] | |
		Low	High
Days of hospital stay	≤ 17	6	0
	≥ 18	2	6

[a] gamma = 0.80; $p < 0.025$.
[b] gamma = 0.66; $p < 0.025$.
[c] Fisher's exact test; $p < 0.01$.

The time elapsed between reported onset of symptoms and the day of hospitalization, which can be labeled "days of delay," may reflect some component of the concept of readiness for medical care. It is therefore interesting to note that "days of delay" are not significantly correlated with: days of hospitalization ($r = -0.04$), Father's Occupational "Overachievement" ($r = 0.12$), Strength of Commitment to a Military Career ($r = $

0.12), and the combined scale of Personal Importance of Leadership and Associations to "Military Career" (r = 0.11). This is thus additional independent evidence that suggests that readiness for medical care does not play an important role in these results.

The final line of evidence bearing on the issue of illness versus illness behavior (severity of illness vs. readiness for medical care) involves the results of the 3 heterophile antibody tests on seroconverters with mild or inapparent disease (41). Cadets whose sera were positive (titer ≥ 1:40) on any of the 3 tests following seroconversion may be viewed as having had a somewhat more severe infection than those whose titers were not elevated. If readiness for seeking medical care is a serious alternative explanation of the results in Tables 4 to 8, then we would expect the cadets with elevated titers to give evidence of being low on readiness, since none of them had sought medical care. The argument here is similar to that above regarding days of hospitalization.

The serological data were available on 124 of the 146 seroconverters with inapparent illness; 64 of these had elevated titers. On the index of Father's Occupational "Overachievement" (used in Table 9), cadets with elevated titers had a slightly higher mean score than the cadets without elevated titers; on Strength of Commitment to a Military Career, the former group had a somewhat higher mean than the latter group. Both of these small differences are in the opposite direction from the prediction involving the readiness for medical care interpretation; instead, the differences favor slightly the severity of illness interpretation, as did the earlier results for days of hospitalization.

Since Table 8 had demonstrated an interaction between motivation and relative academic performance in the development of clinical IM, similar analyses were undertaken with regard to the prediction of presence of elevated titers among all seroconverters with inapparent illness. Table 10 presents the relevant data. The interaction is again in evidence, but the differences are somewhat smaller. The results do suggest that the risk factors for clinical IM among all seroconverters are similar to those for elevated titers among seroconverters with inapparent disease.

In Table 11 we take the data on the first year seroconverters (shown in Table 6) and expand the dichotomous classification (inapparent disease vs. clinical IM) into a 4-step gradient of severity of disease, using also the data from the heterophile antibody tests and length of hospitalization data (16 cadets had missing data on the former). It is readily apparent that a monotonic relationship exists between the level of motivation and this expanded gradient of severity of disease. The table also shows that the seroconverters with inapparent disease but elevated titers are rather like the cases of clinical IM with briefer hospitalization.

TABLE 10. **Interaction of Motivation and Academic Performance as Risk Factors for Elevated Titers among Seroconverters with Inapparent Disease**

| | | Percent with Elevated Titers among Seroconverters with Inapparent Disease[a] | |
| | | Level of Motivation | |
		Low	High
Academic performance	Poor	51.4% (N = 35)	65.4% (N = 26)
	Good	57.7% (N = 26)	41.7% (N = 36)

[a] Interaction p = 0.05.

TABLE 11. Distribution of First Year Seroconverters (in %) by Motivation and Combined Gradient of Severity of Disease [a]

		Development of Heterophile Antibody in Titers of Seroconverters with Inapparent Disease		Days of Hospital Stay Among Cases of Clinical IM		Total
		Not present	Present	≤ 17	≥ 18	
Score on combined scale of personal importance of leadership and associations to "military career"	Low	43	27	0	0	19.4
	Moderate	57	60	100	25	58.3
	High	0	13	0	75	22.2
	N	7	15	6	8	36

[a] gamma = 0.78; $p < 0.001$.

These two groups were also found to be highly similar on the other psychosocial variables discussed above, such as Father's Occupational "Overachievement" or Strength of Commitment to a Military Career. It should be remembered that these same two groups should be maximally *different* on readiness for medical care, were this to be a tenable alternate explanation.

Concluding Comments

The pattern of findings suggests that we have identified a set of interrelated psychosocial risk factors for the development of clinical IM among susceptibles who were infected. Specifically, indicators of greater academic pressure—whether reflected in higher levels of motivation, or poorer academic performance, or the combination of the two—were related prospectively to the development of clinical IM. Because of the additional evidence linking these psychosocial risk factors to length of hospitalization among cases of clinical IM and to presence of positive heterophile antibody in titers of seroconverters with inapparent illness, the interpretation of the results as influences on the expression of clinical versus subclinical illness becomes very compelling. Conversely, the concern over an alternate interpretation of results in terms of readiness for medical care is thereby diminished.

The generalizability of these findings cannot as yet be estimated, since the literature on psychosocial factors in clinical IM is so extremely limited. However, it is interesting to note that in an ongoing pilot study of cadets at the U.S. Coast Guard Academy (42), which uses the prospective sero-epidemiologic design of the West Point study (36), the one set of psychosocial risk factors that predicted the development of clinical IM among the seroconverters was a cluster of interrelated scales from the California Psychological Inventory (CPI) measuring the following traits: aggressive, ambitious, outgoing, intelligent, energetic, enterprising, industrious, mature, efficient. This cluster of traits is encouragingly similar to the general concept of a high level of motivation as a risk factor for clinical IM. It is further interesting to note that the Coast Guard pilot data (42) reveal that seroconverters who go on to develop clinical IM report fewer stressful life events than cadets who have inapparent illness. This is contrary to prediction, but consistent with the Wilder data (33). In view of the accumulated evidence (e.g., Masuda and Holmes (43)) that different groups can experience strikingly different average frequencies of life events, it is thus at least as important to view the level of life events as reflecting a person's chosen lifestyle, as it is to consider such level the amount of stress fate has chosen to heap upon that person. Within this framework, then, highly motivated cadets who go on to develop clinical IM may have an associated lifestyle that precludes a high frequency of life events.

The subjects in our study and the setting, cadets at the U.S. Military Academy, are so highly select and self-selected that our results may not apply to other settings. That is to say, what may be generalizable as risk factors for clinical IM are the broad concepts of level of motivation to meet the goals and demands of a particular role setting and the relative success or failure of one's role performance, but not the specific ways the concepts are measured in this study. Stated concretely, we do not expect, for example, that the Commitment to a Military Career is a predictor of clinical IM among Yale undergraduates, or even among new arrivals to a boot camp. Different study settings, presumably, will demand their own uniquely appropriate measures of the underlying constructs. In this connection, it is worth noting that in our overall results, some motivation variables ceased to be risk factors for clinical IM after the first year, while poor academic performance appeared as a risk factor primarily during the last 2 years. This suggests a further specificity of associations: with passage of time and as the cadets begin to adapt to the environment of the Military Academy, different sources of pressure may become salient, thus calling for different assessments to be made at different points in time. This may also imply that experiencing many stressful life events during the year prior to going away to college is simply not as salient a variable as are the motivational and performance indicators specific to the setting in which the subject currently finds himself.

SUMMARY

In seeking to clarify the role of psychosocial factors in infectious disease, it is desirable to be able to separate out the 4 primary ways in which such factors can exert an influence: 1) on the initial immunity status of the cohort at the start of the study; 2) on the exposure to infection among susceptibles; 3) on the clinical expression of the disease and its course among susceptibles who are infected; and 4) on the treatment-seeking behavior and response to treatment among those with symptoms. Recent advances in the study of infectious mononucleosis (IM) make this a highly appropriate infectious disease in which to examine the above model of the interplay of biological and psychosocial factors in disease.

In a 4-year prospective sero-epidemiological study of one class of some 1400 cadets at the West Point Military Academy, about two-thirds of the subjects were found to be immune to IM, as defined by the presence of antibody to Epstein-Barr virus (EBV) at matriculation. Among the susceptibles (antibody to EBV absent), some 20% per year became infected with EBV, the causative agent for IM. These were seroconverters in whom the antibody to EBV appeared at some point during the 4-year follow-up. About 25% of the seroconverters developed definite clinical IM, while the other seroconverters had presumably only mild or inapparent illness.

While this article does present some data on correlates of initial immunity and of seroconversion among the susceptibles, the primary focus is on identifying risk factors that predict the development of definite clinical IM among those who were known to be infected during the period of observation, the seroconverters. Psychosocial factors that significantly increased the risk of EBV infection being expressed as clinical IM were: 1) having fathers who were "overachievers" (occupational status exceeding own educational level, or wife's education, or her occupational status); 2) having a strong commitment to a military career; 3) ascribing strong values to various aspects of the training and of military career; 4) scoring poorly on indices of relative academic performance; 5) having strong motivation and doing relatively poorly academically.

Two indices of infection or of clinical illness were also examined: development of positive heterophile antibody titers among seroconverters with inapparent disease and length of hospitalization among those with clinical IM. The general finding was that the factors which related to the risk of clinical IM among all seroconverters were also related to these two indices. This strengthens considerably the interpretation that the distinction between cases of definite clinical IM and seroconverters with inapparent disease is one of the severity of disease, rather than reflecting readiness for medical care.

This research was supported by Contract No. DADA 17-69-C-9172 from the Department of the Army, by research grants Nos. AI 08731 and CA 12952 from the National Institutes of Health, and by grant No. NEG-00-3-0009 from the National Institute of Education. The authors wish to express their appreciation to the Office of Institutional Research and to the Medical Department at the U.S. Military Academy for their kind cooperation in this study and the provision of the essential data.

REFERENCES

1. Hill O, ed.: Modern Trends in Psychosomatic Medicine 3. London, Butterworths, 1976
2. Hurst MW, Jenkins CD, Rose RM: The relation of psychological stress to onset of medical illness. Annu Rev Med 27:301−312, 1976
3. Kasl SV, Reichsman F, eds.: Advances in Psychosomatic Medicine, vol. 9. Epidemiologic Studies in Psychosomatic Medicine. Basel, S. Karger, 1977
4. Lipowski ZJ, Lipsitt DR, Whybrow PC, eds.: Psychosomatic Medicine: Current Trends and Clinical Applications. New York, Oxford University Press, 1977
5. Weiner H: Psychobiology and Human Disease. New York, Elsevier, 1977
6. Holmes TH: Psychosocial and psychophysiological studies of tuberculosis, in Physiological Correlates of Psychological Disorders (edited by R. Roessler and NS Greenfield). Madison, The University of Wisconsin Press, 1962, pp. 239−255
7. Sparer PJ, ed: Personality, Stress, and Tuberculosis. New York, International Universities Press, 1956

8. Luborsky L, Docherty JP, Penick S: Onset conditions for psychosomatic symptoms: a comparative review of immediate observation with retrospective research. Psychosom Med 35:187–204, 1973

9. Jacobs MA, Spilken A, Norman M: Relationship of life change, maladaptive aggression, and upper respiratory infection in male college students. Psychosom Med 31:31–44, 1969

10. Jacobs MA, Spilken AZ, Norman MM, Anderson LS: Life stress and respiratory illness. Psychosom Med 32:233–242, 1970

11. Mechanic D: Some implications of illness behavior for medical sampling. N Engl J Med 269:244–247, 1963

12. Marx MB, Garrity TF, Bowers FR: The influence of recent life experience on the health of college freshmen. J Psychosom Res 19:87–98, 1975

13. Rahe RH: Life change and subsequent illness reports, in Life Stress and Illness (edited by EKE Gunderson and RH Rahe). Springfield, Ill., Charles Thomas, 1974, pp. 58–78

14. Rubin RT, Gunderson EKE, Arthur RJ: Life stress and illness patterns in the U.S. Navy. VI. Environmental, demographic, and prior life change variables in relation to illness onset in naval aviators during a combat cruise. Psychosom Med 34:533–547, 1972

15. Wyler AR, Masuda M, Holmes TH: Magnitude of life events and seriousness of illness. Psychosom Med 33:115–122, 1971

16. Friedman SB, Glasgow LA: Psychological factors and resistance to infectious disease. Pediatr Clin North Am 13:315–335, 1966

17. Solomon GF, Amkraut AA: Emotions, stress, and immunity, in Health and the Social Environment (edited by PM Insel and RH Moose). Lexington, Mass., Lexington Books, 1974, pp. 193–205

18. Ader R: Behavioral influences on immune responses. Presented at the First Annual Meeting of the Academy of Behavioral Medicine Research, Snowbird, Utah, June 3–6, 1979

19. Amkraut A, Solomon GF: From the symbolic stimulus to the pathophysiologic response: immune mechanisms, in Psychosomatic Medicine (edited by ZJ Lipowski, OR Lipsitt, and PC Whybrow). New York, Oxford University Press, 1977, pp. 228–250

20. Rogers MP, Dubey D, Reich P: The influence of the psyche and the brain on immunity and disease susceptibility: a critical review. Psychosom Med 41:147–164, 1979

21. Stein M, Schiavi RC, Camerino M: Influence of brain and behavior on the immune system. Science 191:435–440, 1976

22. Canter A: Changes in mood during incubation of acute febrile disease and the effects of pre-exposure psychological status. Psychosom Med 34:424–430, 1972

23. Greene WA, Betts RF, Ochitill HN, Iker HP, Douglas RG Jr: Psychosocial factors and immunity: preliminary report (abstr). Psychosom Med 40:87, 1978

24. Palmblad J, Cantell K, Strander H, Froberg J, Karlsson C-G, Levi, L, Granstrom M, Unger P: Stressor exposure and immunological response in man: interferon-producing capacity and phagocytosis. J Psychosom Res 20:193–199, 1976

25. Totman R, Reed SE, Craig JW: Cognitive dissonance, stress, and virus induced common colds. J Psychosom Res 21:55–63, 1977

26. Luborsky L, Mintz J, Brightman VJ, Katcher AH: Herpes simplex virus and moods: a longitudinal study. J Psychosom Res 20:543–548, 1976

27. Locke SE, Heisel JS: The influence of stress and emotions on the human immune response (abstr). Biofeedback Self-Regulation 2:320, 1977

28. Gruchow HW: Catecholamine activity and infectious disease episodes. J Hum Stress, in press

29. Mason JW, Buescher EL, Belfer ML, Artenstein MS, Mougey EH: Urinary corticosteroid, epinephrine and norepinephrine levels before and after onset of adenovirus respiratory illness in Army recruits. J Hum Stress, in press

30. Evans AS: Infectious mononucleosis and related syndromes. Am J Med Sci 276:325–339, 1978

31. Evans AS, Niederman JC: Epstein-Barr virus, in Viral Infections of Humans (edited by AS Evans). New York, Plenum Publishing Corp., 1976, pp. 209–233

32. Greenfield NS, Roessler R, Crosley AP Jr: Ego strength and length of recovery from infectious mononucleosis. J Nerv Ment Dis 128:125–128, 1959

33. Wilder RM, Hubble J, Kennedy CE: Life change and infectious mononucleosis. J Am Coll Health Assoc 20:115–119, 1971

34. Hendler N, Leahy W: Psychiatric and neurologic sequelae of infectious mononucleosis. Am J Psychiatry 135:842−844, 1978

35. Schulhof E, Roy RS, Trickett PC: The emotional climate of mononucleosis. Am J Orthopsychiatry 36:306−307, 1966

36. Hallee JT, Evans AS, Niederman JC, Brooks CM, Voegtly JH: Infectious mononucleosis at the United States Military Academy. A prospective study of a single class over four years. Yale J Biol Med 3:182−195, 1974

37. Kasl SV: Serum uric acid and cholesterol correlates of achievement in West Point cadets. Final report on Project 8-0082 to the National Institute of Education, 1976

38. Kasl SV, Cobb S: Effects of parental status incongruence and discrepancy on physical and mental health of adult offspring. J Pers Soc Psychol Monogr 7 (No. 2, Whole No. 642):1−15, 1967

39. Krauss I: Sources of educational aspirations among working-class youth. Am Sociol Rev 29:867−879, 1964

40. McGrath JE, ed.: Social and Psychological Factors in Stress. New York, Holt, Rinehart, and Winston, 1970

41. Evans AS, Niederman JC, Cenabre LC, West B, Richards VA: A prospective evaluation of heterophile and Epstein-Barr virus-specific IgM antibody tests in clinical and subclinical infectious mononucleosis: specificity and sensitivity of the tests and persistence of antibody. J Infect Dis 132:546−554, 1975

42. Shaskan EG: Psychosocial and biochemical risks for mononucleosis. 1 RO1 AI/MH 15901 Grant application submitted to NIH from the Department of Psychiatry, University of Connecticut Health Center, 1978

43. Masuda M, Holmes TH: Life events: perceptions and frequencies. Psychosom Med 40:236−261, 1978

44

THE WHITE BLOOD CELLS IN DEMENTIA PRAECOX AND DEMENTIA PARALYTICA

William Dameshek

The white blood cells are derived from three systems: the bone marrow, which produces the polymorphonuclear cells; the lymphoid tissue, which produces the lymphocytes; and the reticuloendothelial tissue, which produces the monocytes. It was thought that these systems could be observed clinically by careful study of the blood smear. Cover slip preparations were used; from 250 to 500 white cells were counted; note was made of: the presence of immature forms of polymorphonuclear cells (according to the Schilling method); "toxic" changes in the polymorphonuclear cells; plasma cells; histiocytes, etc. There were no essential differences in the total white cell counts or their relative proportions in the blood from various situations (brachial, basilic, carotid, jugular, finger or ear).

In seventy cases of dementia praecox, normal conditions were present in 70%. In 30% there was a triad of low polymorphonuclear count, lymphocytosis and an eosinophilia of over 4%. This occurred especially in the catatonic cases. Eosinophilia up to 20% occurred in about 10% of the cases.

In seventy cases of dementia paralytica a monocytosis of over 10% occurred in 52%; histiocytes were present in 20%; plasma cells in 27%; toxic changes in 80%, and an increase in immature forms of polymorphonuclears in 12%. The appearance of histiocytes and plasma cells is linked with the pathology of dementia paralytica. In one remarkable case in which several convulsions occurred each night, there was a monocytosis of 40% or more with the appearance of a large number of histiocytes, many containing phagocytosed particles and vacuoles. These occurred with convulsions and disappeared when convulsions were stopped, to recur when convulsions again started. It was thought that the convulsions in some way caused the discharge of monocytes and histiocytes from the abnormal tissue in the brain.

No definite criteria as to diagnosis or prognosis could be found from the study of the white blood cells.

45

THE "ANTIBRAIN" FACTORS IN PSYCHIATRIC PATIENTS' SERA

I. Further Studies with a Hemagglutination Technique

W. J. Fessel

In preliminary reports [1,8] it was shown that sera of some psychiatric patients had a greater effect than did control sera upon latex particles coated with brain extracts. Because in further experience with the latex particle system there were difficulties in reproducing the results, a red cell agglutination reaction that is both easier to read and more reproducible has been developed. The results obtained with this system confirm the original findings in a general way, but also cast doubt upon the interpretation, mentioned in the previous report as possible, of a circulating brain antibody in the sera of mentally ill patients.

The Departments of Psychiatry and Medicine, University of California School of Medicine, and the Langley Porter Neuropsychiatric Institute, California Department of Mental Hygiene.

Supported by a grant (MY4581) from the National Institutes of Health.

Materials and Methods

A. *Patient Material.*—Psychiatric patients' sera were obtained from several institutions of the California Department of Mental Hygiene, the majority coming either from the patients with acute mental disturbances on the acute treatment service of the Langley Porter Neuropsychiatric Institute or from those with chronic mental disturbances on chronic wards of the Napa State Hospital. The diagnoses of representative samples from these two groups of patients are shown in Table 1.

The sera of patients in the Napa State Hospital were divided into several groups, as indicated in Table 2.

About 50 patients in Napa State Hospital had been used in another research program, and extensive clinical data about them were available. The clinical correlations for this and other groups of subjects will be reported later.

The patients at Ypsilanti State Hospital had been on a controlled diet for from two to four months. The composition of this group of patients is shown in Table 3. The diagnoses of these patients were unknown to us at the time their sera were tested.

TABLE 1.—*Diagnoses of Representative Samples of the Langley Porter Institute Patients (Acute Mental Illnesses) and Napa State Hospital Patients (Chronic Mental Illnesses) Tested With the Brain-Hemagglutination Reaction*

	Langley Porter Institute	Napa State Hospital
Schizophrenic reaction	38	136
Manic-depressive reaction	7	1
Psychotic-depressive reaction	3	9
Involutional psychotic reaction	12	1
Epilepsy with psychotic reaction	0	2
Mental deficiency with psychotic reaction	0	4
Psychoneurotic reaction	18	0
Personality trait disturbance	6	1
Personality pattern disturbance	3	0
Adjustment reaction of adolescence	3	0
Psychophysiological musculoskeletal reaction	1	0
Chronic brain syndrome (other than associated with alcoholism)	3	6
Acute brain syndrome	1	0
Alcoholism with psychotic reaction	0	9
Paralysis agitans	2	0
	97	163

erythematosus and others with severe rheumatoid arthritis, scleroderma, and dermatomyositis.

The 105 sera with raised levels of 7S γ-globulin, mesoglobulins, or macroglobulins,[3] provided by The Institute of Medical Physics, had been sent from various parts of the United States for analytical ultracentrifugation. The mean levels of the various classes of proteins found in this group were greatly raised, as shown in Table 4.

All sera were kept frozen at −15 to −20 C until required for analysis.

B. *Tissue Antigens.*—The brain was obtained, about four hours after death, from a seven-year-old girl who had died after an operation for correction of congenital heart disease. Specimens of kidney, liver, and thyroid were obtained within 24 hours of their deaths from patients dying of diseases not involving these organs. All tissues were stored at −15 to −20 C.

Extracts were made by homogenizing tissue in 0.85% saline in the ratio of 1:10 (weight/volume) and centrifuging at 14,000 rpm for 40 minutes. These procedures were done at 0-4 C. The supernatants, used to sensitize the sheep red cells, were adjusted to have a protein content of 0.25 mg/ml.

TABLE 2.—*Groups of Patients*

Group	No.	Pos (%)	Doubtful Reaction (%)	Neg (%)
Blood bank donors	157	10 (6.4)	5 (3.2)	141 (90.4)
Napa State Hospital (over-all results on the four subgroups tested)	358	112 (31.3)	38 (10.6)	208 (58.1)
Napa State Hospital (blood drawn in 1959)	169	44 (26.0)	25 (14.8)	100 (59.2)
Napa State Hospital (blood drawn in 1962)	79	14 (17.8)	9 (11.4)	56 (70.8)
Napa State Hospital (includes 65 FII + patients)	92	48 (52.2)	4 (4.3)	40 (43.5)
Napa State Hospital (childhood schizophrenias)	18	6 (33.3)	0	12 (66.6)
Ypsilanti State Hospital (on controlled diet: tested "blind"; see Table 3 for breakdown of figures)	39	7 (17.9)	0	32 (82.1)
Langley Porter Neuropsychiatric Institute (patients on acute treatment service)	245	18 (7.3)	24 (9.8)	203 (82.9)
Sonoma State Hospital (postencephalitic brain damage)	25	10 (40.0)	0	15 (60.0)
Sonoma and Porterville State Hospitals (clinical diagnoses of Schilder's disease)	21	4 (19.0)	0	17 (81.0)
University of California Hospital (various connective tissue diseases)	47	8 (17.0)	7 (14.9)	32 (68.1)
Institute of Medical Physics (sera with raised levels of 7S globulins, mesoglobulins, or macroglobulins)	105	28 (26.7)	15 (14.3)	62 (59.0)
Multiple sclerosis	4	1	1	2

Sera were obtained from patients at Sonoma State Hospital who had suffered brain damage after encephalitis of either infectious or allergic etiology. Another group of patients, from Sonoma and Porterville State Hospitals, had clinical diagnoses of Schilder's disease.

A group of 47 sera were from patients with various collagen diseases of sufficient severity to require hospitalization at the University of California Hospital. These included 12 patients with systemic lupus

TABLE 3.—*Overlap Between Rheumatoid Factor Test (FII Latex) and Brain-Hemagglutination Test Findings in 88 Psychiatric Patients*

	FII +	FII −
Brain-hemagglut. +	42 (64.6%)	6 (26.1%)
Brain-hemagglut. −	23 (35.4%)	17 (73.9%)
Total	65	23

Behavior and Immune Function

Group	No.	Pos (%)	Doubtful Reaction	Neg (%)
Total schizophrenic patients	26	6 (23.0)	0	20 (77)
Paranoid schizophrenia	7	1 (14)	0	6 (86)
Chronic undifferentiated schizophrenia	16	3 (19)	0	13 (81)
Nonpsychotic patients with character disorder or chronic brain syndrome	13	1 (8)	0	12 (92)

C. *Hemagglutination Test.*—1. Tannic Acid Cells and Their Sensitization: The procedure of Stavitsky [15] was followed. Sheep red cells were washed three times in saline, and a 2½% suspension was made in pH 7.2 phosphate-buffered saline. One volume of the cell suspension and one volume of a 1:40,000 dilution of tannic acid in saline were incubated at 37 C for ten minutes. The tannic-acid-treated cells were washed once in pH 7.2 buffered saline and reconstituted to a 2½% suspension in saline. Four volumes of pH 6.4 phosphate-buffered saline, one volume of the brain extract, and one volume of the tannic-acid-treated cells were mixed in that order and kept at room temperature for ten minutes. The sensitized, or coated, cells were then washed in two volumes of saline containing 1% of normal rabbit serum and were reconstituted to a 2½% suspension in this same saline. The last two washings were made at 4 C to avoid undue hemolysis of the sensitized cells.

2. Testing the Sera: All sera were complement inactivated at 56 C for 30 minutes and then absorbed of heterophil antibodies by being mixed with an equal volume of packed, washed sheep cells and left overnight at 4 C. Immediately before testing them the sera were again heated at 56 C for ten minutes. The same procedures were applied to the normal rabbit serum before it was mixed with the saline.

Serial doubling dilutions of 0.5 ml amounts of the sera were made, in the saline which contained 1% rabbit serum, starting with a dilution of 1:2 and ending with a dilution of 1:64. To each serum dilution was added 0.05 ml of sensitized cells. The tubes were left overnight at room temperature; next morning the settling patterns were read twice, about an hour apart, for the presence or absence of hemagglutination. At the second reading the end points were usually sharpened, and many initial, equivocal results were clearer. Hemagglutination in any tube was regarded as a positive result. Most titers were in the range of 1:4 to 1:64. The settling patterns and their grading are illustrated in the paper by Stavitsky.[15] For this study, agglutination illustrated in that paper as ± or more was called positive. Observer-to-observer reproducibility was excellent in most cases. Where some doubt existed as to whether the pattern represented a positive or negative result, it was called doubtful. Although the issue would usually be settled upon retesting the serum, in some groups there were high incidences of doubtful reactions, because often insufficient serum was available to make more than two tests (Table 2). It is emphasized that an attempt was made to underestimate the positivity of patients' sera and to overestimate the positivity of the blood donors' control sera. This might have contributed to the high incidence of doubtful reactions in some groups of patients—with less stringent reading of results most of these doubtful reactions would probably have been called positive.

When testing patients' sera, a few normal sera were always included, so that the 157 blood donors' sera were tested over the entire experimental period, thereby eliminating subjective differences in reading the agglutination patterns. Other appropriate controls included the use in each run of a serum known to be positive and the testing of the effects of tannic-acid-treated red cells which had not been exposed to tissue extracts. All sera reported were run on at least two and sometimes three separate occasions.

For several patients, sera taken over a three-year period were available. In all cases the brain-hemagglutination reactions found in the initial samples were the same as those in the later ones.

3. Specificity Studies: A limited number of sera positive in the brain-hemagglutination reaction were studied to determine whether the addition to the dilutions of a known positive serum, before brain-coated red cells had been added, of brain or liver extracts or of Cohn's fraction II (FII) could cause inhibition of the hemagglutination. Inhibition was considered to have occurred if the titer dropped by two or more doubling dilutions as compared with the titer of a simultaneously made test to which no inhibiting material had been added.

A few additional sera were tested for their ability to agglutinate tannic-acid-treated red cells coated with extracts of kidney, liver, or thyroid.

Results

The results of the hemagglutination tests with brain-coated cells are summarized in Table 2. The various groups are so disparate that tests for statistical significance have not been applied. But it is apparent that the results on blood bank donors' sera differ considerably from the results on state hospital patients (Napa and Ypsilanti state hospitals), on patients with postencephalitic brain damage or with the clinical diagnosis of Schilder's disease, on patients with serious connective tissue diseases, and on patients whose sera showed abnormal ultracentrifuge protein patterns. The differences from the control group would be even more striking were the doubtful reactions added to the positive ones.

Of particular interest are the following aspects: (1) Although the incidence of positive tests was rather variable among the subgroups at the Napa and Ypsilanti state hospitals (Table 2), even the lowest incidence (17.8%) was almost three times that seen in the blood donors. (2) Incidences of positive tests in the Napa State Hospital patients were, in general, similar to those in the patients with known brain damage, patients with connective tissue disease, and patients with abnormal ultracentrifugal protein patterns. (3) The highest incidence (52.2%) was at Napa State Hospital in the subgroup of 92 which had been selected to include 65 patients with positive rheumatoid factor tests. This high incidence was due to a partial overlap between the results of the two test systems (Table 3). Positive brain-hemagglutination tests occurred in 64.6% of the psychiatric patients previously found [4] to have positive FII latex tests for rheumatoid factor; positive brain-hemagglutination tests were seen in 26.1% of the psychiatric patients with negative FII latex tests. The latter figure agrees with the general trend of results in the state hospital patients and suggests that these results were not greatly influenced by the presence of rheumatoid factor activity (Table 5). (4) Schizophrenic patients on a controlled diet at Ypsilanti State Hospital had a similar incidence to the patients at Napa State Hospital (Table 4). (5) The incidence of positive results in the group of acutely ill mental patients at the Langley Porter Neuropsychiatric Institute, of whom a high proportion were first hospital admis-

TABLE 5.—*Inhibition Tests on 30 Psychiatric Patients' Sera*

| | | Inhibition by | | |
	Total	Brain	Liver	FII
No inhibition	22	0	0	0
Inhibition	8	8	2	0
	30			

sions for mental disease, was similar to that in the control group. But the percentage of doubtful results was about three times as high—perhaps a reflection of the abnormal proteins which are already present in such patients' sera.[1,2,5,6] The discrepancy between these results and the previous finding of a significantly increased incidence ($P<0.001$) of brain-latex tests in this group of patients [1] cannot be explained.

Inhibition tests were made, by using both brain and liver extracts, and FII, on the sera of 30 psychiatric patients that were positive in the brain-hemagglutination reaction; 0.1 ml of a solution containing 0.25 mg/ml of the inhibiting reagent was added. A parallel test using brain-coated red cells but no inhibiting reagent was made. The results of these tests are shown in Table 5. Inhibition by brain extract was seen in only 8 of the 30 sera; in two of these eight, inhibition also occurred with the liver extract but not with FII reagent. In another six psychiatric patients inhibition tests were made as above except that FII was not used because insufficient serum was available. Inhibition, which was by both brain and liver extracts, was seen in only one of these six sera. In all the inhibition experiments, tests were also made with uncoated tannic-acid-treated cells; significant agglutination of these cells—ie, to a titer equivalent to that found with brain-coated cells—was seen in only one instance.

Inhibition studies were made upon 15 sera, positive in the brain-hemagglutination reaction, from the group of sera known to have abnormal ultracentrifugal protein patterns (Table 6). Although the amounts of brain extract added were 0.25 ml of a solution containing 2.5 mg protein per milliliter,

	Total	Inhibited by		
		Brain	Liver	FII
No inhibition	13	0 '	0	0
Inhibition	2	0	1	2
	15			

and the amounts of liver extract and FII added were 0.1 ml of a solution containing 10 mg protein per milliliter (in each instance 25 times that added for inhibition studies in the psychiatric patients' sera), inhibition was seen in only 2 of the 15 sera. In neither case did brain extract cause inhibition; in one instance both liver extract and FII were inhibitory and in the other only FII was inhibitory. Significant agglutination of uncoated tannic-acid-treated cells was seen in 3 of the 15 sera.

Five psychiatric patients' sera were tested for their ability to agglutinate red cells coated with brain, thyroid, liver, and kidney extracts and, also, a brain extract which had been dialyzed against 6 M urea for 18 hours. (Treatment with urea had been found by George and Vaughan [9] effectively to increase hemagglutination titers in a different antigen-antibody system.) In only one instance was hemagglutination of the brain-coated cells greater than that of the cells coated with other tissue extracts; in this case there was no difference between the effects of the urea-treated and untreated brain extract..

Comment

Some general interpretations of these findings are discussed here. Clinical correlations of the positive test results will be presented and commented upon later.

The findings presented here can be interpreted as evidence either in favor of an antibody-like substance or of a merely altered physical state of the serum resulting from the abnormal proteins known to be present.[2] The incidence of positive tests in general medical patients whose sera had very high levels of

Table 7.—*Results in General Medical Patients
Whose Sera Had High Levels of 7S
Globulins, Mesoglobulins, or
Macroglobulins*

Group	No.	7S (Gm %)	Meso-globulins (Gm %)	Macro-globulins (Gm %)
Seronegative (includes 15 doubtful results)	77	3.3	0.24	0.95
Seronegative (excludes 15 doubtful results)	62	3.4	0.20	0.99
Seropositive	28	3.2	0.30	1.09

7S globulins, mesoglobulins, or macroglobulins [3] was similar to those incidences seen in the state hospital patients and could be taken to imply that the mere presence of abnormal globulins is sufficient to cause a positive test. However, there was little difference between the 28 positive and the 77 negative sera in this group in the mean values of the variously sedimenting classes of proteins. When the 28 positive sera were compared with the 62 definitely negative sera—ie, excluding the 15 doubtfully reacting sera—there was still little difference in the mean levels of the ultracentrifugal findings (Table 7).

Tests were made upon the sera of patients with various collagen diseases of sufficient severity to have caused hospital admission, because these diseases—particularly systemic lupus erythematosus—have a high incidence of serum globulins with strong tissue affinities. It is surprising that the incidence of definitely positive tests was even lower in this group than that in the state hospital patients. Notably, only 2 of 12 sera from patients with systemic lupus erythematosus were positive, a result which might further suggest that the positive reactions were caused by a physicochemical change in the serum, not by a tissue antibody. Yet patients with collagen diseases tend to have severe serum protein disturbances, and it is remarkable that these patients and also those with known abnormalities in the ultracentrifugal findings had incidences of positive tests which were even comparable to those in psychiatric patients. Whatever may be the physicochemical or immunological abnormality causing positive tests in psychiatric patients, it resembles in severity that found in patients with very serious medical illnesses. This supports the suggestion made in a previous paper that the so-called functional psychoses should be regarded as but one facet of a generalized metabolic disturbance.[7]

If a tissue antibody were involved in the hemagglutination reaction, it would be expected to have been inhibited by previous incubation of a positive serum with the appropriate antigen. The results of the few inhibition experiments made were equivocal; the general trend was to find no inhibition, whether by extracts of brain, liver, or kidney, or by FII. However, inhibition was seen twice as frequently in the 30 psychiatric patients' sera so tested as in the 15 sera of patients with abnormal ultracentrifuge protein patterns (Table 5 and 6). Moreover, when inhibition did occur it resulted mainly from brain extract with the psychiatric patients' sera—this suggested a brain-antibody as responsible for hemagglutination in these instances—and from FII in other patients' sera —this suggested rheumatoid factor activity as responsible for hemagglutination in these instances.

Support for the view that these hemagglutination reactions are due, at least in some cases, to brain antibodies is obtained from the findings in patients considered to have brain damage resulting from allergic encephalitis (eg, following vaccination or mumps) and from patients thought to have Schilder's disease (Table 2). Unfortunately insufficient serum was available from these patients to allow for inhibition experiments.

Although most of the evidence from this study points towards a physicochemical alteration of the serum rather than an immunological factor as responsible for the observations, yet some of the results are consistent with the presence of a brain antibody. It is possible that an antibody may in some cases occur in addition to the physicochemical alteration. Further data are required to clarify this point.

Two reports in the literature offer limited support to the suggestion of a brain antibody

TABLE 8.—*Presence of Ganglioside and Asialoganglioside Antibodies in Sera as Modified From Yokoyama, Trams, and Brady*[16]

Group	No. Sera Exam.	Sera Containing Antibodies to:	
		Gang.	Asialogang.
Normal	42	0	0
Schizophrenia	14	1(7.1%)	3(21.4%)
Multiple sclerosis	42	8(19.0%)	0
Tay-Sachs disease	14	0	5(35.7%)
Japanese B encephalitis	14	0	6(42.9%)

in sera of some psychiatric patients. Some recent data of Yokoyama, Trams, and Brady[16] are summarized in Table 8. These workers studied ganglioside and asialoganglioside antibodies in sera of patients with various conditions by using a hemagglutination technique. The asialoganglioside antibodies were found in 3 sera of 14 patients with schizophrenia, in 6 sera of 14 patients with Japanese B encephalitis, and in 5 sera of 14 patients with Tay-Sachs disease. Ganglioside antibodies were seen in 1 serum of the 14 patients with schizophrenia and in 8 sera of 42 patients with multiple sclerosis. Although their figures are smaller, they follow the general trend of those reported here. The titers which they obtained were also similar to those in this study. The findings of Kuznetzova and Semenov,[11] by a complement fixation technique using brain extracts, are consistent with an antibody to a brain protein and are summarized in Table 9. It is remarkable how closely their findings resemble those of this study (Table 2). According to their data, the sera of neuropsychiatric patients reacted, with few exceptions, with antigen only from the brain but not from other organs. Also, in one experiment serum of a schizophrenic patient lost its ability to cause complement fixation after absorption with brain but was unaffected by absorption with liver.

It is an important observation that in almost every instance so tested, psychiatric patients' sera did not cause agglutination of uncoated tannic-acid-treated red cells, even when red cells coated with various tissue extracts were quite strongly agglutinated (eg,

TABLE 9.—*Complement-Fixing Antibodies to Brain as Modified From Kuznetsova and Semenov* [11]

Group	No.	Pos (%)	Doubtful Reaction	Neg (%)
Healthy persons	34	1(2.9)	2(5.9)	31(91.2)
Schizophrenia	84	22(26.2)	9(10.7)	53(63.1)
Paraphrenia, post-traumatic brain injury, arteriosclerotic brain disease, chronic alcoholism, neurosyphilis	30	9(30.0)	6(20.0)	15(50.0)
Collagen diseases	13	2(15.4)	2(15.4)	9(69.2)

1:128). This contravenes previous experience with latex particles where it was found that most sera causing positive tests with brain-extract-coated latex particles did not cause agglutination of kidney-extract-coated latex particles; in those instances where kidney-extract-coated particles were affected, plain latex particles were usually also agglutinated.[1] Although results from systems using different particles are not entirely comparable, the finding of agglutination by psychiatric patients' sera of coated, but not of uncoated, red cells may explain some findings reported in the literature. The statements by Malis [12-14] that a virus may be present in serum of acute schizophrenic but not in chronic schizophrenic patients were based mainly upon positive tests in an agglutination system comprising bacteria which had been previously treated with serum of acute schizophrenic patients. Malis' finding might rather mean that the bacteria were coated by some of the abnormal proteins which are ·present in sera of these acutely ill patients [1,2,5,6]; the same phenomenon as caused agglutination of the brain-coated red cells might have caused agglutination of Malis' bacteria. Another finding with perhaps a similar basis is that of Goodman, Rosenblatt, and their co-workers,[10] who saw a higher incidence of thyroid autoantibodies in schizophrenic females than in controls. The hemagglutination results of Yokoyama and his co-workers have been mentioned above. It is unfortunate that Yokoyama and co-workers did not make inhibition tests,[17] because some of their findings might have been due to a general tendency by sera of those groups of patients to agglutinate any coated particles.

A previous study showed a higher incidence in psychiatric patients' sera than controls' sera of positive FII latex and nucleoprotein latex tests.[4] It is likely that at least some of the FII test results reflected rheumatoid factor activity rather than a non-specific agglutination of coated particles, because several sera of psychiatric patients, having high rheumatoid factor activity, were negative in the brain-hemagglutination test. Moreover, as mentioned previously, although the concordance between positive brain-hemagglutination tests and rheumatoid factor activity was high (Table 3), the incidence of positive brain-hemagglutination tests in psychiatric patients who had negative tests for rheumatoid factor approximated the incidences in other state hospital patients.

Conclusion

The most probable interpretation of the results presented above is that psychiatric patients' sera have some physicochemical abnormality, presumably related to the presence of abnormal serum proteins, which causes the agglutination of red cells coated with various tissue components. Evidence for the importance of this finding is that its incidence in psychiatric patients is as high as in severely ill medical patients.

However, the evidence is not conclusive that a tissue antibody is not responsible for some of the results; further work seems warranted, particularly in the light of Kuznetzova and Semenov's results [11] with a complement fixation method.

Summary

The effect of sera from psychiatric and other patients was tested upon red cells coated with a brain extract.

Hemagglutination occurred with 30.7% of state hospital patients' sera as compared with 6.4% of blood donors' sera, 26.7% of sera having abnormal ultracentrifugal protein patterns, and 17.0% of sera from patients with connective tissue diseases.

Inhibition by brain antigen of hemagglutination occurred in 26% of psychiatric patients' sera and in 13% of other sera so tested.

In the few instances so tested, psychiatric patients' sera caused hemagglutination about equally of red cells coated with brain, liver, kidney, or thyroid antigens.

The most likely interpretation of the findings is that of a physicochemical change in psychiatric patients' sera of equal degree to that seen in severely ill medical patients. The possibility of a brain antibody in some psychiatric patients' sera has not, however, been completely excluded.

The physicians at the Langley Porter Neuropsychiatric Institute and the University of California Hospital and the physicians at the Napa, Sonoma, and Porterville state hospitals allowed me to study their patients. Drs. R. W. Gerard and A. Yuwiler provided sera from their patients at Ypsilanti State Hospital. The Irwin Memorial Blood Bank, San Francisco, supplied blood donors' sera, and The Institute of Medical Physics made a gift of 105 sera together with their ultracentrifugal analyses. Miss Clara Nagano provided technical help.

REFERENCES

1. Fessel, W. J.: Autoimmunity and Mental Illness: A Preliminary Report, Arch Gen Psychiat 6: 320-323 (April) 1962.

2. Fessel, W. J.: Blood Proteins in Functional Psychoses: A Review of the Literature and Unifying Hypothesis, Arch Gen Psychiat 6:132-148 (Feb) 1962.

3. Fessel, W. J.: Clinical Analysis of 142 Cases With High Molecular Weight Serum Proteins, Acta Med Scand 173 (suppl 391) :1-32, 1963.

4. Fessel, W. J.: Disturbed Serum Proteins in Chronic Psychosis: Serological, Medical, and Psychiatric Correlations, Arch Gen Psychiat 4:154-159 (Feb) 1961.

5. Fessel, W. J.: Further Studies on Blood Proteins in Mental Disease, to be published.

6. Fessel, W. J.: Macroglobulin Elevations in Functional Mental Illness, Nature (London) 193: 1005 (March 10) 1962.

7. Fessel, W. J.: Mental Stress, Blood Proteins, and the Hypothalamus: Experimental Results Showing Effect of Mental Stress Upon 4S and 19S Proteins; Speculation That the Functional Behavior Disturbances May Be Expressions of a General Metabolic Disorder, Arch Gen Psychiat 7:427-435 (Dec) 1962.

8. Fessel, W. J.: Paper read at First American Medical Association Multiple Discipline Research Forum, New York, June 29, 1961.

9. George, M., and Vaughan, J. H.: Observations on the Nature of the Antigen in Tanned Red Cell Hemagglutination, J Immun 88:191-198 (Feb) 1962.

10. Goodman, M.; Rosenblatt, M.; Gottlieb, J. S.; Miller, J.; and Chem, C. H.: Effect of Sex, Age and Schizophrenia on Production of Thyroid Autoantibodies, Fed Proc 21:42 (March-April) 1962.

11. Kuznetzova, N. I., and Semenov, S. F.: [Detection of Antibrain Antibodies in the Blood Serum of Patients With Neuropsychiatric Diseases], Zh Nevropat Psikhiat Korsakov 61:869-874 (June) 1961.

12. Malis, G. Y.: [Immunobiological Diagnosis of Schizophrenia], Zh Nevropat Psikhiat Korsakov 57: 82-87 (Jan) 1957.

13. Malis, G. Y.: K Etiologii Shizofrenii, Moscow: Medgiz, 1959, p 223.

14. Malis, G. Y., and Dolgikh, S. I.: [Viral Factor in Pathogenesis of Schizophrenia], Zh Nevropat Psikhiat Korsakov 54:728-731 (Sept) 1954.

15. Stavitsky, A. B.: Micromethods for the Study of Proteins and Antibodies: I. Procedure and General Applications of Hemagglutination and Hemagglutination-Inhibition Reactions With Tannic Acid and Protein-Treated Red Blood Cells, J Immun 72: 360-367 (May) 1954.

16. Yokoyama, M.; Trams, E. G.; and Brady, R. O.: Sphingolipid Antibodies in Sera of Animals and Patients With Central Nervous System Lesions, Proc Soc Exp Biol Med 111:350-352 (Nov) 1962.

17. Yokoyama, M.: Personal communication to the author, 1962.

46

ABNORMAL LEUKOCYTES IN SCHIZOPHRENIA

W. J. Fessel and Motoe Hirata-Hibi

The purposes of the present paper are: (1) to confirm the finding of abnormal circulating leukocytes in schizophrenic patients; (2) to show their finer cytological details; and (3) to discuss the effect of the finding of these abnormal cells upon our concepts of the etiology of mental disease.

The search for a cellular abnormality in the blood or tissues of psychiatric patients is almost as old as the microscope itself. Already in 1844 Andral [1] had described low red blood cell counts in some neurotic patients and stated that " . . . even in the neuroses the study of the state of the blood may be important." Fifty years ago, in 1914, Itten [46] reported an increase in lymphocyte count in schizophrenia and reviewed a considerable literature concerning the white cells in schizophrenia. He noted improvement when the lymphocyte count fell.

Recent reports have described morphological abnormalities of the lymphocytes of schizophrenic patients. Kamp found that the nucleus in comparison to normal had deeper staining and the chromatin lacked an organized pattern [48] These abnormalities were confirmed by Hollister and Kosek,[45] who described smaller, more pyknotic nuclei with minute indentations of the nuclear membranes and coarser, less evenly distributed chromatin.

Materials and Methods

For the first part of this study, smears were made from the untreated peripheral blood of 17 chronic schizophrenic patients from the Napa State Hospital, 10 acute schizophrenic patients from the Acute Treatment Service, and 15 apparently normal personnel from the research floor of The Langley Porter Neuropsychiatric Institute. These 42 slides were not examined blindly.

In the second part of the study, slides were made from the untreated peripheral blood of 50 chronic schizophrenic male patients at Menlo Park Veterans Administration Hospital and 50 male donors at a blood bank. Slides from patients and donors were paired randomly, except for rough matching according to the subjects' age, and each pair examined blindly.

The slides were quickly air-dried, fixed in 100% methanol for about three minutes and stained by the May-Grünwald Giemsa Method. Each slide was examined under 1,000 times magnification. Slides from each patient were studied for two to three hours, during which time 100 lymphocytes were examined and the presence noted of any other abnormal cells.

Results

The results of the first part of the study are summarized in Tables 1 and 2. The lymphocytes of the normal subjects conformed to the usual description. The cytoplasm was pale blue, and had a structureless, narrow perinuclear clear zone. The nucleus was round or kidney-shaped; lobules, if present, were seldom more than two. The chromatin was coarse and lumpy. The atypical features (Table 2) in normal subjects' lymphocytes

---

Departments of Psychiatry and Medicine, University of California School of Medicine, and The Langley Porter Neuropsychiatric Institute.

Supported in part by USPHS grant MH04581-02 and in part by a grant (61-1-29) from the California Department of Mental Hygiene.

TABLE 1.—*Abnormal Cells in*

Patient Number, Sex, and Age *	Large Size			Medium Size			Small Size		
	Type I	Type II	Type III	Type I	Type II	Type III	Type I	Type II	Type III
1 M, 43	1	—	—	15	—	—	1	—	—
2 M, 52	8	—	—	11	—	—	24	—	—
3 M, 41	1	—	1	13	—	—	16	—	—
4 M, 43	1	3	1	9	1	—	5	—	—
5 M, 43	1	2	1	3	—	—	—	—	—
6 M, 35	—	2	—	8	1	—	3	—	—
7 M, 37	6	2	2	8	—	—	1	2	—
8 M	1	2	—	17	—	—	—	—	—
9 M, 35	1	2	—	12	—	—	7	—	—
10 M	—	—	1	5	2	—	10	—	—
11 M, 52	1	—	—	20	—	—	12	—	—
12 F, 52	1	1	—	15	—	—	6	—	—
13 F, 34	1	—	—	11	—	—	6	—	—
14 F, 39	—	—	1	11	—	—	6	—	—
15 M, 53	1	2	1	1	—	—	5	—	—
16 M, 35	—	2	1	9	—	—	2	—	—
17 F, 55	2	3	1	6	—	—	—	—	—
18 M, 30	2	—	—	8	—	—	—	2	—
19 F, 20	1	—	—	8	—	—	3	—	—
20 M, 23	—	—	—	18	—	—	4	—	—
21 M, 27	—	4	—	2	—	—	2	—	—
22 M, 15	2	2	—	—	8	—	—	—	—
23 M, 23	—	1	—	3	1	—	11	—	—
24 F, 32	11	—	—	40	—	—	14	—	—
25 F, 28	1	—	—	10	—	—	3	—	—
26 F, 28	1	3	—	—	1	—	22	—	—
27 F, 17	5	3	—	3	—	—	9	—	—

* Patients 1 through 17, chronic schizophrenic patients at Napa State Hospital; Patients 18 through 27, acute schizophrenic patient at The Langley Porter Neuropsychiatric Hospital.

† These patients were receiving reserpine alone.

were usually confined to nuclear shape; occasionally lobulation was marked. Chromatin structure was seldom atypical and nucleoli were very rare.

Abnormal leukocytes were seen in all of the schizophrenic patients examined from both Napa State Hospital and The Langley Porter Neuropsychiatric Institute. The abnormal cells, described below (Fig 1-5), comprised as many as 65% of the total count of lymphocytes. In the chronic schizophrenic patients their mean number was 20 (range from 7 to 43), and in the acute schizophrenic patients 13.9 (range from 8 to 65), per 100 lymphocytes.

Cytological Description.—The abnormal cells mostly had characteristics of lymphocytic or reticulum cells. The cell type varied considerably from patient to patient, but the predominant abnormal cell type tended to remain constant for an individual. It is possible to categorize the abnormal cell types roughly as follows:

Type I: This type, seen in both acute and chronic schizophrenic patients, represented the majority of the abnormal cells seen (Fig 1). Type I cells had many features in common with lymphocytes. Their size varied

TABLE 2.—*Atypical Lymphocytes * in Controls*

Control Number	Large	Medium	Small	Total	Plasma Cells Seen During Cell Count
1	—	5	—	5	1
2	—	1	—	1	—
3	—	4	—	4	3
4	2	1	1	4	3
5	—	—	—	—	—
6	—	3	—	3	—
7	—	—	—	—	—
8	—	1	—	1	—
9	—	2	—	2	—
10	—	—	—	—	—
11	1	4	1	6	—
12	—	2	—	—	—
13	—	3	—	3	—
14	—	3	—	3	—
15	1	4	1	6	3

* The atypical features in the controls were confined to nuclear shape.

Behavior and Immune Function

Total Abnormal Cells Per 100 Lymphocytes Counted	Plasma Cells Seen During Cell Count	Previous Ataractic Medication
17	6	+ *
43	5	—
31	3	+
20	3	+
7	4	—
14	2	+
21	5	+
20	0	—
22	4	+
18	3	—
33	3	+
23	2	+
18	2	+ †
18	1	+
10	8	—
14	0	—
12	2	+
12	2	+
12	9	+
22	12	+
8	0	+
12	2	+
16	8	+
65	3	+
14	18	+
27	13	+
20	6	+

from small to medium to large, corresponding approximately to the size of the small, medium or large normal lymphocytes. The cytoplasm was usually more basophilic than the normal adult lymphocyte and, when strongly basophilic, had a stippled appearance. The perinuclear clear zone was prominent, often containing small vacuoles and occasionally showing a faint lamellar structure reminiscent of the lamellar ergastoplasm. In some cells the perinuclear clear zone was so large as to occupy most of the cytoplasm and contained a very well-developed lamellar structure. The nucleus had

minute indentations, deep narrow clefts, or frank lobulations. Sometimes the nuclear cleft gave the cell a binucleate appearance. The chromatin structure of Type I cells varied from fine, delicate, and leptochromatic to coarse, clumped, and pachychromatic. Occasional nuclei showed large areas of leptochromatin side by side with areas of pachychromatin. One or two nucleoli were present in about 60% of the Type I cells.

Type II: This type, the second commonest variety, was seen in both acute and chronic schizophrenic patients (Fig 2, 3, and 4) and had many features in common with reticulum cells. The size of the largest diameter varied from 10μ to 20μ. Depending upon the staining characteristics of their cytoplasm and their nuclear structure, type II cells could be subdivided into three sorts: Type II A cells (Fig 2) had abundant, strongly basophilic cytoplasm without a perinuclear clear zone. In two instances the cytoplasm contained phagocytosed particles. The round or oval nucleus occasionally had small indentations. Superimposed upon a very fine chromatin structure were small patches of clumped chromatin. There was a single, large, faintly basophilic nucleolus. Type II B (Fig 3) resembled the so-called reticulum plasma cell. The cytoplasm was basophilic with a small perinuclear clear zone. The round nucleus sometimes had slight indentations. The clumped chromatin resembled that of normal plasma cells. Some nuclei contained a little fine chromatin in addition to the clumped chromatin.

Type II C cells (Fig 4) were very similar to typical reticulum cells. Their cytoplasm

Fig 1.—Type I cell, small size. Indentation of nuclear outline. Strongly basophilic cytoplasm. May-Grünwald-Giesma stain; × 1,200.

Fig 2.—Type IIA cell. Large cell with cytoplasmic inclusion and fine chromatin structure. May-Grünwald-Giesma stain; × 1,200.

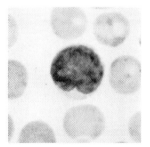

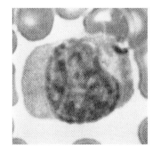

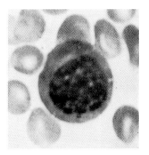

Fig 3.—Type IIB cell. Basophilic cytoplasm. Nuclear structure resembles that of plasma cell. May-Grünwald-Giesma stain; × 1,200.

was faintly staining with poorly defined edges. The nucleus was sometimes indented and the chromatin structure was very fine.

Type III.—These multinucleated giant cells were seen in eight chronic schizophrenic patients (Fig 5) at Napa State Hospital. They were sparse, only about one for every 100 lymphocytes counted. The cytoplasm was pale and structureless. There were up to four separate nuclei, some with the shape and structure of the normal lymphocyte nucleus. These Type III cells appeared mostly with Type I cells.

In addition to the above types of cells, almost all patients had characteristic plasma cells in their circulating blood. In one acute schizophrenic patient, 18 plasma cells were seen during the count of 100 lymphocytes.

Results of Blind Examinations.—In the blind study of coded pairs of slides from 50 schizophrenic patients and 50 controls, 49 pairs were correctly diagnosed.

The following technical note may facilitate confirmation of these blind studies in other laboratories: It is important to make a thin

Fig 4.—Type IIC cell. Marked resemblance to typical reticulum cell. May-Grünwald-Giesma stain; × 1,000.

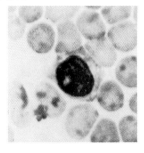

blood smear and rapidly air-dry it. The central portions of the smear should be examined because artifacts may occur at the edges. To distinguish the blood smear of the schizophrenic patient from that of the normal member of the pair, most attention should be paid to the presence in the lymphocytes of a nucleolus and fine chromatin. Although irregularity of nuclear outline is commoner in lymphocytes of schizophrenic patients, this is also seen—contrary to the description in most textbooks—in many lymphocytes of normal subjects.

Effect of Drugs.—Of the 17 chronic schizophrenic patients in the first part of the study, 6 had received no psychotropic medication for at least a month, and 2 were receiving only reserpine (1 mg daily; 1 mg, t.i.d.). The other nine chronic schizophrenic

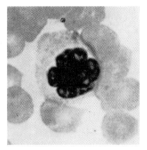

Fig 5.—Type III cell. Note resemblance to Sternberg-Reed cells. Four distinct nuclei clearly discernible in original preparation. Pale abundant cytoplasm. May-Grünwald-Giesma stain; × 1,200.

patients and all the acute schizophrenic patients were receiving various psychotropic drugs, mostly phenothiazine derivatives. The severity of the cytological abnormalities was not linked with the medication or lack of it. Some of the most numerous and severe abnormalities were in patients on no medication (Table 1). This agrees with the conclusion of Hollister and Kosek [45] that abnormalities were as great in patients receiving low doses as in those receiving high doses of psychotropic drugs.

Effect of Institutionalization.—Long hospitalization does not seem to have been a factor in the production of the abnormal cells. This was the first hospital admission for all except one (patient 20, Table 1) of

Table 3.—*Cytological Studies In the Family Studied*

	Abnormal Cells Per 100 Lympho-cytes Counted	Predominant Cell Type		
Father	13	I		
First Mother	Not examined			
Child				
F, 24 * ‡	29	I	II	III
M, 18 †	Not examined			
Second Mother	37	I	II	
Child				
M, 11 *	34	I	II	
F, 10	10	I		
M, 9	29	I	II	
M, 4 *	27	I	II	

* Present diagnosis of schizophrenic reaction.

† Considered to have a mental disorder.

‡ Only this subject was hospitalized at the time of blood examination.

the acute schizophrenic patients. These ten acutely ill subjects had been in hospital for an average of only 17 days before their blood was examined; five of them had been in hospital for less than a week. Patient 24 (Table 1) had 65% of abnormal cells after being in hospital for only five days; a few weeks after discharge from hospital her blood still contained a very high percentage of abnormal cells. Lastly, among the family * studied (Table 3) there were several members with high counts of abnormal cells but only one subject was in the hospital.

There may be a high incidence of parasitic infection and liver disease in chronically hospitalized patients. Our schizophrenic patients did not have an eosinophilia. Moreover, morphological abnormalities of leukocytes similar to those which we observed in schizophrenic patients are not seen in parasitic diseases. Nor are such abnormalities found in liver diseases, aside from occasional, very severe cases of infective hepatitis.

Specificity of the Cytological Abnormality. We limited our present studies in psychiatric patients to those with schizophrenic reactions. In the light of previous findings that

* This family is being studied in collaboration with Dr. M. Persky, Children's Service, Langley Porter Neuropsychiatric Institute, and will be reported upon elsewhere in greater detail.

blood protein abnormalities are not necessarily limited to specific clinical categories,[17,18,20,22,25,26] we anticipate that future surveys will show the abnormal cytology in patients with various psychiatric diagnoses.

We emphasize that we do not yet know how specific these findings will be for psychiatric patients: We suspect that future studies will show similar changes in a variety of general medical diseases. We have already observed mild nuclear abnormalities in two patients with scleroderma and one with systemic lupus erythematosus. The lymphocytic abnormalities which have been reported to occur in various medical diseases will be mentioned in the presentation. The appearance of similar changes in nonpsychiatric patients does not, in our opinion, alter the importance of their occurrence in schizophrenia.

Familial Aspects.—In the family studied,* one child of the first marriage has a schizophrenic reaction and is in a State hospital; the other child of the first marriage has a mental disorder. Two of the four children from the husband's second marriage are being treated as outpatients for schizophrenic reactions. All family members so far tested have abnormal cells, mostly type I, in their blood (Table 3).

Comment

To Kamp [48] goes the credit for making the important observation that circulating lymphocytes in schizophrenia may be abnormal. Our studies have shown reticulum-like cells, giant cells, and plasma cells in addition to abnormal lymphocytes. The cellular abnormality tends to be constant for any individual patient but may vary from patient to patient. The abnormality is quantitatively less severe in acutely than in chronically ill schizophrenic patients; it is not apparently affected by drug therapy. The following is a description of the average cellular abnormalities which we have observed.

The cytoplasm is often strongly basophilic. The perinuclear clear zone tends to be prominent and within it there is sometimes a lamellar structure or some small vesicles.

The nucleus may show lobulation or indentation of its edges. Indentation, when slight, appears to be of the inner nuclear membrane; the outer nuclear membrane retains its normal position, giving the superficial impression of a round nucleus. There may be one or two distinct nucleoli. The chromatin structure shows various phases of maturation from the very fine, leptochromatic, delicate structure seen in reticulum cells or lymphoblasts, to the coarser, pachychromatic structure of the typical small lymphocyte. The cells may be difficult to differentiate from young monocytes or plasma cells and often closely resemble those seen in some patients with Waldenström's disease (Fig 8C of Kappeler, Krebs, and Riva[49]). There are sometimes cells of a type apparently transitional between reticulum cells and lymphoblasts. Unlike the large, so called stress lymphocyte described by Dougherty and Frank[12,13,30,31] the abnormal cell in schizophrenia varies from small to very large in size: further differences from the stress lymphocyte are mentioned below in the section entitled "Endocrinological Dysfunction and Schizophrenia." In five cases enormous reticulum-like cells were seen; in eight other cases, multinucleated giant cells were present.

Occasional atypical cells are seen in normal people. Efrati and Rozenszajn[15] in the examination of the concentrated white cells in peripheral blood of 55 normal adults found atypical mononuclear cells in all the subjects. The mean number was 5 per 1,000 and the highest number was 18 per 1,000 mononuclear cells counted. In our experience with normal persons, we have often observed abnormally shaped nuclei of lymphocytes; nucleoli and fine chromatin were seldom seen.

Efrati and Rozenszajn described the atypical cells as similar to those seen in infectious mononucleosis: the cytoplasm was strongly basophilic; the chromatin structure was coarse and often loose; and a pale nucleolus could be seen. This description suggests only partial similarity to the abnormal cells found in schizophrenia. Examination of the other source of comparison, published photographs of the cell, is difficult because fine details are inevitably lost in the reproduction. Our own studies of normal persons' atypical lymphocytes showed none of the features seen in the abnormal leukocytes of schizophrenia, aside from nuclear indentation or lobulation. Similar cells may be seen in several virus diseases. First described by Downey and McKinlay[14] in infectious mononucleosis, they have since been seen in many other viral diseases, eg, acute viral hepatitis, viral pneumonitis, rubella, rubeola, herpes zoster, roseola infantum, and viral upper respiratory infections.[29,55,63] According to Klima,[51] "reactive lymphocytes" whose description resembles that of the cells presented may also be seen in congenital and acquired syphilis, malaria, tuberculosis, pneumonia, and various hypersensitivity states. Our patients had none of these diseases, to our knowledge. Moreover, blood examined from an otherwise normal subject who had influenza showed none of these abnormal cells but had a few plasma cells.

Whether some of the abnormal cells in schizophrenic patients are the same as those found occasionally in normal people and whatever their genealogy, their incidence in schizophrenia is incomparably higher than in normal persons.

The finding of abnormal leukocytes in schizophrenia raises many questions, particularly about their genealogy, their distribution among other forms of mental disease, and their significance for the total disease process. These questions cannot be presented fully here. The genealogy of even the normal lymphocyte is controversial[71,75,76]; our attempts to trace the lineage of the abnormal cells in schizophrenia, with evidence to support the place of type I cells in the lymphocytic series and type II cells in the reticulum cell series, will be presented elsewhere.[41] Likewise, the distribution of the abnormal cells among the different psychiatric disorders will be surveyed in another paper.[27]

This presentation will be limited to a brief survey of the possible ways in which concepts of the etiology of schizophrenia might be influenced by the finding of abnormal leukocyte morphology. The occurrence of a functional psychosis probably depends upon an appropriate relationship between multiple factors that are interdependent in a complicated way. Yet for clarity the individual factors and their possible involvements in the pathogenetic constellation must be considered separately. Following are some facets of the problem of pathogenesis in relation to the finding of abnormal leukocytes: (1) genetical abnormality; (2) infection; (3) generalized reticuloendothelial system dysfunction; and (4) endocrinological dysfunction. Each of these fits into the theoretical scheme as previously postulated (Fig 3).[23]

The Question of Genetical Influences.— The following facts raise the possibility that the abnormal leukocytes in schizophrenia may be genetically determined: (1) the finding of abnormal blood cells in other diseases known to be hereditary; (2) the fact that many abnormal blood proteins—manufactured by plasma cells and possibly by lymphocytes [3,5,6,39,42-44,53,65,70]—have a familial basis; (3) the observation that while the morphological abnormality of the abnormal cells in individual patients tends to be uniform, the cytology varies from patient to patient; (4) results of studies in the family (Table 3).

Abnormal lymphocytes are seen in Tay-Sachs disease where, as reported by Bagh and Hortling [2] and since confirmed by other investigators,[66,67] the lymphocyte cytoplasm contains vacuoles. In very rare patients there is an apparently familial absence of circulating lymphocytes.[35,47] Abnormal reticuloendothelial cells are found in Gaucher's, Niemann-Pick's and Hand-Schüller-Christian's disease. Erythrocytes are abnormal in hereditary spherocytosis, sickle-cell anemia, and other hemoglobinopathies.

It is reasonable to assume that the abnormal cells—particularly the type I cells—may be a source of the abnormal serum proteins in schizophrenia. Some writers consider that lymphocytes are a source of blood proteins.[5,6,65,68,70] Moreover, cytoplasmic basophilia, which tends to be intense in the abnormal lymphocytes, is an index of the degree of intracellular protein synthesis [7]; and the lamellar structure, prominent in some of the type I cells, probably has similar significance. In many instances immunological abnormalities have a familial, probably genetical, basis. The increased incidence of serum protein abnormalities, such as rheumatoid and lupus factors and hypergammaglobulinemia in members of the families of patients with connective tissue diseases, is well known. Recently spontaneous hereditary diabetes mellitus in Chinese hamsters could be predicted by the presence of high α_2-globulin levels in the serum.[37] The production of many normal proteins, eg, haptoglobin, hemoglobin, and certain γ-globulins, is also known to be under genetical control. Therefore the concept that genetically controlled abnormal cells—particularly those with the lamellar structure in the perinuclear clear zone—produce serum protein changes in schizophrenia is consistent with conditions existing elsewhere.

It must be pointed out, however, that somatic mutation with proliferation of clones of abnormal cells would equally well fit the findings. There are many likely causes of somatic mutation. The observation of chromosomal abnormalities in mammalian cells infected by herpes simplex virus [38] would support the theory of an infectious origin of the leukocyte abnormalities, as will be commented on in a later section. The finding that the abnormal cell type tends to be constant for any particular schizophrenic patient supports the genetical hypothesis but also is consistent with somatic mutation and the proliferation of clones of abnormal cells.

The assumption that the abnormality of the leukocytes is hereditarily determined leads to the question whether the structural abnormality of the cell proteins might be paralleled in cerebral neurones. The cerebral neuronal systems might then be more susceptible to dysfunction as a result of environmental or other pressures. Alternatively or additionally, the abnormal serum proteins presumably produced by these cells could affect the brain in the various ways which we have commented elsewhere.[18,23]

Another, more practical, implication of the assumption of genetical control is the possibility of predicting the liability to future illness on the basis of the leukocyte abnormalities. The vacuolization of the lymphocytes in Tay Sachs disease was shown by Rayner [67] to occur in the apparently healthy family members: this finding probably reflects the presence of a simple recessive gene—both the parents of the probands have abnormal lymphocytes. Studies of schizophrenic patients' families are in progress. Apparently normal members of the family studied have abnormal cells (Table 3). However, because the genetical component in the schizophrenic reaction is probably not a simple recessive gene, the results of cellular studies in the family members are unlikely to be as clearcut as in Tay-Sachs disease.

Infection and Mental Disease.—That no infective agent has been conclusively demonstrated in schizophrenia should not lead to complete rejection of the hypothesis of an infective agent. However absurd this hypothesis might seem in the light of modern genetical analyses, the observations considered to support genetical transmission could equally well be accounted for by vertical transmission of an infection from parent to offspring. This was implied in a thoughtful paper by Vaillant,[74] who drew analogies between schizophrenia and tuberculosis. It is well to remember that the infectious agents responsible for the common cold, serum hepatitis, and infectious mononucleosis, have not yet been isolated. Certain infectious agents like pleuropneumonia-like organisms may remain dormant for many years only to be awakened by circumstances, including nonspecific stress, that cause a breakdown in the defense mechanisms of the host. Other infectious agents like endemic lymphocytic choriomeningitis of mice may be transmitted from mother to offspring in utero.[73] In this instance immunological tolerance prevents a host antibody reaction to the infectious agent, which, apparently nontoxic to the host, remains undisturbed in the tissues for life. It is easy to visualize a situation in which a virus, transmitted in utero, infects the brain. Lying dormant for many years, it becomes activated by unknown circumstances and acts as "infectious nucleic acid".[40] The effect would be to change the desoxyribonucleic acid template and alter the neuronal proteins—and thus behavior—in a way undetectable by present neuropathological techniques. How would such a process differ from orthodox genetical inheritance? In no way except that the blame shifts from forebears to virus.

In previous publications we have suggested several ways by which the serum protein abnormalities in schizophrenia might be involved in pathogenesis. A further possibility is that the abnormal proteins reflect the sort of above-mentioned infection which is an important member of the primary constellation of events leading to schizophrenia, rather than a secondary effect of the disease.

Few attempts have been made to isolate a viral-etiology of schizophrenia. Those that have been published,[8,56-58] have been contested.[8,50,59] Mastrogiovanni [60] repeatedly passaged schizophrenic patients' spinal fluid in chick embryo cultures and finally isolated virus-like particles, but their pathogenicity was not examined.

Finally, there is the possibility in schizophrenia of a hypersensitivity analogous to that of the streptococcal causation of rheumatic fever. Most of the immunological abnormalities seen in schizophrenia [17-26,54] are also seen in rheumatic fever. Although the streptococcus is not proposed as an etiological agent in schizophrenia, we do suggest rhumatic fever as an interesting model. It is pertinent that rheumatic chorea may occur several months after the streptococcal infection [72] and according to most authors is not associated with any specific histological changes in the brain. An autoimmune component in the pathogenesis of mental disease was previously proposed,[18] but the experimental evidence for this is scanty.[17,24,25]

Reticuloendothelial System (RES) Dysfunction and Schizophrenia.—Several reports from this laboratory have confirmed the finding of increased serum macroglobulin levels in schizophrenia.[18-20,22,26,54] A wide clinical survey led to the conclusion that high serum macroglobulin levels reflect reticuloendothelial system (RES) dysfunction.[19] Although type I cells in schizophrenia have been termed lymphocytes, their precise geneology is open to question—our reasons for calling them lymphocytes are discussed elsewhere.[41] To some extent the difficulty is artificial, depending upon whether or not lymphocytes and plasma cells are included in the RES. Similar controversy surrounds the origin of the abnormal cells in infectious mononucleosis: most authors consider them as derived from lymphocytic cells [51,55,63]; others give them a monocytic origin.[4] The reticulum-like cells termed type II and the multinucleated giant cells termed type III, all have morphological features highly suggestive of RES origin. Such cells are never seen in normal blood and, even in disease, their presence in the circulation is very unusual. Therefore, it is tempting to speculate that they belong to the same cell line as is responsible for the abnormal circulating lymphocytes.

The RES has long been considered abnormal in schizophrenia. The evidence was reviewed in great detail by Meyer [62] who stated that in acute schizophrenia there is activation of the RES as shown by round cell infiltration in viscera. Meyer also summarized his extensive experience with two methods which he considered to reflect function and responsiveness of the RES: the retention of intravenously injected Congo red and the cantharides vesicle test. In the cantharides vesicle test the volume of exudate and the number of cells—particularly of histiocytes—in the vesicle induced by cantharides is examined. Meyer saw RES dysfunction in schizophrenia, manic depression, neurosyphilis, and epileptic seizures. Other authors reported these changes in senile and presenile psychoses and multiple sclerosis. Using the Congo red test in manic depressive patients, Meyer found 100% dye retention (ie, increased RES activity) during the manic phase but normal or subnormal retention during the depressive phase, and he could also differentiate between patients with schizophrenia and patients with schizoid personalities. It is of considerable interest that chlorpromazine has been found to depress RES function. For example, a diminished rate of disappearance of intravenously injected colloidal carbon was noted by Meier, Boroff and Heller [61] in chlorpromazine-treated mice. Chlorpromazine also reduced the ability of the mice to withstand a calibrated infection. Clodi [9] noted impaired Bromsulphalein † excretion in chlorpromazine-treated rats.

The finding of Reichard and co-workers [69] that RES function affects resistance to stress, is noteworthy. Rats subjected to traumatic shock in a tumbling apparatus had considerably lowered resistance to this stress after RES blockade by a colloidal suspension of thorium dioxide and saccharated iron oxide. Zweifach and co-workers [77] reported that RES blockade caused an exacerbation of the vascular effects from the endotoxin of *Escherichia coli*. On the other hand, an enhanced tolerance to shock was seen after RES activity had been stimulated by repeated injections of certain colloids. Fine and co-workers [28] also saw a lowered tolerance to both hemorrhagic and endotoxic shock after RES blockade. In addition, they reported that adrenergic activity played an important role in endotoxic shock and death because this could be prevented by the adrenergic blocking agent Dibenamine.‡

Reichard and coworkers found that in normal animals traumatic shock led to increase of the serum lactate/pyruvate ratio. However, animals could be conditioned to be resistant to this form of stress which then caused only a slight increase of the serum lactate/pyruvate ratio. A humoral factor, probably a protein, could be extracted from the spleen and plasma of trauma-resistant animals which could protect against the systemic effects of drum trauma. These findings

† Proprietary name for a brand of sulfobromophthalein used for quantitative evaluation of liver function.

‡ Proprietary name for dibenzyl-β-chlorethylamine hydrochloride.

are reminiscent of those of Frohman and co-workers. They showed that when red blood cells are incubated in serum, the resulting lactate/pyruvate ratio is higher in serum from schizophrenic patients than in serum from controls.[32-34] The serum factor affecting cellular metabolism is an α- or β-globulin. The lactate/pyruvate ratios are maximal after exercise stress. One could speculate that this serum factor in schizophrenia is related to the stress-protection factor extracted from spleen and plasma by Reichard and co-workers and reflects RES dysfunction in schizophrenia.

The RES plays an important role in homeostasis, although the mechanisms are not well understood. There is some evidence of RES dysfunction in schizophrenia. The answer to whether the abnormal cells in the peripheral blood are an anatomical expression of this dysfunction or whether another explanation holds, will depend upon the results of further study.

Endocrinological Dysfunction and Schizophrenia.—Lymphoid tissue is profoundly affected by hormones, a long known fact. This was extensively reviewed by Dougherty,[11] who concluded that acute involution of lymphatic tissue is produced by enhanced endogenous secretion or administration of a wide variety of androgenic, estrogenic, and adrenocortical steroid hormones. Adrenocortical preparations are most potent in this regard; they appear to act both by causing lymphocytolysis and by inhibiting heteroplastic and homoplastic lymphocytopoiesis.

We have previously provided evidence, based upon blood volume and total red blood cell volume data, that growth hormone secretion might be increased in schizophrenia.[21] Feldman[16] has found that growth hormone given to hypophysectomized rats caused overgrowth of lymphoid elements and splenic enlargement. The involved cells had large, pale nuclei and abundant cytoplasm that was variably either basophilic or acidophilic. Dougherty concluded from his review of the evidence that growth hormone could maintain the weight of lymph nodes of hypophysectomized animals to a greater extent

than it could the weight of other lymphatic organs. Moon, Simpson, Li, and Evans[64] injected rats with growth hormone for periods up to 485 days; lymphosarcomas appeared in 6 of 15 rats so treated.

Another hormone considered to have a stimulating influence upon lymphatic tissue is thyroid hormone. This appears to have an even greater effect than growth hormone. However, as indicated by Dougherty,[11] lymphatic tissue is maintained by the opposing effects, both stimulating and destructive, of various hormones; the state of the lymphatic tissue at any time depends upon the existing interrelationship between the hormones.

Kumagai and Dougherty[52] noted that lymphocytosis followed a variety of stressful stimuli (histamine injection, anaphylactic shock, starvation) administered after splenectomy and adrenalectomy in mice. Stress in both humans and animals resulted in morphological changes in lymphocytes, according to Frank and Dougherty,[30,31] who coined the term stress-lymphocyte. Aside from their nuclear lobulation, these changes do not seem to correspond to the majority of abnormal cells found in schizophrenia. In schizophrenia the cells are of any size from small to very large; the cytoplasm is very basophilic and granular and may contain vacuoles and a lamellar structure; the chromatin structure may be very fine or coarse. The stress lymphocytes were described as being large cells, having increased cytoplasmicnuclear ratio, poorly basophilic and hyalinized cytoplasm, round, bilobed or polymorphous nuclei, and aggregated, clumped chromatin, changes not thought to be mediated by adrenocortical activity. In a later report Dougherty, Berliner, and Berliner[12] pointed out that hydrocortisone inhibits mitosis of lymphocytes and enhances maturation but cortisone is ineffective. Dougherty and co-workers presented evidence that the lymphocyte contains a redox system (11β OH-dehydrogenase) which, depending on the concentration or availability of oxidized or reduced coenzymes, determines the rate of oxidation of hydrocortisone to cortisone and thus the state of maturity of the lymphocyte itself. This raises the question whether the cell abnormality in schizophrenia might reflect a change in the state of certain cell enzyme systems.

Conclusions and Summary

Abnormal leukocytes of three types were present in the peripheral blood of almost all schizophrenic patients studied. Type I cells seemed to be of the lymphocytic series: important features were a polymorphous nuclear outline, a distinct nucleolus and a finer than normal chromatin structure. Type II cells were of the reticulum cell series: the cytoplasm was variably basophilic and sometimes contained inclusions; the chromatin structure tended to be very fine. Type III cells were multinucleated giant cells with a nuclear structure usually resembling that of normal lymphocytes.

In a blind study of coded pairs of slides from 50 schizophrenic patients and 50 controls, 49 pairs were correctly diagnosed.

The finding of these cellular changes raises many questions about the pathogenesis of schizophrenia. Genetical, infectious, endocrinological and reticuloendothelial system influences could produce the observed abnormalities. Present evidence is inadequate for a definitive evaluation of the meaning of the cellular abnormalities, which may be important clues for future research.

Dr. Leo E. Hollister aroused our interest in this work. Our colleagues at The Langley Porter Neuropsychiatric Institute, Napa State Hospital, and Menlo Park Veterans' Hospital allowed us to study their patients.

REFERENCES

1. Andral, G.: An Essay on the Blood in Disease, translated by J. F. Meigs, and A. Stillé, Philadelphia: Lea and Blanchard, 1844.
2. Bagh, K. V., and Hortling, H.: Blodfynd vid juvenil amaurotisk idioti, Nord Med 38:1072-1076, 1948.
3. Bernhard, W., and Granboulan, N.: Ultrastructure of Immunologically Competent Cells, in Cellular Aspects of Immunity, edited by G. E. W. Wolstenholme, and M. O'Connor, London: J. & A. Churchill, Ltd., 1960.
4. Bessis, M.: Cytology of the Blood-Forming Organs, translated by E. Ponder, New York: Grune & Stratton, Inc., 1956.
5. Bessis, M. C.: Ultrastructure of Lymphoid and Plasma Cells in Relation to Globulin and Antibody Formation, Lab Invest 10:1040-1067, 1961.
6. Burtin, P.: A Study of Serum Proteins Related to Immunity and their Cellular Origin, in Cellular Aspects of Immunity, edited by G. E. W. Wolstenholme and M. O'Connor, London: J. & A. Churchill, Ltd., 1960.
7. Chantrenne, H.: The Biosynthesis of Proteins, New York: Pergamon Press, 1961.
8. Chubinets, N. F., and Shilman, R. M.: K Laboratornoi Diagnostike Shizofrenii, Lab Delo 5:21-22, 1957; Abstracted in Sovet Med 3:459-460, 1959.
9. Clodi, P. H., and Schnack, H.: Tierexperimentelle Untersuchungen and Ratten über die Beeinflussung der Bromsulfophthaleinausscheidung durch Chlorpromazin, Gastroenterologia (Basel) 95: 176-181, 1961.
10. Donohue, W. L.: Alymphocytosis, Pediatrics 11:129-139, 1953.
11. Dougherty, T. F.: Effect of Hormones on Lymphatic Tissues, Physiol Rev 32:379-401, 1952.
12. Dougherty, T. F.; Berliner, M. L.; and Berliner, D. L.: Hormonal Influence of Lymphocyte Differentiation From RES Cells, Ann NY Acad Sci 88:78-82, 1960.
13. Dougherty, T. F., and Frank, J. A.: The Quantitative and Qualitative Responses of Blood Lymphocytes to Stress Stimuli, J Lab Clin Med 42:530-537, 1953.
14. Downey, H., and McKinlay, C. A.: Acute Lymphadenosis Compared With Acute Lymphatic Leukemia, Arch Intern Med 32:82-112, 1923.
15. Efrati, P., and Rozenszajn, L.: The Morphology of Buffy Coat in Normal Human Adults, Blood 16:1012-1019, 1960.
16. Feldman, J. D.: Endocrine Control of Lymphoid Tissue, Anat Rec 110:17-39, 1951.
17. Fessel, W. J.: Autoimmunity and Mental Illness: A Preliminary Report, Arch Gen Psychiat 6: 320-323, 1962.
18. Fessel, W. J.: Blood Proteins in Functional Psychoses: A Review of the Literature and Unifying Hypothesis, Arch Gen Psychiat 6:132-148, 1962.
19. Fessel, W. J.: Clinical Analysis of 142 Cases With High Molecular Weight Serum Proteins, Acta Med Scand 173:1-32, 1962.
20. Fessel, W. J.: Disturbed Serum Proteins in Chronic Psychosis: Serological, Medical, and Psychiatric Correlations, Arch Gen Psychiat 4: 154-159, 1961.
21. Fessel, W. J.: Further Observations and Remarks on the Blood Proteins in Psychiatry, to be published.
22. Fessel, W. J.: Macroglobulin Elevations in Functional Mental Illness, Nature 193:1005, 1962.

23. Fessel, W. J.: Mental Stress, Blood Proteins, and the Hypothalamus: Experimental Results Showing Effect of Mental Stress Upon 4S and 19S Proteins; Speculation That the Functional Behavior Disturbances May Be Expressions of a General Metabolic Disorder, Arch Gen Psychiat 7: 427-435, 1962.

24. Fessel, W. J.: Paper read at the First American Medical Association Multiple Discipline Research Forum, New York, June 29, 1961.

25. Fessel, W. J.: The "Antibrain" Factor in Psychiatric Patients' Sera: I. Further Experience With a Hemagglutination Technique, Arch Gen Psychiat 8:614-621, 1963.

26. Fessel, W. J., Grunbaum, B. W.: Electrophoretic and Analytical Ultracentrifuge Studies in Sera of Psychotic Patients: Elevation of Gamma Globulins and Macroglobulins, and Splitting of Alpha₂ Globulins, Ann Intern Med 54:1134-1145, 1961.

27. Fessel, W. J., and Hirata-Hibi, M.: In Preparation.

28. Fine, J.; Rutenburg, S.; and Schweinburg, F. B.: The Role of the Reticulo-Endothelial System in Hemorrhagic Shock, J Exp Med 110:547-569, 1959.

29. Fisher, B.; Ranier, A.; and Crawford, F. L.: The Lymphocyte in Virus Diseases, Amer J Med Technol 16:188-193, 1950.

30. Frank, J. A., and Dougherty, T. F.: Evaluation of Susceptibility to Stress Stimuli Determined by "Stress" Lymphocytes, Fed Proc 12:45-46, 1953.

31. Frank, J. A., and Dougherty, T. F.: The Assessment of Stress in Human Subjects by Means of Quantitative and Qualitative Changes of Blood Lymphocytes, J Lab Clin Med 42:538-549, 1953.

32. Frohman, C.; Latham, K.; Czajkowski, N.; Beckett, P.; and Gottlieb, J.: Study of a Serum Factor in Schizophrenia, Fed Proc 19:83, 1960.

33. Frohman, C. E.; Latham, L. K.; Beckett, P. G. S.; and Gottlieb, J. S.: Evidence of a Plasma Factor in Schizophrenia, Arch Gen Psychiat 2: 255-262, 1960.

34. Frohman, C. E.; Goodman, M.; Beckett, P. G. S.; Latham, L. K.; Senf, R;. and Gottlieb, J. S.: The Isolation of an Active Factor From Serum of Schizophrenic Patients, Ann NY Acad Sci 96: 438-447, 1962.

35. Glanzmann, E., and Riniker, P.: Essentielle Lymphocytophthise. Ein neues Krankheitsbild aus der Säuglingspathologie, Ann Peediat 175:1-32, 1950.

36. Good, R. A.: Discussion of paper by Burtin.⁶

37. Green, M. N.; Yerganian, G.; and Gagnon, H. J.: Prediction of Spontaneous Hereditary Diabetes Mellitus in Chinese Hamsters by Means of Elevated Alpha-2 Serum-levels, Nature 197: 396, 1963.

38. Hampar, B., and Ellison, S. A.: Chromosomal Aberrations Induced by an Animal Virus, Nature 192:145-147, 1961.

39. Harris, T. N.: Discussion of paper by W. Bernhard, and N. Granboulan.³

40. Herriott, R. M.: Infectious Nucleic Acids: A New Dimension in Virology, Science 134:256-260, 1961.

41. Hirata-Hibi, M., and Fessel, W. J.: The Leukocyte in Schizophrenia, to be published.

42. Hirata, M.: Cytological Studies of Tissue Anaphylaxis: III., Acta Haemat Jap 11:1-9, 1948.

43. Hirata, M.: Studies on the Specific Cell Reactions of Adventitia Plasma Cell System Upon Nucleic Acid and Nucleoprotein, appendix, "Functional Aspect of Adventitia Birth of Plasma Cells," Acta Path Jap 2:101-111, 1952.

44. Hirata, M.; Fujii, A.; Masuda, K.; and Ando, M.: A New Protein Crystal in the Plasma Cell, Med Biol (Tokyo) 10:24-26, 1946.

45. Hollister, L. E., and Kosek, J. G.: Personal communication to the author.

46. Itten, W.: Zur Kenntniss hämatologischer Befunde bei einigen Psychosen, Z Ges Psychiat Neurol 24:341-377, 1914.

47. Jeune, M.; Larbre, F.; Germain, D.; and Freycon, F.: Lymphocytophtisie, Alymphocytose et Hypogammaglobulinémie, Arch Franc Pediat 16: 14-34, 1959.

48. Kamp, H. V.: Nuclear Changes in the White Blood Cells of Patients with Schizophrenic Reaction: A Preliminary Report, J Neuropsychiat 4: 1-3, 1962.

49. Kappeler, R.; Krebs, A.; and Riva, G.: Klinik der Makroglobulinämie Waldenström: Beschreibung von 21 Fällen und Ubersicht der Literatur; V. Cytologischhämatologische Befunde bei der Makroglobulinämie Waldenström, Helv Med Acta 25:101-152, 1958.

50. Kerbikov, O. V.: Immunological Reactivity in Schizophrenia As Influenced by Some Modern Drugs, Ann NY Acad Sci 92:1098-1105, 1961.

51. Klima, R.: Zur Morphologie und Klinischen Pathologie der lymphatischen Reaktion, Schweiz Med Wschr 91:1165-1169, 1961.

52. Kumagai, L. F., and Dougherty, T. F.: Stress-Induced Lymphocytosis in Adrenalectomized Mice, Fed Proc 10:76-77, 1951.

53. Kunkel, H. G.: Discussion of paper by P. Burtin.⁶

54. Kurland, H., and Fessel, W. J.: Distinctive Protein Patterns in Functional Psychoses, Proc Soc Exp Biol Med, to be published.

55. Litwins, J., and Leibowitz, S.: Abnormal Lymphocytes ("Virocytes") in Virus Diseases Other than Infectious Mononucleosis, Acta Haematol 5:223-231, 1951.

56. Malis, G. Yu.: Immunobiologicheskaya Diagnostika Shizofrenii, Zh Nevropat Psikhiat Korsakov 57:82-87, 1957.

57. Malis, G. Yu., and Dolgikh, S. I.: Virusyi Faktor v Patogeneze Shizofrenii, Zh Nevropat Psikhiat Korsakov 54:728-731, 1954.

58. Malis, G. Yu.: K Etiolgii Shizofrenii, Moscow, Medgiz, 1959.

59. Mamedov, K. M.: O Diagnosticheskom Znachenii Reaktsii A. V. B. Pri Shizofrenii, Zh Nevropat Psikhiat Korsakov 60:1176-1182, 1960.

60. Mastrogiovanni, P. D.: Investigation on the Inoculation of Biological Materials From Schizophrenic Patients in Chick Embryos, in Guinea Pigs, in White Mice and in Monkey Kidney Tissue Culture, Confin Neurol 18:112-114, 1958.

61. Meier, R. M.; Boroff, D. A., and Heller, J. L.: Reticuloendothelial Effects of Some Ataractic Agents, Fed Proc 16:425, 1957.

62. Meyer, F.: Die Bedeutung des Reticuloendothelialen Systems für die Pathogenese und Therapie der Geistekrankheiten, Psychiat Neurol Med Psychol (Leipzig) 8:365-371, 1956.

63. Miale, J. B.: Nonleukemic Lymphocytosis: Diseases and Mechanisms, in The Lymphocyte and Lymphocytic Tissue, edited by J. W. Rebuck, New York: Paul B. Hoeber, Inc., 1960.

64. Moon, H. D.; Simpson, M. E.; Li, C. H.; and Evans, H. M.: Neoplasms in Rats Treated with Pituitary Growth Hormone: I. Pulmonary and Lymphatic Tissues, Cancer Res 10:297-308, 1950.

65. Ortega, L. G., and Mellors, R. C.: Cellular Sites of Formation of Gamma Globulin, J Exp Med 106:627-640, 1957.

66. Plum, C. M.: Lymphocyte Degeneration in Amaurotic Idiocy, Danish Med Bull 4:156-157, 1957.

67. Rayner, S.: Juvenile Amaurotic Idiocy: Diagnosis of Heterozygotes, Acta Genet (Basel) 3:1-5, 1952.

68. Rebuck, J. W., and LoGrippo, G. A.: Characteristics and Interrelationships of the Various Cells in the RE Cell, Macrophage, Lymphocyte, and Plasma Cell Series in Man, Lab Invest 10:1068-1093, 1961.

69. Reichard, S. M.; Gordon, A. S.; and Tessmer, C. F.: Humoral Modification of the Function of the Reticuloendothelial System, Ann NY Acad Sci 88:213-231, 1960.

70. Seligmann, M.: Discussion of paper by P. Burtin.[6]

71. Sundberg, R. D.: Lymphocytes: Origin, Structure, and Interrelationships, in The Lymphocyte and Lymphocytic Tissue, edited by J. W. Rebuck, New York: Paul B. Hoeber, Inc., 1960.

72. Taranta, A.: Relation of Isolated Recurrences of Sydenham's Chorea to Preceding Streptococcal Infections, New Eng J Med 260:1204-1210, 1959.

73. Traub, E.: Factors Influencing the Persistence of Choriomeningitis Virus in the Blood of Mice after Clinical Recovery, J Exp Med 68:229-250, 1938.

74. Vaillant, G. E.: Tuberculosis: An Historical Analogy to Schizophrenia, Psychosom Med 24:225-233, 1962.

75. Yoffey, J. M.: The Present Status of the Lymphocyte Problem, Lancet 1:206-211, 1962.

76. Yoffey, J. M., and Courtice, F. C.: Lymphatics, Lymph and Lymphoid Tissue, London: Edward Arnold Ltd., 1956.

77. Zweifach, B. W.; Benacerraf, B.; and Thomas, L.: The Relationship Between the Vascular Manifestations of Shock Produced by Endotoxin, Trauma, and Hemorrhage. II. The Possible Role of the Reticulo-Endothelial System in Resistance to Each Type of Shock, J Exp Med 106:403-414, 1957.

Abnormal Leukocytes in Schizophrenia

47

EFFECT OF AGE, SEX, AND SCHIZOPHRENIA ON THYROID AUTOANTIBODY PRODUCTION

Morris Goodman, Melvyn Rosenblatt, Jacques S. Gottlieb, Jacob Miller, and Calvin H. Chen

The investigation which this report will deal with was initially motivated by the hypothesis that in schizophrenia there is a heightened tendency to produce antibodies against certain of the endocrine and other tissue constituents of one's own body. In particular, glands such as the pituitary, adrenals, and thyroid which are involved in adaptive responses to stress were thought to be likely targets for the autoantibodies of schizophrenic patients. So far our investigation has centered on thyroglobulin, the major protein constituent of the thyroid gland; first because of the large number of reports in the literature of abnormal functioning of the thyroid gland in schizophrenic patients in the absence of overt thyroid disease,[1-5] and second because very good serological procedures have been developed for detecting autoantibodies to human thyroglobulin.[6,7]

The most sensitive of these procedures, the tanned cell hemagglutination test, has now been used in our laboratory to determine the incidence of autoantibodies to thyroglobulin in over 1,000 subjects, including 396 schizophrenic patients.

Methods

I. *Preparation of Human Thyroglobulin.*—This protein was prepared by the method of Derrien et al.[8] from human thyroids obtained at autopsy. Thyroglobulin is known to have the electrophoretic mobility of an α-globulin and to have a large molecular weight in the order of 650,000. Each preparation used in this study was checked for these characteristics by comparing its mobilities in either paper or agar-paper electrophoresis[9] and in starch-gel electrophoresis[10] with the mobilities of serum protein components. An example of the electrophoretic analyses is presented in Figure 1. Note that thyroglobulin migrates in agar-paper electrophoresis between the α_2- and α_1-globulins and in starch-gel electrophoresis just ahead of the α_2-macroglobulin. Its relatively slow migration in starch-gel is due to its large molecular weight. (The occasional preparation failing to show these mobilities was discarded.) The purified thyroglobulin, meeting our criteria, was stored in the frozen state in small vials. An aliquot

The Lafayette Clinic, Wayne State University College of Medicine, and Northville State Hospital.

Supported by grant MY-2476 from the National Institute of Mental Health.

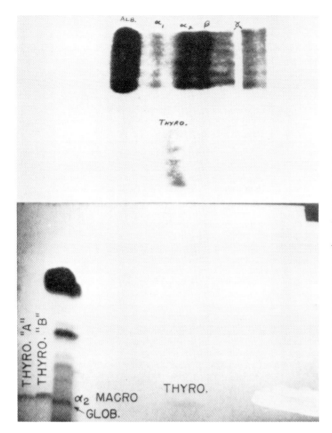

Fig. 1.—Electrophoretic comparison of purified human thyroglobulin to human serum components. In the upper photograph the agar-paper electrophoretic method of Zak et al.[9] was employed. Note that the purified thyroglobulin (*Thyro.*) has a mobility intermediate to that of α_2 and α_1 components of human serum. The lower photograph is a starch-gel in which two preparations (*A* and *B*) of purified thyroglobulin were run alongside of human serum. Note that they migrated just ahead of the α_2 macroglobulin. Purified thyroglobulin was also analyzed by two-dimensional zone electrophoresis, paper electrophoresis followed by starch-gel electrophoresis. Again its relatively slow mobility in starch-gel is evident.

at a time was thawed out as antigen was needed for the following serological procedures.

II. *Tanned Cell Hemagglutination Test.*—A slightly modified version of the method of Witebsky and Rose[6] and Roitt and Doniach[7] was employed. Human Type O, Rh⁻ red blood cells were used within 7 days after being drawn into citrate-dextrose solution. A 2.5% suspension of the washed cells in saline buffered at pH 7.2 was treated with an equal volume of tannic acid (1:20,000) for 10 minutes at room temperature. The tanned cells were washed once and packed. Then the packed tanned cells recovered from each milliliter of the original 2.5% suspension were coated by resuspending them in 2 ml. of saline buffered at pH 6.4 and containing 1 mg. of purified thyroglobulin. After incubation for 15 minutes at 37 C the cells were washed and then brought back to a 2.5% suspension with saline containing 1% normal rabbit serum (previously inactivated and absorbed with human O, Rh⁻ cells) and buffered at pH 7.2. The coated cells were used as antigen in the following testing procedures:

A. Screening of Human Sera: 0.1 ml. of each serum sample was diluted with 1.9 ml. of the saline containing 1% normal rabbit serum and then inactivated at 60 C for 2 minutes to remove complement activity; 0.5 ml. of this 1:20 dilution of serum was pipetted into each of 2 Pyrex test tubes (75×

100 mm). Then 0.05 ml. of the coated cells was added to one of the tubes, and 0.05 ml. of cells treated with tannic acid but not coated with thyroglobulin was added to the other tube. The latter served as a control for false positives. The tubes were shaken and the cells allowed to sediment for

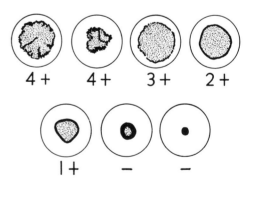

Hemagglutination Patterns (viewed from below)

Fig. 2.—The strengths of reaction from 4+ to − observed in the tanned cell hemagglutination test.

two hours. The hemagglutination reactions were then graded according to Stavitsky.[11] Figure 2 presents an illustration of the various strengths of hemagglutination observed in the tests. Since 1+ and ± reactions are sometimes difficult to distinguish from negative reactions, a serum had to yield at least a 2+ reaction to be recorded as positive. False positives were not accepted. The rare serum showing nonspecific agglutination was absorbed with the O, Rh⁻ cells and then rerun with the next group of samples. In this screening procedure, the human sera (identified only by code numbers) were tested in blocks of 40 to 100 at a time. At least one known positive serum and one negative serum were run with each set of determinations.

B. End Point Titers: These were determined on all sera showing at least a 2+ reaction at the 1:20 screening dilution. Using a single pipette per sample of serum, tenfold dilutions ranging from 10^{-1} to 10^{-5} were made. As before, 0.05 ml. of coated cells was added to 0.5 ml. of serum dilution; 0.05 ml. of tanned uncoated cells was also added to 0.5 ml. of a 10^{-1} serum dilution, as the control for false positives. The titer of a serum was considered the last dilution showing a 2+ reaction. Almost all of the positive sera were subsequently retitered, and those which had been positive at 10^{-5} were also tested at 10^{-6}. All the sera detected as positive in the original screening gave positive titers that could be repeated within two tube dilutions.

C. Inhibition Tests for Serological Specificity: The organ specificity of the autoantibodies to thyroglobulin was examined as follows: 0.05 ml. of each human organ extract (thyroid, liver, kidney, adrenal, lung, ovary, brain, and spleen) containing 0.05 mg. protein was added to 0.5 ml. of a 10^{-2} dilution of serum sample. These serum-extract mixtures were incubated for ten minutes. Then 0.05 ml. of the tanned cells coated with human thyroglobulin was added to each of these mixtures, and the hemagglutination test was carried out as before. Organ specificity was demonstrated if hemagglutination was inhibited by the thyroid extract but not by the other organ extracts. About a third of all the positive sera were so tested.

The species specificity of the autoantibodies to human thyroglobulin was examined by the same procedure, using thyroid extracts from man, chimpanzee,* rhesus monkey, and beef for the prior incubation with the serum samples. Species specificity was demonstrated if the inhibition of the hemagglutination reaction by the prior absorption with heterologous thyroid extract decreased on going from chimpanzee to rhesus monkey to beef. About three-fourths of all the positive sera were so tested.

---

* Dr. Arthur J. Riopelle, Director of the Yerkes Laboratory of Primate Biology, supplied the chimpanzee thyroid.

III. *Subject Groups Surveyed.*—These were: (1) chronic schizophrenic patients, both male and female, at Northville State Hospital; (2) a deteriorating organic brain group of males and females—this was a geriatric group whose mental condition could be attributed to cerebrovascular accidents and other central nervous system organic factors; (3) the female nursing personnel at the hospital; (4) male and female subjects under examination at the Yates Cancer Detection Clinic in Detroit, and finally (5) the members of the Sophomore Medical Class of Wayne State University College of Medicine.

Blood samples from all subjects were taken aseptically using B-D Vacutainer disposable venipuncture sets. After the samples stood overnight in the refrigerator, the serum was separated from the clot and frozen at —20 C in tightly sealed containers.

Results and Comment

I. *Effect of Age and Sex.*—In analyzing the results of the survey, striking age and sex effects on the autoantibody incidence were observed. Figure 3 summarizes these effects for all the subjects in the survey with the exception of the sophomore medical students. They yielded atypical results which will be described later in this report. It can be noted that the incidence of positive reactions is almost two to three times larger in the female group (549 subjects) than in the male group

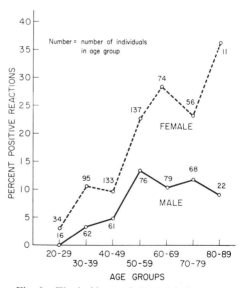

Fig. 3.—The incidence of thyroglobulin autoantibodies compared in males and females as a function of age. All subjects tested with the exception of the sophomore medical students are included in this comparison.

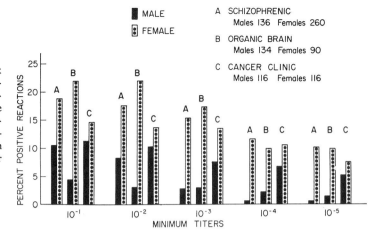

Fig. 4.—Effect of sex on the incidence and potency of thyroglobulin autoantibody production are compared in the schizophrenic patients, the deteriorated organic brain patients, and the cancer clinic subjects.

(386 subjects) and that in both groups the incidence jumps markedly after age 50. In the females the incidence rose from an average of about 9% below age 50 (268 subjects) to an average of about 25% above age 50 (281 subjects). In the males the rise was from an average of about 3.5% (139 subjects) to 11% (247 subjects).

In three of the clinical groups the age distribution within each group between the males and the females was sufficiently close to merit comparing the effect of sex alone on the thyroglobulin autoantibody production. This comparison is presented in Figure 4. In the schizophrenic group the incidence of positive reactions was 19% among the females and 10% among the males. In the

organic brain group the incidence was 22% among the females and 4.5% among the males. In the cancer clinic group the incidence was 15% among the females and 11% among the males. This figure also compares the females and males in terms of the potency of their autoantibodies to thyroglobulin. When this is done the sex effect is even more striking. For example in the schizophrenic group, about 10% of the females showed titers of better than 10^{-5}, whereas less than 1% of the males showed such high titers. In the organic brain group, 10% of the females again showed these high titers, whereas only 1.5% of the males showed such titers. In the cancer clinic group, close to 8% of the fe-

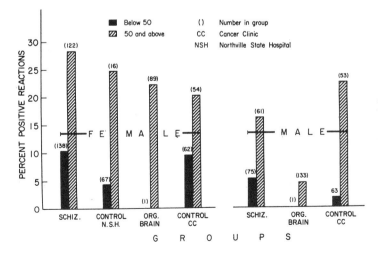

Fig. 5.—The incidence of thyroglobulin autoantibody production above age 50 to that below age 50 is compared in the various female and male subject groups.

males showed the titers of at least 10^{-5}, and about 5% of males showed such high titers.

A marked age effect on the incidence of thyroglobulin autoantibodies was observed in all the female groups and in certain of the male groups. It can be noted in Figure 5 that the autoantibody incidence increased from 11% in the younger to 28% in the older schizophrenic females, from 4% in the younger to 25% in the older nursing personnel, and from 10% in the younger to 20% in the older cancer clinic females. The incidence increased from 5.5% in the younger to 16% in the older schizophrenic males, and from 1.5% in the younger to 23% in the older cancer clinic males. However the age factor was not evident in the deteriorated brain-damaged males. This geriatric group showed only a 4.5% incidence of positive reactions. Thus the effect of age on the thyroglobulin autoantibody incidence appears to be more subtly indicated in males than in females.

II. *Possible Effect of Emotional Stress.*—The findings on the sophomore medical students suggest that stressful situations may be a factor in the production of thyroglobulin autoantibodies. It can be noted in Table 1 that over 8% of the student males were positive compared to about 3.5% of all other males in the group under age 50. There were only seven females in the class, and three of these (or 43%) were positive compared to about 9% of all other females in the group under age 50. It is perhaps of significance that the bloods were drawn from the sophomore students at the height of their final examination period last January and that these students were showing typical signs of "examination stress." Thus the finding of a rather high incidence of thyroglobulin autoantibodies in this student group suggests the possibility that anxiety may heighten the tendency to produce such antibodies. In this connection Wolff [12] has reported that subjects exposed to stressful interviews show rapid and marked increases of thyroid hormone secretion as measured by protein-bound iodine (PBI) determinations.

Another aspect of the data which points to emotional stress as a possible factor in thyroid autoantibody production is that in the older female groups the highest incidence of positive reactions (28%) was developed by the schizophrenic patients. Furthermore, in the younger females, the lowest incidence of positive reactions (4%) was given by the nursing personnel, and in this group of younger females there was no reason to suspect an unusual incidence of acute emotional stress as a characteristic feature of the group. In contrast the younger schizophrenic females showed an 11% incidence of thyroglobulin autoantibody reactions, and the younger females at the cancer detection clinic showed a 10% incidence. With respect to the latter, it may be mentioned that many of these subjects, perhaps a majority, came to the cancer detection clinic with the type of symptoms that created fear and anxiety of cancer. (Most of the subjects, however, did not have cancer.) A surprisingly high incidence of strong autoimmune reactions to thyroglobulin was also observed among the older men who came to the cancer detection clinic.

III. *Clinical Conditions of the Subjects.*—The incidence of positive reactions among the cancer clinic males could be correlated to some extent with certain findings of the medical records of these subjects. For example 23% of the positive males of this group had a record of either goiter or thyroidectomy, whereas only 4% of the negative males had such a record. In contrast, 12% of the positive cancer clinic females had a record of goiter or thyroidectomy, and 7%

TABLE 1.—*Comparison of the Thyroglobulin Autoantibody Incidence of the Sophomore Medical Students and Other Subjects Below Age 50*

Subject Groups	Total No.	No. Positive	% Positive
Males below age 50 (minus students)	139	5	3.6
Male Students	114	9	8.3
All males below age 50	253	14	5.9
Females below age 50 (minus students)	268	24	9.3
Female students	7	3	43.0
All females below age 50	275	27	9.8

of the negative females had such a record. Hypertension, peptic ulcer, and neurodermatitis were also more frequent in the positive cancer clinic males than in the negative cancer clinic males. This correlation did not hold for the females who showed in general a lower incidence of these conditions. On the other hand, 24% of the positive females had shown two or more spontaneous abortions, whereas 13% of the negative females had such a record.

Clinical symptoms of thyroid disorder (judged by questionnaires filled out by the students and by over half of the nursing personnel) were presented by 11% of the positive male student group (1 out of 9 subjects) and by 1% of the negative male student group (1 out of 105 subjects), also by 20% of the positive nursing personnel (1 out of 5 subjects) and by 9% of the negative nursing personnel (5 out of 53 subjects). An examination (still in progress) of the medical records of positively reacting subjects in the Northville patient group has revealed a history of frank thyroid disorder in only 6% of these subjects with thyroid autoantibodies (the records of 51 of the positive subjects have been examined up to now).

IV. *Serological Specificity of the Auto-antibodies.*—Since most of the positively reacting sera in all groups were from subjects without overt thyroid disease, we felt it important to clearly establish the serologic specificity of these presumed autoantibodies. Previous work of Roitt and Doniach [7] on the autoantibodies of patients with Hashimoto's

TABLE 2.—*Inhibition Test for Organ Specificity of Autoantibodies to Thyroglobulin*

Absorption with Extract of	% of Sera * Inhibited
Human liver	0
Human kidney	0
Human adrenal	0
Human lung	0
Human ovary	0
Human brain	0
Human spleen	0
Human thyroid	100

* A total of 42 positively reacting sera of various titers were tested against tanned cells coated with human thyroglobulin after the above absorptions.

TABLE 3.—*Inhibition Test for Species Specificity of Autoantibodies to Thyroglobulin*

Absorption with Extract of	% of Sera Inhibited		
	High Titered *	Medium Titered †	Low Titered ‡
Human thyroid	100.0	100.0	100.0
Chimpanzee thyroid	90.6	100.0	92.8
Rhesus monkey thyroid	43.7	75.6	78.5
Beef thyroid	0	5.4	14.2

* A total of 32 sera having titers of 10^{-6} and 10^{-5} were tested against tanned cells coated with human thyroglobulin after the above absorptions.
† A total of 37 sera having titers of 10^{-4} and 10^{-3} were so tested
‡ A total of 28 sera having titers of 10^{-2} were so tested. (Since the test is carried out with the serum at 10^{-2} dilution, sera having titers of less than 10^{-2} were not tested.)

disease had demonstrated that in this thyroid disease the autoantibodies are highly organ-specific and also species-specific. The type of autoantibodies detected in our survey also show marked organ- and species-specific properties.

The data summarized in Table 2 show that human liver, kidney, adrenal, lung, ovary, brain, and spleen failed to inhibit the reaction for thyroglobulin, whereas human thyroid did.

The species specificity data are summarized in Table 3. It can be noted that human thyroid completely inhibited the reaction for human thyroglobulin of the sera which were tested. Chimpanzee thyroid inhibited 91% of the very high titered sera and 93% of the low titered sera. Rhesus monkey thyroid inhibited 44% of the very high titered sera and 79% of the low titered sera, whereas bovine thyroid failed to inhibit any of the very high titered sera and only inhibited 14% of the low titered sera. Thus these autoantibodies characteristically showed species specificity in that a significant proportion of the antibodies were directed to the phylogenetically new part of the thyroglobulin molecule. The frequent occurrence of such autoantibodies in individuals without overt thyroid disease suggests that there is a strong tendency to produce autoantibodies in our species and that this is somehow related to the distinctive course taken by our biological evolution.

V. *Other Population Surveys of Thyroid Autoantibody Incidence.*—The striking sex and age effects on thyroid autoantibody incidence observed in this study agree with the findings of others.[13,14] Goudie et al.[13] surveyed a hospital population of 486 patients free of overt thyroid symptoms for the incidence of complement-fixing thyroid antibodies. They found a much higher incidence of these antibodies in elderly women than in other age and sex groups. The incidence was 16% for women over 50 as compared to only 3% for women under 50 as well as for younger and older males. Another significant finding was that hepatic necrosis or cirrhosis occurred more frequently in the positive females than in the other groups. Goudie et al.[13] considered the presence of thyroid antibodies in patients without frank thyroid disease to be a sign of subclinical thyroid lesions in these patients. In this connection degenerative thyroid changes were subsequently found at the autopsy of subjects who had shown in the survey strong antibody reactions for the complement-fixing antigen of the thyroid. This antigen is not the same as thyroglobulin, but like thyroglobulin, it strongly expresses its autoantigenicity in individuals with severe thyroid disease such as lymphadenoid goiter or primary myxedema.

Hackett et al.[14] determined the incidence of antibody production to thyroglobulin in 102 blood donors and 387 hospital patients who were without clinical disease of the thyroid gland. They used a tanned cell hemagglutination method for detecting the autoantibodies, but their procedure for performing this test was not the same as ours. They reported that in the blood donor group 4% of the males and 14% of the females yielded positive reactions. In the hospital patient group 11% of the males and 26% of the females were positive. Under age forty, 12% of the males and 19% of the females were positive, and over age forty, 9% of the males and 30% of the females were positive. Thus in their study as in ours the incidence of thyroid autoantibodies was two to three times greater in females than in males

and also greater in the older group of females than in the younger.

Using the tanned cell hemagglutination test, Roitt and Doniach[15] obtained 10 positive autoantibody reactions for thyroglobulin out of 148 hospital controls. However 2 of the 10 positive subjects revealed a history of thyroid disease on further examination. Owen and Smart,[16] using this test, report 3 positives out of 52 nonthyroid hospital cases or a 6% incidence. The 3 positives were given by females at ages 42, 45, and 70. Rose,[17] also using this test, surveyed over 1,000 sera drawn in a Wassermann laboratory and found that the incidence of antithyroglobulin reactions was approximately 3% for the males and 7% for the females. Furthermore, about a third of the positive subjects showed some record of thyroid disease, and many of the other positive subjects were patients entering the psychiatric wards. This latter observation[17] supports the suggestions of our data that severe emotional stress heightens the tendency to produce thyroid autoantibodies.

IV. *Interpretation of Our Findings.*—We might now ask what the significance is of autoantibody production to thyroid proteins in individuals without obvious thyroid pathology and also how emotional stress and age and sex could relate to the production of thyroid autoantibodies. In order to explore these questions we must first have in mind a theoretical rather than strictly operational definition of the phenomenon of autoimmunization. The key premise, supported by the experimental elucidation of the phenomenon of immunological tolerance,[18,19] is that during fetal life most endogenous proteins come in contact with the mesenchymal precursors of the organism's immunological system and so affect this system that when it matures it can not respond to these proteins as antigens. Conversely, there is an absence of immunological tolerance for proteins which fail to enter the precursor cells of the immunological system during fetal life. In later life antibodies will be produced against such proteins if they come in contact with the immunological system. Not only is immunological tolerance lacking for the proteins of foreign organisms, but also for endogenous proteins that failed to gain access to the blood circulation during fetal life due to their immobilization in tissues and in some instances their late appearance in ontogeny. These endogenous proteins only express their autoantigenic properties if released into the circulation. They can then provoke an autoimmunization by entering the antibody producing cells.

The release of autoantigens from a particular tissue is apt to occur when the tissue is stressed or injured or undergoing cyclic proliferative and involutional changes. Clearly, in man emotional stress profoundly influences the activity of such endocrine tissues as the thyroid, the pituitary, and the adrenals. Further, the thyroid gland shows greater cyclic activity in females than in males. If during this activity the membrane integrity of the thyroid cells were to decrease, thyroglobulin and perhaps other potential autoantigens could escape into the circulation and initiate an autoimmune response. Thus we can develop a scheme which implicates the stresses of life in the causation of autoimmune processes and which explains why thyroid autoantibodies are more frequently produced in females than in males. These autoantibodies, if chronically produced, could gradually destroy the metabolically active cells of the thyroid; in other words, they could cause an aging of the thyroid gland. This process should then accelerate as the integrity of cellular membranes decreases with advancing chronological age. Indeed, one of the characteristic features of the aging process is the absolute decrease of metabolically active cells and the relative increase of inert fibrous tissue such as may be observed in more acute form as the aftermath of an inflammation. If the tissues of man are rich in autoantigens (a rationale for expecting this to be the case is presented elsewhere [20]), it follows from the argument developed here that the production of autoantibodies is a key factor in the aging process.

In extending our investigation, we are attempting to more thoroughly evaluate the possible role of emotional stress in the causation of autoimmune reactions to the thyroid gland and by this general approach to further determine if schizophrenia can be characterized as a "stress" disease. It would also seem important to explore the hypothesis that autoimmune reactions to a variety of tissue and glandular proteins increase in frequency with advancing chronological age. Perhaps autoimmune reactions to the adrenal gland are involved in the poor adaptive responses of the chronic schizophrenic patient to stressful situations. Conceivably an autosensitivity to a variety of glandular proteins could be a factor in the deterioration of schizophrenic patients. Fessel [21] has proposed that in schizophrenia an autoimmune process is directed against the brain. This hypothesis certainly deserves to be thoroughly investigated.

Another avenue of research suggested by our data lies in the possibility that autoimmune processes in a pregnant female (which are postulated to increase with the age of the female) can injure the developing fetus, since in our species maternal antibodies are readily transported across the placenta into the fetus. Indeed, some evidence for an association between the birth of cretins and the presence of maternal autoantibodies to thyroid proteins has been presented.[22,23] Similarly, if pregnant females were producing autoantibodies to brain proteins, this too could lead to mentally deficient or distorted offspring.

However, progress is not likely to be made in elucidating the full range of autoimmune reactions in man until fractionation procedures are developed for the separation and purification of tissue proteins. The relative ease by which autoantibodies to thyroglobulin are detected is perhaps due to the preponderance of this protein in saline extracts of the normal thyroid gland.

Conclusions

The tendency to produce autoantibodies to thyroglobulin is more marked in females than in males. This may possibly be related to the greater cyclic activity of the thyroid gland in females.

There is a much higher incidence of thyroid autoantibody production in the human population over age 50 than in the population below age 50. This finding suggests that autoantibody production may be a factor in the aging process.

There are some suggestions from the data that emotional stress heightens the tendency to produce thyroid autoantibodies.

Finally, the data are not inconsistent with the hypothesis that the process of schizophrenia involves physiological reactions characteristic of emotional stress and that such reactions as stated in the previous conclusion can augment the production of autoantibodies to the thyroid.

REFERENCES

1. Hoskins, R. G.: The Biology of Schizophrenia, New York, W. W. Norton & Co., 1946.

2. Cranswick, E. H.: Tracer Iodine Studies on Thyroid Activity and Thyroid Responsiveness in Schizophrenia, Amer. J. Psychiat. 112:170-178, 1955.

3. Sands, E. D.: Endocrine Changes in Schizophrenia, in Schizophrenia: Somatic Aspects, edited by D. Richter, New York, The Macmillan Company, 1957, pp. 77-91.

4. Rawson, R. W.; Koch, H., and Flock, F. F.: The Thyroid Hormones and Their Relationships to Mental Health, in Hormones, Brain Function, and Behavior, edited by H. Hoagland, New York, Academic Press, Inc., 1957, pp. 221-234.

5. Bullmore, G. H. L.; Kay, W. W.; Smith, D. W., and Stott, H. J.: Investigations of Thyroid Function of Mental Patients and the Possible Use of Some Results for Rational Treatment Procedure, in Psychoendocrinology, edited by M. Reiss, New York, Grune & Stratton, Inc., 1958, pp. 52-72.

6. Witebsky, E., and Rose, N. R.: Studies on Organ Specificity: IV. Production of Rabbit Thyroid Antibodies in the Rabbit, J. Immun. 72:408-416, 1956.

7. Roitt, I. M., and Doniach, D.: The Incidence, Nature, and Significance of Autoantibodies in Thyroid Diseases, in Mechanisms of Hypersensitivity, edited by J. H. Shaffer; G. A. Lo Grippo, and M. W. Chase, Boston, Little, Brown & Company, 1959, pp. 325-347.

8. Derrien, Y.; Michel, R., and Roche, J.: Recherches sur la preparation et les propriétés de la thyroglobuline pure, Biochem. Biophys. Acta 2:454-470, 1948.

9. Zak, B.; Volini, F.; Briski, J., and Williams, L. A.: Combined Agar Gel-Paper Electrophoresis, Amer. J. Clin. Path. 33:75-82, 1960.

10. Smithies, O.: Zone Electrophoresis in Starch Gels and Its Application to Studies of Serum Proteins, in Advances in Protein Chemistry: XIV, edited by C. B. Anfinsen, Jr.; M. L. Anson; K. Bailey, and J. T. Edsall, New York, Academic Press, Inc., 1959, pp. 65-113.

11. Stavitksy, A. B.: Micromethods for the Study of Proteins and Antibodies: I. Procedure and General Applications of Hemagglutination and Hemagglutination-Inhibition Reactions with Tannic Acid and Protein-Treated Red Blood Cells, J. Immun. 72:360-375, 1954.

12. Wolff, H. G.: Stress and Disease, Springfield, Ill., Charles C Thomas, Publisher, 1953.

13. Goudie, R. B.; Anderson, J. R., and Gray, K. G.: Complement-Fixing Antithyroid Antibodies in Hospital Patients with Asymptomatic Thyroid Lesions, J. Path. Bact. 77:389-400, 1959.

14. Hackett, E.; Beech, M., and Forbes, I. J.: Thyroglobulin Antibodies in Patients Without Clinical Disease of the Thyroid Gland, Lancet 2:402-404, 1960.

15. Roitt, I. M., and Doniach, D.: Human Auto-Immune Thyroiditis: Serological Studies, Lancet 2:1027-1033, 1958.

16. Owen, S. G., and Smart, G. A.: Thyroid Antibodies in Myxoedema, Lancet 2:1034-1035, 1958.

17. Rose, N. R.: Personal communication to the authors.

18. Hasek, M.; Lengerová, A., and Hraba, T.: Transplantation Immunity and Tolerance, in Advances in Immunology: I, edited by W. H. Taliaferro and J. H. Humphrey, New York, Academic Press, Inc., 1961, pp. 1-66.

19. Smith, R. T.: Immunological Tolerance of Non-Living Antigens, in Advances in Immunology: I, edited by W. H. Taliaferro and J. H. Humphrey, New York, Academic Press, Inc., 1961, pp. 67-129.

20. Goodman, M.: The Role of Immunochemical Differences in the Phyletic Development of Human Behavior, Hum. Biol. 33:131-162, 1961.

21. Fessel, W. J.: Autoimmunity and Mental Illness, Arch. Gen. Psychiat. 6:320-323, 1962.

22. Beierwaltes, W. H.; Dodson, V. N., and Wheeler, A. H.: Thyroid Autoantibodies in Families of Cretins, J. Clin. Endocrinol. 19:179-182, 1959.

23. Blizzard, R. M.; Chandler, R. W.; Landing, B. H.; Pettit, M. D., and West, C. D.: Maternal Autoimmunization to Thyroid as a Probable Cause of Athyrotic Cretinism, New Engl. J. Med. 263:327-336, 1960.

48

CEREALS AND SCHIZOPHRENIA DATA AND HYPOTHESIS

F. C. Dohan

Data and speculation bearing on the possibility that specific foods may play a role in the pathogenesis of schizophrenia are presented in this article. The data were assembled and speculations made on the basis of the following assumptions: (1) the pathogenesis is basically the same in the majority of those diagnosed schizophrenia, (2) the possibility of developing the disease is inherited (i. e. a genotype exists), and (3) the occurrence of the manifest disease (i. e. the phenotype) depends largely, but possibly not entirely, on environmental factors.

An environmental factor of importance may be the kinds and quantities of foods eaten over a relatively long period. The general hypothesis that ingestion of a sufficient quantity of certain foods may be the environmental factor necessary for the phenotypic manifestation of some genotypes has been well supported by studies of certain inherited abnormalities (e. g. phenylketonuria and galactosemia) and suspected in others of less well-defined inheritance (e. g. coronary atherosclerosis).

Because of a possible relationship between schizophrenia and celiac disease, an apparently hereditary defect which is made symptomatic by eating wheat and certain other cereals, I have collected data on admissions to mental hospitals and on wheat and rye consumption in various countries at a time when changes were likely to be relatively great—World War II. If analyzed on the basis of per cent change from the prewar mean, there is a positive correlation between per cent change in numbers of admissions for schizophrenia and per cent changes in "consumption" data for wheat during World War II; not only within countries but between countries. There also appears to be a crude relationship between types of cereals in the diet and the estimated "morbid risk" for schizophrenia in various cultures. Although the morbid risk estimates are generally higher for cultures eating large amounts of wheat, they also demonstrate that schizophrenia occurs among populations eating other cereals but no wheat.

Reprinted from *Acta Psychiat. Scand.* **42**, 125–152, 1966.

These considerations suggest to me that a possible role of cereals deserves consideration in studies on the pathogenesis of schizophrenia.

METHODS AND RESULTS

Data from original sources and the literature have been assembled on: (1) the changes in the annual number of admissions of patients with schizophrenia (and other psychoses) in Finland, Norway, Sweden, Switzerland, Canada and the United States before, during and after World War II. (The sources of original data, methods and results were previously presented (1966.) (2) the calculated "morbid risk" of developing schizophrenia in various cultures, (3) the possible relationships of schizophrenia and celiac disease.

The various estimates of the "frequency" of schizophrenia have been compared with official estimates or other reports of the "consumption" of various cereals and other foods. The collection and interpretation of "consumption" data are discussed in the section on Results and in the Appendix, Part 1; and the methods employed in estimating "morbid risk" and further information on the findings and the dietary habits of the populations at risk in the Appendix, Part 2.

PART 1. INTRA-COUNTRY COMPARISON OF ANNUAL NUMBERS OF ADMISSIONS FOR SCHIZOPHRENIA AND THE ANNUAL "CONSUMPTION" OF WHEAT AND OF RYE

The relationship of the annual number of admissions of women for schizophrenia in Finland and Sweden and the annual number of patients with schizophrenia in Norwegian mental hospitals (*Statistisk Årbok for Norge*) to wheat "consumption" data (*Statistisk Årbok for Norge, Statistisk Årbok för Sverige, Statistisk Årbok för Finland*) is shown in Figures 1, 2 and 3 and the relationship to rye "consumption" (from the same references), in Figures 4, 5, and 6.

Figures 1 and 2 demonstrate relatively good temporal and quantitative concordance of the changes in admissions for schizophrenia and changes in estimated "consumption" of wheat in Finland and Sweden despite the vagaries in annual estimates of "consumption" discussed below and in the Appendix. The admission data for Norway were published by *Ödegård* (1954) in 5 year periods, but the numbers of schizophrenics in Norwegian mental hospitals are available on an annual basis over a limited period (*Statistisk Årbok for Norge*). These data are compared in Figure 3 to the published data on wheat consumption.

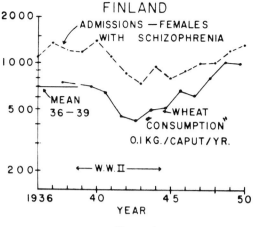

Figure 1

Temporal relationship of changes in *admissions* (first admissions plus readmissions) for schizophrenia and changes in "consumption" of wheat in Finland. The numbers of admission and "consumption" data are plotted in relation to the logarithmic scale of the ordinate. Thus, the same per cent change in the variables is represented by an equal vertical distance on the graph. The marks designating the year-numbers on the arithmetic scale of the abscissa indicate the end of the calendar year. The numbers of admissions are plotted at the end of the calendar year and "consumption" at the approximate position of the end of the "harvest year". The "harvest year" in Finland for wheat and for rye was September 1st to August 31st.

   See text and Appendix, Note 1 for discussion of difficulties in interpretation of annual "consumption" data. See Figure 4 and text of previous publication (1966) for further information on admission data.

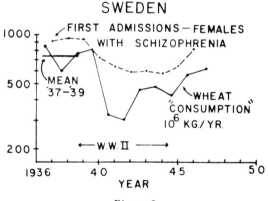

Figure 2

Temporal relationship of changes in first admissions for schizophrenia and changes in "consumption" of wheat in Sweden. See legend Fig. 1. The "harvest year" in Sweden for wheat and for rye was August 1st to July 31st.

Cereals and Schizophrenia

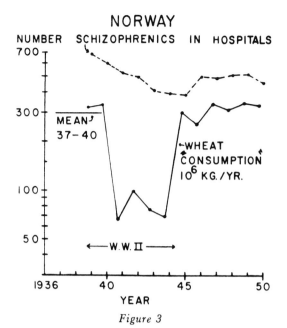

Figure 3

Temporal relationship of changes in number of schizophrenics in hospitals and changes in "consumption" of wheat in Norway. See legend Fig. 1. The "harvest year" for wheat and for rye in Norway was October 1st to September 30th.

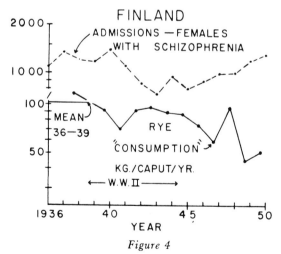

Figure 4

Temporal relationship of changes in admissions for schizophrenia and changes in "consumption" of rye in Finland. See legend Fig. 1.

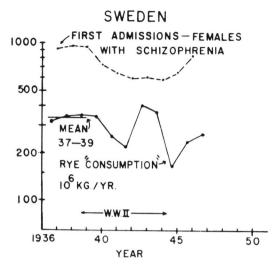

Fig. 5

Temporal relationship of changes in first admissions for schizophrenia and changes in "consumption" of rye in Sweden. See legend Fig. 2.

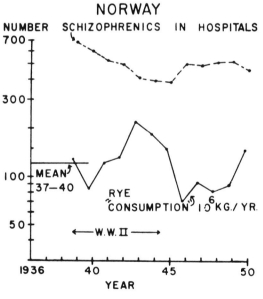

Figure 6

Temporal relationship of changes in number of schizophrenics in hospitals and changes in "consumption" of rye in Norway. See legend Fig. 3.

Cereals and Schizophrenia

Figures 4, 5 and 6 show the lack of correlation between the annual data on schizophrenia and the "consumption" of rye. It may be hypothesized, however, that rye is also pathogenic for the genotype for schizophrenia but much less so than wheat. Some support for this possibility is presented in Part 2.

PART 2. INTER-COUNTRY COMPARISONS OF PER CENT CHANGE IN ADMISSION FOR SCHIZOPHRENIA AND PER CENT CHANGE IN WHEAT CONSUMPTION

Figure 7 shows the wartime changes in admission for schizophrenia and reported "consumption" of wheat for each country. These are expressed as per cent deviation from the prewar mean of the two 3 years periods (i. e. 1940–42, 1943–45) except in the case of Norway there is only one period,

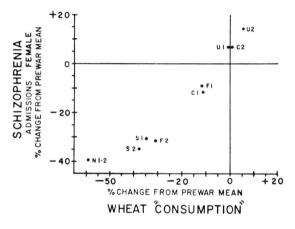

Figure 7

Changes in wheat "consumption" versus changes in admissions for schizophrenia during World War II. The changes in wheat "consumption" and in numbers of females admitted to mental hospitals with schizophrenia in 5 countries have been expressed as the per cent change from the respective prewar means. These values have been plotted for the means of the two periods: Period 1 = 1940–42 and Period 2 = 1943–45 except in the case of Norway the period is Period 1–2 = 1941–45 (because annual data on admissions were not available). The per cent change in numbers of first admissions is plotted for Norway (N), Sweden (S), Canada (C) and United States (U) and of *admissions* (first admission plus readmissions) for Finland (F). The prewar means for the "consumption" of wheat and of rye covered approximately the same years as the admissions data; except that in the case of the United States it was a longer period. The prewar mean number of admissions was calculated from the available annual data; these were—Finland: 1936–39, Norway: 1936–40 (see above), Sweden: 1937–39, Canada: 1936–39, and the United States: 1939. See text for discussion of significance and interpretation og "consumption" data and previous publication (1966) for details on admission data.

1941–45. The per cent change in wheat consumption exhibits a good positive correlation with the per cent deviation from prewar means of the numbers of admissions of women with schizophrenia.

The statistical relationship of changes in admission to change in wheat consumption appears to be true "within" as well as "between" countries. If lines are drawn between the 2 time periods for each country as charted in Figure 7 (Canada, C_1 and C_2; United States, U_1 and U_2; and Finland, F_1 and F_2, either for *admissions*, or estimated first admissions—not shown), the slopes are fairly similar. The two values for Sweden are close together. Since the first admission data for Norway was published as total first admissions by diagnostic classes for 5 year periods (*Ödegård* (1954)), only one period during the war may be plotted.

The per cent changes in first admissions are plotted in Figure 7 with the exception of Finland. No data on first admissions were available for this country so *admission* data (i. e. the sum of first admissions plus readmissions) were employed. Because the per cent decreases in first admissions have been previously shown to be somewhat greater than per cent decreases of *admissions* in countries for which both types of data were available (Canada, Sweden and Norway), it is believed probable that the per cent decreases in first admissions in Finland were greater than indicated in Figure 7. Estimates from a plot (not shown) of the relationship of per cent change in first admissions to per cent change in *admissions* in Canada, Sweden and Norway indicate that Finland probably experiences about a 19 per cent decrease in first admissions of women during 1940–42 (point F 2 for *admissions* in Fig. 7 $= -9.1$ per cent) and about 45 per cent decrease in 1943–45 (point F 2 for *admissions* in Fig. 7 $= -31.6$ per cent). The correlation coefficient of the per cent change in wheat consumption with the per cent change in first admissions for schizophrenia (using the estimated per cent change in first admissions for Finland) is: $r = 0.908$, 7 d. f. $P < 0.01$.

As indicated in Part 1, the possibility that changes in rye consumption might also be related statistically to changes in first admissions for schizophrenia must be considered. Rye "consumption" was about 30 to 60 per cent of the combined "consumption" of wheat plus rye during the prewar period in the three Scandinavian countries and less than 1.4 per cent in Canada and the United States (*Aykroyd & Sukhatme* (1960)). The per cent changes in Canada and the United States in rye "consumption" have been assumed to be zero because of the small absolute change. The multiple regression equation for the per cent change in first admissions (ΔS) as related to the per cent change in wheat (ΔW) and in rye "consumption" (ΔR) is expressed as follows: $\Delta S = + 5$ percent $+ 1.04$ (ΔW) $+ 0.48$ (ΔR). The correlation coefficient of per cent change in first admissions with the per cent change in wheat and in rye consumption is: $r = 0.961$, 6 d. f., $P < 0.01$.

Admission data for women were selected rather than those for men, since it was thought probable that men in the armed service and those civilians doing heavy labor (mostly male) might have received a disproportionate amount of the wheat available for consumption. The data previously presented (1966), are believed to be compatible with this possibility.

The changes in admissions for schizophrenia of men and of women in Finland, Sweden and Norway were similar; this was not true for Canada and the United States. The male admissions (not charted) show a lesser correlation with wheat "consumption" primarily because of the lesser decrease in admissions of Canadian males than of females and the marked, but unexplained (*Pugh & MacMahon* (1956)), increase in admissions of men with schizophrenia in the United States. The figures on food "consumption" changes in Canada and the United States pertained to the civilian populations (*United States Department of Agriculture* (1946)). A high proportion of the men in the age period of maximal risk for developing schizophrenia were in the armed services. It seems highly unlikely that the 52 per cent increase in admissions of males in the United States was primarily "due to" an increased consumption of wheat even though the mean caloric intake was high (*Schor & Swain* (1949)) in the United States army.

Postwar Changes. The marked increase in admissions for schizophrenia which occurred during and after the reconstruction period (1945–50) in Finland (Fig. 1) was not as rapid as increases in apparent "consumption" of wheat. This, in association with the experience in Norway (Fig. 3), if not entirely due to change in diagnostic customs (*Ödegård* (1954)), suggests that if wheat ingestion and admissions for schizophrenia are, in fact, etiologically related, that duration and degree of decrease in wheat ingestion as well as possible effects of the postwar decrease in rye intake must be considered.

The experience with celiac disease may be compared to the proportionately greater postwar increase in wheat "consumption" than in the indices of the frequency of schizophrenia demonstrated in Figures 1 and 3. As discussed more fully in Part 4, a "gluten-free diet" for one or three years followed by a return to gluten-containing cereals resulted in the production of celiac symptoms in only one-fourth of the children, while lesser intervals of abstinence appear to be followed within a few days to months by symptoms. Although a truly gluten-free diet is not comparable to the relatively low wheat diet in the Scandinavian populations, it has been observed in adults with celiac disease that many individuals are able to maintain a clinical remission with repeated minor violations of diet.

COMMENTS

Since an understanding of the economic term "consumption" is necessary for evaluation of these results, a brief discussion is given below. See Appendix for details.

"Consumption" data from the Scandinavian countries as reported for wheat and separately for rye in the respective statistical yearbooks, were based on trade transactions and estimates of harvests and are for grain (not for flour). These estimates were not corrected for waste and animal feeding and no data on these were provided. In contradistinction, the data for the United States and Canada pertained to flour from wheat plus rye available for "human consumption" at the retail level by civilians and were reported by chronilogic year in weight units and per cent of prewar mean.

Despite the problems of interpretation of "consumption" data, the per cent change from the prewar mean is believed to be an appropriate index of the degree of change, especially if considered over a few years (as in Fig. 7), in the actual human consumption of products of these grains. It is not a direct measure and the change in actual amounts eaten each year is probably distorted in annual "consumption" estimates. *Farnsworth* (1961), an authority in the field, stated "National Food balance estimates are at their worst when constructed for individual years and accepted as evidence of year to year changes in consumption" ... "only the largest indicated annual changes, say 20 per cent or more, can be relied on as reflection of actual variations in food consumption in most cou..tries and even these only as indicators of direction, not the magnitude of change." The decreases in wheat "consumption" in the Scandinavian countries were more than 20 per cent during much of the war period (Fig. 7).

The "consumption" data for Finland are of particular interest since *Roine* (1948) has published an analysis of the rations "distributed" each year to consumers (i. e. the two thirds of the people who were not "self-providers") during 1941 through 1946. The wheat flour "distributed" to the "normal consumer," in grams per day, for these six years was 47, 27, 16, 49, 58 and 76, respectively.

Evidence in addition to the "consumption" data from the statistical yearbook for a shortage of wheat flour in Sweden is found (*Bergström* (1964)) in (1) the relatively low bread ration alloted the normal consumer starting in the Summer of 1940, (2) the addition of barley flour (5–15 per cent) to wheat flour from October 16, 1941 to March 1945, (3) the small reduction in the total of wheat plus rye flour consumed in 1942, 1943, 1944 (in association with the 12.7 per cent reduction in rye "consumption" and the decrease of 36.1 per cent in wheat "consumption" for the war period). The survey of *Boalt* & *Zotterman* (1943) demonstrated that clerical workers and women "lived within their rations," including a relatively low bread ration, while lumbermen did not.

A survey of food intake of employees and their families in Oslo by *Ström* (1948) indicated a bread and cereal intake in these Norwegian families similar to prewar values, but other reports indicate that the bread in Norway was quite dark due to the use of high flour extraction ratios (*Toverud* (1949)), and rye flour in much greater quantities, or entirely (*Council of the British Societies for Relief Abroad* (1945)).

Considerable other information on wartime rationing, food supplies and food surveys from other sources has been reviewed (*League of Nations* (1942, 1944, 1946), *Statistisches Jahrbuch der Schweiz* (1947), *Fleisch* (1947), *Rosen* (1947), *Brandt* (1953), *Farnsworth* & *Timoshenko* (1945)). With the exception of Switzerland, the "consumption" data as published in the yearbooks were in good accord with this information. The available food consumption data from Switzerland are not used in this article (for admission data see *Dohan* (1966)) because there is good evidence presented in the publications by *Fleisch* (1947) and by *Rosen* (1947) that the official estimates of bread grain supplies were considerably less than those actually available. See Appendix, Note 1 for details and a discussion of the collection and interpretation of "consumption" data.

In addition to the results presented above, some less complete information is also available on admissions for schizophrenia and wheat "consumption." Denmark experienced a marked reduction in wheat "consumption" during the war (*Iversen* (1948)). The available data (*Svendsen* (1952)) on admissions for schizophrenia (sum of first plus readmissions) also shows a marked decrease. However, the *admission* data extends only through 1944. *Svendsen* (1952) considered the possibility that the introduction of insulin shock therapy might have resulted in longer remissions.

Wheat was reported to have been in abundant supply in Australia during the war (*Crawford et al.* (1954)). The sum of the numbers of men and women admitted for schizophrenia in Western Australia plus New Wales during that period did not decrease (*Dohan* (1966)).

PART 3. ESTIMATED "MORBID RISK" OF DEVELOPING SCHIZOPHRENIA IN VARIOUS CULTURES VERSUS DIETARY INTAKE OF CEREALS

Differences in the prevalence of schizophrenia in various cultures have not been established unequivocally. However, there is a fair amount of evidence indicating that schizophrenia is less likely to occur in some than in others. The problems involved and some of the results achieved have been clearly presented by *Lin & Standley* (1962), *Böök* (1953), *Lin* (1953), and *Lemkau, Tietze & Cooper* (1943). The nature of the problem makes the acquisition of entirely satisfactory evidence a practical impossibility. Nevertheless, it is my belief that examination of these less than perfect data may possibly provide some useful clues concerning the pathogenesis of schizophrenia.

Böök (1953) and *Lemkau* (1943) have presented in table form the results of calculations of the "morbid risk" ("expectancy") of developing schizophrenia as determined from published studies, including their own. The calculations are based on the age distribution of the population at risk and the number and ages of the individuals with past or present illness from schizophrenia discovered within that population.

Table 1 shows these estimates of "morbid risk" of developing schizophrenia and adds an estimate of the "morbid risk" in Taiwan aborigines calculated by me from the data of *Rin & Lin* (1962) and a gross approximation of the "morbid risk" in two non-westernized African populations surveyed by *Carothers* (1948) and *Tooth* (1950). These are compared with the approximate intake of various cereals by the populations at risk.

The technics employed in census surveys, proband and cohort studies, the "correction" for age distribution and the many problems involved in execution and interpretation are briefly outlined in the Appendix, Note 2. The Appendix, Note 2, also supplies details and comments on the studies in Japan, Taiwan, and Africa and gives some reasons why it is probable that *Brugger*'s estimations of the "morbid risk" in several areas of Germany, were considerably too low.

TABLE 1

Estimated "morbid risk" for schizophrenia vs. approximate "consumption" of cereals*)

Reference	Group—Place	Country	"Risk"	Wheat	Rye	Rice	Barley
					kg/caput/yr		
			Europe				
Kaila (1942)	12 % of Fin. Population	Finland	1.18	46	67	4	9
Böök (1953)	Isolate-Finnish Border	Sweden	2.39				
Sjögren (1948)	Island (A:Bo)	Sweden	0.83	58	27	2	5
Sjögren (1935)	Two Isolates North	Sweden	0.87				
Bremer (1951	West Coast	Norway	1.0	70	37	2	5
Strömgren (1938)	Bornholm Island	Denmark	0.65	43	43	2	2
Lemkau (1943)	Swiss-3, German-12	Germany	0.77				
Schade (1950)	Schwalm	Germany	0.52	61	47	3	1
Brugger (1931)	1 Thüringea, 2 Bavaria	Germany	.36–.41[1]	(Prewar—Western Germany)			
			Asia				
Uchimura (1940)	Isolate-Hachijo Island	Japan	0.91				
Akimoto (1942)	Komoro (small town)	Japan	0.50	9	–	135	12
Tsuwaga (1942)	Tokyo	Japan	0.49				
Lin (1953)	3 Chinese towns	Taiwan	0.59	6	–	92	–
Rin & Lin (1962)	Aborigines 4 tribes	Taiwan	(< 0.27[2])	"Sweet potatoes", rice, millet, corn			
			Africa				
Carothers (1948)	Native reserves	Kenya	(< 0.10[3])	Maize major food—rice, small amount			
Tooth (1950)	Native towns in North	Gold Coast	(< 0.21[4])	Millets, sorghums, yams			

*) See text and Appendix, Note 2 for details on sources of data. The morbid risk estimates without parentheses are from the tables, including footnotes, published by *Böök* (1953); *Lemkau* (1943); and *Lin* (1953).

[1]) See Appendix note for reasons why these values are believed to be about one-half or less of the actual morbid risk as indicated by *Brugger's* proband study (1933 b) and other data.

[2]) Estimate made by present author from age and prevalence data in original article (see Appendix, Note 2).

[3]) Crude estimate made by present author from data in original articles plus assumption of age distribution which would favor a high "morbid risk" (see Appendix, Note 2).

The estimates of consumption of various cereals in the European countries, in Japan, and by the Chinese in Taiwan are those reported for the immediate prewar period in the "Food Supply Time Series" published by the Food and Agriculture Organization of the United Nations (*Aykroyd* & *Sukhatme* (1960)). Most of the European and Japanese morbidity studies were made about that time, and the Taiwan studies shortly after the end of World War II. The information on diets of the African populations was obtained from the summary of various reports provided in the Ethnographic Survey of Africa (*Middleton* (1953) and *Manoukian* (1951)) and that on the food habits of the aborigines in Taiwan from a leading surgeon and medical educator practicing in that country (*Hsu* (1964)) and reports of anthropologists (*Hsu* & *Pang* (1957)). Also, see Appendix, Note 2. Estimates of food intake by diet survey (other than a contemporaneous one of the population at risk), commodity utilization study and other technics provide at best an "index of likelihood" that the foods were eaten on the average in approximately the quantities estimated by the various technics (*Bulletin National Research Council* (1949) and *Farnsworth* (1961).

Thus, two imperfect sets of data are compared in Table 1. It shows that, in general, "morbid risk" estimates are highest in Europe where wheat is eaten in relatively large quantities, usually lower in Japan and among the Chinese in Taiwan, where small amounts of wheat and large amounts of rice are eaten, still less among the aborigines of Taiwan, who apparently eat considerably less rice and no wheat; and probably least schizophrenia in Kenya and the Northern Gold Coast (Ghana) where maize or sorghums and yams are the staple foods. There are, of course, many other observed differences in diet as well as in other environmental factors.

The evidence from such a series is certainly no more than suggestive, but it does indicate that schizophrenia is *not* confined to peoples who regularly use wheat as food. However, it also indicates that the "morbid risk" for schizophrenia is apparently 3 times or more as great in populations eating large amounts of wheat as in those eating none. These data would thus suggest that if wheat, in fact, has a causal relationship to schizophrenia, that it is possibly the most noxious member of a hierarchy of potentially noxious substances which probably must be eaten for many years by an individual genetically susceptible to schizophrenia before symptoms appear.

Differences in gene frequency might, of course, account for differences in the estimated "morbid risk" for schizophrenia. However, the great increase in psychoses in association with acculturization of the African (see Appendix, Note 2) suggests this is not a major factor in Africa as does the relatively high incidence of schizophrenia in the non-white population of the United States. The high morbid risk figures for the population studied by *Böök* (1953) in the north of Sweden and the isolate on Hachijo Island in Japan (*Uchi-mura et al.* (1940)) in relation to other studies in the same countries, have been attributed to genetic factors by the investigators.

PART 4. CELIAC DISEASE AND SCHIZOPHRENIA
COMMENTS

Celiac disease has recently been called "gluten enteropathy" since gluten proteins in wheat are involved in the pathogenesis of the disease. It has been the subject of a number of reviews (*Sheehy & Flock* (1964), *Benson, Kowlessar & Sleisenger* (1964) and *Sheldon* (1959)). The term celiac disease will be used for both the childhood and the adult form, which in the past was called non-tropical sprue and, less specifically, the "malabsorbtion syndrome." Patients with the adult form frequently give a history of attacks of classical childhood celiac disease: emotional disturbances, a peculiar diarrhea, and the malabsorbtion syndrome including poor growth.

The epidemiologic and cereal consumption studies were made because of reports that: (1) a history of childhood celiac disease occurs more frequently than would be expected by chance in adults with manifest schizophrenia, (2) psychoses are more frequent in adults with celiac disease than might be expected by chance association, (3) peculiarities of behaviour are a common occurrence in children and adults with celiac disease and behavioral disturbance may be produced by administration of wheat flour and relieved by a "gluten-free" diet, (4) exacerbations of celiac disease often occur in association with psychic stress and acute infections, situations which have been associated by some with exacerbations of schizophrenia.

Graff & Handford (1961) have reported that four (10.8 per cent) of the 37 schizophrenics admitted for the first time during a period of one year to the Institute of the Pennsylvania Hospital had a history of celiac disease in childhood. The childhood period-prevalence of celiac disease in the United States is not known, but undoubtedly the proportion of adults with this history must be far less than 10.8 per cent of the general population. Evidence, other than clinical experience, in support of this is contained in the report by *Black* (1964) that the incidence of celiac disease in Glasgow children varied between about 3 and 8/10,000 live births per year for the period 1941 to 1956 and was even lower in other studies. In further studies confirm the findings of *Graff & Handford*, a genetic relationship of celiac disease and schizophrenia must, among other possibilities, be considered.

Sleisenger (1964) found 3 subjects with schizophrenia among 32 adults with celiac disease. A total of 11 patients exhibited "emotional disturbances," and in 5, the degree of disturbances was serious (*Benson, Kowlessar &*

Sleisenger (1964)). *Bossak, Wang & Adlersberg* (1957) reported that of 94 adults with "idiopathic sprue" (celiac disease), severe mental symptoms occurred in 11 patients. In 5 instances there was "frank psychosis" and the other 6 patients exhibited varying degrees of depression, anxiety or character disorders.

The peculiar behavior of children with celiac disease has been noted by many authors. *Prugh* (1951) stated that such patients appear to be "passive, often withdrawn, definitely inhibited personalities, commonly exhibiting certain aspects of the obsessive-compulsive trends seen in their mothers. Between episodes of illness they were described by their mothers as very good children."

Daynes (1956) has reported instances of naughtiness, depression (and, in some, petit mal-like episodes), as well as somatic symptoms in children, and similar episodes in adults. Symptoms were relieved and then brought on again by ingestion of wheat flour products. He has called this type of episode, which tends to occur after acute infections, the pre-celiac syndrome. The symptoms disappeared after a month or two if left untreated. *Haas* (1951) has also pointed out the high frequency of emotional disturbances in children with celiac disease and the important fact that these symptoms improve before the intestinal symptoms do when treated by proper diet. *Weijers, van de Kamer & Dicke* (1957) have commented: "moreover hypotonia, instability of the autonomic nervous system and disturbed psyche—the typical celiac triad—point much more strongly to a metabolic disorder than to disturbed absorbtion."

The pathogenesis of the behavioral changes is unknown but they are not the result of the major chemical abnormalities associated with severe malabsorbtion. In fact, *Rubin et al.* (1962) have reported mild behavioral changes and return of other celiac symptoms in an adult celiac disease patient (previously on a gluten-free diet) after three or four days of instillation into the ileum of 50 grams of high gluten wheat flour three times per day. In addition, most authors have commented on the tendency for gastrointestinal symptoms to reappear following emotional stress and acute infections, situations, to which some have attributed a precipitating role in the relapse of patients with schizophrenia.

Since celiac disease is employed as a model to help understand the possible relationship of schizophrenia to the ingestion of wheat and other cereals, a short discussion of some of the current knowledge on the clinical relationship of celiac symptoms and cereals is presented below.

There is evidence that celiac disease is an hereditary disease (*Carter, Sheldon & Walker* (1959)). The gluten fraction from wheat flour will produce an attack in susceptible individuals. Apparently considerably less attention has been given to the pathogenic effect of grains other than wheat. However, it appears to be a general practice to advise avoidance of all products of wheat, rye, barley and often buckwheat, but oats, at least in some countries, appear not to be harmful (*Collins & Isselbacher* (1964)). The possible role of rice in peoples who habitually eat large amounts of rice has apparently not been examined. Most, but not all patients, who rigorously follow a "gluten-free" diet have a remission of symptoms within a few days, weeks, or months, but as long as two years may be needed (*Benson et al.* (1964)). When wheat is again eaten, symptoms may not reoccur, may return within a few days, or not until after some 3 to 6 weeks, and, under some circumstances, may be brought on by "traces" of wheat (*Sheldon* (1956) and *Weijers et al.* (1957)). It seems that duration of a gluten-free diet before refeeding may be an important determinant of the response.

Since it also appears to be recognized that some patients with celiac disease do not improve on a gluten-free diet until milk (*Sewell et al.* (1963)) is also removed from the diet, and it appears probable that there may be a hierarchy of pathogenicity of the various cereals in celiac disease, the suggestion of *Weijers* and his colleagues (1957) that the pathogenic substance may be found in a variety of proteins in varying amounts continues to deserve investigation.

The varied immunologic reactions (not discussed here), the variation in time of recovery on a "gluten-free" diet, and the variation in time required to produce a relapse by return to a normal diet, noted above, plus the spontaneous improvement which may occur despite the continuation of a gluten containing diet, and the ability of many celiac patients to remain asymptomatic on a gluten containing diet after a period on a "gluten-free" diet and the reports that "traces" may cause symptoms (*Sheldon* (1959), and others) all suggest some peculiar interaction of the protein pathogen (or its products) and the host reminiscent of immunologic disorders.

If, in fact, the symptoms of schizophrenia are in some fashion due to an immunologic reaction to ingested wheat (and to a lesser degree to other cereals), the brief outline above of the vagaries of the time and dose relationships of cereals to celiac disease should alert us not to expect dramatic and immediate responses to a "gluten-free" diet, and also to the necessity of eliminating all traces of possible pathogenic proteins in testing this hypothesis in patients with a relapse or an acute initial attack of schizophrenia.

DISCUSSION

The epidemiologic data presented above lend some support to the hypothesis that the kinds and quantities of cereals usually eaten may play a role in the pathogenesis of symptoms in those with the genotype for schizophrenia. This hypothesis may be schematically presented as follows:

Genotype for schizophrenia + (cereals × Pc × time) → Phenotype

Pc = pathogenicity factor—wheat highest, millets and sorghums low?

The types of supporting evidence may be briefly summarized as follows:

1. A positive inter- and intra-country correlation of wheat "consumption" and admissions for schizophrenia in 5 countries during World War II.

2. In general, estimates of the "morbid risk" for schizophrenia are the lowest where little rice and no wheat are eaten; in the middle range in populations consuming large amounts of rice and relatively small amounts of wheat; and the highest in wheat (or wheat plus rye) eating countries.

3. A history of childhood celiac disease in those with schizophrenia and the occurrence of schizophrenia in those with adult celiac disease appear to be

far greater than expected by chance alone. Celiac disease is made symptomatic by eating wheat and certain other cereals through mechanisms which may have an immunologic and genetic basis.

There also are a number of descriptive reports of change in the apparent frequency of schizophrenia which are found to be associated with restrictions in diet (*Dohan* (1966)). In addition, there is apparently agreement (*Murphy* (1961)) that there is an increase in incidence of psychoses in non-western peoples during acculturization to Western civilization (see Appendix, Note 2), a process which is frequently associated with adoption of western food habits including white bread as demonstrated by *Poleman* (1961) in Ghana.

There are also reports suggesting more rapid recovery from schizophrenia when wheat ingestion decreased (Sweden and Norway during World War II (*Dohan* (1966)), two Europeans in a Japanese prison camp, reported by *Poynton* (1947) or was not eaten (Taiwan aborigines, reported by *Rin & Lin* (1962)).

Some of the problems in collection and interpretation of the data which support the hypothesis have been discussed above and in the appropriate sections in Results and in the Appendix. In this portion of the paper I shall briefly outline some of the current information which does *not* support the hypothesis.

1. The estimates of "morbid risk" for schizophrenia in the 5 European countries (Table 1) do not show a good correlation with the "consumption" of wheat in kg/caput/yr or of wheat plus rye, even if the high morbid risk of 2.39 per cent in the population studied by *Böök* is considered to be due to genetic factors and the German "morbid risk" is considered as 0.77 per cent. However, the grossness of the "morbid risk" estimates and the varying pattern in quantities of wheat consumed in various sections of the countries (of Germany in particular) make meaningful comparisons of these incomplete data almost impossible as does the possibility that rye may also be pathogenic, but considerably less so than wheat. (See Results, Part 2.)

2. The low "morbid risk" estimates as calculated from the apparent prevalence in Kenya and the Gold Coast (Table 1) were associated with a lesser frequency of other psychoses. This phenomenon has often been attributed in various studies to a low rate of discovery of or hospitalization of psychotic individuals. The outstanding studies of Lin (1962) on the Taiwan Chinese and aborigines do, however, demonstrate a low prevalence rate for schizophrenia not associated with a low rate for psychoses in general.

4. The annual consumption of wheat flour in the United States is reported by *Trulson* (1959) to have decreased from a "consumption" of 97 kg/caput/yr in 1910 to about 56 kg/caput/yr in 1955, yet there appears to be no evidence indicating a considerable decrease in the annual incidence of schizophrenia, and in fact, *Malzberg* (1955) reported that it may have increased.

If the epidemiologic evidence is accepted at face value, one must consider the possibilities that the reponse of the genotype population is near maximum, at or below the 1955 levels of wheat flour consumption; that other pathogenic factors or gene density may have increased; or that the ingestion of wheat has no effect. However, the long term trend in nosocomial and threshold factors affecting indices of frequency of schizophrenia must also be considered. It may be fruitful to examine wheat "consumption" data and the age specific rates for new cases of schizophrenia in those countries with good statistical records. Comparison of the mean age specific rates with mean consumption data for various foods by 2 or 3 year periods over 30 years and the degree of co-variation of the deviations of such data from the long term trend line for each variable may help determine if a relationship exists.

4. Although there was a good positive correlation between changes in admissions for schizophrenia and changes in wheat "consumption" three obvious possibilities and their combinations must be considered: hypothesis 1— the variables are completely unrelated and the positive correlation was due to chance alone; hypothesis 2—the co-variation of the two variables is not due to one causing the changes in the other, but is due to an immediate or remote common cause or set of causes affecting both; hypothesis 3—the variables are causally related. The high correlation ($r = 0.908$, 7 d. f. $P <$ 0.01) between the per cent change in admissions and in wheat "consumption" (Fig. 7) indicates that the co-variation is not likely to be due to chance alone so we should therefore tentatively reject hypothesis 1 above and assume that there may be a common cause or set of causes of the changes in both variables (hypothesis 2) or a direct causal relationship (hypothesis 3).

In regard to the "common factor hypothesis," evidence has been presented in a previous publication (1966) that the nosocomial and threshold factors, war status of the country and the increased availability of employment during war were apparently not the cause or causes of the changes in admissions for schizophrenia in these countries. On the other hand, many changes in food consumption other than those of wheat and rye also occurred. Between country comparisons suggest such changes were not primarily responsible for the changes in admissions. For example, meat consumption was decreased during much of the war period in the 3 Scandinavian countries but increased an average of 10 per cent in Canada during the first 3 years of the war, the period during which first admissions and wheat consumption decreased in Canada (C_1—Fig. 7). Consumption of fats and oils also decreased in the 3 Scandinavian countries but increased about 7 per cent during the first 3 year period in Canada. Similar inter-country disparities apparently occurred in the consumption of eggs, milk, cheese and fish as judged by the data available (usually on production) in the statistical yearbooks and on "consumption" in the U. S. Department of Agriculture publication (1946.).

Cereals and Schizophrenia

Thus the changes in "consumption" of the other major foodstuffs, at least as judged by these criteria, appear not to correlate with the change in admissions when an inter-country comparison is made.

If one examines the obvious major causes for the decreased "consumption" of wheat, it appears that the decreases in the Scandinavian countries were primarily due to the wartime conditions which interferred with shipping so that it was not possible to import adequate amounts of supplementary wheat supplies (particularly in Norway and Finland) as well as decreased harvests (particularly in Sweden). Sweden was almost "self-sufficient" in regards to wheat in the decade prior to World War II and Norway depended heavily on imports.

It is difficult, even on a theoretical basis, to relate some recognized or unrecognized "set of war conditions" which caused a decrease in shipments (Norway and Finland) and in harvests (Sweden) of wheat, and independently and contemporaneously caused proportionately as great decreases in admissions for schizophrenia because: (1) a decrease in admissions for schizophrenia and a decrease in consumption of wheat occurred in combatant Canada and in neutral Sweden, as well as in German-occupied Norway and in Finland fighting on home soil, (2) the decreases commenced and ended at different times in Sweden and adjacent Finland, (3) both admissions and wheat consumption increased in the United States (also a combatant nation) which borders on Canada.

It also seems unlikely that the common factor is weather or climate, which affect the growth of wheat, and "might" also affect the incidence of schizophrenia. This possibility appears to be remote because of the differences in time of onset of the decreases in admissions and return to prewar values in adjacent Sweden and Finland, and for many other reasons.

Therefore, my conclusions are: (1) that the positive correlation between the changes in admissions for schizophrenia and the changes in "consumption" of wheat is probably due to a causal relationship, and (2) that the probability is sufficient great to justify careful and extensive studies of the effects of diet on the behaviour of acute or acutely relapsed schizophrenics. The complete and possibly prolonged omission of all foods which have been reported to produce symptoms in patients with celiac disease would seem advisable as would the subsequent refeeding of the major cereals customarily eaten by the patients.

SUMMARY

It is believed that sufficient evidence exists to suspect that some cereals, and possibly other foods, may play a role in the production of symptoms in those with the genotype for schizophrenia. This hypothesis is based on the following facts:

1. There is a good inter-country correlation between the per cent change from the prewar mean in the number of admissions of women with schizophrenia during World War II and the per cent change from the prewar mean in the published values for wheat "consumption" (r = 0.908, 7 d. f., P < 0.01.

2. The changes in the annual "consumption" of wheat within each of these countries exhibited a fairly good temporal and proportional relationship to changes in the annual number of women admitted with schizophrenia in each of these countries during World War II.

3. In general, the published estimates of prevalence, and of the "morbid risk," of developing schizophrenia are highest—in populations which eat large amounts of wheat (Europe); in the middle range—in populations eating relatively little wheat and large amounts of rice (Japan, Taiwan Chinese); quite low in a population whose staple foods are primarily sweet potatoes, millet, corn and some rice (Taiwan aborigines); and may possibly be even lower in two populations of non-westernized Africans whose staple foodstuffs were maize or millets and sorghums.

4. Celiac disease, a disorder made symptomatic by the ingestion of wheat and certain other cereals, has been reported to be associated with a high frequency of schizophrenia and emotional disorders and to have been experienced in childhood by an unusually high proportion of those with schizophrenia.

The hypothesis is one that may be tested. It is suggested that those with an initial attack of schizophrenia or an acute relapse from a relatively normal state be the subjects of such trials. Absolutely complete and continuous omission of all of those substances which have been reported to produce symptoms in patients with celiac disease would seem advisable as would the refeeding of such substances if substantial improvement in unbiased psychiatric ratings of the patients occurs. The vagaries in time and intensity of the response of the patient with celiac disease to a "gluten-free" diet and refeeding of wheat and the reported effect of "traces" may serve as a model in planning and interpreting similar observations in patients with schizophrenia.

APPENDIX—NOTE 1

A. *Estimation of Actual Intake of Specific Foods Before, During and After World War II.*

The actual mean annual consumption of specific foodstuffs by various large segments of the population has probably never been determined with a high degree of specificity and accuracy. Approximate estimates may be made in several ways (*Bulletin National Research* Council (1949)).

1. *Survey of "Small Samples"*

Fairly accurate estimates of the actual food intake of small, presumably representative samples of a population may be made at representative times by a variety of technics, (e.g. food diary, household purchases, etc.). Such studies have the advantages of relative accuracy and time specificity but may be unrepresentative, reflect local conditions (e.g. rural villages near primary producers of some foodstuffs and possibly distant from the sources of fish) and require the execution of special projects, which seem to have been largely neglected in wartime. The excellent wartime small sample studies of *Ström* (1948) in Oslo, and *Boalt* & *Zotterman* (1943) in Sweden and those in Switzerland discussed by *Fleisch* (1947) are exceptions but have the limitations of restricted locale and time.

2. Food Supply Balance Calculations

If quantitative annual information is available on total population and on production, imports, exports, waste, net changes in storage and non-food uses (e.g. animal feed, seed, etc.) of specific foodstuffs, a gross approximation of the "consumption"/person/year may be obtained. Besides the inaccuracies inherent in the collection of such information (e.g. unreported consumption by farm families), a sizeable error may occur if such consumption data are considered an accurate estimate of food eaten because of lack of knowledge of changes in storage of foods ready for purchase at the ultimate consumer level. Thus, grain storage data may be available but relatively little may be known of storage of flour at the wholesale, retail or consumer levels. The problems of estimating food intake from calculations of "consumption" obtained from food balance studies have been clearly discussed by *Farnsworth* (1961).

The published "consumption" data for the United States and Canada were estimated from trade data indicating supply at the retail level (*United States Department of Agriculture* (1946)). The report stated: "In interpreting the supply picture as shown by the statistics at the retail level, it must be borne in mind that there is always a considerable margin between the supplies of food available and the actual consumption of food. This margin, which is not taken into account in this study, includes losses in preparation, cooking and on the table." The consumption data for the Scandinavian countries were based on less complete balance information. "Consumption" in the case of grain in the Scandinavian countries has been estimated from data on harvests, imports, exports and seed use and reported in the Statistical Yearbooks of Norway, Sweden and Finland.

Other sources of "consumption" data based on national records are available for pre- and postwar years (but not for the war years) in publications of the Food and Agriculture Organization of the United Nations, and various publications of the United States Department of Agriculture (unlisted references).

3. Legal Ration Allowances

All of the six countries rationed some foods. Food limitation was most severe in Finland, apparently somewhat less in Norway, moderate in Switzerland and Sweden and relatively slight in Canada and the United States. A report from the *League of Nations* (1946) summarized the legal rations by quarters and the general information on available food supply in European countries during World War II. Two earlier publications (*League of Nations* (1942, 1944)) provide additional information.

The excellent report of *Roine* (1948) summarizes on an annual basis the daily rations of the most important foodstuffs "distributed to the consumers during the years 1941–46 in Finland." *Fleisch* (1947) provided a monograph detailing the food supply, legal rations and food studies made in Switzerland during World War II.

4. Miscellaneous Sources of Information

The Food Research Institute of Stanford University has issued comprehensive monographs on food production and supply, with some comments on human consumption. These include monographs on wartime food in Switzerland by *Rosen* (1947), the countries of Europe under German occupation or control, Norway and Finland, plus others by *Brandt* (1953), and comments in "World Grain Review and Outlook 1945" by *Farnsworth* and *Timoshenko* (1945) on grain supplies and probable "consumption".

The "consumption" data for wheat and rye used in this report were those published in the Statistical Yearbooks of Norway, Sweden and Finland. These reported data have been cross checked with the information provided by the League of Nations publications, the publications of the Food Research Institute and other sources noted above. However, it is again emphasized that "consumption" data from such calculations are approximate estimates and that stocks of food ready for consumption may be carried over into the following years, yet reported as "consumption" (e. g. flour milled in 1944 and considered "consumed" in that year may be sold to the housewife and eaten in 1945).

B. *Food Consumption in Switzerland During World War II*

Estimates of food "consumption" in Switzerland during World War II have not been used in this report because of considerable evidence that actual consumption of bread was considerably greater than "consumption" estimated from production and import data. No adjustment were made in the *Statistisches Jahrbuch* reports on bread grains for changes in stocks. *Rosen* (1947) estimated that "on September 1, 1939 the total supplies in all positions were almost certainly sufficient to cover the countries estimated 'bread grain' requirements for a full year or longer". Over 90 per cent of "bread grain" was wheat in the prewar period (*Aykroyd & Sukhatme* (1960)).

It appears probable that a gradual release of stocks on hand may have occurred (as well as increased extraction ratios of grain, yielding up to about 25 per cent more flour per kilogram of grain and, additions of potatoes and non-wheat grains to bread flour). This supposition is supported by calculations from the report in the 1957 *Statistisches Jahrbuch* (pp. 368, 369) which demonstrate that the consumption of bread in 1943, the only year reported, was 11.7 per cent greater in "workers families" and 19.8 per cent greater in "employees families" than before the war. In addition, the official bread rations indicate a bread consumption of up to 26 per cent above prewar intake. Further evidence, that flour supplies were larger than "apparent consumption" calculations would indicate, is presented in the monographs by *Rosen* (1947) and that by *Fleisch* (1947).

APPENDIX—NOTE 2: "MORBID RISK" AND DIET

Estimates of the prevalence of individuals who have, or have had, a "specific" mental disease have been made by (1) census surveys seeking evidence of present and past disorders, (2) cohort studies (histories of individuals starting with a random sample of those born in particular years), (3) proband studies (histories of a group of individuals supposedly chosen at random and of their relatives within defined limits).

"Corrections" are made (as described below) from the age distribution of the population at risk. In this fashion an estimate is provided of the probability of an individual experiencing a specific psychosis if he lives through the "risk period" for that particular disorder. This probability has been variously termed the "morbid risk", "lifetime prevalence", "lifetime expectancy" and "expectancy". *Böök* (1953) and *Lin* (1953) and, for an earlier period, *Lemkau* (1943) have summarized much of the literature on the subject. The values provided in their publications are employed in this paper, including corrections indicated in their footnotes.

COMMENT

Obviously, the age distribution of the population at risk will, in part, determine the crude rates developed from incidence and prevalence data. Corrections for differences in age distribution, or calculation of rates for specific age groups must be made in order to permit intergroup comparisons. Various formulae have been employed to "correct" for variations in the age distribution of the populations studied. *Böök* (1953), *Lin* (1953) and *Lemkau* (1943) employed Weinberg's abridged formula for this purpose. It may be expressed as follows:

$$\text{"Morbid Risk"} = \frac{N}{A + 0.5\,B} \times 100$$

A = Total number of population beyond maximum age susceptibility
B = Those in age period of susceptibility
N = Number of individuals with disease plus those who have had one or more attacks in the past.

The "age period of susceptibility" to schizophrenia has been considered as 15 to 45 years in some studies, and lesser intervals in others, but *Böök* (1953) considers the differences "not important" for purposes of comparison.

The proband technic has also been extensively employed, particularly in Europe. This entails the random selection of an appropriate number of "probands" who are *not* known to have mental disease (e. g. husband and wife in every eighth house in a particular region). The probands and their relatives within a certain range of consanguinity are then investigated to determine the number who are psychotic or who have had a psychotic episode. The "morbid risk" can then be determined from the number of identified cases and the number and age distribution of the population at risk. Cohort studies (i. e. detailed history of a random sample of individuals born in a particular year or years) have also been used. Data from such studies bearing on "the morbid risk" for schizophrenia are also presented in Table 1 (*Lemkau* (1953)) and the footnotes (*Brugger* (1933 b)) to it.

Probably the most important sources of error of all these technics are (1) the thoroughness and accuracy of the empiric observations, (2) size of samples and (3) failure to include "recovered" cases in the original count.

European Data

Brugger's census studies in Thuringia (1931), the Allgäu (1933 a) and Rosenheim, Germany (1938), by the *census* technic provided estimates that were from one-half to one-quarter of those he made by the *proband* technic in the Allgäu (1933 a). Since *Brugger*'s census studies gave results so much lower than his own proband study and those of other investigators in Germany (*Lemkau* (1943)), I believe they are not representative of the general experience in that country at that time, and therefore, are not used in the discussion of the possible relationship of food to schizophrenia. *Kaila* (1942) has stated (and I agree) that it is difficult to be certain if *Brugger* actually included those with a history of a past attack of schizophrenia in his final count (even though he included such a classification on his summary cards). *Lemkau* has also discussed some of the problems in *Brugger*'s pioneering studies.

Japan

Estimates of "morbid risk" for schizophrenia were made by various Japanese investigators during 1940–41 in Tokyo (*Tsuwaga* (1942)), Komoro, a small town (*Akimoto* (1942)) and in rural Hachijo Island (*Uchimura* (1940)), which is part of the Tokyo prefecture. The last is of particular interest. The expectancy rate for schizophrenia of the 8,330 individuals surveyed on Hachijo Island was calculated to be 9.1/1,000 compared to 5.0/1,000 for Komoro, and 4.9/1,000 for Tokyo. The Island remained relatively isolated until after World War II. The high expectancy rate of 9.1/1,000 was considered to be on a genetic basis.

Taiwan

The two studies of *Lin* supply some of the best available evidence supporting the thesis that the age corrected true prevalence (and "morbid risk") of schizophrenia are not the same in various cultures. *Lin* has made outstanding studies of samples of the Chinese (1953) and aborigines (*Rin & Lin* (1962)) in Taiwan. His studies showed a significantly lower prevalence (p < .01) of schizophrenia among the aborigines compared with the Chinese sample (Table 1). I have made an estimate by Weinberg's technic of the "morbid risk for schizophrenia" from the information on prevalence and age in his article and used this estimate in Table 1.

The relatively short duration of those cases of schizophrenia which had developed among the aborigines is of considerable interest. Among the 11.442 individuals, 10 had schizophrenia either before or during the study years, 1949–1952. Of these, two became inactive within three months of onset of symptoms; one within one year; three during the second year, and two had lasted more than two years. Only one showed signs of deterioration. The other two schizophrenics had had symptoms for only three months at the time of the study. *Rin & Lin* wrote: "The fact that the schizophrenic reaction differed little from the other types of psychoses in respect of duration and outcome, deserves attention. If left alone untreated in the aborigine communities, a large proportion of schizophrenic cases recovered within two years. Though small in sample, such a picture of spontaneous recovery was as good as, if not better, than most reports of the outcome of schizophrenia using modern treatments."

These findings: the very low calculated expectancy rate and the benign course of schizophrenia (relative to schizophrenia in the western world) may be compared with the marked differences in diets. The diet of the aborigines has been described as follows by *Hsu* (1964), a surgeon and medical educator, a native of Taiwan: 'The aborigines grow mainly sweet potato, millet and upland rice. They do not grow wheat, take no food made from wheat and drink no milk. Their major food is sweet potato instead of rice. They procure very little from outside and are, generally self-sufficient." Anthropologists have reported essentially the same information *Hsu & Pang* (1957). The information on the main foods other than meat and fish of the 4 tribes of aborigines as kindly translated from the Chinese by Wen-lang Li is as follows: Taval tribe—rice, sweet potato and corn; Saisiat tribe—rice, corn; Paiwan tribe— rice (20 per cent), taro (20 per cent), millet (20 per cent), sweet potato (40 per cent); Ami tribe—rice (50 per cent), millet (20 per cent), sweet potato (30 per cent).

African Studies

Apparently only two fairly systematic studies of the prevalence of psychoses among African natives living more or less in their tribal state have been published. Modified census-type surveys were made in Kenya by *Carothers* (1948) and in the northern Gold Coast (Ghana) by *Tooth* (1950). Both studies indicated the point prevalence of active cases of psychoses to be far less then values reported for western countries.

Kenya

Carothers (1948) made a survey of three native reserves in Kenya. Among a total population of 616,000 natives, 205 psychotic individuals were found living in the reserves, and 25 from the reserves were in the only mental hospital in Kenya. Thus, the point prevalence rate for psychoses was 37/100,000, about one-tenth (or less) of that in western nations. No specific diagnoses were given.

This exceptionally low point prevalence might be due to failure to recognize and count all the psychotic individuals. The study was begun by enlisting the help of the District Commissioners and Chiefs in the reserves. All the local chiefs were required to make a census of the insane in the location. The failure to count a person recognized by the chief as psychotic seems unlikely, since there was a head tax from which "the infirm may be exempt", thus "a census of the insane might well give rise to opportunities for tax reduction". As to the detection of the insane by the

Cereals and Schizophrenia   **419**

African, *Carothers* wrote: "There is no reason to believe that mentally deranged persons are more likely to pass unnoticed in Kenya than elsewhere."

The past occurrence and point prevalence of schizophrenia and the age distribution of the population at risk were not determined as such in the survey. However, *Carothers* reported that 28.6 per cent of admissions to the only mental hospital in Kenya during a 5 year period (1939–1943) were diagnosed as schizophrenia, a proportion similar to that in European experience. The annual rate of all admissions of all types was 3.4/100,000, a figure about one-tenth to one-thirtieth of *first* admissions rates in western countries. This low figure is undoubtedly in part due to threshold and nosocomial factors, as well as the very low admission rate for psychoses of ageing.

If one assumes that about 50 per cent of the 228 psychotic individuals found in the point prevalence study of 616,000 surveyed in the native reserves had schizophrenia and that 50 per cent of the active and inactive schizophrenics actually present had recovered or were so mild as to be undetected, one arrives at an estimate of 228 individuals who "had" active or remitted schizophrenia. Assuming the age distribution was similar to that of India in 1931, about 32 per cent of the population at risk had not yet reached the "risk period for schizophrenia" (15–45 years), and about 13 per cent were older than age 45, one can estimate that the probable morbid risk for schizophrenia was 0.09 per cent, as calculated by Weinberg's abridged formula. The assumptions above probably erred considerably in a direction which would increase the estimated risk. This rough estimate is used in Table 1.

Carothers also reported a relationship of the incidence of admissions to the mental hospital and detribalization. The "mean" certification rates/100,000/year to the mental hospital were reported by *Carothers* to be: 2.3 for Africans living in reserves; 2.5 for African living in native fashion as "squatters" on "estates"; and 13.3 for detribalized Africans, employed or living away from home.

The author emphasized that the psychotic squatter was more likely to be certified as insane than the native in a reserve since "he is not likely to be tolerated for long by the European residents on the estate (farm) yet the rates are essentially the same." The group with the highest rate was the detribalized group. Most of this group were men within the age range most susceptible to schizophrenia (15–45) and a higher rate of psychoses would be expected on this basis alone (in a population with a small proportion of individuals in the senile and arteriosclerotic age groups). Nevertheless, the fact that the certification rate of the "squatters" was 19 per cent of that for the "detribalized" group suggest (in association with the comment on certification of squatters) that the partial acquisition of European culture may have increased the likelihood of developing a psychoses. African natives in contact with Europeans tend to adopt some of their food habits as well as other aspects of the culture. The eating of bread has been shown to increase with income in several African groups (*Poleman* (1961)). Many authors have commented on the apparent increase in prevalence of psychoses in the non-western man undergoing acculturization to western societies (*Murphy* (1961)).

Quantitative information on the actual food intake of the natives included in the survey by *Carothers* is apparently not available. However, about 70 per cent of the Africans in Kenya are Bantus, of which about one-half belong to the Kikuyu tribes. 'n the Ethnographic Survey of African, East Central African, Part V, *Middleton* (1953) reported as follows: "In the past the main crops of the Kikuyu were sorghum vulgare, various millets and perhaps beans and sweet potatoes. Today maize is by far the most important crop both for subsistence and for sale. Other crops grown are pigeon pea, European potatoes, manioc (cassava), bananas, sugar cane, arum lily and various fruits ..." "Among the Northern tribes the staple crops were, and to a great extent still are, millets and black and tree beans. Supplementary foods are maize, yams, bananas, sweet potatoes, manioc, sugar cane and many kinds of peas and beans."

Gold Coast

Tooth (1950) studied four areas in the northern territories of the Gold Coast (now Ghana) in 1948. The study was done by a modified census technic with the help of chiefs, subchiefs and census enumerators. A total of 160 insane individuals were found among 166,269 natives; thus the point prevalence was 96/100,000. Of these, *Tooth* personally examined 99.

In another table, *Tooth* summarized the diagnoses established on examining 88 psychotic individuals in the north and 60 in the south. In the northern sample there were 9 schizophrenics among 88 psychotics and in the southern sample, there were 24 schizophrenics among 60 psychotic individuals. This difference is of interest because the southern portion of the Gold Coast at that time was much more westernized than the relatively remote northern regions and presumably western type foods were more available in the south.

From personal observation, it can be stated that the men in this part of Africa had considerably greater contact with European culture (and presumably with western foods) than the women. The male to female ratio in *Tooth*'s combined north and south series was 5.6 to 1 for cases diagnosed as schizophrenia, compared to 1.8 to 1.6 for organic psychosis, 1.5 to 1 for delusional state, and 1 to 1.6 for affective psychoses.

In the northern territories of the Gold Coast, the chief foods were millets and sorghum, and in the southeastern portion of this section, yams and maize were also eaten (*Manoukian* (1961)). Perhaps the outstanding feature of the southern Gold Coast was its contact, chiefly in the larger towns and cities, with European culture.

In the northern sample, those diagnosed as suffering from schizophrenia composed 10 per cent of the psychotics compared to 41 per cent of the psychotics in the southern Gold Coast. However, the diagnosis of delusional state was also used. The sum of those diagnosed as delusional state plus the schizophrenics, was 46 per cent of the psychotics in the north and 52 per cent in the south.

In estimating the "morbid risk" I have made the following assumption: (1) that the age distribution of the population at risk was similar to that of India in 1931; (2) that all of the psychotics diagnosed as "delusional" were schizophrenics; and (3) that only 50 per cent of those who had or had had an attack of schizophrenia, as so defined, were discovered. Using these assumptions and Weinberg's abridged formula, the "morbid risk" was calculated to be 0.21 per cent. I believe all the assumptions erred in the same direction, so that the "morbid risk" is considerably overestimated. If calculations are made on the basis of those diagnosed schizophrenia, the estimate of the "morbid risk" is 0.05 per cent.

ACKNOWLEDGEMENTS

This work was supported in part by General Research Support Grant 1801-FR-05415-01 from the U. S. Public Health Service to the University of Pennsylvania, School of Medicine.

Grateful acknowledgement was made in the previous article of the invaluable help of many individuals in obtaining data used in this and the previous article (1966). In addition, I wish to express gratitude to Professor *Johannes Ipsen*, Professor of Medical Statistics, School of Medicine, University of Pennsylvania, who kindly performed the statistical analyses presented in Part 2 of this article.

REFERENCES

Akimoto, H. (1942): Demographische und psychiatrische Untersuchung der abgegrenzten Kleinstadtbevölkerung. Psychiat. Neurol. Jap. 47, 351–374. Cited by Lin 1953.

Aykroyd, W. R., & *P. V. Sukhatme* (1960): Food Supply, Time Series. Food and Agriculture Organization of the United Nations, Rome.

Benson, G. D., O. D. Kowlessar & M. H. Sleisenger (1964): Adult Celiac Disease with Emphasis upon Response to the Gluten-Free Diet. Medicine *43*, 1–40.

Bergström, S. (1964): Department of Nutrition and Food Hygiene, National Institute of Public Health, Stockholm. Personal Communication.

Black, J. A. (1964): Possible Factors in the Incidence of Coeliac Disease. Acta paediat. (Stockh.) *53*, 109–116.

Boalt, C., & Y. Zotterman (1943): Rations and Food Consumption in Sweden During 1942–43. Nature (Lond.) *152*, 635–636.

Böök, J. A. (1953): A Genetic and Neuropsychiatric Investigation of a North-Swedish Population. Acta genet. (Basel) *4*, 1–100, 133–139, 345–394.

Bossak, E. T., C. I. Wang & D. I. Adlersberg (1957): Clinical Aspects of the Malabsorption Syndrome (Idiopathic Sprue), in: Malabsorption Syndrome, Ed. D. I. Adlersberg, New York.

Brandt, K. (1953): Management of Agriculture and Food in the German-occupied and Other Areas of Fortress Europe. Stanford University Press, Stanford.

Bremer, J. (1951): A Social Psychiatric Investigation of a Small Community in Northern Norway. Acta psychiat. scand. suppl. *62*, 1–166.

Brugger, C. (1938): Psychiatrische Bestandesaufnahme im Gebiet eines medizinisch-anthropologischen Zensus in der Nähe von Rosenheim. Z. ges. Neurol. Psychiat. *106*, 189–207.

Brugger, C. (1933 a): Psychiatrische Ergebnisse einer medizinischen, anthropologischen und soziologischen Bevölkerungsuntersuchung. Z. ges. Neurol. Psychiat. *146*, 489–524.

Brugger, C. (1933 b): Psychiatrische-genealogische Untersuchungen an einer Allgäuer Landbevölkerung in Gebiet eines psychiatrischen Zensus. Z. ges. Neurol. Psychiat. *145*, 516–540.

Brugger, C. (1931): Versuch einer Geisteskrankenzählung in Thüringen. Z. ges. Neurol. Psychiat. *133*, 352–390.

Carothers, J. C. (1948): A Study of Mental Derangement in Africans. Psychiatry *11*, 47–86.

Carter, C., W. Sheldon & C. Walker (1959): Inheritance of Coeliac Disease. Ann. hum. Genet. *23*, 266–278.

Collins, J. R., & K. J. Isselbacher (1964): Treatment of Adult Celiac Disease (Nontropical Sprue). New Engl. J. Med. *271*, 1153–1156.

Crawford, J. J., C. M. Donald, C. P. Dowsett, D. B. Williams & A. A. Ross (1954) Wartime Agriculture in Australia and New Zealand, 1939–50. Stanford University Press, Stanford.

Daynes, G. (1956): Bread and Tears—Naughtiness, Depression and Fits Due to Wheat Sensitivity. Proc. roy. Soc. Med. *49*, 391–394.

Dohan, F. C.(1966): Wartime Changes in Hospital Admissions for Schizophrenia. A Comparison of Admissions for Schizophrenia and Other Psychoses in Six Countries During World War II. Reference Acta psychiat. scand. *42*, 1–23.

Farnsworth, H. C. (1061): Defects, Uses and Abuses of National Food Supply and Consumption Data. Stanford University Food Research Institute Studies *2*, *179*–201.

Farnsworth, H. C., & V. P. Timoshenko (1945): World Grain Review and Outlook, 1945. Stanford University Press, Stanford.

Fleisch, A. (1947): Ernährungsprobleme in Mangelzeiten. Schwabe Verlag, Basel.

Graff, H., & A. Handford (1961): Celiac Syndrome in the Case Histories of Five Schizophrenics. Psychiat. Quart. *35*, 306–313.

Hass, S. V., & M. P. Haas (1951): Management of Celiac Disease. J. B. Lippincott Company, Philadelphia.

Hsu, C-t. (1964): Taipei Medical College, Taipei. Personal Communication.

Hsu, T-w., & K-t Pang (1957): Taiwan Today *1*, 86–88 (In Chinese).

Iversen, K. (1948): Temporary Rise in the Frequency of Thyrotoxicosis in Denmark, 1941–1945, Rosenkilde & Bagger.

Kaila, M. (1942): Über die Durchschnittshäufigkeit der Geisteskrankheiten und des Scwachsinns in Finnland. Acta psychiat. scand. 17, 47–67.

Lemkau, P. V., C. Tietze & M. Cooper (1943): A Survey of Statistical Studies on the Prevalence and Incidence of Mental Disorders in Sample Populations. Publ. Hlth. Rep. 58, 1909–1927.

Lin, T-y. (1953): A Study of the Incidence of Mental Disorder in Chinese and Other Cultures. Psychiatry 16, 313–336.

Lin, T-y., & C. C. Standley (1962): The Scope of Epidemiology in Psychiatry. Wld. Hlth. Org. Publ. Hlth. Pap. 16.

Malzberg, B. (1955): Trends of Mental Disease in New York State 1920–1950. Proc. Amer. philos. Soc. 99, 174–183.

Manoukian, M. (1951): Tribes of the Northern Territories of the Gold Coast, in: Ed., D. Forde, Part V in the Ethnographic Survey of Africa, Western Africa, International African Institute, London.

Middleton, J. (1953): The Central Tribes of the North-Eastern Bantu, in Ed., D. Forde, Part V in the Ethnographic Survey of Africa, East-Central Africa, International African Institute, London.

Murphy, H. B. M. (1961): Social Change and Mental Health, in: Causes of Mental Disorders. A Review of Epidemiological Knowledge. Milbank Memorial Fund. New York, 280–329.

Ödegård, Ö. (1954): The Incidence of Mental Diseases in Norway During World War II. Acta psychiat. scand. 29, 333–353.

Poleman, T. T. (1961): The Food Economics of Urban Middle Africa—The Case of Ghana. Stanford University Food Research Institute Studies 2, 121–174.

Poynton, O. (1947): Some Observations on the Psychological and Psychiatric Problems Encountered in a Singapore Prison Camp. Med. J. Aust. 2, 509–511.

Prugh, D. G. (1951): A Preliminary Report on the Role of Emotional Factors in Idiopathic Celiac Disease. Psychosom. Med. 13, 220–241.

Pugh, T. F., & B. MacMahon (1962): Epidemiologic Findings in United States Mental Hospital Data. Little, Brown Company, Boston.

Rin, H., & T-y Lin (1962): Mental Illness Among Formosan Aborigines as Compared with the Chinese in Taiwan. J. ment. Sci. 108, 134–146.

Roine, P. (1948): The Amounts and Adequacy of Food Rations in Finland During 1941–1946. Maataloustieteellinen Aikakauskirja, 20, 1–30.

Rosen, J. (1947): Wartime Food Developments in Switzerland, War–Peace Pamphlet No. 9. Stanford University Press, Stanford.

Rubin, C. E., L. L. Brandborg, A. L. Flick, P. Phelps, C. Parmentier & S. van Niel (1962): Studies of Celiac Sprue. III. The Effect of Repeated Wheat Instillation into the Proximal Ileum of Patients on a Gluten Free Diet. Gastroenterology 43, 621–641.

Schade, H. (1950): Ergebnisse einer Bevölkerungsuntersuchung in der Schwalm. Abh. math.-nat. Kl. Akad. Wiss (Mainz) 16, 419–491. Cited by Böök, 1953.

Schor, H. C., & H. L. Swain (1949): Simultaneous Surveys of Food Consumption in Various Camps of the United States Army. J. Nutr. 38, 51–62.

Sewell, P., W. T. Cooke, E. V. Cox & M. J. Meynell (1963): Milk Intolerance in Gastrointestinal Disorders. Lancet 2, 1132–1135.

Sheehy, T. W., & M. H. Flock (1964): Diffuse Lesions of the Intestinal Mucosa, in: The Small Intestine, Harper & Row, New York.

Sheldon, W. (1959): Celiac Disease. Pediatrics 23, 132–145.

Sjøgren, T. (1948): Genetic-statistical and Psychiatric Investigations of a West Swedish Population. Acta psychiat. scand. suppl. 52, 1–102.

Sjögren, T. (1935): Investigations of the Heredity of Psychoses and Mental Dificiency in Two North Swedish Parishes. Ann. eugen. 6, 253–318.

Sleisenger, M. H. (1964): New York Hospital, New York. Personal Communication.

Ström, A. (1948): An Examination of the Diet of Norwegian Families During the War. Acta med. scand. suppl. 214, 1–47.

Strömgren, E. (1938): Beiträge zur psychiatrischen Erblehre. Acta psychiat. scand. *19,* 1–259.

Svendsen, B. B. (1952): Psychiatric Morbidity Among Civilians in Wartime. Acta Jutlandica, Aarskrift for Aarhus Universitet 24, Suppl. A., Medicinsk Serie *8,* 1–163, Ejnar Munksgaard, Copenhagen.

Tooth, G. (1950): Studies in Mental Illness in the Gold Coast. Colonial Res. Publ. No. 6, H. M. Stationary Office, London.

Toverud, G. (1949): Decrease in Caries Frequency in Norwegian Children During World War II. J. Amer. dent. Ass. *39,* 127–136.

Trulson, M. F. (1959): The American Diet—Past and Present. Amer. J. clin. Nutr. *7,* 91–97.

Tsuwaga, T. (1942): Über die psychiatrische Zensus – Untersuchung in einem Stadtbezirk von Tokyo. Psychiat. Neurol. Jap. *46,* 204–218. Cited by Lin 1953.

Uchimura, Y. et al. (1940): Über die vergleichend-psychiatrische und erbpathologische Untersuchung auf einer japanischen Insel. Psychiat. Neurol. Jap. *44,* 745–782. Cited by Lin 1953.

Weijers, H. A., J. H. van de Kamer & W. K. Dicke (1957): Celiac Disease. Advanc. Pediat. *9,* 277–318.

The Council of British Societies for Relief Abroad (1945): Nutrition and Relief Work. Oxford.

League of Nations (1946): Food, Famine and Relief, 1940–1946. Geneva.

League of Nations (1944): Food Rationing and Supply 1943–44. Geneva.

League of Nations (1942): Wartime Rationing and Consumption. Geneva.

National Research Council, Food and Nutrition Board (1949): Nutrition Surveys: Their Techniques and Value, by the Committee on Nutrition Surveys. Bull. Natl. Res. Council, No. 117. Washington.

Statistisches Jahrbuch der Schweiz: (1947), Tables pp. 130, 131, 284, 285), (1957, Tables pp. 368–369). Eidgenössisches Statistisches Amt, Bern.

Statistisk Årsbok för Finland: ("Consumption" of cereals: 1950, tab. 86 & 222). Statistiska Centralbyrån, Helsinki.

Statistisk Årbok for Norge: ("Consumption" of cereals: 1946–48, tab. 87; 1949, tab. 72; 1950, tab. 65; 1951, tab. 85); (Insane in the hospitals by diagnosis: 1943–45, tab. 48; 1946–48, tab. 49; 1949, tab. 33; 1950, tab. 39; 1951, tab. 41). Statistisk Sentralbyrå, Oslo.

Statistisk Årsbok för Sverige: ("Consumption" of cereals: 1939, tab. 79; 1943, tab. 75; 1944, tab. 75; 1946, tab. 81; 1948, tab. 79). Statistiska Centralbyrån, Stockholm.

United States Department of Agriculture (1946): Food Consumption Levels in the United States, Canada and the United Kingdom, Third Report of a Special Joint Committee set up by the Combined Food Board, Washington.

49

GLOBULINS AND BEHAVIOR IN SCHIZOPHRENIA

George F. Solomon [+], *Rudolf H. Moos* [++], *W. Jeffrey Fessel* [+++],
and Elwood E. Morgan [++++]

ABSTRACT

Because of several reports of gamma globulin and 19S macroglobulin elevations and of various immunological disturbances in conjunction with mental illness, this study attempted: first, to relate specific parameters of behavior with the levels of gamma globulin and 19S macroglobulin in chronic schizophrenic patients; second, to study the effect of an immunosuppressive antimetabolite drug, chlorambucil, on abnormal behavior. A slight positive correlation between the severity of general psychotic symptoms and 19S macroglobulin levels were found. The administration of chlorambucil to 8 schizophrenic patients with high levels of gamma globulin, macroglobulin or both, led neither to clinical improvement nor to significant change in the levels of these proteins. Extreme caution in dosage may account for the negative results, and it is suggested that careful behavioral studies be carried out on schizophrenic patients who develop leukemia and who are treated with conventional doses of antimetabolites.

This study had two purposes: first, an attempt to relate specific parameters of behavior with the levels of gamma globulin and 19S macroglobulin in chronic schizophrenic patients; second, a study of the effect of an immunosuppressive drug on abnormal behavior.

Several groups of investigators have reported an elevation of gamma globulin levels in chronically psychotic state hospital patients. [1, 2, 3, 4] Fessel [5] found significant elevation of the mean levels of 19S ultracentrifugal class serum proteins in the sera of acutely mentally disturbed patients studied within 24 hours of hospital admission and before the institution of definitive therapy. The 19S level was used to make a blind differentiation between sera of schizophrenic patients and sera of normal subjects. [6, 7] Sapira [8] obtained confirmatory evidence of abnormal macroglobulin by immuno-electrophoresis. Malis [9] and Haddad and Rabe [10] found that sera of schizophrenic patients contained unidentified abnormal antigens. Further evidence for possible immunological disturbance in mental illness were the findings that (1) mentally ill pa-

* This work was supported in part by a grant from the VA and in part by USPHS Grant MHO 4581-03.

+ Asst. Prof. Dept. of Psychiatry, Stanford Univ. School of Medicine, Palo Alto, Calif., and Chief, Psychiatry Training and Research Section, VA Hospital, Palo Alto.

++ Asst. Prof of Psychology, Dept. of Psychiatry, Stanford Univ. School of Medicine, Palo Alto, Calif.

+++ Univ. of Calif. School of Medicine and Langley Porter Neuropsychiatric Institute, San Francisco, Calif., present address, Kaiser Foundation Hospital, San Francisco.

++++ Clinical Instr., Dept. of Psychiatry, Stanford Univ. School of Medicine, San Francisco, Calif.

Acknowledgment: Authors are grateful to Florence Weis, R.N. and Sheldon Starr, Ph.D., who took part in behavioral ratings of patients. Analytic ultracentrifugation was carried out at the Institute of Medical Physics, Belmont, Calif.

From *Intern. J. Neuropsychiat.* 2, 20–26, 1966.

tients had a serum substance which agglutinated particles coated with a brain constituent [11, 12] or gave positive complement fixation tests with a brain antigen; [13] (2) the sera of psychotic state hospital patients showed increased incidences of positive F11 latex ("rheumatoid factor") and nucleoprotein latex ("lupus factor") agglutination tests [14] and (3) schizophrenic patients' lymphocytes showed morphological abnormalities. [15, 16] Vaughn and co-workers [17] found that schizophrenic patients produced a significantly lower titer of antibodies than did healthy controls after hyperimmunization with pertussis vaccine. Similarly deficient antibody responses by schizophrenic patients to administered antigen were found by Kerbicov [18] and Shvedskia. [19] Several extensive reviews of immunological dysfunctions in schizophrenia have appeared. [20, 21, 22]

There have been several attempts to find an association between serum proteins and specific types or features of mental illness. For example, in three different hospitals, sera from manic-depressive and schizophrenic patients could be differentiated by their 19S macroglobulin levels, the mean level of the schizophrenic group being almost double that of the manic-depressive group. [6, 7] Pospisilova and Janik [23] found beta globulin especially elevated in paranoid schizophrenic, manic-depressive and postpartum psychoses and in amentia; and the alpha$_2$ globulin was highest in patients with psychomotor agitation and lowest in patients with psychomotor retardation. Grunbaum, Forrest and Kirk [24] found an increase of alpha$_1$ globulin in non-catatonic schizophrenics, an increase of beta globulin in the same group and in alcoholics, and an increase of gamma globulin in catatonic (but not "other" schizophrenic or alcoholic) patients. Heath's experiments with the effect upon behavior of the "taraxein" fraction of blood have been summarized elsewhere. [25]

Although the evidence is rather weak that the abnormal proteins have some role in producing disturbed behavior, this possibility is of great theoretical importance. In addition to possible direct effects on the CNS, such proteins conceivably might act via binding essential metabolites. 19S macroglobulin generally behaves as antibody, [26] and some auto-antibodies such as rheumatoid factor [27] fall in this class. The hypergammaglobulinemia may reflect an autoimmune process. [3] Therefore, we decided to study the effect upon disturbed behavior of the cytotoxin chlorambucil. This agent belongs to the class of anti-metabolite drugs which particularly affect lymphocytes, plasma cells and other rapidly dividing tissue, and which have been shown in several studies to be capable of reducing plasma immunoglobulin levels when these are high. [28]

METHODS

Eighty male chronic schizophrenic patients below the age of 55, not alcoholic nor suffering from known medical disease, were surveyed by means of serum electrophoresis and analytical ultracentrifugation. The patients were listed in order of the highest to the lowest levels of gamma and macroglobulins. From a two dimensional consideration of these protein levels, twenty of the patients with the highest combined levels of these proteins were transferred in two sequential groups of ten to a research ward. Descriptive data are contained in Table I. Each group was divided into five pairs, the members of each pair matched as closely as possible for age, length of illness, duration of present hospitalization, severity of illness, and amount of phenothiazine medication. Pairings were done by the psychologist investigator (R.H.M.), who was not directly involved in any clinical aspect of the study.

One patient of each pair received chlorambucil, the other placebo (aspirin). Chlorambucil was chosen because it has less myelotoxicity than some other antimetabolites. For ethical reasons we used rather low doses, namely, 4 mg. per day for one week and then 2 mg. per day for five weeks. Because we saw neither toxic reactions nor improvement of behavior in the first experimental group, the second experimental group was given 4 mg. chlorambucil per day for 3 weeks and then 2 mg. per day for 3 weeks.

Each patient had a complete medical examination. Laboratory studies included chest film, urinalysis, and three white blood cell and platelet counts. When on medication all patients, including placebo group, were evaluated medically each week, especially for evidence

TABLE I

TABLE I

DESCRIPTIVE DATA

	No. of Patients	Age *	Duration of Illness * (Years)	Length of Present Hospitalization * (Years)	Illness of Severity	Dosage of Phenothiazine
Chlorambucil Group	10	38.8 (27-53)	15.1 (5-30)	10.1 (2-20)	Severe 2 Moderate 6 Mild 2	High 2 Medium 2 Low 6
Placebo Group	10	37.5 (23-54)	12.9 (6-21)	10.3 (3-20)	Severe 2 Moderate 6 Mild 2	High 4 Medium 3 Low 3

* Figures in columns marked with an asterisk represent the mean values and figures in parentheses their ranges.

of infection or ecchymoses. All patients had white blood cell counts of over 5000/cu.mm. and platelet counts of over 100,000/cu.mm. on three occasions before institution of drug. During the course of the study if any patient's whit cell count fell to fewer than 3500/cu.mm. or platelet count to fewer than 100,000/cu.mm. (the latter never occurred), medication was to be temporarily discontinued and daily

TABLE II

DIMENSIONS OF PSYCHIATRIC RATING SCALE

1. Depression
2. Elation
3. Anger
4. Anxiety
5. Distress
6. Hyperactivity
   a. In interview or group
   b. On the ward
7. Motor Retardation
   a. In interview or group
   b. On the ward
8. Disorganization of concepts
9. Hyperorganization of concepts
10. Unusual thought content
11. Suspiciousness
12. Disengagement—withdrawal
    a. In interview or group
    b. On the ward
13. Self-depreciation
14. Grandiosity
15. Physical appearance
16. Degree of mental illness
17. Improvement
18. Regression
19. Likeability

counts made. When the white cell count had again risen to at least 5000/cu.mm., medication was resumed. If a second drop occurred, dosage on reinstitution was halved.

A behavioral rating scale was derived from Overall and Gorham's [29] factor analysis of the Inpatient Multidimensional Psychiatric Scale. [30] The dimensions of this scale, some of which are mutually exclusive, are listed in Table II. A clinical psychologist and psychiatrist rated the patients weekly following a group meeting, and the ward charge nurse rated the patients weekly on the basis of their ward behavior. We had previously shown a high degree of inter-rater reliability. All patients were rated for three weeks before receiving active drug or placebo. All previous medications were withdrawn during these three weeks, and there was at least a week completely without drugs. A two week post-treatment followup period was provided.

RESULTS

Seventeen patients received the full course of treatment; eight received drug and nine placebo. Two subjects were dropped from the study because of unmanageable behavior and one because of severe infection (with normal leukocytic response).

Complications: During the study four patients had a transient leukopenia that subsided on withdrawal of drug for three to four days. The patient with the severest leukopenia (1500/cu.mm.) was receiving placebo. Hollister and others [31] have noted a

Schizophrenia: Globulins and Behavior

few instances of marked leukopenia in schizophrenic patients during phenobarbital-placebo administration in controlled studies of phenothiazines. No patient experienced such a severe reaction that chlorambucil had to be permanently discontinued. No patient developed splenomegaly, hepatomegaly or bleeding diathesis.

Tables III and IV summarize the alterations in the values of the 19S and gamma-globulin fractions in the experimental and control groups. The 19S fraction in the experimental group was decreased in five, increased slightly in two, and was unchanged in one of the patients. In the control group, the 19S fraction decreased in five, increased in three, and was unchanged in one of the patients. The mean 19S values showed a small decrease in the experimental group, and a slight increase in the control group, a difference in the expected direction but not of significant degree. Gamma globulin levels were decreased in six patients and increased in two patients in the experimental group. However, all nine patients in the control group showed decreased gamma-globulin levels. The mean decrease in gamma globulin, contrary to expectation, was larger in patients receiving placebo.

Analysis of behavioral ratings demonstrated no significant amelioration in any parameter of illness in patients receiving chlorambucil as compared to patients receiving placebo. The general trend was toward clinical deterioration in both groups, though some improvement occurred in a few

TABLE III

DRUG GROUP

Patient	19 S mgm/100 ml			Gamma Globulin gm/100 ml		
	Initial	Final	Change	Initial	Final	Change
79	319	248	— 71	1.06	0.90	— 0.16
83	287	254	— 33	1.15	1.09	— 0.06
84	183	189	+ 6	1.44	1.11	— 0.33
69	333	287	— 46	1.30	1.36	+ 0.06
71	280	319	+ 39	1.39	1.42	+ 0.03
74	222	215	— 7	1.48	1.36	— 0.12
75	248	248	0	1.44	1.33	— 0.11
68	469	450	— 19	1.83	1.77	— 0.06
Mean	293	276	— 17	1.39	1.29	— 0.10

TABLE IV

PLACEBO GROUP

Patient	19 S mgm/100 ml			Gamma Globulin gm/100 ml		
	Initial	Final	Change	Initial	Final	Change
86	274	326	+ 52	1.11	0.75	— 0.36
80	222	215	— 7	1.26	1.01	— 0.25
82	202	163	— 39	1.23	0.74	— 0.49
64	222	228	+ 6	1.49	1.15	— 0.34
70	326	287	— 39	1.36	0.87	— 0.49
72	254	209	— 45	1.52	1.48	— 0.04
73	267	267	0	1.30	1.29	— 0.01
63	333	456	+ 123	1.30	1.12	— 0.18
66	215	202	— 13	1.47	0.70	— 0.77
Mean	257	261	+ 4	1.34	1.01	— 0.33

individuals from each group. There was a most prominent increase in thought disorder and withdrawal with deterioration of personal appearance. Activity in group sessions was the only scale to show any substantial improvement in both groups.

Efforts were made to correlate changes in bood protein fractions with clinical psychiatric rating scores. There were no correlations between changes in 19S and gamma-globulin fractions and any of the clinical parameters except for distress and degree of mental illness. The distress scale is a measure of any noxious affect (anxiety, depression, fear, pain, worry). Generally (Tables V and VI), when there was a change in the 19S protein levels, there was a change in the same direction in the measured levels of both distress and degree of mental illness, though there were several exceptions to this. The patient (# 63 placebo group) with by far the greatest increase in 19S macroglobulin showed the most clinical deterioration.

There was, as indicated, a general trend toward decrease of gamma globulin, and

TABLE V

RELATIONSHIP BETWEEN CHANGES IN 19 s PROTEINS AND DEGREE OF MENTAL ILLNESS

| Mental Illness | 19 s Proteins | | |
	Rise	No change	Drop
Increase	2*	2	1[+]
No change	1	3*	4
Decrease	0	3	1*

* Change in expected direction
[+] Change contrary to expected direction

TABLE VI

RELATIONSHIP BETWEEN CHANGES IN 19 s PROTEINS AND DISTRESS

| Distress | 19 s Proteins | | |
	Rise	No change	Drop
Increase	3*	3	1[+]
No change	0	2*	2
Decrease	0	3	3*

* Change in expected direction
[+] Change contrary to expected direction

most patients showed worsening of clinical symptoms, suggesting an inverse relationship between these behavioral and physiological parameters. However, of the total of seventeen patients, the four who showed some clinical improvement also had small drops in gamma globulin level. In an earlier unpublished study similar results were obtained in attempts to correlate behavior and serum proteins in a general psychiatric ward population of both sexes having mixed diagnoses, both acute and chronic illnesses. It was found that in eight out of ten patients studied serially during a period of three months, there was an inverse relationship between change in degree of mental illness and change in level of gamma globulin. One of the exceptions to the trend occurred in a patient with an organic brain disease and the other in a patient with ulcerative colitis.

EPICRISIS

The administration of the antimetabolite drug chlorambucil to eight schizophrenic patients with high levels of gamma globulin, macroglobulin or both, led neither to clinical improvement nor to significant change in the levels of these proteins. There was a slight positive correlation between the severity of general psychotic symptoms and 19S macroglobulin levels, and there was a tendency to a negative correlation of these symptoms with gamma globulin levels.

The lack of effect of this antimetabolite upon the gamma globulins and macroglobulins, when the levels of these proteins are not greatly increased, is consistent with recent findings of other authors. Levin, Landy and Frei [32] gave 6-mercaptopurine in conventional doses to six medical patients for twenty eight days. There was no substantial effect upon the levels of pre-existing antibodies, gamma globulins or immunoelectrophoretic precipitin lines. They cited evidence that prolonged chemotherapy is necessary to lower gamma globulin levels which were originally within the normal range. Our patients received very cautious therapy for only a short period, which caution may be why the proteins did not change. This conservatism could also account for the absence of notable change in the patients' behavior; however, we have advanced reasons elsewhere [33] why it might be necessary to change simultaneously several of the determinants in order to affect behavior. We suggest that ethical problems in treatment would be avoided if schizophrenic patients who developed leukemia were treated with conventional doses of antimetabolites and the concomitant effect upon behavior observed.

REFERENCES

1. Cepulic, P., Domac, V. and Ruzic, I.: Aenderungen im Verhältnis der Serumwisse bei Schizophrenie. *Neuropsihijatrija,* 2:211, 1954.

2. Milhaud, F., Chatagnon, C., Sandor, M. and Sandor, G.: Une enquete humorale chez les psychopates: analyse statistique des resultats obtenu. *Ann. Inst. Pasteur,* 96:114-119, 1959.

3. Fessel, W. J. and Grunbaum, B. W.: Electrophoretic and analytical ultracentrifuge studies in sera of psychotic patients; elevation of gamma globulins and macroglobulins and splitting of alpha$_2$ globulins. *Ann. Int. Med.,* 54:1134-1145, 1961.

4. Lando, L. J.: Electroforetische issledovanie belkovikh fraktsii syvorotki provi bol'nikh shizofreniei i ikh dinamiki pod bliyaniem lecheniya neirolepticheskimi veshchestvami. *Zh. Nevropat. Psikhiat. Korsakov,* 59:135, 1959.

5. Fessel, W. J.: Macroglobulin elevations in functional mental illness. *Nature,* 193:1005, 1962.

6. Kurland, H. D. and Fessel, W. J.: Distinctive protein patterns in functional psychoses. *Proc. Soc. Experi. Biol. and Med.,* 113:249-251, 1963.

7. Fessel, W. J., Kurland, H. D. and Cutler, R. P.: Serological distinction between functional psychoses. *Arch. Int. Med.,* 113:669-671, 1964.

8. Sapira, J. D.: Immunoelectrophoresis of the serum of psychotic patients. *Arch. Gen. Psychiat.,* 10:196-198, 1964.

9. Malis, G. Yu.: Etiologii shizofrenii. *Medgiz,* p. 223, Moscow, 1959.

10. Haddad, R. K. and Rabe, A.: An antigenic abnormality in the serum of chronically ill schizophrenic patients. In: *Serological Fractions in Schizophrenia,* ed. by R. G. Heath, Hoeber-Harper, New York, 1963.

11. Fessel, W. J.: Autoimmunity and mental illness: a preliminary report. *Arch. Gen. Psychiat.,* 6:320-323, 1962.

12. Fessel, W. J.: The "antibrain" factors in psychiatric patients' sera. I. Further studies with a hemagglutination technique. *Arch. Gen. Psychiat.,* 8:614-621, 1963.

13. Kusnetsova, M. I. and Semenov, S. F.: (Detection of antibrain antibodies in the blood sera of patients with neuropsychiatric diseases). *Zh. Nevropat. Psikhiat. Korsakov,* 61:869, 1961.

14. Fessel, W. J.: Serum protein abnormalities in psychosis: a preliminary report. *J. Nerv. and Ment. Dis.,* 132:89-90, 1961.

15. Fessel, W. J. and Hirata-Hibi, M.: Abnormal leucocytes in schizophrenia. *Arch. Gen. Psychiat.,* 9:601-613, 1963.

16. Hirata-Hibi, M. and Fessel, W. J.: The bone marrow in schizophrenia. *Arch. Gen. Psychiat.,* 10:414-419, 1964.

17. Vaughn, W. J., Jr., Sullivan, J. C., and Elmadjian, F.: Immunity and schizophrenia; survey of ability of schizophrenic patients to develop active immunity following injection of pertussis vaccine. *Psychosom. Med.,* 11:327-333, 1949.

18. Kerbicov, O. W.: Immunological reactivity in schizophrenia as influenced by some modern drugs. Pavlovian Conference on Higher Nervous Activity, Joint Meeting between New York Academy of Sciences and the Academy of Medical Science of the U.S.S.R., New York, Oct. 13-15, 1960.

19. Schvedskia, A. G.: O nekotorykh osobennostiakh bezuslovnykh spetsificheskikh immunologicheskikh reactskii pri shizofreni. *Zh. Nevropat. Psikhiat. Korsakov,* 54:741, 1954.

20. Fessel, W. J.: Blood proteins in functional psychoses. A review of the literature and unifying hypothesis. *Arch. Gen. Psychiat.,* 6:132-148, 1962.

21. Vartanian, M. E.: Immunobiologicheskie issledovaniia shizofrenii (Immunobiological investigations of schizophrenia), *Zh. Nevropat. Psikhiat. Korsakov,* 63:457-465, 1963.

22. Solomon, G. F. and Moos, R. H.: Emotions, immunity and disease: a speculative theoretical integration. *Arch. Gen. Psychiat.,* 11:657, 1964.

23. Pospisilova, U. and Janik, A.: The relation of the blood serum protein fractions to the clinical picture in psychoses and psychotic states, determined by paper electrophoresis. *Rev. Czech. Med.,* 4:29-39, 1958.

24. Grunbaum, B. W., Forrest, F. M. and Kirk, P. L.: The serum proteins in the alcoholic and mentally ill treated with chlorpromazine. Unpublished manuscript.

25. Heath, R. G., Martens, S., Veach, B. E., Cohen,

M. and Feigley, C. A.: Behavioral changes in nonpsychotic volunteers following the administration of taraxein, the substance obtained from serum of schizophrenic patients. *Am. J. Psychiat.,* 114:917-919, 1958.

26. Kunkel, H. G., Fudenberg, H. and Ovary, Z.: High molecular weight antibodies. *Ann. N. Y. Acad. Sci.,* 81:966-973, 1960.

27. Ziff, M.: Possible clinical and pathological associations of rheumatoid factor. *Arth. and Rheumat.,* 6:481-489, 1963.

28. Bayrd, E. D.: Continuous chlorambucil therapy in primary macroglobulinemia of Waldenström: Report of four cases. *Proc. Staff Meet. Mayo Clinic,* 36:135-147, 1961.

29. Overall, J. E. and Gorham, D. R.: The brief psychiatric rating scale. *Psychol. Reports,* 10:799-812, 1962.

30. Lorr, M.: Multidimensional scale for rating psychiatric patients. 1. *Hospital Form Veterans Administration, Technical Bulletin,* TB10-507, Nov. 1953.

31. Hollister, L. E., Caffey, E. M and Klett, C. J.: Abnormal symptoms, signs and laboratory tests during treatment with phenothiazine derivatives. *Clin. Pharm. and Ther.,* 1:284-293, 1960.

32. Levin, R. H., Landy, M. and Frei, III, E.: The effect of 6-mercaptopurine or immune response in man. *New Eng. J. Med.,* 271:16-22, 1964.

33. Fessel, W. J.: Interaction of multiple determinants of schizophrenia. A tentative synthesis and review. *Arch. Gen. Psychiat.,* 11:1-18, 1964.

50

SCHIZOPHRENIA AS AN IMMUNOLOGIC DISORDER
III. Effects of Antimonkey and Antihuman Brain Antibody on Brain Function

Robert G. Health, Iris M. Krupp, Lawrence W. Byers, and Jan I. Liljekvist

OBSERVATIONS in our laboratories that sera of schizophrenic patients contain a unique globulin (probably antibody) capable of attachment to specific sites of the brain (antigen) support our postulate that schizophrenia is an immunologic disorder.[1-3] The findings, however, do not establish a cause-and-effect relation between the globulin and clinical symptoms of the disease.

We have injected serum globulins of schizophrenic patients, normal healthy control subjects, and control subjects with diseases other than schizophrenia into the ventricles of rhesus monkeys prepared with depth and cortical electrodes and intraventricular cannulas.[3-5] Abnormal electroencephalograms (EEG) from the septal region and basal caudate nucleus with concomitant abnormal behavior were induced consistently by serum globulins of acute schizophrenic patients, and sometimes by globulins of chronic schizophrenic patients. Similar aberrations followed intravenous injection of the serum globulins. Fluorescent antibody techniques showed that the brains of the monkey recipients, which were killed at the height of response to the globulin, had a globulin attached to neural cell nuclei at the site of the abnormal EEGs. From these data we concluded that some schizophrenic patients have a serum fraction that affects brain function at specific focal sites at which globulin is attached.[3] Although these data are again suggestive, they do not provide clear evidence that the globulin tested is antibody.

The present study was planned to answer crucial questions generated by earlier studies and to close some gaps in the immunologic hypothesis of schizophrenia. If the protein fraction in schizophrenic serum is indeed antibody against precise regions of the brain, it should be possible experimentally to produce antibodies against parts of the brain, and these antibodies should then interact with brain tissues of the homologous animal to produce the same physiologic and behavioral changes caused by serum globulin from schizophrenic patients. The characteristics of this globulin should be those of the unique fraction in serum of schizophrenic patients, which we named taraxein.[6,7] In the present experiments, the method of Mihailovic and Jankovic[8] was modified to create antibodies in sheep against parts of monkey and human brain and against fractions obtained by submitting a high-speed supernatant from homogenates of specific parts of human brain to diethylaminoethanol (DEAE)-cellulose chromatography. Globulins were removed from sheep sera by fractionation methods used previously for human sera,[3] and were introduced into the ventricles of rhesus monkeys prepared with electrodes implanted for prolonged studies to learn whether antibody produced against specific regions of monkey and human brains could alter electrical activity at these sites when reintroduced into an intact monkey. We further wished to know whether changes in electrical activity of the brain at these sites were associated with behavioral aberrations, as occurred when psychoactive serum fractions of schizophrenic patients were introduced into monkey brains. Fluorescent antibody techniques were used to determine if the antibody attached to brain sites in the same

Submitted for publication June 22, 1966.
From the Department of Psychiatry and Neurology, Tulane University School of Medicine, New Orleans.
Reprinted with permission from *Arch. Gen. Psychiat.* **16**, 24–33. Copyright © 1967, American Medical Association.

way that globulins attached to neural cell nuclei at focal sites of brains of schizophrenic patients, and of brains of monkeys that received psychoactive serum fractions of schizophrenic patients.

Other characteristics of sheep antisera were compared with those for fractions of serum of schizophrenic patients. Our rationale was that if the known antibody against brain behaved in the same way as taraxein, the unique globulin in schizophrenic serum, then taraxein was more likely to be antibody against brain and the in vivo antigen-antibody combination to be responsible for the clinical symptoms of schizophrenia.

Experimental Studies

Preparation of Antigens.—By methods previously described,[1] antigen was prepared from the septal region, caudate nucleus, brain stem, cerebellum, cerebral cortex, substantia nigra, putamen, hippocampus, and hypothalamus of rhesus monkeys exsanguinated without anesthesia, and of patients who had died from various diseases but who had no neurologic or psychiatric disorders. Ages of the patients ranged from 17 to 65 years. After brains had been dissected, homogenized in phosphate buffer, sonicated, and centrifuged at 34,000 times gravity for 30 minutes, protein values were determined on the supernatant by the Biuret method.[9] Antigens were adjusted to 25 mg protein/ml and were mixed with an equal volume of Freund's adjuvant and 1:10,000 merthiolate for intramuscular injection into sheep. All procedures were conducted at 4 C.

Soluble proteins of the human septal region and caudate nucleus were separated on a DEAE-cellulose column by the method of Sober and associates.[10] The tissues of the septal region and caudate nucleus were pooled, homogenized in 0.005 M phosphate buffer pH 7.0, and centrifuged at 100,000 times gravity for 60 minutes. Stepwise elution was done with the following buffers: 0.005 M sodium phosphate pH 7.0 (first fraction); 0.05 M plus 0.1 M NaCl pH 6.0 (second fraction); 0.075 M sodium phosphate plus 0.25 M NaCl pH 6.0 (third fraction); and 0.1 M sodium phosphate plus 0.5 M NaCl pH 6.0 (fourth fraction). The four fractions thus obtained were mixed with Freund's adjuvant for injection into sheep by the same procedure used for monkey brain and whole human brain antigens.

Antibody.—*Production of Antimonkey Brain Antibody.*—Of 17 pure-bred, young adult Montadale sheep[1] in this series of experiments, four received monkey antigen-adjuvant mixtures of septal region, four of caudate nucleus, two of cerebellum, two of brain stem, two of hippocampus, and two of cerebral cortex; one received an antigen-adjuvant mixture of septal region and caudate nucleus combined. The sheep received intramuscular injections of 2.0 ml of antigen-adjuvant mixtures (25 mg protein) in the hip at weekly intervals for three weeks, and booster injections with double the original protein content one month later. One monkey was killed to provide material for each of the first three injections, and two monkeys were killed to provide material for the booster injections. The sheep were bled before the antigen-adjuvant mixtures were injected to provide normal sheep globulin for control studies.

Production of Antihuman Brain Antibody.—Of nine sheep in this series, two received human antigen-adjuvant mixture of septal region and caudate nucleus combined (total of 25 mg protein, 12.5 mg from each region), one of cerebral cortex, one of cerebellum, one of putamen, two of substantia nigra, one of brain stem, and one of hippocampus. Because fresh human brain tissues could not be obtained as regularly as monkey brain tissues, injection and inoculation schedules were necessarily irregular; otherwise the procedures were identical with those used to produce the antimonkey brain antibody.

One of the four fractions of human septal-caudate homogenate obtained by DEAE-cellulose fractionation and mixed with Freund's adjuvant was injected into each sheep. Inoculation schedules were again irregular, depending on availability of fresh human brain tissues. Protein content of the fractions varied from 0.35 to 14.0 mg/ml.

Responses of Sheep to Monkey and Human Antigen-Adjuvant Mixtures.—Paraplegia developed in sheep that received monkey antigen-adjuvant mixtures of septal region, caudate nucleus, hippocampus, and brain stem. Histologic examination of their brains indicated experimental allergic encephalomyelitis. The sheep that received monkey antigen-adjuvant mixtures of cortex and cerebellum remained asymptomatic after having received two booster injections. All sheep that received human antigen-adjuvant mixtures showed clinical symptoms of experimental allergic encephalomyelitis before the scheduled inoculations were completed.

Fractionation of Sheep Sera for Clinical Tests.—Globulins were prepared from sheep sera by procedures previously described for human serum:[3] (1) salting out with 50% ammonium sulfate, (2) salting out with 33% ammonium sulfate, (3) chloroform-ethanol technique, (4) exclusion chromatography on Sephadex G-200 equilibrated with 0.15 M sodium chloride, and (5) DEAE-Sephadex column fractionation.

The ammonium sulfate methods were always used to fractionate the test sera (most frequently, the 50% method), and sometimes the chloroform-ethanol, Sephadex G-200, and DEAE-Sephadex methods were also used to characterize the psychoactive component further, and to relate present methods of fractionation with methods used previously to fractionate taraxein. Some fractions were obtained only by Sephadex G-200 fractionation, which separated proteins by molecular weight. These fractions were sometimes fractionated further by the DEAE-Sephadex method to obtain specific globulin fractions, for example, pure γ-G immunoglobulin (IgG). The findings obtained by fractionation with chloroform-ethanol, Sephadex G-200, and DEAE-Sephadex are presented with the immunoelectrophoretic data.

Total protein content of the serum fractions was determined by either the Biuret[9] or Lowry[11] methods. For routine testing of 50% ammonium sulfate fractions, the total protein content was kept

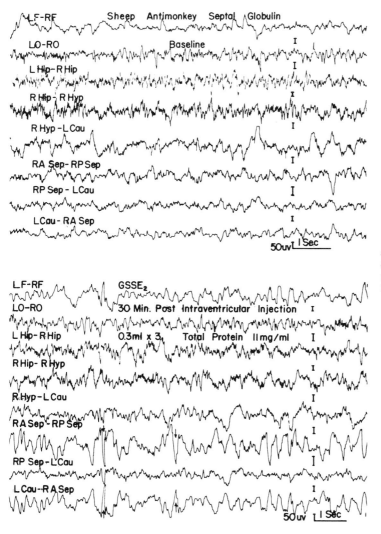

Fig 1.—Surface and depth EEGs of a monkey that received antimonkey septal globulin.

at an arbitrary maximum of 12 mg/ml. In an effort to quantitate the activity, we sometimes tested these 50% ammonium sulfate fractions with notably lower total protein content, but only when they were known to be active at concentrations of 12 mg/ml. The protein content of fractions obtained by salting out with 33% ammonium sulfate and by DEAE-Sephadex column fractionation was below 12 mg/ml. These fractions were tested at the lower levels without concentrating them up to 12 mg/ml.

For control of nonspecific effects of intraventricular injections of serum globulins of sheep, similarly prepared globulins in the same protein concentration (12 mg/ml) from uninoculated (normal) sheep were given in the same quantity and by the same procedure. On the few occasions when higher concentrations of globulins were tested, they were controlled with preparations of normal globulins in the same concentration.

Immunoelectrophoretic analysis (IEA) was done to identify the globulins present in the material used for intraventricular inoculations. All serum fractions were sterilized through a cellulose acetate filter (0.2μ pore size) before injection.

The Assay Animal.—Macaca rhesus monkeys were prepared with depth and cortical electrodes and with intraventricular cannulas by methods of Heath and associates.[4-7,10] The preparation was the same as that used for testing globulins of various human sera,[3] except that monkeys that received fractions of anticortex sheep serum also had cannulas implanted over the cortical sites from which tissue for antigen was obtained, and monkeys that received anticerebellum fractions had a second cannula implanted over the cerebellar site from which tissue had been removed.

While EEGs were being obtained, the globulin was introduced through the intraventricular cannula in increments of 0.3 ml at three hourly

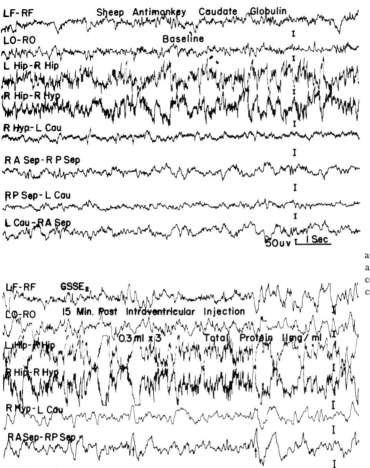

Fig 2.—Surface and depth EEGs of a monkey that received antimonkey caudate globulin.

intervals each day. Monkeys that received monkey and human anticortex and anticerebellum fractions were simultaneously given an additional 0.3 ml of the specific antiserum fraction over the cortical and cerebellar sites. The series of three injections were given for a maximum of three successive days. If EEG and behavioral changes appeared on the first or second day of injections, the procedure was stopped. All sera were fractionated and tested on multiple occasions in different monkeys.[3]

Rating of Monkey Responses to Injections of Globulins.—Electroencephalographic changes were graded from a minimal response consisting of generalized subcortical slowing (GSS) localized to the septal region, hippocampus, and caudate nucleus, to increasing focal epileptogenic spiking in the septal region (GSSE$_1$ to GSSE$_3$) based on the number of spike discharges per 10-second epoch. Behavioral ratings from 1+ (minimal re-

duction of awareness) to 4+ (maximal catatonia) were subjective estimates by the examiner of the monkey's reduced awareness. When fractions contained protein concentrations of 12 mg/ml or more, diffuse (nonfocal) slowing predominantly in the cortex associated with reduced awareness of the monkey sometimes appeared during testing, in contrast to the gradual accentuation of the specific psychoactive effect. This nonspecific response was also noted by Mihailovic and Jankovic.[8]

Results of Testing Antibrain Serum Fractions in Monkeys.—All serum fractions were tested intraventricularly and some were also tested intravenously. Fractions that were psychoactive by intraventricular injections were also psychoactive when tested intravenously.

Antimonkey Brain Serum Fractions.—Monkeys that received injections of antimonkey septal globulins fractionated by the 50% ammonium sulfate

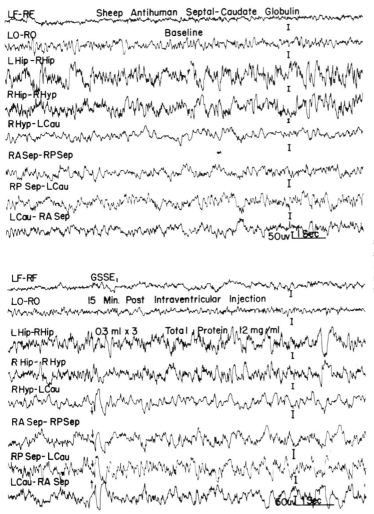

Fig 3.—Surface and depth EEGs of a monkey that received antihuman septal-caudate globulin.

method (eight preparations) or the 33% method (two preparations) consistently showed EEG changes characterized by spiking and slow-wave activity confined almost exclusively to recordings from the septal region and rated as GSSE$_2$ or GSSE$_3$. In some monkeys the abnormal activity spread to the caudate nucleus and hippocampus, and generalized subcortical slowing developed (Fig 1). Associated behavior, rated 2+ to 4+, resembled catatonia: the monkeys were dazed, out of contact, and sometimes could be postured because of waxy flexibility. The EEG and behavioral changes persisted for 30 to 90 minutes after full development.

Monkeys that received antimonkey caudate globulins fractionated by the 50% ammonium sulfate method (twice) or the 33% ammonium sulfate method (once) showed diminished awareness, spiking, and slow-wave activity most prominent in recordings from the septal region but also present in those from the caudate nucleus (GSSE$_1$ to

GSSE$_3$) (Fig 2). Behavioral changes were not as remarkable, however, as those observed in recipients of antimonkey septal globulin; they were usually graded as 1+ to 2+.

Monkeys that received sheep antimonkey combined septal-caudate globulins obtained by 50% ammonium sulfate fractionation (three times) also consistently showed transient changes in EEGs (GSSE$_1$ to GSSE$_3$) and behavior (1+ to 3+) that closely resembled those noted after use of antimonkey septal globulins.

In contrast, EEGs and behavior of monkeys that received sheep antimonkey globulins of all other brain regions tested and fractions of sera of uninoculated sheep were unaffected. Each fraction containing antisera against each brain region was tested at least twice in the monkeys.

Antihuman Brain Serum Fractions.—Injections of sheep antihuman septal-caudate serum fractions obtained by 50% ammonium sulfate fractionation (once) or the 33% method (twice) consistently

Schizophrenia as Immune Disorder

caused notable changes in EEGs (GSSE$_1$ to GSSE$_3$) and behavior (1+ to 3+) in the monkeys (Fig 3).* Fractions of sheep sera containing antibodies against other parts of human brain, on the other hand, failed to induce changes.

Sheep Antisera Against DEAE-Cellulose Column Fractions of Human Septal-Caudate Tissues.—Serum fractions of sheep inoculated with the first, third, and fourth column fractions of septal-caudate brain tissues were active in the monkeys (GSSE$_1$ to GSSE$_2$ EEGs and 1+ to 2+ behavior), whereas serum fractions of sheep inoculated with the second column fraction were inactive. Serum containing antibody against each brain fraction was processed twice by the 33% ammonium sulfate method.

Relation of Protein Content of Serum Fractions to Method of Fractionation.—An arbitrary maximal protein concentration of 12 mg/ml was adopted for the early serum fractions we tested that were obtained by salting out with 50% ammonium sulfate; dilution was usually required to obtain this concentration. The same fractions obtained by salting out with 33% ammonium sulfate sometimes contained as little as 0.6 mg/ml total protein (although usually ranging from 2 to 7 mg/ml), but they retained full activity. Total protein content of fractions obtained by Sephadex G-200 was 1.9 mg/ml, and that of DEAE-Sephadex fractions was 2.5 mg/ml. Content of fractions obtained by the chloroform-ethanol procedure was usually as high or higher than that of fractions obtained by the 50% ammonium sulfate procedure, and some required dilution to 12 mg/ml before testing. Sheep sera from which very active fractions were obtained by ammonium sulfate precipitation, Sephadex G-200, or DEAE-Sephadex procedures sometimes yielded inactive fractions by the chloroform-ethanol method if IgG was absent, or was present in only trace amounts. Activity was shown to be related to the presence of IgG rather than to quantity of total protein, as discussed.

Stability of Serum.—Aliquots of sheep antimonkey globulins were tested for stability in the same way that we tested human sera,[3] and characteristics closely resembled those we found with human sera. Active globulins stored at 4 C consistently lost activity within 24 to 48 hours, but those stored at −20 C retained demonstrable activity for 15 to 50 days. Aliquots of whole serum frozen at −20 C were fully active as long as one year after original storage.

Fluorescent Antibody Studies.—To determine whether antibody had combined with elements in brain tissues after intraventricular injections of the globulin fractions, we did fluorescent antibody studies on the brains of seven monkeys which

---

* To determine whether the phenomenon being studied transcended species, we recently created antibodies against human brain tissues in 16 rabbits: four received antigen-adjuvant mixture of septal region, four of caudate nucleus, four of cerebellum, and four of cerebral cortex. The antigen-adjuvant mixtures (25 mg protein) were injected in the same quantity and by the same procedure as used for the sheep. Responses of the monkeys to intraventricular injections of rabbit antihuman septal serum fractions were identical to those obtained when sheep antihuman septal-caudate serum fractions were used. The findings of this study will be detailed in another paper.

Cellular Fluorescence of Monkey Brain Tissues Removed After Injection of Sheep Antimonkey Brain Tissue Globulins * *and Stained in Vitro With FTA-Sheep γ-Globulin*

Sheep Globulin Injected †	No. Positive/Total Number Brains				
	Septal	Caudate	Cortex	Cerebellum	Stem
None	0/1	0/1	0/1	0/1	0/1
Normal	0/1	0/1	0/1	0/1	0/1
Antimonkey septal †	3/3	1/3	0/3	0/3	0/2
Antimonkey caudate	1/2	2/2	0/2	0/2	0/2
Antimonkey cortex	1/1 ‡	0/1	1/1 ‡	0/1	0/1
Antimonkey cerebellum	0/2	1/2 ‡	0/2	0/2	1/2 ‡
Antimonkey stem	1/1 ‡	0/1	0/1	0/1	1/1 ‡

* Fractionated by ammonium sulfate precipitation.

† One monkey received antimonkey septal globulin intravenously; all other globulins were injected intraventricularly.

‡ Minimal fluorescence.

received antimonkey brain globulins against tissues of five brain regions (septal region, caudate nucleus, cerebral cortex, cerebellum, and brain stem), on the brain of one monkey that received normal sheep globulin, and of one that received no globulins. Twenty minutes after the last intraventricular injection, the eight monkeys receiving the globulins were exsanguinated (the control monkey that had received no globulins was also exsanguinated), the brains were promptly removed, and the various parts were dissected and quick-frozen for histologic study. To relate the results of intravenous testing clearly to those of intraventricular testing, another monkey was also exsanguinated while it was showing maximal effects of an intravenous injection of antiseptal globulin, and the brain was removed for study. Frozen tissues were prepared and stained with fluorescein-tagged antisheep γ-globulin (FTA-Sgg) for detection of sites of in vivo attachment. Serial sections were made completely through each tissue; every 20th section was stained and the interjacent ones were discarded. It was essential to obtain serial sections of tissues that were not homogeneous, such as septal region tissues, since random sections are sometimes devoid of neural cell bodies and antigenic sites might therefore be missed.

Antibody was demonstrated most prominently on the septal region and to a lesser extent on the medial caudate nucleus of monkeys that received antimonkey septal globulin; it was localized in the neural cells, with staining more prominent in nuclei. Antibody was detected in insignificant concentration on tissues of other parts of the brains of recipients of sheep antimonkey septal globulin. These findings were essentially the same whether the antimonkey septal globulin was administered intravenously or intraventricularly (Color Plate 2, Fig 2).

Antibody was demonstrated predominantly on the caudate nucleus and septal regions of monkeys that received antimonkey caudate globulin; again, it was most pronounced in the nuclei of the neural cells. Fluorescence of some neural cell nuclei, not

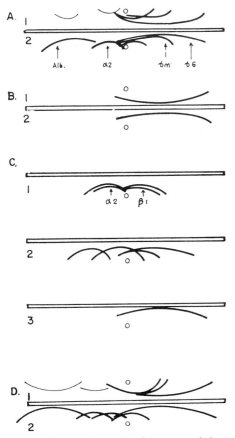

Fig 4.—Immunoelectrophoretic patterns of sheep antimonkey and antihuman brain globulins; anti-sheep serum used in troughs. (A) 50% ammonium sulfate precipitation method: (1) sheep antimonkey septal serum, active and (2) sheep antimonkey cortex serum, inactive. (B) 33% ammonium sulfate precipitation method: (1) sheep antihuman septal-caudate sera, active and (2) sheep antihuman cortex serum, inactive. (C) Sephadex column fractionation of sheep antimonkey septal serum: (1) Sephadex G-200—first peak, inactive; (2) Sephadex G-200—second peak, active and (3) DEAE-Sephadex fraction obtained from second peak of Sephadex G-200 (C2), active. (D) Chloroform-alcohol method: (1) sheep antimonkey precipitate of septal sera, active and (2) Sheep antimonkey supernatant of septal sera, active.

particularly of the homologous region, was present in the brains of the monkeys receiving antimonkey cerebellar, cortical, and stem globulins (Table).

Histopathologic examination of adjacent sections of brain tissues stained with Luxol fast blue-cresyl violet showed no structural changes except those associated with electrode and cannula implantations.

Immunoelectrophoretic Analysis of Antibrain Sera.—Apparatus (LKB) was used for IEA of fractions as previously described.[3] The patterns obtained were not related to the presence or absence of psychoactivity of the serum, but rather to the fractionation method used. Fractions of all sheep sera obtained by the 50% ammonium sulfate method showed almost a total serum protein pattern; all globulins were present and sometimes even a trace of albumin (Fig 4, A). Fractions obtained by 33% ammonium sulfate precipitation showed IgG predominantly, but sometimes weak α_2- or β-precipitin arcs as well (Fig 4, B). Sephadex G-200 fractions showed a β_1- and two α_2-arcs in material from the first peak, IgG, IgA, β_1-, and three α_2-arcs in the second peak, and fractions obtained by DEAE-Sephadex column separation contained the IgG (Fig 4, C). When sera known to contain activity were fractionated by the chloroform-ethanol method and tested in monkeys, some were active and others inert. The inert fractions contained principally β- and α-globulins and albumin, and IgG was either absent or present in trace amounts. In contrast, active fractions always showed a heavy IgG precipitin arc in addition to the others (Fig 4, D).

When a psychoactive fraction was obtained from antiseptal serum by the 33% method, the residual constituents (the supernatant after ammonium sulfate precipitation had removed most or all IgG) were further fractionated over Sephadex G-200 columns to obtain the macroglobulins. Aliquots of whole serum from which active fractions had been obtained (antiseptal and anticaudate) by ammonium sulfate fractionation were twice fractionated by the Sephadex G-200 method. Both times the first peak containing the macroglobulins was inactive in the monkey, whereas the second peak, which was further fractionated over DEAE-Sephadex columns and shown by IEA to contain pure IgG, was active in the monkey (Fig 4, C). The data indicate, therefore, that psychoactivity was present in the fractions of sheep antiseptal or anticaudate serum that contained IgG regardless of the method used to obtain the IgG. However, IgG fractions from antisera against other brain regions were inert (Fig 4, A-2 and B-2).

Agar Diffusion Studies.—Antigen preparations of both human and monkey brains were the same as those used to immunize the sheep. Double diffusion tests were done with use of 1% ion agar in pH 7.0 phosphate buffer (0.1 M) on 3×1 inch microscopic slides. Agar (3 ml) was used for each slide, and antigen wells were 3 mm from the antiserum trough. Slides were incubated, dried, and stained as described for IEA.[3] Precipitin arcs were observed when the double diffusion tests were done with monkey and human brain antigens and sheep antimonkey and antihuman brain sera. These findings contrast with the results obtained when fractions of sera from schizophrenic patients and control subjects were used.[3] (Details of these studies will be presented in another paper.)

Comment

To explore the concept that serum of schizophrenic patients contains antibody that reacts against specific sites of their own brains in an auto-immune mechanism to cause the clinical disorder, we created antibody against various brain tissues of monkeys and humans in sheep. Antibodies to the septal region and adjoining basal caudate nucleus were psychoactive in the monkeys. These antibodies, within the range of IgG, were demonstrated by the fluorescent antibody technic to combine chiefly with neural cells of the septal region and basal caudate nucleus. In contrast, antibodies to other brain regions were not psychoactive, although their presence in some brain sites was demonstrated by fluorescent antibody technics. These results suggest that the septal region and basal caudate nucleus possess a unique antigen capable of producing antibody with psychoactive properties. Studies of the known antibody produced in sheep showed that both its physical characteristics and mode of action resembled those for the unique psychoactive fraction, taraxein, obtained from serum of schizophrenic patients.[6,7] These observations support our hypothesis that taraxein is antibody against brain.

The following earlier observations in our laboratories, which provided basic information and some support for our postulate of an immunologic basis for schizophrenia, prompted the present studies.

1. Focal abnormalities are consistently recorded in EEGs from the septal region of schizophrenic patients during periods of psychosis.[12-14]

2. Intravenous injection of a serum fraction of schizophrenic patients, which we named taraxein, alters EEGs of the septal region and basal caudate nucleus of rhesus monkeys and induces symptoms of schizophrenia in human volunteer-subjects.[6,7]

3. Fluorescent antibody studies show that in vivo globulins, principally in neural cell nuclei of the septal region and basal caudate nucleus, are detectable on the brains of schizophrenic patients.[1,2] Furthermore, sera of schizophrenic patients contain globulin capable of binding in vitro to neural cell nuclei of the septal region and basal caudate nucleus of the brains of both schizophrenic and nonschizophrenic control subjects.[3]

4. Sera of all patients with acute schizophrenia and of some with chronic schizophrenia, when fractionated by ammonium sulfate precipitation or over a DEAE-Sephadex column to obtain IgG and injected intraventricularly or intravenously into monkeys, cause abnormalities in EEGs from the septal region and basal caudate nucleus concomitant with catatonic behavior.[3] Taraxein obtained from sera of schizophrenic

patients by the chloroform-ethanol procedure always contained the IgG when the fraction was psychoactive in the monkey assay.

5. Brains of monkeys that were killed while displaying aberrations in EEGs and behavior after intravenous use of IgG fractions of schizophrenic patients showed fluorescing neural cell nuclei of the septal region and basal caudate nucleus similar to fluorescing nuclei noted on the brains of schizophrenic patients.[1,2]

Production of antibody against column fractions of human brain tissues (septal-caudate) was preliminary to identification of the exact antigenic sites within the septal region and basal caudate nucleus capable of producing the specific antibody in sheep. Activity was not localized. Further studies are required to identify the specific antigenic sites.

Except for cortex and cerebellum all brain tissues potentiated with adjuvant caused experimental allergic encephalomyelitis in the sheep; production of this antibody was thus stimulated by almost all brain tissues. In distinct contrast, production of antibody that induced EEG and behavioral changes was stimulated only by tissues of the septal region and basal caudate nucleus, which therefore presumably contain a unique antigen. Unquestionably, antibody against other common constituents of other tissues was also produced, although not demonstrable by these technics.

We speculate that the less notable EEG and behavioral activity in the monkey given sheep antihuman septal-caudate serum fraction was due to the irregular inoculations of human brain tissues. Conceivably, antibody against myelin was produced so rapidly that the sheep became fatally ill before antibody that affects the monkey, by the assay used in this study, reached high levels.

Other mutual characteristics of serum globulins of sheep antimonkey and antihuman brain tissues and serum fractions of schizophrenic patients have been demonstrated.[3] Globulins of sheep antiseptal-caudate sera obtained by ammonium sulfate precipitation, when tested in the monkey, produced physiologic and behavioral aberrations like those induced by similarly prepared serum fractions of schizophrenic patients. Immunoelectrophoretic patterns of the two serum fractions were also similar, particularly when both were obtained by salting out with 33% ammonium sulfate precipitation; both fractions showed predominantly or solely IgG, and the psychosis-inducing activity of both was related to the presence of IgG. All psychoactive fractions from sera of acute schizophrenic patients and from sheep sera containing antibody against the septal region and basal caudate nucleus contained IgG regardless of the fractionation method used, whereas inactive fractions did not contain IgG. However, the presence of IgG did not necessarily indicate activity, since inert fractions obtained by the same fractionation procedures also showed this precipitin arc. The inert fractions containing IgG were from sheep sera containing antibody against brain regions other than the septal region and basal caudate nucleus, or from human sera of nonschizophrenic control subjects.

Instability of the sheep antimonkey and antihuman brain globulins paralleled our findings with taraxein. The instability of taraxein, the varying amounts of it in the starting serum, and inconsistencies in fractionation procedures were factors responsible for the failure of other researchers to confirm our early taraxein studies.

Although the sheep antimonkey and antihuman septal-caudate serum fractions displayed some of the characteristics described by Mihailovic and Jankovic [8] for the anticat caudate fraction produced in rabbits, there were significant differences. Our test monkeys responded promptly, usually on the first day of injections, whereas the cats of Mihailovic and Jankovic usually did not respond until the third day of injections. Moreover, the response in our monkeys was transient, usually disappearing within 1½ hours, whereas focal abnormalities in the cats were progressive, usually increasing for at least several days after three days of injections.

The finding by agar diffusion studies, that precipititin arcs developed when sheep antisera were reacted with brain homogenates from homologous and other brain regions of monkeys and man, parallels the observation of Mihailovic and Jankovic,[8] who found precipitin arcs when rabbit anticat caudate sera were reacted with homologous brain tissues. Our findings in the present study contrast with our failure to obtain a precipitant when we reacted sera of schizophrenic patients and control subjects with homogenates of various brain regions. Jensen and associates [15] and Rubin [16] were also unsuccessful in demonstrating a precipitant reaction when sera of schizophrenic patients were reacted with homogenates of whole brain or tissues of brain parts. The many mutual characteristics which sheep antisera to brain share with schizophrenic serum fractions suggest that the two sera have common denominators, possibly antibodies against one or more antigens, but the response on agar diffusion against brain tissue antigen indicates they also have different components. It is reasonable to assume, since the homogenates of whole brain tissue which the sheep received contained many antigens, that the sheep developed many antibodies, some having the same characteristics as the globulins of human schizophrenic sera and others with different properties such as the ability to form a precipitation with homogenates of whole brain.

Data obtained in our laboratories and by other investigators support that aspect of our hypothesis which attributes the physiologic abnormality recorded from the septal region of patients during psychotic behavior to impaired neurohumoral activity at the synaptic junction. We have observed similar impaired function and behavior when histamine or atropine was injected intraventricularly into the septal region, or when atropine, a known anticholinergic, was injected into the anterior horn of the lateral ventricle.[12] Other researchers have shown that histamine may be released or acetylcholine activity may be impaired by antigen-antibody combination. Mihailovic and associates,[17] for example, noted increased amounts of histamine in the caudate nucleus of the cat when anticaudate antibody was injected into the lateral ventricle. Strauss and associates [18] found antibody on muscle striations associated with impaired cholinergic activity in patients with myasthenia gravis.

Summary

Antibodies against specific parts of monkey brain, human brain, and column fractions of human septal-caudate tissue were produced by injecting potentiated homogenates of the tissues into sheep. Serum fractions obtained by several methods were tested by injection into the cerebral ventricles of intact rhesus monkeys prepared with depth and surface electrodes for prolonged study. Fractions of antisera against monkey septal region and caudate nucleus induced spiking and slow-waves in electroenoephalograms

(EEGs) from homologous brain sites concomitant with catatonic behavior. Recordings resembled those for monkeys that received the psyshoactive serum fraction (taraxein) of schizophrenic patients obtained by identical fractionation methods as well as those for schizophrenic patients during psychotic episodes. Other characteristics of the antibrain serum fractions resembled those of taraxein.

Fluorescent antibody studies showed that sheep antibrain serum fractions had attached to neural cell nuclei of the septal region and basal caudate nucleus of recipient monkeys whose EEGs and behavior had been altered by the injections.

Psychosis-inducing activity was identified by the presence of γ-G immunoglobulin (IgG) regardless of the fractionation method used to obtain the active fraction from sheep sera containing antibody against the septal region and basal caudate nucleus. Although the active serum fraction migrated with IgG the two fractions were not the same, since inert fractions similarly obtained from sheep sera containing antibody against other brain parts also contained IgG.

We conclude that the septal-basal caudate region of the brain contains a unique antigen against which antibody can be created and which is capable of combining with neural cell nuclei of the septal-basal caudate region to induce, possibly through impairment of neurohumoral conduction, aberrations in EEGs associated with schizophrenic behavior. Since sera of schizophrenic patients contains globulin (taraxein) with essentially the same characteristics, we postulate that taraxein may be antibody and that schizophrenia may represent an auto-immune disorder.

This study was supported by a grant-in-aid from the Edward G. Schlieder Educational Foundation, New Orleans.

Charles J. Fontana gave technical assistance, and Drs. Charles W. DeWitt and Curtis A. Williams gave technical advice.

REFERENCES

1. Heath, R.G., and Krupp, I.M.: "The Biologic Basis of Schizophrenia: An Autoimmune Concept," in Walaas, O. (ed.): *NATO Advanced Study Institute, The Molecular Basis of Some Aspects of Mental Activity,* Academic Press, 1966, to be published.

2. Heath, R.G., and Krupp, I.M.: Schizophrenia as an Immunologic Disorder: I. Demonstration of Antibrain Globulins by Fluorescent Antibody Techniques, *Arch Gen Psychiat* 16:1, 1967.

3. Heath, R.G., et al: Schizophrenia as an Immunologic Disorder: II. Effects of Serum Protein Fractions on Brain Function, *Arch Gen Psychiat* 16:10, 1967.

4. Heath, R.G., and Founds, W.L.: A Perfusion Cannula for Intracerebral Microinjections, *Electroenceph Clin Neurophysiol* 12:930-932 (Nov) 1960.

5. Heath, R.G.; John, S.; and Foss, O.: Stereotaxic Biopsy, *Arch Neurol* 4:291-300 (March) 1961.

6. Heath, R.G.; Leach, B.E.; and Byers, L.W.: "Taraxein: Mode of Action," in Heath, R.G. (ed.): *Serological Fractions in Schizophrenia,* New York: Paul B. Hoeber Inc., Medical Division, Harper & Row Publishers, 1963, pp 107-125.

7. Heath, R.G., et al: Effect on Behavior in Humans With the Administration of Taraxein, *Amer J Psychiat* 114:14-24 (July), 1957.

8. Mihailovic, L., and Jankovic, B.D.: Effects of Intraventricularly Injected Anti-N. Caudatus Antibody on the Electrical Activity of the Cat Brain, *Nature* 192:665-666 (Nov 18) 1961.

9. Gornall, A.G.; Bardawill, C.J.; and David, M.M.: Determination of Serum Proteins by Means of the Biuret Reaction, *J Biol Chem* 177:751-767 (Aug) 1949.

10. Sober, H.A., et al: Chromatography of Proteins: II. Fractionation of Serum Protein on Anion-Exchange Cellulose, *J Amer Chem Soc* 78:756-763 (Feb 20) 1956.

11. Lowry, O.H., et al: Protein Measurement With the Folin Pheno Reagent, *J Biol Chem* 193:265-275 (May 28) 1951.

12. Heath, R.G.: Schizophrenia: Biochemical and Physiologic Aberrations, *Int J Neuropsychiat,* to be published.

13. Heath, R.G., et al: *Studies in Schizophrenia,* Cambridge, Mass: Harvard University Press, 1954.

14. Heath, R.G., and Mickle, W.A.: "Evaluation of Seven Years' Experience With Depth Electrode Studies in Human Patients," in Ramey, E.R., and O'Doherty, D.S. (eds.): *Electrical Studies of the Unanesthetized Brain,* New York: Paul B. Hoeber, Inc., Medical Division, Harper & Row Publishers, 1960, pp 214-247.

15. Jensen, K.; Clausen, J.; and Osterman, E.: Serum and Cerebrospinal Fluid Proteins in Schizophrenia, *Acta Psychiat Scand* 40:280-286 (July) 1964.

16. Rubin, R.T.: Investigation of Precipitins to Human Brain in Sera of Psychotic Patients, *Brit J Psychiat* 111:1003-1006 (Oct) 1965.

17. Mihailovic, L., et al: Effect of Intraventricularly Injected Anti-Cerebral Antibodies on the Histamine-Like Substance and Potassium Content of Various Regions of the Brain of the Cat, *Nature* 203:763-765 (Aug 15) 1964.

18. Strauss, A.J.L., et al: Immunofluorescence Demonstration of a Muscle Binding, Complement-Fixing Serum Globulin Fraction in Myasthenia Gravis, *Proc Soc Exp Biol Med* 105:184-191, 1960.

51

ASPECTS OF HUMORAL AND CELLULAR IMMUNITY IN SCHIZOPHRENIA

M. E. Vartanian, G. I. Kolyaskina, D. V. Lozovsky, G. Sh. Burbaeva, and S. A. Ignatov

The concept of autoantigenic properties of brain tissue was formed at the end of the 19th century when Metchnikov demonstrated the cytotoxic effect of sera against brain tissues [1].

Later on, Khoroshko [2] assumed a possible participation of autoimmune mechanisms in the development of neuropsychiatric diseases.

The interest in autoimmune aspects of psychoneurologic diseases practically disappeared for some period of time. Occasional studies were made concerning the participation of autoimmune mechanisms in the development of psychoneurologic diseases. In the 1930s Lehman-Facius [3–5], applying the method of lipoid flocculation, discovered an antibrain factor in the blood of schizophrenic patients.

In the 1960s there appeared again an interest in immunologic research in the field of mental disease. Fessel [6] and Heath [7–9] in the USA and a group of Soviet researchers [10–13] made an attempt to demonstrate the presence of antibodies to brain antigens in schizophrenic patients.

Nowadays, the significance of some of the above studies is mainly of historic interest. Others, however, need further replication and more profound developments.

Nevertheless, these studies served as a good stimulus for more intensive investigation of the immunopathology of schizoprenia.

On the one hand, detailed investigations were started on brain tissue antigens for the purpose of identifying those antigens whose antibodies were being detected in schizophrenic patients. On the other hand, an intensive study of directly immunologically competent cells of schizophrenic patients was begun.

Reprinted from "Neurochemical and Immunologic Components of Schizophrenia" (D. Bergsma and A. L. Goldstein, eds.), pp. 339–364. Alan R. Liss, Inc., New York.

As can be seen in Table 1, a series of brain-specific proteins have been isolated. However, there are no data whatsoever on their role in pathology.

Proceeding from this, and based on the fact that autoimmune components in schizophrenia can be assumed, we have been studying the organ-specific

Table 1. Summary of Isolated Brain-Specific Proteins

Proteins	Characteristics	Localization
S−100	Heterogenous protein MW 15,000−71,000 EM prealbumin	Glia
14−3−2	Protein MW 40,000 EM α-globulin	Neuron
α-Antigen	Protein MW 39,000 EM α-globulin	Neuron
10B Bogoch, 1969	Glycoprotein EM α-globulin	Glia
α_2-Glycoprotein	Glycoprotein MW 45,000−50,000 EM α_2-globulin	Glia
GFA	Protein MW 43,000 EM α-globulin	Glia
NP-ribonucleoprotein	Nucleoprotein MW 25,000	Glia
GP−350	Sialoglycoprotein MW 11,600	Neuron
Protein unique to the olfactory bulb,	MW 20,000	
$D_1 D_3$ C_1 (synaptin)		Neuron Synaptosomal membranes Synaptosomal vesicles
NS−1, NS−2 NS−3 NS−4		Glia surface Neuron membranes
GM−1 GM−2 GM−10 GM−11	γ-Globulin β_2-γ-Globulin α_2-Globulin α_1-Globulin	

MW−Molecular weight
EM−Electrophoretic mobility

cytoplasmatic antigens of the human brain for the past several years [14, 15].

We used cerebral cortex of normal individuals who died in accidents. The brain samples were obtained not later than 8 hours after death.

An extract of water soluble proteins in phosphate buffer obtained by homogenization and centrifugation at 100,000 g was the source of antigens.

Separation of brain proteins was carried out with the help of anion-exchange chromatography on DEAE-cellulose [15].

As you can see in Figure 1 the proteins having an isoelectric point above pH 7.0 leave the column in the form of 4 or 5 clear-cut fractions which are designated as 1, 2, 3, 4, 5. In certain experiments there were 1 or 2 more peaks containing trace amounts of proteins. The proteins with an isoelectric point below pH 7.0 could be divided into 4 or 5 fractions which are designated here as 10, 11, 12, 13, 14.

Rabbit antisera to protein extract from human cortex absorbed by human liver proteins and blood sera were used in studies of the antigen composition of these fractions. Furthermore, for identification of brain specific antigens in some experiments we used antibrain antibodies obtained from immune sera by the method of affinity chromatography [16].

To strengthen the precipitative arches immunodiffusive preparations were processed by using [125] I sheep antibodies to rabbit globulins followed by autoradiography [17].

Using double diffusion and immunoelectrophoresis it has been shown that the brain specific antigens are to be found only in fractions 1, 2, 10, and 11 (Fig. 1).

Immunoelectrophoresis with the use of absorbed antisera revealed in fraction 10 two antigens with the mobilities of α_2-globulin (which always gave a typical coloration when stained for the presence of glycoproteins) and α_1-globulin, and in fraction 11 only α_1-globulin.

In fractions 1 and 2 the antigens were detected only by autoradiography. There is always an antigen with the mobility of β_2-γ-globulin. In certain experiments we could detect one more antigen with the mobility of γ-globulin.

Comparison of the properties of the antigens detected by us with the antigens of the soluble brain-specific proteins described in the literature led us to the following conclusion. The antigen with the electrophoretic mobility of α_2-globulin detected by us is not identical to the previously reported nonglycoproteins S–100, 14–3–2, α-antigen, GFA, NP-ribonucleoprotein, or DNA-110. The α_2-glycoprotein and α_1-globulin described by Warecka [16], in spite of certain differences in the methods of preparation of the total extract of brain proteins and antigens isolation, proved to be similar to our α_2- and α_1-globulins in immunophoregrams with antibrain antibodies isolated by affinity chromatography. The 10B-glycoprotein described by Bogoch [18] is an α_2-globulin, and the fraction containing it was isolated under almost the same conditions as our

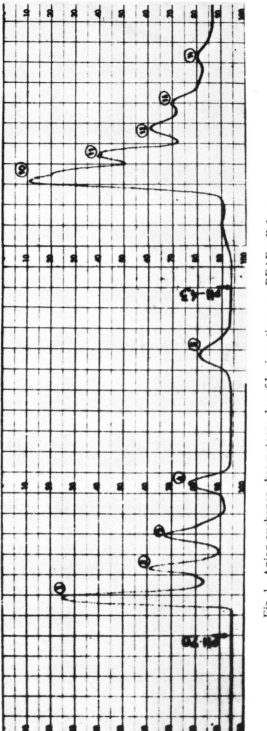

Fig. 1. Anion exchange chromatography of brain antigens on DEAE-cellulose.

Behavior and Immune Function

fraction 10. All this allows the conclusion that Warecka, Bogoch, and we could be dealing with the same antigen.

As for the 2 antigens with the mobilities of β_2-γ- and γ-globulins detected both in the total protein extract and in fractions 1 and 2, we have not come across any data on these human brain antigens in the literature. Some indications as to the presence of antigens with such electrophoretic mobility were encountered only in studies of rat, cat, and bovine brain [19–21].

More comprehensive and comparable data on brain-specific human antigens allowing their systematization will require study based on unified immunochemical testing.

The first stage was to evaluate the antigen activity of all isolated fractions in the complement fixation test (CFT) with sera of schizophrenic, multiple sclerosis (MS), and lateral amyotrophic sclerosis (LAS) patients. The major antigenic activity was found in fractions 2 and 10 although the reaction was positive in low titer in fraction 11 and sometimes in fraction 1. Therefore, the sera of the patients and of normal individuals was studied with these 2 most active fractions. The results are given in Table 2 and Figure 2.

As can be seen in Table 2, the comparison of the groups shows that in schizophrenic patients the antibrain antibodies are detected on interaction with fraction 10 much more frequently than with fraction 2 and more often than after interaction with the protein extract. Whereas in the MS and LAS cases and in normal individuals it is fraction 2 that gives positive CFT most frequently.

TABLE 2. Frequency of Antibrain Antibodies Among Groups of Individuals

Groups examined	N	Positive complement fixation test with different preparations of antigens		
		Protein extract (PE)	Fraction 2[a]	Fraction 10[a]
Schizophrenia	50	44.0	20.0	70.0
		'''NS[b]	'''NS	'''p < 0.001
		"NS	"NS	'p < 0.01
		0.05 < p < 0.08	'NS	'p < 0.001
Multiple sclerosis	29	37.9	48.3	20.7
		"NS	"NS	"NS
		'NS	'NS	'NS
Lateral amyotrophic sclerosis	43	32.6	58.1	37.2
		'NS	'NS	'p < 0.1
Normals	22	13.6	22.7	4.5

''' – compared with sera of patients with multiple sclerosis
" – compared with sera of patients with lateral amyotrophic sclerosis
' – compared with sera of normal patients

[a]See Figure 1
[b]NS = not significant

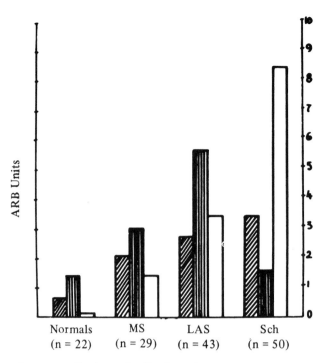

Fig. 2. Titers of serum antibrain antibodies in patients with schizophrenia (Sch), multiple sclerosis (MS), and lateral amyotrophic sclerosis (LAS).

▨ — protein extract (PE); ☐ — fraction No 10; ▥ — fraction No 2

Of the same nature were the results of comparison of average CFT titers expressed in arbitrary units (that is, titer 1:10 corresponds to 1.0, titer 1:20 to 2.0, etc) as shown in Figure 2. Attention should be paid to the fact that between MS patients and normal individuals there is a similarity in the ratios of average antibody titers with the protein extract, fraction 2, and fraction 10.

In LAS patients this similarity somewhat decreases due to the increase of CFT titers with fraction 10.

In schizophrenics, the ratio of average CFT titers with different preparations of brain antigens is quite different. There is a significant increase in the titer with fraction 10 and very low titer with fraction 2 resembling that in normal individuals.

The results obtained with schizophrenics indicate that the antigens to which there are antibodies in sera from schizophrenic patients and which may prove to be in some way associated with autoimmune processes are mostly found in fraction 10. Besides, as was indicated above, antibrain antibodies in sera from schizophrenics produce positive CFT also with fraction 11. This accords with the presence in this fraction of α_1-glycoprotein whose identity with that in fraction 10 is confirmed by the identity of the corresponding lines in the double diffusion test. This also gives grounds for believing that a higher antigenic activity of fraction 10 in CFT with sera from schizophrenics, as compared to

Behavior and Immune Function

fraction 11, may be due to the α_2-glycoprotein component of fraction 10 which is absent in fraction 11.

Thus, the data obtained by us favor the assumption that antibrain antibodies in sera from schizophrenics are directed preferentially against α_2-glycoprotein antigen. However, to fully confirm this conclusion, the study of individual glycoproteins of fraction 10 and/or the glycoprotein fraction binding with concanavalin A will be necessary.

The study of peripheral lymphocytes of schizophrenic patients yielded the following results. Figure 3 demonstrates the results of thymidine incorporation in cellular DNA of phytohemagglutinin (PHA)-stimulated peripheral lymphocytes. As can be seen in Figure 3 the rate of labeled cells in the lymphocyte culture of normal controls was 40.9% after PHA addition. The functional activity of lymphocytes of schizophrenic patients was considerably reduced and averaged 27.2%. The reduced response to PHA was observed in 68% of the patients.

Futher investigations demonstrated that the reduced response of peripheral blood lymphocytes of schizophrenic patients to PHA was conditioned by at least 2 factors: 1) prolongation of the mitotic cycle as seen by a 1-day delay of the peak of the mitotic index (MI) from the peak of the labeled nuclei (Fig. 4A, B) and 2) by the reduction of the volume of the proliferative pool, as shown in Figure 5.

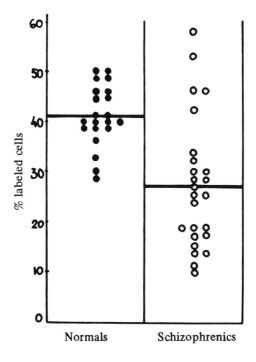

Fig. 3. Percent of labeled cells of PHA culture of patient and normal blood lymphocytes. Cultures were pulsed for 1 hour with titrated-thymidine on 3rd day.

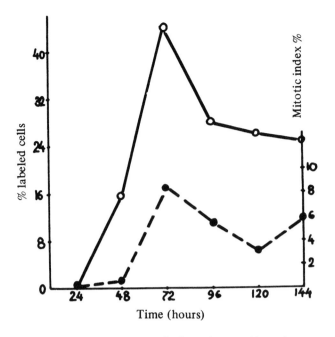

Fig. 4a. Kinetics of titrated-thymidine uptake by cultures of lymphocytes stimulated with PHA. Cultures were pulsed for 1 hour with titrated-thymidine on 1st, 2nd, 3rd, 4th, 5th and 6th day. ○——○ Labeled nuclei, ●——● mitotic index.

If the cell culture consists of a single cell population of proliferating cells (no resting reserve), all the cells should be labeled if titrated–thymidine is made constantly available for a period longer than the generation time. During this time all the cells should have entered or passed through the phase of DNA synthesis and therefore should have incorporated the label. If, on the other hand, not all the cells are cycling because a dormant fraction or resting reserve exists, it should not be possible to obtain labeling of all the cells of the culture, and the percentage of the labeled cells should reach a plateau at some level less than 100%.

The results of the study of the proliferative pool in PHA-stimulated lymphocyte cultures of 2 normal individuals and 2 schizophrenics are demonstrated on Figure 5.

With the aid of the obtained data the saturation curves were constructed (a dependence of the labeled cell portion on the incubation time with H^3-thymidine). The proliferative pools of the lymphocytes of 2 normal individuals were 76% and 63%, and the proliferative pools of schizophrenics were 31% and 32%.

It is apparent from these data that a 100% labeled condition was not obtained in the lymphocyte cultures of either patients or normal individuals, ie all the lymphocyte cultures (stimulated by PHA) consisted of at least 2 populations of cells, one of which was in a state of continuous cycles and the other in a condition of dormancy or resting reserve. The portion of resting cells in the cul-

Behavior and Immune Function

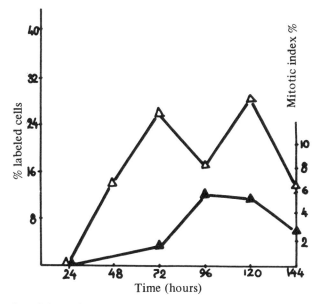

Fig. 4b. Kinetics of titrated-thymidine uptake by cultures of lymphocytes stimulated with PHA. Cultures were pulsed for 1 hour with titrated-thymidine on 1st, 2nd, 3rd, 4th, 5th, and 6th day.   △— △ Labeled nuclei, ▲___▲ mitotic index.

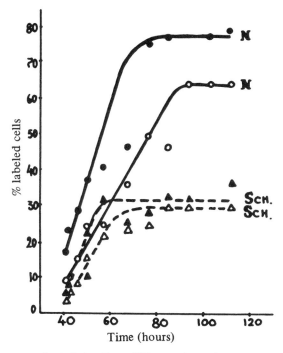

Fig. 5. Mean percent of labeled cells at different time of harvest following continuous ^{3}H-thymidine exposure in lymphocyte cultures of normals and schizophrenics stimulated with PHA.

ture of schizophrenic patients' lymphocytes was considerably larger.

Further investigations were aimed at the study of the quantitative proportion of T and B lymphocytes in the peripheral circulation of schizophrenic patients.

An application of the immunofluorescence technique [22] permitted demonstration that the proportion of B lymphocytes in schizophrenic patients significantly increases and averages 44% as compared to 22% found in normal individuals (p < 0.001) (Fig. 6). At the same time the number of T lymphocytes capable of spontaneous rosette formation [23] with sheep red blood cells is reduced. A further analysis of the various forms of rosettes showed that the lymphocytes in schizophrenic patients form a large number of so-called "incomplete" rosettes, ie rosettes in which 4–7 sheep red blood cells are joined to a lymphocyte (Table 3). At the same time, as can be seen, the number of complete rosettes of the "morula" type is significantly less in schizophrenic patients than in normal individuals.

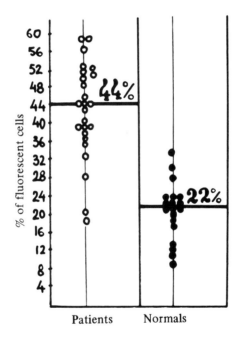

Fig. 6. B lymphocytes (immunofluorescent staining).

The following experiments (cultivation of normal lymphocytes in medium containing serum from schizophrenic patients) demonstrated that blood serum from schizophrenic patients contains a substance which reduces the number of DNA-synthesizing cells in the PHA-stimulated culture of the peripheral blood lymphocytes of normal individuals (Fig. 7). As can be seen in Figure 7 the number of labeled cells in the cultures of normals is significantly reduced after addition

Behavior and Immune Function

TABLE 3. E Rosettes in Schizophrenia

	E rosettes (%)	Incomplete rosettes (%)	Morula type rosettes (%)
Normals	65.9 ± 2.2	32.4 ± 3.1	22.7 ± 3.5
Schizophrenics	49.8 ± 2.4	48.6 ± 2.8	12.4 ± 2.6
	p < 0.001	p < 0.002	p < 0.05

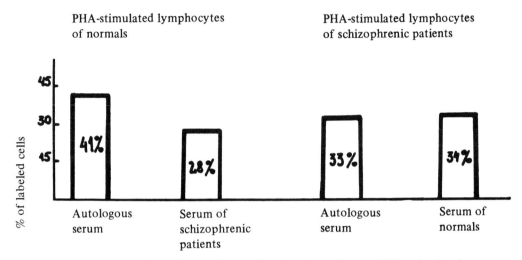

Fig. 7. Inhibitory effect of serum from schizophrenic patients on PHA-stimulated lymphocytes of normals.

into the medium of serum from schizophrenic patients. At the same time, the number of labeled cells in cultures of lymphocytes from schizophrenic patients did not increase after incubation with serum from normal individuals. This inhibiting substance is contained in the blood serum of 81.2% of schizophrenic patients. Similar results were obtained in the application of both the autoradiographic method and the method of total radioactivity in liquid scintillation counter measuring (Fig. 8).

Thus, the above studies resulted in distinguishing 3 groups of facts: 1) The detection of antibodies to brain proteins in schizophrenic patients, 2) the reduction of the functional activity of peripheral blood T lymphocytes in schizophrenic patients, 3) the presence of a factor in the blood serum of schizophrenic patients which reduces the PHA response of peripheral lymphocytes of normal individuals.

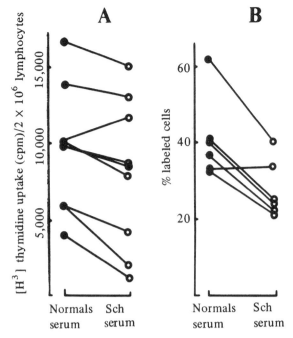

Fig. 8. Inhibitory effect of serum from schizophrenic patients on phytohemagglutinin-stimulated lymphocytes of normals. A) Method of total radioactivity in liquid scintillation counter. B) Autoradiographic method.

Antibodies to T lymphocytes appear to be one of the substances which produce such an inhibiting effect. These antibodies can block, damage, and even lyse T lymphocytes. The data concerning the presence of shared organospecific antigens in the brain and thymus of a whole number of animals and humans allow us to assume that antibodies to brain antigens may possess the same capacity. Some cytotoxic properties of blood serum from schizophrenic patients towards thymus-dependent lymphocytes substantiate this fact.

We investigated the cytotoxic effect of the blood sera on thymocytes of CBA mice, basing our studies on literature [24–27] and our own data [28] which prove the presence of shared antigens between the thymus and the brain of mouse and human. In order to study these shared organospecific antigens of the brain and the thymus of human and mouse, rabbit antiserum against human thymocytes absorbed by the tissue of mouse liver and mouse bone marrow was used. It was found that this serum was highly cytotoxic towards mouse thymocytes. Human brain tissue and human thymocytes completely absorbed the cytotoxic activity of this serum towards mouse thymocytes (Figs. 9 and 10). Using these data we can make an assumption that the human brain possesses antigenic determinants identical or very close to those of human thymocytes. In a similar way the cytotoxicity of antiserum against human thymocytes was completely eliminated after absorption by the mouse brain tissue and the mouse

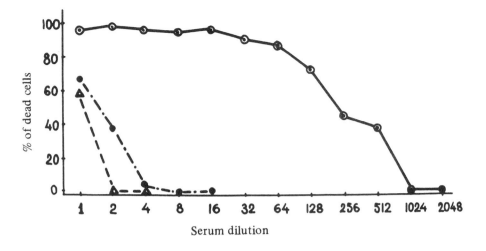

Fig. 9. Absorption of a rabbit antihuman thymocyte antiserum with human brain.

⊙——⊙ Antiserum was not absorbed

●— · — ● Antiserum was absorbed with mouse liver, mouse bone marrow
and human brain once

Δ - - - Δ or twice

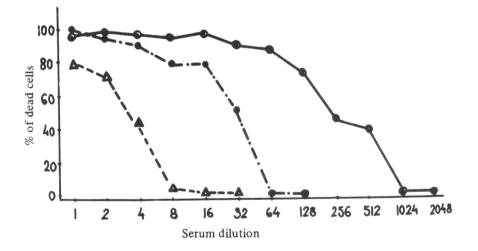

Fig. 10. Absorption of a rabbit anti-human thymocyte antiserum with human thymus.

⊙—⊙ Antiserum was not absorbed

●— · —● Antiserum was absorbed with mouse liver, mouse bone marrow and human
thymus once

Δ - - - Δ or twice

thymocytes (Figs.11 and 12). These results demonstrated the presence of shared antigens between the human and mouse tissues. In this connection, using the mouse thymocytes in cytotoxic tests, we can study the action of serum antibodies against human tissues.

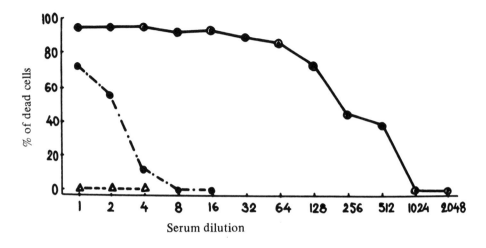

Fig. 11. Absorption of a rabbit antihuman thymocyte antiserum with mouse brain.
⊙—⊙ Antiserum was not absorbed
●—·—● Antiserum was absorbed with mouse liver, mouse bone marrow and mouse brain once
Δ - - - Δ or twice

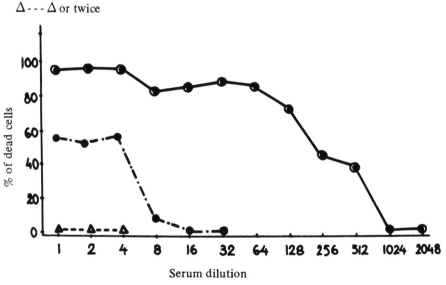

Fig. 12. Absorption of a rabbit antihuman thymocyte antiserum with mouse thymus
⊙—⊙ Antiserum was not absorbed
●—● Antiserum was absorbed with mouse liver, mouse bone marrow and mouse thymocytes once
Δ - - - Δ or twice

The results of these investigations are given in Figure 13. An analysis of the obtained data demonstrated that the blood serum of both schizophrenic patients and normal individuals possesses antithymic activity. The level of the cytotoxic index defining the given activity varies over a wide range in both examined groups, fluctuating from 0.0 to 0.85 in the control groups of normal individuals and from 0.0 to 0.97 in the group of schizophrenic patients. However, the average level of antithymic activity in the group of schizophrenic patients is considerably higher than in the group of normal individuals with averages of 0.52 and 0.26, respectively ($p < 0.001$). Further detailed analysis of the distribution of individuals with different levels of blood serum antithymic activity among the schizophrenic patients and normal individuals allowed us to establish the presence of 2 or more subpopulations in the examined groups (Fig. 14). In this connection a further analysis was made concerning the distribution of all the studied individuals who were classified into 3 groups depending on the level of their serum antithymic activity: the first with a low (from 0.0 to 0.26), the second with a mean (from 0.27 to 0.55), and the third with a high (from 0.56 to 0.97) cytotoxic index. The analysis of the distribution of schizophrenic patients and normal individuals in these groups showed that 61.7% of the sera possessed a low antithymic activity and only 23.4% of the sera a high level in the control group of normal individuals. In the group of schizophrenic patients the

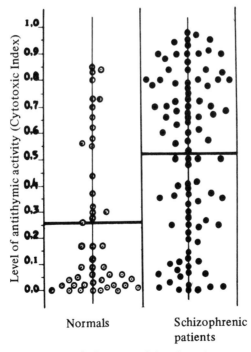

Fig. 13. Serum antithymic activity.

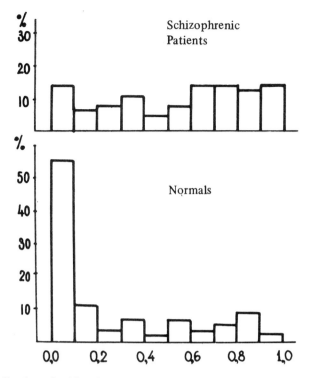

Fig. 14. Distribution of schizophrenic patients and normals depending on levels of their serum antithymic activity.

situation was quite opposite: 26.5% of the sera possessed a low antithymic activity and 53.1%, high. As in the group of schizophrenic patients, there was an accumulation of persons whose blood serum possessed high antithymic activity; the mean level of the blood serum antithymic activity in schizophrenic patients was significantly higher than in controls.

However, further investigations showed that a high level of antithymic activity is a phenomenon characteristic not only of schizophrenia. As can be seen on Figure 15, similar levels of antithymic activity are found in the blood serum of manic-depressive psychotic patients and patients with a thyrotoxic goiter. The level of the cytotoxic index in the given groups was 0.54 and 0.51 respectively. These groups significantly differed from the control group of normal individuals in the level of the blood serum antithymic activity ($p < 0.05$) whereas there was no difference from the group of schizophrenic patients ($p > 0.05$). Compared to the named groups, the level of the blood serum antithymic activity of patients with hernia, acute appendicitis, and senile dementia did not considerably differ from that of the blood serum of normal individuals. The average level of the cytotoxic index in the groups mentioned above was 0.17 and 0.27, respectively, permitting them to be distinguished from the group of schizophrenic patients ($p < 0.001$).

Behavior and Immune Function

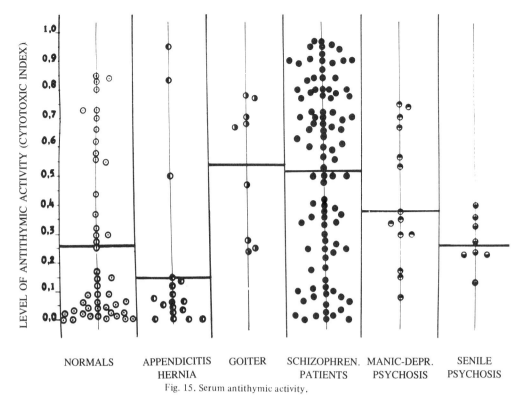

Fig. 15. Serum antithymic activity.

On the basis of a series of biologic studies carried out by the Institute of Psychiatry of the Academy of Medical Sciences of the USSR, the most adequate classification of schizophrenia appears to be one based upon the course of this disease [29]. In this respect the level of the blood serum antithymic activity was analyzed in 2 groups of schizophrenic patients: the continuous and the shift-like forms of schizophrenia. An analysis carried out in these groups showed that there is no definite relation between the clinical peculiarities of the development of the disease and the level of the serum antithymic activity (Fig. 16). The level of the serum antithymic activity for both groups was practically the same: 0.50 and 0.53 for the groups with continuous and shift-like schizophrenia, respectively. Insofar as the level of the blood serum antithymic activity varied considerably in each group of schizophrenic patients, there arose the question as to whether there is an interconnection of these variations with other clinical parameters and in particular with the duration of the disease. The analysis demonstrated that the group of patients whose sera possess low antithymic activity contains 84% individuals with duration of the disease over 5 years and only 16% with duration less than 5 years. A somewhat different picture is observed in the group of patients with high serum antithymic activity: the percentage of patients with the disease lasting over 5 years was 57% and individuals with a schizophrenic process less than 5 years 43%. Comparing the distributions in the mentioned

Schizophrenia: Humoral and Cellular Immunity   **459**

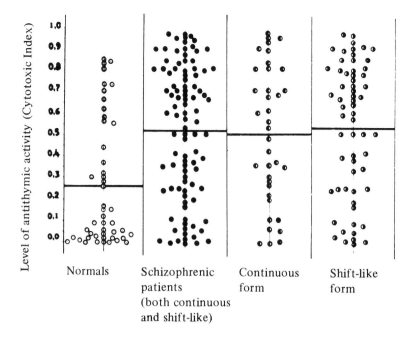

Fig. 16. Serum antithymic activity.

groups we obtained a significant difference (p < 0.05). In other words, at the initial period of the disease there is an accumulation of persons with a high level of blood serum antithymic activity. The maximum frequency of the detection of sera with a high level of antithymic activity is observed in patients with duration of the disease under 5 years. It shows that the longer the disease, the less expressed is the antithymic activity and vice versa, the shorter the schizophrenic process, the more probable that the patient's blood will possess high antithymic activity.

The following investigations were devoted to the genetic determination of the antithymic factor. The antithymic factor was studied in 44 relatives of schizophrenic patients.

The replicated determinations of the antithymic factor in the same patient showed an insignificant variability of the cytotoxic index (CI). At the same time, interindividual differences were expressed much more clearly (Table 4). In evaluating these results we may assume that the interindividual differences in patients of a relatively homogeneous group are partially determined by genetic factors.

It is a well-known fact that the mechanisms producing autoimmunne processes are controlled by a polygenic system. Taking this into consideration, an attempt was made to check whether our data corresponded to a model of

TABLE 4. Analysis of Variance: One-Way Classification

Source	Sum. sqr	Mean sqr	Freedom	F	Factorial portion of variation (%)
Between persons	37.79	1.18	32.0	11.50	77.24
Within persons	6.88	0.10	67.0		

polygenic inheritance with a threshold manifestation [30, 31]. Figure 17 shows the frequency distribution of the level of the CI for 3 basic groups of subjects: a) normal controls, b) schizophrenics, c) the relatives of these schizophrenic patients. As is evident from the graphs (and confirmed by statistical analysis) all 3 distributions markedly deviate from the normal gaussian distribution which is usually expected for polygenic traits. Nevertheless, by using approximate formulas derived by Edwards [31], we attempted to determine the heritability of the CI by choosing different threshold levels for this index with the interval of 0.5–2.5 standard deviations higher than the mean level for normal individuals. Figure 18 shows the theoretic distributions for a polygenic trait in the general population and in the population of relatives of probands with a given trait. The threshold beyond which lie all the persons manifesting a given trait is marked on the right side of the distribution.

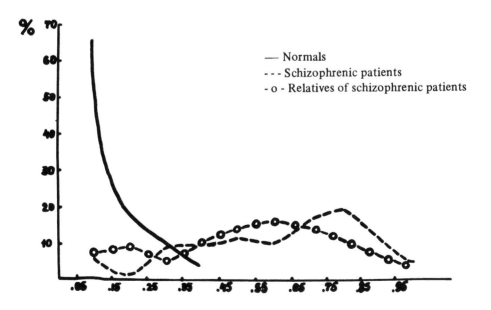

— Normals
- - - Schizophrenic patients
- o - Relatives of schizophrenic patients

Fig. 17. Frequency distribution of CI in different groups

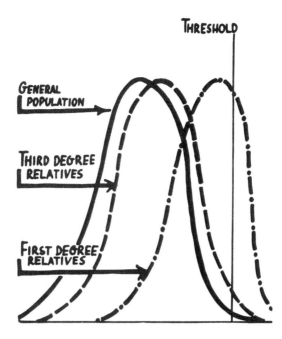

Fig. 18. Model of polygenic inheritance (after Falconer [30] and Edwards [31].

We found that even for the most extreme threshold level beyond which there is no healthy group the percentage of relatives exceeding the threshold is large (approximately 75%).

Thus, the coefficient of heritability exceeds 100%. These results do not correspond to the threshold (polygenic) model. The fact that in comparison with the general population hereditary loading for the CI is sufficiently high suggests the possibility of a monogenic control of antithymic antibody production. Up to the present we have studied a sample of families for which we have data for the parents and sibs of our probands. Data from several of these families are shown in Figure 19. It may be sensible to interpret these data within the framework of a monogenic model with 3 alleles and 6 corresponding genotypes.

This may account for the rather large interindividual variability of the cyto-toxic index among the patients with functional psychoses. The current family data do not oppose such a hypothesis.

On a comparatively small family material another attempt was made to evaluate quantitatively the contribution of genetic factors for the determination of interindividual differences in the level of antithymic activity (CI). We consider this to be a preliminary attempt. Therefore we used the data of 31 "parent-proband" pairs.

In this sample the correlation coefficient (r_{op}) was equal to 0.35. In the same

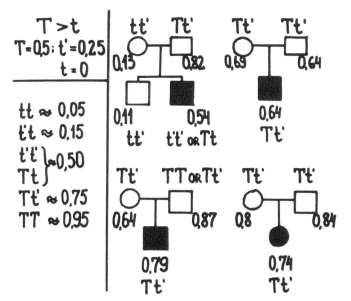

Fig. 19. A possible monogenic model of inheritance.

material for the sample of 24 marital pairs (proband parents) the correlation co-efficient (r_{pp}) was –0.003, indicating that correlation was practically absent. Thus, there were no grounds for finding a special correction of the correlation "parent-child" for possible primary or secondary marriage assortativity. In accordance with the formula of coefficient heritability in a "narrow sense" ($h^2 = 2 r_{op}$), a possible contribution of genetic factors can be evaluated at 0.70 due only to the additive interaction of alleles. It is a rather high evaluation taking into account the fact that it is not possible to exclude a contribution of various nonlinear genetic factors: dominance and epistasis. For this contribution, side indications can be derived from the character of population distributions in CI level in samples of parents and their relatives and a group of normal individuals. Hence we must admit that the studied trait is rather strictly determined by genetic factors.

Actually, the above-mentioned gene locus is only one of several loci involved in a complex oligogenic system controlling the predisposition to schizophrenic spectrum disease. Obviously, our family material is still insufficient, and the above-mentioned model will need a more weighty proof for this hypothesis.

The following results serve as another example of a considerable interfamily variability in schizophrenia. As can be seen in Table 5, the frequency of detection of antibodies against brain tissue in relatives amounted to 46.6% in cases when probands possessed similar antibodies. In contrast to this such antibodies could be detected in only 3.2% of relatives whose proband did not possess antibodies. This was the same as the frequency in the control group.

TABLE 5. Frequency of Serum Antibrain Antibodies Among Relatives of Schizophrenia Patients

Group examined	Positive complement-fixation test (%)	P (to normals)
Relatives of "antibody-positive" probands	46.6 ± 12.8	< 0.01
"Antibody-negative" probands	3.2 ± 3.2	< 0.1

TABLE 6. Interpair Differences in 42 Pairs of MZ and DZ Twins (%)

		MZ	DZ	P
Normal twins	blast cells	34.9	33.5	> 0.1
	miototic cells	38.9	32.8	> 0.1
Schizophrenic twins	blast cells	23.3	66.5	< 0.001
	mitotic cells	33.9	51.8	< 0.001

MZ – monozygotic twins

DZ – dizygotic twins

The number of mitotic and blast cells in PHA-stimulated cultures of lymphocytes is also controlled by genetic factors. It was proved on the twin model. Interpair comparisons of normal twins did not show significant differences between MZ and DZ. At the same time, the analysis of similar criteria in twin pairs of schizophrenic patients demonstrated significant differences between MZ and DZ (Table 6).

REFERENCES

1. Mechnikov II: Kletochnii jadi (cytotoxini). Russ Arch Pathol 11:101, 1901.
2. Khoroshko VK: "Reactii Zivotnogo Organizma na Vvedenie Nervnoi Tkani (Nevrotoxini, Anaphylaksia, Endotoxini)." Moscow. 1912.
3. Lehman-Facius H: Über die Liquordiagnose der Schizophrenien. Klin Wochenschr 16:1646–1648, 1937.
4. Lehman-Facius H: Liquoruntersuchungen bei destructiven Erkrankungen des Nerwensystems besonders bei Schizophrenien. Z Neurol Psychiatr 157:109–115, 1937.
5. Lehman-Facius H: Serologischanalytische Versuche mit Liquoren und seren von Schizophrenien. Allg Z Psychiatr 110:232–243, 1939.

6. Fessel W: Autoimmunity and mental illness. A preliminary report. Arch Gen Psychiatry 6:320, 1962.
7. Heath RG, Krupp IM: Schizophrenia as an immunologic disorder. 1. Demonstration of antibrain globulins by fluorescent antibody techniques. Arch Gen Psychiatry 16:1–9, 1967.
8. Heath RG, Krupp IM: Schizophrenia as an immunologic disorder. 2. Effects of serum protein fractions on brain function. Arch Gen Psychiatry 16:10–23, 1967.
9. Heath RG, Krupp IM, Byers LW, Liljekvist JJ: Schizophrenia as an immunologic disorder. 3. Effects of antimonkey and antihuman brain antibody on brain function. Arch Gen Psychiatry 16:24–33, 1967.
10. Kouznetzova NI, Semenov SF: Le décèlement d'anticorps du nerveaux dans le sérum des malades d'affections neuropsychiques. Zh Nervopathol Psikhiatr 6:869, 1961.
11. Semenov SF, Morosov GV, Kouznetzova NI: L'évaluation de la portée clinique des anticorps anticérébraux dans la sérum des malades de schizophrénie et d'autres affections neuropsychiques. Zh Nervopatol Psikhiatr 8:1210, 1961.
12. Kolyaskina GI, Kushner SG: Principles governing appearance of brain antibodies in serum of schizophrenics. Neuroscience Translation, 1970, vol 13, p 1.
13. Kolyaskina GI, Vartanian ME: The genetic aspects of immunopathological mechanisms in schizophrenia. Br J Psychiatr, Special Publication no. 10, ch 8, p 48.
14. Burbaeva GSh, Lozovsky DV: K immunohimicheskomu issledovaniu belkov mozga cheloveka. Vestn Akad Med Nauk SSSR 1:50–55, 1971.
15. Ignatov SA, Vedernikova L, Burbaeva GSh, Lozovski DV: Antigenni sostav belkovich phraczi kori golovnogo mozga cheloveka, poluchennich chromatographiei na DEAE-celluloze. Zh Nervopatol Psikhiatr. (In press)
16. Warecka K, Möller HJ, Vogel HM, Tripatziz J: Human brain-specific alpha$_2$-glycoprotein: Purification by affinity chromatography and detection of a new component; localization in nervous cells. J Neurochem 19:719–725, 1972.
17. Elgort D, Abelev G: Immunoavtoradiographicheskoe opredelenie α_1-phretoproteina givotnich i cheloveka. Byull Eksp Biol Med 71:119–120, 1971.
18. Bogoch S: Proteins. In Lajtha J (ed): "Handbook of Neurochemistry." New York: Plenum Press, 1969, vol 1, pp 75–91.
19. Shtilman NS, Piven NV, Shtark MB: K issledovaniu antigennogo spektra razlichnih struktur golovnogo mozga kris. Dokl Akad Nauk SSSR 224:1198–1200, 1974.
20. Orosz A, Falus A, Madarâsz E, Gergely I, Adäm G: A brain-specific water-soluble antigen in homogenates of cat cerebral cortex. Acta Biochim Biophys Acad Sci Hung 9:319–326, 1974.
21. Hatcher BV, MacPherson CF: Studies on brain antigens II. Water soluble antigenic proteins of bovine brain. J Immunol 192:877–883, 1969.
22. Fröland SS, Natvig JB: Surface-bound immunoglobulin as a marker of β-lymphocytes in man. Nature (London) New Biol 234:251, 1971.
23. Jondal M, Holm G, Wigzell H: Surface markers on human T- and B-lymphocytes. I. A large population of lymphocytes forming nonimmune rosettes with sheep red blood cells. J Exp Med 136:207, 1972.
24. Takada A, Takada Y, Iti I, Minowada J: Shared antigenic determinants between human brain and human T-cell line. Clin Exp Immunol 18:491–498, 1974.
25. Reif AE, Allen JM: The AKR thymic antigen and its distribution in leukemias and nervous tissues. J Exp Med 120:413–433, 1964.
26. Raff MC, Wortis HH: Thymus-dependance of θ-bearing cells in the peripheral lymphoid tissue of mice. Immunology 18:931–942, 1970.

27. Golub ES: The distribution of brain-associated θ-antigen cross-reactive with mouse in the brain of other species. J Immunol 109:168–170, 1972.
28. Maznina TP, Kushner SG: Studies on human brain-thymus cross-reactive antigens. J Immunol 117:818, 1976.
29. Snezhnevsky AV, Vartanian ME: The forms of schizophrenia and their biological correlates. In Himwich HE (ed): "Biochemistry, Schizophrenia, and Affective Illness." Baltimore: William & Wilkins, 1970, pp 1–28.
30. Falconer DS: The inheritance of liability to certain diseases, estimated from the incidence among relatives. Ann Hum Genet 29:51–76, 1965.
31. Edwards JH: Familial predisposition in man. Br Med Bull 25:58–64, 1969.

DISCUSSION

Dr. Strahilevitz: I want to ask just a short question. In view of all the data that you presented, what would you think about the use of the thymus lymphocyte-stimulating factor to see if it may be therapeutic in some of the schizophrenics?

Dr. Vartanian: I am sorry, I cannot answer your question, because up to now we do not know the real importance of the factor for the pathogenesis of schizophrenia. I guess according to our data at the moment we can assume that probably this is a secondary effect of the disease affecting the processes of the brain.

Dr. Maricq: I find your work extremely interesting because a number of years ago I studied the PHA response in lymphocytes of schizophrenics whom I selected on the basis of capillary criteria which we believe to be a genetic trait. This trait was present in about 70% of chronic hospitalized schizophrenics, and we found a significantly decreased response to PHA stimulation in them. We also found that differential white blood cell counts were slightly different in these patients. Have you observed any such differences?

Dr. Vartanian: Differences of what?

Dr. Maricq: Differential white counts; those patients tended to have fewer lymphocytes.

Dr. Vartanian: We counted 300 patients and it was done by Dr. Prilipko, and they could not find any significant difference between schizophrenics and the control population in counting the lymphocytes.

Dr. Naum: Since you have demonstrated antithymic acitivity in sera of the schizophrenic patients, I think it would be interesting to see if these sera have any effects on MLC reactions.

Dr. Vartanian: It is a fascinating area. At the moment we have only data concerned in the MIF, and I think it is a little bit preliminary to talk about. But there is some macrophage inhibitory activity.

Dr. Munson: I would like to congratulate you on a fine piece of work. I have been very interested in the fact that the antigen on the T lymphocyte exists in the brain. Antitheta serum is made by injecting brain into rabbits or goats. Is there any relationship between the theta antigen on the T lymphocyte and the fraction 10 that you have isolated?

Dr. Vartanian: It is a very important question. We started this project with the hope that we can isolate the antigen to identify these antibodies against a particular antigen, but unfortunately, we met with a lot of difficulties. Regretfully we do not have a pure antigen available.

Dr. Munson: One other very short question. Concanavalin A has a different receptor site on the T lymphocyte than does PHA. By any chance, did you try Con A as a stimulant?

Dr. Vartanian: Yes, this is the subject of Dr. Prilipko's presentation.

Dr. Witz: Two technical questions concerning the antibrain activity of schizophrenic patients' sera. What were the target cells? Were these mouse or human cells? Second, I am not clear as to the exact meaning of your values. What dilutions of the sera were used in the charts presented, and did the lowest serum dilution used still give a measurable cytotoxicity index?

Dr. Vartanian: I did not understand clearly your first question.

Dr. Witz: What were the target cells?

Dr. Vartanian: The experiments were designed so that we could absorb from the serum, which we used for testing this antithymic activity, with human brain and human thymus tissues, and vice versa, with mouse thymus and mouse brain. This was done to prove the existence of shared antigens. In each case the serum was adsorbed by different extracts.

Dr. Witz: You showed cytotoxicity data in terms of antithymic activity. What were the target cells in these assays?

Dr. Vartanian: Thymocytes from CBA mice.

Dr. Witz: Do you still find a higher antithymus antibody activity in schizophrenic sera as compared to sera of normal individuals?

Dr. Vartanian: Yes.

Dr. Witz: I am sure you know of the paper that appeared in the Journal of Immunology a few months ago, in which the investigators could not find any elevated titers of antimouse thymus antibodies in the serum of schizophrenic patients. I would be interested in hearing your comments concerning this point.

Dr. Vartanian: Yes, we know about this Canadian paper, and we have analyzed it in detail (I have a slide showing this analysis), which compares our data with this group. When we compared indices obtained in our study with those of the Canadian group, we found that the level of activity in our schizophrenic samples and in the Canadian group were absolutely the same. I think the differences were related primarily to the control group. In the Canadian control group, they had a higher antithymic activity than we have found. Another difference may be that they absorbed their sera with erythrocytes. We are presently repeating our studies using coded serum samples from the NIMH, from London, from Copenhagen, and from Basel. We will see if we can extend our original findings.

Dr. Papermaster: I would like to congratulate you on a thorough and far-reaching study including the genetic approach. I really do not think that the facts are as important as the leadership that your group has provided in looking at biologic approaches to the immunogenetic aspects of patient populations. I would be interested in whether we could clarify two topics that I think will ultimately become contentious. The first problem includes the sera about which Dr. Witz spoke and the second regards the patient. Hopefully, an international workshop could be organized at some point along the lines of the HLA histocompatibility workshops. At such workshops participants exchange sera, test a panel of blood lymphocytes, and work out differences in techniques and interpretation. Nevertheless, I must add that regardless of the final outcome of such a workshop, it would still have to focus on the lines of immunologic and genetic analyses pioneered at your institution.

Subject Index

A

Academic performance, and mononucleosis, 347–348, 352–354, 357

Acceleration stress, effect on spleen and peritoneal cells, 122, 123–129, 136

ACTH. *See* Adrenocorticotropic hormone (ACTH)

ACTH-RF, 38

Adaptation
  decrease in cortisol levels with, 219
  infantile stimulation and, 221–224
  in malaria, 305
  to predator-induced stress, 248
  in rheumatoid arthritis, 329–330

Adenohypophysis, thymus as target organ of, 105–108

Adenosine 3',5'-cyclic monophosphate (cyclic AMP)
  in antibody formation, 40
  and hormone function, 158

Adrenal cortical extract, effect on lymphocytes, 71–74

Adrenal corticosteroids. *See* Corticosteroids

Adrenalectomy
  ACTH effect after, 70, 71, 136–140
  hypothalamic response after, 52
  lymphocyte response to stress after, 79–85, 198–199
  and skin transplantation immunity, 90, 92–96
  and spleen weight, 163
  and sympathectomy, 57, 58–59

Adrenaline. *See* Epinephrine

Adrenals
  after acceleration stress, 123, 130
  in anaphylaxis, 23
  in avoidance learning stress, 195
  cholesterol in, 68–69
  in glyconeogenesis, 76–77
  grouping effect on, 211–213
  in immunocompetence, 165
  infantile stimulation effect on, 221
  interferon production by, 254
  in predator-induced stress, 243–249
  after sound stress, 199
  sympathetic stimulation of, 296

α-Adrenergic agonist, 57, 60–61, 62

α-Adrenergic blocker, in alloantigen response testing, 186–190

Adrenergic system, posterior hypothalamus and, 40

Adrenocortical hormones. *See* Corticosteroids

Adrenocorticotropic hormone (ACTH)
  alloantigen effect on, 186–190
  in anaphylaxis, 23
  hypothalamic control of, 18, 38
  in lymphocyte regulation, 65–78
  in skin transplantation immunity, 88, 92–94, 100–101, 102
  and somatotropic hormone, 261
  in stress-induced immunosuppression, 130, 133–142, 231

Adrenocorticotropic hormone-releasing factor (ACTH-RF), 38

Adrenotrophic hormone. *See* Adrenocorticotropic hormone (ACTH)

African Burkitt lymphoma, 343

Age
  and streptococcal infection, 309–310, 315
  and thyroid autoantibody production, 389–391, 393

Allergic reaction. *See* Anaphylaxis; Arthus reaction; Delayed hypersensitivity reaction

Alloantigens, tolerance to, 171–180

Allografts. *See* Skin transplantation immunity

Amygdaloid complex, electrolytic lesion of, 34–36

Amyotrophic lateral sclerosis, antibrain antibodies in, 447–448

Anaphylaxis
  anterior lesions and, 21–24
  with conditioned reflex, 274–275
  passive, 3–4, 195, 198, 275
  posterior lesions and, 21–24
  small intestine in, 22
  stress effect on, 195, 198
  tuberal lesions and, 1–6, 21

Anesthesia
  effect on spleen and peritoneal cells, 122, 128–129, 136
  under hypnosis, 322

Angina, personality factors in, 326

Antibody, *see also* Antibrain antibody; Autoantibodies

streptococcal infections in, 307–316
tuberculosis in, 287–297
vigil stress in, 251–256
Humoral immunity. *See* Anaphylaxis; Antibody
 response; Arthus reaction; B lymphocytes;
 Immunoglobulin G (IgG); Immunoglobulin
 M (IgM)
Hydrocortisone
 and lymphocytes, 382
 and skin transplantation immunity, 87, 91, 95–
 96, 196
 stress effect on, 217–219, 254–255, 259–260
17-Hydroxycorticosteroids
 with avoidance stress, 209
 with overcrowding, 231–232
6-Hydroxydopamine-hydrochloride (6-OH-DA),
 in sympathectomy, 56–59, 62
5-Hydroxytryptophan, in development of immune
 response, 149–153, 186–190
Hymenolepis nana, predator stress and resistance
 to, 243–249
Hypersensitivity reaction
 delayed. *See* Delayed hypersensitivity reaction
 immediate. *See* Anaphylaxis; Antibody response; Arthus reaction
Hypertension, personality factors in, 326
Hypnosis, in inhibition of Mantoux reaction,
 319–323
Hypophysectomy
 ACTH effect after, 138–140, 141–142
 humoral antibody production after, 152
 5-hydroxytryptophan effect after, 150–153
 somatotropic hormone effect after, 140–141,
 142
Hypophysis. *See* Pituitary
Hypothalamus
 and anaphylactic shock, 1–6, 21–24
 anterior, 17–18, 21–24, 37–39
 in antibody production, 11–19, 23–24, 36, 231
 in Arthus reaction, 34
 changes during immune response, 51–53, 160–
 161
 in delayed hypersensitivity, 34–36
 and endocrine glands, 23, 36–40, 179–180
 grey paraventricular substance of, 13, 16
 mamillary region of, 21, 22
 posterior, 13–16, 21–24, 40
 in serotonin effect on immune response, 151–
 152
 in thermoregulation, 16–17
 thymus in maturation of, 183
 tuberal lesion of, 1–6, 21, 24
 ventromedial nucleus of, 51

I

IgG. *See* Immunoglobulin G (IgG)
IgM. *See* Immunoglobulin M (IgM)
Immunity
 conditioned reflexes in, 263–267

early experience and, 221–224
 pregnancy effect on, 99
Immunization, reinfection after, 246–248
Immunocompetence
 adrenals in, 165
 somatotropic hormone in, 112–114
 space flight effect on, 239–242
 thyroxine in, 113–114
Immunoenhancement, *see also* Resistance
 with acceleration stress, 121–130
 with sound stress, 259–261
 with sympathectomy, 55–60
Immunoglobulin G (IgG)
 antibody to Epstein-Barr virus, 343
 anti-synaptic membrane, 49
 and 5-hydroxytryptophan, 149–153
Immunoglobulin M (IgM)
 antibody to Epstein-Barr virus, 343
 and 5-hydroxytryptophan, 149–153
Immunological maturation
 ACTH effect on, 133
 adrenals in, 165
 autoantigens in, 393–394
 corticosteroid effect on, 133
 critical period in, 115–117, 180
 and endocrine system maturation, 109, 156–
 157, 172, 178–179
 genetic control of, 180
 hypothalamus in, 179–180
 pituitary in, 105–108, 172
 somatotropic hormone effect on, 108–115, 133
 thyroxine in, 109–111, 112–115
Immunospecificity
 corticosteroids in, 163
 endocrine system in, 162–164
 of thyroid autoantibody, 392–393
Immunosuppression
 acceleration stress effect on, 121–130
 ACTH in, 130, 133–142, 231
 with avoidance learning, 195–196
 conditioned reflex in, 269–276, 279–285
 corticosterone in, 130, 135–142
 cortisone in, 261
 with 5-hydroxytryptophan, 149–153, 186–190
 with noradrenaline and clonidine, 60–61
 with overcrowding, 227–232
 with predator-induced stress, 243–249
 with sound stress, 259–261
Immunotolerance
 critical period for, 171, 173–175, 176
 endocrine status and, 164–165, 171–180, 183–
 190
 hypothalamus in, 179–180
 prolongation of, 176, 178
 thyroid proteins in, 393–394
Impulse control, in rheumatoid arthritis, 329
Influenza, psychosocial influences in, 299–306,
 342
Inhibition tests, on sera of psychiatric patients,
 368–369, 370, 389, 392
Inpatient Multidimensional Psychiatric Scale, 427

Monocytes, *see also* Lymphocytes
    conditioned response of, 264–266
    in dementia, 363
    endocrine status and, 165–166
    hypnotic effect on, 322
    phagocytic rate of, 252–256
    in tuberculin reaction, 322, 323
Mononucleosis, infectious
    ego strength in, 305, 344
    etiology of, 343–344
    incidence of, 343
    lymphocytes in, 378
    psychosocial risk factors in, 341–360
    and stress, 344
Mood. *See* Emotional state
Morale-Loss index, in influenza, 300, 303, 304
Motivation, and mononucleosis, 347–354, 356–359
Mourning. *See* Bereavement
Mouse
    acceleration stress effect in, 121–130
    ACTH effect in, 65–78, 133–142
    adrenalectomy and stress in, 79–85
    developmental hormones in, 105–118
    environmental stressors in, 259–261
    ether stress effect in, 121–130
    somatotropins in immune response in, 183–190
    grouping effect on, 211–213
    5-hydroxytryptophan effect in, 149–153, 186–190
    immunological development in, 171–180
    predator-induced stress in, 243–249
    skin transplantation immunity in, 87–102, 195–196
    viral susceptibility in, 197–200, 201–207
Multiple sclerosis, antibrain antibodies in, 370, 447–448
Muscarinic agents, 145–147
Myasthenia gravis, antibody in, 441
Myocardial infarction, personality factors in, 326

N

Nasopharyngeal carcinoma, 343
Neuronal antigens, cross-reactivity with thymocytes, 45–49
Nicotinic agents, 145–147
Norepinephrine, in immune response, 40, 55–63; *see also* Catecholamines
Nucleic acid synthesis, space flight effect on, 239–242
Nucleus caudatus. *See* Caudate nucleus

O

Obsessive-compulsive syndrome, 329
Ontogeny. *See* Immunological maturation

Opsonin production
    adrenaline and glucose effect on, 288–297
    excitement and, 287–288
    and phagocytosis, 256
    in tuberculosis, 287–288, 294
Ovalbumin, sensitivity to, 21–22
Ovariectomy, ACTH effect with, 92–94
Overachievers, and mononucleosis, 348–349, 356, 357
Overcrowding
    antibody response to, 228–230
    corticosteroid response to, 231–232
    and resistance, 232, 261

P

Parasite infestation, after exposure to predator stress, 243–249
Parasympathetic nervous system, anterior hypothalamus effect on, 24
Paresthesia, under hypnosis, 322
Parity, and skin transplantation immunity, 96–99
Passive transfer
    of allogenic and syngeneic spleen cells, 178
    with tuberal lesion of hypothalamus, 2–3
Penicillin, in streptococcal infections, 314, 315
Pepsinogen secretion, personality factors in, 326–327
Peripheral nerves, in immunomodulation, 161
Peritoneal cells, stress effect on, 121–130
Personality factors
    in acute respiratory infections, 305
    in coronary heart disease, 326
    in hypertension, 326
    in influenza, 299–306
    in malaria, 305
    in mononucleosis, 305
    in rheumatoid arthritis, 325–334
    in schistosomiasis, 304, 305
    in ulcers, 326–327
Phagocytosis
    adrenaline and glucose effect on, 288–296
    stress effect on, 252–256
Phenothiazine derivatives, in schizophrenia, 376
Phentolamine, in alloantigen response testing, 186–190
Phytohemagglutination titers
    in bereavement, 338–339
    in schizophrenia, 449–454
    space flight effect on, 242
Pituitary
    in antibody production, 18, 36, 138–142
    hypothalamus and, 37–38
    in immunological development, 172, 179
    in serotonin effect on immune response, 140–142, 151–152
    in stress response, 23
    thymus and, 105–108

in thyroid-stimulating hormone secretion, 23
Plaque-forming cells
    after adrenalectomy, 163
    and hormone levels, 159
    and hypothalamic changes, 51–52
    stress effect on, 121, 123, 128, 136
    after sympathectomy, 57, 60
Plasma cells
    in dementia, 363
    in schizophrenia, 375, 376
Poliomyelitis, avoidance stress and susceptibility
    to, 209–210
Polymorphonuclear leukocytes
    ACTH effect on, 67, 70, 71, 76
    conditioned response of, 264–266
    in dementia, 363
    phagocytotic rate of, 252–256
    in tuberculin reaction, 323
PPD. *See* Purified protein derivative
Precipitin level
    with conditioned stimulus, 271, 272
    with psychological stress, 218
    with tuberal lesion of hypothalamus, 2
Predator stress, 243–249
Pregnancy, and skin transplantation immunity,
    88–89, 96–99, 101
Progesterone, in skin transplantation immunity,
    87, 91–92, 175–178
Prolactin, response to alloantigen, 175, 177, 186
Properdin, 207
Propyl-thiouracil, and immune system develop-
    ment, 114–115
Prostaglandins, in gonadotropin release, 189–190
Psychosocial influences
    in acute respiratory infections, 305
    bereavement, 337–340
    in coronary heart disease, 326
    in hypertension, 326
    in influenza, 299–306
    in inhibition of Mantoux reaction, 319–323
    in malaria, 305
    in mononucleosis, 305, 341–360
    in rheumatoid arthritis, 325–334
    in schistosomiasis, 304, 305
    in streptococcal infections, 307–316
    in tuberculosis, 287–297
    in ulcers, 326–327
Purified protein derivative (PPD), hypnotic in-
    hibition of reaction to, 319–323

R

Rabbit
    antibrain antibody in, 25–30
    conditioned response in, 269–276
    5-hydroxytryptophan effect in, 149–153
    hypothalamic lesions in, 11–19
Rat
    ACTH effect in, 65–78

antigenic stimulation of, 51–53
behaviorally conditioned immunosuppression
    in, 279–285
brain-lymphocyte antigen system in, 45–49
early experience and immunity in, 221–224
hypothalamic lesions in, 21–24, 31–40
lymphocyte-mediated cytotoxicity in, 145–147
neuroendocrine regulatory functions in, 155–
    166
reticular formation lesions in, 34, 36, 40
stress and antibody response in, 227–232
sympathectomy in, 55–63
Reserpine, in schizophrenia, 376
Resistance
    to cancer, 222
    to Coxsackie B virus, 201–207
    in diabetics, 296
    early experience effect on, 221–224
    to encephalomyocarditis, 222
    to helminth infestation, 243–249
    to herpes virus, 197, 201, 206, 342
    to infectious disease, 342
    to leukemia, 222
    to mononucleosis, 341–360
    overcrowding effect on, 232
    to poliomyelitis, 209–210
    to streptococcal infections, 307–316
    to *Trichinella spiralis*, 211
    to vesicular stomatitis, 227, 228
    to viral infection, 197–200
Respiratory infections
    catecholamines in, 342
    psychosocial factors in, 305, 307–316
Reticular formation
    in antibody production, 36
    in Arthus reaction, 34
    in delayed hypersensitivity, 36
    and endocrine glands, 40
    integrative activities of, 18
    sympathoadrenal system regulation of, 11
Reticuloendothelial cells, hereditary abnormalit-
    ies of, 379
Reticuloendothelial system
    and central nervous system, 333
    corticosteroid effect on, 165–166
    hypothalamic connection to, 18
    and schizophrenia, 380–382
    stress effect on, 195, 256
Reticulum cells, in schizophrenia, 374, 375–376,
    381
Rheumatic fever, 380
Rheumatoid factor
    brain-hemagglutination test with, 328, 368, 371
    personality factors and, 325–334
    in psychiatric patients, 368, 371, 426, 439–440
Risk factors. *See* Resistance
RNA synthesis, space flight effect on, 239–242
Rosette formation
    in bereavement, 340
    5-hydroxytryptophan effect on, 149–153

in schizophrenia, 452, 453
space flight effect on, 337
Runt disease, 109–114, 188, 189
Rye consumption, and schizophrenia, 397, 400–402, 403

S

Schilder's disease, brain-hemagglutination test in, 368, 370
Schistosomiasis, psychosocial influences in, 304, 305
Schizophrenia
  antibody response in, 426
  antibrain antibodies in, 370, 433–442, 443–449, 463–464
  as autoimmune disorder, 442
  cereals and, 397–421
  chlorambucil in, 425–430
  cultural differences in, 406–409, 412, 418–421
  endocrine dysfunction and, 382–383
  genetic factors in, 379–380, 397, 408–409, 411, 460–464
  globulins in, 425–430, 433–442
  infective agents in, 371, 380
  lymphocytes in, 373–383, 449–454, 467
  reticuloendothelial system in, 380–382
  thymocytes in, 454–463, 467–468
  thyroid autoantibodies in, 371, 387–395
Schultz-Dale test, with tuberal lesion of hypothalamus, 1, 2
Seasonal variations, in streptococcal infection, 310, 315
Self-recognition. See Immunotolerance
Seminal vesicles, with stress, 246
Seroconversion, in mononucleosis, 347–358
Serotonin
  in ACTH release, 162
  in immune response, 149–153
  in neuroendocrine function, 162
Sex, and thyroid autoantibody production, 389–391, 393, 394
Shock, anaphylactic. See Anaphylaxis
Shock stress, antibody response to, 227–230, 236
Skin reactions. See Delayed hypersensitivity reaction
Skin transplantation immunity
  ACTH effect on, 88, 92–94, 100–101
  cortisone effect on, 87–88, 90–91, 99–100
  and endocrine differentiation, 174–180
  gonadotropin effect on, 183–190
  pregnancy effect on, 88–89, 96–99, 101
  species differences in, 101–102
  stress effect on, 195–196
Sleep deprivation
  antibody response to, 228–231
  and delayed hypersensitivity reaction, 235
  and interferon production, 251–256
  and phagocytosis, 251–256

Social rank
  and antibody titer, 211–213, 248
  in mononucleosis, 345–346, 348
Somatotropic hormone (STH)
  and ACTH, 261
  alloantigen response of, 175, 177, 186–190
  after hypophysectomy, 140–141, 142
  hypothalamic control of, 18, 39, 40
  and immunological maturation, 133
  and insulin, 115
  in lymphoid cell development, 117
  in runt disease, 109–112
  in schizophrenia, 382
  in stress reaction, 142
  and thymocytes, 112–114
  as thymotropic hormone, 108–109, 114
  and thyroxine, 114–115
Somatotropic hormone-releasing factor (STH-RF), 39
Sound stress, 197–200, 217, 259–260
Space flight, and immune function, 239–242, 337
Spleen
  after adrenalectomy, 163
  denervation of, 56, 58
  norepinephrine content in, 59–60, 62–63
  somatotropic hormone effect on, 114–115
  in stress response, 195, 199, 207, 246
Spleen cells
  induction of tolerance in, 173–174, 176
  and runt disease, 109–111
  stress effect on, 121–130, 259–261
Staphylococcus filtrate, conditioned response to, 266
Stereotype, dynamic, 270–276
Sternberg-Reed cells, in schizophrenia, 376
STH. See Somatotropic hormone (STH)
STH-RF. See Somatotropic hormone-releasing factor
Streptococcal infections, psychosocial influences in, 307–316
Stress
  with adrenalectomy or hypophysectomy, 133–142
  antibody response to, 211–213, 227–232
  in bereavement, 337–340
  and blastogenic activity of mitogens, 259–261
  chronic vs. acute, 210, 259–261
  corticosteroid response to, 199, 215–219, 316
  and delayed hypersensitivity, 235–238
  and helminth reinfection, 243–249
  in hypertension, 326
  and interferon production, 251–256
  lymphocyte response to, 79–85, 239–242, 382
  in mononucleosis, 344, 352–353, 359
  neonatal, 221–224, 261
  and phagocytosis, 251–256
  and poliomyelitis susceptibility, 209–210
  reticuloendothelial system function and, 381–382
  in rheumatoid arthritis, 327

in schizophrenia, 394
and skin transplantation immunity, 195–196
spleen and peritoneal cell response to, 121–130
and streptococcal infection, 311–314, 315
and thyroid autoantibody production, 391, 394
ulcers from, 248, 326–327
and viral susceptibility, 197–200, 201–207
Stress lymphocytes, 79–85
vs. abnormal lymphocytes in schizophrenia, 378, 382
Stressors
acceleration, 122, 123–129, 136
achievement motivation as, 352–353
ACTH, 130, 134–142
acute family crisis, 311–313, 315
anesthesia, 122, 128–129, 136
avoidance learning, 195–196, 201–207, 209–210
bereavement, 288, 337–340
chronic family stress, 311–314, 315
episodic, 231
grouping, 211–213, 232
irregular feeding, 217
lights, 217
overcrowding, 228–232, 261
predator, 243–249
shock, 227–230, 236
sleep deprivation, 228–231, 251–256
sound, 197–200, 217, 259–260
space flight, 239–241, 337
transportation, 123
vertical movement, 217
vigil, 251–256
Superior colliculus, electrolytic lesion of, 34–36
Susceptibility. See Resistance
Swine flu vaccine, 342
Sympathetic nervous system
immunomodulation by, 55–63
posterior hypothalamus effect on, 24
Sympathoadrenal system, and reticular formation, 11
Synaptic membranes, and thymocytes, 45–49
Synaptic transmission, in schizophrenia, 440
Systemic lupus erythematosus, serum protein abnormalities in, 368, 369–370, 379

T

Tanned cell hemagglutination test, 388–389
Tannic acid cell test, 367
Taraxein, in schizophrenia, 433–442
Taste aversion, conditioning of, 279–285
Tay-Sachs disease
abnormal lymphocytes in, 379, 380
asialoganglioside antibodies in, 370
Temperature regulation, hypothalamus in, 12, 16–17
Testosterone, in skin transplantation immunity, 87, 91–92, 175–178

Tetanus toxin, with conditioned response, 273–274
Tetramethylammonium chloride, in lymphocyte-mediated cytotoxicity, 146–147
Thalamus, in immune response, 16, 18, 34–36
Thermoregulation, hypothalamus in, 12, 16–17
Theta antigen, 48, 467
Thymectomy
endocrine function disturbances after, 157
immunological deficiencies after, 117
somatotropic hormone effect with, 113
Thymocytes
in schizophrenia, 454–463, 467–468
somatotropic hormone effect on, 112–114
and synaptic membranes, 45–49
Thymosin, 118
Thymus
corticosterone effect on, 77
effect of hypothalamus, 183
in immunological maturation, 37, 165, 172, 179
sensitivity to somatotropic hormone, 108–109
after stress, 123, 195, 199, 207
as target organ of adenohypophysis, 105–108
Thyroglobulin, in schizophrenia, 387–395
Thyroid
in anaphylaxis, 23
in immunological maturation, 116
and somatotropic hormone, 114
Thyroid autoantibodies
age and sex differences in, 389–391, 393, 394
in schizophrenia, 371, 387–395
Thyroid hormone. See Thyroxine
Thyroid-stimulating hormone (TSH)
alloantigen response by, 186
hypothalamic regulation of, 23, 39
Thyroid stimulating hormone-releasing factor (TSH-RF), 39
Thyroxine
alloantigen response by, 175–177
after antigenic stimulation, 51
and cyclic AMP, 40
hypothalamic control of, 39, 40
immune response effect on, 158–160
in runt disease, 109–111
in schizophrenia, 382
somatotropic hormone and, 114–115
T lymphocytes
in bereavement, 339–340
chemical mediators released by, 162
cholinergic receptor of cytotoxic, 145–147
concanavalin A stimulation of, 259–260
differentiation of, 179, 183
in schizophrenia, 452–454, 467
space flight effect on, 239–242
Tolerance. See Immunotolerance
Trichinella spiralis, grouping and resistance to, 211
TSH. See Thyroid-stimulating hormone (TSH)
TSH-RF. See Thyroid-stimulating hormone-releasing factor

Tuberal lesion, of hypothalamus, 1–6, 21, 24
Tuberculin test, hypnosis effect on, 319–323
Tuberculosis
    autoinoculation in, 297
    corticosteroids in, 316
    psychosocial influences in, 287–297
d-Tubocurarine, in lymphocyte-mediated cyto-
    toxicity, 146

U

Ulcers
    personality factors in, 326–327
    from stress, 248
Urea, and hemagglutination titers, 369

V

Varicella, corticosteroids in, 316
Vasoactive amines, effect on interferon, 254; *see also* Histamine; Serotonin
Ventromedial nucleus, of hypothalamus, 51
Vesicular stomatitis, stress effect on, 227, 228
Vigil, effect on immune response, 251–256
Viral infection
    Epstein-Barr, 343–358
    herpes, 197, 201, 206, 342
    in schizophrenia, 380
    stress and susceptibility to, 197–200

W

Weight changes, with stress, 202–207, 245, 248
Wheat consumption, and schizophrenia, 397–421